The Days of
Henry Thoreau

ALSO BY WALTER HARDING

THOREAU: A CENTURY OF CRITICISM

AN ESSAY ON TRANSCENDENTALISM

A CHECKLIST OF THE EDITIONS OF WALDEN

THOREAU'S LIBRARY

THE CORRESPONDENCE OF HENRY DAVID THOREAU
(edited with Carl Bode)

THE NEW THOREAU HANDBOOK
(with Michael Meyer)

BRONSON ALCOTT'S ESSAYS ON EDUCATION

THOREAU: MAN OF CONCORD

A THOREAU PROFILE
(with Milton Meltzer)

THOREAU'S MINNESOTA JOURNEY

THE VARIORUM WALDEN

SOPHIA THOREAU'S SCRAPBOOK

THE THOREAU CENTENNIAL

HENRY DAVID THOREAU: A PROFILE

The Days of
Henry Thoreau
A Biography

Walter Harding

Princeton University Press
Princeton, New Jersey

Published by Princeton University Press,
41 William Street,
Princeton, New Jersey 08540
In the United Kingdom by Princeton University Press,
Chichester, West Sussex

A clothbound edition of this book published in 1982 was
an enlarged and corrected republication of the sixth (1970)
printing of the work originally published by Alfred A.
Knopf, Inc., New York, with an addition of notes that
appear at the end of the book. The 1982 afterword has been
replaced by the new afterword for the Princeton Paperback
edition, 1992.

Library of Congress Cataloging-in-Publication Data

Harding, Walter Roy, 1917–
The days of Henry Thoreau: a biography / Walter Harding.
p.   cm.
Includes bibliographical references (p.   ) and index.
ISBN 0-691-02479-0 (PB: acid-free paper)
1. Thoreau, Henry David, 1817–1862—Biography.
2. Authors, American—19th century—Biography. I. Title.
PS3053.H3   1992
818'.309—dc20
[B]   92-28836

First Princeton Paperback printing,
with a new afterword, 1992

Princeton University Press books are printed on acid-free
paper, and meet the guidelines for permanence and
durability of the Committee on Production Guidelines for
Book Longevity of the Council on Library Resources

1   3   5   7   9   10   8   6   4   2
Printed in the United States of America

for
MARTIN LUTHER KING, JR.
and
EDWIN WAY TEALE,
who although they lead widely disparate lives have
both found inspiration in Henry David Thoreau

Portions of this book have already appeared in slightly different form as follows: Chapter Three in the *Harvard Alumni Bulletin* (March 21, 1964) under the title "Thoreau at Harvard"; Chapter Five in *The Educational Forum* (November 1964) under the title "Henry D. Thoreau, Instructor," used by permission of Kappa Delta Pi, An Honor Society in Education; Chapter Six in the *South Atlantic Quarterly* (Winter 1965) under the title "Henry Thoreau and Ellen Sewall," used by permission of the Duke University Press, copyright © 1965 by the Duke University Press; Chapter Ten in *Horizon* (Autumn 1964) under the title "The Camper in the Back Yard"; and Chapter Twenty in *American Heritage* (December 1962) under the title "This is a beautiful world; but I shall see a fairer."

Preface to the 1992 Edition

The bibliographical notes on pages 479–485 were added to the 1982 edition, and are keyed to the text by page and line number. Thus ''16–34'' means that the accompanying note glosses page 16, line 34 of the text. An asterisk has been placed in the margin next to each line of the text for which a note has been added.

Contents

ILLUSTRATIONS

[ix]

ILLUSTRATIONS

[x]

Introduction

A HUNDRED YEARS AGO Henry David Thoreau was looked upon as a minor disciple of Ralph Waldo Emerson. Fifty years ago he was thought of as an "also-ran" who was rapidly and deservedly being forgotten. Yet today he is widely rated as one of the giants in the American pantheon and his fame is on an upward rather than a downward curve. It is universally agreed that he speaks more to our day than to his own.

Nature lovers find solace and beauty in his works. Critics of our times find in him one of the great satirists of our foibles and follies. Conservationists look upon him as the pioneer in their battle to save our natural resources. Litterateurs hail him as one of the great modern prose stylists. Reformers have seized upon his theory of civil disobedience as their most effective weapon. Advocates of the simple life see in his philosophy the solution of some of the most pressing problems of our day.

Leaders in many fields have hailed his influence. Robert Frost has said: "In Thoreau's declaration of independence from the modern pace is where I find most justification for my own propensities"; Mahatma Gandhi: "There is no doubt that Thoreau's ideas greatly influenced my movement in India"; Henry Miller: "There are barely a half-dozen names in the history of America which have meaning for me. Thoreau's is one of them"; Frank Lloyd Wright: "The history of American Architecture would be incomplete without Thoreau's wise observations on the subject"; Justice William O. Douglas of the United States Supreme Court: "Thoreau lived when men were appraising trees in terms of board feet, not in terms of watershed protection and birds and music. His protests against that narrow outlook were among the first heard on this continent"; Sinclair Lewis: "*Walden* [is] one of the three or four unquestionable classics of American literature"; and President John F. Kennedy has paid tribute to "Thoreau's pervasive and universal influence on social thinking and political action."

Unfortunately the chorus of praise in recent years has tended to embalm Thoreau the man in apocryphal legend. The man in the street knows that Thoreau went to Walden Pond to live and went to jail, but has a vague notion that he spent one half of his life doing the one and the other half the other. And so I have written this biography. I have tried to present Thoreau as he really was. Elsewhere I have discussed his writings and charted the course of his fame. Here I am writing about Thoreau the man.

In writing this biography I have tried wherever possible to pin my statements down to specific facts and to cite the sources of my facts in footnotes, reducing speculation to a minimum. However, I have not hesitated at times to introduce what I was almost certain was apocryphal, keeping in mind Thoreau's own statement in his sketch of Sir Walter Raleigh—"It does not matter much whether the current stories are true or not, since they at least prove his reputation"—but I have labeled all such statements as apocryphal or legendary. On a few occasions I have quoted conversations in these pages. The words therein are not the product of my imagination but in every case direct quotations cited by the participants in or witnesses of these conversations. On occasion I have borrowed words and phrases, particularly from Thoreau himself, without benefit of quotation marks simply because I had revised slightly the phrasing to fit better into my own sentences.

I have not attempted to prove any particular thesis in this book, but rather to present the facts and let them speak for themselves. As a result, at times Thoreau not only appears inconsistent —he is inconsistent. At times, we can ascribe this inconsistency to a natural growth and development of his thought over a period of years. At other times, we can attribute it only to the fact that he was a very human human being. He, like most of us, could be sweet, gentle, and thoughtful one moment and a stubborn curmudgeon the next; I have tried to gloss over neither the thoughtfulness nor the stubbornness. In his journal for March 25, 1842, Thoreau said, "Great persons are not soon learned, not even their outlines, but they change like the mountains in the horizon as we ride along." I have tried here to present the opportunity of riding by and observing a particularly notable mountain.

As I have said, in writing this book I have had no thesis to present, no axe to grind. But I do think the wealth of new material that I have had the good fortune to use does modify at least the popular concept of Thoreau. It shows that while he was by no means lionized, he was more widely recognized in his own time than has been supposed; that he was more the townsman and neighbor and less the solitary and eccentric than he has been portrayed; that he was not the cold, unemotional stoic that some have believed, but a warm-blooded human being; and that rather than being bitter and disappointed in his last years, he was vibrant, creative, and happy to the very end. I have not gone out of my way to italicize these differences in my text, for it would be easy to overstate them, but I believe the evidence is here for all to see.

Emerging from this long study of Thoreau, I find myself most impressed by Thoreau's aliveness. All his senses were thoroughly awake and he was able to examine the worlds of both man and nature with a keenness and clarity that have made him one of the great observers of the American scene. It is that aliveness above all that I hope I have captured in these pages.

In writing this biography I have been exceedingly fortunate in the assistance I have received, both intellectual and, to be mundane, financial. The State University of New York granted me a sabbatical leave for the academic year 1962–3 and the American Council of Learned Societies appointed me a fellow for that year, enabling me to devote my full time to work on the book. The Research Foundation of the State University of New York has also given me two summer fellowships and numerous grants-in-aid.

I am even more indebted to both the individuals and the institutions who have opened their doors to me and have given me access to books, papers, and manuscripts that in many cases have not been available to previous biographers of Thoreau. I am particularly indebted to the children and grandchildren of Ellen Sewall—Mr. George L. Davenport, Jr., of Los Angeles, the late Mrs. Louise Koopman of Cambridge, Mass., Mrs. Gilbert Tower and Mrs. Frances Collier of Cohasset, Mass., and Mr. Theodore Abbot of Forty-Fort, Pa.—for granting me access to the Sewall-

Ward-Osgood papers and to Mr. Davenport and Mr. Clayton Hoagland of Rutherford, N.J., for providing me with transcripts of many of these documents. I am also greatly indebted to Mr. and Mrs. Raymond Emerson of Concord, Mass., for permitting me to use Dr. Edward Emerson's manuscript notes on Thoreau and John Shepard Keyes' diary. I am also indebted to the Abernethy Library of Middlebury College (Mrs. Grace Davis); the Boston Public Library (Mr. John Alden); the Cary Memorial Library of Lexington, Mass. (Mrs. Harry Erdman); the Colby College Library (Mr. Richard Cary); the Concord Free Public Library (Mrs. Marcia Moss, Mr. David Little, and Mrs. Dorothy Nyren); the Fruitlands Museum (Mr. William Henry Harrison); the Harvard College Library (Dr. William Bond, the late Dr. William Jackson, and Miss Caroline Jakeman); the Charles Robert Autograph Collection of the Haverford College Library (Mrs. Marjorie F. Davis); the Huntington Library, San Marino, Calif.; the Kentucky Historical Society (Mrs. Wilburn B. Walker); the Library of Congress; the Lilly Library of Indiana University; the Louisville, Kentucky, Free Public Library (Mrs. Arthur S. Ricketts); the Massachusetts Historical Society; the Medford, Mass., Public Library (Miss Helen G. Forsyth); the Milne Library of the State University of New York College at Geneseo (Dr. James Eberhardt and Miss Alice Fedder); the Pierpont Morgan Library (Mr. Herbert Cahoon); the New Bedford Free Public Library (Miss Loretta E. Phaneuf); the New Hampshire State Library (Mr. Paul K. Goode); the New York Public Library (Mr. John Gordan of the Berg Collection); the University of Notre Dame Library; the Paulist Archives of New York City (Rev. Vincent Holden, C.S.P.); the Portland, Maine, Public Library (Miss Eugenia M. Southard); the Sawyer Free Library of Gloucester, Mass. (Mrs. Alan G. Hill); the Springfield, Mass., Library (Miss Margaret Rose); the University of Texas Library; the Clifton Waller Barrett Library of the University of Virginia Library (Mr. John Wyllie and Mr. Kendon Stubbs); the Silas Bronson Library of Waterbury, Conn.; and the Yale University Library.

I am equally indebted to Professor Raymond Adams of Chapel Hill, N.C. (for the use of unpublished manuscripts in his collection); Mr. T. L. Bailey; Mr. C. Waller Barrett; Mr. Daniel J. Bernstein; Mrs. Millicent Todd Bingham of Washington, D.C. (for the use of the Wilder and Loomis family papers); Mr. Jacob Blanck; Mrs. Robert Bowler; Prof. Kenneth Walter Cameron; Miss Gladys Clark of Concord, Mass.; Mr. William Cummings; Professor Robert Gorham Davis; Mr. David Dean; Mr. August Derleth; Mr. Thomas de Valcourt of Craigie House, Cambridge, Mass.; Mrs. Edmund Fenn of Concord, Mass. (for searching through the archives of the First Parish of Concord for me); Professor William Gilman; Professor James Greaves; Miss Edith Guerrier; the late Mr. Cephas Guillet; Professor Benjamin Hickok; Professor Hubert Hoeltje; Mrs. Herbert Hosmer; Professor Anton M. Huffert; Professor Rudolf Kirk; Mr. Leonard Kleinfeld of Forest Hills, Long Island; Mr. Anton Kovar; President Evald B. Lawson of Upsala College; Mr. Albert E. Lownes of Providence, Rhode Island (for the use of many books and manuscripts in his collection and for giving me various details about the publication of Thoreau's first book); the late Mr. Horace Mann; Professor Frederick T. McGill, Jr., of Short Hills, N.J. (for lending me the manuscript of his unpublished biography of Ellery Channing and transcripts of Channing's unpublished journals); Mr. Milton Meltzer; Mr. Robert Rulon Miller of Bristol, Rhode Island (for the use of manuscripts in his collection); Dr. John Mould (for discussing with me some of the medical problems of Thoreau's life); Mr. Truman Nelson; Mr. Paul Oehser; Mr. Laurence Richardson (for sharing with me his findings in his voluminous reading of Concord records and manuscripts); Mrs. Mary Sherwood; Professor William Slavick; Mr. Noel Stevenson (for checking the United States Census records of 1850 and 1860); Professor Leo Stoller (for sharing with me his discoveries in Thoreau research); the late Mr. Robert L. Straker; Mr. Edwin Way Teale (for calling to my attention many of his discoveries in Thoreau research and for checking for me some of the natural history data); Professor Eleanor Tilton; Mrs. Caleb Wheeler of Concord, Mass. (for needling me until I wrote this book and then for both providing me with a wealth of material from her researches into Concord history and doing a great deal of special research in answer to my inquiries); Mrs. Henry J. Wheelwright; and Mr. Herbert P. Wilkins (for permitting me to examine the architecture of the Thoreau-Alcott House).

Portions of this volume have appeared previously elsewhere in print: the section on Thoreau at Walden Pond in *Horizon* for

Autumn, 1964; on Ellen Sewall in the *South Atlantic Quarterly* for Winter, 1965; on Thoreau's school in *Educational Forum* for November 1964; and on Thoreau's death in *American Heritage* for December 1962. I am indebted to the editors of these journals for permission to reprint.

For the illustrations I am indebted to the Concord Free Public Library, Mrs. Gilbert Tower, Eastman House of Rochester, New York, Mr. Roger Smith, Mrs. Caleb Wheeler, Mr. Albert E. Lownes, and particularly to my old friend and collaborator, Mr. Milton Meltzer.

I am of course also indebted to the multitude of scholars who have written on Thoreau in recent years—my specific acknowledgments to them are given in my footnotes. My work on this volume has extended over so long a period that I have undoubtedly overlooked some names that should have been included in this list—to them my apologies and my thanks. I want also to express my appreciation to my secretary, Miss Freda Hark, who patiently and painstakingly typed the manuscript.

Walter Harding

State University College, Geneseo, New York
February 25, 1965

The Days of
Henry Thoreau

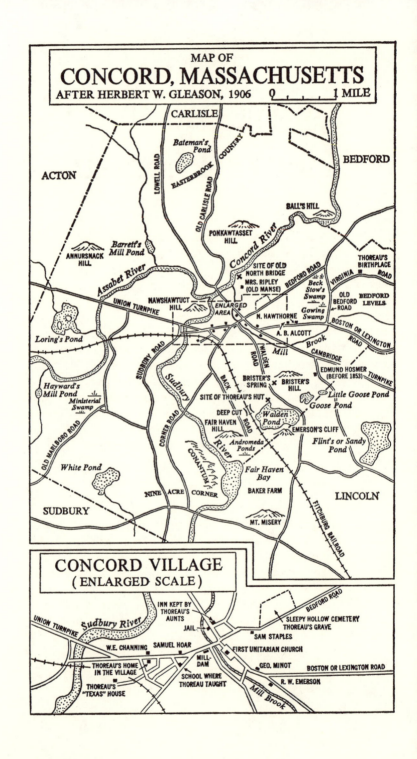

MAP OF
CONCORD, MASSACHUSETTS
AFTER HERBERT W. GLEASON, 1906

0 __ 1 MILE

CARLISLE

BEDFORD

ACTON

Bateman's Pond

EASTERBROOK COUNTRY

LOWELL ROAD

OLD CARLISLE ROAD

BALL'S HILL

Concord River

PONKAWTASSET HILL

Barrett's Mill Pond

ANNURSNACK HILL

Assabet River

SITE OF OLD NORTH BRIDGE

MRS. RIPLEY (OLD MANSE)

BEDFORD ROAD

Beck Stow's Swamp

THOREAU'S BIRTHPLACE

VIRGINIA ROAD

OLD BEDFORD ROAD

BEDFORD LEVELS

NAWSHAWTUCT HILL

UNION TURNPIKE

ENLARGED AREA

N. HAWTHORNE

Gowing Swamp

A. B. ALCOTT

BOSTON OR LEXINGTON ROAD

Loring's Pond

Mill Brook

CAMBRIDGE

SUDBURY ROAD

WALDEN ROAD

BRISTER'S SPRING

BRISTER'S HILL

EDMUND HOSMER (BEFORE 1853)

TURNPIKE

Little Goose Pond

Hayward's Mill Pond

Ministerial Swamp

Sudbury

BACK ROAD

SITE OF THOREAU'S HUT

DEEP CUT

FAIR HAVEN HILL

Goose Pond

CORNER ROAD

Walden Pond

EMERSON'S CLIFF

OLD MARLBORO ROAD

River

Andromeda Ponds

Flint's or Sandy Pond

White Pond

CONANTUM

Fair Haven Bay

NINE ACRE CORNER

BAKER FARM

LINCOLN

SUDBURY

MT. MISERY

FITCHBURG RAILROAD

CONCORD VILLAGE
(ENLARGED SCALE)

INN KEPT BY THOREAU'S AUNTS

BEDFORD ROAD

UNION TURNPIKE

Sudbury River

JAIL

SLEEPY HOLLOW CEMETERY
THOREAU'S GRAVE

SAM STAPLES

W.E. CHANNING

SAMUEL HOAR

FIRST UNITARIAN CHURCH

THOREAU'S HOME IN THE VILLAGE

MILL DAM

GEO. MINOT

BOSTON OR LEXINGTON ROAD

THOREAU'S "TEXAS" HOUSE

SCHOOL WHERE THOREAU TAUGHT

R. W. EMERSON

Mill Brook

CHAPTER ONE
(1817–1823)

I

H ENRY DAVID THOREAU was born in Concord, Massachusetts, on July 12, 1817, in what he thought "the most estimable place in all the world, and in the very nick of time, too."[1] His birthplace was the easternmost upper chamber of his maternal grandmother's house, a gray, unpainted farmhouse on Virginia Road, which winds almost deserted along the eastern outskirts of the village, in the center of a great tract known as the Bedford levels.

Concord, some twenty miles northwest of Boston, is located on the plains surrounding the juncture of the Assabet and Sudbury Rivers which forms the Concord River, one of the principal tributaries of the Merrimack. In 1817 it was a quiet little town of two thousand, devoted chiefly to agriculture. Its stores and hotels were the stopping places for farmers and travelers en route from Boston to southern New Hampshire or western Massachusetts, and the fact that it then shared with Cambridge the seat of Middlesex County meant that its village square was often enlivened at the time of court sessions.

The town's citizens knew neither great wealth nor extreme poverty. At one end of the social spectrum were families like the Hoars in their square, white-frame Greek Revival homes on Main Street; at the other, a few ne'er-do-wells and former slaves who lived in shanties near Walden Pond on the outskirts of the village. The town was essentially a democracy, and no man felt the need of kneeling to his neighbor. The townspeople were almost exclusively of White Protestant stock whose ancestors had emigrated from England or Scotland long before the Revolution. The Reverend Dr. Ezra Ripley, minister of the First Parish in Concord,

---

1. Henry David Thoreau, *Journal* (Boston, 1906), IX, 160

dominated the religious life of the community just as the steeple of his church dominated the town.

What was true of Concord then was true of most of the nation. It had primarily a rural, agricultural economy. The country was recovering rapidly from the misfortunes of the War of 1812. The threatening clouds of strife between the North and the South were not even on the horizon. With the inauguration of James Monroe in 1817, Thoreau's birth year, the nation was entering that long period of peace and prosperity known popularly as "the era of good feeling." The Thoreau family, however, had experienced a series of misfortunes, physically, politically, and financially, and were trying quite unsuccessfully to regain their former status.

II

The first of the Thoreaus to come to America was Jean (later Anglicized to John) Thoreau, Henry's grandfather, who was born in St. Helier on the Isle of Jersey in the English Channel about 1754, the son of Philippe Thoreau, a wine merchant. The family, originally of French Protestant ancestry, had taken refuge in Jersey after the revocation of the Edict of Nantes in 1685 and its name is said to have appeared frequently in the records of Tours, France, during the late Middle Ages.[2]

Jean Thoreau came to America in 1773. He was apparently a member of the crew of a Jersey privateer that had been shipwrecked, and when rescued after suffering severe privations, he was brought to the colonies without any intention on his part of going there.[3] Arriving in Boston, Massachusetts, he worked first in a sail loft and then as a cooper. When the Revolutionary War threw him out of work, he went back to privateering after participating briefly in the defense of Boston, and served for a time under Paul Revere, sharing in the booty seized from the *Minerva Cartet*.[4]

2. Raymond Adams, "A Thoreau Family Tree," *Thoreau Society Bulletin*, XVII (1946), 2

3. F. B. Sanborn, *Henry D. Thoreau* (Boston, 1882), 6

4. John Thoreau et al., Receipt for sale of goods from *Minerva Cartet*, Castle Island, June 8, 1779. MS, Massachusetts Historical Society

After the war he established a shop on Long Wharf in Boston with a single hogshead of sugar as his entire stock. But his store rapidly prospered and he moved to Kings (now State) Street, where he entered a successful partnership with a Mr. Hayse. For a time he was also in business with a Mr. Phillips.

In 1781 he married Jane (Jennie) Burns,[5] had ten children (several of whom died in infancy), and for many years lived at 51–53 Prince Street in a house he had purchased from his wife's family. His first wife died in 1796, and a year later he married Rebecca Kettell. On October 30, 1799, he purchased what is now the north end of the Colonial Inn on the square in Concord, next door to his sister-in-law and her husband, Deacon John White, and moved there in 1800. He died in 1801, at the age of forty-seven, after contracting a cold while patrolling the streets of Boston in a severe rainstorm when it was thought an anti-Catholic riot was imminent.[6] (For some years he had suffered from tuberculosis). He left an estate worth $25,000, including his homes in Boston and Concord and some $12,000 in cash and securities. But when his widow died in 1814, it was discovered that not only had all his estate, except for the houses, disappeared, but her own personal estate had been encumbered in the care of her stepchildren.[7] There was a great deal of whispering about the high-handedness of an executor who was said to have paid himself exorbitant fees for his work.

Jane Burns, Thoreau's paternal grandmother, was the daughter of a Scotch gentleman and Sarah Orrok, a Boston Quaker. Burns had had to give up his rich apparel of gems and ruffles and conform to the more simple garb of the Orrok family before he could gain their consent to the marriage, which occurred about 1750. He died during a return visit to Scotland, leaving a large estate which his heirs never succeeded in claiming.[8] Sarah Orrok was the daughter of David Orrok and Hannah Tillet, both from old Quaker families. Hannah, in turn, was the daughter of Edward

5. Sanborn, *Henry D. Thoreau*, 5
6. Annie Russell Marble, *Thoreau: His Home, Friends and Books* (New York, 1902), 35
7. F. B. Sanborn, *The Life of Henry David Thoreau* (Boston, 1917), 31
8. Sanborn, *Henry D. Thoreau*, 7–8

[5]

Tillet, a Boston sailmaker, who lived in a mansion on Prince Street and owned a number of slaves.[9]

Thoreau's maternal grandfather, Rev. Asa Dunbar, was born in Bridgewater, Massachusetts, in 1745, and attended Harvard College, where in 1767, in his senior year, he led a rebellion against the food served in the college dining hall. When he was threatened with expulsion, his classmates called a meeting and announced that they would "resent it in a proper manner" should Dunbar be punished. The college administration capitulated after the students walked out of chapel, and Dunbar became the hero of his class.[1] After graduation, he taught school for a time in Mystic, preached at Bedford, and eventually settled in Salem, Massachusetts, as the colleague of Rev. Thomas Barnard.[2] He married Mary Jones, of a wealthy Tory family in Weston on October 22, 1772, and the marriage brought Dunbar himself under so much suspicion that he was obliged once or twice to declare publicly his sympathies for the American cause.[3] Plagued by chronic illness, he resigned his church in April 1779, and turned to the study of law under Joshua Atherton, later attorney-general of New Hampshire.[4] Settling down in Keene, New Hampshire, he was soon elected to the office of town clerk and admitted to the bar. He died on June 22, 1787, at the age of forty-one, after an illness of only thirty-six hours and, as a charter member of the Rising Sun Lodge No. 4 in Keene, was buried with full Masonic honors.[5]

Mary Jones Dunbar, his wife, was born in 1748, the ninth of fifteen children, and lived until 1830, the only grandparent that Henry Thoreau was to know. When her Tory brothers were arrested during the Revolution and placed in Concord jail, she brought them food in which files were concealed, and with the help of horses which she had captured for them, they were successful in making

9. Henry David Thoreau, MS laid in front of Vol. XIV, MS Journal, Morgan Library
1. William C. Lane, "The Rebellion of 1766 in Harvard College," *Publications of the Colonial Society of Massachusetts*, X (1904), 33
2. E. Harlow Russell, *Thoreau's Maternal Grandfather: Asa Dunbar* (Worcester, 1908), 8
3. Sanborn, *The Life of Henry David Thoreau*, 9, 522
4. Charles H. Bell, *The Bench and Bar of New Hampshire* (Boston, 1894), 323
5. Russell, *Thoreau's Maternal Grandfather*, 12

their escape to Loyalist Canada.[6] After Asa Dunbar's death, she for a time operated a tavern in her home in Keene. But in 1798 she married Captain Jonas Minott and settled on his farm on Virginia Road in Concord, Massachusetts. She was left a widow a second time in 1813. Most of the captain's possessions were sold at public auction and she was assigned half of his house as her widow's third.[7] She promptly mortgaged the building to Josiah Meriam for $129 and moved into the village to occupy part of the house at 47 Lexington Road. Falling upon hard times, in 1815 she persuaded Rev. Ezra Ripley to petition the Grand Lodge of Masons in Massachusetts for financial aid.[8]

Her father, Col. Elisha Jones, had lived in a fine old mansion in Weston, Massachusetts. He owned land in Adams, Pittsfield, Washington, Partridgefield, and Weston, Massachusetts, and was a slaveowner and an outspoken Loyalist. For ten years he represented his town in the Provincial Assembly and in January 1774 persuaded his townsmen to turn down Samuel Adams's plans for Committees of Correspondence and a Continental Congress. In May of that year he was chosen to represent the town at Governor Gage's Assembly, but with the growth of the revolutionary spirit in Weston, he soon lost his popularity and was forced to keep a military guard around his house for fear of being attacked. Eventually he took up residence in Boston under the protection of British troops. After his death in 1776, his estate was confiscated and eight of his sons were forced to flee into exile in Loyalist Canada, where several joined the British army. Henry David Thoreau thus came from a sturdy stock of men and women of principle who had the courage to stand up for their convictions even when they were in the minority.

III

John Thoreau, Henry's father, was born on Richmond Street in Boston, Massachusetts, on October 8, 1787, and moved to Concord with his father in 1800. After attending Lexington

6. Sanborn, *The Life of Henry David Thoreau,* 11–12
7. John Thoreau, Deed of Virginia Road property. MS, Morgan Library
8. Sanborn, *Henry D. Thoreau,* 10–11

Academy for a year, he entered Deacon White's store in Concord as a clerk, and later clerked for a time in Salem. When he came of age in 1808, he mortgaged his share of his father's estate to his stepmother for one thousand dollars and opened a store of his own next to the hill burying-ground on the town square in Concord; he lived in quarters above the store.[9] He prospered until he took in Isaac Hurd, a son of the local physician, as a partner. They soon quarreled and their partnership was dissolved with John Thoreau winning the case when the dissolution was challenged in court. For a time he tried selling things to the Indians in Bangor, Maine, with his brother-in-law, Caleb Billings, but then returned to Concord and on May 11, 1812, married Cynthia Dunbar. During the War of 1812 he was commissary at Fort Independence in Boston harbor, and later received a bounty of 160 acres for his services.[1] In 1814, in financial difficulties, he sold land adjacent to his mother-in-law's farm on Virginia Road, which he had purchased five years before.[2] Eventually he took over the management of the Jarvis store in Concord center.[3]

John Thoreau took great pleasure in music and often played the flute in the parish choir as a young man. He liked to read, particularly the classics, and handed many good books on to his son. He was active in the Concord Fire Society, a volunteer fire company, and in the early 1840s acted as its secretary. His neighbors thought of him as "an amiable and most lovable gentleman, but far too honest and scarcely sufficiently energetic for this exacting yet not over scrupulous world of ours."[4] His favorite occupation was to sit by the stove in his little shop and chat by the hour. Throughout his married life he lived quietly, peacefully, and contentedly in the shadow of his wife, who towered a full head above him.

He was a quiet mousey sort of man and there is little evidence that he had much direct influence on his famous son. The two

9. John Thoreau, Deed to Rebecca Thoreau, Concord, Mass., October 11, 1808. MS, Massachusetts Historical Society
1. Sophia Thoreau, Letter to George M. Brooks, March 15, [1871]. MS, Concord Free Public Library
2. Jonas Minott, Documents pertaining to division of estate of. MS, Concord Free Public Library
3. Leonard Jarvis, Letter of June 24, 1818. MS copy, Mrs. Caleb Wheeler
4. Irving Allen, "American Women to Whom the World is Indebted," *Independent*, XLVII (1895), 988

got along together well enough on the surface, but they had little understanding of each other's interests. Their relationship was one based more on toleration than on enthusiasm.

Mrs. Thoreau, however, was a much more dynamic person and she dominated not only her meek spouse, but, to a certain extent, the whole household. She had been born just thirty days before the death of her father in Keene, New Hampshire, on May 28, 1787. She moved to Concord with her mother and stepfather in 1798, and later often recalled for her son her quiet childhood on the Virginia Road farm. She had the reputation among her neighbors of being an excellent mother and housewife.[5] In the midst of poverty she brought up her children to all the amenities of life and it was said that "if she had but a crust of bread for dinner, she would see that it was properly served."[6] Poor as they were, each year at both Thanksgiving and Christmas she invited her poorer neighbors in for dinner. Throughout her life she showed compassion for the downtrodden, whether Negro, Indian, or white. Always active in the affairs of the town, in 1825 she joined the Concord Female Charitable Society (the "chattables" as her son Henry called them), which devoted itself to the care of the town's needy, and later served as its vice-president. She was also a member of the Bible Society and a founder of the Concord Women's Anti-Slavery Society. She saw to it that the family took its part in the social life of the village and often entertained with parties and sociables for the young people of the church or the town.

Mrs. Thoreau had a strong personality. The town shopkeepers learned that if they sent her anything but the best butter and flour, she would promptly return it. She never took a second grade of anything willingly.[7] She was noted for speaking her mind frankly, particularly when she thought some moral issue was at question. She was a born reformer, and reformers are not always the easiest people to live with. There were numerous persons in Concord, her son's two biographers Ellery Channing and Frank Sanborn among them, who could not abide her and did not hesitate to say so. They complained that her tongue wagged from morning till night. There is

---

5. Edward Emerson, Notes on Thoreau. MS, Raymond Emerson
6. Mrs. Jean Le Brun, "Henry Thoreau's Mother," *Boston Daily Advertiser*, February 14, 1883
7. Edward Emerson, Notes on Thoreau

no question about it; she was a born talker, but all agreed she was neither mean nor malicious.

She and her husband had a common interest in nature, an interest they were later to share with all their children. In the early days of their marriage they could often be found in their spare time, at almost any season of the year, exploring the banks of the Assabet, the cliffs at Fairhaven, or the shores of Walden Pond. One of their children, it is said, narrowly escaped being born on Lee's Hill, the site of one of their favorite rambles.[8]

As Mrs. Thoreau grew older, she developed a regal presence that many who knew her commented upon. Old Dr. Shattuck used to say, "Cynthia would have graced a court if she had been born to it."[9] And there are many hints that she often wished her social position higher than it was. Her husband's quiet, easygoing ways did not bring her the status she sought. But she was not an ungrateful woman, and there is every indication that theirs was a happy marriage.

Henry was the third of the four children of John and Cynthia Thoreau. Helen, the eldest, was born on October 22, 1812, a short five months after her parents' marriage. She was so quiet and retiring that few seem to have remembered her. Apparently she shared some of Henry's intellectual interests, because his few extant letters to her are more concerned with books and learning than those to other members of the family. After attending Concord Academy, she taught for a time in both Taunton, Massachusetts, and in Roxbury. Later she gave music lessons and taught painting in Concord, where the parents of her pupils are said to have particularly valued her "as an example of politeness" to their children.[1]

John, Junior, born in 1815, has been aptly described as "his father turned inside out."[2] He had charm and geniality—characteristics possessed by few of the Thoreaus—and an easy gregariousness. Although he displayed some intellectual interests, he lacked the deep seriousness of his younger brother. It was John who first

8. Jones, *Thoreau: A Glimpse* (Concord, 1903), 31
9. Sarah Storer, Letter to T. W. Higginson of October 18, 1891. MS, Raymond Adams
1. Sanborn, *The Life of Henry David Thoreau*, 197
2. Edward Emerson, *Henry Thoreau as Remembered by a Young Friend* (Boston, 1917), 125

showed an interest in ornithology and Henry later learned much of his bird lore from John's notebooks. Interestingly enough, most of Concord thought John the more promising of the two Thoreau boys.

Henry Thoreau, as has been said, was born on his maternal grandmother's farm on Virginia Road. Mrs. Minott had repaid the mortgage and Henry's father, still in financial difficulties, was attempting to run the farm and manage the Jarvis's store as well. His health however had deteriorated under the strain and he often found himself unable to walk the two miles into the village to the store.[3] To add to his troubles, Joseph Hurd, who had already exacted exorbitant fees in his years as executor of the Thoreau family estate, now demanded further compensation for the final settlement. Only a few weeks after Henry's birth, his father was forced to sign over his share in the family home in Boston that he had mortgaged years before. It is said that in his proud honesty he even sold his gold wedding ring to satisfy his creditors.[4]

Six weeks after Henry's birth, his twenty-three-year-old paternal uncle David Thoreau died. And so when the three-month-old baby was christened on October 12, 1817, by Rev. Ezra Ripley of the First Parish Church, he was named David Henry—a name he was to reverse when he reached maturity.[5] Proud of his early stoicism, Henry often boasted in later years that he did not cry at the ceremony.

In March of 1818 his father gave up the farm on Virginia Road (a few months later the Virginia Road house was sold by court order to settle the Minott estate) and moved his family into the village, renting from Josiah Davis the western half of the "Red House" at 201 Lexington Road in which his mother-in-law resided.[6] Here at the age of fourteen months Henry was taught to walk by his Aunt Sarah Thoreau and was tossed by a cow as he played near the door in a red flannel dress.

In the fall of 1818 John Thoreau, improved in health, determined to go into business for himself once again. He rented the

3. Jarvis, Letter of June 24, 1818
4. Marble, *Thoreau: His Home, Friends and Books*, 36
5. Hubert H. Hoeltje, "Thoreau in Concord Church and Town Records," *New England Quarterly*, XII (1939), 350
6. *Middlesex Gazette & Advertiser*, September 19, 1818

Proctor house next to the church in Chelmsford, a tiny village about ten miles north of Concord, and armed with a certificate from Rev. Ezra Ripley stating that he had sustained a good character and correct morals and was "a man of integrity accustomed to store-keeping," he rented Spaulding's shop there on November 10, 1818, and five days later opened a grocery store.[7] Cynthia Thoreau waited on customers while her husband painted signs and dealt out liquor.

Of his Chelmsford days, Henry recalled chopping off his toe with an axe he had picked up when no one was looking, being knocked over by a hen with its chickens, the bursting of a bladder his brother John was playing with on the hearth, a cow wandering into the entry after pumpkins, and falling down the stairs and faint-ing. "It took two pails of water to bring me to," he boasted, "for I was remarkable for holding my breath in those cases."[8]

He was much distressed by thunderstorms as a child and in-sisted on taking refuge in his father's room, announcing, "I don't feel well." But his health improved rapidly as soon as he felt his father's reassuring arms around him. When he was three or four years old he announced, coming in from coasting, that he did not want to die and go to heaven, because he could not carry his sled to so fine a place, for the boys had told him that it was not shod with iron and so not worth a cent.[9] He and his brother John slept to-gether in a trundlebed. John would go to sleep at once, but Henry often lay long awake. When his mother once found him so, she asked, "Why, Henry dear, don't you go to sleep?" "Mother," he replied, "I have been looking through the stars to see if I could see God behind them."[1]

Sophia, the youngest member of the family, was born in Chelmsford, Massachusetts, on June 24, 1819. After attending Phoebe Wheeler's dame school and studying Latin at the Concord Academy, she too later taught school. Fond of music, she sang and played the piano well, and dabbled in painting. But her only known extant attempt at portraiture—that of her brother John in the Concord Antiquarian Society—reveals her to have been a rank amateur. (Reportedly, she also did a portrait of Henry, but if she

7. Sanborn, Henry D. Thoreau, 26–7; Thoreau, *Journal*, VIII, 65; Sanborn, *The Life of Henry David Thoreau*, 34
8. Thoreau, *Journal*, VIII, 93–4
9. Sanborn, *Henry D. Thoreau*, 49
1. Edward Emerson, Notes on Thoreau

Thoreau in 1856
From a daguerreotype by B. W. Maxham

Thoreau in 1854
From a crayon portrait from life by Samuel Worcester Rowse

did, it has apparently disappeared—which may be just as well.) A number of her sketches in watercolor and in oil have been preserved, and pleasant sentimental bits they are. She was especially fond of flowers, filling the home with potted plants, the yard with flower gardens, and a herbarium with pressed specimens. She had many of her mother's qualities and like her was remembered as one of the greatest talkers ever seen. But she was also remembered as a vital and fascinating woman who "possessed charm far ahead of any possible beauty."[2]

She, like her brother, was quite capable of genuine independence of thought and action. She is known to have marched out of church rather than accept communion when she could not believe in it.[3] After the death of her father and the illness and death of Henry, she took over the family business and managed it capably herself for some years despite the then current prejudice against women in business. And it was she who loyally edited her brother's unpublished manuscripts after his death.

John Thoreau, Sr., conducted the Chelmsford store for a little more than two years. But this venture was no more successful than his earlier tries at storekeeping and he closed up shop on March 21, 1821. His business flaw was apparently his good nature. He did not have the heart to turn down anyone's request to purchase on credit and he could not bring himself to insist that the bills be paid.

Once again he was impelled to move his family. This time he decided to try his fortune in his native Boston, but tarried first for a while in Concord once more. By late spring the family was living in Mr. Pope's house, a "ten-footer" in the South End of Boston, and then on September 10 they moved to the Whitewell house at 4 Pinckney Street. For a time at least, Thoreau's father taught in a school at 6 Cornhill Court.[4] And Thoreau himself, at the age of five, started school.

While they were living in Boston, Thoreau, brought out to Concord to visit his grandmother, paid his first remembered visit to Walden Pond. It became, he said:

---

2. Mabel Loomis Todd, *The Thoreau Family Two Generations Ago* (Berkeley Heights, N.J., 1958), 15
3. Mabel Loomis Todd, Diary for June 2, 1874. MS, Mrs. Walter Bingham
4. *Boston Directory for 1822*

. . . one of the most ancient scenes stamped on the tablets of my memory. . . . That sweet solitude my spirit seemed so early to require at once gave the preference to this recess among the pines, where almost sunshine and shadow were the only inhabitants that varied the scene, over that tumultuous and varied city, as if it had found its proper nursery.[5]

Thus, early did he associate Walden Pond with his happiest hours.

5. Thoreau, *Journal*, I, 380–1

CHAPTER TWO
(1823–1833)

I

AFTER so many years of misfortune in business, a turn for the better at last came for John Thoreau. Paradoxically, it was instigated by the most undependable of his relatives, his brother-in-law Charles Dunbar. Uncle Charles, a perennial bachelor, was born with wandering feet. He was constitutionally unable to hold a job for any length of time or even to stay put in one locale. It was said of him that when his stepfather, Jonas Minott, was anxious that he should cast a vote for Thomas Jefferson, Minott deeded him a small farm in a neighboring town to give him the right to vote there; and when after the election Minott asked for the deed back, Charles refused to give it up and with court approval held on to it for the rest of his life.[1]

So long as his mother was alive, Charles made his headquarters with her. But after her death in 1830, he moved in with the Thoreaus. He would stay with his sister's family for months on end and then would suddenly disappear. Weeks or even months later they would learn that he was cutting hay on a farm in northern Vermont or that he had been seen wandering through a village on the coast of Maine. Then one morning they would come down for breakfast and find him asleep by the kitchen stove, and for a few months he would be with them again. Henry reveled in his uncle's idiosyncracies and often jotted down anecdotes about him in his journal. It was Uncle Charles to whom Thoreau referred when in *Walden* he spoke of having an uncle "who goes to sleep shaving himself, and is obliged to sprout po-

---

1. William S. Robinson, *"Warrington" Pen-Portraits* (Boston, 1877), 69–70

tatoes in a cellar Sundays, in order to keep awake and keep the Sabbath."[2]

In 1821 Uncle Charles in his wanderings about New England stumbled upon a plumbago (i.e., graphite) deposit in the town of Bristol, New Hampshire, and staked out a claim. About ten years before, William Munroe of Concord had successfully manufactured the first American pencils. Although he had found great difficulty in producing a pencil that would write smoothly, Munroe eventually established a business so profitable that he gave up his regular profession of cabinetmaking.

Uncle Charles, in one of the few practical moments of his life, upon finding the mine decided to embark upon pencil manufacturing. With Cyrus Stow of Concord as a partner, he established the firm of Dunbar & Stow and began working the claim.[3] So good was the quality of their graphite that James Freeman Dana, Professor of Chemistry and Mineralogy at Dartmouth College,[4] and a Dr. Mitchell of New York City both issued certificates stating that it was far superior to graphite found anywhere else in the United States.[5] But unfortunately Uncle Charles soon reverted to type. In staking his claims he neglected to file all the necessary papers. Instead of obtaining permanent mineral rights to the land, he obtained mining rights for only seven years. His lawyer, Samuel Hoar of Concord, wisely advised him to mine all he could before the time was up.[6] It was perhaps for this reason that John Thoreau was soon asked to move back to Concord from Boston and join the business.

In March 1823 John Thoreau established his family in a brick house (since torn down) on the corner of Main and Walden Streets. The pencil-making business was conducted until 1830 in a little shop which now forms the ell of the house on the southwest corner of Walden and Everett Streets. Stow, for some unknown reason, dropped out of the business and was followed soon after by Uncle Charles. The firm was then renamed John Thoreau & Co. By 1824 he had so improved the quality of his pencils that

2. Henry David Thoreau, *Writings* (Boston, 1906), II, 285
3. Social Circle in Concord, *Memoirs* (Boston, 1882–1940), II, 297–8
4. *Middlesex Observer*, November 9, 1822
5. J. Farmer and J. B. Moore, *Collections, Historical and Miscellaneous* (Concord, N. H., 1823), II, 30–1
6. Social Circle in Concord, *Memoirs*, II, 297–8

he received a special citation from the Massachusetts Agricultural Society and he began to find a steady market for their sale. Slowly over the years they managed to build up a firmer financial footing no longer chronically threatened by bankruptcy.

By the early 1830s the Munroes began to feel the Thoreau competition. Both firms had their plumbago ground at Ebenezer Wood's mill in nearby Acton. Munroe, who had originally established Wood in the business, tried to persuade him to boycott the Thoreaus, but the scheme backfired because the Thoreaus were the more lucrative customers and the mill went into their sole employ. There are rumors that the Munroes then filed suit against the Thoreaus for theft of their pencil-lead formula, but the suit, if brought, was apparently unsuccessful. The Thoreau business continued to prosper and the Munroes turned to other fields. When the Thoreaus were no longer able to obtain graphite from the Bristol mine, they found a new source of supply in the Tudor mine at Sturbridge, Massachusetts. And when that mine eventually closed, they turned to importing graphite from Canada. E. Harris and Hugh Cash of Acton, Hayward's Mill in Factory Village, and Warren Miles at a mill on Nut Meadow Brook later did the grinding for them.[7]

II

Once he was re-established in his native Concord, young Henry Thoreau settled down to the life typical of any small-town American boy of the early nineteenth century. He was enrolled in Miss Phoebe Wheeler's private "infant" school, kept in the old Peter Wheeler home, an unpainted, weather-beaten house in the shade of the buttonwoods on Walden Street. There he learned his A B C's tied by his apron strings to Miss Wheeler's knee. When he was tired, he could take a nap on a made-up bed in the corner. If he were bad, he would be shut into a dark garret stairway for punishment. It was remembered that he once asked Miss Wheeler "Who owns all the land?" and that after he won a medal

7. Edward Emerson, Notes on Thoreau

for geography, he asked his mother "Is Boston in Concord?"[8] He thought that if he had remained at Miss Wheeler's a little longer he would have received the chief prize book—*Henry, Lord Mayor.*

From Miss Wheeler's Thoreau went on to the public grammar school, the brick schoolhouse (now the Masonic Hall) on the common where some years later he himself was to teach. The school was conducted in a packed little amphitheater of wooden benches facing the teacher's desk on three sides of the tiny first-floor room. Boys and girls of all grades and abilities were of course grouped together. The subjects of study were few and the work in large part was devoted to rote learning of passages from the Bible and such English classics as Shakespeare, Bunyan, Johnson, and the Essayists. When the public school was not in session (its school year was appallingly short), Mrs. Thoreau often sent her two boys to Phoebe Wheeler's school for girls to get a little extra learning.

Although Thoreau was by no means a poor scholar, many of his classmates considered him "stupid" and "unsympathetic" because he would not join their games.[9] They could not recollect his ever playing with them, for he preferred to stand on the sidelines and watch. He was so quiet and solemn that their favorite nickname for him was "Judge," but when they wanted to tease him, they called him "the fine scholar with the big nose."[1] His quietness stood out all the more because of the gaiety and gregariousness of his brother John, who would sit by the hour on the fence outside the schoolhouse and regale them all with stories and jokes until their sides ached from prolonged laughter. On the few occasions when Henry tried to match his brother's storytelling, the results were remembered as "most improbable."[2]

Henry early developed a reputation for Stoicism. When he took some pet chickens to the inn to sell, the innkeeper thoughtlessly wrung their necks before the poor boy's eyes, but he neither budged nor murmured.[3] When he was accused of stealing a knife

8. Henry David Thoreau, *Journal,* VIII, 94–5
9. A[lfred] M[unroe], "Concord Authors Continued," *Richmond County Gazette* [Stapleton, N. Y.], August 15, 1877
1. William Ellery Channing, *Thoreau, the Poet-Naturalist* (Boston, 1873), 11
2. A[lfred] M[unroe], "Concord Authors Continued"
3. Channing, *Thoreau, the Poet-Naturalist,* 11–12

from a schoolmate, he replied only, "I did not take it." When after a few days the culprit was found, he then said that he had known all the time who had taken it and that the day it was stolen he was in Newton with his father. When asked why he did not say so at the time he was accused, he replied quietly, "I did not take it." On another occasion a schoolmate complained that Henry would not whittle a bow and arrow for him though his whittling skill was known to be superior. Later it came out that the reason for his refusal was that he had no knife and did not want to admit it.

When Mrs. Samuel Hoar, the *grande dame* of Concord, invited him over to play with her children, he failed to appear. When his mother asked him how she could explain his absence, he replied, "Tell her because I did not want to."[4] Although other children flocked to watch the street parades and bands, he preferred to stay home, but in later years he was to recall vividly Lafayette's visit to Concord in 1824, and the semi-centennial celebration of the Concord Fight in 1825.[5]

He remembered even more vividly the occasional arrival of canal boats on the Concord River and joining his schoolmates along the banks to admire the barges with their loads of brick, iron ore, and wheelbarrows. To be invited upon their decks was an almost unbelievable thrill. He remembered too the joy of those rare occasions when he was permitted to stay home from school and spend the day picking huckleberries on a neighboring hill to make a pudding for the family dinner. Such days he thought "like the promise of life eternal."[6]

His mother, eager to foster a love of nature in her children, often took them out into the dooryard to call their attention to the songs of the wild birds. On bright afternoons she would gather them together and walk out to Nashawtuc Hill, the Cliffs at Fairhaven, or the "little woods" between the river and Main Street, and there, after building a rough fireplace, would cook their supper while they enjoyed the flowers and bird songs.[7] A chowder

4. Sarah Hosmer Lunt, "Memories of Concord." MS, Evald B. Lawson
5. Sanborn, *Henry D. Thoreau,* 47
6. Thoreau, *Journal,* II, 308
7. Edward Emerson, Notes on Thoreau

boiled on the Walden Pond sandbar when he was seven stood
out particularly in her son's mind.

Although the family was poor, their table was always attractive and the food abundant and appetizing. They often did without tea, coffee, sugar, and other luxuries, so that Mrs. Thoreau
could spend the little money they could spare on music lessons
for the girls. Henry regretted only that he often had to wear hand-
me-down or cut-down clothes and recalled that the pockets for his
pants made from his father's old fire-bags—the date of the forma-
tion of the society, 1794, still on them—were "rotten."[8]

The only days to be dreaded were the long Puritan Sundays,
which he was compelled to spend in the house without even the
aid of interesting books. He would then spend hours looking out
from an attic window at the martins soaring around their box. And
it was a thrill indeed when an occasional hawk appeared in the
heavens to take his thoughts, as he said, from earthly things.[9]

But earthly things were what he most remembered of his
youth—being kicked by a passing ox, catching an eel with his
brother John, trying to smoke dried pond-lily stems, proudly going
to bed with new boots and cap on, and peeping through a keyhole
at a pet chicken he was given to see that all was right. He recalled
finding a sprouting potato and, at his mother's suggestion, planting
it in the garden, only to have it dug up first by his brother and
then by his older sister to plant in their gardens. But when he protested volubly that he was the original discoverer of that particular potato, it was restored to his corner of the garden. And when
he dug it up in the fall, it provided a dinner for the whole
family.[1]

Years later he told his publisher, James T. Fields, of driving
the cows daily in his bare feet to a pasture out the Walden road
some distance from the village. He spoke particularly of a favorite
cow, and "if she had been his own grandmother," Fields said, "he
could not have employed tenderer phrases about her."[2]

8. Thoreau, *Journal*, X, 227
9. Ibid. III, 427
1. Ibid. VIII, 94–5
2. James T. Fields, "Our Poet-Naturalist," *Baldwin's Monthly*, April,
1877

III

The return to Concord meant a closer association with their kin for the Thoreaus. Henry's aunts Sarah and Betsey Thoreau continued to maintain the family homestead on the village square where they ran a genteel boarding house. One of their customs was to dip the sugar spoon in water so that more sugar would stick to the spoon than would fall in the boarders' cups.[3] Upon their deaths in 1829 and 1839 respectively, Aunt Sarah and Aunt Betsey each willed their nephew Henry ten dollars as tokens of their affection.[4]

Aunt Maria and Aunt Jane Thoreau maintained a home of their own, first in Boston and later in Cambridgeport, but they were frequent visitors in Concord and, as the years passed by, spent more and more of their time with their brother and his family. Aunt Jane has been remembered as "a saintly character with a placid and lovable nature, most winning to a child." Aunt Maria, on the other hand, was "a sharp and brilliant soul, a great talker, with very decided opinions upon religion, politics, and the world in general."[5] Like her sister-in-law Cynthia Thoreau, Aunt Maria had a deep social concern and was active in many "causes," particularly those devoted to anti-slavery. She was an inveterate, if ungrammatical, letter writer and her various correspondences that have survived add much to the vividness of our picture of the Thoreau household. Both Aunt Jane and Aunt Maria outlived their nephew. Indeed Aunt Maria, at her death in Bangor, Maine, in 1881, was the last remaining descendant of the John Thoreau who had immigrated to Boston in 1773.

Aunt Louisa Dunbar, Cynthia's maiden sister, joined the Thoreau household in 1830 when her mother died, and lived with them until her own death some years after Henry's. At the opposite pole from her brother Charles, she had been converted to Calvinism

---

3. Charles E. Brown, et al., *Complimentary Dinner to Mr. Thatcher Magoun*, (Concord, 1894)
4. Kenneth Walter Cameron, "The Thoreau Family in Probate Records," *Emerson Society Quarterly*, XI (1958), 17
5. Mabel Loomis Todd, *The Thoreau Family Two Generations Ago* (Berkeley Heights, N. J., 1958), 11–13

by Daniel Webster, who had wooed her unsuccessfully when she had taught in Boscawen, New Hampshire, in 1805–6, and continued to call on her whenever he visited Concord. She devoted most of her energies to "flitting away to some good meeting, to save the credit of you all," as Henry once reminded his family.[6]

Mrs. Thoreau, shortly after their arrival in Concord, and perhaps taking her cue from her sisters-in-law on the square, began to add boarders to her household to add to the family income. Occasionally she took in transients if they were recommended by someone she knew. Eventually she began to take in permanent boarders, such as Mrs. Joseph Ward and her daughter Prudence, who were old friends of Aunt Maria. Thus there was a constant stream of people through the Thoreau household. It was a rare occasion that the family was alone in its own home. At times the constant hubbub was unquestionably enervating and Sophia, Henry's sister, once complained to her diary that the din was "enough to drive a man to Nova Zembla for quiet."[7] But she would have been the first to admit that life there was rarely dull.

Certainly, despite the interruptions of boarders and visitors, the Thoreaus were a closely knit family. There was a warmth about it to give the young Henry and his brothers and sisters the feeling of security so essential to a happy childhood. There has only recently come to light a letter written by brother John about the family Christmas traditions that gives us a good insight into the family circle:

> When I was a little boy I was told to hang my clean stocking with those of my brother and sister in the chimney corner the night before Christmas, and that "Santa Claus," a very good sort of sprite, who rode about in the air upon a broomstick (an odd kind of horse I think) would come down the chimney in the night, and fill our stockings if we had been good children, with dough-nuts, sugar plums and all sorts of nice things; but if we had been naughty we found in the stocking only a rotten

6. Henry David Thoreau, *Correspondence* (New York, 1958), 131
7. George Hendrick, "Pages from Sophia Thoreau's Journal," *Thoreau Society Bulletin,* LXI (1957), I

potato, a letter and a rod. I got the rotten potato once, had the
letter read to me, and was very glad that the rod put into the
stocking was too short to be used. And so we got something every
year until one Christmas day we asked a girl at school what
"Santa Claus" had left her the night before, but she did not
understand us, and when we told her about all the nice things
which he had left us, and showed her some candy, she said she
did not believe it; that our mother had purchased the candy at
her father's shop the night before, for she saw her. We ran
home as fast as we could scud to enquire about it, and learned
that what the girl had said was true, that there was no "Santa
Claus," and that our mother had put all those good things into
our stockings. We were very sorry, I assure you, and we have
not hung up our stockings since, and "Santa Claus" never gives
us anything now . . .

I determined one night to sit up until morning that I might get
a sight at [Santa Claus] when he came down the chimney. . . . I
got a little cricket and sat down by the fireplace looking sharp up
into the chimney, and there I sat about an hour later than my
usual bed time, I suppose, when I fell asleep and was carried off
to bed before I knew anything about it. So I have never seen
him, and don't know what kind of a looking fellow he was.[8]

In the spring of 1826 John Thoreau moved his family once more.
This time it was to the Davis house, a large white frame house
(now number 166) next to Samuel Hoar's on Main Street. Almost
exactly a year later they moved across the street to the Shattuck
house, another large white frame building, where they settled
down for the remarkably long period—for the Thoreaus, at least—
of eight years.

IV

In 1826, for the first time in its peaceful history, the town
of Concord was split by a schism in its church. For some years
many of the leaders of the Congregational churches throughout

8. John Thoreau, Jr., Letter to George Sewall of December 31, 1839.
MS, George L. Davenport, Jr.

New England had been gradually moving from Trinitarianism to Unitarianism under the benevolent leadership of William Ellery Channing of Boston. Ezra Ripley had made the change in Concord, but so gradually and so gently that many of his parishioners were hardly aware that any such change had been made. First he persuaded them to drop the shorter catechism and then the doctrine of the Trinity from the church creed. But in 1826 the stricter Calvinists in the church finally protested by withdrawing and forming a Trinitarian Church of their own. On May 7, nine members petitioned to be dismissed from the First Parish Church; among them were three of Thoreau's aunts—Elizabeth, Jane, and Maria Thoreau. For two weeks the church postponed action, hoping that the nine would reconsider, but on the 21st it grievingly complied.[9] On June 5, the new Trinitarian Congregational Church in Concord was formed at a council with the Reverend Lyman Beecher of fire and brimstone notoriety presiding, and the three Thoreau sisters signed as charter members. When a ladies sewing society was formed for the new church in 1828, it held its first meeting as guests of Maria Thoreau.[1]

Thoreau's parents were caught in the very center of the controversy. Cynthia had joined Dr. Ripley's church in 1811. Her husband apparently had never formally joined the church, but he acted as an agent for his sisters and advertised, unsuccessfully, their pew—No. 43 "pleasantly situated on the lower floor"—for sale in the Yeoman's Gazette for three months beginning July 15, 1826. Three years later, on September 26, 1829, he again started advertising it for sale in the same paper, and again was unsuccessful. Finally, on November 20, 1832, he purchased it from them for $75.00, and the next day sold it to Nathan Brooks for $99.49.[2]

On April 22, 1827, Cynthia, won over by her sisters-in-law, requested permission to transfer her membership to the Trinitarian society, and the church voted to comply. But to her chagrin and dismay, the Trinitarians refused to accept her; apparently either she was unwilling to accept verbatim their orthodoxy or

9. Hubert H. Hoeltje, "Thoreau in Concord Church and Town Records," New England Quarterly, XII (1939), 350–2
1. H. M. Grout, Trinitarian Congregationalism in Concord (Boston, 1876), 21
2. First Parish Church in Concord, MS records

they were unwilling to accept her staunch independence.[3] She returned to the First Parish fold and Ezra Ripley, who had been deeply hurt by the schism in his church, noted in the margin of the parish records, with some satisfaction:

Our sister Cynthia Thoreau changed her mind, and did not offer herself for communion with the Trinitarian church, and is still a member in this church. Notice of this given by the pastor, July 6, 1828.[4]

Mrs. Thoreau remained faithful to the First Parish Church for the rest of her days.

V

"I was fitted, or rather made unfit, for college, at Concord Academy & elsewhere, mainly by myself, with the countenance of Phineas Allen, Preceptor," Thoreau wrote to his college class secretary in 1847.[5]

In 1822, four of the more prominent citizens of Concord—Col. William Whiting, Samuel Hoar, Dr. Abiel Heywood, and Nathan Brooks—dissatisfied with the public schools of the town, had joined together in establishing the Concord Academy. At the cost of twenty-four hundred dollars they purchased land and erected a schoolhouse on what is now Academy Lane. It was planned primarily as a college preparatory school for boys, but girls were permitted to attend. Among the early instructors was Richard Hildreth, later to achieve renown as a historian. Phineas Allen became the instructor in the fall of 1827. Born in 1801 in Medfield, Massachusetts, he had graduated from Harvard in 1825 and taught in Brookline for two years before going to Concord. He remained in charge of the Concord Academy for eight years, and resigned under fire when he alienated the school's proprietors in 1834 by being elected town clerk on the Anti-

---

3. Edward Emerson, Notes on Thoreau
4. Hoeltje, "Thoreau in Concord Church and Town Records," 349
5. Thoreau, *Correspondence,* 186

Masonic ticket.[6] In 1836 he left Concord and taught elsewhere in Massachusetts for the rest of his long life.

Allen was said to have been "a perfect encyclopedia of information to all inquiring minds" with "an exact knowledge of five languages besides English" and one "whose every thought seemed given to the pursuit or giving of knowledge."[7] It was his announced intention as a teacher to be a shining example of all those things he wished his pupils to be. The ideal instructor he thought, should be neat, conscientious, obliging, polite, mild, gentle, patient, forbearing, and always smiling.[8] But unfortunately his practice did not always keep up to his theory and one of his pupils, John Shepard Keyes, thought Allen kept the worst school he ever knew anything about, adding that he had studied seven long years under him without learning anything.[9] Thoreau's own opinion of Allen, though not enthusiastic, was not as harsh as Keyes's.

Thoreau and his brother John were enrolled in the Concord Academy under Allen's tutelage in the fall of 1828, when Thoreau was eleven. Allen seems to have boarded with the Thoreaus for a time—probably a factor in the brothers' enrollment in the school. But even more important, undoubtedly, was Cynthia Thoreau's abiding desire that her children receive the best possible education within their reach—even though the tuition fee of five dollars a quarter per pupil must have loomed large in the family budget of the time.

Allen's emphasis in the curriculum was on the classics and he taught Virgil, Sallust, Cicero, Caesar, Euripides, Homer, Xenophon, Voltaire, Molière, and Racine in the original languages as well as geography, history, grammar, spelling, astronomy, botany, algebra, trigonometry, geometry, natural philosophy, and natural history. Allen took a particular interest in composition and required frequent themes. Among the few papers from the school that have survived is one by Thoreau, probably written when he was eleven or twelve, which has never been collected into his works:

6. Gladys Hosmer, "Phineas Allen, Thoreau's Preceptor," *Thoreau Society Bulletin*, LIX (1957), I
7. Ibid.
8. *Concord Freeman*, September 21, 1838
9. Social Circle in Concord, *Memoirs*, V, 73

THE SEASONS

Why do the seasons change? and why
Does Winter's stormy brow appear?
Is it the word of him on high,
Who rules the changing varied year.

There are four seasons in a year, Spring, Summer, Autumn, and
Winter, I will begin with Spring. Now we see the ice beginning
to thaw, and the trees to bud. Now the Winter wears away, and
the ground begins to look green with the new born grass. The
birds which have lately been to more southern countries return
again to cheer us with their morning song.

Next comes Summer. Now we see a beautiful sight. The trees
and flowers are in bloom. Now is the pleasantest part of the year.
Now the fruit begins to form on the trees, and all things look
beutiful.

In Autumn we see the trees loaded with fruit. Now the farmers
begin to lay in their Winter's store, and the markets abound with
fruit. The trees are partly stripped of their leavs. The birds
whith visited us in Spring are now retireing to warmer countries, as they know that Winter is coming.

Next comes Winter. Now we see the ground covered with snow,
and the trees are bare. The cold is so intense that the rivers and
brooks are frozen.

There is nothing to be seen. We have no birds to cheer us
with their morning song. We hear only the sound of the sleigh
bells.[1]

Despite the weaknesses in spelling, this little essay gives ample
indication of the direction in which the young Thoreau's interests
had already turned and which he was to follow the rest of his life.

The end of each twelve-week quarter in the Concord Academy
was marked by declamatory exercises. Thoreau regularly participated and among his recitations were such pieces as Croly's "The
Death of Leonidas," "Lines written in 1821 on hearing that the
Austrians had entered Naples" by Moore, Everett's oration at Plymouth, Massachusetts, Wirt's letter from the *British Spy,* Sheridan's
"Sir Anthony and Captain Absolute," Shakespeare's "Prince Henry
and Falstaff," Bonaparte's "Address to his Army" and the "Speech

---

1. Henry David Thoreau, *The Seasons* (Ysleta, Texas, n.d.)

in the National Convention of France." Thoreau was among the
few to receive his instructor's commendation of "Good."[2]

As an extracurricular activity, Allen organized the Concord
Academic Debating Society. Here again young Thoreau participated
frequently, but hardly covered himself with glory. On October 9,
1829, taking the affirmative, he lost a debate with Rockwood Hoar
on the topic "Does it require more talents to make a good writer
than a good extemporaneous speaker?" The secretary, George
Moore, recorded that "the debate was not very animated on account
of some misunderstanding of the question."[3] On November 5, taking
the negative, Thoreau debated Edward Wright on "Is a good
memory preferable to a good understanding in order to be a distinguished scholar at school?" The secretary complained:

> The affirmative disputant through negligence, had prepared
> nothing for debate, and the negative not much more. Accord-
> ingly . . . the President decided in the Neg. . . . Such a debate,
> if it may be called so, as we have had, this evening, I hope never
> again will be witnessed in this house or recorded in this book.
> It is not only a waste of *time,* but of paper to record such pro-
> ceedings, of wood and oil.[4]

On December 17, Moore being absent, Thoreau was chosen
secretary pro tem. But he did no better in his recording than in his
debating and Moore complained when he returned that Thoreau
"neglecting to perform his duty by recording the proceedings, it
falls to the lot of the Sec. to record, by hearsay, what was done."[5]
On December 24, Moore, J. G. Davis, and Thoreau, taking the
negative, debated Edward Wright and Rockwood Hoar on "Ought
lotteries to be granted for any use?" and won.[6] It was Thoreau's
last appearance before the Concord Academic Debating Society, for
a month later it was disbanded, having been superseded by the newly
founded Concord Lyceum.

---

2. Hubert H. Hoeltje, "Thoreau and the Concord Academy," *New
England Quarterly,* XXI (1948), 105–6
3. Cameron, "Young Henry Thoreau in the Annals of the Concord
Academy," *Emerson Society Quarterly,* IX (1957), 6
4. Ibid.
5. Ibid. 7–8
6. Ibid. 8

The Concord Lyceum was not limited to students in the academy, but was open to all the townsfolk, young and old.[7] The lyceum movement had started in the mid-1820s chiefly through the efforts of Josiah Holbrook. It was a pioneer attempt at community education, and its activities centered chiefly around lectures and debates on scientific, moral, and historical topics in those small locales that had little other intellectual stimulus and outlet. The lectures at first were given chiefly by local talent, although as the movement grew neighboring lyceums began to exchange speakers, and eventually complex lecture circuits were established. Thoreau himself in later years was to find the lyceum both a source of income and, more important, an opportunity to be heard.

The Concord Lyceum, destined to be one of the largest, strongest, and longest-lived of all the lyceums, was established on January 7, 1829, with fifty-seven charter members under the leadership of Rev. Ezra Ripley. In the course of the next half century it sponsored 784 lectures, 105 debates, and 14 concerts. Just when Thoreau joined the lyceum is not known; its early membership lists are no longer extant. But it seems likely that he started attending meetings as soon as it was established, for there is ample evidence that the children of the community attended.[8] And Thoreau, even in childhood, was never one to neglect such an opportunity for learning more about the world around him. The numerous lectures he heard on geology, botany, and ornithology—for Concord even more than the typical New England town of the day was blessed with numerous citizens actively interested in natural history—undoubtedly were an important factor in developing just such interests in Thoreau himself.

Among Thoreau's schoolmates at the Concord Academy were a surprisingly large number who later achieved prominence. George Heywood served seven terms in the Massachusetts legislature and as a member of the governor's council. Rockwood Hoar became a justice of the Massachusetts Supreme Judicial Court and Attorney

---

7. Charles H. Walcott, *Semi-Centennial Proceedings of the Fiftieth Anniversary of the Organization of the Concord Lyceum* (Concord, 1879) Ibid. 10
8. Walter Harding, "Thoreau and the Concord Lyceum," *Thoreau Society Bulletin*, XXX (1950), 2

General in Grant's cabinet; his brother, George Frisbie Hoar, a United States Senator. John Shepard Keyes, judge of the Middlesex District Court and a founder of the Republican Party, was a United States marshal who protected Lincoln on the occasion of the Gettysburg Address, and Moses Prichard, a distinguished lawyer in New York City. Edward J. Stearns, who boarded for a time with the Thoreau family, taught at St. John's College in Annapolis, Maryland.[9] And William Whiting was Solicitor General for the War Department during the Civil War, a presidential elector in 1868, and a member of the United States Congress. But closest to Thoreau of all his schoolmates was Charles Stearns Wheeler, a native of nearby Lincoln who attended the district school in Lincoln winters and the Concord Academy in milder seasons.[1] The two quickly struck up a friendship which was to continue on into their college years.

Wheeler, now almost forgotten, was once thought of by Emerson and his friends as one of the most promising of the younger Transcendentalists. After graduating from Harvard, he replaced the eccentric Jones Very as a tutor of Greek there. Later he edited the works of both Thomas Carlyle and Tennyson for their first publication in America. In 1842 he went abroad to do graduate work in the German universities, but contracted gastric fever and died in Leipzig in June 1843 at the age of twenty-six.

For the most part Thoreau made little impression on his schoolmates—and they little on him. One thought Thoreau "an odd stick, not very studious or devoted in his lessons, but a thoughtful youth and very fond of reading . . . not given to play or to fellowship with the boys; but shy and silent."[2] On the other hand, it has been reported that the boys used to assemble about Thoreau as he sat on the school fence to hear him talk.[3]

Thoreau himself was seemingly more interested in the outdoors than in school and spent all his spare time in Concord's woods and meadows and on her rivers and ponds. He was known among the

---

9. Cameron, "Memorabilia of Thoreau's Concord Academy Friends," *Emerson Society Quarterly*, XI (1958), 41
1. John Olin Eidson, *Charles Stearns Wheeler: Friend of Emerson* (Athens, Ga., 1951), 4
2. George W. Cooke, "The Two Thoreaus," *Independent*, XLVIII (1896), 1671
3. William Ellery Channing, *Thoreau, the Poet-Naturalist*, 5

boys of his age as the one "who did not fear mud or water, nor paused to lift his followers over the ditch."[4] Despite his later qualms about the use of rod and gun, he was an ardent sportsman as a youth and thought "few tools to be compared with a gun for efficiency and compactness." He boasted that he could carry a gun in his hand all day on a journey and not feel it to be heavy, though he did not use it once.[5]

In the summer of 1833, after his last quarter at the Academy, he devoted his spare time to the building of his first boat, a rowboat christened "The Rover," and in it further explored the ponds and rivers of Concord.[6] He spent, as he said, many an hour floating over Walden Pond's surface as the zephyr willed, paddling his boat to the middle and then, lying on his back across the seats, dreaming awake until he was aroused by the boat's touching the sand and he arose to see what shores the fates had impelled him to. On such days, he thought, "idleness was the most attractive and productive industry."[7]

---

4. Ibid. 6
5. Henry David Thoreau, *The First and Last Journeys* (Boston, 1905), I, xviii; Edward Emerson, Notes on Thoreau
6. William Ellery Channing, *Thoreau, the Poet-Naturalist,* 13
7. Thoreau, *Writings,* II, 213

CHAPTER THREE
(1833–1837)

I

With the completion of his schooling in the Concord Academy, it was decided that Thoreau should go on to Harvard College. He himself was not particularly enthusiastic about the venture.[1] Since he was so adept with his hands, the family for a time talked of apprenticing him to a carpenter instead. But Cynthia Thoreau was anxious that at least one of her sons follow in her father's footsteps and matriculate at Harvard. And despite the fact that their contemporaries thought John the more promising of the two, it was unquestionably Henry who was the more scholarly. Besides, the family pencil business was now beginning to prosper; Helen and John could contribute from their schoolteaching salaries; and even the aunts promised to help out of their small incomes. Total expenses, according to the college catalog, would come to about $179.00 a year. Through scraping and skimping the family could handle that.

Thoreau took his entrance examinations in the summer of 1833 and barely squeezed through. He was conditioned in Greek, Latin, and mathematics.[2] (In fairness to Thoreau it should be noted that better than ninety per cent of the students were conditioned in at least one subject.) "One branch more," President Quincy, who conducted the examinations, warned him, "one branch more, and you had been turned by entirely. You have barely got in."[3] But get in he did and on August 30, 1833, he and Charles Stearns Wheeler journeyed the fifteen miles to Cambridge, moved into Hollis Hall 20 and settled down as roommates.

1. Annie Russell Marble, *Thoreau: His Home, Friends and Books*, 60
2. Harvard University Admissions Records. MS, Widener Library
3. Kenneth Walter Cameron, "The Solitary Thoreau of the Alumni Notes," *Emerson Society Quarterly*, VII (1957), 2

Harvard College in those days consisted chiefly of that small group of ancient brick buildings that still stand on the west side of the yard along Massachusetts Avenue, just north of Harvard Square. It included Massachusetts Hall for classes, Hollis, Holworthy, and Stoughton Halls for dormitories, Harvard Hall for the library, and the chapel. Cambridge itself was still a small, almost rural town, its streets lined with elms, lindens, and horse chestnuts. Open fields and woods were only a short distance off in * almost any direction one wandered.

Josiah Quincy had become president of Harvard in 1829. For many years a representative to Congress and later a reform mayor of Boston, he had been brought to Harvard to rescue it from a precarious financial position. He quickly became notorious among the undergraduates for fostering an intricate marking system whereby instructors granted points for class and chapel attendance, recitations, and compositions, and deducted them for misbehavior. The system put a premium on memory work and passive acceptance of the status quo, while it discouraged discussion or even lectures and generally made the class periods inordinately dull under any but the most inspired teachers. So strong were the feelings of the students against this system that in March 1834 all four classes unsuccessfully petitioned the faculty to abolish it because it "fostered jealousy" and "encouraged superficial scholarship." Thoreau was one of the thirty-eight members of his class to sign the petition.[4]

Harvard's faculty in Thoreau's day numbered only thirty-five. But it included such distinguished figures as Cornelius Conway Felton, professor of Greek and later president of Harvard (he later remembered Thoreau as "a scholar of talent, but of such pertinacious oddity in literary matters, that his writings will never probably do him any justice"[5]); Charles Beck, professor of Latin and a political refugee from Germany who has been termed largely responsible for introducing German scholarship into American colleges; Benjamin Peirce, professor of astronomy and mathematics, generally recognized as the leading American mathematician of his day; Henry Ware, who had once been Ralph Waldo Emerson's colleague in the ministry of the Second Church in Boston and

4. Kenneth Walter Cameron, "Freshman Thoreau Opposes Harvard's Marking System," *Emerson Society Quarterly*, VIII (1957), 17–18
5. Walter Harding, "Thoreau's Professor Has His Say," *Thoreau Society Bulletin*, XLVI (1954), 3

who taught the required undergraduate theology courses (Thoreau thought sufficiently well of him that when he came to Concord on November 4, 1840, to preach at the First Parish Church, Thoreau attended—one of the rare occasions in his adult years that he went inside a church); Henry Wadsworth Longfellow, who joined the faculty as professor of the French and Spanish languages and literatures in the spring of Thoreau's senior year (Thoreau dropped
✱ out of his seminar in German after only a few meetings); Thaddeus William Harris, college librarian, whose extracurricular interest in entomology soon attracted Thoreau's attention and who became a lifelong friend (Harris once complained that Thoreau would have been a splendid entomologist if Emerson had not spoiled him[6]); and Edward Tyrrell Channing, professor of rhetoric and oratory, brother of Rev. William Ellery Channing, uncle of Thoreau's later friend Ellery Channing, and the teacher of a remarkable list of outstanding writers including Emerson, Lowell, Holmes, Edward Everett Hale, Thomas Wentworth Higginson, Charles Sumner, James Freeman Clarke, and Richard Henry Dana, Jr.

Harvard in Thoreau's day presented a program of studies that
✱ had been little modified since pre-Revolutionary days. The emphasis was primarily on classics and the training was perhaps better for theology than for any other profession. Thoreau studied Greek (composition, grammar, "Greek antiquities," Xenophon, Demosthenes, Aeschines, Sophocles, Euripides, and Homer) under Cornelius Felton and Christopher Dunkin for eight of his eleven terms in college; Latin grammar for eight terms (composition, "Latin antiquities," Livy, Horace, Cicero, Seneca, and Juvenal) under Charles Beck and Henry S. McKean; mathematics for seven terms (geometry, algebra, plane trigonometry, analytic geometry, topography, differential and integral calculus, mechanics, optics, electricity, magnetism, and electromagnetism) with Benjamin Peirce and Joseph Lovering; history, three terms; English, eight terms (grammar, rhetoric, logic, forensics, criticism, elocution, declamations, and themes) with Edward Tyrrell Channing assisted by Joel Giles, William Simmons and George Simmons; and courses in mental philosophy (Paley and Stewart) with Joel Giles; natural philosophy (astronomy) with Joseph Lovering; intellectual phi-

---

6. Joseph Wade, "Friendship of Two Old-time Naturalists," *Scientific Monthly*, XXIII (1926), 152

losophy (Locke, Say, and Story) with Francis Bowen; and theology (Paley, Butler, and the New Testament) two terms with Henry Ware.[7]

Modern languages, still not quite considered academically respectable, were offered on a "voluntary" basis, which meant not that one did not have to take them, but that he could choose between four terms of German, Italian, Spanish, French, *or* Portuguese. ✿ Credits in these courses were worth only half those in any other course. Thoreau, intensely interested in languages, took five terms of Italian with Pietro Bachi, four of French with Francis Surault, four of German with Hermann Bokum, and two of Spanish with Francis Sales. Natural history, first offered in Thoreau's senior year by Harris, was the only science course he took. For some unknown reason he did not register with the rest of his class for Webster's course in chemistry. In the final semester of his senior year, he elected to attend voluntary lectures on German and Northern literature by Longfellow, on mineralogy by Webster, on anatomy by John C. Warren, and on natural history by Harris.

Of all Thoreau's professors, Edward Tyrrell Channing probably made the most lasting impression. Channing demanded themes on assigned topics such as "Imagination as an Element of Happiness"; "Characteristics of Milton's Poesy"; "The Sublimity of Death"; "Conformity in Things Unessential"; "Various Means of Public Influence"; and "Social Reforms and Restraints." The results from Thoreau's hand were a group of papers perhaps a cut above the usual level of college themes. Now and then there can ✿ be found sentences that sound like the later Thoreau, but they are few and far between. On the whole, Thoreau's college essays are pretty cut and dried. (They still are not included in his collected works.) It was not until he could write on topics of his own choosing that he began to develop his own personal prose style. Nonetheless, his training under Channing gave him the all-important experience of applying his pen to paper and trying to achieve a worthwhile style. He readily admitted later that it was under Channing's tutelage that he first learned to express himself.

Despite his poor showing in his entrance examinations, Thoreau was consistently an above-average student at Harvard.

---

7. Kenneth Walter Cameron, "Chronology of Thoreau's Harvard Years," *Emerson Society Quarterly*, XV (1959), 1–108

Grading at Harvard in his day, as has been pointed out, was entirely on Josiah Quincy's rank system. Some of Quincy's rank sheets for Thoreau's class are now missing, but enough are left to show a distinct pattern. The class varied in number from term to term from forty-three to fifty. At the end of Thoreau's second term he was ranked sixteenth. At the end of the first year he was awarded twenty-five dollars as "exhibition money" for his high grades. At the end of the first term of his sophomore year he was rated sixth (although here he profited slightly from a mathematical error on President Quincy's part) and was awarded a "detur," a specially bound volume, for achieving good grades.[8] He ended the second term in seventh place, and the third term in eleventh. At the close of the year he was awarded another twenty-five dollars as "exhibition money" and was asked to take part in a class honors exhibition on July 13, 1835, where he and Manlius S. Clarke gave a Greek dialogue on "Decius and Cato." At the end of the first term of the junior year he was fourteenth in his class. By taking advantage of a new college regulation, he dropped out for the entire second term to earn a little money by teaching in a country school. Since the only "rank work" he did that term consisted of two compositions, he slipped down to twenty-second position. Before the third term he was forced to leave campus because of illness. To add to his misfortunes President Quincy made another mathematical error— this time not in Thoreau's favor—and he slipped to twenty-third place. He missed more school, again because of illness, the first part of his senior year and so remained in twenty-third place for the first two terms. But his final term, by dint of attending a large number of voluntary lectures, he was able to raise his rank to the nineteenth place. He thus received another twenty-five dollars as "exhibition money" on June 15, 1837, and was asked to take part in an honors "conference" with Henry Vose and Charles Wyatt Rice on "The Commercial Spirit of Modern Times" at graduation. Thus, except for the three terms immediately after his prolonged absences for teaching and illness, when he was ranked almost exactly at the midpoint in his class, he was decidedly in the upper ranks. And were it not for the fact that the rank scores were always cumulative (and so those absences counted against him for the

---

8. Frederick T. McGill, "Thoreau and College Discipline," *New England Quarterly*, XV (1942), 350

rest of his college career), he would have ended with a much
higher rank than he did.

II

A student's life at Harvard in the 1830s was not exactly one
of ease and luxury. Andrew Peabody, one of Thoreau's near contemporaries, has complained:

> Morning-prayers were in summer at six; in winter, about half
> an hour before sunrise in a bitterly cold chapel. Thence half of
> each class passed into the several recitation-rooms in the same
> building, . . . and three-quarters of an hour later the bell rang
> for a second set of recitations, including the remaining half of
> the students. Then came breakfast, which in the college com-
> mons consisted solely of coffee, hot rolls, and butter, except when
> members of a mess had succeeded in pinning to the nether sur-
> face of the table, by a two-pronged fork, some slices of meat
> from the previous day's dinner. Between ten and twelve every
> student attended another recitation or a lecture. Dinner was at
> half-past twelve,—a meal not deficient in quantity, but by no
> means appetizing to those who had come from neat homes and
> well-ordered tables. There was another recitation in the after-
> noon, except on Saturday; then evening prayers at six, or in win-
> ter at early twilight; then the evening meal, plain as the breakfast,
> with tea instead of coffee, and cold bread, of the consistency of
> wool, for the hot rolls. After tea the dormitories rang with song
> and merriment till the study-bell, at eight in winter, at nine in
> summer, sounded the curfew for fun and frolic, proclaiming
> dead silence throughout the college premises, under penalty of a
> domiciliary visit from the officer of the entry, and, in case of a
> serious offense, of private or public admonition.[9]

Thoreau's daily program was undoubtedly similar.

Thoreau, however, was not one to confine his education to the
classroom. Harvard offered him, for the first time, access to a
good library, and he made the most of it. He soon found that the
demands of classes and homework by no means consumed all his
time and so he devoted many hours to browsing in the college

---

9. Andrew P. Peabody, *Harvard Reminiscences* (Boston, 1888), 197–8

library. There were fifty-thousand volumes there, and access to them was almost completely unlimited. He consumed a goodly portion of the twenty-one large volumes of Chalmers's anthology, *The English Poets.* He read Goldsmith, Southey, Shakespeare, Chaucer, Milton, Cowper, Johnson, Gray, Homer, the Greek poets, and the travel books of Hall, McKenney, Barrow, Bracken-ridge, and Back, among others. A good many of the books that he withdrew undoubtedly were required or supplementary reading for his courses, but even more seem to have been chosen simply because they interested him. Throughout his lifetime Thoreau could never resist reading a good book when it was available. And just before his death he counseled young Edward Emerson, who was about to enter Harvard, that the library was the best gift the college had to offer.[1]

Systematic, as usual, about everything, and realizing that he would not always have ready access to such a library, Thoreau soon adopted what was to become a lifelong habit—the keeping of a series of commonplace books—notebooks into which he copied quotations that hit his fancy or that might later be of use. Nearly twenty of these notebooks are still extant, and their five or six thousand pages are filled with what must be close to one million copied words—fantastic testimony to the zeal with which Thoreau carried out his studies both in college and afterwards. The commonplace books he kept in college are devoted for the most part to extracts from the English poets from the Anglo-Saxons to the Romantics, but he also included bits from Cooper, Irving, and Longfellow. There is little order to these earlier notes, he simply jotted down what he liked as he came across it. Nonetheless, he later found them useful and many of the quotations used in his essays in the forties are culled from these notebooks.

When Thoreau was not in the library or the classroom, he was often wont to slip off by himself out into the fields of Cambridge and along the banks of the Charles. To his surprise he found more wildlife than he had seen in Concord. It seemed to flourish despite the presence of man. Birds there were a-plenty and small mammals too. All one winter he visited daily the nest of a weasel in a hollow apple tree. And each spring—until his roommate demolished it—

1. Edward Emerson, *Henry Thoreau as Remembered by a Young Friend,* 18

there was a flicker's nest that could easily be watched in the grove on the east side of the college yard. Wildlife was everywhere, he learned, if one but bothered to observe it. And the observations offered a welcome alternative to study.

III

Approximately two hundred and fifty students were enrolled at Harvard in Thoreau's day, fifty of them in his Class of 1837. Two of them at least—Charles Stearns Wheeler and Henry Vose— he was already acquainted with, for they had been fellow students at the Concord Academy. Vose later became a prominent lawyer in Western Massachusetts and eventually a justice of the Massachusetts Superior Court. Among the other members of his class were John Weiss (later a prominent Unitarian clergyman), Charles H. A. Dall (who married the minor Transcendentalist Caroline Healey and became a Unitarian missionary to India), Horatio Hale (who while still a student at Harvard published a pamphlet on the Penobscot Indians and went on to become an outstanding authority on the American Indian) and David Greene Haskins (Ralph Waldo Emerson's cousin and later dean of the University of the South). Professor Channing thought the most promising author in the class to be Horace Morison—his later sole contribution to our literary heritage was a children's book entitled *Pebbles from the Seashore.*

Richard Henry Dana, author of *Two Years Before the Mast,* originally entered Harvard with the Class of 1835, but dropped out because of eye trouble, took his famous voyage around Cape Horn, and joined the Class of 1837 at the close of the autumn term in 1836. Harrison G. O. Blake, later one of Thoreau's most devoted disciples, and E. Rockwood Hoar, Thoreau's Concord neighbor, were in the Class of 1835. Jones Very the eccentric sonneteer and Samuel Gray Ward, Emerson's friend, were in the Class of 1836. James Russell Lowell and William Wetmore Story were members of the Class of 1838, and Edward Everett Hale and Marston Watson, the latter another devoted friend of Thoreau, were in the Class of 1839.

[39]

Some of Thoreau's classmates thought him standoffish. John Weiss, the most vocal of these, complained:

> He passed for nothing, it is suspected, with most of us; for he was cold and unimpressible. The touch of his hand was moist and indifferent, as if he had taken up something when he saw your hand coming, and caught your grasp upon it. How the prominent, gray-blue eyes seemed to rove down the path, just in advance of his feet, as his grave Indian stride carried him down to University Hall! . . .
> He did not care for people; his classmates seemed very remote. This reverie hung always about him, and not so loosely as the odd garments which the pious household care furnished. Thought had not awakened his countenance; it was serene, but rather dull, rather plodding. The lips were not yet firm; there was almost a look of smug satisfaction lurking round their corners. It is plain now that he was preparing to hold his future views with great setness, and personal appreciation of their importance. The nose was prominent, but its curve fell forward without firmness over the upper lip; and we remember him as looking very much like some Egyptian sculptures of faces, large-featured, but brooding, immobile, fixed in a mystic egotism. Yet his eyes were sometimes searching, as if he had dropped or expected to find, something. It was the look of Nature's own child learning to detect her wayside secrets; and those eyes have stocked his books with subtle traits of animate and inanimate creation which had escaped less patient observers. For he saw more upon the ground than anybody suspected to be there. . . .[2]

Not all of Thoreau's classmates however were of the same opinion. When he was absent from the campus on occasion, he received warm, friendly letters from A. G. Peabody and Charles Wyatt Rice telling of extracurricular pyrotechnic experiments in the Davy Club and "laughing gas" binges on the banks of the Charles, hardly the type of letter one would write to the cold, standoffish individual Weiss thought Thoreau to have been[3] And John Shepard Keyes tells of visiting Thoreau's dormitory room as an entering freshman in Thoreau's senior year and finding a convivial scene:

---

2. John Weiss, "Thoreau," *Christian Examiner*, LXXIX (1865), 98
3. Thoreau, *Correspondence*, 4–6

A burst of Thoreau's classmates into his room, headed by
Charles Theodore Russell, Trask and others who chaffed Thoreau
and his Freshman in all sorts of amusing ways, and took down
some of our local pride and Concord self-conceit for which I soon
found that my host was as distinguished in college as afterwards.
These roaring seniors fresh from vacation's fun and with no
more college duties to worry about made a sharp contrast to a
Sunday evening at home. . . . It was startling and novel to hear
"Old Prex" and other nicknames familiarly applied to such
dignitaries as Concord had almost worshipped, and I fear that
the introduction wasn't of the most useful sort to just such a
boy as I was.[4]

Still further evidence of Thoreau's at least comparative geniality
is found in the fact that he was one of the five members of his
class voted into membership in the Institute of 1770, a private
fraternity and debating society, on July 3, 1834, at the end of
his freshman year. The following October, Thoreau paid his entrance fee of two dollars, attracted no doubt by the Institute's
1400-volume library which supplemented the college library with
more popular books. Indeed, Thoreau donated a book to the
Institute so that he might win the privilege of withdrawing more
than two books at a time and then took advantage of that privilege
regularly. He also took part frequently in the Institute's debates
on such topics as "Is political eminence more worthy of admiration than literary?"; "Ought there to be any restrictions on the
publications of opinions?"; and "Ought capital punishment to be
abolished?"

At the end of Thoreau's freshman year the last major student
revolt on Harvard campus took place. An insignificant incident lit
the fuse and a full-scale rebellion exploded. In the words of the
official Harvard University report on the famed Dunkin Rebellion:

On the 19th of May last [1834], the Instructor of the Freshman Class in Greek [Christopher Dunkin], reported to the President that one of that Class, when reciting to him, stopped and
refused to recite farther; on being told by his Instructor that
when "he directed any thing to be translated, he expected it
would be done," the student replied, "I do not recognize your

4. Raymond Adams, "Thoreau at Harvard," *New England Quarterly,*
XIII (1940), 32

authority," shut his book and paid no attention to his recitation afterward.[5]

When the student was asked to apologize to Dunkin, he instead withdrew from the college.

> On that night, (Wednesday) between the hours of ten and one, the room occupied by the Greek Instructor, above-mentioned, as a recitation room, was torn in pieces by some students, all its furniture broken, and every window dashed out. . . .
> The morning and evening daily prayers were, on the next day, (Thursday) interrupted by scraping, whistling, groaning and other disgraceful noises. . . .
> On this night a watch was set for the protection of the College property. It was attacked with stones by several students. An affray ensued. . . .
> On [the next] evening, about midnight, the Chapel bell was rung, (a cord having been attached to it,) accompanied by great noises in the yard.[6]

At this point President Quincy stepped in and broke all collegiate tradition by announcing that he would "turn over the violators of the public peace and destroyers of the property of the University to the animadversion of the civil tribunals."[7] When the riots continued, the faculty dismissed (with three exceptions) the entire sophomore class and told them that they would not be readmitted until after the next commencement, late in August, and then only after taking new examinations and offering certificates of good conduct. Fourteen members of the other classes were dismissed and three sophomores were indicted in Middlesex Court for trespass and assault on the college watch.[8]

Where was Thoreau in the midst of all the excitement? John Weiss, who was one of the leaders of the rebellion, says:

> He [Thoreau] had no animal spirits for our sport or mischief. We cannot recollect what became of him during the scenes of the Dunkin Rebellion. He must have slipped off into some "cool retreat or mossy cell." We are half inclined to suppose that the

5. Harvard University, *Proceedings of the Overseers Relative to the Late Disturbance in That Seminary* (Boston, 1834), 21
6. Ibid. 22–3
7. Ibid. 5
8. Ibid. 17

tumult startled him into some metamorphose, that corresponded to a yearning in him of some natural kind, whereby he secured a temporary evasion till peace was restored. . . . Thoreau disappeared while our young absurdity held its orgies, stripping shutters from the lower windows of the buildings, dismantling recitation rooms, greeting tutors and professors with a frenzied and groundless indignation which we symbolized by kindling the spoils of sacked premises upon the steps. It probably occurred to him that fools might rush in where angels were not in the habit of going. We recollect that he declined to accompany several fools of this description, who rushed late, all in a fine condition of contempt, with Corybantic gestures, into morning prayers,—a college exercise which we are confident was never attended by angels.[9]

But, contrary to Weiss's recollection, Thoreau did not stay completely aloof. On June 30 Dr. Henry Ware complained that offensive noises had been made in chapel by members of the freshman class. The faculty conducted a personal interview of each freshman to determine who was guilty. As a result, Giles Henry Whitney was dismissed from the college for five months. He however pleaded innocent and asked the faculty for a re-examination of Thoreau and Charles Stearns Wheeler in relation to Whitney's conduct at prayers. The faculty refused to reopen the case, whereupon Whitney's father wrote asking for a new hearing and enclosing letters written by Thoreau and Wheeler testifying on behalf of his son. But once again the request was denied.[1] Unfortunately the two letters have disappeared from the records, so we have no clue as to the nature of Thoreau's testimony. But it is obvious that though he was unwilling to commit civil (or collegiate) disobedience himself, he was not unwilling to come to the rescue of one whom he felt unjustly charged.

It is interesting to note in this connection that of the sixty-three boys who were at one time or another members of the Class of 1837, forty-four were at some time subject to disciplinary action on the part of the faculty. Thoreau was one of the nineteen who never got into trouble. Although it has often been remarked that he wore a green coat on the campus when regulations demanded black, he was never prosecuted for that offense. The truth of the

9. Weiss, "Thoreau," 101
1. McGill, "Thoreau and College Discipline," 350–1

matter was probably not, as was supposed, that he wore green because the college rules required black, but because he could not afford a new coat. And this fact the faculty apparently recognized, for when the well-to-do James Russell Lowell appeared in a brown coat, he was immediately referred to President Quincy for a remonstrance.

IV

Concord was always in the back of Thoreau's mind throughout his four years at Harvard, and whenever he had the opportunity, he returned home to visit. In October of his freshman year he walked home from Cambridge with Charles Stearns Wheeler and blistered his feet so badly that he hiked the last two miles in his stockings and was three hours going the last few miles from Lincoln to Concord.[2] It was only the first of many such visits home. In 1835 the Thoreaus moved into the family homestead on the square to live with Aunt Betsey. In the spring of 1837 they moved once again —this time to the Parkman house, a large white frame house on Main Street, near Sudbury Road, approximately where the Concord Free Public Library now stands.

In the spring of 1836 Thoreau took an unwanted vacation. About May 21 he was forced to withdraw from college because of illness.[3] Unfortunately there seem to be no contemporary reports detailed enough to tell us the exact nature of his illness, but it seems likely that it was the first attack of the tuberculosis of the lungs that was to plague his adult life. Year after year the Concord town reports recorded more deaths from consumption than any other cause. The fact that they did not then realize its contagious nature and so made no attempt to isolate those who suffered from it served of course only to spread it more widely. The Thoreau family was particularly prone to the disease. It was the cause of Grandfather John Thoreau's death in 1801, a contributing factor in brother John's death in 1842, and the cause of sister Helen's death in 1849. The remarkable thing is that Henry recovered from this first attack and from several later ones. His penchant for an outdoor life was unquestionably a factor in prolonging his days.

2. Kenneth Walter Cameron, "Young Henry Thoreau in the Annals of the Concord Academy," *Emerson Society Quarterly*, IX (1957), 16
3. Cameron, "Chronology of Thoreau's Harvard Years," 17

Thoreau in 1861
From an ambrotype by E. S. Dunshee

*Thoreau as recalled
by Daniel Ricketson's
son, Walton*
From the bust in the
Concord Free Public Library

Thoreau in profile as recalled by Walton Ricketson

Thoreau as he presented himself at the door of Brooklawn, New Bedford, December 25, 1854
From a pencil sketch by Daniel Ricketson

THOREAU AS SEEN BY HIS FRIENDS

Although at the time of his illness some members of his family wondered if he should not drop out of college completely because "there are some constitutions that will not bear study,"[4] Thoreau himself was anxious to return to classes and as early as July 5 wrote to make arrangements for a room in the fall. He spent the summer building himself a new boat, "a kind of oblong bread-trough" as he described it, equipped with sails and christened the *Red Jacket.*   *
Then he made a brief trip to New York City with his father to peddle their pencils in the stores and thus raise money for his college expenses. But when he returned to the campus in September,   *
he was plagued by recurring incidents of illness—fortunately none of them serious enough to send him back to Concord.

Meanwhile just before his illness Thoreau briefly left his classes for another reason. On November 2, 1835, the Harvard faculty adopted a new regulation permitting students to take a thirteen-week leave of absence if they wished to teach school to help finance their college education.[5] Since Thoreau's financial situation throughout his college career was perennially precarious, he took advantage of the new ruling at the earliest possible moment—just one month later, when the new term began. He applied for a teaching position in Canton, Massachusetts, and was interviewed by Rev. Orestes A. Brownson, the Unitarian minister in Canton, who not only was a member of the school committee but also had children of his own in the school. Brownson was one of the most voluble of the New England intellectuals of the time. A whirligig in religion, he managed to embrace successively Presbyterianism, Universalism, Unitarianism, the Society for Christian Union and Progress (a church he himself established), and finally Roman Catholicism. He was a keen thinker—and knew it. When asked to name the three profoundest men in the United States, he included his own name among the three. But despite his egotism, Thoreau found him stimulating and the two that first night sat up until midnight talking. Brownson informed his committee that the young man would indeed do and Thoreau was hired.

It is not now certain how long Thoreau remained in Canton. He was absent from Harvard more than three months, from

4. Caroline Sewall, Letter to Prudence Ward of June 6, 1836. MS, George L. Davenport, Jr.
5. Anton Huffert, *Thoreau as a Teacher, Lecturer and Educational Thinker* (New York University, 1951, unpublished doctoral dissertation), 62

* December 6, 1835, to March 20, 1836, but he later wrote to Brownson of "the short six weeks I passed with you."[6] It has been said that he taught with "poor success."[7] But if that report is true, perhaps it was because as a beginning teacher he had seventy pupils imposed on him at once.[8] That in his own mind he thought he performed adequately is indicated by the fact that he later asked Brownson for a recommendation as a teacher.

Thoreau and Brownson made the most of their time together. They embarked on a joint study of German. And since Brownson was probably engaged at the moment in writing his *New Views of Christian Society and the Church,* one of the seminal books in American Transcendentalism, it seems inevitable that they discussed many of the new ideas then circulating among New England intellectuals. Brownson's influence on Thoreau at this formative moment in his career has generally been overlooked. Thoreau himself later wrote Brownson of those weeks:

> They were an era in my life—the morning of a new *Lebenstag*. They are to me as a dream that is dreamt, but which returns from time to time in all its original freshness. Such a one as I would dream a second and third time, and then tell before
* breakfast.[9]

Brownson, on his side, was impressed with the young man, and when he later met Thoreau's brother John in Boston he went out of his way to express his great regard for Henry.[1]

V

Thanks to his good grades, as we have seen, Thoreau occasionally won small "exhibition money" grants from the Harvard

---

6. Thoreau, *Correspondence,* 19
7. Daniel Huntoon, *History of the Town of Canton* (Cambridge, 1893), 143
8. Huffert, *Thoreau as a Teacher,* 63
9. Thoreau, *Correspondence,* 19
1. John Thoreau, Jr., Letter to Helen Thoreau of June 24, 1836. MS, George L. Davenport, Jr.

Corporation. He also held a small scholarship, the income from an old Chelsea estate, granted by the Second Church, Unitarian, of Boston—a scholarship which Emerson had once held as a student. The beneficiary was expected to collect his own rents and Thoreau later told Sanborn of the obstacles and delays he had encountered while gathering his rents.[2]

Shortly before Thoreau's graduation, Ralph Waldo Emerson, who had recently moved to Concord, wrote to President Quincy recommending further financial aid. Quincy replied on June 25, 1837:

> Your view concerning Thoreau is entirely in consent with that which I entertain. His general conduct has been very satisfactory and I was willing and desirous that whatever falling off there had been in his scholarship should be attributable to his sickness.
>
> He had, however, imbibed some notions concerning emulation & College rank, which had a natural tendency to diminish his zeal, if not his exertions.
>
> His instructors were impressed with the conviction that he was indifferent, even to a degree that was faulty and that they could not recommend him consistent with the rule, by which they are usually governed in relation to beneficiaries. I have, always, entertained a respect for, and interest in, him, and was willing to attribute any apparent neglect, or indifference to his ill-health rather than to wilfulness. I obtained from the instructors the authority to state all the facts to the Corporation, and submit the result to their discretion.
>
> This I did, and that body granted *Twenty-five dollars,* which was within *ten,* or at most *fifteen* dollars of any sum, he would have received had no objection been made.
>
> There is no doubt that from some cause an unfavorable opinion has been entertained, since his return, after his sickness, of his disposition to exert himself. To what it has been owing, may be doubtful. I appreciate very fully the goodness of his heart and the strictness of his moral principle; and have done as much for him, as under the circumstances was possible.[3]

---

2. Sanborn, *The Life of Henry David Thoreau,* 153
3. Josiah Quincy, Letter to Ralph Waldo Emerson of June 25, 1837. MS, Morgan Library

By that time though, the financial struggle was nearly over. In a few weeks he would graduate and be on his own.

VI

Under the system then prevailing at Harvard, commencement occurred the last Wednesday in August, preceded by a six weeks' vacation. This vacation enabled Thoreau to attend the dedication of the original monument at old North Bridge in Concord on July 4. For more than a dozen years the citizens of Concord had been quarreling over the erection of a suitable marker commemorating the battle of April 19, 1775. Rev. Ezra Ripley, hoping to resolve the argument, donated some land at the site on condition that it be fenced with heavy stone and a marker erected by July 4, 1837. Ceremonies were planned for April 19, 1836, but the committee could not agree on the wording of the inscription. The event was postponed for more than a year. Ralph Waldo Emerson, newly resident in the town, was asked to prepare a hymn for the occasion and composed the well-known "Concord Hymn" to be sung to the tune of "Old Hundred," though when the dedication ceremonies finally took place, he was out of town. John Shepard Keyes, who with Henry Thoreau sang in the choir, has recalled the occasion:

> It was a very hot, sunny, July day. After the noon salute and bell ringing the village became as quiet as of a Sunday. About three o'clock the procession, escorted by the military companies, but a straggling advance, consisting mainly of the townspeople, men, women, and children, came slowly along the Common and passed up the road to the old North Bridge. There were assembled about the Monument two or three hundred, seated on the grass, who listened to a prayer by Mr. Frost, an oration by Samuel Hoar, and then Mr. Emerson's hymn was sung by all who could join in full chorus. The hymn was printed on slips of paper about six inches square and plentifully supplied to the audience. . . . Rev. John Wilder prayed, and Dr. Ripley gave a very solemn benediction—for was not his life's work and effort accomplished in this Monument, erected and dedicated on the spot he had selected?[4]

4. Social Circle in Concord, *Memoirs* (Boston, 1882–1940), V, 77–8

A year later, on April 19, 1838, when the committee for the erection of the monument asked the townspeople to donate trees to beautify the site, the Thoreau family was among the contributors.

It was probably also during this summer vacation of 1837 that Thoreau spent six weeks sharing with Charles Stearns Wheeler a hut that Wheeler had built on the shores of Flint's Pond in nearby Lincoln. It was little more than a shanty, with bunks of straw, and built, as Ellery Channing scoffed, "in the Irish manner." The two ate their meals with the Wheeler family, spending their time at the hut in reading, loafing, and sleeping and providing a period of rest that must have helped to stabilize Thoreau's precarious health. Thoreau often looked back fondly on that vacation and it undoubtedly served as an inspiration for his later experiment at Walden Pond.

The Valedictory Exercises, or Class Day, were held on July 18. It is not certain that Thoreau even bothered to attend. It seems even less likely that he was interested in the Class Supper of mock turtle soup, turkey, pig, oyster pies, squabs, and so on that followed the ceremonies. The Class of 1837 was an ebullient one and Charles Russell confessed many years later that the group "celebrated its class day so vehemently in the old fashioned coarser style, that the faculty from and after that day put an extinguisher upon that kind of celebration."[5]

The graduation itself took place on August 30. Levi Farwell, the college steward, having certified to President Quincy that Thoreau and his classmates had settled all their college dues, announced that they were entitled to the degree of bachelor of arts.[6] Thoreau's rank in the class entitled him to a part in the commencement exercises and he joined with Charles Wyatt Rice and Henry Vose in a "conference" on "The Commercial Spirit of Modern Times, Considered in Its Influence on the Political, Moral, and Literary Character of a Nation." Thoreau, in his part, expounded a philosophy that he was to follow the rest of his life:

We are to look chiefly for the origin of the commercial spirit, and the power that still cherishes and sustains it, in a blind and

5. Charles Russell, Speech delivered on Alumni Day, 1897. MS, Berg
6. Cameron, "The Solitary Thoreau of the Alumni Notes," 22

unmanly love of wealth. Wherever this exists, it is too sure to become the ruling spirit; and, as a natural consequence, it infuses into all our thoughts and affections a degree of its own selfishness; we become selfish in our patriotism, selfish in our domestic relations, selfish in our religion.

Let men, true to their natures, cultivate the moral affections, lead manly and independent lives; let them make riches the means and not the end of existence, and we shall hear no more of the commercial spirit. The sea will not stagnate, the earth will be as green as ever, and the air as pure. This curious world which we inhabit is more wonderful than convenient; more beautiful than it is useful; it is more to be admired and enjoyed than used. The order of things should be somewhat reversed; the seventh should be man's day of toil, wherein to earn his living by the sweat of his brow; and the other six his Sabbath of the affections and the soul,—in which to range this widespread garden, and drink in the soft influences and sublime revelations of nature.[7]

One of the most persistent of the many apocryphal legends about Thoreau is that at the end of his four years at Harvard he refused to accept his diploma—persistent despite the fact that the diploma still exists and facsimile reproductions of it have been widely distributed. The legend probably had its beginnings in a letter Thoreau wrote to Emerson on November 14, 1847. Speaking of a new science school that had been established at Harvard, Thoreau said: "They have been foolish enough to put at the end of all this earnest the old joke of a diploma. Let every sheep keep but his own skin, I say."[8] What is more, Thoreau did refuse *a* diploma, but it was a master's degree rather than a bachelor's. In those days, Harvard automatically granted the master of arts degree to all who proved their physical worth by being alive three years after graduating, and their having five dollars to give the college. Although twenty-seven of the forty-seven graduating members of his class paid out the five dollars, Thoreau himself would have no part of such a fraudulent degree.

On August 31 the commencement was made particularly memorable by Ralph Waldo Emerson's delivery of his "American Scholar" before the Phi Beta Kappa society. With its stirring call for a truly American literature, it is quite rightfully known as our

7. Thoreau, *Writings*, VI, 8–9
8. Thoreau, *Correspondence*, 190

intellectual declaration of independence—and no writer fulfilled its prophecies better than Henry David Thoreau. But unfortunately we cannot be certain that he even attended Emerson's lecture. A week later his classmate James Richardson wrote him:

> After you finished your part in the Performances of Commencement (the tone and sentiment of which by the way I liked much, as being of sound philosophy,) I hardly saw you again at all. Neither at Mr. Quincy's levee, neither at any of our Classmates' evening entertainments, did I find you.[9]

The Harvard commencement of Thoreau's day was a gala carnival occasion, more like a country fair than an academic ceremony. Such festivities unquestionably attracted the crowds, but Thoreau, not one for crowds, quickly headed back home to Concord, and quite likely missed hearing Emerson's lecture.

In his later years Thoreau was wont to disparage the importance of his college training. When Emerson once boasted that most of the branches of learning were taught at Harvard, Thoreau retorted, "Yes, indeed, all the branches and none of the roots."[1] . . . Yet unquestionably Harvard had a profound influence on Thoreau's thought. Although German Transcendentalism had not reached the Harvard curriculum in his day, the so-called Scottish "common sense" philosophers Thomas Reid, Dugald Stewart, and Thomas Brown had. These Scottish philosophers suggested the inadequacy of Locke's then prevalent theory of knowledge, especially with regard to moral values, and thus provided for Thoreau and some of his contemporaries a transition to the newly discussed philosophy of Transcendentalism. Coming just as it did at the most intellectually formative years of his life, his Harvard training broadened his horizons in many ways as they never could have been broadened in Concord alone. It made him aware of the world of books, of ideas, of thought. And it helped hone his intellect to its razor sharpness—even if, paradoxically, he later used some of that sharpness in striking back at his alma mater.

---

9. Thoreau, *Correspondence*, 11
1. John Albee, *Remembrances of Emerson* (New York, 1903), 33

CHAPTER FOUR
(1837–1838)

I

A COLLEGE GRADUATE in Thoreau's day had four roads open to him—the ministry, law, medicine, or teaching. Thoreau did not hesitate in his choice; schoolteaching was almost a family tradition. Both his father and his grandfather Asa Dunbar had taught for a time. Aunt Louisa Dunbar, who lived with them now, had taught for years. Brother John and sister Helen had taught to help Henry out financially while he was in college and were even now teaching in Taunton, Massachusetts. What is more important, no sooner had Henry graduated from Harvard than the Concord school committee offered him a position as a teacher in the Center School, the same little brick schoolhouse on the village square that he himself had attended as a child ten and more years before, with a salary of five hundred dollars.[1] The country was in the midst of a severe economic depression and Thoreau was one of the few members of his college class lucky enough to have a position ready at hand. He accepted and started work immediately.

Physically the school was much too small for the ninety scholars enrolled. It was perhaps just as well that the average attendance that winter was only fifty-two, for even then they must have crowded the tiny room.[2] Although theoretically the Center School was aimed primarily at college preparatory work, all the better students had been siphoned off into the private Concord Academy, just as Thoreau himself had been as a student. What was left were chiefly farm boys who had little interest in learning and spent most of their time in creating disciplinary problems.

At the end of the second week of Thoreau's teaching, Deacon

---

1. *Yeoman's Gazette*, April 14, 1838
2. Ibid.

Nehemiah Ball, one of the three members of the school committee, dropped in to see how the new teacher was getting along.[3] Observing that Thoreau was using no corporal punishment and that the classroom was not as quiet as he would have liked, he called Thoreau out into the corridor and insisted that it was his duty to flog the students on occasion or "the school would spoil"—this despite the fact that the Concord School Regulations specified that corporal punishment was to be excluded "as much as practical."[4]

Always one to keep his side of the bargain and wishing to dramatize the preposterousness of Deacon Ball's request, Thoreau returned to the room, called out several of the pupils, including the Thoreau family maid, and feruled them. The students were baffled. One later complained that in the district school he had been taught to put his books away and fold his hands when he had finished his lessons; now when he did this Thoreau whipped him for "doing nothing."[5] Thoreau had never seemed severe before, so the unexpected whippings were more surprising. Quite understandably it was many years before some of the astonished pupils forgave him. (Daniel Potter years later said: "When I went to my seat, I was so mad that I said to myself: 'When I'm grown up, I'll whip you for this, old feller.' But I never saw the day I wanted to do it.—Why, Henry Thoreau was the kindest hearted of men."[6]

That evening Thoreau handed his resignation in to the committee. If he could not teach the school in his own way, he would have none of it. He told his family that it would be impossible to keep the school as still as the committee would require on his plan; he would prefer to teach in an academy or private school where he could have his own way.[7] He was replaced immediately in the Center School by his friend and college classmate, William Allen. The next spring, Rev. Barzillai Frost, in making his annual report for the school committee, complained about an interruption

---

3. Ruth R. Wheeler, "Masonic Building Has Long History," *Concord Journal,* November 30, 1961
4. Anton Huffert, *Thoreau as a Teacher, Lecturer and Educational Thinker* (New York University, 1951, unpublished doctoral dissertation), 68
5. Edward Emerson, Notes on Thoreau
6. Allen French, Interview with Daniel Potter. MS, Walter Harding
7. Prudence Ward, Letter to Caroline Ward Sewall of September 25, 1837. MS, George L. Davenport, Jr.

in the fall term of the Center School "which was occasioned by a change of masters and produced the usual evil attendant on that event."[8] And thus Thoreau's brief career in public-school teaching came to an end.

Unquestionably Thoreau's action was not well received by his townsmen. It was hard for them to understand someone throwing up a good job, as he did, particularly in the midst of a depression. Children had always been whipped in school; they did not see what he had to protest about. There must be something odd about him to do such a thing, they thought.

Their opinion of his oddity was confirmed by another incident —his changing his name. Throughout his childhood and college years he had consistently signed his name as he had been christened —David Henry Thoreau. But now suddenly he reversed it and began signing it Henry David Thoreau. His family had always called him Henry and he apparently thought that "Henry David" was more euphonious than "David Henry." Quite characteristically he did not go through the then required legal formality of petitioning the state legislature to change his name; he just went ahead and changed it by himself.[9] His neighbors did not approve. To them "David Henry" was his God-given name and he should be satisfied with it. Even long after Thoreau's death one of the Concord farmers was heard to say:

> Henry D. Thoreau—Henry D. Thoreau. . . . His name ain't no more Henry D. Thoreau than my name is Henry D. Thoreau. And everybody knows it, and he knows it. His name's Da-a-vid Henry and it ain't never been nothing but Da-a-vid Henry. And he knows that![1]

And to the end of his life some of his townsmen persisted in calling him David Henry. But Thoreau could be just as persistent himself and went on signing himself as Henry David and correcting them when they differed.

8. *Yeoman's Gazette*, April 14, 1838
9. Kevin H. White, Secretary of the Commonwealth of Massachusetts, Letter to Walter Harding of February 28, 1963. MS, Walter Harding
1. Mrs. Daniel Chester French, *Memories of a Sculptor's Wife* (Boston, 1928), 94–5

II

Giving up a school proved easier for Thoreau than finding a new one. He was not at all anxious to leave Concord. When his mother suggested he could buckle on his knapsack and roam abroad to seek his fortune, tears came to his eyes and he was not consoled until his sister Helen put her arm around him, kissed him, and said, "No, Henry, you shall not go: you shall stay at home and live with us."[2] But there were no positions available in Concord, and so at last he began to write to his classmates to learn if they knew of vacancies elsewhere. Their replies were discouraging. Teaching jobs everywhere were scarce that year.

Recalling his brief experience in Canton, Thoreau then wrote Rev. Orestes Brownson:

> My apology for this letter is to ask your assistance in obtaining employment. For, say what you will, this frostbitten 'forked carrot' of a body must be fed and clothed after all. It is ungrateful, to say the least, to suffer this much abused case to fall into so dilapidated a condition that every northwester may luxuriate through its chinks and crevices, blasting the kindly affections it should shelter, when a few clouts would save it. . . .
>
> I seek a situation as teacher of a small school, or assistant in a large one, or, what is more desirable, as private tutor in a gentleman's family.
>
> Perhaps I should give some account of myself. I would make education a pleasant thing both to the teacher and scholar. This discipline, which we allow to be the end of life, should not be one thing in the schoolroom and another in the street. We should seek to be fellow students with the pupil, and we should learn of, as well as with him, if we would be most helpful to him. . . .
>
> I have even been disposed to regard the cowhide as a nonconductor. Methinks that, unlike the electric wire, not a single spark of truth is ever transmitted through its agency to the slumbering intellect it would address. I mistake, it may teach a truth in physics, but never a truth in morals.[3]

---

2. William Ellery Channing, *Thoreau, the Poet-Naturalist,* 18
3. Henry David Thoreau, *Correspondence,* 19–20

But he was no more successful with this letter than with his earlier ones.

Since there were no more promising opportunities available, Thoreau went to work in his father's pencil factory. It at least gave him the chance to earn his living and it was pleasant to work alongside his father. But he was not satisfied to do just routine work. He wanted a challenge and soon found it. The major problem that faced the early American pencil makers—the Thoreaus, the Munroes, the Dixons, and all the others—was that they could not seem to attain the quality of lead found in the Faber pencils imported from Germany. The lead in the American pencils was gritty, greasy, or brittle—and sometimes all three. Thoreau soon concluded that it was the filler used with the graphite that was causing the difficulties, for their graphite was unquestionably of first quality. American pencil manufacturers had always mixed graphite with bayberry wax, glue and spermaceti, pressed the mixture into a paste, warmed it, and poured it into the pencil grooves soft. Hunting around in the Harvard Library, Thoreau found an encyclopedia published in Edinburgh which revealed that the German manufacturers mixed their lead with a certain fine Bavarian clay and then baked it. He also learned that this same clay was regularly imported into this country by the New England Glass Company and the Phoenix Crucible Company of Taunton, Massachusetts, for other purposes, and so was readily available.

Using this new method, Thoreau immediately obtained a harder and blacker lead, but one that was still gritty. He then reasoned that he must grind the graphite finer in order to secure its more regular distribution throughout the clay. Probably at his father's suggestion, although it was Henry himself who worked out all the mechanical details, he designed a new grinding mill for the graphite. It was a narrow churn-like chamber around the millstones prolonged some seven feet high and opening into a broad, closed, flat box, a sort of shelf. Only lead-dust that was fine enough to rise to that height, carried by an upward draft of air, and lodge in the box was used; the rest was ground over. The machine spun around inside a box set on a table and could be wound up to run itself so it could easily be operated by his sisters. The result of these new developments was the first American pencil that was the equal of those produced in Germany. But the effect of that fine graphite

[56]

dust on Thoreau's already deteriorating lungs can readily be imagined.

As a result of the improvements, their pencil business was now extensive enough that a long series of sheds extending towards Sudbury Road was built on the back of the Parkman house. Outsiders were not permitted inside, for the Thoreaus did not want to expend the money necessary to have their new machines patented and thus were forced to resort to secrecy. To supplement their income, they also manufactured stove polish, marbled paper,[4] and sandpaper, and Thoreau himself often went out to Goose Pond to collect sand by the cartload. For a time at least they stocked paper supplies, and it is said that they also repaired clocks.[5] They were not ashamed to pursue any method to earn an honest dollar. But as the pencil business increased, thanks to Thoreau's improvements, they were gradually able to drop the various sidelines and concentrate on the pencil business alone.

III

Meanwhile however Thoreau did not abandon his efforts to find a teaching position. Pencilmaking, despite his capabilities, did not interest him, but teaching positions, in the midst of the depression, were still not easy to find. Granted Helen and John both were teaching in Taunton—and without any collegiate training— yet they had a number of years of experience behind them, and Henry had almost none. Besides, they had not thrown up their jobs in the face of the school committee. It must have been particularly galling to him that winter to pick up the local *Yeoman's Gazette* and to read of a vacancy in Concord's own west school district, but he knew after his experience with the Center School that there was no point in applying there.[6]

As time passed he got more and more restless. On March 6 he complained in his *Journal* that a man could hardly sit down and quietly pare his nails while the earth went gyrating ahead. He

4. Edward Emerson, Notes on Thoreau
5. Ibid.
6. *Yeoman's Gazette,* January 29, 1838

must get up and shake himself, he said.[7] And so on the 17th he wrote his brother John in Taunton and suggested that the two of them start out together for the West. Dr. Edward Jarvis, who had left Concord the year before to establish a medical practice in Louisville, Kentucky, had written that there were at least a dozen vacancies in the area. Travel would be cheap once the canals opened for the spring, and Thoreau thought they could easily borrow what little money they would need to set out. In preparation he obtained a certificate from Josiah Quincy, the president of Harvard, stating that "his rank was high as a scholar in all the branches, and his morals and general conduct unexceptionable and exemplary." It recommended him as "well qualified as an instructor, for employment in any public or private school or private family."[8]

John was enthusiastic about Henry's suggestion and made plans to return to Concord from Taunton in mid-April and, after a week's rest, to set out with him for the West.[9] Mrs. Thoreau busily set about preparing her sons' clothes and packing their luggage.[1] Then on April 13 Thoreau received a letter from President Quincy telling of a vacancy in Alexandria, Virginia. It required a knowledge of Greek and Latin and experience in school keeping and offered six hundred dollars a year besides washing and board. The brothers postponed their Western trip and Henry applied for the job in Virginia. But he was turned down—probably for lack of experience. Meanwhile John had found himself a school in Roxbury, not far from where Helen and Sophia were thinking of establishing a boarding school, and decided not to go West.

Henry then started out on a new tack. He decided to tour the villages in central Maine to look for a school. This time he obtained a recommendation from Rev. Ezra Ripley affirming that he was "well disposed & well qualified to instruct the rising generation . . . modest & mild in his disposition & government, but not wanting in energy of character & fidelity in the duties of his profession."[2]

7. Thoreau, *Journal*, I, 35
8. Thoreau, *Correspondence*, 26
9. Prudence Ward, Letter to Dennis Ward of April 2, 1838. MS, Abernethy Library
1. Prudence Ward, Letter to Mrs. Joseph Ward of April 13, 1838. MS, Abernethy Library
2. Ezra Ripley, Letter of May, 1838. MS, Morgan Library

Ripley also gave him a list of clergymen in Portland, Belfast, Camden, Kennebunk, Castine, and Ellsworth to visit. On May 2 he set out, with a copy of *Phelps & Squire's Travellers' Guide and Map of the United States* under his arm as a guide book, and took the night boat from Boston to Portland, spending most of the night with his head over the rail paying, as he said, his "small tribute to Neptune." (Much to his chagrin, he almost never failed to get seasick.)

For nearly two weeks he toured Bath, Brunswick, Augusta, Gardiner, Hallowell, China, Oldtown, Saturday Grove, Belfast, Castine, and Thomaston, but to no avail. The trip did give him an opportunity to visit with his Bangor cousins for a few days and to hold a memorable conversation with an old Indian brave in Oldtown who talked of his hunting and fishing exploits by the hour, whetting Thoreau's appetite for later visits to the Indians and woods of Maine. But there were no teaching jobs he could find. All the hiring for the summer school term had been done the month before; hiring for the fall term would not be considered for another three months. By May 17 Thoreau was back in Concord. Learning that his classmate Henry Vose was about to give up a tutoring position in Butternuts, New York, he applied for the job but was not accepted.[3] David Greene Haskins told him of still another position, but again he was unsuccessful. Understandably Thoreau was discouraged.[4]

IV

But despite Thoreau's inability to find work that he liked, his first winter out of college was not wasted. It was then, while he was at loose ends, that he developed the most important friendship of his life—that with Ralph Waldo Emerson. Since it was the home of his paternal ancestors, Emerson had long been familiar with Concord. His grandfather had been minister of Concord's First

---

3. H. D. Thoreau, Letter to Henry Vose of May 28, 1838. MS, Barrett Collection
4. David Greene Haskins, *Ralph Waldo Emerson: His Maternal Ancestors* (Boston, 1887), 119

Parish and his step-grandfather, Ezra Ripley, was still the pastor. In October 1834, after having abandoned his own ministerial career, Emerson moved into the Old Manse, Ripley's home, and there wrote his first book, *Nature*. In September 1835, after his marriage to Lydia Jackson, he settled down in the large, square white "Coolidge Castle" on Lexington Road that was to be his own home for the rest of his life. Meanwhile on February 25, 1835, Thoreau had been one of the Harvard sophomores examined on Richard Whately's *Rhetoric* by Emerson as a member of a committee of the Harvard Board of Overseers.[5] And, as we have seen, Emerson wrote Josiah Quincy in June of 1837 recommending Thoreau for a scholarship. Concord was small enough for the two to have a nodding acquaintance, but there is no evidence of anything more. Quite possibly Ezra Ripley, knowing of Emerson's influence at Harvard, had asked him to write the letter to Quincy.

Twice in the spring of 1837, seven months after it was published, Thoreau withdrew Emerson's *Nature* from the Institute library at Harvard. Later he obtained a copy of the first edition for himself and kept it in his library to the end of his days. He also gave a copy to his classmate William Allen in 1837 as a graduation present. Although in later years Thoreau read Emerson rarely, *Nature* appeared at just the critical moment in his life and there is no question that he read it avidly. It was one of the seminal books in his life.

Just when Thoreau and Emerson really became personally acquainted can no longer be accurately determined; there are too many seemingly authentic but essentially conflicting stories. George Hoar reported that it was when Thoreau once walked to Boston and back from Concord to hear Emerson lecture, and Emerson, learning of it, invited him to his house to hear a lecture read there.[6] Emerson himself once said that it was when his sister-in-law Mrs. Brown, who boarded with the Thoreaus, called his attention to some of Henry's manuscript poems.[7] Still another version has it that it was when Sophia or Helen called Mrs. Brown's attention to a passage in one of Henry's journals that appeared to anticipate a

5. Kenneth Walter Cameron, "Chronology of Thoreau's Harvard Years," *Emerson Society Quarterly*, XV (1959), 15
6. George Hoar, *Autobiography of Seventy Years* (New York, 1903), I, 72
7. Sanborn, *The Life of Henry David Thoreau*, 128–9

remark Emerson had made in one of his Concord lectures, and that she in turn called this to Emerson's attention.[8] Which of these is the true version is not known. But the exact date of their first meeting—or even exactly how they met—is not important. What is important is that in the fall of 1837 their acquaintance began to develop into a real friendship.

It is almost impossible to overestimate the importance of that friendship. Although the members of Thoreau's own family and household were unquestionably intelligent, they were, none of them, basically intellectual. And any intellectual who has ever found himself dwelling in a typically rural community knows how lonely life there can be. It has been suggested that in some respects Emerson became a father surrogate for Thoreau. Certainly although Thoreau and his own father got along well on the surface, there was little of interest that they shared in common. Mr. Thoreau could develop little if any enthusiasm for his son's intellectual interests and he probably would have been happier had Henry shown signs of living the conventional everyday sort of life that he himself was happiest with. Emerson, in contrast, was most interested in those very fields that Mr. Thoreau least cared for and Thoreau, once they became acquainted, quickly began to look to him for guidance and leadership. Perhaps Emerson's greatest contribution to Thoreau—and his contributions both intellectual and material were many—was that he kept wide the horizons that Thoreau had found opened for him at Harvard. Emerson opened his large personal library to his young friend, who made regular use of it for the rest of his life, finding many volumes there important in his development that he could not easily have found elsewhere —in particular Emerson's copies of the various translations from the Oriental scriptures. Emerson in many ways acted as a catalyst for Thoreau.

As Emerson's fame spread, his home became a mecca for a constant stream of admirers from all parts of this country and even abroad. He took particular pride in introducing Thoreau to his guests, and much to his amusement a few of these visitors, such as H. G. O. Blake and Thomas Cholmondeley, were so taken with Thoreau that they never came back to see their host.

---

8. Edward Emerson, *Emerson in Concord* (Boston, 1888), 110

Emerson was the nominal leader of the American Transcendentalists. And Thoreau was so much a part of New England Transcendentalism that an understanding of that movement is vital to a clear understanding of Thoreau himself. In late seventeenth-century England, John Locke propounded a new theory of knowledge in his widely influential *Essay Concerning Human Understanding*. It averred that the infant is born without knowledge; his mind is a *tabula rasa*. All knowledge is gained directly through the senses—through touch, sight, hearing, taste, and smell. Therefore only that knowledge which can be proved to the senses is valid. The modern "scientific method" is based entirely on this theory of knowledge as is witnessed by the laboratories in which we test our chemistry, physics, biological and earth sciences. And eighteenth-century rationalism and deism both developed out of Locke's theories.

Locke had a profound influence on the theological leaders of New England shortly after the American Revolution and many began to abandon the trinitarian Christianity (an avowed belief in the Father, Son, and Holy Ghost) for a "more rationalistic" Unitarianism. Indeed Unitarianism, under the leadership of Rev. William Ellery Channing (uncle of Thoreau's friend of the same name) became the predominant sect in the area centering around Boston.

But meanwhile a reaction against Locke's theories had set in. In late eighteenth-century Germany Kant and Hegel began advocating a theory that while Locke's ideas were valid as far as they went, there was a body of knowledge innate within man and that this knowledge transcended the senses—thus the name "Transcendentalism." This knowledge was the voice of God within man—his conscience, his moral sense, his inner light, his over-soul—and all of these terms and others were used by the various Transcendentalists. But it was central to their belief that the child was born with this innate ability to distinguish between right and wrong. Unfortunately however as he grew older he tended to listen to the world about him rather than the voice within him and his moral sense became calloused. Thus did evil come into the world. And therefore it was the duty, the obligation of the good citizen to return to a childish innocence and heed once more the voice of God within him.

[62]

Kant's and Hegel's theories were brought to England by Samuel Taylor Coleridge (particularly in his volume, *Aids to Reflection*) and Thomas Carlyle and gradually spread their way over to New England by the mid 1830s. In 1836 at the celebration of the Harvard College bicentennial in Cambridge, a group of young members of the alumni, most of them Unitarian ministers (for Harvard Divinity School was the chief seminary for the Unitarian church), found that they shared many of these Transcendental ideas in reaction to the "cold rationalism" of the earlier Unitarianism. Enjoying their own discussion more than the formal bicentennial celebrations, they adjourned to a Boston hotel parlor for further talk. So stimulating did they find their talk there that they agreed to meet again whenever the opportunity arose. Included among the members (there was never any formal roster and the make-up of the group changed from time to time) were Emerson, Rev. Frederick Henry Hedge, Rev. George Ripley, Rev. Orestes Brownson, Rev. Jones Very, Margaret Fuller, Elizabeth Peabody, Bronson Alcott, Rev. Theodore Parker, Christopher Pearce Cranch, Rev. John Sullivan Dwight, and Henry David Thoreau. They chose Emerson's home in Concord as their most frequent meeting place. And since most of their meetings were scheduled to coincide with Hedge's visits from his church in Bangor, Maine, among themselves they called the group the "Hedge Club." The meetings of such a group of influential men and women soon attracted the attention of the general public, and the newspapers of the day, seizing upon one of their favorite words, began to call them "Transcendentalists."

The Transcendentalists never had any more formal organization than the highly informal Hedge Club and even that petered out by the mid 1840s. But by bringing together a group of like-minded people it acted as a catalyst in bringing about what Van Wyck Brooks has so aptly called "the flowering of New England."

Thoreau did not join the Hedge Club until the fall of 1837. But he thereafter was a regular attendant whenever the meetings were held at Emerson's home—as they most frequently were by that time. He was younger than most of the others and was in some respects more of a product than a founder of the group. But there is hardly a major principle of the movement that he did not espouse. And in the long run he held more closely to its fundamental principles than did any of the others. He was a true Transcendentalist to the end of his life. Whether he was experimenting in life at Walden Pond, going to jail for refusing to pay his poll tax, or defending John Brown's action at Harpers Ferry, he was operating from a base of Transcendentalist principles.

V

As the winter of 1837–38 progressed, Emerson and Thoreau saw more and more of each other. At the 1837 Harvard commencement, Emerson had delivered his Phi Beta Kappa address on "The American Scholar," describing in it what he thought to be the ideal man. Now he discovered that he had the incredible good fortune to find that ideal come to life right in Concord in the person of young Henry Thoreau. And Thoreau for his part, as he was later to tell Moncure Conway, "found in Emerson a world where truths existed with the same perfection as the objects he studied in external nature, his ideals real and exact as antennae and stamina."[9] When on February 15 Emerson invited a group of his neighbors in for what he called a "teachers' meeting"—an evening of discussion—Thoreau was included. There Edmund Hosmer, after disclaiming any uniquely divine characteristics in Jesus, suddenly proclaimed, "Jesus made the world and was the Eternal God." Thoreau immediately interjected, "Mr. Hosmer, you've kicked the pail over." And Emerson, recording the incident in his journal, commented, "I delight much in my young friend, who seems to have as free and erect a mind as any I have ever met."[1] A week later Emerson noted:

> My good Henry Thoreau made this else solitary afternoon sunny with his simplicity and clear perception. How comic is simplicity in this double-dealing, quacking world. Everything that boy says makes merry with society, though nothing can be graver than his meaning. I told him he should write out the

9. Henry Seidel Canby, *Thoreau* (Boston, 1939), 90
1. Ralph Waldo Emerson, *Journals* (Boston, 1910), IV, 395

history of his college life, as Carlyle has his tutoring. We agreed that the seeing the stars through a telescope would be worth all the astronomical lectures. Then he described Mr. Quimby's electrical lecture here, and the experiment of the shock, and added that "college corporations are very blind to the fact that that twinge in the elbow is worth all the lecturing."[2]

With the coming of warm weather, the two saw even more of each other, often walking out to the Cliffs together or to Walden Pond. When James Russell Lowell, Jones Very, Cornelius Felton, or Margaret Fuller came to call, Thoreau was invited in to meet them. When Thoreau set off on his journey to Maine in May to look for a school, he carried with him a character reference from Emerson:

> I cordially recommend Mr. Henry D. Thoreau, a graduate of Harvard University in August, 1837, to the confidence of such parents or guardians as may propose to employ him as an instructor. I have the highest confidence in Mr. Thoreau's moral character and in his intellectual ability. He is an excellent Scholar, a man of energy & kindness, & I shall esteem the town fortunate that secures his Services.[3]

It is obvious that the two men were more and more attracted to each other. Despite Emerson's greater age (he was fourteen years older than Thoreau) and his already well established fame, the two treated each other as equals. Occasionally there was a touch of condescension on Emerson's part, but for the most part he found Thoreau as stimulating as Thoreau found him.

Unfortunately (and probably inevitably, granted the situation) others failed to see the two on equal terms. They thought of Thoreau not only as a disciple but also as an imitator of Emerson, though nothing could be more foreign to Emerson's professed philosophy of self-reliance. It was a bugbear Thoreau had to live with for the rest of his days, to stand in the shadow of Emerson and have his most independent writings and actions dismissed as "Emersonian." James Russell Lowell's later well-published accusation that Thoreau was stealing literary apples from Emerson's

2. Ibid. IV, 397
3. Ralph Waldo Emerson, Letter of May, 1838. MS, Morgan Library

orchard probably postponed for a whole generation, if not longer, any true recognition of Thoreau's individual genius.

It is amusing how far some went in accusing Thoreau of imitating his neighbor. Lowell, visiting Concord, wrote a friend that Thoreau so imitated Emerson's tone and manner that with his eyes shut he wouldn't know them apart.[4] David Greene Haskins made much the same comment, but added: "I do not know what subtle influences to ascribe it, but, after conversing with Mr. Emerson for even a brief time, I always found myself able and inclined to adopt his voice and manner of speaking."[5] Some even accused Thoreau of "getting up a nose like Emerson's." Mrs. Thoreau, full of pride in her son, looked upon it from another angle. She told Elizabeth Oakes Smith, "How much Mr. Emerson does talk like my Henry."[6]

Emerson from the very beginning of their friendship pointedly and even heatedly denied any imitation on Thoreau's part. To his mind, one of Thoreau's real claims to fame was that he was an "original" in the best sense of the word. Neither would deny the unquestionable fact that the two often had very similar ideas. Given their nearly identical backgrounds, such was to be expected. "In reading [Thoreau]," Emerson said, "I find the same thought, the same spirit that is in me."[7] But he hastened to add that Thoreau also went beyond, into fields of his own. It was typical of Emerson's magnanimity and intellectual honesty that he told his cousin David Greene Haskins in 1838, "When Mr. Carlyle comes to America, I expect to introduce Thoreau to him as *the* man of Concord."[8]

Emerson was unquestionably the most outstanding of the Transcendentalists so far as influence on Thoreau is concerned. But Bronson Alcott was not far behind. Thoreau and Alcott apparently first met at Emerson's house in late April 1839 on one of Alcott's frequent visits to the town.[9] And only a few days later Alcott was invited to conduct one of his so-called "Conversations"

4. Leon Howard, *Victorian Knight Errant* (Berkeley, 1952), 18–19
5. Haskins, *Ralph Waldo Emerson: His Maternal Ancestors*, 121–2
6. Elizabeth Oakes Smith, *Selections from the Autobiography* (Lewiston, Maine, 1924), 140
7. Ralph Waldo Emerson, *Journals*, IX, 522
8. Haskins, *Ralph Waldo Emerson: His Maternal Ancestors*, 119
9. Thoreau, *Correspondence*, 33; Amos Bronson Alcott, MS Journals, Houghton Library

at the Thoreau home on May 3.[1] The Conversation, even to Emerson's friendly eyes, was a miserable failure, but its lack of success did nothing to dampen Alcott's budding friendship with Thoreau.

In March 1840 Alcott, wishing to be nearer Emerson, moved to Concord and settled down with his family in the Hosmer Cottage. By November 4, 1840, they were sufficiently well acquainted that the Thoreaus invited the Alcotts in for Sunday dinner on their way home from church.[2] Thoreau quickly realized that Alcott provided a very different intellectual fare than did even the most stimulating Concord farmer. The two found much in common to talk about, and Alcott often read to Thoreau from his correspondence with his English disciples on theories of education.

Alcott, whose favorite occupation was talking, could never understand Thoreau's penchant for walking. Thoreau often urged Alcott to accompany him on his walks (an honor he accorded to few people indeed), but Alcott invariably perched on the first convenient stump or fence rail they came to and Thoreau could get him no farther into the woods. Not wanting thus to spend his afternoons, Thoreau eventually changed his tack and took to calling on Alcott at his home in the evenings. There the two spent many a happy hour together solving the problems of the world.

While the rest of the world was denouncing Alcott as an impractical dreamer, Thoreau was able to overlook his faults and foibles—of which there were unquestionably many—and see the idealist beneath. He might laugh now and then at Alcott, telling Emerson that Alcott was so good-natured that even "the rats and mice make their nests in him," but it was always a sympathetic, understanding laugh.[3] Alcott on his side found Thoreau a rare companion. He never ceased to be astonished at Thoreau's knowledge of nature and thought he must be able "to see round the corner of himself, to comprehend everything." Like Emerson he was early to recognize Thoreau's genius and his potential. And unlike Emerson, he was too good-natured ever to let Thoreau's irascibility disturb him. When he saw Thoreau striding along, he thought he literally as well as symbolically seemed to cling to the

---

1. Amos Bronson Alcott, *Journals* (Boston, 1938), 127
2. Honoré W. Morrow, *The Father of Little Women* (Boston, 1927) 233
3. Ralph Waldo Emerson, *Journals*, VII, 552

earth.[4] And when he noticed Thoreau's arms were covered with thick dark hair, he thought it appropriately like a pelt.[5]

Margaret Fuller, on the other hand, seemed to have primarily a negative effect on Thoreau. They were each too much of an individualist to get along with the other. Thoreau met her frequently at Emerson's house and once, in February 1839, even helped Emerson—though unsuccessfully—to locate a house for her in Concord. In May 1841 Thoreau took her rowing on Walden Pond and she wrote her brother Richard glowingly of the beauty of the moonlight, the song of the whippoorwills, and the fragrance of the apple blossoms on the air she found there.[6] But if there were momentarily romantic thoughts on her part, there were none on Thoreau's.

When as editor of *The Dial* she considered the poems that Emerson prodded Thoreau to submit, she almost invariably rejected them or insisted on major revisions. When, in turn, Emerson asked Thoreau to read the manuscript of her *Summer on the Lakes,* he found nothing of merit in it, though later readers have suspected it inspired the form of his own first book, *A Week on the Concord and Merrimack Rivers.*[7] Later he apparently reversed himself and through Emerson tried to persuade her to publish the book at her own expense rather than through a commercial publisher, assuring her that she would make more money that way.[8] When Thoreau was living on Staten Island, she visited him briefly and he took her on a tour of his favorite sites, gallantly (for him, at least) paying for a carriage which she ordered and did not use.[9]

There is a tale, unquestionably apocryphal, that once gossip was prevalent that Thoreau and Margaret Fuller were to be married. According to that gossip, someone approached Thoreau to see if it were true, and he supposedly replied, "No, in the first place Margaret Fuller is not fool enough to marry me; and second,

4. Amos Bronson Alcott, Autobiographical Collections. MS, Houghton Library

5. Odell Shepard, *Pedlar's Progress* (Boston, 1937), 506

6. Perry Miller, *Margaret Fuller, American Romantic* (Garden City, 1963), 74–5

7. Ibid. 114, 116

8. Ralph Waldo Emerson, *Letters* (New York, 1939), III, 250

9. William White, "Three Unpublished Thoreau Letters," *New England Quarterly,* XXXIII (1960), 373

I am not fool enough to marry her."[1] Emerson was nearer the truth when he jokingly called Thoreau "Margaret's enemy" and tried to assure her that Thoreau's "perennial threatening attitude" was his "natural relation" and not something he assumed in her presence alone.[2]

VI

Thoreau's lack of success in schoolteaching and his friendship with Emerson, who was already attaining national fame as an author, joined to foster Thoreau's interest in writing as a profession. During his college days he had often written brief essays for his own amusement, among them, for example, a nostalgic little piece about his youth in Concord turned out in the spring of 1835. It is worth quoting in part because it foreshadows his later masterly way with words:

'Twas always my delight to monopolize the little Gothic window, which overlooked the kitchen garden, particularly of a Sabbath afternoon, when all around was quiet and nature herself was taking her afternoon nap, when the last peal of the bell in the neighboring steeple,

"Singing with sullen roar," had
"Left the vale to Solitude and me," and the

very air scarcely dared breathe lest it should disturb the universal calm. Then did I use with eyes upturned to gaze upon the clouds, and, allowing my imagination to wander, search for flaws in their rich drapery that I might get a peep at the world beyond which they seem intended to veil from our view. Now is my attention engaged by a truant hawk, as like a messenger from those ethereal regions, he issued from the bosom of a cloud, and, at first a mere speck in the distance, comes circling onward exploring every teeming creek and rounding every jutting precipice. . . .
In the freshness of the dawn my brother and I were ever ready to enjoy a stroll to a certain cliff, distant a mile or more, where

1. Elbert Hubbard, *Thoreau* (East Aurora, N. Y., 1904), 168
2. Ralph Waldo Emerson, *Letters,* III, 222

we were wont to climb to the highest peak, and seating ourselves on some rocky platform, catch the first ray of the morning sun, as it gleamed upon the smooth, still river, wandering in sullen silence far below. . . .[3]

And he also tried his hand, quite unsuccessfully it must be admitted, at a poem or two—none of them worth quoting. But he made no attempt to publish these juvenile attempts.

Then however in the fall of 1837 he made his first appearance in print. In early November he went down to the Concord poorhouse to interview Anna Jones, one of the last of the Concordians still able to recall vividly incidents in the Revolutionary War. She was on her deathbed and too ill to tell him much, but when she died on November 12, he wrote a brief obituary which was published in the *Yeoman's Gazette* for November 25, 1837:

DIED: In this town, on the 12th inst. Miss Anna Jones, aged 86.

When a fellow being departs for the land of spirits, whether that spirit takes its flight from a hovel or a palace, we would fain know what was its demeanor in life—what of [the] beautiful it lived.

We are happy to state, upon the testimony of those who knew her best, that the subject of this notice was an upright and exemplary woman, that her amiableness and benevolence were such as to win all hearts, and, to her praise be it spoken, that during a long life, she was never known to speak ill of any one. After a youth passed amid scenes of turmoil and war, she has lingered thus long amongst us a bright sample of the Revolutionary woman. She was as it were, a connecting link between the past and the present—a precious relic of days which the man and patriot would not willingly forget.

The religious sentiment was strongly developed in her. Of her last years it may truly be said, that they were passed in the society of the apostles and prophets; she lived as in their presence; their teachings were meat and drink to her. Poverty was her lot, but she possessed those virtues without which the rich are but poor. As her life had been, so was her death.[4]

3. Henry David Thoreau [Childhood reminiscences]. MS, Morgan Library
4. Kenneth Walter Cameron, "Thoreau's Three Months Out of Harvard and His First Publication," *Emerson Society Quarterly,* V (1956), 9

This brief piece appeared anonymously and was only recently un-covered. There are hints that there may be other anonymous pieces by Thoreau in the Concord newspapers, but if so, no one has succeeded as yet in identifying them. Thoreau's newspaper career —if such it can be called—apparently ended as abruptly as it began.

Far more important is the fact that in the fall of 1837 he began making regular entries in a journal. On October 22, 1837, he purchased a blank book, and in it wrote:

> "What are you doing now?" he asked. "Do you keep a journal?" So I make my first entry to-day.[5]

Tradition has it that it was Emerson who asked the question and started Thoreau on a task that was to engage his labors almost daily right up until his fatal illness twenty-four years later. It was his major literary accomplishment, although its very length of nearly two million words or more than seven thousand printed pages has prevented its ever achieving the popularity of *Walden* or "Civil Disobedience." For the connoisseur however it is the best of Thoreau.

From the very beginning it is obvious that the *Journal* was the result of a professional concern with writing as an art. He dis-cussed therein frequently and often at length how to write effec-tively, how to edit, how to revise. What is more important is that he used this journal as both a proving ground and a storehouse of materials for his later essays and books.

In the early years of his writing career, he scissored to pieces his manuscript journals as he culled out from them materials suit-able for his publishable works, then recopied the remainder into a volume which he entitled "Gleanings or What Time Has Not Reaped of My Journal." Thus because the early journal is neither in its original form nor complete, we cannot make a fair judgment of its contents. As it now stands, it consists in a large part of quo-tations from his current reading—Goethe and Virgil, in particular —aphorisms which are sometimes as vapid as the notorious "Or-phic Sayings" of his friend Bronson Alcott, and only the beginnings of those nature notes and those philosophical ponderings that were

---

5. Thoreau, *Journal*, I, 3

to become such a memorable part of his later journal. It is not the masterpiece that the later journal was to become.

Thoreau, like Emerson, soon learned that an equally valuable proving ground for his writing was the lecture platform. As soon as he returned to Concord from Harvard, he renewed his active interest in the Concord Lyceum. On March 14, 1838, he inserted a large number of comments on "Society" into his Journal, and these he later welded into an essay which he read at the Concord Lyceum on April 11, 1838—the first of his many appearances on the lecture platform. The lecture was delivered in the Masonic building—the site of his ill-fated teaching experience of the previous fall.

"Society," he said therein, "was made for man," not man for society. "The mass never comes up to the standard of its best member, but on the contrary degrades itself to a level with the lowest." And striking closer to home, he continued:

> It is provoking, when one sits waiting the assembling together of his neighbors around his hearth, to behold merely their clay houses, for the most part newly shingled and clapboarded, and not unfrequently with a fresh coat of paint, trundled to his door. He has but to knock slightly at the outer gate of one of these shingle palaces, to be assured that the master or mistress is not at home.[6]

Despite these animadversions against his neighbors—or perhaps because of them—Thoreau was elected secretary of the lyceum when it began its new season in the fall on October 18, and three weeks later, he was also elected curator to replace A. H. Nelson who had resigned. Of the two positions, the latter was by far the more important. The secretary merely recorded the minutes of the meetings. The curators, on the other hand, were the general agents to do the business of the society. They prepared the winter's program, arranged for the lectures, and obtained a heated and lighted hall to hear them in. Of the seventeen lecturers that season, Thoreau was perhaps responsible for the obtaining of Emerson, Stearns Wheeler, and possibly A. H. Nelson and George Moore. He was re-elected both secretary and curator on November 6,

6. Ibid. I, 38

1839, and served until December 9, 1840, when he refused re-election.

Encouraged with the success of his first lecture, Thoreau immediately started to work on a second, entitled "Sound and Silence." But for some reason, although he had many ideas on the subject, he could not get them to fit together well enough to suit him. Three years later he was still playing with the topic, but he apparently never completed it for either the lecture platform or the press.

Thoreau readily took part in other social activities of the town and he is remembered as having joined such other young people as Albert Nelson, Henry, Reuben and John Moore, William Whiting, William Prichard, Hiram Dennis, J. F. Barrett, Francis Munroe, Rufus Hosmer, Josiah Davis, Reuben Rice, and his own brother John as "comrades in all the parties, dances, and various schemes of entertainment which occupied the leisure hours of the young people of the village." When two old maids nearby found themselves with a bountiful cherry crop and no way to harvest it, it was Thoreau who volunteered to come to their rescue.

VII

While Thoreau was away at college, there had been an important addition to the family household—Mrs. Joseph Ward and her daughter Prudence. Mrs. Ward was the widow of a colonel in the American Revolutionary army. She had become acquainted with the maiden Thoreau aunts in Boston, and in 1817 Aunt Maria Thoreau had introduced Mrs. Ward's other daughter, Caroline, to a young ministerial student named Edmund Quincy Sewall. The two became engaged and were married in August of 1820—a marriage we shall hear more of. In 1833, Mrs. Ward and Prudence moved to Concord and made their home with Elizabeth, Jane, and Maria Thoreau. When John Thoreau moved his family into the Parkman house in the spring of 1837, the Wards went along too.

Mrs. Ward and her daughter were both active radical abolitionists. When the Women's Anti-Slavery Society was formed in Concord in 1837, not only did they both become charter members, but they were joined by Mrs. Thoreau and both her daughters. Mrs. Mary Merrick Brooks, who was a close friend of both the Wards and the Thoreaus and lived on the corner of Sudbury Road next to the Parkman house, also was an active member of the Anti-Slavery Society, as was Mrs. John Wilder, the wife of the Trinitarian minister, and another friend of the Thoreau and Ward ladies. Although the abolitionist movement was still socially outcast in the North as well as in the South, the Concord ladies nonetheless gathered sixty-one members into their group and eventually numbered more than one hundred. In 1839 they were contributing more to the support of William Lloyd Garrison and his various abolitionist activities than any other local society in New England. It was typical of their interest in the cause of social justice that the Wards and Mrs. Thoreau were the leaders in calling a public meeting in Concord to protest the mistreatment of the Cherokee Indians in Georgia and in persuading Ralph Waldo Emerson to write a public letter to President Martin Van Buren on behalf of the Indians.[7]

When Mrs. Ward died in 1844, one of the Thoreau aunts wrote of her:

> She had a heart full of compassion for the suffering and the tried, which was the cause of her deep interest in the deeply injured, weary, heart-broken slave. For many years she has been a member of our [Women's Anti-Slavery] Society, always aiding us by her purse, her sympathies and her labors. She uniformly and consistently stood by the principles of the old pioneer society; and we feel that indeed a great void is made in our much thinned ranks.[8]

It was unquestionably the Wards, mother and daughter, who aroused the interest of the Thoreau family in the anti-slavery movement and in turn planted the seeds in the young Henry's mind that were later to yield some of his most memorable words and deeds. What is more, it was Prudence Ward who taught the Thoreau sisters how to paint and introduced the whole family to the excitement and pleasures of botanical studies.

7. F. B. Sanborn, "A Concord Note-Book," *Critic*, XLVIII (1906), 410
8. Sanborn, *The Life of Henry David Thoreau*, 467–8

CHAPTER FIVE
(1838–1841)

I

HAVING GIVEN UP HOPE, after nearly a year of concerted effort, of ever obtaining a regular teaching or tutoring position, Thoreau finally decided to create his own. In mid-June of 1838 he opened a private school in the family home, the Parkman house on Main Street.[1] As might be expected, especially after his difficulties with the Concord school committee, the school was slow in getting started, but by the end of the month he had four boys from Boston enrolled and had made arrangements with his mother for them to board and room in the Thoreau home.[2] When the master of Concord Academy resigned his position in the late summer, Thoreau immediately made arrangements with the trustees to rent their building for five dollars a quarter, and take over the name and goodwill of the institution.[3] Accordingly he announced in the *Yeoman's Gazette* for September 15, 1838:

CONCORD ACADEMY. The subscriber opened his school for the reception of a limited number of pupils, of both sexes, on Monday, September the tenth. Instruction will be given in the usual English branches, and the studies preparatory to a collegiate course. Terms—Six dollars per quarter. Henry D. Thoreau, Instructor.

---

1. Anton Huffert, *Thoreau as a Teacher, Lecturer and Educational Thinker* (New York University, 1951, unpublished doctoral dissertation), 61
2. Prudence Ward, Letter to Dennis Ward of June 29, 1838. MS, Abernethy Library
3. Townsend Scudder, *Concord: American Town* (Boston, 1947), 160; Kenneth Walter Cameron, "Thoreau Bills His Pupils at the Concord Academy," *Emerson Society Quarterly*, VII (1957), 48

Samuel Hoar, Nathan Brooks, and John Keyes, the trustees of Concord Academy, and Ralph Waldo Emerson offered their names as referees.

Few new pupils answered Thoreau's advertisements. By October 6 he was so discouraged with his prospects that he applied for a position in the Taunton, Massachusetts, high school, his sister Helen wrote him about, and explained that his private school was not proving sufficiently lucrative to continue. But no offer came from Taunton, and so, having nothing better at hand, he continued with the academy. By the end of the term however the situation had changed. Not only had enough pupils enrolled to justify continuing the school; there were enough to warrant hiring another teacher. And so it was that his brother John gave up his school in Roxbury and came to join Henry at the Concord Academy. On February 9, 1839, John announced in the *Yeoman's Gazette:*

> CONCORD ACADEMY. The Above School will be continued under the care of the subscriber, after the commencement of the spring term, Monday, March 11th. Terms per Quarter: English Branches, $4.00. Languages included, $6.00. He will be assisted in the classical department by Henry D. Thoreau, the present instructor. N.B. Writing will be particularly attended to. John Thoreau, Jr., Preceptor.

Before long the enrollment evidently reached the maximum of twenty-five they wished to handle. Tradition has it that eventually there was even a waiting list to get in, and they were able to refuse any short-term pupils, insisting on a minimum enrollment of twelve weeks. And yet, if they felt the family could not afford to pay, they would grant free tuition.[4] Most of their pupils, quite naturally, came from Concord. Among them were Jerome Bacon, Edward Wood, Joseph Keyes, Sarah, Helen, and Martha Hosmer, Elijah Wood, James and Story Gerrish, George and Joseph Brooks, Benjamin W. Lee, Cyrus Warren, Henry Bigelow, Kilham Flint, George Loring, Charles Kilham, Joseph Dakin, Sidney Rice, Gorham and Martha Bartlett, Sherman and Almira Tuttle, Benjamin Tolman, James Barrett Wood, Samuel Burr, and George

---

4. Edward Emerson, Notes on Thoreau

F. Hoar. Later when the Alcotts moved to Concord, Louisa May
and her sister enrolled. Thomas Hosmer and two of his friends
walked the five miles each way daily from Bedford. Horace Hosmer came in from Acton. And two students, Alexander and Andrew Beath, were from Cuba.

II

One of their prize pupils, the Thoreaus thought, was Edmund
Sewall of Scituate who enrolled for the spring term in 1840.
Edmund was a grandson of Mrs. Thoreau's star boarder, Mrs.
Joseph Ward. On June 17, 1839, he came to Concord with his
mother to visit his grandmother for a week. Henry was immediately attracted to the eleven-year-old lad and in the next few days
took him sailing on the Concord River, hiking out to the Cliffs,
and on a visit to Walden Pond. On the 22nd, Thoreau wrote in
his *Journal:*

> I have within the last few days come into contact with a pure,
> uncompromising spirit, that is somewhere wandering in the at-
> mosphere, but settles not positively anywhere. Some persons
> carry about them the air and conviction of virtue, though they
> themselves are unconscious of it, and are even backward to ap-
> preciate it in others. Such it is impossible not to love; still is
> their loveliness, as it were, independent of them, so that you seem
> not to lose it when they are absent, for when they are near it is
> like an invisible presence which attends you.
> That virtue we appreciate is as much ours as another's. We see
> so much only as we possess.[5]

And several days later, after Edmund's departure, Thoreau wrote
a poem in Gondibertian measure, entitled "Sympathy":

> Lately, alas, I knew a gentle boy.
> Whose features all were cast in Virtue's mould,
> As one she had designed for Beauty's toy,
> But after manned him for her own stronghold.

---

5. Thoreau, *Journal*, I, 80

On every side he open was as day,
That you might see no lack of strength within,
For walls and ports do only serve alway
For a pretense to feebleness and sin. . . .

So was I taken unawares by this,
I quite forgot my homage to confess;
Yet now am forced to know, though hard it is,
I might have loved him, had I loved him less.

Each moment, as we nearer drew to each,
A stern respect withheld us farther yet,
So that we seemed beyond each other's reach,
And less acquainted than when first we met.

We two were one while we did sympathize,
So could we not the simplest bargain drive;
And what avails it now that we are wise,
If absence doth this doubleness contrive?

Eternity may not the chance repeat,
But I must tread my single way alone,
In sad remembrance that we once did meet,
And know that bliss irrevocably gone. . . .

Make haste and celebrate my tragedy;
With fitting strain resound, ye woods and fields;
Sorrow is dearer in such case to me
Than all the joys other occasion yields.

Is't then too late the damage to repair?
Distance, forsooth, from my weak grasp hath reft
The empty husk, and clutched the useless tare,
But in my hands the wheat and kernel left.

If I but love that virtue which he is,
Though it be scented in the morning air,
Still shall we be truest acquaintances,
Nor mortals know a sympathy more rare.[6]

It is to be wondered that the Sewalls were not disturbed that their son was the subject of such a poem with its—to modern eyes at least—quite androgynous overtones. But disturbed they were not in the least. In fact, they delighted in calling Edmund "gentle boy,"

6. Ibid. I, 80–2

and when his younger brother George enviously lamented that he had no poem of his own, they asked Thoreau for one and he obliged with a copy of his "Bluebirds," autographed: "To Master George W. Sewall. In consideration of his love of animated Nature, the following poem is humbly inscribed by the Author H. D. Thoreau."[7] And what is more, less than a year later they enrolled Edmund as a boarding pupil in the Thoreau school for a term—something they surely would not have done had they had even the slightest question about the relationship of their son and Thoreau. Quite rightly they realized Thoreau's admiration of Edmund was intellectual rather than physical, the sort of Platonic idealization rampant among all the Transcendentalists and quite effectively described by Thoreau himself in his essay on Friendship in the "Wednesday" chapter of his first book, *A Week.* As we shall see, when Edmund's seventeen-year-old sister Ellen arrived in Concord a few weeks later, Thoreau immediately forgot entirely about Edmund. And when Edmund enrolled in the Thoreau school the following March, Thoreau was, if anything, a little annoyed, apparently fearing that Edmund's presence might in some way interfere with his pursuit of Ellen.[8]

III

The Thoreau brothers, as might be expected, had their own ideas of how to run a school and how to maintain discipline. When a pupil entered the school, he was immediately taken aside and asked why he wished to enroll. When he replied that he wished to study Latin, Greek, algebra, geometry, and so on, they would reply: "If you really wish to study those things, we can teach you, if you will obey our rules and promise to give your mind to your studies; but if you come to idle and play, or to see other boys study, we shall not want you for a pupil. Do you promise, then, to do what we require? If so, we will do our best to teach you what we know ourselves."[9] Once the boy promised, he was

---

7. Henry David Thoreau, "The Bluebirds." MS, George L. Davenport, Jr.

8. Thoreau, *Journal,* I, 129

9. F. B. Sanborn, *The Life of Henry David Thoreau* (Boston, 1917), 203–4

promptly reminded, if he were idle or mischievous, that he had broken his word. Another device they used was to assign each child his individual duties in the daily school routine to keep him busy in his moments of leisure. By such methods they were able to avoid the use of corporal punishment and yet maintain what all their pupils remembered as an almost military discipline.[1]

The school was started each morning at eight thirty with prayers, followed by a little address to put the scholars' minds in proper trim for the work of the day. Once Henry spoke of the rotation of the seasons and how it worked to the advantage of man, impressing on the children the beauties of summer, autumn, winter, and spring. So engaging was his story, it is said, that one could have heard a pin drop. He had a real faculty, Thomas Hosmer thought, for interesting his charges and winning their respect.[2]

On another occasion he spoke of the certainty of the existence of a wise and friendly power overlooking all. He asked the children: if they should go into a shop and see all the nicely finished wheels, pinions, springs, and frame pieces of a watch lying spread out on a bench and again came to find them put together exactly and working in unison to move the hands on a dial and show the passage of time, whether they could believe that this had come about by chance or rather thought that somebody with thought and plan and power had been there.[3]

When Thoreau once overheard some of the boys swearing, he called them all together and lectured them:

> Boys, if you went to talk business with a man, and he persisted in thrusting words having no connection with the subject into all parts of every sentence—Boot-jack, for instance,—wouldn't you think he was taking a liberty with you, and trifling with your time, and wasting his own?[4]

He then went on to introduce "boot-jack" frequently and violently into a sentence to demonstrate the absurdity of profanity in a striking way.

1. Edward Emerson, Notes on Thoreau
2. Ibid.
3. Ibid.
4. Edward Emerson, *Henry Thoreau as Remembered by a Young Friend*, 128–9

Once when Thoreau in his enthusiasm for the wonders of nature announced that "everything was a miracle," one of the more
skeptical pupils, announcing that he had recently cleaned some fish
and thrown their heads into the garbage, wanted to know if that
act were a miracle. Thoreau replied, "Yes," but refused to make
any further explanation, apparently thus hoping to squelch the
boy's sarcasm. The boy however long remembered and resented
the fact that Thoreau would say no more.[5] So his lectures were
not always successful.

IV

In general, John, using the downstairs room, taught the "English branches" and elementary mathematics; Henry, using the
upstairs hall, taught Latin, Greek, French, physics, natural philosophy, and natural history. A typical day in the Thoreau school
has been recorded by Edmund Sewall in a letter written to his
father on April 23, 1840:

> In the morning I recite Solid Geometry. I draw the figures and
> write down the demonstration on the slate after Mr. Henry has
> taken the book and when I have done carry it to him. He ex-
> amines it to see that it is right. Geography comes next, immedi-
> ately after recess. Smith's geography is the one used. I borrow it
> of one of the boys who has done studying it. Grammar comes
> next. Parker and Fox's is used. It is in two parts. I have been
> through the first part and have begun the second. I borrow it of
> Mr. Thoreau. . . .
> In the afternoon I am exclusively under Mr. Henry's juris-
> diction. I recite in Algebra and Latin generally before recess.
> In the afternoon Mr. Henry's classes go up into the hall over the
> schoolroom to recite. In Latin I am in company with Miss Hine.
> We are now on the life of Alcibiades in Nepos and in the excep-
> tion in conjugation in the grammar.
> Geography is studied by a good many. We draw maps of the
> states. Saturday morning is devoted to writing composition. The
> two that I have written have been on birds and berries.

5. Annie Russell Marble, *Thoreau: His Home, Friends and Books,*
272–3

The school hours are from half past eight to half past twelve in the morning and from two to four in the afternoon. Mr. Thoreau reads [a]loud those compositions which he thinks will please the scholars, which sometimes occasions a great deal of laughter. The boys sometimes write their lives or those of some venerable Aunt Hannah or Uncle Ichabod.[6]

The school was noted for its innovations. It was one of the first in our educational history to operate on the principle of "learning by doing" and to devote a considerable part of its program to field trips. At least once a week, and usually much more frequently, the whole school was taken for a walk in the woods or fields or for a row on one of the rivers or ponds. As one might expect, most such excursions were devoted to the study of natural history. Once Thoreau astonished the boys by plucking a plant so minute they could barely see it and demonstrating with a magnifying glass that it was just then in blossom with a perfect but miniscule flower. He told the boys that he was so well acquainted with the flowers of Concord, Acton, and Lincoln that he could tell by the blooming of the flowers in what month he was. On another occasion he shot a slate-colored junco for them so they could examine it more closely, and when no other game presented itself, he shot at a snowball set up on a post, just for fun.[7]

The children were impressed that he seemed to know the birds, the beasts, and the flowers not as a surgeon who dissected them, but as "one boy knows another with all their delightful little habits and fashions." The pupils used to declare to each other, "If anything happened in the deep woods which only came about once in a hundred years, Henry Thoreau would be sure to be on the spot at the time and know the whole story."[8] They could see no evidence that he wished to display his own superior knowledge; he wanted only to impress them with the wonders of Nature and to impart to them his own skill in such matters.

On their excursions together, he also took the opportunity to acquaint the children with the history of the area, particularly

6. MS, T. S. Abbott
7. Sewall, Diary
8. George Hoar, *Autobiography of Seventy Years* (New York, 1903), I, 70–1

that of the Indians. He showed them where to find the arrowheads, spearheads, pestles, and other stone implements so common then on the Concord fields and meadows—if one knew where and how to look for them. Henry Warren has recalled a time when they were sailing down the Concord River past the Great Meadows and Ball's Hill when Thoreau called their attention to a spot on the river shore which he thought to be the site of an Indian fishing village. A week later he brought them back there, this time armed with a spade. "Do you see," he asked them, "anything here that would be likely to attract Indians to this spot?" One lad pointed out that the river was available for fishing; another, that the woods were nearby for hunting. With Thoreau's help another discovered a spring nearby that made good water readily available, and still another that the nearby hill sheltered the spot from the northern winds of the winter. Then, after careful investigation, Thoreau struck his spade into the soil several times without result. The boys had just begun to think their teacher mistaken when his spade struck a stone. Moving forward a foot or two, he struck another stone, and then another. He soon uncovered a whole circle of red, fire-marked rocks that indicated an ancient Indian fireplace. But having proven his point, he then carefully buried them as he found them, leaving them for someone else to discover at a later date.[9]

Field trips of other types were taken on occasion, too. A group of boys was taken to the office of the local *Yeoman's Gazette* to watch the compositors setting type. Once they were taken to Pratt's gunsmith shop to observe the regulating of gunsights. Each spring Thoreau had the land plowed and, providing each of the boys with a little hoe, set them to work planting their own individual plots. When his boat needed tarring, the children were taken along to watch the process and to play in the shallow water while John and Henry worked.[1]

In the fall of 1840, Thoreau purchased a combination leveling instrument and circumferentor and introduced surveying into the curriculum to give their mathematics a more practical and vivid application. He took his class out to Fairhaven Bay and had them

9. Sanborn, *The Life of Henry David Thoreau*, 205–6
1. Sewall, *Diary*

work out a practice survey of the cliff. Unwittingly he thus stumbled upon an interest that within a few years was to provide a regular source of income for him.

Although inside the classroom both Thoreau brothers could be formal, outside there was much more freedom. They extended the traditional ten-minute recess to half an hour while the school windows were open to ventilate the room and give the children fresh air when they returned from their playing—an almost unheard of innovation. Both teachers would oftentimes go out into the schoolyard at recess and join with the children in their amusements. John was always ready to joke or play with the students, but Henry seemed to be a little more standoffish and on his dignity so long as they were in the vicinity of the school. However, as soon as they got outside the schoolgrounds, he let down the bars and became one of the boys.[2]

On one occasion Thoreau overheard some of the children arguing over the relative merits of their skates. Some of the Concord boys were belittling the old-fashionedness of the skates that Thomas Hosmer and his companions from Bedford had used in skating along the river to school. They in turn argued that their skates, despite the lack of style, would stand up under a test of performance. Thoreau stepped in and suggested that they go down to the river and put the two types of skates to a test. But when young Hosmer argued that the race should begin the moment they knelt on the ice to buckle on the skates, stating that in the quality of the skates should be included the speed with which they could be put on, Thoreau overruled him and insisted that the test should be taken on the original terms.[3]

George Hoar remembered that once when a group of the pupils went on an expedition to Walden woods, old Tommy Wyman, who lived there by himself and did not want the boys to invade the huckleberry fields, tried to frighten them off by telling them that there was an Indian doctor living nearby who caught small boys and cut out their livers to make medicine. Frightened, the boys dashed toward the safety of home, only to meet Thoreau out for his afternoon walk. Hearing their story, he laughed and then reas-

2. Edward Emerson, Notes on Thoreau
3. Ibid.

sured them, as he pulled a key out of his pocket, that if he met that Indian he would ram the key down his throat.[4]

Edmund Sewall, in his diary for April 1, 1840, recorded some further adventures of the pupils:

> I had a nice sail on the river yesterday after school. Messrs. John and Henry T. rowed and Jesse and I were passengers. We went up the river against the wind and then sailed down to the monument where we got out with the intention of all embarking again, but Mr. J and Jesse being near the monument and Mr. H and I near the boat we jumped in and went across to the abutment of the former bridge on the opposite side. I suppose that we should have come back for them if they had staid but they went off with the sail which we had left on the bank. Mr. H. rowed up the river a little way and got out. We had not the keys of the boat and should have been obliged to leave her without being securely fastened or have hauled her upon the shore if Joseph had not come down with the keys. He got two wet feet for his pains.

A week later he recorded another excursion:

> In the afternoon we went off into the woods with a parcel of the boys of the school where we played awhile and drank out [of] a jug of lemonade we had carried with us. We then left the jug till we came back and started for Walden pond. As we were coming back we saw Aunt [Prudence Ward] and Mr. Thoreau, and I went and joined her while the rest of the boys kept on. We went to Goose pond where we heard a tremendous chirping of frogs. It has been disputed whether the noise was caused by frogs so we were very curious to know what it was. Mr. Thoreau however caught three very small frogs, two of them in the act of chirping. While bringing them home one of them chirped in his hat. He carried them to Mr. Emerson in a tumbler of water. They chirped there also. On Sunday morning I believe he put them into a barrel with some rain water in it. He threw in some sticks for them to rest on. They sometimes crawled up the side of the barrel. I saw one of them chirping. He had swelled out the loose skin of his throat like a little bladder. . . .
> . . . At night we heard the frogs peeping and on Monday

---

4. Hoar, *Autobiography of Seventy Years*, I, 57

morning they were nowhere to be seen. They had probably crawled out of some hole in the cover of the barrell and made for the river as Mrs. Thoreau affirmed that when she heard them in the night their voices seemed to recede in that direction. Mr. Thoreau intended to have preserved them in spirits.

The children had their own adventures too. Once Georgie Hoar cut the bell rope and another of the boys climbed up into the belfry and tolled the bell the entire time Henry was walking from his home around the corner to the school—Henry's reaction is not recorded.[5] Another time Nathan Brook's son broke a window in the school, and despite the fact that Brooks was a trustee of the academy, Thoreau sent him a bill for fifty cents—which was paid. On still another occasion Edmund Sewall and some of his fellow boarding pupils started a snowball fight with the "townies" and in their excitement tipped over a bowl of pudding cooling in Mrs. Thoreau's back entry. They were sentenced to salt fish for supper.[6]

The boarding pupils, in general, found life in the Thoreau home pleasant. Horace Hosmer has recalled:

> I never forgot those dinners; the room was shaded and cool, there was no hustle. Mrs. Thoreau's bread, brown and white, was the best I had ever tasted. They had, besides, vegetables and fruit, pies or puddings; but I never saw meat there. Their living was a revelation to me. I think they were twenty years ahead of the times in Concord.
>
> At the house there was nothing jarring. Mrs. Thoreau was pleasant and talkative and her husband was always kind. If I ever saw a gentleman at home, it was he.

In later years the pupils remembered the school and its teachers with "affection," "gratitude," and "enthusiasm." Benjamin Lee thought he would never forget the kindness and goodwill of the Thoreau brothers "in their great desire to impress upon the minds of their scholars to do right always." Horace Hosmer recalled they were "rigid in exacting good work" and remembered Henry's keeping one pupil after school for nearly an hour because he omitted an *et* in reading a Latin sentence—but, Hosmer added,

5. Edward Emerson, Notes on Thoreau
6. Sewall, Diary

it was because Thoreau was a "conscientious teacher" and "wouldn't take a man's money for nothing."[7]

In general the children seemed to favor John over Henry. They thought John the "more human" and "loving." He understood and thought of others, while Henry thought more about himself, they felt. Henry was "rigid" but "not disagreeable." One pupil described him as then having been "in the green apple stage."[8] Another said they "loved" John, but "respected" Henry.[9] On the other hand, George Keyes remembered Henry as "thoroughly alive and a very pleasant talker," and Thomas Hosmer recalled the children catching him by the hand as he went away to walk with him and hear more."[1] George Hoar remembered his taking part in their games, taking them for long walks in the woods and showing them the best places to find huckleberries, blackberries, chestnuts, lilies, and cardinal flowers. He said they used to call him "Trainer Thoreau" because the boys called soldiers "trainers" and he had a long, measured stride and an erect carriage that, despite his short and rather ungainly figure, reminded them of a soldier. At times the children did not hesitate to poke fun at Thoreau. A picture of a booby in the current almanac resembled him so much that it was cut out and circulated among the pupils as a likeness.[2]

The Thoreau school lasted not quite three years. Although it had been prospering, it was brought to an abrupt close on April 1, 1841. John had never been in hearty health. As early as 1833 he had suffered from nosebleeds so violent that he fainted.[3] There were times when what he called "colic" confined him to the house all day. But tuberculosis was the real trouble. Frail and thin—he weighed only 117 pounds—he could stand the strain of teaching no longer.[4] Since Henry did not care to carry on by himself, the

---

7. Edward Emerson, Notes on Thoreau
8. Edward Emerson, *Henry Thoreau as Remembered by a Young Friend*, 23, 127
9. Ralph Waldo Emerson, *Complete Writings* (Boston, 1903), X, 609
1. Edward Emerson, Notes on Thoreau
2. John S. Keyes, Letter to F. H. Underwood of November 15, 1886. MS, Barrett Collection
3. John Thoreau, Letter to George Stearns of October 18, 1833. MS, Massachusetts Historical Society
4. Sewall, Diary

doors of the school were closed and John left immediately on a tour of New Hampshire, hoping vainly that the mountain air would benefit his weakened lungs. A month later the Concord Academy trustees persuaded a James Oliver to reopen the school, but he was not able to make a go of it and the school closed down completely. Thus one of the pioneer experiments in modern education and Henry Thoreau's own schoolteaching days came to an abrupt end.

The Thoreau school was a century ahead of its time. Granted Bronson Alcott's famous Temple School had anticipated some of its innovations by a few years. But Alcott with his experimentation had brought the wrath of the community down on his head. The Thoreaus, on the other hand, although many of their innovations were more radical than those of Alcott, won acceptance and made of their school a considerable and memorable success.

V

Thoreau and his brother John had long planned a vacation from their school together—a boat trip on the Concord and Merrimack Rivers. In the spring of 1839 they spent a week building a new and more seaworthy boat than their old "Rover." It was fifteen feet long by three and a half feet wide at its greatest breadth, and shaped like a fisherman's dory. They christened it the "Musketaquid"—the Indian name for Concord River, painted it green below, with a border of blue, and equipped it with two sets of oars, two masts, and sails. They also provided it with a pair of wheels to roll it around any falls they should encounter, and with several poles for shoving it through shallow places. A cotton cloth tent—with one of the masts to be used for a tent pole —would provide shelter for the night, and a buffalo skin for warmth.

Their vacation was to be between the summer and autumn sessions of their school. They planned to go down the Concord to its confluence with the Merrimack, and then up the Merrimack as far as they could. Then they would journey up to the White Mountains before returning on the rivers. Dr. Josiah Bartlett, the local physician, proposed that his son accompany them, but they wanted the vacation to themselves and so decided against it.[5]

On August 29, to celebrate their planned departure, Thoreau gave one of the first of his melon parties that were later to become annual events on the Concord social calendar. He had developed a reputation for growing the biggest and juiciest melons in town and was exceedingly proud of it. To assure a good crop, he put a hundred melon seeds into every hill, instead of the usual eight or ten. And then, to make even more certain, he planted as many as sixty hills. When they were available, he added exotic species, such as the citron melon, that few Concordians had seen or heard of. Little wonder his neighbors went out of their way to wangle invitations to the annual Thoreau melon party.

The boys of the town too soon learned of the quality of Thoreau's melons. A neighbor told Thoreau that he could not successfully raise melons because his own sons always cut them up before they were fully ripe. A few days later Thoreau, looking out the window, saw one of the man's sons astride the largest and earliest watermelon in the Thoreau patch and brandishing a case knife over it. Thoreau bellowed with such force from the window that the boy scooted for the fence before any damage was done and Thoreau later gave him a lecture that convinced him that watermelon was not in his father's dominions. The watermelon was thus saved and grew to be a remarkably large and sweet one, though bearing to the last the triangular scar of the tap which the thief had designed upon it.

On the afternoon of August 29, 1839, John Shepard Keyes dropped in for a visit, and that evening he reported in his diary:

> Went up to see Henry Thoreau who is about starting on his expedition to the White Mts in his boat. He has all things arranged prime and will have a glorious time if he is fortunate enough to have good weather. He showed me all the minutiae of packing and invited me up there to eat some fine melons in the evening. . . .
>
> I spent . . . the rest of the time getting the fellows ready to go to the Thoreau[']s melon spree. We went about 9 and saw a table spread in the very handsomest style with all kinds and qualities of

melons and we attacked them furiously and I eat [*sic*] till what with the wine & all I had quite as much as I could carry home.[6]

The next evening John and Henry wheeled the boat up to their door and loaded it down with potatoes, melons, and cooking utensils.

On Saturday, August 31, they were ready to leave, but there was a warm, drizzling rain that did not bode well. They thought of postponing the trip, but by afternoon it had cleared off, and with a vigorous shove, they launched their boat and started downstream, waving to their friends, who had gathered to wish them godspeed, as they disappeared around a bend in the river. For a few minutes they paused at Ball's Hill to pick blueberries and seven miles down the river at Billerica they moored their boat. After a supper of cocoa and bread, they pitched their tent for the night. With the novelty of the occasion they found it difficult to get to sleep. A fox stepped daintily through the dried leaves and a muskrat tried unsuccessfully to raid their melons. Later a fire in Lowell brightened up the horizon and they could hear the distant fire bells; eventually sleep overcame them.

A dense fog which obliterated the landscape greeted them in the morning, but it melted away soon after they embarked. Just above Billerica Falls they entered the Middlesex Canal and, by dint of drawing the boat along by a cord from the towpath, covered its six miles in little more than an hour. Churchgoers, disapproving of their Sunday dissipation, looked at them askance. By noon they had been let down through the locks into the Merrimack and started on their way upstream. They rested for lunch on a sandy shore opposite the Glass-house village in Chelmsford, plucked wild plums, and read to each other out of their gazetteer. As they rowed past Wicasuck Island, two rough-looking customers called down from the high banks to learn if they could hire passage to Nashua, New Hampshire, but the Thoreaus, pointing out that their boat was already overloaded, denied them passage and left them to get along the bank as well as they could. That evening, having covered twelve miles, they pitched their tent on the east side of the river, in Tyngsborough, just above some patches of beach plum.

---

6. John Shepard Keyes, Diary. MS, Mrs. Raymond Emerson

On Monday morning, after washing out their boat, they proceeded on their way. Occasionally one would run along the bank, stopping to visit at a farmhouse for a glass of milk or a cool drink from the well, while the other continued boating. When they were both tired, they would beach the boat in the shade of a tree and feast on a melon from their load. At one point they were passed by a fleet of canal boats on their way down the river; at another, they floated along for a time with a scow, exchanging gossip and cooling themselves with a draft of water from the crew's jug. They stopped to explore a miniature desert between Tyngsborough and Hudson and found therein the remnants of an ancient Indian fireplace. At noon they stopped in the shade of some buttonwoods to rest and swim. Later they explored Salmon Brook briefly and got their first good view of Mount Uncannunuc. In the late afternoon they passed Nashua and that night camped by a deep ravine near Penichook Brook in Nashville. There was a high wind that night that ruined many a neighboring cornfield, but protected by the pines, they slept peacefully through it.

Tuesday morning they were up long before daybreak and by three o'clock were on their way. In mid-morning they wheeled their boat around Cromwell's Falls, picking up four Indian arrowheads and a stone tool on their way. A passing canal boatman, thinking they were hunters, inquired if they had shot anything, and Thoreau quipped back that he had "shot a buoy." At noon they boiled rice, ate their lunch on an island about a mile north of the mouth of the Souhegan River, and shot some passenger pigeons to take along for their supper. In mid-afternoon they locked through the canal around Moore's Falls and camped that night by the falls at Bedford, New Hampshire.

On Wednesday they locked themselves as rapidly as they could past the manufacturing city of Manchester. In the upper river, they met a canal boatman who offered to take them in tow for a time—an offer they declined when they discovered he intended to lift their boat onto his. When they stopped at a farmhouse to purchase supplies, the owner's son, entranced with the account of their adventures, asked leave to join them. But though the Thoreaus were willing, the father was not, and so they had to go along without him. They camped that night in Hooksett.

[91]

On Thursday morning they awoke to find it raining. Getting permission to hang their tents and buffalo skins in a corn barn to dry, they started off on foot. They stopped that night in Concord, New Hampshire, to visit friends and were "hospitably entertained."[7] There they abandoned temporarily the gun they had brought with them, thinking it would affect the "innocence of their enterprise."[8]

Friday morning dawned clear and the brothers took a Plymouth-bound stage at 7 a.m. When it stopped over at Sanbornton for lunch, they climbed a nearby hill for exercise and got their first real view of the White Mountains. Arriving in Plymouth in mid-afternoon, they hiked fifteen miles up the Pemigewasset valley through Campton to James Tilton's inn in West Thornton.

On Saturday, September 7, they hiked through Peeling (now Woodstock) to Lincoln, where they visited the Stone Flume and the Basin, and were deeply impressed by the great pot holes worn in the rock. Later in the afternoon they hiked through Franconia Notch and reached Profile Lake, where they paused to look up at the Old Man of the Mountains.

Sunday and Monday they devoted to mountain climbing. They proceeded through Crawford Notch, followed the Amonoosuck River to its source, and finally started up Mount Washington, the highest of the White Mountains, reaching the summit on Tuesday. Returning to the Crawford House, they took the stage, first to Conway, and then on to Concord, New Hampshire, and on Thursday, the 12th, they reached their boat and campsite at Hooksett. Purchasing a watermelon "for ballast" from the friendly farmer who had stored their possessions, they started off down the river, and with wind and current with them, they reached Merrimack, New Hampshire, where they camped for the night.

They had gone to bed on a summer's night; they woke up in the morning to find autumn in the air. Getting under way at five o'clock they continued rapidly downstream. At noon they purchased an apple pie at a country farmhouse and devoured the news in the paper with which it was wrapped as eagerly as the pie

7. Thoreau, *Writings*, I, 322
8. Christopher McKee, "Thoreau's First Visit to the White Mountains," *Appalachia*, XXXI (1956), 199

itself. The wind deserted them when they turned into the Merrimack Canal and they resorted once more to the towrope. Rowing leisurely up the Concord, they found the sun had set and the stars were twinkling in the sky before they reached their native port and discovered to their surprise their keel marks still in the mud and the flags still flattened by their boat. They had traveled fifty miles that day and so brought their journey and their vacation to an end.

The voyage on the Concord and Merrimack on the surface was simply a vacation lark of the two young men. But as the years passed, it had a growing significance in Thoreau's mind. As we shall see, John was soon to die and this voyage through the haze of memory was to become a tangible symbol of Thoreau's love and admiration for his lost brother, a symbol which he eventually metamorphosed into his first book, *A Week on the Concord and Merrimack Rivers*. Although Thoreau kept a diary on the voyage itself, it was not until after his brother's death that he seriously embarked on expanding the brief bare bones we have recorded here into the work of literature that is the book.

CHAPTER SIX
(1839–1842)

I

ELLEN, the oldest of the three Sewall children, was seventeen and her brothers Edmund and George eleven and five respectively when on July 20, 1839, she arrived in Concord for a two-week visit with the Wards and the Thoreaus. Although Henry had unquestionably met her many times before, he suddenly saw her as though for the first time. From all accounts she was a striking young lady—possessing a beauty she was to retain all her life. And Thoreau, at twenty-two, was ripe for such an encounter. He had been slow to develop an interest in the opposite sex. The earliest indication we can find of such an interest is a poem he had written in his journal only the previous winter, which begins:

> We two that planets erst had been
> Are now a double star.[1]

But the object of that particular poem has never been identified. It was apparently a passing infatuation, soon forgotten even by Thoreau.

Ellen, on her arrival in Concord, had a much more striking and lasting effect. Before the first day of her visit was over, Thoreau had fallen completely and, like the love-sick Orlando of *As You Like It,* started writing poems to her. The first was one in which he suggested:

> One green leaf shall be our screen,
>   Till the sun doth go to bed,
> I the king and you the queen

---

1. Thoreau, *Journal,* I, 72

Of that peaceful little green,
Without any subject's aid.[2]

Four days later in another he said:

As 't were two summer days in one,
Two Sundays come together,
Our rays united make one sun
With fairest summer weather.[3]

They were hardly great poetry—Thoreau, after all, wrote few if any great poems—but they clearly conveyed his love for Ellen. By July 25 he was beyond poetry. He could write only one short but emphatic prose sentence in his journal—"There is no remedy for love but to love more."[4]

As for Ellen, she was not unmoved. She wrote her father: "I can not tell you half I have enjoyed here."[5] She spoke of walks with the Thoreau brothers, John and Henry, accounts of which she said would fill half a dozen letters; of Henry's taking her to see a camelopard (i.e. giraffe) that had been brought on tour to Concord; of his taking her out for a sail on the river with Aunt Prudence; of walking out to Fairhaven Bay and Walden Pond with John, Henry, and the inevitable Aunt Prudence; of going berrying up the North Branch, and of riding with the Wards with Henry as the driver.

Evenings the young people entertained themselves. Since phrenology was all the rage at the moment, they tried reading the bumps on each other's heads. When Thoreau announced after feeling Ellen's cranium that she had no bumps at all, the party went into gales of laughter, for apparently he was not aware that his statement could mean she was either a genius or an idiot.[6]

Ellen was with Thoreau almost constantly for two weeks, but recalcitrant as he could be with others, only once did he refuse to carry out her every wish. When on Sunday morning she asked

---

2. Ibid. I, 87
3. Ibid. I, 88
4. Ibid.
5. Ellen Sewall, Letter to her father of July 31, 1839. MS, George L. Davenport, Jr.
6. Louise Osgood Koopman, "The Thoreau Romance," *Massachusetts Review*, IV (1962), 67

him to accompany her to divine services, he adamantly refused. Outdoors was where he worshipped, he announced. Not even Ellen Sewall could get him into a church pew.[7]

John Shepard Keyes was enjoying at the moment a vacation from his classes at Harvard. On August 1 he was visiting Captain Moore when Aunt Prudence brought Ellen to see the Moore gardens. Keyes too was impressed with Ellen and walked her home, talking, according to his diary, "on all manner of things that were interesting."[8] He immediately strolled over to see his friend Henry Fuller and report "what an excellent girl" he thought Ellen was. After dinner he wandered down to the Thoreau's, ostensibly to borrow their boat for a sail, but he was frustrated, for Ellen was not in sight. That evening he was luckier—he was invited to a party at Mrs. Richard's and was delighted to find Ellen there. He, to use his own words, "pounced upon" her and conversed with her so long that the others finally introduced some singing to break up their *tête à tête*. He accompanied her to supper, talked with her about the Athenaeum, and, when the party was over, walked her home. The next day he attended a "tea squall" at Mrs. Brooks's. The Thoreaus entertained with music and he talked for a while with Sophia, Henry's sister, but eventually he was able to get Ellen aside by himself and finally walked her home once more. On the 3rd he made another visit to the Thoreau's to borrow the boat, but to his dismay he discovered that Ellen had returned that morning to Scituate.

Ellen herself was sad at leaving Concord. She cried, she said, all the way to Lexington in the stage coach and, on arriving home in Scituate, wrote Aunt Prudence that the Concord visit had been one of the happiest moments of her life. She asked that "affectionate remembrance" be given to the Thoreaus.[9]

Henry's brother John had been equally attracted to Ellen. When he discovered she had left some Indian relics behind, he forwarded them to her, enclosing a cleverly mounted insect as a joke, and a letter announcing that he and Henry were about to leave on a boating trip to New Hampshire, a vacation from their

7. Ibid.
8. John Shepard Keyes, Diary. MS, Mrs. Raymond Emerson
9. Elizabeth Osgood Davenport and Louise Osgood Koopman, "Henry D. Thoreau 1839–1840." MS, George L. Davenport, Jr.

schoolteaching duties.[1] The excursion was, of course, their memorable journey on the Concord and Merrimack rivers.

When the brothers returned from their trip, John left immediately for Scituate. Aunt Prudence's suggestion that it was not quite proper to visit when Ellen's parents were away on a trip to Niagara Falls was quietly ignored.[2] Ellen, however, was not in the least disturbed at his arrival. When one of her friends, Sarah Otis, called hinting that she would like to stay for a visit, Ellen put her off until after John had gone. George and Edmund, she thought, provided adequate chaperonage.[3]

John and Ellen took a walk to Colman's hill together and John entertained the boys with tales of his recent excursion and stories of wild animals. Georgie thought him quite delightful, but disconcertingly persisted in calling him Henry. When John returned to Concord he brought with him a sermon to appease Aunt Prudence. Laid in was a note from Ellen: "I have enjoyed Mr. John's visit exceedingly though sorry father and Mother were not at home."[4] Her sorrow, however, seemed not to have overwhelmed her.

Henry's spirits, quite understandably, were dampened for some time at the obvious success of his brother's visit. All fall he wrote melancholy notes on maidens and love in his journal, climaxing them with an entry saying:

> But alas! to be actually separated from that parcel of heaven we call our friend, with the suspicion that we shall no more meet in nature, is source enough for all the elegies that ever were written.[5]

By Christmas vacation time, however, he had regained his good spirits and, instead of writing elegies, joined Prudence and John on a visit to Ellen in Scituate.

There is little record of what occurred on that visit, but no sooner was it over than Ellen wrote Aunt Prudence:

1. Ibid.
2. Thoreau, *The First and Last Journeys,* I, 6–7
3. Davenport and Koopman, "Henry D. Thoreau 1839–1840"
4. *An Address delivered before the Teachers and Friends of the Sunday School in the Twelfth Congregational Society, Boston . . . ,* March 29, 1833 (Boston, 1833). Inscribed copy, Abernethy Library
5. Thoreau, *Journal,* I, 108

The house seems deserted since you left us; I never was so lonely in my life as the day you went away, and I have not quite recovered my spirits yet. You will say "how foolish," but I can't help it. . . .

I have wished you and John and Henry here a thousand times this week.[6]

She wanted to know if the Thoreau school had been reopened with due form and wondered, "Does Dr. Thoreau continue to give advice gratis?" adding, "I do not clean my brasses half as quick without the accompaniment of his flute."

After Thoreau returned to Concord, he judiciously sent Ellen's father a gift—a volume of Jones Very's poems—and Ellen soon reported that the whole family had enjoyed them. John, in his turn, sent Ellen some South American opals for her natural-history cabinet, some books for her brother Edmund, and a long letter to little George which ended:

I send you Sir nothing but a letter, and now if sister has read it through to you very carefully you may give her a kiss for me and wish her a Happy New Year!![7]

But Henry was not to be outdone. He in his turn sent Ellen some of his own poems, including one on the Assabet River which suggested:

Up this pleasant stream let's row
  For the livelong summer's day,
Sprinkling foam where'er we go
In wreaths as white as driven snow.
  Ply the oars! away! away![8]

In one of his letters he threw in for good measure a lecture to Ellen against the use of tea and coffee.[9]

Ellen, writing to Aunt Prudence, told of her brother's delight

6. Ellen Sewall, Letter to Prudence Ward of December 26, 1839. MS, George L. Davenport, Jr.
7. John Thoreau, Jr., Letter to George Sewall of December, 1839. MS, George L. Davenport, Jr
8. Davenport and Koopman, "Henry D. Thoreau 1839–1840"
9. Henry Beetle Hough, *Thoreau of Walden* (New York, 1956), 77

in their gifts and her own pleasure in the opals and closed her letter with, "I often wish you three here to walk with me to the beach and hills again. We had pleasant times that week, did we not?"[1] Later she wrote again:

My neglecting to thank Henry for his original poetry was entirely unintentional, and I regret it exceedingly. I wish you would give him to understand that we really were much pleased at receiving it.[2]

Three months later, in March 1840, young Edmund Sewall was enrolled in the Thoreau School and came to live with the Thoreaus in Concord for a term. At the time of Edmund's arrival, Thoreau noted cryptically in his journal, "We will have no vulgar Cupid for a go-between, to make us the playthings of each other, but rather cultivate an irreconcilable hatred instead of this."[3]

In June, Ellen herself came to Concord for another visit and Thoreau once more took her out in his boat, reporting in his journal:

The other day I rowed in my boat a free, even lovely young lady, and, as I plied the oars, she sat in the stern, and there was nothing but she between me and the sky. So might all our lives be picturesque if they were free enough.[4]

(Perhaps he took her down to see her name and his initials carved together on the Red Bridge.)[5] When Ellen returned shortly to Scituate, John immediately followed her there. Henry enviously complained in his journal that no matter how hard he had striven, he had not yet succeeded in really getting to know one member of his own mysterious and undiscoverable race.[6]

In July the Wards made a visit to Scituate and John went with them. When he and Ellen went for a stroll along the beach, Aunt

1. Ellen Sewall, Letter to Prudence Ward of January 21, 1840. MS, George L. Davenport, Jr.
2. Ellen Sewall, Letter to Prudence Ward of February 12, 1840. MS, George L. Davenport, Jr.
3. Thoreau, *Journal*, I, 129
4. Thoreau, *Journal*, I, 144
5. Edmund Sewall, Diary. MS, T. S. Abbot
6. Thoreau, *Journal*, I, 155

Prudence went along as a chaperone. But when Prudence decided to rest on some rocks, John took the opportunity to propose as soon as they got out of hearing. Ellen, in surprise, accepted, but hardly had she returned home when she began to feel that she had made a mistake. She realized, she said, that it was not John but Henry whom she preferred. When her mother learned of the engagement, she insisted that Ellen break it immediately, for she was certain that the news would break Mr. Sewall's heart. He was an old-line conservative Unitarian and disapproved strongly of Emerson and his associates. Both Thoreau boys were too Transcendentalist to please him as potential sons-in-law. John accepted her new decision regretfully and when he returned home, sent her a crystal as a memento of their friendship.

It has been said that Henry did not know at the time of John's proposal and Ellen's rejection. When Prudence Ward mentioned the incident after John's death, Henry is said to have expressed surprise.[7] But his seeming innocence was more than likely only a cover for his embarrassment. It is true that he may never have known *why* Ellen rejected John, for in *A Week* he remarked:

> I heard that an engagement was entered into between a certain youth and a maiden, and then I heard that it was broken off, but I did not know the reason in either case.[8]

But on July 19, 1840, the day of John's return from Scituate, Henry wrote in his journal:

> These two days that I have not written in my Journal, set down in the calendar as the 17th and 18th of July, have been really an aeon in which a Syrian empire might rise and fall. How many Persias have been lost and won in the interim? Night is spangled with fresh stars.[9]

Surely this is evidence that Henry knew why John went to Scituate and what the final outcome was.

It is more likely that Henry, knowing of his brother's love for Ellen, wittingly stepped aside so that John, as the elder, might

7. T. M. Raysor, "The Love Story of Thoreau," *Studies in Philology,* XXIII (1926), 460
8. Thoreau, *Writings,* I, 311
9. Thoreau, *Journal,* I, 170

have the field free. Then, when John was rejected, Henry felt free to speak for himself. Thus the night became "spangled with fresh stars" and a few weeks later he was able to say, "A wave of happiness flows over us like sunshine over a field."[1]

Early in September 1840, the Sewalls, learning of their daughter's continued interest in the Thoreaus, sent her off to Watertown, New York, to visit relatives, hoping that the distance might help her to forget them. They would have been dismayed had they known that Aunt Prudence kept Ellen informed of activities in Concord. Ellen gratefully wrote her on October 26:

> I always think of you when I see any beautiful prospect, or such like, for we have seen so many together. You are not the only person in Mrs. Thoreau's family whom such scenes call to mind. What delightful walks we had together in Concord last summer, to the cliffs, etc. Oh, those were happy times. . . .
> What great work is Henry engaged in now? . . . Will the school go on as usual this winter?[2]

Then early in November Henry himself wrote Ellen. The letter no longer exists, but it seems likely that his journal entry for November 1 is a draft of a portion of it, for it reads:

> I thought that the sun of our love should have risen as noiselessly as the sun out of the sea, and we sailors have found ourselves steering between the tropics as if the broad day had lasted forever. You know how the sun comes up from the sea when you stand on the cliff, and doesn't startle you, but everything, and you too are helping it.[3]

Henry in love could be cryptic, but before the letter was finished, he had proposed marriage. Ellen this time consulted her father first, by letter, before replying. She was summoned back post haste to Scituate and on her way wrote Aunt Prudence from New York City on November 18:

> Last week Tuesday, the day I sent my last letter to you I received one from Father. He wished me to write immediately

---

1. Perry Miller, *Consciousness in Concord* (Boston, 1958), 148
2. Ellen Sewall, Letter to Prudence Ward of October 26, 1840. MS, George L. Davenport, Jr.
3. Miller, *Consciousness in Concord*, 178

in a "*short, explicit* and *cold* manner to Mr. T." He seemed very glad I was of the same opinion as himself with regard to the matter. I wrote to H.T. that evening. I never felt so badly at sending a letter in my life. I could not bear to think that both those friends whom I have enjoyed so much with would now no longer be able to have the free pleasant intercourse with us as formerly. My letter was very short indeed. But I hope it was the thing. It will not be best for either you or me to allude to this subject in our letters to each other. Your next letter may as well be to Mother perhaps, or Edmund. By that time the worst of this will be passed and we can write freely again. I do feel so sorry H. wrote to me. It was such a pity. Though I would rather have it so than to have him say the same things on the *beach* or anywhere else. If I had only been at home so that Father could have read the letter himself and have seen my answer, I should have liked it better. But it is all over now. We will say nothing of it till we meet. . . . Burn my last.[4]

Many years later Ellen told her children that "she had been so distressed and had felt so mortified and worried over her mistaken acceptance of John and the consequent trouble and disturbance that she could only acquiesce in her father's desire with regard to Henry."[5]

But Henry, intuitively perhaps, had already prepared himself for a negative answer. On November 7, two days before Ellen replied to his letter,[6] he wrote in his journal a poem which said:

> I did not think such sober play
> Would leave me in so sad a plight,
> And I should be most sorely spent
> When first I was most innocent.
>
> I thought by loving all beside
> To prove to you my love was wide,
> And by the rites I soared above
> To show you my peculiar love.[7]

And so their romance came to an end.

4. Ellen Sewall, Letter to Prudence Ward November 18, 1840. MS, George L. Davenport, Jr.
5. Davenport and Koopman, "Henry D. Thoreau 1839-1840"
6. Raysor, "The Love Story of Thoreau," 460
7. Miller, *Consciousness in Concord*, 181

Even before Ellen had made her visit to Concord in the summer of 1839, she had met a young man by the name of Joseph Osgood in her father's home. Later he was ordained pastor of the Unitarian Church in Cohasset, Massachusetts, a few miles from Scituate, and their acquaintance blossomed into a courtship. He proposed to her in October 1842; she accepted; and they were married in 1844. Their marriage was a long, fruitful, and happy one. Years later she told her children that she would have married Joseph Osgood even if her parents had objected.[8]

At some point, perhaps at the time of her engagement to Joseph Osgood, Ellen clipped all the pages from her diary for the summer and fall of 1840, apparently not wishing to embarrass him with any reference to Thoreau. However she overlooked a revealing entry of a year later, when after recounting the reading aloud of some of Thoreau's manuscript poems to her friends, she added:

> The favorite was "Up this pleasant stream let's row." That is the first peice [sic] Henry gave me in "days long passed," "in years not worth remembering." I wonder if his thoughts ever wander back to those times when the hours sped so pleasantly and we were so happy. I think they do. I little thought then that he cared so much as subsequent events have proved.—But to quit this painful theme. . . .[9]

And she turned to other subjects. Yet she continued to inquire regularly as to his welfare when she wrote to Prudence Ward. She watched for his writings in *The Dial*.[1] In later years she kept a picture of him on her living-room wall, and her own children presented her with a set of his collected works. When Thoreau made his first visit to Cape Cod in 1849, he stopped off at Cohasset, called on the Osgoods, and took a walk along the beach with Ellen's husband. Together they examined the wreck of the *St. John,* which Thoreau so vividly describes in *Cape Cod,* and he gave Mr. Osgood two geological cases. Later, when Mr. Osgood preached one Sunday in Concord, he and Thoreau took a walk around Walden Pond together. After Thoreau's death, his sister Sophia re-

---

8. Florence Lennon, "The Voice of the Turtle." *Thoreau Society Bulletin,* XV (1946), 2
9. Ellen Sewall, Diary for July 25, 1841. MS, Mrs. Gilbert Tower
1. Ellen Sewall, Diary for January 31, 1841. MS, Mrs. Gilbert Tower

newed her acquaintance with Ellen. They corresponded and visited back and forth frequently. And when Sophia died in 1876, she willed Ellen a thousand dollars and some of her most personal possessions, including a scrapbook which she had made as a memorial to her two brothers.

Neither did Thoreau forget Ellen. Two months later he lamented in his journal: "To sigh under the cold cold moon for a love unrequited, is to put a slight upon nature; the natural remedy would be to fall in love with the moon and the night, and find our love requited." And the next day he added: "Disappointment will make us conversant with the nobler part of our nature." Nine years later, when he published his first book, Thoreau incorporated into it his description of her in his boat on the Concord River in the summer of 1840 and added:

> I could then say with the poet,—
> "Sweet falls the summer air
> Over her frame who sails with me;
> Her way like that is beautifully free,
>   Her nature far more rare,
> And is her constant heart of virgin purity."[2]

He carried the memory of her to the very end. Shortly before his death in 1862, his sister Sophia mentioned Ellen's name in his presence and Thoreau replied: "I have always loved her. I have always loved her."[3]

II

Years later Thoreau was able to sublimate his love for the opposite sex in a worship of the world of nature and, as he once put it, in falling in love with a shrub oak. But now at twenty-three, he found the love of nature insufficient. There were yearnings and desires for companionship that a shrub oak simply could not fulfill. It was only natural therefore that he turned for motherly

---

2. Thoreau, *Writings*, I, 45–6
3. Koopman, "The Thoreau Romance," 66

consolation to a woman whom he had long admired—Emerson's sister-in-law, Mrs. Lucy Jackson Brown.

Born in 1798, Mrs. Brown was nearly twenty years older than Thoreau. She had married Charles Brown, a Boston commission merchant, who, when he became involved in financial difficulties, fled to Europe, abandoning his wife and their two children. Emerson persuaded her to move to Concord. And thus it was that while Thoreau was away at Harvard she and her children had become boarders in the Thoreau household.

Mrs. Brown was somewhat of a bluestocking—or at least Thoreau thought of her as such—and he developed a strong admiration for her. In May 1837, while home for a few days from college, he had gathered a bunch of violets and tossed them in through her window with a copy of his poem "Sic Vita":

> I am a parcel of vain strivings tied
> By a chance bond together,
> Dangling this way and that, their links
> Were made so loose and wide,
> Methinks,
> For milder weather.[4]

It was not a love poem, but an expression of affection for a woman whom he idealized.

Since in 1841 Mrs. Brown was once again living in Concord—this time in a house of her own near Emerson's, it was only natural that he turned to her for consolation. Elizabeth Weir, who was working as a governess in the Emerson household at the time, has said:

He [Thoreau] loved . . . Mrs. Brown and was as a son to her. She depended on him [and] would say, "Run over to Mr. Emerson's and see if H[enry] is there. Get him to come over and see if anything can be done about my stove's smoking." He would look at the damper or latch and mend and fit. While at work at these jobs, he would prolong the conversation. It seemed a favour to him to ask him to do something.[5]

It is said he liked to entertain her by solo dancing.

4. Henry David Thoreau, *Collected Poems* (Baltimore, 1964), 81
5. Edward Emerson, Notes on Thoreau

It seems likely it was Mrs. Brown that Thoreau was thinking of when he wrote in his journal for January 4, 1841:

> I know a woman who is as true to me and as incessant with her mild rebuke as the blue sky—When I stand under her cope, and instantly all pretension drops off—& I am swept by her influence as by the wind and rain, to remove all taint. I am fortunate that I can pass and repass before her (as a mirror) each day—and prove my strength in her glances. She is far truer to me than to herself. Her eyes are like the windows of nature, through which I catch glimpses of the native land of the soul and from them comes a light which is not of the sun.[6]

And the depth of his feeling for her seems to be indicated in his journal entry for February 21: "It is hard to preserve equanimity and greatness on that debatable ground between love and esteem."[7] At any rate, when Mrs. Brown returned to Plymouth in midsummer, Thoreau wrote her:

> I would deluge you with letters, as boys throw feathers into the air to see the wind take them. I should rather fancy you at evening dwelling far away behind the serene curtain of the West,—the home of fair weather,—than over by the chilly sources of the east wind.[8]

And on October 5, he wrote her:

> Pray let me know what you are thinking about any day,— what most nearly concerns you. Last winter, you know, you did more than your share of the talking, and I did not complain for want of an opportunity. Imagine your stove-door out of order, at least, and then while I am fixing it you will think of enough things to say.
>
> What makes the value of your life at present? what dreams have you, and what realizations? You know there is a high table-land which not even the east wind reaches. Now can't we walk and chat upon its plane still, as if there were no lower latitudes?[9]

---

6. Miller, *Consciousness in Concord*, 207
7. Thoreau, *Journal*, I, 219
8. Thoreau, *Correspondence*, 45
9. Ibid. 51

And on that higher table-land his affection for her continued, although, as time at least partially healed the wound of Ellen's rejection, Thoreau found less need of Mrs. Brown's consolation.

III

Meanwhile however Thoreau had found another, younger lady to be of interest. Mary Russell, three years younger than Thoreau, was a resident of Plymouth, Massachusetts, and a close friend of Mrs. Emerson. She was a frequent visitor to the Emerson household and a resident there for the entire summers of 1840 and 1841, when she acted as tutor and governess for young Waldo. In the summer of 1840 John Shepard Keyes had attempted a brief flirtation with her but gave up when he found her monopolized by the Thoreaus. When they took her to visit an encampment of the Penobscot Indians on the bank of the Concord, he tried to entice her off to hunt for cardinal flowers. But she excused herself, first because she did not have a shawl, and then because it looked like a shower. "The Thoreaus were the real cause," Keyes complained that night in his diary.[1]

The summer of 1841, as we shall see, Thoreau too was living with the Emersons, and so the two were thrown into direct contact. When she returned to Plymouth in the fall, he wrote a poem for her, entitling it "To the Maiden in the East":

> Low in the eastern sky
> Is set thy glancing eye;
> And though its gracious light
> Ne'er riseth to my sight,
> Yet every star that climbs
> Above the gnarled limbs
>   Of yonder hill,
> Conveys thy gentle will.
>
> Believe I knew thy thought,
> And that the zephyrs brought
> Thy kindest wishes through,

1. Keyes, Diary

As mine they bear to you,
That some attentive cloud
Did pause amid the crowd
    Over my head,
While gentle things were said. . . .

Still will I strive to be
As if thou were with me;
Whatever path I take,
It shall be for thy sake,
Of gentle slope and wide,
As thou wert by my side,
    Without a root
To trip thy gentle foot

I'll walk with gentle pace,
And choose the smoothest place,
And careful dip the oar,
And shun the winding shore,
And gently steer my boat
Where water-lilies float,
    And cardinal flowers
Stand in their sylvan bowers.[2]

If Thoreau wrote any letters to her that fall, they seem to be no longer extant. However he did inquire about her in his letters to Mrs. Brown, and on December 12, 1841, he made an entry in his journal that seems most certainly to concern Mary Russell:

Now lately I have heard of some traits in the character of a fair and earnest maiden whom I had only known superficially, but who has gone hence to make herself more known by distance. . . . Every maiden conceals a fairer flower and more luscious fruit than any calyx in the field, and if she go with averted face, confiding in her own purity and high resolves, she will make the heavens retrospective, and all nature will humbly confess its queen.[3]

In February 1842 she visited the Emersons briefly and Thoreau noted that talking to her was "like talking to the clouds."[4] Two

2. Thoreau, *Collected Poems*, 38–9
3. Thoreau, *Journal*, I, 292
4. Thoreau, *Correspondence*, 63

Thoreau as recalled by
Edward Emerson in old age

Caricature drawn by
W. H. Furness when Thoreau
visited Philadelphia in 1854

THOREAU AS SEEN BY HIS FRIENDS

John Thoreau,
Henry's father

Cynthia Dunbar Thoreau,
Henry's mother

Helen Thoreau,
Henry's sister. From a daguerreotype
taken at Henry's suggestion
shortly before her death in 1849

John Thoreau,
Henry's brother. From a painting
by his sister Sophia, now in
the Concord Antiquarian Society

THOREAU'S FAMILY

weeks later he made an entry in his journal that reads as though it were possibly the draft of a letter to her:

> It is not easy to find one brave enough to play the game of love quite alone with you, but they must get some third person, or world, to countenance them. They thrust others between. Love is so delicate and fastidious that I see not how [it] can ever begin. Do you expect me to love with you, unless you make my love secondary to nothing else? Your words come tainted as if the thought of the world darted between thee and the thought of me. You are not venturous enough for love. It goes alone unscathed through wildernesses. . . .
>
> Did I ask thee to love me who hate myself? No! Love that I love, and I will love thee that lovest.[5]

The next day he affirmed:

> The only way to speak the truth is to speak lovingly; only the lover's words are heard. The intellect should never speak; it is not a natural sound.[6]

Ten days later he added:

> How insufficient is all wisdom without love! . . . Ignorance and bungling with love are better than wisdom and skill without. Our life without love is like coke and ashes,—like the cocoanut in which the milk is dried up.[7]

By March 26, 1842, he could say only, "Where is my heart gone? They say men cannot part with it and live."[8] But there the record ends and there is no indication of what happened. We can only suppose that she gave him some clear indication that she was not interested.

Mary Russell continued to visit the Emersons occasionally, but she made no more extended stays. Several years later she married Marston Watson of Plymouth, who had known Thoreau at Harvard. Thoreau continued his friendship with the Watsons after their

---

5. Thoreau, *Journal*, I, 329
6. Ibid. 332
7. Ibid. 348
8. Ibid. 350

marriage, as he did with the Osgoods. He never failed to visit them when he was in the vicinity of Plymouth—on occasion being their house guest for more than a week. Watson invited him frequently to Plymouth to lecture, hired him to survey his farm, and occasionally sent him rare plants from his nursery. Twenty years later when Thoreau was on his deathbed, Mary Russell Watson wrote constantly inquiring as to Thoreau's health. Although Thoreau never succeeded in winning the hand of either Ellen Sewall or Mary Russell, he unquestionably did win their lasting goodwill and affection.

IV

So far as is known, the romance—if it can be called such—with Mary Russell was the last in Thoreau's life. By the mid-1840s he slipped into the pattern of the confirmed bachelor—a role that he was to play consistently for the rest of his life. And play the role he did. He delighted in jibing at women and at marriage. When he lost his opportunity to purchase the Hollowell Farm, he blamed the owner's wife because she changed her mind, and added in *Walden*, "Every man has such a wife."[9] In one of his commonplace books, he copied down in the margin with relish a sentence he had come across: "Take your wife's opinion and act in opposition to it."[1] And when David A. Wasson once tried to discuss marriage as an institution with him, Thoreau kicked at a nearby skunk cabbage and said, "There, marriage is like that."[2] (It should be added that perhaps Wasson did not fully realize how much affection Thoreau had for skunk cabbages.)

Thoreau made almost a fetish of belittling attractive women. When Ellery Channing asked him if he knew a certain young lady then noted for her beauty, he replied, "Is she the one with the goggles?"[3] And in 1851, after he found himself trapped into attending a party, he complained:

9. Thoreau, *Writings*, II, 91
1. MS, Library of Congress
2. Frank Preston Stearns, *Sketches from Concord and Appledore* (New York, 1895), 26
3. Channing, *Thoreau: the Poet-Naturalist*, 311

In the evening went to a party. It is a bad place to go to,—thirty or forty persons, mostly young women, in a small room, warm and noisy. Was introduced to two young women. The first one was as lively and loquacious as a chicadee; had been accustomed to the society of watering-places, and therefore could get no refreshment out of such a dry fellow as I. The other was said to be pretty-looking, but I rarely look people in their faces, and, moreover, I could not hear what she said, there was such a clacking. . . .

These parties, I think, are a part of the machinery of modern society, that young people may be brought together to form marriage connections. . . .

Some of my friends make singular blunders. They go out of their way to talk with certain young women of whom they think, or have heard, that they are pretty, and take pains to introduce me to them. . . . I confess that I am lacking a sense, perchance, in this respect, and I derive no pleasure from talking with a young woman half an hour simply because she has regular features. The society of young women is the most unprofitable I have ever tried. They are so light and flighty that you can never be sure whether they are there or not there. I prefer to talk with the more staid and settled, settled for life, in every sense.[4]

As he grew older, Thoreau became more and more firmly established in this pattern of bachelorhood, a pattern he was never to break. He himself has said, and we have no reason to believe he was not telling the truth, "My most intimate acquaintance with woman has been a sister's relation, or at most a catholic virgin mother relation —not that it has always been free from the suspicion of a lower sympathy."[5] His reticence on the subject led his friend Bronson Alcott to believe that he "seemed to have no temptations," that "All those strong wants which do battle with other men's nature, he knew not."[6] But in the privacy of one of his notebooks Thoreau in the spring of 1845 wrote a rather extended essay on the subject of sex relations, saying, in part:

The subject of sex is a most remarkable one—since though it occupies the thoughts of all so much, and our lives & characters

---

4. Thoreau, *Journal*, III, 115–16
5. Canby, *Thoreau*, 162
6. Bronson Alcott [Reminiscences of Thoreau], *Radical*, V (1869), 523

are so affected by the consequences which spring from this source
—yet mankind as it were . . . agrees to be silent about it. . . .
Here is the most interesting of all human facts or relations still
veiled, more than the Elenesian [sic] mystery. . . . I believe it is
unusual for the most intimate friends to impart the pleasures and
anxieties connected with this fact.[7]

He thus revealed that he had not put such matters as far out of his
mind as some of his friends had thought but was Victorianly shy
about speaking of them.

Seven years later, when his friend H. G. O. Blake was about
to be married, Thoreau copied the essay out for him as an odd sort
of Transcendental wedding present with a note confessing that he did
not know how far he spoke to the condition of men generally or how
far he betrayed his own "peculiar defects."[8] But that was virtually
the only time he ever spoke out on the subject. Often he could be
exceedingly old maidish and prudish. Several times when Ellery
Channing attempted to tell him an off-color joke, he haughtily refused to listen and complained in his journal that he could not
"respect the mind that can jest on this subject."[9] And when in
Everett's meadow he discovered a Stinking Morel fungus shaped
unmistakably like a human phallus, he was even ready to denounce
Nature as putting herself "on a level with those who draw in
privies."[1]

While it cannot be said of Thoreau as Sir Winston Churchill
once said of a political opponent, "He was born of a long line of
maiden aunts," it must not be forgotten that he was raised in an
atmosphere of prudish bachelorhood and spinsterhood. Neither
his brother nor his sisters ever married—nor Aunt Jane, nor Aunt
Maria, nor Aunt Louisa, nor Aunt Sally, nor Aunt Betsey, nor
Uncle Charles—and all of these were at one time or another members of the Thoreau household. The unmarried state was an accepted fact and condition for the Thoreaus. It was one of the few
traditions that Thoreau himself did not break.

7. MS, Berg Collection
8. Thoreau, *Writings*, VI, 198
9. Thoreau, *Journal*, III, 335
1. Ibid. IX, 115–7

CHAPTER SEVEN
(1839–1843)

I

I T WAS ONLY a few days after Thoreau's return from his journey on the Merrimack in 1839 that his friends and associates in the Hedge Club—the Transcendentalists—took the step that perhaps more than anything else was to lead him into the profession of writing. For some time they had been disturbed that there seemed to be no outlet for their ideas. The pages of the leading periodicals of the day—such as those of the *North American Review*—were closed to them, for their editors thought the writings of the Transcendentalists nonsensical if not heretical. And there was hardly a publisher in sight who would bring out any of their books unless they themselves underwrote them. Therefore at a meeting of the club at the home of Cyrus Bartol on September 18, 1839, it was proposed that a periodical be established and Margaret Fuller was asked to serve as editor.[1] After months of planning, a prospectus was issued on May 4, 1840, announcing that the first number of a quarterly journal of 136 octavo pages would be published on July 1, 1840. Its name, *The Dial,* was chosen by Bronson Alcott.

Here at last would be an opportunity for the Transcendentalists to express themselves—and Thoreau, like most of the younger members of the group, was quick to take advantage of the opportunity. He immediately sent in his subscription, only to have his money refunded on the grounds that he was expected to be a regular contributor to its pages.[2] He then submitted the poem "Sympathy," which he had written for Edmund Sewall, and it was accepted and printed in the first issue. In February 1840 he had completed a

---

1. George Willis Cooke, *An Historical and Biographical Introduction to Accompany the Dial* (Cleveland, 1902), I, 59
2. Ralph Waldo Emerson, *Letters* (New York, 1938), II, 310

short critical essay on Aulus Persius Flaccus, the Roman poet, and Emerson, when he saw it, urged that Margaret Fuller include it too in the first number. But much to Emerson's astonishment, Thoreau himself balked, saying the essay was poor writing and not worth the time needed to revise it. Emerson however insisted and late in April sent it on to Miss Fuller. Even after she accepted it, Thoreau insisted on revising it further, but his efforts were somewhat in vain, for through a slipup, he never saw proofs of the essay, and when it appeared in the July *Dial* it was marred by a number of typographical errors. Emerson though thought the essay "full of life" and rushed a copy to his friend Carlyle in England.[3] But when he also recommended it to Theodore Parker, Parker complained that the life in it was Emerson's own, not Thoreau's, and recommended that Thoreau write more for the newspapers and less for *The Dial*.[4]

No sooner was the first issue of *The Dial* out than Emerson asked Thoreau for copy for the second. He submitted his poem "Nature doth have her dawn each day," but dillydallied when Emerson asked for revisions, and so it did not appear until the third number. He also submitted the poem "When winter fringes every bough," but then withdrew it and later incorporated it into the text of his essay "A Winter Walk." As a result he had nothing in the second number.

In mid-summer of 1840 Thoreau finally completed an essay on the "brave" or "spheral" man that he had been laboring on for more than a year. Entitling it "The Service," he sent it off to Margaret Fuller for *The Dial* in July. She dallied over the manuscript for five months and then finally rejected it. She wrote Thoreau:

I am to blame for so long detaining your manuscript. But my thoughts have been so engaged that I have not found a suitable hour to reread it as I wished till last night. This second reading only confirms my impression from the first. The essay is rich in thoughts, and I should be *pained* not to meet it again. But then the thoughts seem to me so out of their natural order, that I cannot read it through without *pain*. I never once feel myself

3. Charles Eliot Norton, ed., *The Correspondence of Thomas Carlyle and Ralph Waldo Emerson* (Boston, 1883), I, 290
4. Emerson, *Letters*, II, 324 n

in a stream of thought, but seem to hear the grating of tools on the mosaic. . . .[5]

Surprisingly she closed her letter with a request that he resubmit the essay, adding, "If you see no force in my objections disregard them." But if he did resubmit it (as apparently he did, for it was found among Emerson's papers after Thoreau's death), it was never published in *The Dial*. Why Emerson, who looked much more favorably upon Thoreau's writings than did Margaret Fuller, did not print it when he later took over the editing of *The Dial* is not known. At any rate it did not see print until forty years after Thoreau's death and still is not included in his collected works. It is a short, aphoristic work, much more abstract than Thoreau's later writing and often bordering on the vapid in expression. Nonetheless kernels of ideas that Thoreau was later to extoll can be found in it. Essentially it is a plan for the well-rounded man and in a sense can be considered Thoreau's essay on "self-reliance," though it has none of the trenchancy of Emerson's essay.

Thoreau had no contributions in the April 1841 number of *The Dial*. As a result, Emerson prodded Margaret Fuller to see that he was not omitted in future issues and thus she included the poem "Sic Vita" ("I am a parcel of vain strivings") in the July number. But when Emerson suggested she also use Thoreau's "With frontier strength ye stand your ground," she resisted, returning it several times for revisions, and finally writing Thoreau directly: "I do not find the poem on the mountain improved by mere compression, though it might be by fusion and glow."[6] Thoreau put it back into his portfolio and several years later, by inserting it into the midst of "A Walk to Wachusett," succeeded in publishing it in the *Boston Miscellany* in January 1843. Later Miss Fuller did accept his poem on friendship ("Let such pure hate still underprop") and published it in the October issue.

In March 1842 Miss Fuller, in despair over the low circulation of *The Dial* and the complete lack of any financial remuneration for the hours and days and weeks of labor she was devoting to it, gave up the editorship. Because no one else was willing, Emerson, with many misgivings, took over the burden. Despite constant

---

5. Thoreau, *Correspondence*, 41–2
6. Ibid. 56

prodding by him, in two years of editorship, Miss Fuller had printed only four short poems and one translation by Thoreau. The pattern immediately changed with the change of editors. On April 10, having acquired a set of the newly published natural-history surveys issued by the Commonwealth of Massachusetts—T. W. Harris's *Insects,* Chester Dewey's *Flowering Plants,* D. H. Storer's *Fishes, Reptiles and Birds,* and Ebenezer Emmons's *Quadrupeds* —Emerson put Thoreau to work preparing a review. The resulting essay, "The Natural History of Massachusetts," appeared in the July 1842 *Dial.* It was perhaps Thoreau's first major prose work, a lengthy mosaic of choice excerpts from the best nature writing in his journal, although it hardly mentioned the books he was supposedly reviewing.

Emerson also included Thoreau's poem "My Prayer" in the July issue, using it as an epigraph to his own essay, "Prayers." This circumstance led to an amusing error by Thoreau's editors years later. Knowing the poem was by Thoreau, they assumed the essay was too and included it as such in the first edition of Thoreau's *A Yankee in Canada* in 1866. Thus readers were confused by finding it reprinted in the collected works of both Emerson and Thoreau.

In the October 1842 number of *The Dial* Emerson printed eight of Thoreau's poems—"The Black Knight," "The Inward Morning," "Free Love," "The Poet's Delay," "Rumors from an Aeolian Harp," "The Moon," "To a Maiden in the East," and "The Summer Rain." Thoreau, anxious to help out, canvassed— unsuccessfully—for new subscribers and assisted Emerson with the chore of proofreading. When Margaret Fuller complained of misprints in her review of Tennyson's poems, Emerson teased her that Thoreau had either overlooked them or concluded they were "good Dialese."[7] As a matter of fact, more misprints occurred in Thoreau's own works in that issue, so she could hardly accuse him of partiality.

In mid-November of 1842, Thoreau brought some more of his poems to Emerson for *The Dial.* According to the standards of his time they were roughhewn; lines, meter, and rhymes were all highly irregular. Like Emerson, Thoreau was more interested in

7. Emerson, *Letters,* III, 91

"metre-making argument" than in form. Few of his contemporaries were impressed with the results and even those who view them from the more liberal standards of today's free verse find comparatively little to praise. But Thoreau was more interested in satisfying his own creative urges than his contemporaries, and he continued to write poetry even though only *The Dial* would publish it—and now even Emerson was not overly enthusiastic about it. He complained to his journal: "Their fault is, that the gold does not yet flow pure, but is drossy and crude. The thyme and marjoram are not yet made into honey; the assimilation is imperfect."[8] On some occasion— and perhaps this was it—Emerson so discouraged Thoreau as a poet that he went home and burned many of his manuscripts, an act which he was later much to regret—though if we are to judge by the poems that have survived, their loss was not a great one. Thoreau learned to write great poetic prose, and he learned to make his life poetic:

> My life hath been the poem I would have writ,
> But I could not both live and utter it.[9]

But his poetry was rarely better than third rate.

For the January 1843 number of *The Dial* Emerson ignored Thoreau's poetry and instead asked him to do a translation of *Prometheus Bound* from the Greek. The result was little more than a routine piece of hack work, although there are legends that it was quickly adopted as a "pony" by students at Harvard. Emerson also asked Thoreau to gather some selections from the *Laws of Menu* that he had discovered in Emerson's library and Thoreau thus edited another installment in the series of "Ethnical Scriptures" that Emerson had started in the July 1842 number.

Emerson's lecture schedule that winter was heavier than usual and he found himself forced to neglect his editorial duties on *The Dial*. Thoreau, with Emerson's encouragement, picked up the reins and edited the April 1843 issue by himself, although he consulted freely with Emerson by mail as the occasion arose. When Charles Lane submitted an essay on Bronson Alcott, Thoreau

---

8. Ralph Waldo Emerson, *Journals*, VI, 304
9. Thoreau, *Writings*, I, 365

worked over it, as he wrote Emerson, "just as we pull open the petals of a flower with our fingers where they are confined by its own sweets."[1] He rejected a "notice to the readers of the *Dial*" by Elizabeth Peabody, denouncing it as "not good," and worked over and revised a letter on the German universities by Stearns Wheeler. When the issue went to press, it included an essay by Margaret Fuller on Canova; one by Mrs. Child, "What is Beauty?"; James Freeman Clarke on Keats' American brother and remarks on Milton by Keats; four poems by Ellery Channing; Emerson's "Europe and European Books"; a travel essay on Porto Rico by the late Charles Emerson; and a catalog of books by Bronson Alcott. Thoreau also included his own translation of extracts from Anacreon; three poems—"To a Stray Fowl," "Smoke," and "Haze"; a short essay, "Dark Ages"; and his selections from the sayings of Confucius. This April 1843 issue of *The Dial* stands out only slightly from the other issues. A larger percentage of it, perhaps, than of most issues has stood the test of time. But the distinction, if any, cannot honestly be attributed to Thoreau. For the most part he was simply fortunate in what was submitted to his editorial desk.

Emerson returned to his editorial duties with the July 1843 issue and immediately asked Thoreau to submit material, but Thoreau was so dilatory that by the time he got "A Winter Walk" to Emerson's desk, there was no room for it. In mid-August, in preparing for the October issue, Emerson looked over the manuscript and found himself sadly disappointed with it. He complained to his journal:

Henry Thoreau sends me a paper with the old fault of unlimited contradiction. The trick of his rhetoric is soon learned: it consists in substituting for the obvious word and thought its diametrical antagonist. He praises wild mountains and winter forests for their domestic air; snow and ice for their warmth; villagers and wood-choppers for their urbanity, and the wilderness for resembling Rome and Paris. With the constant inclination to dispraise cities and civilization, he yet can find no way to know woods and woodmen except by paralleling them with towns and townsmen. Channing declared the piece is excellent: but it makes me nervous and wretched to read it, with all its merits.[2]

1. Thoreau, *Correspondence*, 90
2. Emerson, *Journals*, VI, 440–1

Nonetheless, by making some "pretty free omissions," he removed his principal objections and printed it in the October issue along with five pages of Thoreau's selections from the Chinese Four Books. When Thoreau saw "A Winter Walk" in print, he confessed that he had been "very blind" to send the manuscript "in such a state" and thought even now he "could still shake it in the wind to some advantage."[3] But despite Thoreau's misgivings and Emerson's criticism, for the modern reader it is one of Thoreau's best early pieces. Although its first few pages are perhaps a little too effusive and romantic, its sturdy familiarity with nature based obviously on long and loving observation more than redeems its few flaws. It is amusing to note that although Emerson chopped out one entire poem, Thoreau had already inserted another, "When winter fringes every brow," which Margaret Fuller had earlier rejected for *The Dial* when it was submitted alone—and this one survived Emerson's editorial axe.

More impressed than others had been with Thoreau's translations, Emerson suggested he try some from Pindar for the October issue. Thoreau's first reaction was that they were hardly worth the effort and instead offered a translation of Aeschylus' *Seven against Thebes.* Emerson accepted the Thebes manuscript, but never used it. Many years later it was found among his papers and was not published until 1959. Emerson however kept prodding Thoreau for the Pindar and he eventually turned it in in time for the January 1844 issue, along with some selections from the "Preaching of Buddha" and "Hermes Trismegistus" and a short essay titled "Ancient Poets," that is, Homer, Ossian, and Chaucer.

In the April 1844 number of *The Dial* Emerson printed two pieces by Thoreau—some further translations from Pindar and an appreciative essay on the *Herald of Freedom,* an anti-slavery weekly published in Concord, New Hampshire, by Nathaniel P. Rogers. Rogers, unlike the better-known William Lloyd Garrison, believed in an individualistic rather than an organizational approach in anti-slavery activities. He went so far indeed as to advocate the dissolution of all anti-slavery societies because he thought they as institutions impeded the exercise of freedom on the part of individual abolitionists. For this heresy he was removed from the editorship of his paper later in the year by Garrison. But to Thoreau's mind

---

3. Thoreau, *Correspondence,* 145

Rogers was applying principles thoroughly in keeping with Transcendentalism to the major social problem of the day, slavery, and thus praised his efforts and his courage. When Rogers saw the review, he was delighted and not only reprinted the entire article in his issue of May 10, but led it off with a note of thanks:

> I had been praised before—generously and beautifully, but it was by my own outcast fellow-laborers in the forlorn service of Anti-Slavery. —We had cheered one another on, amid the darkness and chill of public contempt, with what outcry we might. But this was not an abolitionist, noticing the Herald of Freedom, nor a personal friend—but a stranger, whose initials gave me no clue to his name,—and I have just been informed, one of those they call "foreigner"—who has been pleased, as a literary reviewer—(a philanthropist too he must be)—to take notice, and such notice, of the most odious and despised publication of the time—so far as it may have become notorious, even. And I don't know to what extent it has. The writer, "H.D.T.," I understand, is mentioned in a paper that comes to our printing office, among the writers of this number of the Dial, as Henry D. Thoreau, probably a German. He cannot have written much in this country, or his name would have reached me, from no farther off than Concord, Mass., though for the last half dozen years, I have been almost a stranger to any but the Anti-Slavery literature. And if he were a practical writer, he could hardly have written so beautifully and freshly. And if he had any reputation, he wouldn't be likely to hazard it, by a notice of our poor, "infidel," "nigger" sheet. . . .
>
> This little notice brief, but very honorable—came as a balm to my outlawed spirit. I give it place here. It will live elsewhere, if it perishes here. I hope the writer will let Anti-Slavery have the
> benefit of his beautiful pen.[4]

Rogers, who died the next year, unfortunately did not live to read Thoreau's greatest anti-slavery writings.

With the April 1844 issue, *The Dial* came to an end. It had never achieved a circulation of more than a thousand nor a subscription list of more than three hundred, most issues falling far below even those small figures. It had never been able to fulfill its

4. Wendell Glick, "Thoreau and the 'Herald of Freedom,'" *New England Quarterly*, XXII (1940), 198–200

original intention of paying its contributors even a nominal sum. In fact, it found great difficulty most of the time in paying even its printing bills. All of the Transcendentalists regularly expressed their disappointment in it and felt that even in quality it fell short of their expectations. The general public, when they paid any attention to it at all, laughed at it rather than admired it. And so at last Emerson decided that it was not worth continuing and there was no one else willing to devote himself to it.

But despite all its shortcomings, *The Dial* served its purpose. It not only was an outlet for the expression of the Transcendentalists' views, but, more important, it aroused the interest of a number of young men and women in professional writing and gave them their first opportunity to get into print. Most important among these was Thoreau. In its sixteen issues *The Dial* had printed a total of thirty-one separate poems, essays, and translations of his. It had given him the confidence that he could write what was worth reading. It had called him to the attention of some of the most influential intellectual leaders of the day. With *The Dial* behind him, now he could try to find his way into periodicals of wider circulation.

The activities of the Transcendentalists had reached their high point in the publication of *The Dial*. With its decease the movement gradually drifted apart. As we have seen, the group had never been large nor highly formalized. They were always more interested in talk than action. By the mid-1840s the older generation of Transcendentalists, such as Hedge and Ripley, were already so well launched on their personal careers or so involved in their own individual activities and interests that they no longer had a vital interest in their meetings and so the Hedge Club slowly faded into non-existence. The younger generation, such as Thoreau, still kept the flame of Transcendentalism burning in their own lives, but their very Transcendentalism had made them so individualistic that they had no interest in even as little formal organization as had existed. Although Emerson still called some of his friends together occasionally at his house on Lexington Road for a weekend of discussion—and invariably included Thoreau in these invitations —these later meetings could hardly be called meetings of the Hedge Club. Their talk was devoted less to a discussion of principles than to reminiscences. Transcendentalism as a formal movement died of old age not more than ten or fifteen years after it had begun.

II

Thoreau's first reaction to the closing of his school in the spring of 1841 had been to look elsewhere for another teaching position. Learning from the newspapers that there was an opening at Samuel Gridley Howe's newly founded Perkins Institute for the Blind in Boston, he applied, but nothing came of it.[5] Nor did he try again elsewhere. Instead he turned to a more prosaic method of earning a living; he noted in his journal on April 20: "To-day I earned seventy-five cents heaving manure out of a pen, and made a good bargain of it.[6]

His health was none too good. In mid-February he had boasted that he had gone thus far through the snowbanks of winter wearing neither greatcoat nor drawers. But a week later he was confined to the house with bronchitis and was worried once more about his lungs. The siege, fortunately, was a short one and he was soon up and about once more. But his health was precarious enough that his friends worried.

For some time he had been thinking of retiring to some lonely spot where he might rest and devote himself to writing. At first he thought that he could attain the necessary solitude merely by ascending to the garret and associating with the spiders and mice, and there "coming face to face" with himself. But gradually he realized that he needed more solitude than that. Even before the school was abandoned, he began looking for an appropriate spot. He thought of either buying an old run-down farm or renting some land and building himself a cabin. He investigated the Weird Dell, the orchard side of Fairhaven Hill, the Cliff, and Baker Farm. On February 10 he asked a farmer if he could rent some of his land and received an affirmative answer, but immediately began to have qualms. He thought he might lose his freedom and feel that his wings were clipped as soon as he became a landholder. And George Ward, Prudence's brother, warned him that he might "hurt himself seasoning" by going off by himself.[7] But by April

---

5. *Lantern,* "Thoreau Applies for a Position," XX (1960), 2
6. Thoreau, *Journal,* I, 250–1
7. Canby, *Thoreau,* 176

5, he had made up his mind to build a lodge on the southern slope of some hill, and "take there the life the gods sent" him.[8] Within a few days he decided to purchase the Hollowell Place, just across Hubbard's Bridge on the Sudbury River, about two miles southwest of Concord village.[9] Its real attractions, he thought, were that the nearest neighbor was a half a mile away and that its owner had permitted the house and barns to become dilapidated and the fields to grow up to birches. He feared that if he did not buy it soon, the owner might "improve" it by cutting down the trees and getting out the rocks that filled the fields. They quickly came to terms and Thoreau was making a wheelbarrow to move his possessions when the owner returned and asked to buy the farm back, since his wife had changed her mind, and offered Thoreau ten dollars for his trouble. Thoreau refused the ten dollars, but with some regret returned the property and began looking elsewhere.

By fall he had given up looking for a farmhouse and was instead seeking a lonely spot to build a cabin. On December 24, he confided to his journal:

> I want to go soon and live away by the pond, where I shall hear only the wind whispering among the reeds. It will be success if I shall have left myself behind. But my friends ask what I will do when I get there. Will it not be employment enough to watch the progress of the seasons?[1]

It was not Walden he was thinking of then, but Sandy Pond in nearby Lincoln where he had spent his college vacation visiting Stearns Wheeler in his cabin. He went to see the Flints who owned the land around Sandy Pond and asked their permission to build a cabin similar to Wheeler's, but much to his disappointment they refused. Some years later Thoreau took his revenge and immortalized Flint in *Walden* as "the unclean and stupid farmer . . . some skin-flint, who loved better the reflecting surface of a dollar, or a bright cent, in which he could see his own brazen face . . . his fingers grown into crooked and horny talons

---

8. Thoreau, *Journal*, I, 244
9. Ellen Sewall, Letter to Prudence Ward of April 8, 1841. MS, George L. Davenport, Jr.
1. Thoreau, *Journal*, I, 299

from the long habit of grasping harpy-like."[2] What Flint thought of his impalement on Thoreau's pike is not recorded.

About this time Thoreau started work on an autobiography —or at least an autobiographical sketch—of which only a fragment remains in a manuscript in the Berg Collection:

> It may be well if first of all I should give some account first of my species and variety. I am about five feet 7 inches in height —of a light complexion, rather slimly built, and just approaching the Roman age of manhood. One who faces West oftener than East—walks out of the house with a better grace than he goes in —who loves winter as well as summer—forest as well as field— darkness as well as light. Rather solitary than gregarious—not migratory nor dormant—but to be raised at any season, by day or night, not by the pulling of any bell wire, but by a smart stroke upon any pine tree in the woods of Concord.

Thoreau became more and more restless. On March 8, 1840, he had complained in his journal:

> Two years and twenty now have flown;
> Their meanness time away has flung;
> These limbs to man's estate have grown,
> But cannot claim a manly tongue.[3]

Now, a year and a half later, he was no more satisfied that he was accomplishing anything. He did not want to feel as though his life were a sojourn any longer. It was time, he thought, that he should begin to live. The whole duty of life was "contained in the question how to respire and aspire both at once."[4]

Thoreau was of course not alone in having to face that problem. It is one to be faced by every creative artist who has not inherited or otherwise acquired an independent income. And at this very moment Emerson's friend George Ripley was sponsoring a new attempt to solve it. Ripley argued that if only a number of creative artists would group together and work communally, they could overcome the need of an independent income. By

---

2. Thoreau, *Writings*, II, 217
3. Thoreau, *Journal*, I, 127
4. Ibid. I, 299–300

pooling their resources, they could in a few hours each day earn enough to meet their needs, and to free the rest of the day for their creative efforts. Thus would the artistic millennium be achieved.

With this plan in mind, Ripley in 1841 purchased a tract of land in West Roxbury, one of the suburbs of Boston, and established the Brook Farm community. Most of the Transcendentalists were invited to join. Thoreau apparently received his invitation —perhaps Ripley had heard of the end of the school—for on March 3, Thoreau replied in his journal:

> As for these communities, I think I had rather keep bachelor's hall in hell than go to board in heaven. Do you think your virtue will be boarded with you? It will never live on the interest of your money, depend upon it. The boarder has no home. In heaven I hope to bake my own bread and clean my own linen. The tomb is the only boarding-house in which a hundred are served at once. In the catacomb we may dwell together and prop one another without loss.[5]

Two years later, when Thoreau was living on Staten Island, Bronson Alcott and his English friend Charles Lane started a community experiment of their own, which they named "Fruitlands," on Prospect Hill in Harvard, Massachusetts. From the very beginning it was a folly of follies. Because they refused to enslave animals in any way, they not only gave up eating meat of any kind, but also renounced the use of oxen to pull their plows, refused to wear woolen clothing, and abstained from using animal manure on their gardens. Their opposition to slave labor led them to refuse to wear cotton. And so in the cold New England climate they tried to content themselves with linen. Going beyond vegetarianism, they refused to eat any such vegetables as potatoes and carrots because they showed their lower nature by growing earthward, and instead ate only those aspiring vegetables, such as corn and melons, that demonstrated their higher nature by growing upward toward heaven. To make matters worse, the soil on the farm was poor and the communitarians were too busy conversing to plant the gardens on time or to weed them when they finally were planted.

Thoreau was invited to join this community too. Early in

---

5. Ibid. I, 227

June 1843 Lane wrote him a lengthy letter romanticizing the future of the community in the most glowing terms and assuring Thoreau that they needed only his mind "to elevate the whole scene to classic beauty."[6] But again Thoreau was not tempted. When Lane needed help in selling his large personal library in New York City to raise funds for the community, Thoreau was willing to step into the breech and to help oversee the arrangements for the sale, but he was not willing to become a member of the community. And since the community, quite understandably, failed that winter before Thoreau had returned to Concord, he never even visited the site.

Nor did Thoreau ever change his mind. Twelve years later he had a conversation with F. A. T. Bellew, the artist, in New York City, and said:

> Talking with Bellew this evening about Fourierism and communities, I said that I suspected any enterprise in which two were engaged together. "But," said he, "it is difficult to make a stick stand unless you slant two or more against it." "Oh, no," answered I, "you may split its lower end into three, or drive it single into the ground, which is the best way; but most men, when they start on a new enterprise, not only figuratively, but really, *pull up stakes*. When the sticks prop one another, none, or only one, stands erect."[7]

Thoreau was far too much the Transcendentalist, far too much the individualist ever to believe that the problems of life could be solved on such a community basis. He believed firmly that reform always began with the individual. He was ready to reform himself, not others, and never joined any of the many community experiments of the time. There seems to be no record that he ever even visited nearby Brook Farm although many of his friends were among its members.

Nonetheless Thoreau did find a solution to his problem, albeit a temporary one. He was invited to live with the Emersons in their home on Lexington Road. The bonds between the two men had continued to grow as they got to know each other better. In the fall of 1840 Emerson had published in *The Dial* his now well-

<hr />

6. Thoreau, *Correspondence*, 115
7. Thoreau, *Journal*, VII, 500

known poem "Woodnotes," which, in telling of a "forest seer" who was so close to nature that

> It seemed as if the breezes brought him,
> It seemed as if the sparrows taught him,[8]

created what is generally accepted as his portrait of Thoreau. Less widely known is the fact that a year later he expressed even more vividly his feeling for his young neighbor in "Forbearance":

> Hast thou named all the birds without a gun?
> Loved the wood-rose, and left it on its stalk?
> At rich men's tables eaten bread and pulse?
> Unarmed, faced danger with a heart of trust?
> And loved so well a high behavior,
> In man or maid, that thou from speech refrained,
> Nobility more nobly to repay?
> O, be my friend, and teach me to be thine![9]

But if Emerson admired Thoreau, he envied even more his practicality. Emerson had always been unhandy around the house and yard. It was a family joke that his little son Waldo watching him working in the garden had warned, "I wish you would not dig your leg." Making minor repairs around the house had always seemed a task. For a time he had solved the problem by having a chore-boy, Alexander McCaffery, but Alex had recently left and so Emerson had turned to Thoreau.[1] Thoreau was as dexterous as Emerson was unhandy. Laughingly, he said he once shut the window of a railroad car when all the other passengers had failed, and was offered a job in a factory on the spot. Emerson marveled at his dexterity, thinking it a miracle that he could select exactly a dozen pencils at every grasp when he was helping his father with packaging, that he could estimate the weight of a calf or a pig like a dealer, and that he could outwalk, outswim, outrun, outskate, and outboat most of his contemporaries. Thus it was that Emerson offered Thoreau his board and room for a year (later extended to two) in exchange for a few hours' service each day around the house and garden, and thus it was that on April 26, 1841, Thoreau moved his few important possessions over to

---

8. Ralph Waldo Emerson, *Complete Works* (Boston, 1903), IX, 44–5
9. Ibid. IX, 83
1. Canby, *Thoreau*, 142

Emerson's house and took over the little bedroom at the head of the front stairs as his own.

Emerson was delighted. His garden got planted, his apple trees grafted, and the chimneys burned out. When Mrs. Emerson needed a place to store her Sunday-go-to-meeting gloves, Thoreau built a special little drawer under the seat of one of the dining-room chairs. When she complained that the hens were invading her gardens and scratching out the flowers, Thoreau, with a straight face but a twinkle in his eye, made gloves for their claws.[2] When Emerson was off on lecture tours—as he was with increasing frequency—he felt assured that his wife and children were in good hands. Lidian, on her side, found both comfort and pleasure in Thoreau's presence in the house and told her husband, "Well as I have always liked [Thoreau], he still grows upon me."[3]

Thoreau took particular joy in Emerson's small children. He chattered babytalk with little Edith and wrote her a special poem:

> Thou little bud of being, Edith named,
> With whom I've made acquaintance on this earth,
> Who knowest me without impediment,
> As flowers know the winds that stir their leaves,
> And rid'st upon my shoulders as the sphere,
> Turning on me thy sage reserved eye,
> Behind whose broad & charitable gaze
> Floats the still true & universal soul
> With the pure azure of the general day,
> Not yet a peopled & a vulgar town,
> Rather a pure untarnished country ground;
> For thou are whole, not yet begun to die,
> While men look on me with their shrivelled rays
> Streaming through some small chink of the broad sky;
> Pure youthful soul, thou hast begun to be,
> To cumulate thy sin & piety.[4]

Emerson was so charmed that he preserved the manuscript of the poem among his choicest papers for the rest of his life.

---

2. Walter Harding, *Thoreau, Man of Concord* (New York, 1960), 72
3. Marble, *Thoreau: His Home, Friends and Books*, 94
4. Kenneth Walter Cameron, "A New Thoreau Poem—'To Edith,'" *Emerson Society Quarterly*, XVIII (1960), 41

Thoreau also won young Waldo's heart by making toys, whistles, boats, and popguns for him, and won his respect by the gentle firmness with which he treated him. Even the household maids were delighted, for Thoreau was always ready and willing to mend what was broken, often effecting his repairs even before they could call them to his attention.

He was given the greatest freedom. There was no time schedule to adhere to. He worked when he wanted to and stopped when he felt like it. When his father needed help, he was free to go home for a few days at a time, although he usually still spent the nights with the Emersons. On occasion, when he wanted a little extra spending money, he was able to put in a few days in the family pencil shop.

But Emerson had much more in mind than merely keeping his garden weeded and his house repaired. He had long thought of Thoreau as a potential writer. As we have seen, he constantly encouraged Thoreau to write for *The Dial*. On September 25, 1841, he wrote Rufus W. Griswold, the editor of the influential *Poets and Poetry of America,* to call attention to Thoreau's poems in *The Dial* and to suggest he be included in the next edition of Griswold's anthology.[5] Griswold did solicit some poems from Thoreau but never included him in his anthology. Emerson thought Thoreau as a scholar and a poet "as full of buds of promise as a young apple tree."[6] If, by taking care of his minimal needs, Emerson could give broader margins to his life, then perhaps Thoreau would devote himself to writing. Emerson had high hopes, and although he wrote Margaret Fuller, "I know that nearly all the fine souls [such as Thoreau] have a flaw which defeats every expectation they excite," he added, "To have awakened a great hope in another, is already some fruit is it not?"[7]

One of the first benefits of Thoreau's residence in Emerson's home was that it gave him full access to Emerson's library. From the very beginning of their friendship Emerson had given Thoreau the liberty of his library. Indeed, he had gone further and had borrowed books from George Bancroft for him and had

---

5. Rufus W. Griswold, *Passages from the Correspondence* (Cambridge, 1898), 99
6. Emerson, *Letters,* II, 402
7. Ibid. II, 447

introduced him as a guest at the Boston Athenaeum. But living right in the same house with a good library was something different. Here the books were always at hand and could be read at one's leisure. Thoreau was an inveterate reader. His reading had by no means stopped with his graduation from college; if anything, it had increased—a fact voluminously documented by the commonplace books which he continued to fill, page after page, with favorite quotations from his reading—from Zoroaster, Ben Jonson, Pythagoras, Cowley, Heraclitus, and from many, many others. In Emerson's library he was particularly attracted to the Oriental books and read deeply in such volumes as the *Heetopades of Veeshnoo-Sarma* and the *Laws of Menu*. It was his introduction to Oriental literature and therein he found a philosophy of life far more akin to his own than any he was able to discover in Occidental literature. For many years he was to read every such work he could lay hands on, even at times doing his own translating from French and German when the books were not available in English. But he was as eclectic as all his fellow Transcendentalists in that he accepted from Oriental literature only that which appealed to him and ignored the rest. The Eastern supernaturalism he dismissed as myth; it was their understanding of the values of solitude and of contemplation and their scorn for the Western standards of a success based on materialistic values that appealed to him.

Despite their innate congeniality of outlook, Thoreau and Emerson did not always find it easy to live together and the fault was unquestionably on Thoreau's side. He could be both prickly and uncompromising even over trivial issues and Emerson readily admitted to Hawthorne that he suffered some inconvenience from having Thoreau as an inmate in his house. Such a person, Hawthorne thought quite rightfully, was easier to meet occasionally out in the open air than to have as a permanent guest at the table and fireside.

When after two years Thoreau's residence with the Emerson's came to a close, he sent them a note saying:

> I will not write . . . to thank you and Mrs. Emerson for your long kindness to me. It would be more ungrateful than my constant thought. I have been your pensioner for nearly two years,

and still left free as under the sky. It has been as free a gift as the sun or the summer, though I have sometimes molested you with my mean acceptance of it,—I who have failed to render even those slight services of the *hand* which would have been for a sign, at least; and, by the fault of my nature, have failed of many better and higher services. But I will not trouble you with this, but for once thank you as well as Heaven.[8]

Later he sent them a thank-you poem:

> This true people took the stranger
> And warm hearted housed the ranger
> They received their roving guest
> And have fed him with the best. . . .

In those two years at Emerson's house the friendship of the two men was at its height. They achieved a special feeling of respect and regard for each other. Thoreau was no longer the pupil, Emerson was no longer the mentor. There was an equilibrium in their relations, an equilibrium that was later, unfortunately, to disintegrate.

III

Meanwhile, in the fall of 1841, recalling Thoreau's experience as a schoolteacher, Margaret Fuller suggested to Emerson that Thoreau be persuaded to tutor her brother Richard. Young Fuller, after trying the business world for a time, had decided to enter Harvard, and his sister thought that with help he might achieve advanced standing. She thought too that a brief residence in Concord might give him a taste for the intellectual. Emerson quickly arranged for the two young men to meet. After taking a walk with Thoreau, Fuller, after some hesitation, moved to Concord, settling down in a room in the home of a farmer on the outskirts of the village. Fourteen hours a day he spent studying and interrupted it only when invited by Thoreau or other friends to take a walk. Thoreau, he recalled later,

---

8. Thoreau, *Correspondence,* 78

furnished me with a good deal of companionship. He was a college graduate of high culture, but still more intimately versed in Nature. He was thoroughly unselfish, truly refined, sincere, and of a true spirit. His minute and critical knowledge of the affairs of Nature as well as his practical appreciation of her fleeting graces not only attracted me but helped my education. Thoreau abounded in paradox. This led me to review the grounds of opinion rather than change them. I saw it was his humor, and his vane would whip around and set in the opposite quarter if the world should conform to his statements. Of Indian relics and history he was a careful student, and of the savage character an inveterate admirer. He had a good deal to say, too, of the Indian over the sea; which I thought better unsaid, as his natural bent apprehended the North American than the Asiatic.[9]

Thoreau enjoyed Fuller's companionship, since there were altogether too few young men with intellectual interests around Concord. Fuller profited from the friendship and on February 28, 1842, he was admitted to Harvard as a sophomore.

In mid-July the two renewed their friendship and set out together on a four-day walk to Wachusett Mountain, twenty-five miles distant to the west. Off to an early morning start, they hiked rapidly through Acton and Stow, stopping on a hilltop in Lancaster at noon for a rest and lunch while they read Virgil aloud to each other. As they continued on their way in the afternoon, they paused at every rill to bathe their aching feet. They spent the night at an inn in Sterling, four miles from the base of the mountain. In the morning they ascended Wachusett, and pitched their tent on the summit, two thousand feet above sea level. They arose early next morning, as soon as the moon had set, and after kindling a fire whose blaze they noted might have been seen for thirty miles around, cooked their breakfast. At noon they descended and proceeding through Swiftwater, Sterling, Lancaster, and Still River, spent the night in the village of Harvard. Next day Fuller returned to his home in Groton and Thoreau to Concord.

In the fall Thoreau worked at length on the notes he had taken on his excursion and, using as an epigraph a poem on Wachusett that Margaret Fuller had refused to accept for The

9. Richard Fuller, *Recollections* (Boston, 1936), 50–6

Dial, submitted the resulting essay, entitled "A Walk to Wachu-sett," to Nathan Hale's new *Boston Miscellany of Literature,* where it was published in the issue of January 1843. Although it lacks the concreteness of his later, better travel essays, it was his first attempt at what he called the "excursion," a form that he was to find particularly suited to his talents. The *Miscellany* had accepted it swiftly, but they dawdled about paying. First, Elizabeth Peabody tried to collect for him; then Thoreau himself made a trip to their office, only to receive an unkept promise that he would be paid within a week. Then Emerson intervened, only to be told that they would gladly pay—in extra copies of the particu-lar issue—an offer which Emerson refused. Thoreau finally wrote off the debt to experience.

Next winter, Fuller sent Thoreau a music box with a view of Lucerne painted on its cover as a memento of their excursion and in appreciation of Thoreau's tutoring. They corresponded sporadically after that for a time but eventually went their separate ways.

Another young man who fell under the influence of Thoreau at about the same time was Isaiah T. Williams. A native of the Berkshires, he began to teach school in Concord in 1840. Here he became acquainted with the Thoreau brothers. After he moved to Buffalo, New York, to study law (a cardinal sin to Thoreau's mind), he missed the intellectual ferment of Concord and started a correspondence with Thoreau asking to be kept informed of the activities "of those whom the Public call Transcendentalists."[1] Thoreau, in reply, reminded Williams that "places are well nigh indifferent" and that one could be as good a Transcendentalist in western New York State as in Massachusetts.[2] When Williams replied that no matter what his future as a lawyer was to be, he would never turn his back on either literature or the principles of Transcendentalism, Thoreau rather haughtily cautioned him that the trades and professions are "so many traps which the Devil sets to catch men in—and good luck he has too, if one may judge."[3] Williams, obviously discouraged, made one more try and asked Thoreau, "Do you think engaged in the practice of law the best way

1. Thoreau, *Correspondence,* 48
2. Ibid. 51–3
3. Ibid. 68

of spending one[']s life?"[4] But by this time Thoreau apparently came to the conclusion that they were talking different languages and never bothered to answer the letter and so their brief correspondence came to an end.

IV

In January 1842 tragedy struck the Thoreau household. On New Year's Day, John Jr. was stropping his razor when it slipped and cut off a little piece from the end of the ring finger of his left hand. It was a very slight cut, just deep enough to draw blood. Replacing the skin, he put on a bandage and paid no more attention to it for several days. Although his health had been precarious enough the spring before for him to abandon teaching, it had not shown any marked deterioration since, and so no one thought seriously of the tiny cut. But by mid-week he noticed pains in the finger and when he removed his bandage on the 8th, he found part of the replaced skin had "mortified." That evening he called on Dr. Bartlett, who dressed the finger but thought nothing unusual of it. On the way home, John had strange sensations and acute pain in various parts of his body, and was barely able to reach the house. He woke the next morning complaining of a stiffness of the jaws. That night he was seized with violent spasms and lockjaw set in. A doctor was called in from Boston, but he said nothing could be done. On being told that he must die a speedy and painful death, he asked, "Is there no hope?" "None," replied the doctor. Then calmly he answered, "The cup that my Father gives me, shall I not drink it?" and bade all his friends good-bye.[5]

Henry took over the care of his brother and became the "most untiring and watchful of nurses."[6] At times John was delirious; at times he was as cheerful and composed "as if only going on a short journey." But the end came quickly. He died at two o'clock on Tuesday afternoon, January 11, in his brother's arms.

4. Ibid. 71
5. William S. Robinson, *"Warrington" Pen-Portraits* (Boston, 1877), 12–13
6. Davenport and Koopman, "Henry D. Thoreau 1839–1840"

Barzillai Frost, the minister of the First Parish Church, delivered the funeral eulogy on the texts "For what is your life? It is even a vapour, that appeareth for a little time and then vanisheth away" (James 4,14) and "Man cometh forth like a flower and is cut down" (Job 14,2):

He had a love of nature, even from childhood amounting to enthusiasm. He spent many of his leisure hours in straying over these hills and along the banks of the streams. There is not a hill, nor a tree, nor a bird, nor a flower of marked beauty in all this neighborhood that he was not familiar with, and any new bird or flower he discovered gave him the most unfeigned delight, and he would dwell with it and seem to commune with it for hours. He spent also many a serene and loving evening gazing upon the still moonlight scene and the blazing aurora, or looking into the bright firmament, radiant with the glory of God. . . .

The benevolence of the deceased appeared in his love of animals, in the pleasure he took in making children happy, and in his readiness to give up his time to oblige all. He had a heart to feel and a voice to speak for all classes of suffering humanity; and the cause of the poor inebriate, the slave, the ignorant and depraved, was very dear to him. . . .

Of his religious opinions I must speak with less confidence. He has been affected no doubt by the revolutionary opinions abroad in society in regard to inspiration and religious instructions, as it is very natural the young should. But there has been a tendency of late in his mind, I have thought, to those views which have fortified the minds of the great majority of the wise and good in all ages. (I may be mistaken in supposing that he adopted the transcendental views to any considerable extent.) But, however his theories *about* religion were unsettled, his principles and religious feelings were always unshaken. The religious sentiment had been awakened, and he manifested it in his tastes, feelings and conversation.[7]

It was a eulogy that twenty years later could have just as appropriately been read for Henry Thoreau.

At the time of John's death, the rest of the family thought Henry strangely calm, but it proved an outward calm only. He

---

7. Barzillai Frost [Funeral Sermon for John Thoreau, Jr.]. MS, George L. Davenport, Jr.

soon became completely passive—sitting, pondering, saying nothing. His sisters, worried, led him outdoors, hoping through his
interest in nature to arouse him, but their efforts were to no avail.
Then to their horror and despair, on January 22 he too became ill,
exhibiting all the symptoms of his brother's disease, lockjaw. The
doctor was baffled. There was no sign of any cut. There seemed
nothing to do but await the end. Then suddenly, on the 24th,
there was a turn for the better and slowly be recovered. He was
confined to his bedroom for a month. Even by mid-April he was
not sufficiently recovered to work in the garden. He continued
silent and depressed and for a long, long while could not be induced
to indulge in one of his favorite pastimes—singing.[8] For several
years he dreamed tragic dreams on the anniversary of John's death.[9]
And many years later he still choked and tears came into his eyes
at the mention of John's name.

Thoreau's was unquestionably a psychosomatic illness
brought on by the tragic death of the brother he loved so much.
Such illnesses are not unknown in the annals of medicine and in
Thoreau's case it well indicates the depth of his emotional involve-
ment in the death of his brother. There are those who feel that
had John lived, his gaiety and gregariousness would have light-
ened some of Henry's deep seriousness and involved him more
directly in the social life of Concord. But such can only be
speculation. Certainly, for a time at least, and an extended time at
that, much of the spark went out of Thoreau's life.

As if the tragedy of John's death were not enough, only
two weeks later tragedy struck with equal force in the Emerson
home. On January 24, Emerson's five-year-old son Waldo was
stricken with scarlatina and died three days later. Thoreau, who
had come to love the boy in his months of close association in the
Emerson household, was as deeply stricken as the Emersons. One
of the few consolations for both was that only a few months
before, John Thoreau had, in a moment of inspiration, taken young
Waldo to a visiting daguerreotypist and had his portrait taken, so
they at least had his image to remember him by. Unquestionably

8. S. E. Rena, "Thoreau's Voice," *Boston Transcript*, February 15,
1896
9. Hildegarde Hawthorne, *Concord's Happy Rebel* (New York,
1940), 73

their mutual grief bound Thoreau and Emerson even more closely together. Although Thoreau had moved back with his parents for a time after John's death, he soon returned to live with the Emersons, and eventually he resumed his normal pattern of life.

V

In July 1842 Nathaniel Hawthorne and his bride came to Concord to live in the Old Manse next to the battleground. With the death of Ezra Ripley in the fall of 1841, the Old Manse had become empty and in May of 1842 Hawthorne came to Concord and made arrangements for renting it. When they moved in on July 8, their wedding day, they found that Thoreau had plowed a garden and planted it for them.[1] Shortly after the newlyweds' arrival, Emerson and Thoreau together paid a formal call of welcome. It was not a success. Each sat on his chair bolt upright and completely ill at ease. Much of the time they sat in embarrassed silence. Hawthorne occasionally propounded a question which Thoreau would answer in a monosyllable. Emerson tried to start a conversation only to have each sentence sound like a royal pronouncement. Finally, in desperation the guests departed. It was one of the few formal calls in Thoreau's life—or Hawthorne's, for that matter.[2]

Despite the inauspicious beginning, however, a friendship between Thoreau and Hawthorne soon flourished. Thoreau was charmed with a music box they owned and came often to hear it played. He was invited for dinner on August 31 and Hawthorne the next day described him in his notebooks:

Mr. Thorow [sic] dined with us yesterday. He is a singular character—a young man with much of wild original nature still remaining in him; and so far as he is sophisticated, it is in a way and method of his own. He is as ugly as sin, long-nosed, queer-mouthed, and with uncouth and somewhat rustic, although courteous manners, corresponding very well with such an ex-

---

1. Louise Hall Tharp, *The Peabody Sisters of Salem* (Boston, 1950), 151
2. George William Curtis et al., *Homes of American Authors* (New York, 1853), 302

terior. But his ugliness is of an honest and agreeable fashion, and becomes him much better than beauty. . . . Mr. Thorow is a keen and delicate observer of nature—a genuine observer, which, I suspect, is almost as rare a character as even an original poet; and Nature, in return for his love, seems to adopt him as her especial child, and shows him secrets which few others are allowed to witness. He is familiar with beast, fish, fowl, and reptile, and has strange stories to tell of adventures, and friendly passages with these lower brethren of mortality. Herb and flower, likewise, wherever they grow, whether in garden, or wild wood, are his familiar friends. He is also on intimate terms with the clouds, and can tell the portents of storms. It is a characteristic trait, that he has a great regard for the memory of the Indian tribes, whose wild life would have suited him so well; and strange to say, he seldom walks over a ploughed field without picking up an arrow-point, a spear-head, or other relic of the red men—as if their spirits willed him to be the inheritor of their simple wealth.

With all this he has more than a tincture of literature—a deep and true taste for poetry, especially the elder poets, although more exclusive than is desirable, like all other Transcendentalists, so far as I am acquainted with them. . . .[3]

After dinner the two went for a row on the Concord River in Thoreau's "Musketiquid." Hawthorne was much impressed that Thoreau "managed the boat so perfectly, either with two paddles or with one, that it seemed instinct with his own will, and to require no physical effort to guide it."[4] Needing money, Thoreau offered to sell the boat to Hawthorne for seven dollars, an offer which Hawthorne immediately accepted, and he expressed the wish that he "could acquire the aquatic skill of its original owner at as reasonable a rate."[5]

Thoreau delivered the boat on the first of September and gave Hawthorne a lesson on its management. He assured Hawthorne that "it was only necessary to will the boat to go in any particular direction, and she would immediately take that course, as if imbued with the spirit of the steersman." But Hawthorne complained:

---

3. Nathaniel Hawthorne, *The American Notebooks* (New Haven, 1932), 165–6
4. Ibid. 166
5. Ibid.

It may be so with him, but certainly not with me; the boat seemed to be bewitched, and turned its head to every point of the compass except the right one. He then took the paddle himself, and though I could observe nothing peculiar in his management of it, the Musketiquid immediately became as docile as a trained steed. I suspect that she has not yet transferred her affections from her old master to her new one.[6]

Hawthorne, despite his misgivings, finally mastered the boat, changed its name to "Pond Lily," and made good use of it as long as he remained in Concord. When he moved to Salem in 1846, he gave it to Ellery Channing, who in turn used it for many years until it finally rotted to pieces.

Hawthorne found Thoreau's unpretentiousness a welcome relief at times, and when life at the Old Manse threatened to become too social, he took off with Thoreau for a boat ride on the river or a stroll to Walden. Julia Ward Howe has told of going for tea, expecting to meet Hawthorne, only to have him disappear out the back door leaving his wife to apologize as best she could by saying he had a "previous appointment" to go out on the river with Thoreau.[7]

When winter came, Hawthorne often joined Thoreau and Emerson in skating on the river and Mrs. Hawthorne was amused to note their varied posture. Thoreau did "dithyrambic dances and Bacchic leaps on the ice" while Hawthorne "moved like a self-impelled Greek statue, stately and grave," and Emerson "closed the line evidently too weary to hold himself erect, pitching headforemost, half lying on the air."[8]

Hawthorne was duly impressed when he read Thoreau's "Natural History of Massachusetts" in *The Dial* and thought it "gives a very fair image of his mind and character—so true, minute, and literal in observation, yet giving the spirit as well as letter of what he sees, even as a lake reflects its wooded banks. . . . There is a basis of good sense and moral truth, too, throughout

---

6. Ibid. 166–8
7. F. B. Sanborn, *Bronson Alcott at Alcott House* (Cedar Rapids, Ia., 1908), 40–1
8. Rose Hawthorne Lathrop, *Memories of Hawthorne* (Boston, 1897), 53

the article, which also is a reflection of his character. On the whole, I find him a healthy and wholesome man to know."[9]

Hawthorne took an active interest in fostering Thoreau's writing career, going out of his way to praise him in the prefaces of both *Mosses from an Old Manse* and *The Scarlet Letter*. He also took more practical and concrete steps to help Thoreau out. In mid-October 1842 when Epes Sargent, the editor of the short-lived *New Monthly Magazine,* wrote to ask Hawthorne to contribute, he suggested in his reply that Sargent also ask for something from Thoreau, whom he described as "a wild, irregular, Indian-like sort of fellow . . . who . . . writes . . . very well indeed," and added, "He is somewhat tinctured with Transcendentalism; but I think him capable of becoming a very valuable contributor to your Magazine." After pointing out the "Natural History of Massachusetts" as a good example of Thoreau's work, Hawthorne said, "The man has stuff in him to make a reputation of; and I wish that you might find it consistent with your interest to aid him in attaining that object."[1] Sargent, however, ignored his advice.

But Hawthorne was not willing to give up so easily. When in mid-January 1843 J. L. O'Sullivan, the editor of the *Democratic Review,* came to call at the Old Manse, Hawthorne pointedly invited Thoreau over to tea. Before he left, O'Sullivan invited Thoreau to write for his magazine. When Thoreau was in New York City the following summer, he looked up O'Sullivan at his office and offered him a review of J. A. Etzler's *The Paradise within the Reach of All Men.* Emerson had originally called the book to Thoreau's attention and asked him to review it for *The Dial,* but Thoreau preferred to submit it to O'Sullivan's magazine with its wider circulation. Much to Thoreau's chagrin, O'Sullivan rejected the review and asked instead that he submit "some of those extracts from your Journal, reporting some of your private interviews with nature, with which I have before been so much pleased." He hinted however that if Thoreau were willing to have the Etzler review modified to bring it more in line with O'Sullivan's own views—he objected primarily to Thoreau's want of

9. Hawthorne, *American Notebooks,* 166
1. Edward C. Sampson, "Three Unpublished Letters by Hawthorne to Epes Sargent," *American Literature,* XXXIV (1962), 102–3

Jane Thoreau,
Henry's aunt

Maria Thoreau,
Henry's aunt

Sophia Thoreau,
Henry's sister

THOREAU'S FAMILY

Ellen Sewall about 1840. From a hitherto unpublished daguerreotype now owned by her granddaughter, Mrs. Gilbert Tower

sympathy for communities—he might accept it. They eventually worked out a compromise and Thoreau's "Paradise (to be) Regained" appeared in the November 1843 *Democratic Review.*

Etzler's *Paradise* is a Utopian propaganda piece that suggests that if man would but harness such available sources of energy as the sun, winds, and tides and introduce mass-production techniques into manufacturing, he would no longer have to exert any appreciable labor and could live in a paradise as happily as Adam and Eve. Etzler accurately foreshadowed many of the inventions of the coming century including the apartment-house life of our large cities. Thoreau, however, was not impressed. "We will not be imposed upon by this vast application of forces," he said. "We believe that most things will have to be accomplished still by the application called Industry." "The chief fault of this book," he continued, "is, that it aims to secure the greatest degree of gross comfort and pleasure merely." Thoreau, true to his Transcendentalist principles, believed that the only true reformation came from within the individual and could not be imposed by society:

> Love is the wind, the tide, the waves, the sunshine. Its power is incalculable; it is many horse-power. It never ceases, it never slacks; it can move the globe without a resting-place; it can warm without fire; it can feed without meat; it can clothe without garments; it can shelter without roof; it can make a paradise within which will dispense with a paradise without.[2]

Such talk could give little comfort to the multitudinous reformers of Thoreau's day—or ours. There is little wonder that O'Sullivan feared the many communitarians among his subscribers might not like it. But it was true to Thoreau's principles, and to those principles he stuck.

Meanwhile, in reply to O'Sullivan's request for other papers, Thoreau submitted a short essay entitled "The Landlord," which O'Sullivan printed in the October 1843 issue. It is one of the few pieces that Thoreau consciously "wrote to sell" and is in the style of the familiar essay or sketch so popular in the mid-nineteenth-century periodicals. Filled with puns—at which Thoreau was a °

2. Thoreau, *Writings*, IV, 297, 302, 304

master—it sketches the popular conception of the ideal landlord. Thoreau himself cared little for the essay after it appeared and refused to pay fifty cents for an extra copy to send home to his parents. Few now would dispute his judgment.

VI

When in the summer of 1842 Emerson proposed to a number of his friends that they establish a public reading room in Concord well stocked with newspapers and periodicals, Thoreau was one of the first to express his enthusiasm. And when the Concord Athenaeum was thus established with a room reserved in the vestry of the First Parish Church, Thoreau joined Emerson in donating subscriptions to the *London Phalanx*, the *Cambridge Miscellany*, *The Dial*, the *New York Weekly Tribune*, the *Anti-Slavery Standard*, the *Albany Cultivator*, the *Lynn Washingtonian*, and the *Boston Miscellany*.[3] The Hoars, the Cheneys, the Keyeses, and even Hawthorne took up membership. For several years the Athenaeum provided both a central meeting place and a good supply of reading material for the intellectuals of the town, and Thoreau apparently used it as much as any.

Meanwhile he continued his active leadership in the Concord Lyceum. On January 27, 1841, he and his brother John had taken the affirmative in debating Bronson Alcott on the topic "Is it ever proper to offer forcible resistance?" Then, on November 18, 1842, over his own protest, he was elected curator of the lyceum. But once elected he set to work to provide a worthwhile course of lectures. He persuaded Emerson to speak on the 30th; his college classmate, James Richardson, now a student at Harvard Divinity School, on December 7; Rev. James Freeman Clarke, on the 14th; Horace Greeley, on the 19th; Wendell Phillips, on the 21st; his old mentor Orestes Brownson, on the 28th; Alcott's English friend Charles Lane, on January 4; M. B. Prichard of Concord, on the 11th; John Shepard Keyes, on the 18th; J. M. Barrett of Boston, on the 25th; Emerson's brother-in-law Charles T. Jackson

3. Kenneth Walter Cameron, *The Transcendentalists and Minerva* (Hartford, 1958), III, 890–1

of Boston, on February 1; a Mr. Knapp of Lexington, on the 15th; Dr. Edward Jarvis, on the 22nd; E. H. Chapin of Charlestown, on March 1; Charles Bowers of Concord, on the 8th; Henry Giles of Ireland, on the 16th; Theodore Parker of Roxbury, on the 22nd; E. W. Bull of Concord grape fame, on the 29th; Emerson again on the 30th; George Bancroft of Boston on April 5; Charles Lane again, on the 12th; Rev. Barzillai Frost of Concord's First Parish on the 19th; and Emerson for a third time, on the 26th. To provide all this, Thoreau received $109.20 from the lyceum treasury. From this he spent $31.25 for rent, lighting, and heat; paid Bancroft, Brownson, Giles, and Jackson, ten dollars each, Chapin, eight, and Parker, three; persuaded the other speakers to donate their services; and at the end of the season, having spent exactly one hundred dollars, returned $9.20 to the lyceum treasury. No wonder then that he boasted:

> How much might be done for a town with $100: I myself have provided a select course of twenty-five lectures for a winter, together with room, fuel, and lights, for that sum,—which was no inconsiderable benefit to every inhabitant.[4]

As for his own lecture on February 8, it was the only one in the entire course that the *Concord Freeman* took notice of. On February 10, it reported:

> *Mr. Thoreau's Lecture,* delivered last Wednesday evening, before the Lyceum, is spoken of as a production very creditable to its author. The subject was the life and character of Sir Walter Raleigh. Raleigh was one of the most remarkable men of a remarkable period, the Elizabethan age. He was learned, brave, and adventurous, and was possessed of such varied intellectual powers, as to be esteemed as a writer, a statesman, and a soldier. Those who are wholly unacquainted with his writings, have yet to explore a mine of intellect which has few equals in point of richness. Like the productions of all those men whom we are accustomed to call the old English prose writers,—and who terminated with the author of the "Urn-Burial,"—they are literally filled with profound thought, which finds its expression in the most

---

4. Walter Harding, "Thoreau and the Concord Lyceum," *Thoreau Society Bulletin,* XXX (1950), 2

nervous language. The public conduct of Raleigh is well known to every historical reader, and no one will be found to question the accuracy of the assertion, that much of it added to the glory of the English name. Yet he had many bad traits of character, and is scarcely deserving of the admiration of which he is the object, and which, it is quite probable, had its origin in his melancholy fate, and has been kept up in these latter days thro' the genius of Scott. Raleigh was a selfish man, and to say that many of his acts were superlatively mean, would be but to utter a simple truth. In adventure, he was but a higher sort of Mike Lambourne, and readily subscribed to the creed of those "jolly fellows" who held that there was no law beyond the line. His conduct in his last voyage was clearly illegal, and Gondomar was right when he called him and his comrades pirates. He was haughty, insolent, and vindictive, an unchivalrous enemy, and too often a deceitful friend. But he is one of the world's favorites, and the closing scene of his life atoned in the opinion of many for all his errors.

The lecture itself, although once printed in a limited edition many years after Thoreau's death, has never been included in his collected works and is chiefly of interest only because it was Thoreau who wrote it.

CHAPTER EIGHT
(1843)

I

As PLEASANT AS life had been at the Emerson's, by the spring of 1843 Thoreau once more began to feel restless. He was twenty-five years old and had little, he felt, to show for it. As early as October 11, 1842, he had begun to look for some new type of employment. And on March 1, 1843, he wrote Emerson, who was then in New York City, asking him to keep his ears alerted for any employment that might be appropriate. He was particularly anxious to further himself as an author.

At the moment, Emerson was visiting with his brother William, the County Judge of Richmond Court on Staten Island, who, with three sons—Charles, an infant; Haven, three years of age; and Willie, seven—was anxious to secure for all three, but particularly Willie, the essentials of a good education. Emerson immediately proposed that Thoreau would make a highly suitable tutor for the children, and, having received the judge's approval, returned to Concord to suggest to Thoreau that if he were anxious to pursue a writing career, such a position would place him admirably near the publishing world of New York City.

On March 13, Emerson wrote to his brother:

> I have to say that Henry Thoreau listens very willingly to your proposition[;] he thinks it exactly fit for him & he very rarely finds offers that do fit him. He says that it is such a relation as he wishes to sustain, to be the friend & educator of a boy, & one not yet subdued by schoolmasters. I have told him that you wish to put the boy & not his grammer & geography under good & active influence that you wish him to go to the woods & to go to the city with him & do all he can for him—This he understands & likes well & proposes to accept[.]

[145]

I have told him that you will give him board, lodging (washing?) a room by himself to study in, when not engaged with Willie, with fire when the season requires, and a hundred dollars a year. He says, it is an object with him to earn some money beyond expenses, which he supposes the above named terms will about cover, and that his health now will not allow him to stipulate any manual labor: he therefore wishes to know if there is any clerical labor from your office or from any other office, known to you—which he can add to his means of support. He is sure that his handwriting is not so careless, but that he can make it legible for such work. He would like to know if there be such employment attainable, pending the time when he shall procure for himself literary labor from some quarter in New York. He further says he shall be ready to come as soon as 1 April, if you wish, & he asks whether it will be convenient to you to advance to him $20. before he comes, in case it is agreed between you that he shall come.—I recite this last proposition as he made it, but I can easily do it myself, if you prefer. You shall write in reply either to H. D. Thoreau or to me. Lidian & Elizabeth are charmed with the project, & think it auspicious on both sides only Lidian cannot spare Henry.[1]

On April 3, Emerson wrote his brother that Thoreau was willing to accept his offer and report to Staten Island on May 1, conditional only that when winter came he be guaranteed the use of a room with fire for his evening's studies; and he reported that he had advanced Thoreau ten dollars already and would pay him ten dollars more when he needed it.

Word soon spread throughout Concord of Thoreau's impending departure. Hawthorne, after talking with Thoreau, confided to his notebook:

I am glad, on Mr. Thoreau's own account that he is going away; as he is physically out of health, and, morally and intellectually, seems not to have found exactly the guiding clue; and in all these respects, he may be benefitted by his removal;— also it is one step towards a circumstantial position in the world. On my account, I should like to have him remain here; he being one of the few persons, I think, with whom to hold intercourse

---

1. Ralph Waldo Emerson, *Letters*, III, 158–9

is like hearing the wind among the boughs of a forest-tree; and with all this wild freedom, there is high and classic cultivation in him too.[2]

On April 11, Thoreau dropped in at the Manse to ask for one last ride in the rowboat he had sold Hawthorne. They rowed up the North Branch, climbed a snowy hillside, and then floated back down the river on a cake of ice, towing the boat behind. Knowing their love of music, Thoreau thoughtfully took the music box Richard Fuller had given him to the Hawthornes and asked that they enjoy it while he was away. As a going away memento of their friendship, Elizabeth Hoar sent him an inkstand and Prudence Ward, a small microscope.

Thoreau left for Staten Island on May 6, accompanying Mrs. William Emerson, who had been visiting in Concord for a month. Emerson's mother, who had originally planned to join them, decided at the last moment to remain behind in Concord. Emerson advanced Thoreau ten dollars more to outfit himself for the journey and seven dollars to pay his traveling expenses. He also sent his brother a letter warning: "He [Thoreau] is a bold & a profound thinker though he may easily chance to pester you with some accidental crotchets and perhaps a village exaggeration of the value of facts. Yet I confide, if you should content each other, in Willie's soon coming to value him for his real power to serve & instruct him. I shall eagerly look, though not yet for some time, for tidings how you speed in this new relation."[3]

En route, Thoreau stopped off long enough in Boston to make a last and once more unsuccessful attempt to collect what Bradbury & Soden owed for his "A Walk to Wachusett." Their boat ran aground briefly in the Thames River near New London, Connecticut, but was luckily released by the next high tide. Docking near Castle Garden, they went immediately to Staten Island without stopping to look at New York City. Thoreau found the "Snuggery," Judge Emerson's home, located on what is now known as Emerson Hill, on Douglas Road not far from Richmond Road, a "long,

2. Hawthorne, *The American Notebooks,* 175
3. Emerson, *Letters,* III, 172

low brown house, standing with its end to the road, with grapevines
on the piazza and box plants in the garden."[4]

Immediately settling down to a routine of work, Thoreau
breakfasted regularly at six thirty, lunched at twelve, and dined at
five. From nine to two he tutored. Willie was his major pupil, but
Charles and Haven were usually around. Later the Wandel boy
who lived across the street and played with the Emerson boys
was added to the class. Thoreau took them all on long walks, often
early in the morning before the elders were astir. On one occasion, Wandel recalled, he took them fishing in the bay and to his
embarrassment succeeded in beaching the boat where only a horse
could pull it off.[5]

Thoreau's happiest moments were in his off-hours when he
could ramble about the island to his heart's content by himself. He
wandered about the interior, visiting the old Huguenot homesteads
and inspecting the lands so closely that a native was certain he was
a land speculator and offered him a bonus if he would sell his farm
for him. The flora and fauna of the area fascinated him, it was so
surprisingly different from that of his native Concord. He had never
seen tulip trees before and thought them particularly beautiful.
Painted cups he noted were common in the meadows and fruit
trees abounded in every direction. In early July, when the seven-
teen-year locusts emerged in one of their spectacular brood years,
he was so excited he wrote his mother:

> Pray have you the Seventeen year locust in Concord? The air
> here is filled with their din. They come out of the ground at first
> in an imperfect state, and crawling up the shrubs and plants,
> the perfect insect burst[s] out through the bark. They are doing
> great damage to the fruit and forest trees. The latter are covered
> with dead twigs, which in the distance look like the blossoms
> of the chestnut. They bore every twig of last year's growth in
> order to deposit their eggs in it. In a few weeks the eggs will be
> hatched, and the worms fall to the ground and enter it—and in
> 1860 make their appearance again.[6]

4. Richard J. Turk, Jr., "Emerson Hill," *Staten Island Historian,* XXI
(1960), 14; Mabel Abbott, *The Life of William T. Davis* (Ithaca,
1949), 16
5. Abbott, *The Life of William T. Davis,* 17
6. Thoreau, *Correspondence,* 121–2

But it was the sea more than all else that impressed him. It was his first and only opportunity to live by the ocean and he made the most of it, spending hours at a time sitting in an old ruined fort watching vessels sail up the coast, take on their pilots, round the Hook and proceed down the narrow channel to Quarantine. He was disillusioned though to discover large packs of wild dogs roaming the beaches, living off the carcasses of horses and oxen that washed up on the shore, and once he rescued a tiny puppy from their attack.

On occasion he journeyed into the city, but was not impressed with what he saw. "Every thing there disappoints me but the crowd," he complained in a letter to Emerson.[7] And later:

> I don't like the city better, the more I see it, but worse. I am ashamed of my eyes that behold it. It is a thousand times meaner than I could have imagined. It will be something to hate,—that's the advantage it will be to me; and even the best people in it are a part of it and talk coolly about it. The pigs in the street are the most respectable part of the population. When will the world learn that a million men are of no importance compared with *one* man?[8]

There were, however, individuals who helped to redeem the city. Emerson had written in advance to Henry James, Sr., the father of the novelist, suggesting that Thoreau's friendship was worth cultivating and adding, "Thoreau is a profound mind and a person of true magnanimity, and if it should happen that there is some village pedantry and tediousness of facts, it will easily be forgotten when you come at what is better."[9] James promptly invited Thoreau to call.[1] A month later Thoreau reported to Emerson:

> I have been to see Henry James, and like him very much. It was a great pleasure to meet him. It makes humanity seem more erect and respectable. I never was more kindly and faithfully catechised. It made me respect myself more to be thought worthy of such wise questions. . . . I know of no one so patient

---

7. Ibid. 107
8. Ibid. 111–12
9. Ralph Barton Perry, *The Thought and Character of William James* (Boston, 1935), 12–13
1. Thoreau, *Correspondence*, 101

and determined to have the good of you. It is almost friendship, such plain and human dealing. I think that he will not write or speak inspiringly; but he is a refreshing forward-moving man, and he has naturalized and humanized New York for me. . . . I had three hours' solid talk with him, and he asks me to make free use of his house.[2]

Thoreau called once or twice more, but then the Jameses left the city for the summer and their brief acquaintance came to an end. Fifteen years later they met once more in Emerson's parlor in Concord at one of Bronson Alcott's conversations. James offended everyone present by dominating the meeting and Thoreau denounced his "*quasi* philanthropic doctrines in a metaphysic dress" as "for all practical purposes very crude."[3] James, in his turn, was offended by Thoreau's comments and years later recalled him as "literally the most childlike, unconscious and unblushing egotist it has ever been my fortune to encounter in the ranks of manhood."[4]

Thanks again to Emerson, Thoreau also met two young Transcendentalists, Giles Waldo and William Tappan, in New York City and surprisingly adjourned with them for an afternoon to the comforts of an English alehouse. He enjoyed their company, but expressed to Emerson his disappointment that though "they are so much better than the great herd, . . . the heavens are not shivered into diamonds over their heads."[5] He was disappointed too with the Rev. William Henry Channing, a young Unitarian minister who was active in many reform movements and at the moment was editing a short-lived journal, *The Present*. Thoreau wrote Emerson that he thought Channing "retreating from himself and from yourself, with sad doubts," adding, "You feel as if you would like to see him when he has made up his mind to run all the risks."[6] Albert Brisbane, the pioneer American Fourierist, made, if anything, even less of an impression on Thoreau, who said of him, "He did not impress me favorably. . . . I barely saw him, but he did not look as if he could let Fourier go, in any case, and throw up his hat."

2. Ibid. 110
3. Sanborn, *Recollections of Seventy Years*, II, 384
4. Perry, *The Thought and Character of William James*, 49
5. Thoreau, *Correspondence*, 111
6. Ibid. 111

Horace Greeley, the Editor of the New York *Tribune,* he found much more exciting. He had already met Greeley the preceding winter at the lyceum in Concord and now thought him "cheerfully in earnest . . . a hearty New Hampshire boy as one would wish to meet [who] says 'now be neighborly.' "[7] Greeley did indeed become neighborly. Taking time out of his overwhelmingly busy life to volunteer his services as Thoreau's literary agent, he not only placed Thoreau's essays in the best periodicals of the day, but also collected his pay for him and then puffed his articles in the pages of his own *Tribune.* Thoreau also took advantage of an opportunity to hear Lucretia Mott, the well-known Quakeress, speak at the Friends Meeting on Hester Street. He was delighted that she did not hesitate to speak out strongly against slavery and thought her talk "transcendentalism in its mildest form."[8] He was impressed too with the ways of the Quakers in general, their plainness, their straightforwardness, their simplicity. Thoreau also tried —but unsuccessfully—to locate some of his mother's distant relatives. He did, however, succeed in locating Prudence Ward's brother George and spent the night at his home. Ward, who had often met Thoreau in Concord, was more favorably impressed with Thoreau than he had been in the past and wrote his sister: "I think he is getting to view things more as others do, than formerly; & he remarked he had been studying books—now he intended to study nature & daily life. It would be well."[9]

One of the advantages of living in the vicinity of New York City, Thoreau discovered, was that it gave him ready access to whole new stores of books. After he learned that H. S. McKean, who had been one of his tutors at Harvard, was now in charge of the Mercantile Library, he obtained from him first a visitor's card for a month and then a perpetual stranger's ticket that gave him the freedom of the library. He was also befriended by Dr. Philip J. Forbes of the New York Society Library, who permitted him to take out some "untake-out-able books," which Thoreau otherwise threatened to read on the spot. Thoreau had a way with librarians when he was anxious to get hold of rare books. The early English poets interested him at the moment and he read all

7. Ibid. 128
8. Ibid. 128–9
9. Canby, *Thoreau,* 176–7

he could find of Ossian, Daniel, Donne, and Lovelace. He became most excited by the work of Francis Quarles, a minor seventeenth-century metaphysical poet, and thought it rare to find one who "was so much of a poet and so little of an artist."[1]

Nor did Thoreau forget that one of his major objects in coming to Staten Island was to acquaint himself with the literary world of the city. Emerson had tried unsuccessfully through Henry James, Sr., to arrange for Thoreau to meet Parke Godwin. But he did get into the offices of Harper's and various other publishers and editors. He found however that Harper's were already making fifty thousand dollars annually and so, taking as their motto "Leave well enough alone," were not interested in risking anything on new and unknown authors.[2] As for the periodicals, he found they were overwhelmed with contributions, even though they paid nothing. Only the *Ladies' Companion* paid anything, but he thought he could "write nothing companionable." He tried unsuccessfully to earn a little selling subscriptions to the *Agriculturist* and traveled up the city as far as Manhattanville in that endeavor.

II

Unfortunately Thoreau was never really happy on Staten Island or in New York City. In the first place, he was in poor health. There seems to be every indication that his tuberculosis had flared up again the previous winter. His friends spoke of it as "bronchitis," but its long duration would seem to indicate that it was something more serious than a temporary inflammation. On his way to Staten Island he had caught a new cold and became ill enough to be confined to the "Snuggery" for most of the month of May. Undoubtedly the moist climate of the island helped his condition little. He developed a chronic sleepiness, like that which haunted his Uncle Charles, and complained that he found it impossible to read or write, except at rare intervals. Even as late as August he counted himself "with the innumerable army of invalids."[3]

1. Thoreau, *Correspondence,* 143–4
2. Ibid. 134–5
3. Ibid. 122, 132–3

To make matters worse, he found himself almost intolerably homesick for both his family and Concord. He mourned in a letter to his mother, "Methinks I should be content to sit at the back-door in Concord, under the poplar-tree, henceforth forever."[4] And he sent a profusion of letters back to his parents, his sisters, and the Emersons in Concord, filled with requests for every tiny item of news.

So lonely did he become that thinking back on his happy days with the Concord Emersons, he wrote two warmly affectionate letters to Mrs. Emerson as a son might to his distant mother. On May 22, 1843, he wrote:

> I think of you as some elder sister of mine, whom I could not have avoided,—a sort of lunar influence,—only of such age as the moon, whose time is measured by her light. You must know that you represent to me woman, for I have not traveled very far or wide,—and what if I had? I like to deal with you, for I believe you do not lie or steal, and these are very rare virtues. I thank you for your influence for two years. I was fortunate to be subjected to it, and am now to remember it. It is the noblest gift we can make; what signify all others that can be bestowed? You have helped to keep my life "on loft," as Chaucer says of Griselda, and in a better sense. You always seemed to look down at me as from some elevation—some of your high humilities—and I was better for having to look up. I felt taxed not to disappoint your expectation; for could there be any accident so sad as to be respected for something better than we are? It was a pleasure even to go away from you, as it is not to meet some, as it apprised me of my high relations; and such a departure is a sort of further introduction and meeting. Nothing makes the earth seem so spacious as to have friends at a distance; they make the latitudes and longitudes.[5]

And on June 20, after receiving a note from her, he replied:

> You seem to me to speak out of a very clear and high heaven, where any one may be who stands so high. Your voice seems not a voice, but comes as much from the blue heavens, as from the paper. . . .

---

4. Ibid. 131
5. Ibid. 103

The thought of you will constantly elevate my life; it will be something always above the horizon to behold, as when I look up at the evening star. I think I know your thoughts without seeing you, and as well here as in Concord. You are not at all strange to me.

I could hardly believe after the lapse of one night that I had such a noble letter still at hand to read—that it was not some fine dream. I looked at midnight to be sure that it was real. I feel that I am unworthy to know you, and yet they will not permit it wrongfully.

I, perhaps, am more willing to deceive by appearances than you say you are; it would not be worth the while to tell how willing—but I have the power perhaps too much to forget my meanness as soon as seen, and not be incited by permanent sorrow. . . .[6]

These two letters reveal to the fullest his heartbreaking loneliness on Staten Island, but they have their amusing side too. When Mrs. Thoreau heard they had been received, she asked to see the news from her son. Mrs. Emerson consented, but said she was almost ashamed to show them because Henry had exalted her by very undeserved praise. "O yes," replied Mrs. Thoreau, "Henry is very tolerant."[7]

To add to Thoreau's feeling of loneliness on Staten Island, word arrived from Leipzig that his college roommate, Stearns Wheeler, who had gone abroad to study in the German universities, had died very suddenly. Thoreau, at first, could not accept word of his passing and hoped that it was only a false rumor. But when confirmation of the tragedy came, Thoreau thought that Wheeler's death had left a gap that could not be filled.

The real crux of Thoreau's unhappiness however was simply the fact that he was not getting along well with his employers. He found them to be neither his "kith nor kin." He was not attracted at all by young Willie, and he soon found that the judge was a very different person from his brother. William was too formal and admittedly "rather antipathetic to Thoreau and the more eccentric Transcendentalists."[8] The judge was far too conventional for

---

6. Ibid. 119–20
7. Ralph L. Rusk, *The Life of Ralph Waldo Emerson* (New York, 1949), 291
8. F. B. Sanborn, *The Personality of Emerson* (Boston, 1903), 22

Thoreau, and Thoreau was too much of the individualist for the judge. Years later Emerson told F. B. Sanborn: "Wm. Emerson and Henry Thoreau were not men that could get along together.— Each would think whatever the other did was out of place."[9] Thoreau's antipathy to William Emerson and his family can be seen in a journal entry he penned at their home on October 21, 1843:

> I have seen such a hollow, glazed life as on a painted floor,— which some couples lead; with their basement, parlor and folding doors, a few visitors' cards and the latest Annual; such life only as there is in the shells on the mantelpiece. The very children cry with less inwardness and depth than they do in the cottage. There they do not *live*, it is there they reside. There is no hearth in the centre of that house. The atmosphere of the apartments is not yet peopled with the spirits of its inhabitants; but the voices sound hollow and echo, and we see only the paint and the paper.[1]

By fall Thoreau was ready to give up. He thought for a time of turning to schoolteaching in the Staten Island area. In the spring his sister Helen had asked him if he could find a teaching position for her there and he made a number of unsuccessful inquiries at the time. Now he looked around again, this time for a school where they could teach together, but he could find nothing that suited him. Meanwhile Sophia reported that she had started a small school in the family home and Helen had turned to giving piano lessons to the neighbors' children, so he abandoned those plans.

Not ordinarily very much concerned with holiday festivities, Thoreau suddenly decided he would like to go home for Thanksgiving. Emerson unwittingly encouraged him by asking him to give a lecture before the Concord Lyceum if he came. He returned to Concord, ostensibly only for a short visit. The lecture he delivered on November 29, 1843, was on "The Ancient Poets"—that is, Homer, Ossian, and Chaucer. Homer and Chaucer had long been his favorites, but his enthusiasm for Ossian was based on his recent discovery of Patrick MacGregor's blank-verse translation of *The Genuine Remains of Ossian.* Thoreau innocently accepted

9. F. B. Sanborn, Journal for March 22, 1878. MS, Morgan Library
1. Thoreau, *The First and Last Journeys,* I, 80–1

James Macpherson's hoax as genuine and thought the poems "of the same stamp with the Iliad itself." He later published a condensed version of his lecture in *The Dial* for January 1844, and still later revised the essay for inclusion in his first book, *A Week*.

The visit to Concord proved too much for the homesick Thoreau. When he left once again for Staten Island on December 3, it was only to gather up his possessions. By the 17th he was back in Concord for good, never to leave the town again except for brief excursions. William Emerson gave him a final purse and they parted company on not unfriendly terms.[2] But the Staten Island experiment on the whole had to be written off as a failure. Thoreau's only success in the literary world during his island stay was his cultivation of a friendship with Horace Greeley—though he was not to reap the benefits of even that friendship for a few years yet. The sea was no substitute for the ponds and rivers of Concord. Staten Island was not Concord.

---

2. Emerson, *Letters*, III, 229

CHAPTER NINE
(1843–1845)

I

Back in Concord once more, Thoreau settled down with his parents in the Parkman house on Main Street. His immediate problem was, of course, a financial one—to pay off his debts—and he settled it by going to work in the family pencil factory. Coming fresh again to the pencil business after an absence of several years, he quickly saw many ways to improve both the manufacturing methods and the product. It had always been the custom, for example, to split open the cedar pencil wood, chisel out a groove, fill it with lead in a paste form, and then glue the two halves together while the paste dried. Thoreau had discovered after a little experimentation that the mixture of graphite and Bavarian clay he had developed was fireproof and could be quickly baked hard. Next he invented a saw that would strip the baked lead to fit into the grooved pencil halves.[1] So absorbed did he become in the project that for weeks, as he complained to Emerson, he could think of nothing else, and even in his dreams he worked at the new machines.[2]

Later he conceived the idea of baking the graphite mixture into cylinders just the exact size for the pencils and dispensed with the necessity of sawing out the individual leads. Then, carrying the process one step further, he invented a new machine which drilled holes in the solid pencil woods the exact size of the leads, thus permitting one to ram them in without having to go to the trouble of splitting the woods open and then gluing them back together again. He also discovered that he could obtain varying degrees of hard-

---

1. Kurt Steel, "Prophet of the Independent Man," *Progressive*, September 24, 1945
2. Ralph Waldo Emerson, *Journals*, VI, 496

ness and softness of the lead simply by increasing or decreasing the amount of clay in the formula—the more clay, the harder the pencil—and was able to offer pencils graded according to their standard of hardness.

Having thus improved their product, the Thoreaus set about advertising it. In the summer of 1844 they issued a broadside announcing that they manufactured "a new and superior drawing pencil, expressly for Artists and Connoisseurs, possessing in an unusual degree the qualities of the pure lead, superior blackness, and firmness of point, as well as freedom of mark, and warranted not to be affected by changes of temperature." It also announced that they manufactured various other kinds of pencils including "the Mammoth Large Round, the Rulers or Flat, and the common of every quality and price" as well as "leadpoints in any quantity, and plumbago Plates for Galvanic Batteries."[3] They also made pencils with red lead and with blue. Appended to their broadside was a testimonial from Emerson's brother-in-law, Charles T. Jackson, stating:

> I have used a number of different kinds of Black-lead Pencils made by you, and find them to be of excellent quality. I would especially recommend to Engineers your fine hard pencils, as capable of giving a very fine line, the points being remarkably even and firm, which is due to the peculiar manner in which the leads are prepared. The softer kinds I find to be of good quality and much better than any American Pencils I have used.[4]

There was also a puff from D. C. Johnston, a prominent artist-engraver in Boston, who said: "Having made a trial of your pencils, I do not hesitate to pronounce them superior in every respect to any American Pencils I have yet met with, and equal to those of Rhodes, or Beekman & Langdon, London." They packaged the pencils by the gross in artistic blue and gold boxes, Elizabeth Peabody stocked a supply of the pencils in her Boston bookstore and sold them for seventy-five cents a dozen.[5] When Emerson called them to the attention there of his friend Caroline Sturgis, she tried

3. Milton Meltzer and Walter Harding, *A Thoreau Profile* (New York, 1962), 138
4. Ibid.
5. Ralph Waldo Emerson, *Thoreau's Pencils* (Cambridge, 1944)

them out in her art work and reported that they were "excellent,—worthy of Concord art and artists and indeed one of the best productions I ever saw from there—something substantial & useful about it." Legend has it that Boston art teachers were soon insisting that their pupils buy only Thoreau pencils. In 1847 they won a diploma from the Massachusetts Charitable Mechanic Association at their annual fair, and in 1849 they won the silver medal for the best lead pencils at the Salem Charitable Mechanic Association.[6] The Thoreau pencils, thanks to Henry's efforts, had become the best on the market. Their success led others to enter the field and by 1850 there were thirteen pencil makers in Concord.[7]

II

On the last day of April 1844, taking a vacation from his pencil work, Thoreau set out with Edward Sherman Hoar by rowboat to explore the upper reaches of the Sudbury River for a few days. Hoar, the younger brother of George, Rockwood, and Elizabeth Hoar, and son of the town's most distinguished citizen, Samuel Hoar, was in his senior year at Harvard and home for a few days' vacation. When Hoar's parents had not allowed him as a lad to use a gun, he had accompanied Thoreau with his old single-barreled flintlock on hunting expeditions through the Concord woods.[8] Later he distressed his family and disturbed the whole town by running off briefly to California with a ne'er-do-well by the name of Worthington. But he eventually found himself and returned to Concord and Cambridge to complete his college degree. He never achieved the fame and position of his brothers, preferring a quiet, retiring life to political office. Thoreau was one of the formative influences of his life as is well implied by the epitaph now carved on his stone in Sleepy Hollow Cemetery: "He cared nothing for the wealth or fame his rare genius might easily have won. But his ear knew the songs of all the birds. His eye saw the

---

6. [Walter Harding], "A Lead Pencil Diploma," *Thoreau Society Bulletin* LXXIV (1961), 8
7. *Middlesex Freeman*, July 25, 1851
8. Edward Emerson, Notes on Thoreau

beauty of flowers and the secret of their life. His unerring taste delighted in what was best in books. So his pure and quiet days reaped their rich harvest of wisdom and content."

But, to return to their boating expedition. They caught a mess of fish sufficient for their noon meal before they had gone a mile up the river, and after borrowing a match, they proceeded to cook them on the shores of Fair Haven Bay. They should have known better. The earth was uncommonly dry, even for a Massachusetts April, and a stray spark soon set the nearby dead grass on fire. They tried first to extinguish it with their hands and feet, and then with a board from their boat, but to no avail. In no time the fire was beyond their control and racing up the hillside through grass and bushes. Realizing that it could not be stopped before it reached the Well Meadow Brook and that it might easily jump that, both young men raced off for help—Hoar down the river by boat, and Thoreau through the woods toward town.

The first farmer Thoreau met declared the fire was "none of his stuff" and drove unheedingly along. (To his chagrin the fire later spread to his own woods.) The next was the owner of the woods then burning and he quickly returned with Thoreau to the scene. Realizing at once that they could do little good alone, the farmer returned for further assistance while Thoreau, by this time spent from running two miles, remained. But when he comprehended the half-mile front of flame before him, Thoreau gave up and walked slowly off through the woods to Fair Haven Cliff, where, climbing to the highest rock, he sat down to observe the progress of the fire. Presently he heard the distant alarm bells ringing in the village, and when sufficient crowds of help arrived, he joined with them in putting out the fire.

The townspeople were understandably angry. Anyone with any sense, they thought, should have realized that it was no time to light a fire. The *Concord Freeman* for May 3, after pointing out that more than three hundred acres had been burned over and more than two thousand dollars damage done to the properties of A. H. Wheeler, Cyrus Hubbard, and Darius Hubbard, editorialized:

> The fire, we understand, was communicated to the woods through the thoughtlessness of two of our citizens, who kindled

it in a *pine stump,* near the Pond, for the purpose of making a chowder. As every thing around them was as combustible almost as a fire-ship, the flames spread with rapidity, and hours elapsed before it could be subdued. It is to be hoped that this unfortunate result of sheer carelessness, will be borne in mind by those who may visit the woods in [the] future for recreation.

An advertisement on another page stated: "Cyrus Hubbard and others, return their thanks to the citizens of Concord for their prompt and unwearied exertions in extinguishing the fire in the woods on Tuesday last." Obviously the thanks applied neither to Thoreau nor to Edward Hoar. Indeed there was talk of court prosecution of the two young men and were it not for the fact that Hoar was a son of the town's leading citizen, something might have been made of it. As it was, Hoar's father is said to have paid some damages to the Hubbards and the Wheelers.[9] Even this did not quiet the irate owners of the woods. For years Thoreau had to endure the whispers of "woods-burner" behind his back. And even on into the twentieth century one of the Wheeler girls was frequently heard to say, "Don't talk to me about Henry Thoreau. Didn't I all that winter have to go to school with a smootched apron or dress because I had to pitch in and help fill the wood box with partly charred wood?"[1]

Six years after the fire, Thoreau wrote his misadventure up at length in his journal to rationalize his behavior:

> I had felt like a guilty person,—nothing but shame and regret. But now I settled the matter with myself shortly. I said to myself: "Who are these men who are said to be the owners of these woods, and how am I related to them? I have set fire to the forest, but I have done no wrong therein." . . . I settled it with myself and stood to watch the approaching flames. It was a glorious spectacle, and I was the only one there to enjoy it.[2]

But unfortunately his protests do not ring true. The mere fact that six years after the event he could devote five pages in his journal to the topic is ample indication of how much his conscience still

9. Henry David Thoreau, *Walden* (Boston, 1909), II, 94 n
1. Mary Hosmer Brown, *Memories of Concord* (Boston, 1926), 105
2. Thoreau, *Journal,* II, 22–4

disturbed him. To his townsmen he might answer he was not guilty, but underneath it still rankled that he was.

III

In April 1844 young Isaac Thomas Hecker arrived in Concord. Hecker was a New York City baker and miller two years younger than Thoreau. Attracted by Transcendentalism, he went to Boston and joined the Brook Farm community in January 1843, but six months later, dissatisfied, he moved along to Bronson Alcott's Fruitlands community, where he remained only two weeks. Still searching for a more satisfactory way of life (his friends jokingly called him "Earnest the Seeker"), he came under the influence of Orestes Brownson, who was at the moment contemplating embracing Roman Catholicism. Hecker decided to study the classic languages in order to understand better the doctrines Brownson advanced.

Emerson's Plymouth friend George Bradford had just opened a small private school in Concord and Emerson suggested he might be willing to help Hecker in his spare time. Bradford readily agreed to tutor Hecker during his noon hours and set out with him to find a suitable rooming house. Hecker was discouraged when the first landlady demanded seventy-five dollars a year.[3] But searching further they happened upon Mrs. Thoreau, Henry's mother, and quickly came to terms. On the evening of April 24 Hecker wrote his mother from the Thoreau home:

> This evening I can say that I am settled, comfortably settled in every particular. All that is needed for my comfort is here— a good straw bed—a large table—carpet—washstand—bookcase —stove—chairs—looking glass—all, all that is needful; and this for 75 cents a week, including lights; wood is extra pay. . . . The lady of the house, Mrs. Thoreau, *is a woman* about whom the only fear I have is that she is too much like dear Mother: she will take too much care of me. She has told me how she used to sit up nights and wait until a young man whom she had to board with her came home, a stranger to her, still she insists

3. Isaac Hecker, Letter to his parents of April 19, 1844. MS, Paulist Archives

that she must treat all the same as her own, and even with greater care. If you were to see her, Mother, you would be perfectly satisfied that I have fallen into good hands and met with a second mother, if that is possible.[4]

The whole Thoreau family took a friendly interest in Hecker and when they learned he had lost his trunk en route from New York, Mr. Thoreau checked both of the Boston depots for him.[5] Hecker spent most of his time in study and quiet contemplation, interrupted only by Mrs. Thoreau's coming to make his bed in the morning and Bradford's tutoring at noon.[6]

Thoreau and Hecker soon became acquainted. Charles Lane of Fruitlands had tried to arrange their meeting in New York City the winter before—successfully or not, it is not known, but at least they were familiar with one another's names. Once he learned of Thoreau's knowledge of the classics, Hecker regretted that he had not turned to him for tutoring and complained in his diary:

> If I had known that Henry Thoreau had been taught the Greek and Latin languages, I should have selected him instead of Mr. Bradford. . . . Mr. Thoreau has a better knowledge of languages, has more leisure, takes a delight in languages. Mr. Bradford comes here when he has been tired out by his school, simply hears me recite, gives me scarcely any valuable information on the structure and the nature of the languages, and does not awaken any new interest in my study; whereas from H.T. a few moments' conversation gave me more instruction and delight than all that G.P.B. has ever said to me on the subject. G.P.B. has so much other business that takes up his mind that when he comes here I feel as if he felt his time was lost, and that he is desirous to get away as soon as he can. . . . Would he accept willingly that H.T. should take his place? I cannot say. I fear not, or he would have told me of Thoreau, situated as he is.[7]

Fortunately Bradford's interest in his tutoring shortly picked up and his pupil was happy to continue with him.

---

4. Isaac Hecker, Letter to his mother of April 24, 1844. MS, Paulist Archives
5. Isaac Hecker, Letter to his parents of May 13, 1844. MS, Paulist Archives
6. Isaac Hecker, Letter to his mother of April 24, 1844
7. Isaac Hecker, Diary. MS, Paulist Archives

Hecker nonetheless continued to be intrigued by Thoreau. On May 14, undoubtedly thinking of him, he wrote in his diary: "He who lives in the closest accord with nature, in the completest harmony with all the laws of God, is the most poetic-natured man; in other words, the most Godlike-natured man is the beautifullest and the best."[8] Yet, he felt, Thoreau's way was not his own. He became convinced his only salvation was in the doctrines of an established church and he pondered whether it should be "the Roman or the Anglican, the Presbyterian or the Baptist, &c. &c."[9] By mid-June he had decided on Roman Catholicism, and when he told Thoreau of his decision, Thoreau's contemptuous reply was: "What's the use of your joining the Catholic Church? Can't you get along without hanging to her skirts?"[1]

But Hecker's mind was made up. On June 17 he left Concord for his native New York. After six weeks of talking with his family, his friends, and various priests, he was baptized into the Roman Catholic Church at the cathedral in New York City on July 31. The evening before, he had suddenly been seized with an idea—he would set out as soon as possible on a pilgrimage to Rome and he would ask, of all people, Henry Thoreau to accompany him! He proposed in his diary:

> I should not hesitate to start tomorrow on the journey. I mean to write to Henry Thoreau on the subject. We know of no pleasanter, better way both for soul and body than to make such a pilgrimage in the old middle age fashion. Suffer hunger, storm, cold [,] heat, thirst, all that can affect the body of flesh. If we receive hard usage, rough knocks, &c., so much the better will it be for us. . . . We have a good constitution, can live on bread and water, why can't we take a walk over the fairest portions of this earth planet, and make it ours by seeing it? It would be so, for more than that the owners cannot do. We say again, go.
>
> We would say, if H.T. should consent to go, therefore it was we were sent to Concord. Who knows? . . . "God works by mysterious ways." We will write to Henry Thoreau. Nothing is impossible.[2]

8. Ibid.
9. Ibid.
1. Walter Elliott, *The Life of Father Hecker* (New York, 1891)
2. Isaac Hecker, Diary

And two days later he wrote Thoreau, significantly saying not a word of the religious nature of his pilgrimage:

> I have been stimulated to write to you at this present moment on account of a certain project which I have formed in which your influence has no slight share I imagine in forming. It is to work our passage to Europe, and to walk, work, and beg, if needs be, as far when there as we are inclined to do. . . . The heavens shall be our vaulted roof, and the green Earth beneath our bed, and for all other furniture purposes. These are free and may be so used. What can hinder us from going but our bodies, and shall they do it[?] We can as well deposit them there as here. Let us take a walk over the fairest portions of the planet Earth and make it ours by seeing them. . . . We shall prove the dollar is not almighty and the impossible moonshine. The wide world is before us beckoning us to come let us accept and embrace it. Reality shall be our antagonist and our lives if sold sold not at a good bargain for a certainty. . . .
>
> Will you accept this invitation? Let me know what your impressions are. As soon as it is your pleasure.[3]

But Thoreau was at the moment off on an excursion to the Berkshires. Even after he returned he meditated a while, but finally answered:

> I am strongly tempted by your proposal and experience a decided schism between my outward and inward tendencies. Your method of travelling expecially—to *live* along the road—citizens of the world, without haste or petty plans—I have often proposed this to my dreams, and still do—But the fact is, I cannot so decidedly postpone exploring the Farther Indies, which are to be reached you know by other rout[e]s and other methods of travel. I mean that I constantly return from every external enterprise with disgust to fresh faith in a kind of Brahminical Artesian, Inner Temple, life. . . .
>
> I remember you, as it were, with the whole Catholic Church at your skirts—and the other day for a moment I think I understood your relation to that body, but the thought was gone again in a twinkling, as when a dry leaf falls from its stem over our heads, but instantly lost in the rustling mass at our feet.
>
> I am really sorry that the Genius will not let me go with you,

---

3. Thoreau, *Correspondence,* 154-5

[165]

but I trust that it will conduct to other adventures, and so if nothing prevents we will compare notes at last.[4]

On August 15, not having yet received Thoreau's letter, Hecker fired off another, urging him in even stronger terms to join on the pedestrian excursion to Europe. But on the 18th he noted in his diary receipt of Thoreau's refusal and added, "I am set upon my wits again what to do." On the 22nd he noted receipt of a second refusal, in reply to his own second letter, and added regretfully, "We could go but we are not very anxious to go." And so the pilgrimage was given up.

Within a year Hecker did go abroad and joined the Redemptorist Fathers at St. Trond in Belgium. But his thoughts still continued on Thoreau and on May 15, 1847, he wrote him from Holland (addressing him as "Henry Thorough"!):

My interest in your greatest welfare compels me to write you a few lines, perhaps they may aid you in your progress. I have found my centre and of course my place in the Roman Catholic Church. . . .

Tho now my friend within cloistered walls in my cell I am infinitely freer than I was when breathing the air on Concord cliffs. . . . We don't want the middle ages, but we want its inspiration. It is here my friend, it is here. Mon Dieu could you see & feel it once.[5]

Thoreau, not surprisingly, was not convinced. But Hecker was not one to give up easily. Two years later, in the summer of 1849, he wrote Thoreau again, this time from London.

. . . I would like marvellously to free your soul by placing it in the light of Catholicity that hectic dissension has robbed it of. . . . Why indeed my brother, should you beat out your brains against the prison bars of error or sink back into helpless inanity or utter despair on finding this fountain source of all truth? . . . Ah my dear brother, could I induce you to bend your knees once in solitude & silence before God then new life would spring up into yr. heart, then would yr. Soul be kindled afresh with vigor

---

4. Ibid. 155–6
5. Isaac Hecker, Letter to Thoreau of May 15, 1847. MS, Paulist Archives

& virtue & the heavens open above yr. head, and Angels be seen who chant, & a sun of love & glory appear that never is or shall be obscured.

. . . I embrace you with a hearty hug & undeminished [sic] affection.[6]

But this letter was no more successful.

Hecker returned to the United States in the spring of 1851 and settled down at the Church of the Most Holy Redeemer in New York City. On a trip to Boston a few weeks later he made an effort to get out to Concord to see Thoreau once again, but failed. And so on July 6 he wrote him from New York, "Where art thou and what art thou doing? . . . What are your hopes, what of the future? You have not rec'd yr souls in vain," and suggested that Thoreau drop in to see him should he ever be in New York City.[7]

So far as is known, the two never met nor corresponded again. When, in the fall of 1854, Hecker ran across a copy of *Walden,* he wrote Orestes Brownson, who had meanwhile joined the Roman Catholic Church himself:

> Do give in y[ou]r next Review a notice of "Thoreau[']s Life in the Woods." He places himself fairly before the public and is a fair object of criticism. I have not read all his book through, & I don[']t think anyone will except as a feat. I read enough in it to see that under his seeming truthfulness & frankness he conceals an immense amount of pride, pretention & infidelity.
>
> This tendency to solitude & asceticism means something, and there is a certain degree of truthfulness & even bravery in his attempts to find out what this something is; but his results are increased pride, pretention & infidelity, instead of humility, simplicity & piety.[8]

But Brownson did not take the hint to review *Walden.* Hecker eventually went on to found the Paulist Fathers and establish the *Catholic World.* As the years went by, he turned strongly against the

---

6. Isaac Hecker, Letter to Thoreau of Summer, 1849. MS, Paulist Archives
7. Isaac Hecker, Letter to Thoreau of July 6, 1851. MS, Paulist Archives
8. Isaac Hecker, Letter to Orestes Brownson of October 29, 1854. MS, University of Notre Dame

Transcendentalism of his youth and often denounced it in the pages of the *World,* saying on one occasion of Thoreau:

> He was the only man among the Transcendentalists that allowed their theories the fullest play in him, and the incompleteness and failure of his life cannot be concealed by all the verbiage and praise of his biographers.[9]

In 1882 Rev. Walter Elliott, interviewing Hecker for the official Paulist biography, asked him his final opinion of Thoreau. "Consecrated crank—rather be crank than president," was his answer.[1] Thoreau's final opinion of Hecker is unfortunately not recorded.

IV

The last Wednesday of May each year every able-bodied man of military age in Massachusetts was required to turn out for military training and inspection. Thoreau's thoughts at the requirement can well be imagined, but turn out annually he apparently did. Occasionally there were redeeming features and one was that at the 1844 Muster Day he met a newcomer to Concord, George William Curtis.[2] Curtis, the son of a well-to-do Providence businessman, had, with his brother Burrill, been attracted to the Brook Farm community in 1842. But eventually they had tired of the experiment, had tried life in New York City for a time and, now attracted by Ralph Waldo Emerson, had decided to settle in Concord. On Emerson's recommendation they rented rooms from Captain Nathan Barrett on a farm out beyond the Battleground and settled down to a simple life of their own, living on vegetables when Mrs. Barrett, in her motherly way, didn't insist on plying them with the products of her ample stove. Half of each day they spent working on the farm, the other half they devoted to boating on the river, walking, talking, and writing—a life very close to that which Thoreau was soon to pursue at Walden. Thoreau and

---

9. *Catholic World* (1878), 296
1. Elliott, *The Life of Father Hecker,* 82
2. Gordon Milne, *George William Curtis and the Genteel Tradition* (Bloomington, Ind., 1956), 23

Curtis quickly struck up a conversation in the muster field and then continued their acquaintance in the fields and woods of Concord. In later years Curtis was to say:

> One of my most vivid recollections of my life in Concord is that of an evening upon the shallow river with Thoreau in his boat. We lighted a huge fire of fat pine in an iron crate beyond the bow of the boat and drifted slowly through an illuminated circle of the ever-changing aspect of the river bed. In that house beautiful you can imagine what an interpreter he was.[3]

They kept up their intercourse for the two years the Curtises remained in Concord. Curtis it was, undoubtedly, who saw to it that Thoreau was invited each year to attend the Brook Farm reunion picnics on Minot Pratt's farm in Concord. In later years, as we will see, Curtis took an interest in Thoreau's literary career and as an editor of *Putnam's* was to prove of some assistance to him. In 1853 Curtis wrote an article on Emerson for the *Boston Commonwealth* which he soon after expanded into a chapter for the *Homes of American Authors,* published by Appleton in New York. In it he recalled his Concord friend:

> Henry Thoreau's instinct is as sure towards the facts of nature as the witch-hazel toward treasure. If every quiet country town in New England had a son, who, with a lore like Selborne's and an eye like Buffon's, had watched and studied its landscape and history, and then published the result, as Thoreau has done, in a book as redolent of genuine and perceptive sympathy with nature, as a clover-field of honey, New England would seem as poetic and beautiful as Greece.[4]

But, ironically, he had to write Emerson before he could publish the essay because he simply could not remember the title of Thoreau's book he so glowingly described.

But far more important for Thoreau than the friendship with Curtis was his friendship with William Ellery Channing the Younger. Ellery Channing, as he was known to distinguish him from his uncle William Ellery Channing, the great Unitarian divine, was one of the

---

3. Samuel Arthur Jones, "A Belated Knight-Errant," *Inlander,* February 1895
4. (New York, 1853), 247–8

most capricious and undependable of souls—outstanding in these respects even in such a highly individualistic movement as American Transcendentalism. He had been spoiled from childhood by an overindulgent father, had dropped out of Harvard after only a brief trial, and for a time had lived alone in a cabin on the Illinois prairie. He and Thoreau first met at Emerson's home in December 1840 and frequently renewed their acquaintance on Channing's numerous visits to Concord. In 1842 Channing, now married to Margaret Fuller's sister Ellen, thought of settling down in Concord. Emerson suggested that they board with the Thoreaus, but Margaret Fuller countered that they might find a pleasanter place, suggesting first that they try Mrs. Prichard's home overlooking the meadows and river, and then the Hawthornes, who might be interested in taking boarders at the Manse. But Hawthorne quickly countermanded the latter suggestion and the Channings gave up for the time.

In the spring of 1843 Thoreau, at Channing's request, did some house-hunting and finally arranged for them to rent the little "Red Lodge" out the Cambridge Turnpike beyond the Emersons for fifty-five dollars a year. Channing looked over the house and sent Thoreau a long list of repairs to supervise—sanding the cellar, building new stairs, banking the house, sodding the lawn, painting and whitewashing the interior, putting new locks on, cleaning the well and adding a new pump, fencing the land, and moving and whitewashing the privy. On May 1 he wrote to thank Thoreau for his labors and in recompense offered to let him live with them. Thoreau replied that he had already accepted William Emerson's offer on Staten Island. Channing was unhappy to learn that Thoreau was leaving town just as he was moving in and lamented to Emerson, "I hear with regret that this, our man of the world, fleeing afar from his beloved woods, will no longer pick the first of the spring flowers."[5] It is amusing to note that when Hawthorne learned of Channing's impending arrival and Thoreau's departure, he thought Channing but a poor substitute for Mr. Thoreau. Mrs. Hawthorne thought the reverse; to her, Channing had "a pleasanter way of saying things than Mr. Thoreau, because so wholly without the air of saying anything of consequence."

---

5. Sanborn, *Bronson Alcott at Alcott House*, 35

Channing and his wife settled down in the Red Lodge and Mrs. Channing opened an infant school with the older Emerson daughter as a star pupil. When Thoreau returned from Staten Island, he and Channing resumed their friendship. Channing and his wife moved from the Cambridge Turnpike to Lexington Road in April 1844, and there his wife gave birth to their firstborn on May 2. Soon after, Channing accepted a position on Horace Greeley's *Tribune* and left for New York City. In mid-summer, he and Thoreau decided to go on an excursion together and agreed to meet at the foot of Saddleback Mountain (now better known as Greylock) in the northwestern corner of Massachusetts.

On his way Thoreau camped out for a night on Mount Monadnock, the first of many visits to what was to become one of his favorite mountains. Wending his way alone, he tramped over the hills, plucking raspberries by the wayside, occasionally buying a loaf of bread at a farmer's house, carrying a staff in his hand and a knapsack filled with books and clothing on his back. Reaching the Connecticut River, he started up the Deerfield River valley, dipping his feet occasionally in the stream or, when he could find a deep enough pool, bathing briefly. At nightfall he rented a room at the home of a Mr. Rice in the last and highest of the valleys.

In the morning Thoreau crossed Hoosack Mountain, trekked down through North Adams and started up the long valley known as the Bellows toward the top of Greylock. At one of the last houses on the road he stopped to talk with a "frank and hospitable young woman," who unconcernedly combed her long black hair as she asked him news of "the lower world" from which he had just come. Thoreau was charmed with her "lively, sparkling eyes" and the way she tossed her head with each sweep of her comb and thought of asking if he could return next day and stay a week at her house.[6] But Channing, it turned out, had other plans for him, so he never returned.

Forsaking the paths, Thoreau took out his compass and made a beeline for the summit through dense mountain laurel and trees that had "a scraggy and infernal look."[7] The night he spent sleeping outside the rude observatory that had been built by Williams College students on the peak of the mountain. When it got cold, having no

---

6. Thoreau, *Writings*, I, 191–2
7. Ibid. I, 193

blanket, he covered himself with boards—of all things—to keep warm, even managing to place one on top of himself with a stone to keep it in position, and later boasted that he slept comfortably. Quite understandably he awoke before dawn and, when the sun came up, found that his lone peak surmounted a sea of fog which covered all the surrounding landscape.

Descending the mountain, Thoreau met Channing at the Pittsfield railroad station and, as Channing later recalled, "He had no shirt-collar perceptible, carried a small leather wallet belonging to the late Charles Emerson on his back and looked as if he had slept out in the fields as he was unshaved & drest [sic] very poorly."[8] Together they journeyed westward to the Hudson River, where they took an excursion boat down to the Catskills, spending the night on deck watching the moonlight on the mountains. A passenger mistaking Thoreau in his hiking clothes for a deckhand, tried unsuccessfully to borrow a chew of tobacco from him.

Leaving the river, the two hiked up into the Catskill Mountains through the blueberries and raspberries and rented a room for the night at the home of the miller of Kaaterskill Falls. A small tarn on the side of Bald Mountain particularly impressed Thoreau and reminded him of Walden. On their return trip on the excursion boat, Thoreau, surprisingly enough, shocked Channing when he stalked the deck chewing hungrily on a half-loaf of bread because he had had no dinner.

More usually the shoe was on the other foot, it was Channing's behavior that disturbed Thoreau. Thoreau was an individualist all right and undoubtedly many of his contemporaries thought of him as an eccentric. But his behavior was usually marked by a consideration for others. Channing, on the other hand, was not so thoughtful—and his behavior often disturbed Thoreau. An old Concord resident told F. B. Sanborn that when she was a child of ten she passed the Channing cottage on her way from school and Mrs. Channing asked her to go through the woods to Walden and tell Mr. Channing that he had a guest who had come out from Cambridge to make a call. She found Thoreau and Channing out on the pond in a boat and shouted the message to them. Channing made some indifferent reply, but Thoreau, she noted, immediately

---

8. William Ellery Channing, Annotations in his copy of Thoreau's *Week*, 197, Berg Collection

returned the boat to shore and walked alone to the Channing cottage to report that his companion would be returning soon.[9]

There are those who think, and probably quite rightfully, that Channing's boorishness served as a check on Thoreau—a constant reminder that he must not permit himself Channing's excesses. But despite their differences of opinion, the two became firm friends— indeed theirs was the most intimate and most lasting friendship of Thoreau's life. And Channing, on his side, was to look upon it as *the* great event of his life. Five years after Thoreau's death he mourned, albeit somewhat melodramatically but unquestionably with true feeling in his journal, "I [cannot] expect anything like a single moment of satisfaction again. I have never had such a moment since H[enry] left me."[1]

It was Channing who, in 1873, published the first biography of Thoreau, a book as eccentric as its author, but in it he gives us a memorable picture of the Thoreau he knew striding through the fields and woods of Concord:

> In height, [Thoreau] was about the average, in his build, spare, with limbs that were rather longer than usual, or of which he made a longer use. His face, once seen, could not be forgotten. The features were quite marked: the nose aquiline or very Roman, like one of the portraits of Caesar (more like a beak, as was said); large, overhanging brows above the deepest set blue eyes that could be seen, in certain lights, and in others gray, —eyes expressive of all shades of feeling, but never weak or near-sighted; the forehead not unusually broad or high, full of con-centrated energy and purpose; the mouth with prominent lips, pursed up with meaning and thought when silent, and giving out when open a stream of the most varied and unusual instructive sayings. His hair was a dark brown, exceedingly abundant, fine and soft. . . . His whole figure had an active earnestness, as if he had no moment to waste. The clenched hand betokened pur-pose. In walking, he made a short cut if he could, and when sitting in the shade or by the wallside seemed merely the clearer to look forward into the next piece of activity. Even in the boat he had a wary, transitory air, his eyes on the outlook,—perhaps

---

9. Sanborn, *The Life of Henry David Thoreau*, 329
1. William Ellery Channing, Diary. Transcript, Frederick T. McGill, Jr.

there might be ducks, or the Blondin turtle, or an otter, or sparrow.[2]

Emerson, delighted to have so many stimulating young men gath ered around him, decided in the fall of 1844 to organize a weekl discussion group, which was to meet Monday evenings in hi library. Alcott, Hawthorne, Thoreau, George Bradford, the Curti brothers, and Channing were all invited to attend. The first Mon day evening there was an uneasy silence as though, as Georg Curtis recalls, each were asking, "Who will now proceed to sa the finest thing that has ever been said?" Finally Alcott made on of his most orphic sayings. Silence. Thoreau made a brief observa tion. More silence. Emerson beamed and said nothing. Hawthorn shrunk further into the shadowed corner of the room. Finally bowl of apples was brought in and each munched in silence. Whe the end of the long evening came, each disappeared his own wa into the darkness. Two more Monday evenings they assembled bu with no more success. Their place of conversation, they had dis covered, was not the parlor but the woods, and their club dis appeared into oblivion.[3]

V

On August 1, 1844, the very day Thoreau returned from hi jaunt to the Berkshires with Channing, the anti-slavery women o Concord and thirteen surrounding towns conducted their annua fair in the corridors of the county courthouse in Concord. The had asked for permission to use the various church vestries i town but had been turned down. Hawthorne volunteered the us of his front lawn at the Old Manse, but a rainstorm prevente their accepting.[4] Mrs. Thoreau and some of her friends had per suaded Emerson to deliver an address commemorating the tent

2. Channing, *Thoreau, the Poet-Naturalist*, 25
3. George William Curtis et al., *Homes of American Authors*, 251–2
4. Wendell Glick, "Thoreau and the 'Herald of Freedom,'" *New England Quarterly*, XXII (1949), 201

nniversary of the emancipation of the slaves in the British West
Indies. Although all of Emerson's close friends knew that his
sympathies were with the abolitionists, they had long been disturbed that he had not spoken out publicly against slavery and
so added the growing prestige of his name to their cause. His acceptance now therefore gave particular joy to the abolitionists.
Thoreau was delighted and personally made the arrangements for
Emerson to speak in the courthouse hall and went from door to
door to urge the villagers to attend the meeting.[5] The sexton of the
First Parish Church however refused to ring the town bell in the
church steeple to announce the meeting. He wanted nothing to do,
he said, with such "irresponsible" activities. The selectmen of the
town, equally conservative, refused to order him to do it. One
person after another was asked to assume the task, but all were too
timid. Then Thoreau heard of the impasse. He rushed to the
church, grasped the rope vigorously in his hands, and set the
bell to ringing merrily until it had gathered a whole crowd for
Emerson's speech. Anna Maria Whiting of Concord, one of the
leaders of the anti-slavery women, wrote up the whole incident
and sent her report off to Nathaniel Rogers, who, remembering
Thoreau's passionate defense of his publishing activities, published it in full in his *Herald of Freedom* for September 27, 1844.[6]
Later Thoreau acted as agent for the anti-slavery women and ne-
gotiated successfully with James Munroe & Co. of Boston to
have Emerson's address printed in pamphlet form.[7]

Abolition was not a popular topic of discussion among the
more conservative elements in Concord. For some time the Concord Lyceum had been split by dissension over the question.
Wendell Phillips of Boston was the center of the controversy. At
Thoreau's invitation he spoke before the Concord Lyceum on
December 21, 1842, and his open and forthright remarks on the
topic shocked many of the town's leaders. When he was asked to
speak again the next winter, John Keyes, describing his earlier

5. James Elliott Cabot, *A Memoir of Ralph Waldo Emerson* (Boston,
1887), II, 430; Sanborn, *The Personality of Emerson,* 88
6. Glick, "Thoreau and the 'Herald of Freedom,' " 200
7. Henry David Thoreau, Letter to James Munroe & Co., of September 17, 1845. MS, Charles Roberts Autograph Collection, Haverford
College Library

speech as "vile, pernicious, and abominable," asked that he be instructed to speak on some topic other than slavery.[8] But Keyes's motion was defeated and Phillips was invited. Again he was so forthright that this time the town's conservatives called a meeting to discuss and censure him. Warned in advance by Thoreau, Phillips attended their meeting and sat quietly in a back seat until Keyes and Samuel Hoar had spoken their pieces. Then, rising, he demolished their arguments one by one and was promptly invited back to speak the next year. The Hoars were so distressed at Phillips's performance that years later, at the time of his death, one of them, when asked if he were going to attend the funeral, snapped back, "No, but I heartily approve of it."[9]

The battle lines between the conservatives and the abolitionists were drawn once again in the Concord Lyceum in the spring of 1845 when the question was raised of inviting Phillips to speak. Finding themselves outvoted when they opposed extending an invitation, the conservative curators resigned and were speedily replaced by Emerson, Samuel Barrett, and Thoreau on March 5. The new curators immediately issued the invitation and Phillips spoke on the 11th. The very next day a triumphant Thoreau sent off his first and only known "letter to the editor"—an epistle to William Lloyd Garrison of the anti-slavery *Liberator* eloquently and vigorously defending Phillips's right to speak. Garrison printed the lengthy letter in its entirety in the *Liberator* for March 28, 1845, and Helen Thoreau boasted in a letter to a friend that the battle for freedom of speech in the Concord Lyceum had been won.[1] Thoreau, exulting in the victory, delivered the next lecture before the lyceum, on March 25, 1845. It was an uncontroversial familiar essay, "Concord River," that he was later to revise and incorporate into his first book, *A Week on the Concord and Merrimack Rivers,* and perhaps served to heal the wounds between the two factions.

---

8. Sanborn, *The Life of Henry David Thoreau,* 471
9. Moncure Conway, *Autobiography, Memories and Experiences* (Boston, 1904), I, 145 n.
1. Annie Russell Marble, "Where Thoreau Worked and Wandered," *Critic,* XL (1902), 512

VI

So quickly did the Thoreau pencil business prosper thanks to Henry's recent improvements that by the late summer of 1844 Mrs. Thoreau was convinced the family could afford a house of their own. She had long since tired of living in rented houses. Yet, she fully realized, only through concerted effort on the part of the whole family could they afford a house. Her son promptly indicated his willingness to do his share and set himself to work longer hours in the pencil shop, giving up or reducing for a time his excursions to the fields.[2] Although rumors have long been rampant that Thoreau sponged on his family, there is ample documentary evidence that such gossip was anything but true. Scattered among the extant Thoreau manuscripts are numerous receipts for the board money he regularly and conscientiously paid his father throughout his adult life.[3] Thoreau, self-conscious perhaps because of the criticism of his financial matters that he heard muttered constantly by his neighbors, was always scrupulously exact in pecuniary affairs, if anything leaning over backwards to see that he owed not a man a cent.

David Loring had recently purchased the old Heywood farm and opened up Texas Street (now Belknap Street), just west of the station on the newly built Fitchburg Railroad, to development. Mr. Thoreau was skeptical, but his wife had made up her mind; on her own she picked out a lot, marked out the house site exactly, and made a plan for the house with a carpenter.[4] Bowing to the inevitable, on September 10, 1844, Mr. Thoreau paid Loring twenty-five dollars for the three-quarters-acre lot, and two days later mortgaged it, together with a note in hand, for five hundred dollars to Augustus Tuttle, to buy the lumber and supplies for the house.[5]

Henry immediately pitched in, dug the cellar, and stoned it

---

2. Edward Emerson, Notes on Thoreau
3. F. B. Sanborn, *The Personality of Thoreau* (Boston, 1901), 28; Stephen Wakeman [Sale Catalog], (New York, 1924), #983
4. Edward Emerson, Notes on Thoreau
5. *Middlesex County Registry Records,* CCCCXLIX, 297

himself. Then with his father he did the actual building. They soon discovered that both Mrs. Thoreau and the carpenter who had drawn up the plans had forgotten to put any stairs in the house and so they had to remedy that defect themselves. The final result was a two-story square building with the front door off to one side and quite lacking in distinction of any sort. The Fitchburg Railroad conducted an auction that summer to sell off the shanties the Irish laborers had lived in while building the railroad. The Thoreaus acquired one or two and from them constructed a lean-to shed on the house in which to conduct their pencil business. The completed house and lot were valued by the town assessors at $1100.[6]

Built out in the middle of the fields, the Texas house (as the Thoreau family always called it) looked bare and lonely, so Thoreau set to work again, made a bank around the house, and then planted about forty trees, including fourteen apple trees, a grapevine, and a syringa bush among others. Fourteen years later he was able to boast that he had harvested between ten and eleven barrels of apples from the trees. And a century later some of his plantings still lingered on. With the yard thus beautified, the Thoreau family was at last content to settle down in a house of their own and so gave up the Parkman house.

---

6. Town of Concord, *Assessors Record Book*

CHAPTER TEN
(1845–1847)

I

IT WAS in the early spring of 1845 that Henry David Thoreau went out to the shores of Walden Pond, a little glacial lake, three quarters of a mile in length and half a mile in width, two miles south of Concord village, and began cutting down the tall, arrowy pines to build the cabin that was to make him famous around the world. He wanted to get down to work seriously on a book he had long planned to write about the voyage he and his brother John had taken on the Concord and Merrimack Rivers in 1839. And unless he could "get away from it all," it seemed as though that book would never be written.

There was plenty of precedent for Thoreau's going to the woods. After all, this was the period of the great migration west. Men, women, and children were pulling up stakes by the hundreds and thousands and moving to new territory to start life anew. But such a move could not satisfy Thoreau. He realized that he needed to change something more vital than his mere geographical location. He needed to change his way of life. He was going to stay in Concord and simplify his life there. Remembering what he had said so boastfully at his college graduation, he determined to reverse the Biblical instruction and, after working one day a week, to rest six—though rest would be merely a euphemism. Those six days of each week he would devote to writing and the observation of nature.

In 1845, when he was twenty-seven, his opportunity had come and he did not let it go by. The preceding fall, Ralph Waldo Emerson had purchased some land on the shores of Walden Pond. Ostensibly he bought it to save its trees from the woodcutter's axe, for it was a spot he loved, and already one landowner there had permitted many trees along the shore of the pond to be felled.[1] But he had also long thought of building himself a rural study on the shores of the pond if the opportunity arose. And he thought, too, of giving the land to either his sister-in-law Lucy Jackson Brown or to Bronson Alcott to build houses for their families. (Alcott, incidentally, was so enthusiastic about this idea that he immediately extended an invitation to Thoreau to live with them long before even a plan was made and then, as with so many of Alcott's plans, it came to nothing.) Neither house was ever started at the pond.

Then on March 5, 1845, Ellery Channing wrote Thoreau from New York City and suggested that he go out to Walden Pond, there build himself a hut, and begin the grand process of devouring himself alive.[2] Thoreau took the hint and, after obtaining permission from Emerson, went out to the pond late in March of 1845 and began to chop down those arrowy pines. Just how long he intended to live at the pond, he had not decided, but it would be at least until he finished writing the book. He went to Walden, he said, because he wished to live deliberately, to front only the essential facts of life, and to see if he could not learn what it had to teach, so that when he came to die, he would not discover that he had not lived.[3]

Thoreau began his work at the pond with a borrowed axe. It probably belonged to Bronson Alcott, though as its fame spread, it was later claimed for both Emerson and Channing.[4] But from whomever he obtained it, he returned it later, he boasted, sharper than he had borrowed it. He hewed the main timbers, he said, "six inches square, most of the studs on two sides only, and the rafters and floor timbers on one side, leaving the rest of the bark on, so that they were just as straight and much stronger than sawed ones."[5] By mid-April he had every stick mortised and tenoned and the house framed, ready for raising. Meanwhile, for $4.25, he had purchased an old shanty from James Collins, an Irish laborer

1. Caroline Ticknor, "Some Early Letters of George William Curtis," *Atlantic Monthly*, CXIV (1914), 366
2. Thoreau, *Correspondence*, 161
3. Thoreau, *Writings*, II, 100–1
4. Henry David Thoreau, *The Variorum Walden* (New York, 1962), 276
5. Thoreau, *Writings*, II, 46

on the Fitchburg Railroad. In a few hours Thoreau had dismantled the shack, to spread out the boards in the sun to bleach and warp themselves back into shape, and to draw the nails. Those nails, however, disappeared into the capacious pockets of one neighbor Seeley, who helped himself when Thoreau's back was turned.

It took Thoreau but two hours to dig a cellar hole six feet square and seven deep in the soft, sandy soil, two hundred feet up a gentle slope from the shore of a cove on the north side of the pond and in the shade of some small pines at the edge of a briar field. It was not a lonely spot. The well-traveled Concord-Lincoln road was within sight across the field. The Fitchburg Railroad steamed regularly past the opposite end of the pond. Concord village was less than two miles away, and the Texas house was less than that along the railroad right-of-way.

In early May, adopting the old country custom, Thoreau invited some of his neighbors to set up the frame of the house and raise the roof—both tasks that took more than one pair of hands. His assistants were a distinguished crew, including Emerson, Bronson Alcott, Ellery Channing, George William Curtis and his brother Burrill, and Thoreau's favorite Concord farmer, Edmund Hosmer, and his sons John, Edmund, and Andrew.

Thoreau was in no hurry to move in. Once the frame was up, he did the remaining carpentry slowly and lived the meanwhile with his parents. He walked back and forth to the pond each day, carrying his luncheon, wrapped in a paper, with him. When warmer weather came, he cleared the briarfield and planted two and a half acres, chiefly with beans and potatoes for money crops, and some corn, peas, and turnips for his own use.

On July 4, 1845—Independence Day, appropriately enough —he borrowed a hay rigging, carted his few articles of furniture out to the cabin, and moved in. As yet he had no chimney nor fireplace, and the walls, still unplastered, had wide chinks that let the cool air circulate through at night. Later, when he had completed the cabin, Thoreau described it as a tight shingled and plastered house, ten feet wide by fifteen long, and eight-feet posts, with a garret and a closet, a large window on each side, two trapdoors, one door at the end, and a brick fireplace opposite. Out back was a woodshed. Nearby—Thoreau was too much the Victorian to say exactly where—was a privy. The pond was his bathtub and refrigerator, and the spring under nearby Brister's Hill provided his drinking water when the pond was too warm.

The cabin cost Thoreau exactly $28.125. His only extravagance was $3.90 for nails. Despite his boasted dexterity, he was apparently a bad shot with a hammer; when the site of the Walden cabin was excavated a hundred years later, the cellar hole was found filled with hundreds of bent nails.

Ellery Channing, who visited the cabin often, has aptly described it as a wooden inkstand on the shores of Walden Pond. "Just large enough for one . . . a durable garment, an overcoat, he had contrived and left by Walden, convenient for shelter, sleep, or meditation."[6]

The inside of the cabin was as simple as the outside. Thoreau's total furniture, much of it homemade, consisted of a caned bed, a table, a desk, three chairs, a looking-glass three inches in diameter, a pair of tongs and andirons, a kettle, a skillet and a frying pan, a dipper, a wash bowl, two knives and forks, three plates, one cup, one spoon, a jug for oil, a jug for molasses, and a japanned lamp. For a time he kept three pieces of limestone on the desk, but threw them out when he found they required daily dusting. When a friend offered a mat for the floor, he declined it, saying he wanted neither to spare the room for it nor to take the time to shake it out.

In the fall of 1845 he built a fireplace and chimney in his cabin. With a thousand secondhand bricks and stones and sand from the shore of the pond in his mortar, he worked slowly at his task, doing a few rounds of bricks a day. It was November before the task was completed. Meanwhile he took in a guest for two weeks—his friend Ellery Channing. They found the tiny cabin so crowded that Channing spent the nights sleeping on the floor below Thoreau's low-slung cot.[7]

With the coming of cold weather, Thoreau set about making the cabin more snug. He lathed the interior and then, gathering clean white sand from the opposite shore of the pond, he plastered all the walls. The previous winter he had burned a few clamshells to prove to himself that he could manufacture his own lime, but

6. Channing, *Thoreau, the Poet-Naturalist*, 7–8
7. Edward Emerson, Notes on Thoreau

now having satisfied himself that he could, he bought two casks of lime for $1.20 each. From November 12 until December 6, while he was applying the plaster and letting it dry, he lived at home with his parents. It is a wonder that, having left the plaster to dry in a cold building, he did not find it frozen and disintegrated upon his return.

Thoreau ate simply and plainly while he lived at the pond. Joseph Hosmer, who spent a Sunday in September of 1845 with him, said Thoreau's hospitality and manner of entertainment were unique and peculiar to the time and place. The cooking apparatus was primitive and consisted of a hole made in the earth and inlaid with stones, upon which the fire was made, as at a clambake.

Their bill of fare included roasted horned pout, corn, beans, bread, salt. Hosmer gave the bill of fare in English and Thoreau rendered it in French, Latin, and Greek. The beans had been previously cooked. The meal for their bread was mixed with lake water only, spread upon the surface of a thin stone, and baked. When the bread was sufficiently brown, the stone was removed and the fish were placed over the hot stones and roasted—some in wet paper and some without. When seasoned with salt, they were delicious.[8]

Thoreau experimented frequently with his bread making and soon learned that an unleavened variety was simplest. When he added raisins to the dough, it was said that he became the inventor of raisin bread. Concord housewives were reportedly shocked at the innovation.[9]

When his fireplace was completed, Thoreau moved his cooking indoors. In his second year at the pond, he gave up the fireplace and installed a small stove. It was not as poetic as the fireplace and he felt that he had lost a companion. But he did not own a forest to burn, he said, and the stove was much more efficient.

At the end of his first eight months at the pond he found that he had spent a total of only $8.74 for food—an average of twenty-

8. Joseph Hosmer, "Henry D. Thoreau," *Concord Freeman, Thoreau Annex*
9. Ann Batchelder, "Line-a-Day," *Ladies' Home Journal,* September 1943

seven cents a week. Clothing for the same period cost him only $8.4075 and fuel $2.00. From an economic standpoint the experiment at Walden was a complete success.

There were those who complained that he balanced his budget only through sponging on his friends and relatives. Some Concordians claimed that "he would have starved, if it had not been that his sisters and mother cooked up pies and doughnuts and sent them to him in a basket."[1] It is true that his mother and sisters made a special trip out to the pond every Saturday, carrying with them each time some delicacy of cookery which he gladly accepted.[2] And it is equally true that he raided the family cookie jar on his frequent visits home. But any other behavior on his part would have hurt his mother's feelings—she prided herself on her culinary accomplishments and dearly loved to treat her son.

The Emersons, too, frequently invited him to dinner as did the Alcotts and the Hosmers. They had all done so before he went to Walden Pond and continued the custom after he left. Rumor had it that every time Mrs. Emerson rang her dinner bell, Thoreau came bounding through the woods and over the fences to be first in line at the Emerson dinner table. The fact that a mile and a half was a pretty exceptional distance to hear a dinner bell was ignored by the gossips. And in *Walden* Thoreau has explained: "If I dined out occasionally, as I had always done, and I trust shall have opportunities to again, it was frequently to the detriment of my domestic arrangements."

Thoreau found plenty to do at the pond. He learned to love a broad margin to his life. On summer mornings he would sometimes sit in his sunny doorway from sunrise until noon, rapt in revery, while the birds sang around or flitted noiselessly through his house. He grew, he thought, on such occasions, like corn in the night and said they were not time subtracted from his life, but so much over and above his usual allowance. Other mornings he devoted to his housework, setting all his furniture out of doors on the grass, dashing water on the floor, and scrubbing it with white sand from the pond and a broom; when it had dried, he returned his furniture to its place before the villagers had had their breakfast.

1. Harding, *Thoreau, Man of Concord*, 72
2. Marble, *Thoreau: His Home, Friends and Books*, 129

But most mornings he devoted to his garden. His bean rows added up to more than seven miles in length and required constant weeding. Concord farmers laughingly christened his garden "The Paradise of Beans."[3] What is worse, the woodchucks nibbled the bean sprouts faster than he could pull the weeds. "My enemies," he said, "are worms, cool days, and most of all woodchucks. They have nibbled for me an eighth of an acre clean. I plant in faith, and they reap."

Thoreau was at a loss for a time what to do. The woodchucks, he felt, had prior claims as residents, but if they remained, there would be no garden. He finally consulted a veteran trapper for advice. "Mr. W., is there any way to get woodchucks without trapping them with—" "Yes; shoot 'em, you damn fool," was the reply.[4] But Thoreau ignored that sage advice and matters got worse instead of better. Finally, in desperation, he procured a trap and captured the grandfather of all the woodchucks. After retaining it for several hours, he delivered it a severe lecture and released it, hoping never to see it again. But it was a vain delusion. Within a few days it was back at its old stand, nibbling as heartily as ever at his beans. Accordingly he set the trap again, and this time when he caught the villain he carried it some two miles away, gave it a severe admonition with a stick, and let it depart in peace.[5] He never saw that woodchuck again, but what the farmers in *that* area thought is not recorded.

On a later occasion when another woodchuck trifled with his garden, Thoreau was more bloodthirsty. Abandoning his not-too-strongly-held vegetarian principles, he trapped, killed, and ate it as a culinary experiment; he found the meat to be surprisingly good.

Despite the woodchucks, the worms, the cool weather, and the weeds, Thoreau's garden was a success. His expenses for tools, plowing, seeds, and cultivator totaled only $14.725. The garden yielded twelve bushels of beans, eighteen bushels of potatoes, and some peas; the sweet corn and turnips failed to mature. Keeping enough for his own needs, he sold beans, potatoes, grass, and

---

3. Thoreau, *Journal*, I, 423
4. Kenneth Walter Cameron, *Emerson, Thoreau and Concord in Early Newspapers* (Hartford, 1958), 86
5. Hosmer, "Henry D. Thoreau"

stalks for a total of $23.44. Thus he had his food for a year and a profit of $8.71½. Few other Concord farmers, comparatively speaking, he thought, did as well.

The second summer at Walden, Thoreau decided he had had enough of agriculture and planted only a third of an acre—just enough for his own use. "I learned from the experience of both years," he explained, "that if one would live simply and eat only the crop which he raised, and raise no more than he ate, and not exchange it for an insufficient quantity of more luxurious and expensive things, he would need to cultivate only a few rods of ground."[6]

In the colder seasons he found other methods of earning a living. For a dollar a day he worked as a fence builder, painter, gardener, and carpenter. Once he built a fireplace for a man who would not accept his protests that he was not a professional mason. On another occasion he built a woodshed "of no mean size" for the Kettles for six dollars and cleared half that sum by close calculation and swift working. Going home from one task, he suffered a misfortune. As he was about to clamber into a hay rigging, he inadvertently frightened the horse with his ubiquitous umbrella. Feet flew; the bucket on Thoreau's arm was smashed, and Thoreau himself was stretched out on his back on the ground. The sudden bending of his body backwards strained his stomach. He did not feel strong there for several years and had, for a time, to give up hard manual labor.[7]

He also tried his hand at surveying, making use of both borrowed instruments and those left over from his schoolteaching days. He found the work both satisfying and remunerative. It enabled him simultaneously to earn a living and to spend most of his time out of doors in the fields and woods he loved. Its only flaw was that his surveying was all too often a preliminary to woodcutting on the part of his employers, and thus he was playing his part in the destruction of the Concord woods. That fact was to disturb his conscience for some time.

From all these various sources Thoreau found he was easily able to support himself at the pond by working at the most some six weeks a year. "In short," he wrote his friend Horace Greeley,

6. Thoreau, *Writings*, II, 61
7. Thoreau, *Journal*, X, 61–3

"I am convinced, both by faith and experience, that to maintain one's self on this earth is not a hardship but a pastime, if we will live simply and wisely. . . . It is not necessary that a man should earn his living by the sweat of his brow, unless he sweats easier than I do."

A good part of his newfound free time he was able to devote to his writing. The first work he completed at the pond was an extended essay on Thomas Carlyle. As early as 1842 he had begun making notes on Carlyle's works, but it was probably not until he got to the pond that he gathered the notes together and wrote the essay. The essay he then tried out as a lecture before the Concord Lyceum on February 4, 1846. Although it was apparently a success, it was not what his townsmen expected or wanted to hear. They wanted to know why he, a college graduate, had given up conventional life and had gone to live in a cabin in the woods. That was what interested them, and they told him so. He then started writing the series of lectures that eventually grew into his masterpiece, *Walden, or Life in the Woods.* Thoreau was careful to explain on the first page of that book that he had written it, not out of egotism, but because "very particular inquiries" had been made by his townsmen concerning his mode of life.

"Some," he said, "have asked what I got to eat; if I did not feel lonesome; if I was not afraid; and the like. Others have been curious to learn what portion of my income I devoted to charitable purposes; and some, who have large families, how many poor children I maintained."[8] And those were some of the questions he attempted to answer in his lectures and in his book.

It was a full year later, February 10, 1847, before he delivered the first of those Walden lectures to his townsmen. That evening he read a paper entitled "A History of Myself," a portion of what was eventually to become the "Economy" chapter of *Walden,* and it was received so well that, quite out of keeping with the regular practice of the lyceum, he was asked to repeat it a week later for those who had missed it. Prudence Ward reported:

Henry repeated his lecture to a very full audience. . . . It was an uncommonly excellent lecture—tho, of course few would

8. Thoreau, *Writings,* II, 1

adopt his notions—I mean as they are shown forth in his life. Yet it was a very useful lecture, and much needed.[9]

And Emerson wrote to Margaret Fuller:

Mrs. Ripley & other members of the opposition came down the other night to hear Henry's account of his housekeeping at Walden Pond, which he read as a lecture, and were charmed with the witty wisdom which ran through it all.[1]

The favorable reactions to this and his following lectures persuaded Thoreau that it would be worthwhile to write a book-length account of his life at the pond. So earnestly did he set to work that by September 1847 he had completed the first draft. It was seven years and eight complete revisions later before the book was finally published, but that is another story.

Meanwhile Thoreau had not forgotten that his original purpose in going to Walden Pond was to write another book, the account of his voyage on the Concord and Merrimack Rivers. Work on that book too had progressed so rapidly with his newfound leisure that just a year from the time he moved to the pond the first draft was completed. Emerson immediately urged him to submit it to a publisher, but Thoreau insisted on taking further time to polish the manuscript. He spent a great deal of time at the cabin reading various drafts aloud to his friends, such as Alcott and Emerson, to get the benefit of their criticism, and it was 1849 before that book was published. But the bulk of both it and *Walden* was written in his two years at the pond.

By no means all of his time was spent at the desk. Afternoons he spent strolling through the woods and fields of Concord or boating on its ponds and rivers. Evenings he often rowed out on the pond in his boat and played his flute or fished. He became, in his own words, "self-appointed inspector of snow-storms and rain-storms, . . . surveyor, if not of highways, then of forest paths and all across-lot routes." He "looked after the wild stock of the town" and "had an eye to the unfrequented nooks and corners of the farms."[2] In the fall he often went graping to the river meadows

9. Prudence Ward, Letter to Caroline Sewall of February, 1847. MS, George L. Davenport, Jr.
1. Ralph Waldo Emerson, *Letters,* (New York, 1939), III, 377–8
2. Thoreau, *Writings,* II, 19–20

[1 8 8]

or hunting for nuts in the chestnut groves of Lincoln. In the cold weather he dragged home old logs and stumps to burn in his fireplace.

He became fascinated with the phenomena of the pond. In the spring of 1846, before the ice broke up, he surveyed carefully the size and depth of the pond. He cut holes in the ice and charted his findings with a cod line and a pound-and-a-half stone, a compass, and a chain. Native Concordians had sworn that the pond had no bottom, but he quickly put an end to their stories and proved that Walden has a reasonably tight bottom at a not unreasonable, though an unusual, depth. When, a century later, a trained limnologist checked Thoreau's findings with the latest complex instruments, he was astounded at the accuracy of Thoreau's findings.

In February 1847, Frederic Tudor, the "king" of the New England ice industry, took over the pond for a time. He and his former partner, Nathaniel Jarvis Wyeth, had quarreled. For years they had garnered huge profits together by cutting ice on the ponds near Boston and shipping it to warmer climates from New Orleans to Calcutta. Now Wyeth gained control of the ice-cutting rights on most of the ponds they had been using. Rather than give in, Tudor moved farther from his base and acquired rights on new ponds. He purchased the rights to Walden Pond from Emerson and the Fitchburg Railroad.[3] Shortly afterward a hundred Irish laborers and their Yankee supervisors came from Cambridge daily on the railroad. They often harvested as much as a thousand tons a day, stacking it up in a pile thirty-five feet high, banking it with hay, and covering it with boards. Thoreau was delighted. Here was one commercial venture that could do no harm to his pond or his woods, and the ice cutters, he thought, a merry race, full of jest and sport. When he talked with them, they gleefully invited him to saw the ice pit-fashion with them, he taking the position underneath. When they fell into the water—which they did frequently—he invited them to use his cabin for a dressing-room.

Inspired by their activities, he began a study of the temperature of Walden and the various nearby ponds, rivers, and springs. It was the first of the many statistical studies that were to become

---

3. Emerson, *Letters*, III, 383; *Boston Transcript*, July 23, 1927

so much a part of his life. Like so many of his contemporaries, he found himself developing a mania for charts of temperatures, heights, depths, weights, and dates. It disturbed him, but he was never able to free himself from the habit. As for the ice, Tudor's men returned briefly in July and removed a small part of it, but Tudor had won his war and the pile was soon abandoned; it did not melt away completely until September of the following year.

Hardly a day went by that Thoreau did not visit the village or was not visited at the pond. His very first morning, a drunk hobbled up to his door and asked for a drink of water. "I knew," Thoreau said, "that rum or something like it was the only drink he loved, but I gave him a dish of warm pond water, which was all I had, nevertheless, which to my astonishment he drank, being used to drinking."[4] Not long after, five of the workmen on the nearby Fitchburg Railroad dropped in to see what he was doing. When he told them of his plans, one replied:

> Sir, I like your notions. I think I shall live so myself. Only I should like a wilder country, where there is more game. I have been among the Indians near Appalachicola. I have lived with them. I like your kind of life. Good day. I wish you success and happiness.[5]

Before the second day was over, his sister Sophia arrived for a visit. She had so worried about him that she had not slept the previous night and now used the excuse of bringing out some food to reassure herself that he had survived what she thought of as the rigors of the wilds. But she soon got over her worries and he made a point of stopping off regularly at his parents' house to reassure them all.[6]

One of his most frequent visitors was Alek Therien, the French-Canadian woodchopper he later immortalized in *Walden*. Therien, almost exactly Thoreau's age, had come down from Canada in his teens. Although their backgrounds were very different, they found much in common. Thoreau admired Therien's

---

4. Thoreau, *Journal*, II, 188
5. Ibid. I, 366
6. Edward Emerson, Notes on Thoreau; Edward Emerson, *Henry Thoreau as Remembered by a Young Friend*, 60

overflowing happiness and the thorough way he went about his work with his axe. Therien delighted in stealing up in back of Thoreau's cabin, firing off a stout charge in his gun, and laughing at Thoreau's surprise.[7] Although Therien had had little formal education, he was keen and alert. The two often talked of books. Quite naturally their discussion turned to one of Thoreau's favorite authors, Homer. And when Therien told Thoreau that he thought Homer a great writer, "though what his writing was about, he did not know," Thoreau took his *Iliad* down and translated portions for him. Therien was so delighted that he later quietly borrowed Pope's translation from the cabin and forgot to return it. Thoreau was to wonder in *Walden* where it had gone to.

Emerson was, of course, a frequent visitor at the cabin. He made out a new will, naming him heir to the land on which the cabin was built.[8] When there was a threat of further woodcutting at the pond, Emerson purchased another forty-one acres of land on the Lincoln side of the pond and Thoreau was asked to witness the signing of the deed.[9]

Meanwhile Emerson frequently asked Thoreau to come in to the village to help him. When he found he was to be out of town for a few days, he asked Thoreau to supervise the building of a home for Mrs. Brown near his own. When he purchased two acres adjacent to his home, he asked Thoreau to survey it for him and gave him a dollar for his trouble. When he wanted the yard beautified, Thoreau dug up seventy-three pines, hemlocks, and junipers in the Walden woods and transplanted them around Emerson's house. It was then that Emerson said:

> It is worth while to pay Henry surveyor's wages for doing other things. He is so thoughtful and he does so much more than is bargained for. When he does anything I am sure the thing is done.[1]

But not all was work between them. On pleasant summer days Thoreau would often join the Emerson family on a picnic or a

---

7. J. Lyndon Shanley, *The Making of Walden* (Chicago, 1957) 172
8. Rusk, *The Life of Ralph Waldo Emerson*, 307
9. Kenneth Walter Cameron, "Thoreau Witnesses Emerson Purchase Land at Walden," *Emerson Society Quarterly*, XI (1958), 15
1. Emerson-Channing manuscript notes. MS, Morgan Library

blueberrying party. Emerson would drive a carryall with his mother and Mrs. Brown; Thoreau would follow in a hayrack loaded with the Emerson children and their friends, the mothers, and the Emerson servants. While Emerson and the ladies sat in the shade, Thoreau would lead the children from one berry bush to another.[2]

Nathaniel Hawthorne too, so long as he remained in Concord, frequently came out to the pond for a visit. With his almost painful shyness, he sometimes found Thoreau's cabin a welcome relief from the stream of visitors at home. Bronson Alcott also was a frequent visitor. He purchased a farm on Lexington Road and set about restoring it. Thoreau helped him transplant evergreens and vines from the Walden woods and climbed a tree to assure him that the site he planned for a new summerhouse would have a good view. Thoreau often attended Alcott's "Conversations" in town. And Alcott, in his turn, spent nearly every Sunday evening for several months in the winter of 1846-7 visiting with Thoreau at his cabin.

Louisa May Alcott was but a child at the time of Thoreau's residence at Walden, but he made an indelible impression on her and years later she recalled:

[He] used to come smiling up to his neighbors, to announce that the bluebirds had arrived, with as much interest in the fact as other men take in messages by the Atlantic cable. On certain days, he made long pilgrimages to find "the sweet rhodora in the wood," welcoming the lonely flower like a long-absent friend. He gravely informed us once, that frogs were much more confiding in the spring, than later in the season; for then, it only took an hour to get well acquainted with one of the speckled swimmers, who liked to be tickled with a blade of grass, and would feed from his hand in the most sociable manner.[3]

The Alcotts often took their friends out to the pond to see Thoreau. Once it was an escaped Negro who was stopping over with them on his way to Canada.[4] Another time it was the seventeen-year-old Frederick L. H. Willis, who is said to be the original of the Laurie of Louisa May Alcott's *Little Women*. He

2. Rusk, *The Life of Ralph Waldo Emerson*, 311
3. Louisa May Alcott, "Merry's Monthly Chat with His Friends," *Merry's Museum*, March, 1869
4. Bronson Alcott, Journals. MS, Houghton Library

visited Thoreau in July 1847, and in his old age rather romantically recalled:

> Thoreau . . . gave us a gracious welcome, asking us within. For a time he talked with Mr. Alcott in a voice and with a manner in which, boy as I was, I detected something akin with Emerson. He was a tall and rugged-looking man, straight as a pine tree. His nose was strong, dominating his face, and his eyes as keen as an eagle's. He seemed to speak with them, to take in all about him in one vigorous glance.
>
> He was talking to Mr. Alcott of the wild flowers in Walden woods when, suddenly stopping, he said: "Keep very still and I will show you my family." Stepping quickly outside the cabin door, he gave a low curious whistle; immediately a woodchuck came running towards him from a nearby burrow. With varying note, yet still low and strange, a pair of gray squirrels were summoned and approached him fearlessly. With still another note several birds, including two crows, flew towards him, one of the crows nestling upon his shoulder. I remember it was the crow resting close to his head that made the most vivid impression upon me, knowing how fearful of man this bird is. He fed them all from his hand, taking food from his pocket, and petted them gently before our delighted gaze; and then dismissed them by different whistling, always strange and low and short, each little wild thing departing instantly at hearing its special signal.
>
> Then he took us five children upon the Pond in his boat, ceasing his oars after a little distance from the shore and playing the flute he had brought with him, its music echoing over the still and beautifully clear water. He suddenly laid the flute down and told us stories of the Indians that "long ago" had lived about Walden and Concord; delighting us with simple, clear explanations of the wonders of Walden woods. Again he interrupted himself suddenly, speaking of the various kinds of lilies growing about Walden and calling the wood lilies, stately wild things. . . . Upon our return to the shore he helped us to gather . . . flowers and laden with many sweet blossoms, we wended our way homewards, rejoicingly.[5]

The children of Concord were always happy to go out to Walden Pond and Thoreau was equally happy to have them. Mary Hosmer Brown some years ago recorded her mother's memories of her visits there:

---

5. Frederick L. H. Willis, *Alcott Memoirs* (Boston, 1915), 91–3

On a Sunday afternoon the children loved to go to the Walden shack. Thoreau sat at his desk, Grandfather was given a chair, while they arranged themselves along the edge of the cot bed, the youngest child still remembering that her feet couldn't quite reach the floor. If the conversation grew too abstruse, or they were tired of sitting still, one by one they slipped out to amuse themselves in the woods. They might be rewarded later by a glimpse of friendly animals, or Mr. Thoreau would give them a row on the pond.

To take a walk with Thoreau, one must rigidly adhere to the manners of the woods. He could lead one to the ripest berries, the hidden nest, the rarest flowers, but no plant life could be carelessly destroyed, no mother bird lose her eggs.[6]

And George Keyes, who had been a pupil in the Thoreau school, has said:

We boys used to visit him on Saturday afternoons at his house by Walden and he would show us interesting things in the woods nearby. . . . He was never stern or pedantic but natural and very agreeable and friendly, but a person you would never feel inclined to fool with.

He was light haired, better looking than his portraits, had a healthy complexion with a bright color [though] rather pale for an out-of-doors man; had a strong, prominent nose and good eyes, a face that you would long remember and, though short in stature and inconspicuous in dress, a man you would not fail to notice in the streets as more than ordinary.[7]

Thoreau's way with wildlife continually astonished his visitors. Mrs. Edwin Bigelow, too, has recalled:

Henry would tell all to sit absolutely quiet and close together —then he would go forward cautiously, sprinkle crumbs before them and then retreating, seat himself a little before the others and begin a sort of rolling or humming sound and so would draw squirrels to come and eat at last out of his hands.[8]

The favorite of all his wild pets was a mouse, which Thoreau said had a nest under his house, and came when he took his luncheon to pick the crumbs at his feet. It had never seen the race of man

6. Brown, *Memories of Concord,* 98
7. Edward Emerson, Notes on Thoreau
8. Ibid.

before, and so the sooner became familiar. It ran over his shoes and up his pantaloons inside, clinging to his flesh with its sharp claws, and it would run up the side of the room by short impulses like a squirrel, which it resembled. When he held it a piece of cheese, it came and nibbled between his fingers, and then cleaned its face and paws like a fly.

Like the Pied Piper, Thoreau could summon the mouse out of hiding with his flute and display it to his friends.[9] One of the few decorations he permitted in his cabin was a drawing, made on the closet door, of himself and his pet mouse.[1]

For the sake of science Thoreau was willing, occasionally, to sacrifice a specimen or two. Louis Agassiz, who had arrived in Boston from Europe in the fall of 1846, was anxious to catalog all of the flora and fauna of America. James Elliot Cabot enlisted Thoreau's aid and in the spring of 1847 he shipped a number of specimens into Agassiz's laboratory. Among them, Agassiz found a number of new species, including breams, smelts, and shiners. Thoreau also sent a live young fox, which Agassiz promptly caged in his back yard, and offered to put the hunters and trappers of Concord to work collecting snapping turtles if Agassiz would pay seventy-five cents to a dollar apiece for them. But that offer was not accepted.

Occasionally whole groups of Thoreau's friends came out together to the pond and swarmed into his little cabin. It became quite the fashion to hold picnics on his front doorstep. When it rained, his visitors took refuge inside. He had as many as twenty-five or thirty people inside the tiny cabin at one time. On August 1, 1846, the anti-slavery women of Concord held their annual commemoration of the freeing of the West Indian slaves on his doorstep and Emerson, W. H. Channing, and Rev. Caleb Stetson spoke to the assembled group.[2] Afterward a picnic lunch was served to all the guests.[3]

Although Thoreau was devoted to the abolitionist cause and was a frequent conductor on the Underground Railroad, the Walden cabin, despite tradition, was rarely used as a station. Mrs. Edwin Bigelow, the leader of the Concord unit, has testified that slaves

---

9. Hosmer, "Henry D. Thoreau"
1. S. R. Bartlett, "Walden," *Concord Monitor*, I (1862), 33–4
2. *Concord Freeman*, August 7, 1846
3. Alcott, *Journals*

were occasionally brought there, but since there was no place for concealment, Thoreau always smuggled them into town to his mother's house under cover of darkness, and from there helped them along their way to Canada, often giving them money from his limited funds.[4]

The only guests that Thoreau did not welcome were the curious—and there were plenty of them. They would use any excuse to see the inside of his cabin. When they asked for a glass of water, Thoreau, knowing their real intent, would point to the pond and offer to lend them his dipper. When two young ladies thus borrowed his dipper and failed to return it, he fumed in his journal: "I had a right to suppose they came to steal. They were a disgrace to their sex and to humanity. . . . They will never know peace till they have returned the dipper. In all worlds this is decreed."[5] Even less welcome were two young men he found one day attempting to seduce a young lady. Somehow he collared them both and marching them into town, turned them over to the proper authorities, who promptly took care of them.[6]

But despite all the visitors, despite all his visits to Concord village and to his parents' home, despite his surveying and fence-building and carpentry, and despite the hours devoted to writing, it must not be forgotten that the experiment at Walden was primarily a period of solitude and of communion with nature for Thoreau. It was a period of observing the loons and geese on the pond, the foxes and hawks in the woods, the woodchucks and meadow larks in the fields, the stars and the clouds overhead, the ants and the grasses under his feet, the flowers and trees all around him. And his contemplation was one akin to religious devotion. Frank Sanborn once told Thoreau that when he first moved to Concord in 1855, he was told there were three religious societies in town—the Unitarian, the Orthodox, and the Walden Pond Society.[7] The latter consisted of those who spent their Sunday mornings out walking around Walden Pond enjoying the beauties of nature. Thoreau was unquestionably the high priest of that sect and spent a good part of each day at his devotions. He himself

4. Edward Emerson, Notes on Thoreau
5. Thoreau, *Journal*, III, 198
6. Anna and Walton Ricketson, *Daniel Ricketson and His Friends* (Boston, 1902), 252–3
7. Thoreau, *Journal*, IX, 331

once said, "What in other men is religion is in me love of nature."[8] And Edwin P. Whipple, the literary critic, after meeting Thoreau while visiting in Concord on March 3, 1847, commented, "Thoreau seemed to me a man who had experienced Nature as other men are said to have experienced religion."[9] Some of his townsmen however viewed his devotion to Nature with a jaundiced eye. Madame Hoar said, "Henry talks about Nature just as if she's been born and brought up in Concord,"[1] and another neighbor used to chide him, "You always talk about Nature as if she were your mother-in-law!"[2]

Although he was never basically to change the pattern of life he adopted at Walden Pond, by 1847 he began to feel that he had exhausted the particular benefits of his life there. He had fulfilled his original purpose in coming to the pond—not only had he completed the manuscript of *A Week*, but he had written the first draft of *Walden*. It was time to turn to other fields, he thought, before his life turned into a time-worn rut.

In May, Emerson, learning of Thoreau's restlessness, wrote to his brother-in-law, Dr. Charles T. Jackson, urging that Thoreau be included as an assistant on his government expedition to survey the mineral lands of Michigan.[8] Thoreau would have been admirably suited for the position and wanted very much to go along, but the appointments proved to be political plums over which Jackson had no control, and so the opportunity was lost.

Then in the late summer of 1847 Emerson himself decided to go abroad for the winter. His English friends had arranged a lecture tour for him. Mrs. Emerson was in poor health and the children were too young to travel. Emerson was worried about leaving them alone, but she quickly proposed a solution, suggesting that Thoreau be invited to join them for the winter. His presence would not inconvenience them in the least, for he required no ceremony, and it would assure her husband that his family had

---

8. Henry David Thoreau [Miscellaneous notes]. MS, W. Stephen Thomas
9. Edwin Percy Whipple, *Recollections of Eminent Men* (Boston, 1886), 134
1. Sanborn, *Henry D. Thoreau*, 96
2. John Shepard Keyes, Letter to F. H. Underwood of November 15, 1886. MS, Barrett Collection
3. Emerson, *Letters*, III, 397

the protection and assistance he felt they needed. Emerson quickly agreed to her suggestion and Thoreau readily accepted their joint invitation.

And so it was that Thoreau left the pond, on September 6, 1847, exactly two years, two months, and two days after he had moved in. He explained in the pages of *Walden:*

> I left the woods for as good a reason as I went there. Perhaps it seemed to me that I had several more lives to live, and could not spare any more time for that one.[4]

But in the confidence of his journal he later confessed:

> Why I left the woods I do not think I can tell. I have often wished myself back. I do not know any better how I ever came to go there. Perhaps it is none of my business, even if it is yours. Perhaps I wanted a change. There was a little stagnation, it may be. . . . Perhaps if I lived there much longer, I might live there forever. One would think twice before he accepted heaven on such terms.[5]

But he had no regrets over his experiment. It was, he concluded, one of the real high points of his life. In *Walden* he boasted: "I learned this, at least, by my experiment; that if one advances confidently in the direction of his dreams, and endeavors to live the life which he has imagined, he will meet with a success unexpected in common hours."[6] It was not a success that could be measured in monetary terms or according to conventional values. But then Thoreau himself once said:

> If the day and the night are such that you greet them with joy, and life emits a fragrance like flowers and sweet-scented herbs, is more elastic, more starry, more immortal,—that is your success.[7]

On such terms, and they were, after all, Thoreau's terms—the Walden experiment was a resounding success.

---

4. Thoreau, *Writings*, II, 355
5. Thoreau, *Journal*, III, 214–15
6. Thoreau, *Writings*, II, 356
7. Ibid. II, 239

CHAPTER ELEVEN
(1846–1847)

I

O NE EVENING late in July of 1846, probably the 23rd or 24th, Thoreau walked in to Concord village from Walden Pond to pick up a shoe he had left at the cobbler's shop to be repaired. He was stopped on the street by Sam Staples, the local constable, tax collector, and jailer, and asked to pay his poll tax for the last several years. "I'll pay your tax, Henry, if you're hard up," Staples said.[1] He also offered to try to persuade the selectmen to reduce the tax if Thoreau thought it too high, but Thoreau replied that he had not paid it as a matter of principle and didn't intend to pay it now. When Staples asked what *he* should do about it, Thoreau suggested that if he didn't like it, he could resign his office.[2] But Staples, not taking kindly to that suggestion, replied, "Henry, if you don't pay, I shall have to lock you up pretty soon." "As well now as any time, Sam," was the answer. "Well, come along then," said Staples, and took him to jail.[3]

This was not Thoreau's first brush with the tax authorities in Concord. It had been the custom in Massachusetts for the churches to assess their members for financial support and to have the town treasurers collect for them along with the town assessments. The First Parish Church, apparently assuming that Thoreau was a member both because he had been brought up in the church and because his family owned a pew there, added his name to their tax rolls in 1840.[4] When Thoreau received his church tax bill, he

1. Edward Emerson, *Henry Thoreau as Remembered by a Young Friend*, 64
2. Thoreau, *Writings*, IV, 371
3. Ralph Waldo Emerson, *Complete Writings*, X, 612
4. John C. Broderick, "Young Thoreau Asserts Himself," *Thoreau Society Bulletin*, LIII (1955) 2

marched down to the town office and announced he would refuse to pay it. "Pay or be locked up in jail," they replied.[5] But before the issue could be decided, someone else paid the tax over Thoreau's protest and the town officials were ready to drop the matter. Not so Thoreau however for he knew the subject would be raised another year. He demanded that his name be dropped from the church tax rolls and, at their suggestion, filed with the town selectmen a statement saying, "Know all men by these presents, that I, Henry Thoreau, do not wish to be regarded as a member of any incorporated society which I have not joined."[6] He also informed them that if they would provide him with a list of all societies which he had never joined, he would sign a specific denial of membership in each one of them. But they, unable to produce such a list, informed him they were willing to let the matter drop and he was never again billed for the church taxes. Thoreau however had one more parting shot. In examining the tax records of the town, he noted that he was listed as David H. Thoreau and promptly informed them that he had changed his name to Henry D. Thoreau three years before and insisted successfully that the clerk then and there change the records.[7] Thoreau thus won his first campaign of civil disobedience.

Nor was Thoreau the first to be arrested in Concord for nonpayment of his poll taxes. More than three years before, on January 17, 1843, Staples had arrested Bronson Alcott on the same charge. The Massachusetts poll tax (not a voting tax, but a head tax imposed on every male between the ages of twenty and seventy) had long been unpopular and the Abolitionists seized upon protesting against paying it as a dramatic way of demonstrating their abhorrence of a government that supported slavery. Although Alcott was arrested, he was never jailed, for Squire Hoar, the town's leading citizen, paid Alcott's taxes himself rather than permit such a blot on the town escutcheon. And in the succeeding years, despite his pleas for "the privilege of non-payment of taxes," his wife's family paid his taxes in advance to avoid the embarrassment of having a relative in jail. In December 1843 Alcott's English friend, Charles Lane, also refused to pay his poll tax in Con-

5. Thoreau, *Writings*, IV, 374
6. Ibid. IV, 374-5
7. Broderick, "Young Thoreau Asserts Himself," 2

cord and was arrested. Again Squire Hoar paid the tax and Lane was quickly released.

The examples of Alcott and Lane set Thoreau to thinking. The agitation against slavery had grown in recent years from the work of a few rare individuals to that of the beginnings of a mass movement. William Lloyd Garrison was beginning to become a household name. Ex-President John Quincy Adams through his constant barrage of petitions and speeches in the national House of Representatives was slowly making more and more people aware of the vast gap between the democratic principles the country vocally avowed and the slavery legally practiced in the South. The anti-slavery movement had by no means attained respectability (ironically it was not to attain that until after the Civil War when the need for its activities no longer existed) and Garrison could still be dragged through the streets of Boston with a noose around his neck. But at least it was causing twinges in the American conscience.

Thoreau himself was made particularly aware of the issues involved by the anti-slavery activities of the members of his own household—his mother, his sisters, and Prudence Ward—by the anti-slavery periodicals they regularly subscribed to, and by the fact that the anti-slavery agitators who visited Concord invariably put up for the night in his mother's boarding house. It is safe to say that there was probably hardly a single prominent New England abolitionist of those times that Thoreau did not meet at least once across his mother's dining table.

The abolitionists had, in recent years, split, philosophically at least, into two groups. Those led by William Lloyd Garrison were activist. They denounced loudly and vehemently those institutions such as the church, the state, and the press which they felt were the most ardent defenders of the status quo on the slavery question. Feeling their only weapon against these institutions to be mass action, they stressed the development of larger and more aggressive anti-slavery societies. The other group, which until his recent death had been led by Nathaniel P. Rogers, believed the only possible solution was the reformation of mankind. They feared that Garrison's plans would lead to the institutionalizing of the anti-slavery societies themselves and argued that a utopian society could be achieved only through self-reformation of each individual in a society. This kind of a philosophy was inevitably attractive to a Transcendentalist such as Thoreau. As we have seen, he had already endorsed Rogers's principles in the pages of *The Dial*. Now that he felt called to action himself, he quite naturally took the individualistic rather than the organizational approach, and adopting the ideas and actions of Lane and Alcott, he refused to pay his own poll tax.

Unfortunately for Thoreau's principles, Staples for several years simply ignored Thoreau's tax resistance. Although Staples, like many of the "more practical" townspeople, was pretty skeptical of the "Transcendentalist crowd" (he used to say of Emerson, "I suppose there's a great many things that Mr. Emerson knows that I couldn't understand; but I *know* that there's a damn sight of things that I know that he don't know anything about"[8]), he always had a high opinion of Thoreau.[9] Therefore, if Thoreau chose to ignore paying his taxes, Staples chose to ignore his non-payment.

Why Staples suddenly decided to take action in the summer of 1846 is not known for certain. He was about to give up his position as tax collector and so might have been faced with the prospect of paying Thoreau's taxes himself to clear the books. Or it might have been that the recent declaration of war against Mexico had inflamed a patriotism that demanded the collection of all taxes. At any rate, he gave Thoreau several warnings before finally arresting him[1] and said afterwards that he was not worried about Thoreau's running off; he knew he could get him when he wanted to.[2]

The Concord jail, now long since torn down, was no small-town lock-up. Concord was the shire town of Middlesex County and this was the county jail. It stood just off the Mill Dam, behind the stores, near the present site of the Roman Catholic rectory, and was built of granite, three stories high, sixty-five feet long, thirty-two feet wide, and surrounded with a brick wall about ten feet high, mounted with iron pickets. It had eighteen cells, each

8. Rusk, *The Life of Ralph Waldo Emerson*, 256-7
9. Edward Emerson, *Henry Thoreau as Remembered by a Young Friend*, 64
1. Edward Emerson, Notes on Thoreau
2. S[amuel] A. J[ones], "Thoreau's Incarceration," *Thoreau Society Booklet*, IV (1946), 99

twenty-six feet long and eight-and-a-half feet high. Each cell had two double-grated windows.[3] A formidable jail indeed.

The prisoners were enjoying a chat and the evening air in the prison yard when Thoreau and Staples entered. Staples told the men it was time to return to their cells and introduced Thoreau to his cell mate. When the door was locked, he showed Thoreau where to hang his hat and how to manage matters there. After inquiring about Thoreau's arrest, he explained that he had been accused of burning down a barn and had been waiting three months for his trial—although since he was given free board and room and was permitted to go out and work in the hayfields by the day, he thought he was being well treated and was contented.

Thoreau made the most of what he thought to be a rare opportunity and pumped his cell mate for all he was worth about the history of the jail and its occupants and its gossip, which he realized never circulated outside, but eventually his informant tired of the inquisition and went to bed, leaving Thoreau to blow out the lamp. Thoreau however was much too excited to sleep and stood at the window for some time, looking out through the grating and listening to the activities in the nearby hotel. Later in the night a prisoner in a nearby cell began calling out with painful monotony, "What is life? So this is life!" Finally tiring of the repetition, Thoreau put his head to the window bars and called out himself in a loud voice, "Well, what *is* life, then?" His only answer was silence and his reward a quiet night's sleep.[4]

Meanwhile word of Thoreau's arrest had rapidly spread through the village. When his mother heard of it, she rushed to the jail to ascertain the truth of the rumor and then back home to tell the family the news.[5] Sam Staples had gone out for a while that evening, and on his return his daughter Ellen informed him that someone had knocked at the door in his absence and, passing in a package, had said, "Here is the money to pay Mr. Thoreau's tax."[6] Staples had taken off his boots and was sitting by the fire when his daughter told him, and he declared that he wasn't going

3. *Yeoman's Gazette*, April 28, 1827
4. Edward Emerson, Notes on Thoreau
5. Sanborn, *The Life of Henry David Thoreau*, 513
6. J[ones], "Thoreau's Incarceration," IV, 99

to take the trouble to put them back on. Thoreau could just as well spend the night in jail and be released in the morning.

Just who the person was who knocked on Staples's door and handed in the package has never been absolutely ascertained. Some have claimed that it was Emerson, others Aunt Jane Thoreau, Elizabeth Hoar, Rockwood Hoar, or Samuel Hoar. Staples himself told so many stories in later years—that it was a man, a young woman, an old woman, two women—that his word, as he readily admitted to one of his inquisitors, was not to be depended on.[7] As a matter of fact, neither he nor his daughter probably ever knew, for tradition has it that the person was heavily veiled. But the preponderance of evidence points to Aunt Maria Thoreau. And Eben J. Loomis, who was an old friend of the Thoreau family, was almost certain in his old age that Aunt Maria had once admitted to him that she was the one.[8]

Probably what happened is that when Thoreau's mother returned home with the news, Aunt Maria was understandably upset to learn that her nephew was in jail. It seems likely that Thoreau had extracted a promise from his mother not to interfere with his plans. But Aunt Maria was bound by no such promise and so stepped in and paid the tax. And regularly thereafter, possibly even until the time of Thoreau's death, she or others paid his tax in advance so that the incident could not occur again.[9]

When morning came, the prisoners were fed their breakfasts of bread and a pint of chocolate, and Thoreau's cell mate, leaving for his day's stint in the hayfields, bade him good-bye, saying that he doubted if he would see Thoreau again. (Later Thoreau was to find out that when his cell mate came to trial, he was found innocent of the charges and released.[1] Apparently he had fallen asleep in the barn while smoking and so had inadvertently burned it down.)

When Staples came to release Thoreau, he was astounded to discover that Thoreau was not willing to leave the jail, the only prisoner he ever had who did not want to leave as soon as he could. In fact, said Staples, Thoreau was "as mad as the devil" at

7. Ibid. 102
8. Ibid. IV, 101
9. Emerson, *Complete Writings*, X, 458
1. J[ones], "Thoreau's Incarceration," IV, 100

being released.[2] It had been the whole purpose of his refusal to pay taxes to get arrested and so to call dramatically to the attention of his fellow citizens the cause of abolitionism that he had espoused. When Aunt Maria paid his taxes, she had destroyed the whole point of his campaign, and, to put it mildly, he was not pleased. Since he himself had not paid those taxes, he felt he had the right to stay in jail and said so. But Staples said, "Henry, if you will not go of your own accord I shall put you out, for you cannot stay here any longer." Capitulating, Thoreau finally went on his way, picked up his shoe at the cobbler's, and within a half an hour was picking huckleberries on a hill two miles off where, as he said rejoicingly, "the State was nowhere to be seen."

Word of his arrest and release had, of course, spread rapidly throughout the town. Many stared at him, he noticed, as though he had been on a long journey. And little Georgie Bartlett said that he thought from the excitement he was seeing a Siberian exile or John Bunyan himself.[3] Many of his townsmen of course did not agree with or approve of Thoreau's action. James Garty, who readily admitted that Thoreau "was a good sort of man" and "would pay every cent he owed to any man," complained at the time that "it wouldn't do to have everybody like him, or his way of thinking." Emerson himself complained to Bronson Alcott that Thoreau's action was "mean and skulking, and in bad taste," but Alcott in reply defended it as a good example of "dignified noncompliance with the injunction of civil powers."[4] Emerson then sputtered in his journal: "The State is a poor, good beast who means the best: it means friendly. A poor cow who does well by you,—do not grudge it its hay. . . . As long as the state means you well, do not refuse your pistareen. You have a tottering cause: ninety parts of the pistareen it will spend for what you think also good: ten parts for mischief. . . . In the particular, it is worth considering that refusing payment of the state tax does not reach the evil so nearly as many other methods within your reach. . . . The prison is one step to suicide."[5] And when Emerson next met Thoreau, he asked him why he had gone to jail, only to have

---

2. J[ones], "Thoreau's Incarceration," IV, 100
3. Edward Emerson, Notes on Thoreau
4. Alcott, *Journals* (Boston, 1938), 183–4
5. Ralph Waldo Emerson, *Journals*, VII, 220–3

Thoreau aptly reply, "Why did you not?"[6] Emerson, on further thought, finally admitted in his journal that Thoreau's position was at least stronger than the Abolitionists who denounce the war and yet pay the tax.[7]

As for Sam Staples, his relations with Thoreau continued as amiable as ever. There is a legend that Alcott once, when pestered by Staples for his taxes, picked all the potato bugs off his own vines and dumped them into Staples's garden in retaliation. But Thoreau carried no such grudge. In later years he often hired Staples as his assistant when he was surveying. And Staples, in his turn, often boasted that Thoreau was his most distinguished prisoner.[8]

So many of Thoreau's townsmen expressed a curiosity about his actions and wanted to know the rationale for his trying to go to jail that Thoreau finally wrote out an explanation and delivered it as a lecture on "the relation of the individual to the State" at the Concord Lyceum on January 26, 1848. He found an attentive audience and Bronson Alcott, at least, "took great pleasure" in the lecture.[9] Three weeks later, he gave the second part of the lecture again so others of his townsmen could hear.

In the spring of 1849 Elizabeth Peabody suddenly wrote to ask Thoreau for permission to publish that lecture. She was establishing a new periodical to be called *Aesthetic Papers* to carry along the Transcendentalist message where *The Dial* had dropped it, and wanted to include his lecture in the first (and what later turned out to be the only) issue. Thoreau at the moment was busy correcting proofs of his first book and replied that he hardly had time left for bodily exercise, let alone copying out an old lecture. Nonetheless he promised to send the manuscript along within a week, but he cautioned her that it was offered for use in her first volume only. He had had, as we shall see, enough of delaying actions on the part of editors.

Miss Peabody however kept her word and six weeks later, on May 14, 1849, published her magazine containing pieces by Emerson and Hawthorne along with Thoreau's essay, now entitled "Resistance to Civil Government."[1] (It did not receive its more widely

6. John Weiss, "Thoreau," *Christian Examiner*, LXXIX (1865), 105
7. Emerson, *Journals*, VII, 219
8. Social Circle in Concord, *Memoirs* (Boston, 1882–1940), IV, 137
9. Alcott, *Journals*, 201
1. Bronson Alcott, Journals. MS, Houghton Library

known title of "Civil Disobedience" until it was collected into his *Yankee in Canada, with Anti-Slavery and Reform Papers* in 1866, four years after his death.)

"Civil Disobedience" is Thoreau's most powerful and most influential political essay. Its fundamental principle is the Transcendentalist one that there is a higher law than civil law—the law of conscience—and that when these laws are in conflict, it is the citizen's duty to obey the voice of God within rather than that of civil authority without. If he will go to prison rather than obey an evil law, he will through his courage and his martyrdom arouse the conscience of his people to rebel *en masse* and through their resistance they will clog the machinery of tyranny by filling the courts and the jails and thus bring about repeal of the offensive law. Aunt Maria's action in paying Thoreau's tax prevented his personally testing these principles. But they have long since been proven effective by such courageous moral leaders as Mahatma Gandhi in India and Martin Luther King in Alabama.

At the time of its publication however, the essay produced scarcely a ripple. Although *Aesthetic Papers* was noticed here and there, the reviewers generally ignored Thoreau's contribution. They were more interested in the essays by the better-known Emerson and Hawthorne in the same issue. The one exception was a review by Sophia Dobson Collet in the *People's Review* in London, England. She quoted several of the meatiest paragraphs and prefaced them with the comment that "as it is not likely to be much known in England, we give the following extracts, premising that it ought to be read as a whole to be thoroughly appreciated." But except for Miss Collet's comment, the essay was ignored.

Thoreau had one more brief brush with the tax gatherers of Concord before he was through. In 1855 they called him into their office to get an inventory of his property. Did he have any real estate? No. Any notes at interest or railroad shares? No. Any taxable property? None that he knew of; he admitted though he owned a rowboat. They scratched their heads and thought for a time they might consider that a pleasure carriage and so tax it. But they finally decided they had no case and permitted Thoreau to go tax free. There were undreamed of advantages, he found, to the simple life. But tax exemption was of course not his major aim in his civil disobedience. What he really wanted, as he said in the closing passage of his essay, was a state which could "afford to be just to all men, and to treat the individual with respect as a neighbor; which even would not think it inconsistent with its own repose if a few were to live aloof from it, not meddling with it, nor embraced by it, who fulfilled all the duties of neighbors and fellow-men." And to earn such a state, he for one was ready and willing to go to jail if necessary. Out of his experience in jail came one of our great documents of human freedom.

II

There was one other brief interlude in Thoreau's stay at Walden Pond. At the invitation of his Bangor cousin, George Thatcher, he took his first extensive excursion into the Maine Woods. Thatcher, who was in the lumber business, wished to look over some property on the West Branch of the Penobscot River and, knowing Thoreau's interest in both the Indians and the woods of Maine, asked him to accompany him.

Thoreau left Concord on August 31, 1846, and, traveling by rail and boat, reached Bangor on the morning of September 1; he started off immediately in a buggy with Thatcher for Mattawamkeag Point, some sixty miles distant. At the Indian village of Oldtown, they stopped long enough for Thoreau, always interested in crafts, to watch for a while the manufacturing of batteaus, the sharp-ended canoe-like boats especially designed for running the rocky Maine rivers. At Lincoln they stopped again, this time to hire an Indian guide, for Thoreau was intent upon climbing Mount Katahdin, Maine's highest peak, which few men had climbed before. They learned that Louis Neptune, one of the leaders of the Oldtown community, and some of his friends were leaving the next morning for a month's moose hunt up the river, and promptly arranged to meet them at the West Branch dam. At Mattawamkeag, while they waited for two of Thatcher's Bangor friends to join them, Thoreau discovered Greenleaf's latest map of Maine on the wall. Having no map of his own, he oiled a sheet of paper and made a tracing—only to find once he was in the wilderness that it was a labyrinth of errors.

Early the next morning they mounted their packs and started

off up the river. Eighteen miles upstream they came to "Uncle George" McCauslin's house in the midst of a clearing and spent the night there. Although bad weather held them there an extra day, they saw no sign of the Indians and persuaded McCauslin himself to join them as a guide. With a strip of cotton cloth for a tent, a few blankets, fifteen pounds of hard bread, ten pounds of pork, and a little tea, they felt they had provisions enough for six men for a week—along with whatever they picked up in the forest or streams along their way.

At the mouth of the Millinocket River they hired a batteau and persuaded Thomas Fowler, who lived there, to join them since they needed two men to guide and to carry the boat. After a short portage, they packed their baggage in the bow of the boat, and with Uncle George in the stern and Tom in the bow, each using a twelve-foot spruce pole, they shot up the rapids like a salmon, grazing rocks by the hundreds until Thoreau felt he was the *Argo* passing through the Symplegades and confessed he had never experienced any boating half so thrilling before. Reaching the dam, they were at the last human habitation of any kind in this direction. Beyond, there was no trail, and traveling by batteaus on the rivers and lakes was the only practicable route.

They camped that night on the north end of North Twin Lake, where they had hardly pitched their cotton-cloth tent when the wind carried sparks on to it from the fire and burned it. They hastily drew the batteau up into the woods, propped up one side three or four feet high, and went to sleep with their heads and bodies under the boat and their feet and legs sticking out toward the fire. The next day they poled, rowed, and portaged across lakes, streams, and carries to Sowadnehunk Deadwater, about twelve miles from the summit of Katahdin. The following morning, swinging their baggage and provisions up to the tops of saplings out of reach of the bears, they mounted their packs and started off on a compass hike toward the highest peak. All day long they climbed, until at four o'clock, in view of the summit, they camped. While others prepared the site, Thoreau continued along alone, following up the course of the stream which occupied the ravine, pulling himself up the side of perpendicular falls of twenty or thirty feet by the roots of firs and birches, and then walking a level rod or two until he reached the next falls. He soon found himself above the tree line, and, after stopping long enough to look back over the countryside, returned to find his companions camping miserably on a damp shelf of rock.

In the morning, after breakfasting on pork, bread, and "a dipper of condensed cloud or waterspout," they again headed for the summit. Thoreau soon left his less enthusiastic companions by the wayside and continued on alone. He shortly found himself deep within the clouds on the thousand-acre tableland that makes up the summit of the mountain—probably the fifth or sixth man in history to reach it. All he could see was a vast and fearful aggregation of loose rocks and clouds. For once he felt that "vast, Titanic, inhuman Nature" had got him at a disadvantage and seemed to say to him, "Why came ye here before your time. This ground is not prepared for you." This was not the gentle kindly Nature he knew on the banks of Walden Pond and he did not like it. Remembering conveniently that his companions were anxious to return, he turned back without reaching the highest point of the tableland and quickly and happily descended to friendlier regions.

By two o'clock the party reached their batteau and by four had started on their return voyage. They made their way back to civilization rapidly and when they reached Tom Fowler's house at Millinocket, found to their disgust their Indians, Louis Neptune and his companions, delayed by a drunken frolic and not yet fully sober. After spending a night at Uncle George's, Thoreau and his companions made the long buggy journey back to Bangor in one day, and by six the next morning Thoreau was on his way back home by boat. Thus ended his first journey into wilderness country. Here at last he had experienced nature in the raw, uncontaminated by civilization. He found it could be at times fearsome and cruel, but he found it also had a fascination that was to bring him back again and again.

III

With the additional time at his command at Walden, Thoreau was able to produce a great deal more writing. Not only did he do a major part of the work on his first two books, but he had time

or articles as well. As we have seen, he gathered together materials for a lecture on Thomas Carlyle and delivered it before the
Concord Lyceum on February 4, 1846. Now he determined to ❋
revise the lecture for the printed page. And while working on the
essay, he noted in his journal the techniques he had evolved and
that he was to follow for the rest of his life:

> From all the points of the compass, from the earth beneath
> and the heavens above, have come these inspirations and been
> entered duly in the order of their arrival in the journal. There-
> after, when the time arrived, they were winnowed into lectures,
> and again, in due time, from lectures into essays.[2]

And this was exactly the procedure he followed with his Carlyle
essay. The embryo notes were scattered over four years of his
journal. They were gathered together and worked into his lecture.
On the basis of the audience's reactions to the lecture and his own,
he sat down and rewrote it in essay form. Then, recalling that
Horace Greeley of the New York *Tribune* had graciously offered
his services should Thoreau ever want help in placing an article in
the periodicals of the day, he sent the essay off to Greeley in mid-
summer of 1846.

On August 16 Greeley replied that he would do his best to
place it, but warned Thoreau that the article was far too long to
be printed in one issue of a magazine and that editors shunned
like a pestilence the words "To be continued." He also thought
the article "too solidly good" to be profitable—Thoreau needed
to write down to his audience if he wanted to be popular.[3] A week
later Greeley offered the essay to G. R. Graham of *Graham's Magazine,* pointing out frankly that while Emerson would have been
the best one to write on Carlyle, Thoreau was Emerson's apt pupil
and the "second-best" man in the country to do it.[4] He was confident, he said, that the article would attract many new readers to
the magazine and promised to puff it loudly in the pages of the
Tribune if Graham would print and pay for it. He closed his letter
with a not-too-subtle threat that if it were not accepted he would
offer it to Graham's rival, Godey, and give him the publicity.

2. Thoreau, *Journal,* I, 413
3. Thoreau, *Correspondence,* 169–70
4. Griswold, *Passages from the Correspondence,* 206–7

On September 30 Greeley wrote Thoreau that the article had been accepted by Graham. On October 26 he wrote to say that it was in type and to promise that Thoreau would be paid liberally. On November 21 he wrote Rufus Griswold, Graham's current editor, to suggest that he commission Thoreau to write a similar article on Emerson. On December 16, he wrote Griswold again, this time wondering what had happened to the Carlyle essay since it had not yet appeared in print.[5] Early in February, Thoreau lost patience and wrote Greeley to ask if he could get the essay back so that he could use it as a lecture. Greeley replied on the 5th that not only was the essay in type, but it would appear as the lead article in the March issue and would be concluded in the April number; therefore it would be folly now to withdraw it. He added that now the Carlyle article's place in print was assured, Thoreau should sit down and write similar articles about his friends Emerson and Hawthorne. Greeley promised to see that they would be printed and suggested that in a year or two, Thoreau would thus have enough material to gather into a volume. Thoreau played around with the idea briefly, jotting down a few brief notes on Emerson and on Bronson Alcott in his journal, but then, apparently feeling he would be presuming upon his friendships, abandoned the project. He did however accede to Greeley's request that he leave the article with Graham, and the essay finally appeared as promised, but Thoreau's troubles with it were not over. A whole year later, on March 31, 1848, he wrote Greeley that although the article had appeared, he had never been paid for it. Greeley apologized immediately for the delay and promised to see that he collected. Two weeks later he wrote that he had been unsuccessful in locating Graham in his office in Philadelphia. A month later he sent Thoreau fifty dollars and said that in order to collect it he had had to locate a copy of the article and, after making out a bill to accompany it, had had to draw a draft on Graham for the amount. Thoreau, in thanking him, confessed that such a technique had never occurred to him, but that it had a peculiar advantage—it permitted the author to determine the amount he should be paid. Thoreau then went on to tell Greeley briefly of his life at Walden Pond. Greeley was so delighted with his account that he took the liberty of publishing

---

5. Griswold, *Passages from the Correspondence*, 212–13

it in his New York *Tribune* for May 25, 1848, and set it off with an explanatory editorial:

We are continually receiving letters from young gentlemen who deem themselves born to enlighten the world in some way—to "strike the sounding lyre," or from the Editorial tripod dispense wisdom and guidance to an instructed and admiring world. These generally want to know why they cannot be employed in our establishment, or find a publisher for their poems, or a chance in some shape to astonish mankind and earn a livelihood by letters. —To this large and increasing class, we wish to propound one question: "Suppose all who desire to live by Literature or Trade could find places, who would hoe the needful corn or dig the indispensable potatoes?" —But we purposed in beginning to ask their attention to the following extract from a private letter we have just received from a very different sort of literary youth—a thorough classical scholar, true poet (though he rarely or never wrote verses,) and never sought to make a livelihood by his writings, though there are not six men in America who can surpass them. We feel indeed honored by his friendship; and in the course of a private letter we have just received from him he casually says:

"For the last five years, I have supported myself solely by the labor of my hands. I have not received one cent from any other source, and this has cost me so little time—say, a month in the Spring and another in the Autumn—doing the coarsest work of all kinds, that I have probably enjoyed more leisure for literary pursuits than any contemporary. For more than two years past, I have lived alone in the woods, in a good plastered and shingled house of my own building, earning only what I wanted, and sticking to my proper work. The fact is, Man need not live by the sweat of his brow—unless he sweats easier than I do—he needs so little. For two years and two months, all my expenses have amounted to but 27 cents a week, and I have fared gloriously in all respects. If a man must have money—and he needs but the smallest amount—the true and independent way to earn it is by day-labor with his hands at a dollar a day. I have tried many ways and can speak from experience.

"Scholars are apt to think themselves privileged to complain as if their lot were a peculiarly hard one. How much have we heard about the attainment of knowledge under difficulties—of poets starving in garrets—of literary men depending on the patronage of the wealthy, and finally dying mad! It is time that men sang another song. —There is no reason why the scholar, who professes to be a little wiser than the mass of men, should not do his work in the ditch occasionally, and, by means of his superior wisdom, make much less suffice for him. A wise man will not be unfortunate. How otherwise would you know that he was not a fool?"

—We trust our friend will pardon the liberty we have taken in printing the foregoing, since we are sure of effecting signal good thereby. We have no idea of making a hero of him. Our object is simply to shame the herd of pusillanimous creatures who whine out their laziness in bad verses, and execrate the stupidity of publishers and readers who will not buy these maudlin effusions at the paternal estimate of their value, and thus spare them the dire necessity of doing something useful for a living. It is only *their* paltriness that elevates our independent friend above the level of ordinary manhood, and whenever they shall rise to the level of true self-respect, his course will be no longer remarkable.

"What!" says one of them, "Do you mean that every one must hoe corn or swing the sledge?—that no life is useful or honorable but one of rude manual toil?" —No, Sir; we say no such thing. —If any one is sought out, required, demanded, for some vocation specially intellectual, let him embrace it and live by it. But the general rule is that Labor—that labor which produces food and clothes and shelter—is every man's duty and destiny, for which he should be fitted, in which he should be willing to do his part manfully. But let him study, and meditate, and cultivate his nobler faculties as he shall find opportunity; and whenever a career of intellectual exertion shall open before him, let him embrace it if he be inclined and qualified. But to coin his thoughts into some marketable semblance, disdain useful labor of the hands because he has a facility of writing, and go crying his mental wares in the market, seeking to exchange them for bread and clothes—this is most degrading and despicable. Shall not the world outgrow such shabbiness?

Greeley then wrote Thoreau an apology: "Don't scold at my publishing part of your last private letter . . . in this morning's paper. It will do great good."[6] Thoreau was delighted and decided to insert the paragraphs Greeley had quoted into his *Walden* manuscript, where they became a part of the first chapter.

6. Thoreau, *Correspondence*, 228

"Thomas Carlyle and His Works" is Thoreau's one extended piece of literary criticism. As one might expect, he approves highly of Carlyle and hails him as the one who "alone, since the death of Coleridge, has kept the promise of England." Typically, Thoreau admires those very characteristics of Carlyle's style and content that the twentieth-century reader finds most admirable in Thoreau's work. He "wonders how so much, after all, was expressed in the old way, so much here depends upon the emphasis, tone, pronunciation, style, and spirit of the reading." He praises Carlyle's humor, but emphasizes that it is always subordinate to a serious purpose. And he concludes that "Carlyle is a critic who lives in London to tell this generation who have been the great men of our race." Carlyle himself was understandably pleased when he received a copy and wrote Emerson, "I like Mr. Thoreau very well; and hope yet to hear good and better news of him."[7]

After all his trials and tribulations with the article, Thoreau must seriously have questioned whether the effort was worth it. His reaction for a time at least was a negative one. He wanted nothing more to do with the magazines. When on April 14, 1847, Emerson called thirteen of his friends—Theodore Parker, Alcott, George Bradford, and Thoreau among them—to a meeting at his house to discuss the possibility of establishing a successor to *The Dial,* Thoreau immediately threw cold water on the project by asking if there were any present who found difficulty in publishing in existing journals anything that they had to say.[8] When the group went on to establish the *Massachusetts Quarterly Review* and chose Parker as the editor, Thoreau lost what little interest he had in the project and never contributed to it. It could be, of course, that he knew Parker's opinion of his worth, for one of the first steps Parker had taken as editor was to make up a list of possible contributors, divide them into three categories—"Certain and Valuable," "Valuable but not Certain," and "Certain but not Valuable"—and place Thoreau's name in the last category.[9] Later, when the *Review* was foundering (it lasted only through three volumes),

7. Norton, *The Correspondence of Thomas Carlyle and Ralph Waldo Emerson,* II, 130-1
8. James Elliott Cabot, *A Memoir of Ralph Waldo Emerson* (Boston, 1887), II, 497
9. Henry Steele Commager, *Theodore Parker* (Boston, 1936), 132

Emerson suggested that Thoreau be urged to write for it and so help save it, but he still would have nothing to do with it.

For several years Emerson tried, unsuccessfully, to establish a transatlantic magazine. When John A. Heraud in England expressed some interest, Emerson quickly suggested Thoreau as a possible contributor.[1] But Thoreau, when approached, only replied, "I am more interested in the private journal than the public one," and thought there was no certainty that anything valuable would be written by anyone for such a publication. Thus Emerson's efforts for him went to waste. There is no question about it: Thoreau could be most caustic and unco-operative at the very moment his friends were doing their best to help him—particularly if his pride had been hurt.

IV

In the summer of 1846 Emerson, envious of Thoreau's quiet retreat at Walden, thought seriously of constructing one of his own on the opposite shore of the pond where the eminence Thoreau had named Emerson's Cliff rose high above the water. He could use it for an occasional study and from it look out not only over the waters of the pond but to Mount Monadnock and Mount Wachusett on the distant horizon. At Emerson's request, Thoreau surveyed the site, chose a likely spot, and drew up the plans for a lodge. When Alcott saw the plans, he insisted on adding a second story to the design.[2] But there, for some unknown reason, the plans were dropped and nothing more was ever done about it.

In the summer of 1847, just before Thoreau left Walden, Emerson purchased two and a half acres of land on the eastern side of his property on Lexington Road and, tearing down the boundary fence, hired Bronson Alcott for fifty dollars to build a summerhouse.[3] It was undoubtedly one more example of Emerson's kindly ingenuity in providing an income for the improvident Alcott's family. Alcott was to be the architect of the projected

1. Emerson, *Letters*, III, 370
2. Alcott, Journals
3. Sanborn, *The Personality of Emerson*, 73

summerhouse, but Emerson readily recognized that it would need Thoreau's practicality if it ever were to get built.

The building of the summerhouse from the very beginning became a comedy of errors if ever there was one. On July 15 Alcott, Thoreau, and Emerson trekked out to Emerson's Walden woodlot and cut down and brought home twenty hemlock posts for the frame. Alcott, inept as ever, dreamily felled a tree without looking where it was going, and Thoreau, seeing that it was about to land in some neighboring trees, rushed at it while it was falling and by main strength carried out the trunk until it fell where he wanted it to.[4]

On August 12 Alcott, with Thoreau's assistance, laid the timbers for the floor and some of the planks. The next day, having completed the planking, they set up nine corner joists—nine not for any practical purpose but because Alcott wished to honor the nine muses. As the work progressed, Emerson understandably became skeptical and expressed to his wife his wonder that the whole structure did not collapse. He thought he would christen it "Tumbledown-Hall."[5] Mr. Wetherbee, the village carpenter, examined it and commented that Alcott would undoubtedly use more nails in building a fence than any other man would require to construct a two-story house, shingles included. "A few more spikes driven would to all appearance," Emerson thought, "shatter the supporters."[6]

As the structure grew, so did Alcott's plans. He kept Thoreau busy searching the woods for strangely gnarled branches and shoots, for they made up most of its skeletonic structure. By August 29, Emerson was writing Margaret Fuller of the summerhouse's "alarming dimensions" with all its peristyle gables and dormer windows.[7] Nearly a month later Thoreau's Aunt Maria reported to Prudence Ward:

H—— is building an arbour for Mr. Emerson, but H—— says, A—— pulls down as fast as he builds up, (quite characteristic) but it is rather expensive [and] somewhat tedious to poor Henry, to say nothing of endangering life and limbs for if there had not

4. Sanborn, *Henry D. Thoreau,* 279
5. Emerson, *Letters,* III, 411
6. Ibid. 57
7. Emerson, *Letters,* III, 413

been a comfortable haystack near that he availed himself of by jumping into, when the top rafter was knock'd off, it might have been rather a serious affair. I do not know but I exaggerate a little, but at any rate jump he had to, and I believe it *was* in a hay mow. I hope they will find as soft a landing place, one and all, when they drop from the clouds.[8]

And Thoreau complained to Emerson that he felt as though he were "nowhere doing nothing."[9]

But Alcott was not perturbed in the least. Despite all the appended bric-a-brac and gingerbread, he boasted in his journal that the one merit of the structure was its simplicity. So enthralled with the project was he that he seldom reached home before dark, dreamed about it all night long, and awoke in the morning filled with an urgency to get immediately back to the task.[1] On November 14 Thoreau reported to Emerson, who by then was in England:

Alcott has heard I laughed, and so set the people laughing, at his arbor, though I never laughed louder than when I was on the ridge-pole. But now I have not laughed for a long time, it is so serious. He is very grave to look at. But, not knowing all this, I strove innocently enough, the other day, to engage his attention to my mathematics. "Did you ever study geometry, the relation of straight lines to curves, the transition from the finite to the infinite? Fine things about it in Newton and Leibnitz." But he would hear none of it,—men of taste preferred the natural curve. Ah, he is a crooked stick himself. He is getting on now so many *knots* an hour. There is one knot at present occupying the point of highest elevation,—the present highest point; and as many knots as are not handsome, I presume, are thrown down and cast into the pines. Pray show him this if you meet him anywhere in London, for I cannot make him hear much plainer words here. He forgets that I am neither old nor young, nor anything in particular, and behaves as if I had still some of the animal heat in me. As for the building, I feel a little oppressed when I come near it. It has no great disposition to be beautiful; it is certainly a wonderful structure, on the whole, and the fame of the architect will endure as long as it shall stand.[2]

---

8. Canby, *Thoreau,* 243–4
9. Emerson, *Journals,* VII, 499
1. Alcott, *Journals,* 197
2. Thoreau, *Correspondence,* 189–90

And Ellery Channing laughingly reported:

> Now for the summer-house, that all-important feature. You know to what I refer—the chapel of ease which our great philosopher is erecting on the lawn; is erecting and has been erecting. There it is, or the idea of it. This eternal pancake, which not even the all-powerful rays of the Alcott sun have quite baked, has finally drawn on its double nightcap. First a wickerwork skull; then a head of moss, affirmed by those who have seen it to be admirable; lastly, a straw night-cap. Even the thermometer at sixteen below zero cannot pinch its ears. In other words, the building of this microscopic Cathedral of Cologne realizes eternity.[3]

It became the standard amusement of the townsfolk to make a daily examination of the weird progress of the building and even Alcott could overhear their comments to one another—"Odd," "The Strangest thing I ever saw," "A log cabin," "A whirligig."[4] But they did not deter him in the least. Only the coming of cold weather brought the project to a stop. Then he resumed work in the spring, and it was mid-summer before he was finally satisfied that it was completed. Emerson's mother promptly dubbed it "The Ruin" and the name stuck. The open architecture kept out neither the rain nor the mosquitoes, so it was never used. Thoreau planted a goodly supply of evergreens around it to make it look a little more presentable. But passersby could still see the front gable from the road and often wondered aloud what the structure could be for. Despite everyone's forebodings, it did not collapse immediately. In fact, as much as fifteen years later, Emerson was still hiring Alcott and Thoreau on occasion to repair it. Were not Alcott so completely guileless, one might almost suspect that he knew a good thing when he saw one. And Thoreau unquestionably got his time's worth of laughs out of it all.

1847 marked the tenth anniversary of Thoreau's graduation from Harvard. His class planned a celebration and in the spring, Henry Williams, the class secretary, sent out a form letter asking routine questions about life since graduation. It was seven months later, on September 30, 1847, before Thoreau got around to

3. William Ellery Channing, *Poems of 65 Years* (Philadelphia, 1902), xxxi
4. Alcott, *Journals,* 197

answering and his letter showed hardly the enthusiasm that a class secretary would like to see:

> I confess that I have very little class spirit, and have almost forgotten that I ever spent four years at Cambridge. That must have been in a former state of existence. It is difficult to realize that the old routine is still kept up. However, I will undertake at last to answer your questions as well as I can in spite of a poor memory and a defect of information. . . .
>
> I am not married.
>
> I dont know whether mine is a profession, or a trade, or what not. It is not yet learned, and in every instance has been practised before being studied. The mercantile part of it was begun *here* by myself alone.
>
> —It is not one but legion, I will give you some of the monster's heads. I am a Schoolmaster—a private Tutor, a Surveyor—a Gardener, a Farmer—a Painter, I mean a House Painter, a Carpenter, a Mason, a Day-Laborer, a Pencil-Maker, a Glass-paper Maker, a Writer, and sometimes a Poetaster. If you will act the part of Iolas, and apply a hot iron to any of these heads, I shall be greatly obliged to you.
>
> My present employment is to answer such orders as may be expected from so general an advertisement as the above—that is, if I see fit, which is not always the case, for I have found out a way to live without what is commonly called employment or industry attractive or otherwise. Indeed my steadiest employment, if such it can be called, is to keep myself at the top of my condition, and ready for whatever may turn up in heaven or on earth. For the last two or three years I have lived in Concord woods alone, something more than a mile from any neighbor, in a house built entirely by myself. . . .
>
> I beg that the Class will not consider me an object of charity, and if any of them are in want of pecuniary assistance, and will make known their case to me, I will engage to give them some advice of more worth than money.[5]

But Williams was more fortunate this time with Thoreau than most. Although Thoreau was regularly invited to attend the annual dinners of the class and to contribute his photograph to the class archives, this is the only time he even bothered to respond. College, so far as he was concerned, was something to be forgotten.

---

5. Thoreau, *Correspondence*, 185–6

CHAPTER TWELVE
(1847–1849)

I

On October 5, 1847, Emerson sailed from Boston on the packet *Washington Irving* for London. Thoreau, who was at the wharf to see him off, thought his stateroom no better than a carpeted dark closet with a keyhole for a window and was happy that he was remaining where he could walk in Walden woods rather than on a wooden deck. If he were to go anyplace, he told Emerson, he would rather it were Oregon than London. But instead he returned to Concord and settled down once again in the Emerson home on Lexington Road to act as man of the house. He banked the trees against winter, repaired the palings in the fence, put up shelves in the closet, took care of Emerson's railroad shares, and helped to straighten out the confused status of the ownership of the land at Alcott's ill-fated Fruitlands community in Harvard, of which Emerson had been appointed a trustee. When spring came, he carefully manured the fields and planted the garden, including, at Emerson's request, a goodly share of his famous melons.

Thoreau's great joy was the children. Ellen Emerson was now eight; Edith, six; and Edward, three. He would carry Eddy around on his shoulders, make pan's pipes for the girls from pumpkin stalks, onion tops, or willow shoots, or gather them all around the fire and tell them stories of the adventures of his childhood or of a duel between turtles he had observed in the river or of the battle of the ants he had seen at his Walden cabin. When they tired of stories, he would make pencils and knives disappear and redeem them magically from their ears and noses. And then he would rescue a heavy copper warming-pan from the garret and would unweariedly shake it over the fire while they listened to the explosions within, until finally he would open it and the white-blossoming popcorn would cascade over them. In season he would help them to gather high-bush blueberries, chestnuts, barberries, or wild grapes. On other occasions he would take them out in his boat on Walden Pond and show them how, by striking the side of the boat with an oar, to make a crash that would reverberate back and forth from shore to hill and fill the whole atmosphere with its echoes. At other times he would help them to gather wild-flowers or show them that a snake was a friend to be petted rather than an enemy to be destroyed. Little wonder that one day Eddy, almost forgetting his own father abroad, said, "Mr. Thoreau, will you be my father?"[1] And little wonder that Emerson, hearing of these adventures, wrote his wife, "Our Spartan-Buddhist Henry is a *Père* or *bon-homme malgré lui,* and it is a great comfort daily to think of him there with you."[2]

Hugh Whelan, the Emerson's Irish gardener, raised a problem for Thoreau, though. When Thoreau left the pond, Emerson had purchased the Walden cabin and had in turn sold it to Whelan, who wished to move it a bit farther back from the pond and to convert it into a cottage for his family. On December 15 Thoreau wrote Emerson:

Hugh's plot begins to thicken. He starts thus. 80 dollars on one side—Walden field & house on the other. How to bring these together so as to make a garden & a palace.

$80 . . . . field □ house

1st let *10* go over to unite the two last □

70

6 for Wetherbee's rocks to found your palace on.

64 So far indeed we have already got.

4 to bring the rocks to the field

60

save 20 by all means to manure the field, and you have left 40 to complete the palace, build cellar—& dig well. Build the cellar yourself—& let well alone—& now how does it stand?

$40 to complete the palace somewhat like this

—for when one asks ["] What do you want? Twice as much room more," the reply—Parlor kitchen & bedroom—these make

1. Thoreau, *Correspondence,* 189
2. Ralph Waldo Emerson, *Letters* (New York, 1939), III, 455

the palace.—Well Hugh, what will you do? Here are forty dollars to buy a new house 12 feet by 25 and add it to the old.—Well, Mr. Thoreau, as I tell you, I know no more than a child about it. It shall be just as you say.—Then build it yourself—get it roofed & get in. Commence at one end & leave it half done, and let time finish what money's begun.

So you see we have forty dollars for a nest egg—sitting on which, Hugh & I, alternately & simultaneously, there may in course of time be hatched a house, that will long stand, and perchance even lay fresh eggs one day for its owner, that is, if when he returns he gives the young chick 20 dollars or more in addition by way of "swichin"—to give it a start in the world.[3]

But unfortunately Hugh's addiction to the bottle interfered with his glorious plans. On January 12, 1848, Thoreau reported his downfall to Emerson:

I thought you needed to be informed of Hugh's progress. He has moved his house, as I told you, and dug his cellar, and purchased stone of Sol Wetherbee for the last, though he has not hauled it; all which has cost sixteen dollars, which I have paid. He has also, as next in order, run away from Concord without a penny in his pocket, "crying" by the way,—having had another long difference with strong beer, and a first one, I suppose, with his wife, who seems to have complained that he sought other society. . . . He writes back to his wife from Sterling, near Worcester, where he is chopping wood, his distantly kind reproaches to her, which I read straight through to her (not to his bottle, which he has with him, and no doubt addresses orally). He says that he will go on to the South in the spring, and will never return to Concord. . . . He dug his cellar for the new part too near the old house, Irish like, though I warned him, and it has caved and let one end of the house down. Such is the state of his domestic affairs. . . .

In that sorry state, tilted over and slanted down into its cellar hole, the cabin was abandoned. Thoreau suggested to Emerson:

I think that if an honest and small-familied man, who has no affinity for moisture in him, but who has an affinity for sand, can be found, it would be safe to rent him the shanty as it is, and

---

3. Thoreau, *Correspondence*, 196–7

the land; or you can very easily and simply let nature keep them still, without great loss.[4]

But no purchaser was interested and so the cabin remained there until the late summer of 1849, when it was purchased by James Clark. On September 3, 1849, he and Daniel Brooks Clark, using an ox team, moved it across town to a site on the Clark farm on the old Carlisle Road, where it was used for grain storage for a number of years.[5] It was not taken care of and gradually fell into a ruinous condition. In 1868 the roof was removed and used to cover a pig pen. "Such is fame," Ellery Channing lamented when he reported this outrage to the neglected cabin.[6] In 1875 the remaining floor and timbers were made into a stable shed on the south side of the Brooks Clark barn.[7] Still later the shed collapsed, the timbers were used to patch up the barn, and their identity was completely lost. By happy coincidence, though, that barn is now owned by Emerson's grandson.

In England Emerson was doing his bit to spread the word of Thoreau. Wherever he went, he spoke to such young people as George Searle Phillips and Henry S. Sutton of his young neighbor, his characteristics, and his achievements and boasted to his English listeners that Thoreau was one whom they would "hear of by and by." Thoreau would not remain unknown long if Emerson were to have his way. When in 1855 Phillips published a biography of Emerson, he took pains to emphasize Emerson's friendship with Thoreau.

II

While Emerson was still abroad, Thoreau had an unwonted adventure. It is amusing to us now, but he did not find it so at the time. On November 14, 1847, he wrote Emerson:

4. Ibid. 203–4
5. Daniel Brooks Clark, Diary for September, 1849. MS, Gladys Clark
6. William Ellery Channing, Annotations in his copy of Thoreau's *Walden,* 256–7, Berg Collection
7. William E. Griswold, After Walden: a Biography of Thoreau's Hut. MS, Gladys Clark

I have had a tragic correspondence, for the most part all on one side, with Miss Ford. She did really wish to—I hesitate to write—marry me. That is the way they spell it. Of course I did not write a deliberate answer. How could I deliberate upon it? I sent back as distinct a *no* as I have learned to pronounce after considerable practice, and I trust that this *no* has succeeded. Indeed, I wished that it might burst, like hollow shot, after it had struck and buried itself and make itself felt there. *There was no other way.* I really had anticipated no such foe as this in my career.[8]

Sophia Ford (or Foord, as she sometimes spelled it) was born in Milton, Massachusetts, on June 8, 1802, and was thus fifteen years older than Thoreau. She was active in various Transcendentalist and Abolitionist circles and spent two years in the early 1840s, as a member of the Northampton (Massachusetts) Association of Education and Industry, a community experiment similar to Brook Farm.[9] Bronson Alcott, in 1846, thought for a time of establishing a private school in Concord and, having been impressed with her way with children, hired her as a teacher. Since this school like so many of his plans failed to materialize, she was then asked to tutor the Alcott children instead. Later the Emerson and the Ellery Channing children were added to her fold and a school and bedroom was created for her in Emerson's barn. Thoreau was hired by Emerson to build a chimney so that the room might be kept warm.[1]

The children in general found her a delightful teacher and Louisa May Alcott boasted in a letter to one of her young friends of a walk they had taken to Flint's Pond:

Now if you won't laugh, I'll tell you something—if you will believe it, Miss F—— and all of us waded across . . . a great big pond a mile long and half a mile wide, we went splashing along making the fishes run like mad before our big claws, when we got to the other side we had a funny time getting on our shoes and unmentionables, and we came tumbling home all wet and

8. Thoreau, *Correspondence*, 191
9 Charles A. Sheffield, *The History of Florence, Mass.* (Florence, 1895), 103
1. Thoreau, *Correspondence*, 195

muddy; but we were happy enough, for we came through the woods bawling and singing like crazy folks.[2]

In October 1846 Miss Ford became ill and was forced to give up
* her teaching. She returned later for a while, but left Concord
* permanently in March 1847. It was six months later she proposed to Thoreau.

Emerson was no more pleased than Thoreau at Miss Ford's unconventional proposal and wrote him, "You tell me in your letter one odious circumstance, which we will dismiss from remembrance henceforward."[3] But the "odious circumstance" was not destined to be so easily forgotten. On February 28, 1849, two years later, Aunt Maria Thoreau wrote a friend:

> By the way, have you heard what a strange story there was about Miss Ford, and Henry, Mrs. Brooks said at the convention, a lady came to her and inquired, if it was true, that Miss F—— had committed, or was going to commit suicide on account of H—— Thoreau, what a ridiculous story this is. When it was told to H—— he made no remark at all, and we cannot find out from him anything about it, for a while, they corresponded, and Sophia said that she recollected one day on the reception of a letter she heard H—— say, he shouldn't answer it, or he must put a stop to this, some such thing she couldn't exactly tell what.[4]

The suicide attempt—if there ever were one—proved abortive. Thoreau's only comment was a remark in his journal three years later:

> Hearing that one with whom I was acquainted had committed suicide, I said I did not know when I had planted the seed of that fact that I should hear of it.[5]

On November 15, 1849, Aunt Maria wrote her friend again in a letter that has just come to light:

---

2. Annie Clark, *The Alcotts in Harvard* (Lancaster, Mass., 1902), 41
3. Thoreau, *Correspondence,* 195
4. Canby, *Thoreau,* 258
5. Thoreau, *Journal,* IV

Do you recollect what I told you of Miss Ford and H—— well I do believe she must be crazy, a month ago H—— had a letter commencing, British steamer fourteen days later—and Sophia says it was a most incoherent letter, she seems to have as much the spirit of reform as ever, telling H—— she hoped he would join that society which is about forming to ascertain the cause of so many dreadful shipwrecks on the ocean where so many lives are sacrificed, and last week while I was at Brother's, Henry had another letter from her which he read to himself and then put into the fire. When I asked to see it, he answered it was secret. I wonder if her friends know anything about these letters they come by mail, tho I believe H—— does not answer them.[6]

Miss Ford eventually regained her balance, but she never lost her love for Thoreau. In the mid-1850s, she worked for a time in Valley Falls, Rhode Island, as the governess for the family of the well-known abolitionist, the Elizabeth Buffum Chaces. The Chace children later remembered her as "a dark-skinned, pudgy featured woman who always remained a spinster," and said she confided to Mrs. Chace her conviction that Thoreau's soul was a twin to hers and that in "the other world" her spirit and his would be united.[7]

Miss Ford kept up her friendship with the Alcott family and through them kept in touch with Thoreau's activities. At the time of Thoreau's death, Louisa May Alcott sent her a long letter with details about the funeral and burial ceremonies.[8] In 1869 Sophia Thoreau wrote Ellen Sewall that she had recently happened upon Miss Ford at a meeting in Boston and had been greeted with the words, "You don't know me, Miss Thoreau."[9] When Channing's biography of Thoreau appeared, Miss Ford purchased a copy and presented it to a friend. Earlier she had acquired a copy of Thoreau's *A Week* for herself.[1] She died in 1885, at the age of eighty-two, and Louisa May Alcott paid tribute to her in the *Woman's Journal:*

6. Maria Thoreau, Letter to Prudence Ward of November, 1849. MS, George L. Davenport, Jr.
7. B. C. Lillie and Arthur Wyman, *Elizabeth Buffum Chace* (Boston, 1914), I, 130–1
8. Louisa May Alcott, *A Sprig of Andromeda* (New York, 1962)
9. Sophia Thoreau, Letter to Ellen Osgood of February 23, 1869. MS, George L. Davenport, Jr.
1. Now owned by Leonard Kleinfeld

Sophia Foord was one of those who, by an upright life, an earnest sympathy in all great reforms and the influence of a fine character, made the world better while here, and left a sweet memory behind her.

She is one of the most prominent figures in my early Concord days, when she kept school for the little Emersons, Channings and Alcotts in the poet's barn. Many a wise lesson she gave us there, though kindergartens were as yet unknown; many a flower-hunt with Thoreau for our guide, many a Sunday service where my father acted as chaplain, and endless revels where young and old played together, while illustrious faces smiled on the pretty festivities under the pines.

The warmth and vigor of her own nature were most attractive, and sincerity made her friendship worth having, and her life-long desire for high thinking and holy living won for her the regard of many admirable persons, of which she was too modest to boast.[2]

It is idle to speculate how Thoreau's career might have been changed had Miss Ford been successful in her assault. But it is interesting to note that she was not the only woman who wanted to ensnare him. Annie Russell Marble, after interviewing many of Thoreau's close friends, has reported that there were *two* women "quite willing, even anxious, to link their lives with his."[3] The identity of that second woman has been lost, but she too was obviously not successful. Thoreau, despite his feminine foes, managed to retain his bachelorhood untarnished to the end.

III

On January 5, 1848, Thoreau delivered a lecture to a large audience at the Concord Lyceum on the excursion he had taken to Mount Katahdin two summers before. Bronson Alcott thought it "a very lively picture" of Thoreau's adventures.[4] Encouraged with its reception, Thoreau worked it over and on March 31, offered it to Greeley for publication in the *Tribune*. Greeley im-

2. Walter Harding, "Thoreau's Feminine Foe," *PMLA*, LXIX (1954), 115
3. Marble, *Thoreau: His Home, Friends and Books*, 218
4. Bronson Alcott, Journals

mediately sent him twenty-five dollars for it, but said he would try to place it elsewhere because it was "too fine for the million."[5] On May 19, describing it as an essay "full of Poetry and Nature," he submitted it to C. Chauncey Burr.[6] It was finally placed in *Sartain's Union Magazine,* where it was published as "Ktaadn" in five installments from July through November 1848. John Sartain paid Greeley seventy-five dollars for it, and Greeley sent twenty-five dollars along to Thoreau.

The Katahdin piece is a woodsy, outdoors essay filled with the odor of pine trees and the rushing waters of mountain streams. Thoreau concludes:

It is a country full of evergreen trees, of mossy silver birches, and watery maples, the ground dotted with insipid small, red berries, and strewn with damp and moss-grown rocks,—a country diversified with innumerable lakes and rapid streams, peopled with trout and various species of *leucisci,* with salmon, shad and pickerel, and other fishes; the forest resounding at rare intervals with the note of the chickadee, the blue jay, and the woodpecker, the scream of the fish hawk and the eagle, the laugh of the loon, and the whistle of ducks along the solitary streams; at night, with the hooting of owls and howling of wolves; in summer, swarming with myriads of black flies and mosquitoes, more formidable than wolves to the white man. Such is the home of the moose, the bear, the caribou, the wolf, the beaver, and the Indian. Who shall describe the inexpressible tenderness and immortal life of the grim forest, where Nature, though it be midwinter, is ever in her spring, where the moss-grown and decaying trees are not old, but seem to enjoy a perpetual youth; and blissful, innocent Nature, like a serene infant, is too happy to make a noise, except by a few tinkling, lisping birds and trickling rills?[7]

Emerson reading over the essay decided it was the first piece of American literature he had seen in ten years that was worth binding.[8] But Thoreau, with a more cynical eye, simply noted sixty-six typographical errors in the printing.[9]

---

5. Thoreau, *Correspondence,* 218
6. *Thoreau Society Bulletin,* LXII (1958), 3
7. Thoreau, *Writings,* III, 89–90
8. Emerson, *Journals,* VII, 526
9. His marked copy is in the Berg Collection

To help call the essay to the attention of the reading public, Greeley ran four columns of extracts in his November 17, 1848, *Tribune* and another column and a half on the 18th. He remarked on "all the freshness and odor of the pine-forests about them" and called the conclusion "as fine a piece of unrhymed poetry as we have ever read." In January 1849 *The Student,* "a Family magazine and monthly School reader," ran another long excerpt, with "The Backwoods of Maine" as title, a watered-down vocabulary, and simplified sentence structure for juvenile readers. Whether the article was pirated or arranged for by Greeley is not known. The essay was not published in book form until 1864, after Thoreau's death, when it, along with his other accounts of excursions into the wilderness of Maine, was gathered into the volume *The Maine Woods.*

Although Greeley had given his public stamp of approval to the Katahdin essay, privately he warned Thoreau that if he wished to be published in the periodicals, he should write shorter pieces and suggested specifically that he write an essay on the literary life. Thoreau, never very amenable to suggestions, replied that he was too busy working on his books. Greeley in turn answered that it was more important for his fame to get into the periodicals, "ten years hence will do for publishing books."[1] Once more Thoreau replied in the negative and Greeley countered with the suggestion that he send along some passages from his books for advanced publication, but it was some time before Thoreau got around to accepting even that invitation.

IV

On March 14, 1848, Bronson Alcott in conversation with Thoreau asked "if it were not proof of our inefficiency that we had not as yet attracted some fine soul, some maid from the farmer's hearth or youth from farm or workshop, to our houses, and there found a proof undeniable of having a positive and real existence here in this world."[2] Certainly it was true that Emerson had at-

1. Thoreau, *Correspondence,* 232
2. Bronson Alcott, *Journals,* 204

racted disciples by the dozens if not hundreds, a constant stream of cranks and geniuses beating a path to his door, while Thoreau attracted none—although Emerson was by now well known around the country and Thoreau was not. It was an odd coincidence that Alcott should have made that remark just then, for only a few days later Thoreau found in his mail a letter from Harrison Gray Otis Blake of Worcester, Massachusetts, who asked him to "speak to me in this hour as you are prompted."[3] And thus he acquired his first major disciple and began the most important correspondence of his life.

Thoreau had known Blake, slightly at least, for many years. Blake had been two years ahead of him at Harvard and then had been a member of the Harvard Divinity School class that had invited Emerson to speak at their graduation, the occasion for the famed "Divinity School Address." For a time he held a pastorate in Milford, New Hampshire, but after hearing Emerson's address, he began to question some of the dogmas of the church and ended by resigning his pastorate. He taught school for a while near Boston and then at a private girls' school in his native Worcester, where he spent the rest of his long life. Thoreau occasionally met Blake at Emerson's, for he visited Concord frequently. But theirs was hardly more than a nodding acquaintance until the spring of 1848, when Blake happened upon Thoreau's essay on Aulus Persius Flaccus in an old copy of *The Dial*. Suddenly he was struck with an awareness of Thoreau's genius, sat down and wrote him the letter, and, as Emerson laughingly complained, "never came near my house again."

In the remaining fourteen years of his life, Thoreau wrote at least forty-nine letters to Blake, most of them many pages in length, the longest and most philosophical letters he ever wrote. Typical is a paragraph from the first of them, dated March 27, 1848:

> My actual life is a fact in view of which I have no occasion to congratulate myself, but for my faith and aspiration I have respect. It is from these that I speak. Every man's position is in fact too simple to be described. I have sworn no oath. I have no designs on society—or nature—or God. I am simply what I am, or I begin to be that. I *live* in the *present*. I only remember

---

3. Thoreau, *Correspondence*, 213

the past—and anticipate the future. I love to live, I love reform better than its modes. There is no history of how bad became better. I believe something, and there is nothing else but that. . . . I know that the enterprise is worthy—I know that things work well. I have heard no bad news.[4]

Blake recognized their value and told Bronson Alcott as early as 1859 that he was considering editing them for publication with notes and comments.[5] In later years when autograph collectors asked him for the manuscripts, he was exceedingly generous, but always took care to make verbatim transcriptions of the letters, no matter how trivial, before giving them away. The letters offer, as well might be imagined, an unparalleled opportunity for an examination of Thoreau's philosophical views since Blake knew the right questions to ask. However it must also be admitted that at times they border on the tedious, for Blake seemed to bring out the preacher in Thoreau as no one else did. Blake was conscientious to the point of being humorless. Emerson used to joke that he was the kind of man who would even return a borrowed umbrella. And for many years a story circulated at Harvard that Blake, after greeting one of his classmates at a reunion with the words, "Very glad to see you," went back in all seriousness and corrected the phrase to "glad" without the "very."[6] Fortunately most of the time Thoreau was able to ignore that side of Blake.

Whatever Blake's failings, he was unquestionably one of Thoreau's most ardent admirers and most devoted disciples. He gathered around him in Worcester a small circle of friends including Theo Brown, Thomas Wentworth Higginson, Seth Rogers, Henry Harmon Chamberlin, David Atwood Wasson, and Edward Everett Hale, and whenever he received a letter from Thoreau he would send a messenger around to each bearing an invitation to join him at breakfast the next morning at his home at 3 Bowdoin Street to hear extracts from the letter. Later, as we shall see, when Blake learned that Thoreau occasionally offered himself as a lecturer, he saw to it that he was regularly invited to lecture in Worcester, even if it meant making all the arrangements, including

---

4. Ibid. 216
5. Alcott, Journal
6. Daniel Gregory Mason, "Harrison G. O. Blake, '35, and Thoreau," *Harvard Monthly*, XXVI (1898), 94

rounding up an audience, himself. And frequently he went to Concord to visit Thoreau.

Blake in later years admitted that their relationship was a strangely impersonal one. He said that Thoreau's physical appearance did not interest him and that when together they rarely if ever talked of personal matters.[7] Their conversation was conducted on as high and philosophical a level as their correspondence. Nonetheless Blake's discipleship must have done much to sustain and encourage Thoreau through those long years when little other concrete evidence of fame came to him. Thoreau might occasionally quip that his lack of fame gave him a privacy that he relished, but deep down underneath there must have been a wondering if recognition would ever come.

V

In the late summer of 1848 Thoreau and Ellery Channing took another of their brief excursions together, this time a four-day walking trip through southern New Hampshire. At Tyngsborough, where they stopped at a farmhouse to ask for water, Thoreau recognized the same bucket he had seen there in 1839, and when he pointed it out to the housewife, she leaped to the conclusion that he was a peddler who had been traveling the roads the intervening nine years. At Dunstable, wishing to examine a copy of Charles J. Fox's *History of the Old Township of Dunstable,* which had been published only two years before, he amused Channing by simply knocking at the door of the best house in town and asking the young lady who made her appearance, if she had the book in question and if he might consult it. Finding it particularly interesting to read and realizing that it would be helpful in writing up his 1839 voyage on the rivers, he then asked if he might buy it. When the young lady recovered from her surprise, she agreed, and after he produced a coin from his wallet, Thoreau went on his way rejoicing with the book under his arm.[8]

---

7. Henry Salt, *The Life of Henry David Thoreau* (London, 1890), 144–6
8. Channing, *Thoreau, the Poet-Naturalist,* 26–7

At Moore's Falls, they stopped to lunch beside the rapids and ate, as they boasted, crusts of bread that the farmers had refused, hen's eggs for which they had waited until they were laid, and hasty pudding boiled on the rocks amidst the roar of the waters, for while their appetites were great, their means were small, and they "studied economy as well as the landscape."[9] Climbing Mount Uncannunuc, they were able to view not only Agamenticus Hill on the Maine coast, but Gunstock, Kearsarge, and the dim peaks of the White Mountains in the distance to the north. It was Sunday and on their way to the mountaintop they were passed by a minister driving his horse to the meetinghouse, who, learning of their destination, reproved them for "breaking the Lord's fourth commandment" and enumerated for them in sepulchral tones the disasters that had befallen him whenever he had done ordinary work on the Sabbath.[1] But dismissing his warnings as poppycock and assuring themselves that they would have gone farther than he to hear a true word spoken on that or any other day, they continued happily along their way. Afterward they toured through Goffstown and Hooksett. On their way home they spent a night at Caleb Harriman's tavern in Hampstead and, continuing on through Plaistow and Haverhill, returned to Concord. Aunt Maria Thoreau was not pleased with the adventure. She complained, "I wish [Thoreau] could find something better to do than walking off every now and then."[2]

There was no question but that Thoreau did have financial problems to face. In late July 1848 Emerson had returned from Europe and so on the 30th Thoreau moved back to the Texas house with his parents. That fall he tried various odd jobs—whitewashing, papering, budding, hoeing, and wood sawing—and picked up a little money from each.[3] His father had suffered a severe financial blow a few months earlier when the steam mill in Concord that made the wooden part of his pencils burned down—apparently the work of an incendiary—and he lost four to five

9. Thoreau, *The First and Last Journeys*, I, xxiii
1. Thoreau, *Writings*, I, 76–7; Thoreau, *The First and Last Journeys*, I, xxii
2. Maria Thoreau, Letter to Prudence Ward of September, 1847. MS, George L. Davenport, Jr.
3. Henry David Thoreau [Financial notes], Huntington Manuscript 13182

hundred dollars' worth of uninsured materials. Thoreau worked some in the pencil factory to help him recoup his loss, but he was finding factory work less and less to his taste.

A much more congenial source of income, he discovered, was surveying, and he tried his hand more and more at it. Deciding to turn professional, he made up a list of fourteen books to study, had his compass repaired, acquired a surveyor, a blank journal, and some drawing paper, and inquired about the prices of a drawing instrument.[4]

To drum up more surveying business, Thoreau drew up a broadside and had it printed:

LAND SURVEYING Of all kinds, according to the best methods known; the necessary data supplied, in order that the boundaries of Farms may be accurately described in Deeds; *Woods* lotted off distinctly and according to a regular plan; Roads laid out, &c., &c. Distinct and accurate Plans of Farms furnished, with the buildings thereon, of any size, and with a scale of feet attached, to accompany the Farm Book, so that the land may be laid out in a winter evening.

Areas warranted accurate within almost any degree of exactness, and the Variation of the Compass given, so that the lines can be run again. Apply to Henry D. Thoreau.[5]

By the fall of 1849 he was doing enough surveying to justify purchasing a notebook to keep his records straight; he labeled it "Field Notes of Surveys made by Henry D. Thoreau Since November 1849."[6] But for a time, since his compass was out of order again, he borrowed both compass and chain of Cyrus Hubbard and did not acquire good ones of his own until the spring of 1850.

He also discovered still another source of income—the lecture platform. The lyceum movement which had so long been conducted on a purely amateur basis was gradually becoming professional. More and more speakers were finding that they could acquire a reasonable living by lecturing from town to town. Emerson

---

4. Kenneth Walter Cameron, *The Transcendentalists and Minerva,* (Hartford, 1958), II, 374
5. John D. Gordon, "A Thoreau Handbill," *Bulletin of the New York Public Library,* LIX (1955), 254
6. Kenneth Walter Cameron, *The Transcendental Climate* (Hartford, 1962), II, 413 ff.

had been doing it for some years now and Thoreau saw no reason that he should not try his hand at it too. What was perhaps even more important than the money, it would not only give him a greater opportunity to test out his writings before he put them into print, but it would also serve, he hoped, to create a market for his works when they were published. Thoreau had for years been speaking at the Concord Lyceum, but there, like all his fellow townsmen, he donated his services. Now he wanted to go outside of Concord where he could charge for his lectures.

Emerson, as usual, was the first to help. In the fall of 1848 he did his best to persuade James Freeman Clarke to hire Thoreau to lecture in Boston, assuring him that his audience would prize Thoreau "as a quite new cordial."[7] But Clarke, interested only in hearing Emerson himself lecture, ignored the suggestion. Then on October 21, 1848, Nathaniel Hawthorne, now the corresponding secretary of the Salem Lyceum, wrote to offer Thoreau twenty dollars to lecture before that group. Thoreau immediately accepted though he must have been chagrined to find himself billed in the *Salem Observer* of November 4 as "Henry S. Thoreau of Concord, New Hampshire."[8]

The lecture he delivered on November 22, 1848, in Salem was "Student Life in New England, Its Economy," an early version of the "Economy" chapter of Walden. Mrs. Hawthorne, for one, was delighted. She thought the lecture "so enchanting, such a revelation of nature in all its exquisite details of wood-thrushes, squirrels, sunshine, mists and shadows, fresh, vernal odors, pine tree ocean melodies" that her ear "rang with music" and she "seemed to have been wandering through copse and dingle." Thoreau, she thought, had "risen above all his arrogance of manner" and was "as gentle, simple, ruddy, and meek as all geniuses should be." His "great blue eyes," she confessed, fairly outshone and "put into shade" his long nose, which she once thought "must make him uncomely forever."[9]

The reviewer for the *Salem Observer* was equally pleased and

---

7. Emerson, *Letters*, IV, 119
8. Hubert H. Hoeltje, "Thoreau as Lecturer," *New England Quarterly*, XIX, (1946), 486
9. Rose Hawthorne Lathrop, *Memories of Hawthorne* (Boston, 1897), 92–3

reported on November 25, 1848, that while the lecture was "sufficiently *Emersonian* to have come from the great philosopher himself," and that "in thought, style, and delivery, the similarity was equally obvious," it "furnished ample proof of being a native product, by affording all the charm of an original." It was, he thought, "done in an admirable manner, in a strain of exquisite humor, with a strong under current of delicate satire against the follies of the times," with observations "sufficiently queer to keep the audience in almost constant mirth, and sufficiently wise and new to afford many good practical hints and precepts." The performance, he agreed, had "created quite a sensation."

On his way home, on November 23, at Hawthorne's invitation Thoreau stopped off in Cambridge to have dinner with him, Longfellow, and Ellery Channing at Craigie House. Hawthorne had warned Longfellow in advance that while Thoreau was a man of thought and originality "well worth knowing," he had a "certain iron-pokerishness,—an uncompromising stiffness,—in his mental character, which . . . grows rather wearisome on close and frequent acquaintance."[1] But Thoreau was no stranger to his host, having not only attended some of his classes at Harvard, but having had dinner with him at Emerson's only the week before.

The Gloucester, Massachusetts, Lyceum, hearing word of Thoreau's success in Salem, immediately invited him to repeat his lecture for them on December 20. On the 23rd the *Gloucester Telegraph* reported:

The lecturer gave a very strange account of the state of affairs at Concord. In the shops and offices were large numbers of human beings suffering tortures to which those of the Bramins [sic] are mere pastimes. We cannot say whether this was in jest or in earnest. If a joke, it was a most excruciating one—if true, the attention of the Home Missionary Society should be directed to that quarter forthwith.

The lecturer spoke at considerable length of society, men, manners, travelling, clothing, etc., often "bringing down the house" by his quaint remarks. Now and then there was a hard hit at the vices and follies of mankind, which "told" with considerable effect. There were hits, too, not remarkably hard. . . .

1. F. B. Sanborn, *Hawthorne and His Friends* (Cedar Rapids, Ia., 1908), 28–9

We believe that concerning this lecture there are various opinions in the community. With all deference to the sagacity of those who can see a great deal where there is little to be seen—hear much where there is hardly anything to be heard—perceive a wonderful depth of meaning where in fact nothing is really meant, we would take the liberty of expressing the opinion that a certain ingredient to a good lecture was, in some instances, wanting.

Gloucester, unlike Salem, had had enough of Thoreau. There is no record of his ever having been invited to lecture there again.

But Gloucester's lack of enthusiasm did not stop him. On January 3, 1849, he gave the Concord Lyceum audience another free lecture, "White Beans & Walden Pond," apparently a draft of the "Beanfield" chapter of *Walden*. Then on February 19, Hawthorne invited him to give another lecture in Salem and suggested either a continuation of his earlier talk or one on the American Indian. On the 28th he read there another section of his *Walden* manuscript, apparently the chapters "Reading" and "Sounds," but with little of the success of his earlier lecture. The *Salem Observer* on March 3 reported: "The diversity of opinion is quite amusing. Some persons are unwilling to speak of his lecture as any better than 'tom-foolery and nonsense,' while others think they perceived beneath the outward sense of his remarks, something wise and valuable. . . . This lecture . . . on the whole we thought less successful than the former one."

Meanwhile Thoreau had accepted an invitation to speak in Portland, Maine, on March 21, for twenty dollars, and the *Eastern Argus* on the 23rd remarked: "The lecture was unique, original, comical, and high-falutin. It kept the audience wide awake, and most pleasantly excited for nearly two hours. . . . It was like the dashing out of a comet that had broken loose from its orbit—hitting here and there, a gentle rap at this folly, and a severe one at that—but all in good nature." The Bangor Lyceum, in turn, offered him twenty-five dollars to extend his tour and lecture for them. Thinking that it would offer a good opportunity to run up the Chesuncook River on the ice and to watch the logs running after the ice broke up, Thoreau replied that he would come if they would arrange for two lectures rather than one. That, however, they were unwilling to do and the plan fell through.

Horace Greeley, hearing of Thoreau's lecture tour, decided to give him another puff and so on April 2 ran an editorial in the pages of the *Tribune:*

Henry D. Thoreau of Concord, Mass. has recently been lecturing on "Life in the Woods," in Portland and elsewhere. There is not a young man in the land—and very few old ones—who would not profit by an attentive hearing of that lecture. Mr. Thoreau is a young student, who has imbibed (or rather refused to stifle) the idea that a man's soul is better worth living for than his body. Accordingly, he has built him a house ten by fifteen feet in a piece of unfrequented woods by the side of a pleasant little lakelet, where he devotes his days to study and reflection. . . . If all our young men would but hear this lecture, we think some among them would feel less strongly impelled either to come to New-York or go to California.

Concord was proud that one of its own had achieved such recognition in the nation's leading newspaper and the *Yeoman's Gazette* commented:

OUR TOWNSMAN—MR. THOREAU.

All the good things which the Tribune says of this gentleman are richly deserved. But the Tribune is mistaken in supposing he still continues this course of life, or that he continued in it four years. Mr. Thoreau lived upon the banks of our beautiful Walden Pond for two years, where he wrote some of the most interesting and instructive lectures we have ever heard, and where he became as "conversant with beans" as any man living, because he cultivated them extensively. He is a gentleman [sic] of rare attainments, and now has one or two works in press which all who have heard him lecture are anxious to see.[2]

(It should be recorded that not everyone in Concord was as enthusiastic about Thoreau. Priscilla Rice Edes, one of the dissenters, in her reminiscences, has said:

"David Henry" did not care whether he was decently clothed, or not. The ladies of the charitable society proposed to make

---

2. Clipping in the collection of Raymond Adams

[239]

him some cotton shirts, but thot it best, first to ask his mother if it would be agreeable to him. Dear Mrs. Thoreau at the next meeting said, "I told my David Henry that you would like to make him some unbleached cotton shirts; he said 'unbleached mother, unbleached. Yes, that strikes my ears pleasantly; I think they may make me some.'" A practical farmer's wife with no sentiment said in an aside, "Strike his ears pleasantly, indeed. I guess they will strike his back pleasantly when he gets them on."[3])

The *Youth's Companion,* liking Greeley's precepts, ran his whole editorial in their issue of July 19, 1849, for the edification of their youth. But at least one of Greeley's readers was not so impressed and sent a protest which was published in the *Tribune* on April 7:

I notice in your paper of this morning a strong commendation of one Mr. Thoreau for going out into the woods and living in a hut all by himself at the rate of about $45 per annum, in order to illustrate the value of the soul. Having always found in The Tribune a friend of sociability and neighborly helping-each-other-along, I felt a little surprised at seeing such a performance held up as an example for the young men of this country, and supposed I must have mistaken the sense of your article. Accordingly I called in my wife, Mrs. Thorough, and we studied it over together, and came to the conclusion that you really believed the Concord hermit had done a fine thing. Now I am puzzled, and write in a friendly way to ask for a little light on this peculiar philosophy. Mrs. T. is more clear in her mind than I am. She will have it that the young man is either a whimsy or else a good-for-nothing, selfish, crab-like sort of chap, who tries to shirk the duties whose hearty and honest discharge is the only thing that in her view entitles a man to be regarded as a good example. She declares that nobody has a right to live for himself alone, away from the interests, the affections, and the sufferings of his kind. Such a way of going on, she says, is not living, but a cold and snailish kind of existence, which, as she maintains, is both infernal and infernally stupid.

Yours, truly,   *Timothy Thorough*

Le Roy Place, April 2, 1849.

---

3. Raymond Adams, "Thoreau and His Neighbors," *Thoreau Society Bulletin,* LXIV (1953), 2

But Greeley was not daunted. He replied immediately, in the same issue:

> Mr. Thorough is indeed in a fog—in fact, we suspect there is a mistake in his name, and that he must have been changed at nurse for another boy whose true name was Shallow. Nobody has proposed or suggested that it becomes everybody to go off into the woods, each build himself a hut and live hermit-like, on the vegetable products of his very moderate labor. But there is a large class of young men who aspire to Mental Culture through Study, Reading, Reflection, &c. These are too apt to sacrifice their proper independence in the pursuit of their object—to run in debt, throw themselves on the tender mercies of some patron, relative, Education Society, or something of the sort, or to descend into the lower deep of tapping out a thin volume of very thin poems, to be inflicted on a much-enduring public or to importune some one for a sub-Editorship or the like. Now it does seem to us that Mr. Thoreau has set all his brother aspirants to self-culture, a very wholesome example, and shown them how, by chastening their physical appetites, they may preserve their proper independence without starving their souls. When they shall have conned that lesson, we trust, with Mr. Thorough otherwise Shallow's permission, he will give them another.
>
> *Ed. Trib.*

Such banter, Greeley was fully aware, would get Thoreau's name before the public and create an audience for him. And that at the moment was Greeley's aim.

H. G. O. Blake had also learned of Thoreau's lecture tour and invited him to give a series of three in Worcester. The first was given in Brinley Hall in the City Hall on April 20. On the 25th the *Worcester Palladium*, after admitting that Thoreau's account of his life at Walden Pond was "witty, sarcastic, and amusing," went on, however, to berate him:

> Such philosophers illustrate the absurdities the human mind is capable of. What would a forest of them be good for? Nothing but curiosities for people to look after, as they pay their shilling to see a menagerie. They are watches without any pointers; their springs and wheels are well adjusted, and perform good service;

but nobody is the wiser for it, as they do not tell the time of day. They are a train of carwheels; they run well, and in good time, but can carry no passengers or luggage. A wheel-barrow, with an Irishman for its vitals, renders the world a far better service.

He fared better, however, in the *Worcester Spy,* for not only did they urge their readers on the 26th that his second lecture in Brinley Hall on the 27th would be "intellectual entertainment that should not be neglected," but on the 27th they added that they would be "pleased to see a full house for the occasion." The third lecture, "Beans" (probably the "Beanfield" chapter of *Walden* again), attracted an audience of about a hundred.

Aunt Maria Thoreau, having heard about the *Palladium* account, was sure that Worcester had had enough of her nephew and confessed that she was as disgusted with what he had to say as the *Palladium* had been.[4] But despite her forebodings and the newspaper's harsh words, Thoreau, as we shall see, was invited time and time again to return. Thanks to Blake's enthusiasm he was invited to lecture there more frequently than any other place outside Concord.

---

4. Maria Thoreau, Letter to Prudence Ward of May, 1849. MS, George L. Davenport, Jr.

CHAPTER THIRTEEN
(1845–1849)

I

FOR NEARLY ten years Thoreau had been working on the manuscript of his book about the voyage he and his brother John had taken on the Concord and Merrimack rivers in 1839. It was on June 11, 1840, that he first began expanding his original journey notes, perhaps thinking to make a short travel essay such as his "Walk to Wachusset" out of it.[1] Then, with John's death in 1842, his motives changed. Now it was to be a full-length book and a memorial tribute to John. Until he went out to Walden, the world, as he said, was just too much with him, and he got little done. But there, in a tremendous surge of creative energy, as we have seen, he went to work on *A Week on the Concord and Merrimack Rivers* and *Walden* too.

In the summer of 1845, Evert Duyckinck approached Nathaniel Hawthorne on behalf of a new series of "American Books" that his firm of Wiley & Putnam were establishing. They had determined to launch this new series as a counter to the overwhelming domination of English authors on the American book market and they asked Hawthorne not only if he would contribute a volume, but if he knew of any promising young authors who might have something to offer. Hawthorne immediately suggested Thoreau but warned Duyckinck that he might offer difficulties:

> As for Thoreau, there is one chance in a thousand that he might write a most excellent and readable book; but I should be sorry to take the responsibility, either towards you or him, of stirring him up to write anything. . . . He is the most unmalleable fellow alive—the most tedious, tiresome, and intoler-

---

1. Thoreau, *Journal,* I, 136

able—the narrowest and most notional—and yet, true as all this is, he has great qualities of intellect and character. The only way, however, in which he could ever approach the popular mind, would be by writing a book of simple observation of nature, somewhat in the vein of White's *History of Selborne*.[2]

Thoreau, however, was not ready then to submit his manuscript. Nearly two years later on March 12, 1847, he had Emerson write Duyckinck:

> Mr. Henry D. Thoreau of this town has just completed a book of extraordinary merit, which he wishes to publish. It purports to be an account of "An Excursion on the Concord & Merrimack Rivers," which he made some time ago in company with his brother. . . . I have represented to Mr. Thoreau, that his best course would undoubtedly be, to send the book to you, to be printed by Wiley & Putnam, that it may have a good edition and wide publishing.
>
> This book has many merits. It will be as attractive to *lovers of nature,* in every sense, that is, to naturalists, and to poets, as Isaak Walton. It will be attractive to scholars for its excellent literature, & to all thoughtful persons for its originality & profoundness. The narrative of the little voyage, though faithful, is a very slender thread for such big beads & ingots as are strung on it. It is really a book of the results of studies of years.
>
> Would you like to print this book into your American Library? It is quite ready, & the whole can be sent you at once. It has never yet been offered to any publisher. . . . I am only desirous that you should propose to him good terms, & give his book the great advantage of being known which your circulation ensures.[3]

Duyckinck replied immediately that he would be willing to consider the manuscript, but it was May 28 before Thoreau got around to mailing it. There were corrections and revisions he found that he wanted to make and they took time. And Duyckinck had the manuscript only two weeks when Thoreau asked for it back again to make still further corrections. He returned it to them on July 3 and Duyckinck made a favorable recommendation to Wiley &

2. MS, New York Public Library
3. Ralph Waldo Emerson, *Letters* (New York, 1939), III, 384

Putnam, who in turn wrote Thoreau that they would be happy to publish it—but only at Thoreau's, not their own expense.[4]

Bronson Alcott had listened to Thoreau read a number of passages from the book, and he assured Thoreau that it should easily become a popular book. "The book is purely American, fragrant with the lives of New England woods and streams, and could have been written nowhere else,"[5] Alcott noted in his journal. Emerson too was equally encouraging that the book would find a ready market: Wiley & Putnam should not be so hesitant, he thought. Other publishers would show a more lively interest. And to make good his words, Emerson wrote off to his friend William Henry Furness to ask him to approach the various Philadelphia publishers. Furness tried his best but won only protests that they already had more manuscripts on hand than they could handle.[6]

Thoreau himself sent his manuscript off to James Munroe & Co., a Boston publisher that had brought out several of Emerson's books, and when they made an offer similar to that of Wiley & Putnam, he countered with an offer to reimburse them for half the net cost remaining six months after publication. But that offer they turned down. He next asked William Emerson to approach some of the New York publishers on his behalf.[7] The judge tried Harpers but with no success. Then Crosby & Nichols, like Munroe and Wiley & Putnam, offered to publish it if Thoreau would underwrite the cost. Even though Emerson urged him to accept such terms, telling him he would surely get his money back, for he thought the book bound to sell, Thoreau was completely discouraged and announced that he had given up all idea of attempting to publish the book in the near future. He wanted to revise it heavily.

The thus enforced delay turned out to be fortunate after all—even Thoreau eventually admitted that, for out of it grew a much stronger book. Early in January 1848 he wrote his memorable essay "Friendship," and after reading it aloud to Bronson Alcott,

---

4. H. H. F[urness], *Records of a Lifelong Friendship* (Boston, 1910), 60–1; Thoreau, *Correspondence*, 191
5. Bronson Alcott, *Journals*, 213–14
6. F[urness], *Records of a Lifelong Friendship*, 60–1, 63, 66
7. Emerson, *Letters*, III, 413 n.

who thought it superior to anything he had ever heard, he inserted it into the *Week* manuscript. All spring, summer and fall he worked on the manuscript and assured Greeley, when he inquired, "My book is swelling again under my hands."[8] Finally in February of 1849 he wrote the new Boston publishing house of Ticknor & Co. to offer them *A Week* and assure them that he would soon have a second book, *Walden,* ready too. They replied that they were not interested in the first book but might be willing to publish the second in an edition of one thousand copies at a ten per cent royalty. When Thoreau insisted that they publish *A Week* first, they said they would if he would put up $450 in advance for a thousand copies, half of them bound, half in sheets.

The $450 dollars might as well have been ten thousand, for Thoreau had no such resources available. Reluctantly he turned to James Munroe & Co. once more. They now offered to print *A Week* and let Thoreau pay the costs out of sales so long as he would guarantee that they eventually receive the full amount.[9] Once *A Week* was out, they would follow it with *Walden.* When Thoreau accepted their offer, Aunt Maria Thoreau was unhappy. Parts of the book sounded to her like blasphemy and she feared no one would persuade him to leave those parts out. Mrs. Thoreau thought he was "putting things into his book that never ought to be put there." Even Sophia Thoreau, she claimed, was disturbed about it.[1] Aunt Maria feared too the book would never sell well enough to pay the expenses and she didn't see how Thoreau could reimburse the publisher.[2] But Thoreau went ahead despite her worries. He began to receive galley proofs on March 16 and returned the last sheet to the printer on April 30.[3] The typesetting had been deplorable; he had to make more than a thousand corrections.

Thoreau went in to Boston on May 26 and picked up his author's copies. The book was officially published on May 30, but with only the meagerest amount of advance publicity—a brief

---

8. Thoreau, *Correspondence,* 225
9. Thoreau, *Journal,* V, 521
1. Maria Thoreau, Letter to Prudence Ward of February 28, 1849. MS, George L. Davenport, Jr.
2. Maria Thoreau, Letter to Prudence Ward of March 15, 1849. MS, George L. Davenport, Jr.
3. Maria Thoreau, Letter to Prudence Ward, May 1, 1849. MS, George L. Davenport, Jr.

note in the *Literary World* for May 19 and another in the *Boston Daily Advertiser* on the 30th. Munroe printed one thousand copies, but bound only 450 (and since those 450 exist in eight different bindings, it is apparent that they did not bind even that many at first).[4] The title page ostentatiously announced that it was being published simultaneously also by George Putnam of New York, Lindsay and Blackiston of Philadelphia, and John Chapman of London, but that was merely Munroe's euphemistic way of announcing that these others had promised to carry a few copies of his edition in stock.

Although H. M. Tomlinson once spoke of *A Week on the Concord and Merrimack Rivers* as the best of all travel books, few other critics have been as generous in their criticism. Ostensibly it is an account of the two-week boat and hiking trip Thoreau took with his brother John in the late summer of 1839. (The one week of mountain climbing is covered in a few connective paragraphs.) It is also a memorial tribute to John; although, in the tradition of the elegy, it nowhere mentions him directly by name.

The voyage is narrated in an introductory essay, "Concord River," and in seven chapters, each devoted to one day of the week beginning with Saturday. The narrative occupies perhaps forty per cent of the book and tells fairly straightforwardly how they traveled, what they saw, where they camped, and some of the history of the area they were passing through. Had only this portion of the book been published, it is conceivable that it would have been a success. It is pleasant summer reading, written competently and smoothly. It would not have been a great book, but it might have been popular.

The other sixty per cent of the book however has little connection with the travel narrative. It is a collection of essays, poems, translations, and quotations, dumped in like plums into a pudding, but there is less artistic justification for their presence. Occasionally, as with the extended essay on the fish of New England rivers, the connection with the narrative can be seen. Sometimes Thoreau endeavors to manufacture a connection, even though a tenuous one, as when he introduces his comments on religion into the Sunday chapter. But at other times he drops all

---

4. Albert E. Lownes, Letter to Walter Harding, July 8, 1948

pretense of any connection and simply announces that he will deliver some remarks on such and such a subject.

A great many of these interpolations and digressions were culled from Thoreau's various contributions to *The Dial*—the poems, the translations, the remarks on Chaucer, and so on. A few, such as his remarks on Raleigh, were lecture notes that he had never succeeded in getting into print before. Most of them are good writing in their place, but their place is obviously not in the midst of the narrative of a voyage on the Concord and Merrimack rivers. And a few, particularly the comments on religion, were bound to antagonize the more conservative readers of his day just as they had offended Thoreau's aunt.

The first review to appear in print was probably that in the New York *Tribune* for June 12, 1849, and, if Thoreau is correct, it was written by Horace Greeley himself.[5] The review was printed on the front page and was nearly two full columns long—a remarkable notice for the first book of a virtually unknown writer, but from the very beginning it was obvious the reviewer could muster up only a lukewarm enthusiasm. He praised it as "A really new book—a fresh, original, thoughtful work." Yet he added: "His philosophy which is the Pantheistic egotism vaguely characterized as Transcendental, does *not* delight us. It seems second-hand, imitative, often exaggerated—a bad specimen of a dubious and dangerous school." And after quoting many examples of what he considered the book's dangerous pantheism, he closed his review with a challenge: "Albeit we love not theological controversy, we proffer our columns to Mr. Thoreau, should he see fit to answer. . . . We would have preferred to pass the theme in silence, but our admiration of his book and our reprehension of its Pantheism forbade that course. May we not hope that he will reconsider his too rashly expressed notions on this head?" But the only reply that Thoreau ever gave was a few sentences jotted down in the privacy of his journal nearly three years later: "Horace Greeley found some fault with me to the world because I presumed to speak of the New Testament using my own words and thoughts, and challenged me to a controversy. The one thought I had was that it would give me real pleasure to know that he loved it as sin-

---

5. Thoreau, *Journal*, III, 257

cerely and enlightenedly as I did; but I felt that he did not care so much as I."[6]

Other reviews soon appeared. In July 1849 *Holden's Dollar Magazine* gave it a long paragraph and called it "a rare work in American literature." It said that while "some people have compared it with Emerson's essays, . . . in style and habits of thought they are quite unlike, and we think that Mr. Thoreau may be safely judged, in reference to his own merits, without comparing his name with Emerson's. . . . We advise our readers to procure it. It is full of fine thoughts and pleasant descriptions of nature."

On July 26 an anonymous reviewer in the *New Hampshire Patriot,* a Concord newspaper, thought it "a remarkable volume and its author a remarkable man . . . The author . . . is a man of thought—retired from the busy scenes of life, he turns the mental eye inward and endeavors to read the mysterious page of his own soul. Again looking upon objects around which meet his senses, he reads lessons of wisdom. . . . The thread of his narrative is very simple, but upon it he has strung pearls. . . . On closing the book we find ourselves in love with the author, satisfied with ourselves and at peace with the world." And then apparently recalling the *Tribune* review, he added, "We do not by any means endorse the author's Pantheism, but will let it stand or fall for itself."

In September *Godey's Lady's Book,* after asserting that undoubtedly its author was John Greenleaf Whittier writing under a pseudonym, decided that it was a sort of hammock book, "just the book to read in the idleness of summer, when wishing to enjoy the pleasures of journeying, without the inconvenience which the actual packing up and going off in hot steamboats and dusty cars occasion."

On September 22 the Duyckinck brothers' New York *Literary World* devoted two full pages to the book. For the most part, the review was friendly: "[Thoreau] loves nature, of which he is a careful observer, relishes good books, estimates at their worth the manly qualities of work and endurance. We have read his book backwards, if he is not kind and humane. He has stored his mind with the fruits of much reading and reflection. He is patient of the most minute investigations of insects and fishes;

6. Ibid.

can be reverent over an arrow head turned up from an old Indian field, or respect a voracious pickerel newly taken from the river which runs through it." But like so many others, the reviewer balked at the apparent heresies in the book and concluded: "Yet, when this writer, so just, observant, and considerate, approaches what civilized men are accustomed to hold the most sacred of all, he can express himself in a flippant style which he would disdain to employ towards a mussel or a tadpole. . . . We are not so rash or uninformed in the ways of the world as to presume to give counsel to a transcendentalist, so we offer no advice; but we may remark as a curious matter of speculation to be solved in the future —the probability or improbability of Mr. Thoreau's ever approaching nearer to the common sense or common wisdom of mankind."

Emerson was anxious to see Thoreau's book reviewed in the new *Massachusetts Quarterly Review,* but when Theodore Parker, the editor, asked him to do the review himself, he begged off, saying that he was of Thoreau's "same clan & parish" and that the review should be done by "a good foreigner," E. P. Whipple, Starr King, Henry James, Sr., Parke Godwin, or Charles Dana.[7] Parker replied that he had found the book "full of beautiful things" but that there was "a good deal of sauciness, & a good deal of affectation in the book, the latter . . . from his trying to be R. W. Emerson, & not being contented with his own mother's son." He then added that he was asking James Russell Lowell to do the review.[8]

Parker asked for a review of four to six pages.[9] Lowell was slow at getting at the task, but finally turned in a paper four or five times the length Parker had suggested. It was a curiously mixed review. What he gave with one hand he took away with the other. "The great charm of Mr. Thoreau's book," he thought, "seems to be, that of its being a book at all is a happy fortuity. The door of the portfolio-cage has been left open, and the thoughts have flown out of themselves." But then he complained of the digressions: "We come upon them like snags jolting us headforemost out of our places as we are rowing placidly up stream or drifting

7. Emerson, *Letters,* IV, 151
8. Ibid.
9. Leon Howard, *Victorian Knight-Errant* (Berkeley, 1952), 298

down. Mr. Thoreau becomes so absorbed in these discussions, that he seems, as it were, to *catch a crab,* and disappears uncomfortably from his seat at the bow-oar." And he concludes: " 'Give me a sentence,' prays Mr. Thoreau bravely, 'which no intelligence can understand!'—and we think that the kind gods have nodded." Quite surprisingly when Thoreau's Aunt Maria read the review, she was delighted and wrote Prudence Ward that "Mr. Lowell has written a beautiful review of [Thoreau's] book in the Massachusetts Monthly, it is so just, and pleasant, and some parts of it so laughable that I enjoyed reading it very much."[1] It is not likely that Thoreau himself found it quite so amusing.

The *Pictorial National Library* dismissed the book in three sentences that merely summarized its contents. Several other unidentified reviews have turned up in the personal scrapbooks of Bronson Alcott[2] and Sophia Thoreau.[3] One written in reply to the *Tribune's* criticisms, answered: "We should not more fear the 'dangerous tendencies of this book' to propagate Pantheism than that the image of the Goddess of Liberty on our coin, would tend to revive her Pagan worship." Another said: "The numerous admirers of Carlyle and Emerson will read this book with a relish; for Mr. T. writes in their vein, and to some extent in their dialect . . . yet he is not a servile imitator . . . having his own sphere in which to move, and his own mission to consummate." And a third says: "We could not but admire the tact of the author in seizing upon the most trivial occurences, and building upon them a fabric of beautiful imagery." Still another, by Thoreau's Concord friend and neighbor, William S. Robinson, says: "It may be said of this book as the author says of great poems, '. . . they will yield of their sense in due proportion to the hasty and deliberate reader.' "[4]

Surprisingly the book received considerable notice in England. The *Athenaeum* of October 27, 1849, said: "The matter is for the most part poor enough; but there are a few things in the volume, scattered here and there, which suggest that the writer is a man with a habit of original thinking which with more careful

---

1. Maria Thoreau, Letter to Prudence Ward of December 1849. MS, George L. Davenport, Jr.
2. Houghton Library
3. In the collection of Raymond Adams
4. William S. Robinson, *"Warrington" Pen-Portraits* (Boston, 1877), 576–7

culture may produce a richer harvest in some future season."
Sophia Dobson Collet, in the London *People's Review,* in perhaps
the most favorable contemporary evaluation the book received,
said: "The writer describes the scenery of his voyage with the
vividness of a painter, and the scrutiny of a naturalist. . . . Every
object seen is, with him, an element in a higher vision. . . . The
occasional digressions are . . . not unworthy to stand beside [the
essays] of Emerson himself."[5] Nearly as favorable was a notice
in the *Westminster Review* for January 1850, which said: "Notwithstanding occasional attempts at fine writing, and some rather
long-winded disquisitions upon religion, literature, and other
matters . . . the book is an agreeable book." The *Spectator,* on
the other hand, on October 13, 1849, had dismissed the book as
"rather flat and not of a kind to interest."

Thus, although Thoreau could hardly have been overwhelmed
by its reception, his first book did, nonetheless, receive a re-
spectably wide notice and a comparatively favorable reaction from
the reviewers, considering the fact that it was the first book by
an unknown author.

To assure the book wide attention, Thoreau, Emerson, and
Munroe had sent out seventy-five copies, not only to potential
reviewers but to Hawthorne, Ellery Channing, Bronson Alcott,
H. G. O. Blake, Theo. Brown, Orestes Brownson, Dr. G. C. Shattuck (the Thoreau family physician), William Cullen Bryant, and
in England to Emerson's friends James Anthony Froude, Arthur
Hugh Clough, Walter Savage Landor, Alfred Lord Tennyson,
William Allingham, and Thomas Carlyle.[6] Alcott thought it
"worthy to stand beside Emerson's Essays."[7] Carlyle however

5. Undated clipping in Bronson Alcott's Autobiographical Collections,
Houghton Library
6. John D. Gordan, *First Fruits* (New York, 1951); Stephen Wakeman
[Sale Catalog], (New York, 1924), #995; Alcott, *Journal,* 209; Amer-
ican Academy of Arts and Letters, *The Great Decade in American
Writing* (New York, 1954), 3; Norman Dodge, "First Edition of
Thoreau's First," *The Month at Goodspeed's,* XXVI (1955), 175;
William Harris Arnold [Sale Catalog], (New York, 1924), #1026;
[Leo Stoller], "Henry David Thoreau 1817–1862" (Detroit, 1962), 8;
Charles Eliot Norton, *The Correspondence of Thomas Carlyle and
Ralph Waldo Emerson* (Boston, 1883), II, 185; Kenneth Walter
Cameron, "William Allingham and Emerson," *Emerson Society
Quarterly,* VI (1957), 24
7. Bronson Alcott, *Journals,* 209

found it "too Jean-Paulish" to read,[8] and Landor got only as far as page 73 and left the remainder of the book uncut.[9] Froude wrote Thoreau, "When I think of what you are—of what you have *done* as well as of what you have written, I have a right to tell you that there is no man living upon this earth at present, whose friendship or whose notice I value more than yours"[1] (but a few weeks later he wrote Clough that he thought the book "soda-waterish" and Sylvester Judd's *Margaret* much better).[2] Herman Melville borrowed a copy from Evert Duyckinck. Hawthorne told him that he was thinking of writing a travesty on it to be entitled "A Week on a Work-Bench in a Barn."[3] Ainsworth R. Spofford, who later became Librarian of Congress, was so impressed with the book that he sent Thoreau a check for five dollars as a token of his appreciation. (Thoreau confessed to Emerson that it was the first money he had made on the book.[4]) Thoreau himself, reading over the book two years later, said:

I thought that one peculiarity of my "Week" was its hypaethral character, to use an epithet applied to those Egyptian temples which are open to the heavens above, *under the ether.* I thought that it had little of the atmosphere of the house about it, but might wholly have been written, as in fact it was to a considerable extent, out-of-doors. It was only at a late period in writing it, as it happened, that I used any phrases implying that I lived in a house or led a *domestic* life. I trust it does not smell [so much] of the study and library, even of the poet's attic, as of the fields and woods; that it is a hypaethral or unroofed book, lying open under the ether and permeated by it, open to all weathers, not easy to be kept on a shelf.[5]

But despite the attention it received, *A Week* did not sell. Booksellers returned their stocks to the publisher and the publisher

8. Norton, *The Correspondence of Thomas Carlyle and Ralph Waldo Emerson,* II, 185
9. Dodge, "First Edition of Thoreau's First," 172
1. Thoreau, *Correspondence,* 248
2. Arthur Hugh Clough, *Correspondence* (Oxford, 1957), I, 272
3. Jay Leyda, *The Melville Log* (New York, 1951), I, 407
4. Ralph Waldo Emerson, Letter to Ainsworth R. Spofford of May, 23, 1851. MS, Library of Congress. (Called to my attention by Kenneth W. Cameron)
5. Thoreau, *Journal,* II, 274–5

relegated his stock to the cellar.[6] By the fall of 1849 Thoreau realized that he was in debt for a considerable sum and set about making up the money to pay for it elsewhere. He thought briefly of speculating on the cranberry market, buying wholesale in Boston and selling retail in New York City, only to discover to his dismay that the New York retail price was lower than the Boston wholesale. Finally he went doggedly back to work in his father's factory and manufactured a thousand dollars' worth of pencils. But misfortune continued to dog him. When he took them to New York, he found the market flooded and he had to sell at a loss to get rid of them.

On October 27, 1853, more than four years after the book was published, he confessed, not without a sense of humor, in his journal:

> For a year or two past, my *publisher,* falsely so called, has been writing from time to time to ask what disposition should be made of the copies of "A Week on the Concord and Merrimack Rivers" still on hand, and at last suggesting that he had use for the room they occupied in his cellar. So I had them all sent to me here, and they have arrived to-day by express, filling the man's wagon,—706 copies out of an edition of 1000 which I bought of Munroe four years ago and have ever since been paying for, and have not quite paid for yet. The wares are sent to me at last, and I have an opportunity to examine my purchase. They are something more substantial than fame, as my back knows, which has borne them up two flights of stairs to a place similar to that to which they trace their origin. Of the remaining two hundred and ninety and odd, seventy-five were given away, the rest sold. I have now a library of nearly nine hundred volumes, over seven hundred of which I wrote myself.[7]

And a month later he was at last able to record the last payment on his debt to Munroe. The book had cost him $290. His total income on it had been fifteen dollars. "This," he announced with understandable cynicism, "has been the pecuniary value of the book."[8] Munroe did agree to keep twelve copies of the book to

---

6. Walter Harding, "Notes and Queries," *Thoreau Society Bulletin,* LVIII (1957), 2
7. Thoreau, *Journal,* V, 459
8. Ibid. V, 521

sell on a commission basis and Thoreau was occasionally able to sell a copy from his attic. But otherwise the book had to be written down as a failure. To add insult to injury, someplace along the line he discovered not only that the printer had not made many of the corrections he had requested in the proofs but that on inserting a space he had requested between paragraphs on page 396 they had dropped three lines making complete nonsense of the text. (Although Thoreau sometimes wrote in the missing lines when he sold a copy from his attic, it is an inexplicable oddity that the earliest known copy in which he did this was the one he sent Daniel Ricketson on August 19, 1854.[9] Did such a glaring error escape Thoreau's keen eye all that time?)

The failure of *A Week* had its unfortunate repercussions. Munroe & Co. understandably refused to bring out *Walden* and no other publisher was interested in it. Those people around Concord who had long been certain that Thoreau was little more than a fool leaped upon the failure of the book as conclusive evidence that they had been right all along. So greatly did the local gossips exaggerate the story that James Kendall Hosmer, who often visited Concord as a boy in the 1850s, has recalled:

> This strange man [Thoreau], rumor said, had written a book no copy of which had ever been sold. . . . The edition fell dead from the press, and all the books, one thousand or more, he had collected in his mother's house, a queer library of these unsold books which he used to exhibit to visitors laughing grimly over his unfortunate venture in the field of letters. My aunt sent me one day to carry a message to Mrs. Thoreau and my rap on her door was answered by no other man than this odd son who, on the threshold received my message. He stood in the doorway with hair which looked as if it had been dressed with a pine-cone, inattentive grey eyes, hazy with far-away musings, an emphatic nose and disheveled attire that bore signs of tramps in woods and swamps. Thinking of the forest fire I fancied he smelled of smoke and peered curiously up the staircase behind him hoping I might get a glimpse of that queer library all of one book duplicated one thousand times.[1]

9. Copy owned by Albert E. Lownes
1. James Kendall Hosmer, *The Last Leaf* (New York, 1912), 235–6

When *Walden* was finally published by Ticknor & Fields in 1854, Thoreau persuaded them to take a few copies of *A Week* from his attic on consignment. The next year he tried to persuade them to bring out *A Week* in a new edition, but it was not until a few weeks before his death in 1862 that he finally succeeded, and then they simply sold copies of the 1849 edition with a new title page. It was not until 1868 that a true second edition, embodying the thousand or more additions and corrections he had made in his own copy, was published. Although the book has been in print ever since, it has never achieved anything approximating the success of his masterpiece, *Walden*.

II

Thoreau's older sister Helen had been in poor health for some time. In 1838 she had suffered from a severe skin inflammation that necessitated her giving up teaching in Taunton and returning home for a time.[2] Then, against her family's advice, she had established a private school in Roxbury with her sister Sophia. Eventually she had to give that up and return home. In the spring of 1842 she advertised that she was about to open a private school for young ladies in Concord itself, specializing in needlework, painting, and piano.[3] To help advertise it, both she and Sophia entered paintings in the local cattle show that fall and won prizes of a dollar each.[4] Apparently the school never materialized, for the next spring she asked her brother, then on Staten Island, to try to locate a school for her there. Since he was unsuccessful, she began to give painting and music lessons in the family home. Gradually she became weaker and it became obvious that she had contracted tuberculosis. One by one she was forced to give up her outside activities. By the winter of 1848 she was desperately ill. On February 16, 1849, Thoreau reported to his cousin George Thatcher that he feared she was failing. Twelve days later Aunt

2. Kenneth Walter Cameron, "Helen Thoreau Writes to Dr. Shattuck in 1838," *Emerson Society Quarterly*, VI (1957), 48
3. *Concord Freeman*, April 8, 1842
4. *Concord Freeman*, October 7, 1842

Maria Thoreau wrote Prudence Ward that Helen was weaker.[5] On March 15 she reported:

> As for Helen, last week we thought her failing fast,—she had two or three faint turns, but this week she has been more comfortable again, tho' she thinks herself weaker, she still goes from room to room lying on the sofa to rest. Dr. Bartlett called to see her Sabbath evening, and said she looked better than he expected to find her, as he had heard she was failing. She didn't like to be told so, for she feels . . . anxious to go. She says she has not a gloomy thought about it, and she would not if she could come back again to life to suffer what she had done with ill health, these feelings reconcile us the more to parting with her, but still her loss will be deeply felt by her family. . . . Her mind is cheerful, and at times she is quite sociable. . . . I should not be surprised if she should linger along till quite summer.[6]

And on May 1 she added:

> Helen appears to be failing more rapidly, her feet are much swollen, tho I think it more an indication of her humor than of the last stage of her disease, but some days it seems as if she could not survive a week, and then again it appears that she might live a *number*. This you know is the nature of this insidious disease.
>
> Sophia told me that Sabbath evening she talked all about her funeral saying that to her there was not the least gloom attached to it.[7]

When Thoreau learned at this point that a daguerreotypist was visiting the town, he arranged for him to visit their home and take pictures of both Helen and Sophia. It was a tiring experience for Helen in her weak condition but she was gratified with her brother's thoughtfulness and considered the picture a good one. Sophia, on the other hand, despised hers and insisted on another sitting.[8]

---

5. Maria Thoreau, Letter to Prudence Ward of February 28, 1849. MS, George L. Davenport, Jr.
6. Maria Thoreau, Letter to Prudence Ward of March 15, 1849. MS, George L. Davenport, Jr.
7. Maria Thoreau, Letter to Prudence Ward of May 1, 1849. MS, George L. Davenport, Jr
8. Ibid.

Helen died on June 14, 1849, aged only thirty-six. The funeral was held in the home on the 18th with both the Unitarian and the Trinitarian ministers in attendance. Thoreau sat seemingly unmoved with his family through the service, but as the pall-bearers prepared to remove the bier, he arose and, taking a music box from the table, wound it and set it to playing a melody in a minor key that seemed to the listeners "like no earthly tune." All sat quietly until the music was over.[9] She was buried in the burying ground next to her brother John.

Recalling her lifelong exertions on behalf of the slave, one of the abolitionist papers euologized:

Our friend, Miss Thoreau, was an abolitionist. Endowed by nature with tender sensibilities, quick to feel for the woes of others, the cause of the slave met with a ready response in her heart. She had a mind of fine native powers, enlarged and matured by cultivation. She had the patience to investigate truth, the candor to acknowledge it when sufficient evidence was presented to her mind, and the moral courage to act in conformity with her convictions, however unpopular these convictions might be to the community around her. . . .[1]

Thoreau as his own tribute wrote one of the rare poems of his later years:

Farewell

. . . Regret doth bind
Me faster to thee now
   Than neighborhood confined.
Where thy love followeth me
Is enough society
Thy indelible mild eye
   Is my sky.
Whether by land or sea
   I wander to and fro,
Oft as I think of thee
   The heavens hang more low

---

9. Amanda Mather, Letter to Daniel Gregory Mason of September 13, 1897. MS, Raymond Adams
1. Unidentified clipping in the collection of Raymond Adams

The pure glance of thy eye
Doth purge the summer's sky,
And thy breath so rare
Doth refine the winter's air. . . .[2]

A few weeks later he learned that little Ellen Emerson, who had suffered a severe case of the mumps, had been sent to her uncle's house on Staten Island to recuperate. Remembering how homesick he had been there, he sat down and wrote her a letter to cheer her up:

I think that we are pretty well acquainted, though we never had any very long talks. We have had a good many short talks, at any rate. Dont you remember how we used to despatch our breakfast two winters ago, as soon as Eddy could get on his feeding tire, which was not always remembered, before the rest of the household had come down? Dont you remember our wise criticisms on the pictures in the portfolio and the Turkish book with Eddy and Edith looking on,—how almost any pictures answered our purpose, and we went through the Penny Magazine, first from beginning to end, and then from end to beginning, and Eddy stared just as much the second time as the first, and Edith thought that we turned over too soon, and that there were some things which she had not seen—? I can guess pretty well what interests you, and what you think about. Indeed I am interested in pretty much the same things myself. I suppose you think that persons who are as old as your father and myself are always thinking about very grave things, but I know that we are meditating the same old themes that we did when we were ten years old, only we go more gravely about it. You love to write or to read a fairy story and that is what you will always like to do, in some form or other. By and by you will discover that you want what are called the necessaries of life only that you may realize some such dream.

Eddy has got him a fish-pole and line with a pin-hook at the end, which he flourishes over the dry ground and the carpet at the risk of tearing out our eyes; but when I told him that he must have a cork and a sinker, his mother took off the pin and tied on a cork instead; but he doubts whether that will catch fish as well. He tells me that he is five years old. Indeed I was present at the celebration of his birthday lately, and supplied the

2. Thoreau, *Collected Poems*, 215

company with onion and squash pipes, and rhubarb whistles, which is the most I can do on such occasions. Little Sammy Hoar blowed them most successfully, and made the loudest noise, though it almost strained his eyes out to do it. Edith is full of spirits. When she comes home from school, she goes hop skip and jump down into the field to pick berries, currants, gooseberries, raspberries, and thimbleberries; if there is one of these that has thoughts of changing its hue by tomorrow morning, I guess that Edith knows something about it and will consign it to her basket for Grandmama. . . .

I found a nice penknife on the bank of the river this afternoon, which was probably lost by some villager who went there to bathe lately. Yesterday I found a nice arrowhead, which was lost some time before by an Indian who was hunting there. The knife was a very little rusted; the arrowhead was not rusted at all. . . .

Do not think that you must write to me because I have written to you. It does not follow at all. You would not naturally make so long a speech to me here in a month as a letter would be. Yet if sometime it should be perfectly easy, and pleasant to you, I shall be very glad to have a sentence.[3]

Thoreau seemed to know almost instinctively what a little child would enjoy.

---

3. Thoreau, *Correspondence*, 245–6

CHAPTER FOURTEEN
(1849–1852)

I

ALTHOUGH the pencil business had been prospering since Thoreau had worked out the new methods of perfecting their manufacture, the whole family was both pleased and puzzled suddenly to start receiving large orders for the ground lead itself from the Boston firm of Smith & McDougal. At first they thought the firm might be going into the pencil business themselves, but investigation proved that they were printers. The Thoreaus asked questions, but the firm for some time refused to give any answers. Finally, after swearing the Thoreaus to secrecy, they explained. Electrotyping had been invented and the high quality of the Thoreau's ground lead was ideal for the process. But if the Thoreaus wished to keep their business, they would have to see that no competitor learned the secret.[1]

The Thoreaus went to great lengths to keep their promise and the firm's business. Thoreau himself made the trips to the Acton mill by buggy to pick up the lead.[2] Then it was packaged at home and addressed to Boston only by members of the immediate family. Secrecy prevailed, although they had difficulty explaining to their friends when the lead dust began pervading the entire house. (One guest noted that the keys of the family piano were coated with it when he opened it to play and the effect on Thoreau's delicate lungs can well be imagined.[3]) For a time the Thoreaus continued to manufacture pencils as a cover-up, and then abandoned that subterfuge. When it became apparent that he was

---

1. Edward Emerson, Notes on Thoreau
2. Ibid.
3. Edward Emerson, *Henry Thoreau as Remembered by a Young Friend*, 37

no longer manufacturing pencils, Thoreau put his friends off by saying, "Why should I? I would not do again what I have done once?"[4] His friends and neighbors, not understanding the maneuver, thought him unusually perverse.

At first the Thoreaus received ten dollars a pound for their ground lead and were able to sell as much as six hundred pounds a year. But eventually the secret leaked out and they had to meet the prices of the resulting competition. The price dropped from eight to five and finally to two dollars a pound. Fortunately however the market increased and they were able to do nearly as well even at the drastically lower prices.[5]

By 1854 any attempt at secrecy as to the use of plumbago for electrotyping was abandoned and the Thoreaus began doing business with a large number of firms in Boston, New York, Philadelphia, and even cities in the Middle West. Their business became well enough known so that on one occasion at least a letter addressed simply "Black Lead Works, Concord, New Hampshire" [sic] reached them.[6] So much of their business was centered in New York City, which by this time was becoming the leader in the printing business, that they were urged by many of their customers to open a Manhattan office.[7] They tried to work out arrangements for the electrotyping firm of W. Fulmer & Co., at 128 Fulton Street to handle their business but gave up when Fulmer failed to carry out his side of the bargain.[8] Later, for a time at least, Horace Hosmer, Thoreau's former student, became their New York agent. And C. S. Smith too acted in that capacity.[1] But for the most part the business was conducted from the Main Street house, and as his father grew older and more feeble, Thoreau himself more and more assumed the various chores of the business. With the growth of the black-lead business, the Thoreaus gradually abandoned

4. Harding, *Thoreau, Man of Concord*, 189–90
5. Edward Emerson, Notes on Thoreau
6. Miller & Gilchrist, Letter to Concord, N. H., Express Agency of March 4, 1856. MS, Morgan Library
7. A. H. Jocelyn Co., Letter to John Thoreau of December 20, 1854. MS, Abernethy Library
8. Ibid.
9. Raymond Adams, *Thoreau Newsletter,* April 1937
1. C. S. Smith, Letter to Mr. Thoreau of September 23, 1856. MS, Morgan Library

manufacturing pencils and by 1853 had given it up completely. That was probably just as well, for in the winter of 1853-4, a whole group of German pencil makers established themselves in New York City and very rapidly succeeded in taking over the American pencil business almost completely.

With their growing prosperity, Mrs. Thoreau aspired to be back nearer the center of town and in a more pretentious home than the Texas house. She looked around for a time and finally decided on a yellow-painted frame house at 259 Main Street, a short distance west of the Parkman house they had lived in earlier. John Thoreau purchased it for $1450 on September 29, 1849.[2] The tenants however did not move out until after winter weather had settled in. Then, Mrs. Thoreau decided the house needed extensive repairs.[3] Nathan Hosmer was hired to raise the house so that all downstairs rooms would be nine feet high and all upstairs rooms, eight, to make a sidelighted front door and portico and a "handsome newel and hard rail of mahogany" on the front stairs, to put in more partitions, and new doors throughout, to tear down chimneys and install fireplaces, to put new glass in the windows, a new sink in the kitchen, and new shingles on the roof, to build closets and repair the plastering, to repaint the house and add green blinds.[4] Thoreau himself helped Hosmer to attach the barn to the house; when that was lathed and plastered throughout, a sink, a boiler, and a chimney were added. The resulting ell was to house the family lead business, although the coarse grinding was now done at the mill at Loring's Lead Works in Concord Junction. They also added on a shed moved from the Texas house when they found they needed still more room.

It was August 29, 1850, before the carpentry work was completed and they were able to move into their new house. Mrs. Thoreau, foreseeing a vastly increased amount of housework in the new home, hired two young Irish girls, Margaret Doland, aged

2. Mrs. Caleb Wheeler, "Thoreau Alcott House," *Thoreau Society Bulletin,* XXIV (1948), 1; Middlesex County Registry Records, DLXXXVIII, 300
3. Maria Thoreau, Letter to Prudence Ward of November 15, 1849. MS, George L. Davenport, Jr.
4. Nathan S. Hosmer, Contract with John Thoreau. MS, Concord Free Public Library

eighteen, and Catherine Rioden [sic], aged thirteen, to live in and to assist her.[5] Still further indication of their relative prosperity lies in the fact that they did not sell the Texas house but instead rented it out. The Kendall family for a time rented it for ten dollars a month.[6] Then in the summer of 1854, William S. Robinson, the newspaper man, took it over for twenty-five dollars a quarter so that he and his family might live near his aging mother, and continued to live there until 1857.[7] Thoreau quickly renewed his acquaintance with Robinson, called on him, and invited him to the annual melon party. Mrs. Robinson thought Thoreau a great talker and noticed that he tended to sit with his head bent over as though he were carrying on a conversation all by himself. On one of his visits he was introduced to a visitor who was considered an authority on Indian affairs. Within a very short time, the Robinsons remembered, Thoreau had "talked the fellow dumb" on his own subject.[8] In August 1859 David Wasson, a Worcester clergyman and friend of H. G. O. Blake suffered a breakdown and was forced to give up his church. He moved to Concord, rented the Texas house, and became a fairly frequent companion of Thoreau on his walks. Later, after Thoreau's death, the house was sold and as the neighborhood in general deteriorated, was allowed to run down. A fire seriously damaged it in the 1930s and before any repairs were made, the hurricane of 1938 ripped off the roof. For some years the frame lingered on as a ruin, but it was finally torn down and in 1961 the cellar was filled in. Now only a bronze tablet marks the site.

Thoreau himself, according to Aunt Maria, did not like the idea of moving to Main Street at all, although she protested that he was going to have a pleasanter and more convenient room than he had ever had before.[9] His new room was to be the finished attic of the main portion of the house, with an open stairway coming up into the center of the room, sloping ceilings, and windows a

5. 1850 United States Census, Middlesex County, XV, 218
6. J. Thoreau, Letter to Mr. Kendall of July 29, 1854. MS, Huntington Library
7. Gladys Hosmer, "Some Notable Concord Women," *Concord Journal,* November 9, 1961
8. Robinson, *"Warrington" Pen-Portraits,* 67–8
9. Maria Thoreau, Letter to Prudence Ward of November 15, 1849. MS, George L. Davenport, Jr.

oth ends. He eventually had to admit his new room was very much to his liking. He gathered driftwood boards along the river and made bookshelves. Still later he added sundry pockets, boxes, and bins where he neatly displayed curious rocks and stones, lichens and mosses, and old books filled with preserved flowers. In a bureau he kept his collections of birds' eggs and of Indian relics. In one bookcase he kept his ever-lengthening manuscript journal. On the walls were a few antlers he had picked up in Maine and snowshoes he had purchased from the Indians. Here and there were birdskins, nests, and a few animal pelts. Always available was a supply of nuts picked up in the woods, for he was as fond of them as was a squirrel. An air-tight stove in which he burned odds and ends of wood he picked up on his wanderings in Concord kept him warm. His only other furniture was his Walden cot, a bureau, and two chairs. Here, surrounded by his collections, he could read and write in peace and quiet. Although he often took his own friends up to his room, the family was hesitant to do so. Sophia laughingly apologized when she said that Henry considered dust on his furniture like the bloom on fruits, not to be swept off.[1]

He made no recluse of himself in the attic. Although he was not happy one summer when it was so hot that he was forced to spend *every* evening downstairs with the family, he made it an invariable practice to spend at least part of every evening with the family, and he was sure to be drawn downstairs by the sound of his sister playing the piano. Mrs. Hemans' "Pilgrim Fathers," Moore's "Evening Bells" and "Canadian Boat Song," and Wolfe's "Burial of Sir John Moore" were among his favorites. He would often join with the others in the singing and occasionally would play for them on his flute. As a friend of the family said, "No one could more heartily enjoy his family life than Henry."[2]

One visitor to the house recalled that on the evening of a day too stormy for Thoreau to take his customary outdoor exercise, he came flying down from his study and amazed them all by suddenly breaking into a dance all by himself, "spinning airily around, displaying most remarkable litheness and agility and . . . finally [springing] over the center-table, alighting like a feather on the other side—then, not in the least out of breath [continuing]

1. Thoreau, *Journal*, IX, 83
2. Marble, *Thoreau: His Home, Friends and Books*, 55

his waltz until his enthusiasm abated."[3] His mother boasted to the guest that she had taken care to see that he had had dancing lessons as a child as one of "the usual accomplishments of well bred children."[4]

Thoreau took a particular delight in the family cat, playing with it by the hour and each April making a special walk to pick catnip for it. Dogs he did not particularly enjoy although he did admit that Channing's, when it accompanied them on walks, sometimes served to scare up birds and animals they might not otherwise have seen.

II

In the late fall of 1841 Thoreau had had a brief skirmish with the Harvard College authorities over his use of their library. He had decided to make a further study of early English poetry in preparation for either a lecture or an essay for *The Dial* and, not finding the books readily at hand, journeyed to Cambridge to make use of the facilities there. Much to his disgust he learned that since he was not a resident of Cambridge he was not eligible to withdraw books. He protested to the librarian to no avail and then went over his head directly to President Quincy. Quincy found him a formidable opponent and finally gave in; he sent a note to the librarian instructing him to permit Thoreau to take "the usual number of volumes—and for the usual length of time, on the usual conditions."[5] In the next twelve days Thoreau withdrew twenty-four volumes, but found to his dismay that his tastes had changed and the books seemed utterly dull and dry.

It was not until the fall of 1849 that he made another attempt to use his college library. This time he was interested in Oriental literature and made up a long list of books that he wanted to see and could find nowhere in Concord.[6] Quincy had retired in 1845 and Jared Sparks had taken his place, but Thoreau had learned that both Emerson and Barzillai Frost, the minister of Concord's

3. Anon, "Reminiscences of Thoreau," *Outlook*, LXIII (1899), 820
4. Ibid.
5. Cameron, *The Transcendentalists and Minerva*, II, 474
6. Ibid.

irst Parish, had recently been granted the privilege of withdraw-
ig books from the Harvard Library and so set out to win the
rivilege for himself.[7] He went down to Cambridge on September
I, and obtained permission to take out two books while they
onsidered his case further, and chose the *Harivansa, ou Histoire
e la Famille,* a volume translated from Sanskrit into French by
Alexandre Langlois, and *Histoire de la Littérature Hindoui et
Hindoustani* by Garcin de Tassy. In the former he found a brief
able, "The Transmigration of the Seven Brahmans," which he
arefully translated into English—for what purpose it is not known,
t was found among his unpublished manuscripts years after his
eath.

He had applied directly to President Sparks for a more perma-
ent library privilege. When Sparks explained that library facili-
es were limited to resident graduates, to clergymen who were
lso members of the alumni, and to residents who lived within a
ircle of ten miles' radius from the college, Thoreau immediately
ointed out that the railroad had destroyed the old scale of dis-
ances and Concord was now handier to Harvard than the outlying
istricts of Cambridge had been a few years before. He added that
he one benefit he felt he owed to the college was its library and
hat his need for books was far more imperative now than it had
ver been in his college days. As a result, Sparks too gave in and
n September 13 sent a note to the librarian that gave Thoreau
he privilege of taking books "according to the rules in similar
ases."[8]

But apparently Thoreau had returned to Concord without
ealizing Sparks had capitulated, for on the 17th he addressed a
etter to him:

> I wish to get permission to take books from the College library
> to Concord, where I reside. I am encouraged to ask this, not
> merely because I am an alumnus of Harvard, residing within a
> moderate distance of her halls, but *because I have chosen letters
> for my profession,* and so am one of the *clergy* embraced by
> the spirit at least of her rule. Moreover, though books are to
> some extent my stock and tools, I have not the usual means
> with which to purchase them. I therefore regard myself as one

7. Ibid. 47
8. Ibid. 476-7

whom especially the library was created to serve. . . . I ask only that the University may help to finish the education, whose foundation she has helped to lay. I was not ripe then for her higher courses, and now that I am riper I trust that I am not too far away to be instructed by her. Indeed I see not how her children can more properly or effectually keep up a living connexion with their Alma Mater, than by continuing to draw from her intellectual nutriment in some such way as this.[9]

Then, just to make sure, Thoreau called on Sparks the next time he was in Cambridge, on November 9, and received another note addressed to the librarian granting him library privileges. Although Sparks had written "one year" at the bottom of the letter, Thoreau continued to exercise the privilege for the rest of his life and rarely visited Boston or Cambridge without taking out a book or two from the library. He was not ungrateful for the privilege and when in 1859 as a member of the alumni association he received an appeal for funds for the library, he sent them five dollars, explaining in a letter, "I would gladly give you more but this exceeds my income from all sources together for the last four months."[1]

Almost inadvertently Thoreau won access to another important library, that of the Boston Society of Natural History. In the fall of 1849 Jacob Farmer, one of Thoreau's Concord friends, caught an American goshawk, a large hawk that occasionally drifts into the Concord area from the North and, knowing of Thoreau's interest in anything unusual, brought it over for him to see. Thoreau, recognizing its rarity, took it into Boston and presented it to the Boston Society of Natural History, whose curator of birds, Samuel Cabot, dissected it, stuffed the skin, and preserved the remains in alcohol. As a result, a year later, on December 18, 1850, the society elected Thoreau a corresponding member, an honorary position which required no dues but gave him access to the library. From then on, he visited the society's rooms on nearly every visit to Boston, often consulted with their curators when he found the identification of species difficult, and regularly withdrew books on natural history from the library. Legend says that he often got to the society's rooms before the janitor in the morning

9. Ibid.
1. Ibid. 488

nd did not hesitate to crawl in through a window to use their
ooks.[2]

Although Thoreau paid no dues to the society, he more than
equited the society for its courtesies. In 1854 he presented it
vith a copy each of *A Week* and *Walden;* in 1858, some specimens
f *Pomotis, Esox,* and frogs; and in 1860, a copy of the *Transac-
ions of the Middlesex Agricultural Society,* which contained his
paper on "The Succession of Forest Trees," and also a long letter
n a Canadian lynx killed in Carlisle, Massachusetts. After his
leath in 1862, his mother and sister donated to the society his
ollections of more than one thousand pressed plants, his collection
f New England birds' eggs and nests, and his collection of Indian
ntiquities, consisting of the arrowheads and other implements he
ad picked up in Concord. The society in its turn prepared a long
nemorial notice which was read at their meeting of May 21, 1862,
ent to his mother and sister, and incorporated into the proceedings
f the society.[3]

Although Thoreau liked to scoff at collectors of relics and
t dry and dusty museums and libraries, he nonetheless readily
appreciated their value and did his best to help them when the
pportunity arose. Back in 1840 when Edward Jarvis, a former
Concordian who had settled in Louisville, Kentucky, wrote back
o his home town for appropriate donations to the Kentucky His-
orical Society, of which he was librarian, Thoreau promptly re-
ponded with a donation of ten pamphlets.[4] And when in 1846
ie happened upon a seventeenth-century deed to some land in
Taunton, Massachusetts, he donated it to the Massachusetts His-
orical Society, where it is still treasured in their archives.[5] When
owards the end of his life Thoreau learned that Concord's eccentric
Cummins Davis had started a museum of antiquities, he was among
he few who did not scoff, but instead carefully inspected the collection and reported that it gave him great pleasure to examine
such indications of an earlier simple life.[6] Appropriately enough

---

2. Channing, *Thoreau, the Poet-Naturalist,* 263
3. Cameron, "Emerson, Thoreau, and the Society of Natural History,"
American Literature, XXIV (1952), 23
4. *Concord Freeman,* February 14, 1840
5. Kenneth Walter Cameron, "Thoreau's Gift to the M.H.S. in 1846,"
Emerson Society Quarterly, VI (1957), 48
6. Thoreau, *Journal,* XIV, 87–8

it was Davis who later saved Thoreau's Walden cabin furniture fo posterity.

III

On Tuesday, October 9, 1849, Thoreau and Channing set ou from Concord on an excursion to Cape Cod. Thoreau wished t acquaint himself with the ocean and the seashore, and where, othe than on that hundred-mile sand dune curling out to sea, could ther be a better place to do it? When they reached Boston, they learnee that the Provincetown steamer on which they had planned to sai had not yet reached port because of a violent storm and that a sailing brig, the *St. John,* filled with immigrants from Ireland, hac been wrecked at Cohasset with the loss of 145 lives. Although Thoreau had boasted that he would not go around the corner to see the world blow up, he immediately changed his plans and journeyed down to see the wreck. He called upon Ellen Sewall, now Mrs. Joseph Osgood, and with her husband walked along the shore.[7] They found livid, swollen, and mangled bodies of those drowned, gashed by the rocks or fishes so that the bone and muscle were exposed, strewn hither and yon among the rocks and seaweed. They talked with what survivors they could find, inspected the debris from the wreck, and were appalled at the nonchalance with which the Cohasset natives devoted themselves to harvesting the seaweed as serenely as if there had never been a wreck in the world.

Thoreau and Channing journeyed on to Bridgewater, where after putting up for the night at the Inn, they took the train next morning to Sandwich. There, because it was raining hard, they crowded into a stagecoach, finding themselves, so Thoreau said, forced to time their inspirations and their expirations so as to assist the driver in closing the door. Thoreau pulled a copy of the 1802 *Collections* of the Massachusetts Historical Society and a gazetteer out of his pack and settled down to read the histories of the towns as he passed through them. Keeping to the bay side, they journeyed through Barnstable, Yarmouth, Dennis, and Brewster to Orleans,

---

7. Davenport and Koopman, "Henry D. Thoreau 1839–1840"

here they spent the night in Higgins's Tavern. Thoreau was not impressed with what natives he saw. The women, he thought, "looked exceedingly pinched up," with prominent chins and noses, and since they had lost all their teeth, their profiles could be represented by "a sharp *W*." If they were well preserved, he thought, it was "as dried specimens. Their husbands, however, were pickled," he wryly added.[8]

The next morning, though it was still raining hard, the two set out by foot, hiking around Nauset Harbor and across Jeremiah's Gutter to Eastham. As they struck out cross-country for Nauset Lights, they could hear the roar of the ocean though it was still several miles distant. Walking along the Back Side shore, they found the beach strewn with jellyfish, shells, driftwood, and fragments of old wrecks. At noon they built a fire on the sand and Thoreau cooked and ate a huge sea clam he had picked up. At the time he thought it sweet and savory, but when later he learned he had eaten a supposedly unpalatable portion, his stomach revolted and he was ill for a time.

By late afternoon they had reached the Wellfleet-Truro boundary stone and turned inland to find a place for the night. John Newcomb, an old Wellfleet oysterman, welcomed them in to his cottage, though they had noticed that his wife had rushed out to close up the bulkhead when they approached, and their idiot son kept muttering, "Damn book-pedlers,—all the time talking about books. Better do something. Damn 'em. I'll shoot 'em."[9] But the oysterman himself proved a congenial host and sat with them in front of the fireplace for hours discoursing on the lore of the Cape and the sea. When they finally retired to their bedroom, their host's wife took the precaution of locking them in.

In the morning Thoreau was up before dawn and let out to see the sun come up out of the ocean. He returned to find breakfast being prepared and the old man back at his place in front of the fire, discoursing as volubly as ever and firing tobacco juice right and left into the fireplace without regard to the various dishes that were cooking there. Thoreau avoided the buttermilk cake and the green beans at breakfast because he thought they had been particularly exposed, but later when he compared notes he found that

---

8. Thoreau, *Writings,* IV, 24
9. Ibid. 90

Channing had avoided for the same reason the apple sauce and doughnuts that Thoreau had eaten.

After breakfast Thoreau repaired the old man's clock, for he refused to believe that they were not peddlers or tinkers. It reminded Thoreau that on another excursion someone equally convinced that he was a peddler demanded to see the contents of his knapsack, but when Thoreau finally convinced him he was only hiking, he said, "Well, it makes no difference what it is you carry so long as you carry truth with you."[1] Thoreau unquestionably agreed.

Striking the beach again in the south part of Truro, Thoreau and Channing continued northward until they reached Highland Light early in the afternoon. After arranging to stay for the night, they strolled across the narrow peninsula and inspected the bay side briefly. When the light-keeper ascended to light the lamps they accompanied him into the tower. In the morning, continuing along the shore, they watched the mackerel schooners gathering over the banks and examined the carcass of a whale that had drifted ashore. At noon they ascended Mount Ararat, one of the largest of the sand dunes, and observed, to their delight, a mirage of pools in the sands. At dusk, having nearly reached Race Point, they crossed the Cape once more to enter Provincetown and put up at a hotel. Since the wind came up in the night, they crossed to Race Point again in the morning and spent the day watching the stormiest sea they had ever seen. Their second morning in Provincetown they spent atop a sand dune overlooking the village.

At noon they embarked on the steamer *Naushon* and arrived in Boston at nightfall. At Concord they found enough sand in their shoes to fill the shakers with which everyone in those days dried the ink on their pages, and they could hear the roar of the sea in their ears for weeks. (Later when Emerson and his brother brought back from the Cape some botanical specimens that Thoreau had missed, he was amused that Thoreau could hardly suppress his indignation because he had brought him a berry he had not seen.)[2]

Immediately upon his return Thoreau launched himself on a campaign to read every book he could find about Cape Cod.

1. Edward Emerson, Notes on Thoreau
2. Rusk, *The Life of Ralph Waldo Emerson*, 364

y mid-December Aunt Maria reported to Prudence Ward that
Thoreau had a lecture ready on the subject that she thought would
be "very entertaining, and much liked."[3] He gave it before the
Concord Lyceum on January 23 and 30, 1850. Although James
Barty complained that some of the things Thoreau said were very
polish, even though they were applauded by the audience, and
that some of his plays on words "no man of sense there but knew
them before,"[4] Emerson reported that the lecture was a huge success and people in the audience "laughed until they cried." Thanks
to Emerson's negotiations, Thoreau repeated the lecture in Danvers,
Massachusetts, on February 18 and received expenses and $10.00.[5]
In late May, Blake asked him to lecture again in Worcester, but
remembering the *Palladium* rebuke, Thoreau refused, saying that
his lecture was not "calculated for a promiscuous audience," he
required a "concordant audience."[6]

In June of 1850, apparently wishing to find more writing material, Thoreau made another excursion to Cape Cod, this time alone.
On the 25th he sailed from Boston and spent the night in a
Provincetown hotel. The next day, sitting on the sand dunes overlooking the village, he found his meditations interrupted by the
noise of a preacher "who shouted like a boatswain," and ardently
wished the tithing-man would stop him from "profaning the quiet
atmosphere." Thoreau stopped for a time at Highland Light once
again and was astonished to discover that forty feet of the em-
bankment had washed out to sea since he had been there in October.
He visited the Wellfleet oysterman once more and learned that
when a Provincetown bank had been robbed a day or two after
their previous visit, suspicion had rested upon them, and that the
policemen who had traced their route all the way down the back
side of the Cape concluded they had come that way on foot in
order to discover a way to get off the Cape once they had committed
their robbery.

At Eastham, Thoreau explored the pine groves near the camp-
grounds and at Chatham watched sloops dragging for lost anchors
and chains. When he returned to Provincetown to sail for Boston,

3. Maria Thoreau, Letter to Prudence Ward of December, 1849. MS,
George L. Davenport, Jr.
4. Edward Emerson, Notes on Thoreau
5. Thoreau, *Correspondence*, 255
6. Ibid. 260

he found that the steamer could not get up to the wharf at lo
tide and he was conveyed thirty rods out through the waves in
two-wheeled horse cart, surrounded by a troop of boys wading
the water. Although it was a brief visit, it at least enabled him
add a few interesting bits to his Cape Cod essay.

IV

By the spring of 1850 Thoreau had acquired an adequa
compass of his own and was being asked to do more and mo
surveying. His cousin C. H. Dunbar of Haverhill arranged fc
him to survey the estate of Nehemiah Emerson there and divide
into sixty house lots. Thoreau boarded for the time with a Mr
Webster, a stiff, old-fashioned Methodist, who did her best to co
vert him to her way of religion, but he sloughed her off with th
remark, "I am too hard a nut to crack." He was much more inte
ested in young Samuel A. Chase, one of his fellow boarders, an
spent some time showing him how to observe the birds of th
area. Thoreau expounded to him on his beliefs and said, "Fift
years from now the majority of people will believe as I do now.
Chase thought Thoreau personified all purity and goodness, an
later said he could not believe he ever did a wrong thing in h
life. He noted particularly the respect and affection with whic
Thoreau held his mother and said a tear would come to his eye
whenever he spoke of her. "He was a loving man," Chase cor
cluded.[7]

In his spare time in Haverhill Thoreau visited many of th
ancient houses and historical sites. He was disappointed to lear
that the site of Hannah Dustin's home could not be positivel
identified, but an old garrison house owned by the Ayer fami
he found worth investigation and was much impressed by fire
places so huge that he could walk into them and look directly u
into the sky. A row of old buttonwoods planted in 1739 on th
banks of the Merrimack attracted his attention and he carefull
measured the circumference of the largest.

When he returned to Concord, he surveyed the new yello\

7. Harding, *Thoreau, Man of Concord*, 190

ouse lot for his father. In June he was hired to survey the new
ourthouse and town house lots—the first of many such jobs he
was to do for the town. Summer and fall he was hired to do one
urveying task after another. By December he had notations on
nore than twenty surveys for the year in his field book, including
uch tasks as squaring Mrs. Keyes's cellar, laying out a street in
Acton, surveying the West Burying Ground, drawing a plan for
David Loring's barn, and measuring stonework at the court-house.[8]
ames Barrett Wood who hired him to survey a wood lot in North-
oro in November found him very pleasant and talkative to work
vith. On one particular day they had great trouble finding the
ounds and it was dark before they were ready to run the final line.
Wood wondered how they would be able to see the last bound to
ake the bearings, but Thoreau quietly continued to work and,
vhen he had his compass set, pulled a candle and a match from
is pocket, lighted it, and told Wood to hold it on top of the
tick on the last bound. In that way he finished the work and
aved Wood not only the trouble of journeying out to the wood lot
gain but the three dollars he would have paid for another's day's
vork.[9]

As word spread of Thoreau's proficiency at surveying, the
lemand for his services rapidly increased. In 1851, for example,
e worked on Daniel Shattuck's new house on January 7, John
Hosmer's wood lot on February 5, White Pond for the new official
own map on the 17th, Cyrus Stow's swamp lot on the 20th and
27th, his wood lot in east Concord on March 3, then James McCaf-
erty's farm, Timothy Brooks's estate, and a new street across the
ailroad tracks for Francis Monroe, land near the factory for
Thomas Ford on April 12, a new street and house lots for Cyrus
tow on the 19th, the new courthouse property on the 29th, a new
oad for the town on May 3, the courthouse lawn, then the West
Center School property on May 24 and a boundary line for Mrs.
Barber on June 2, a field for James Wood on the 9th, a road in
Acton on the 19th and 20th, Edmund Hosmer's farm on the 18th
nd 21st, a boundary for F. R. Gourgas on the 28th, a new road
o Bedford on July 12 and 14, the courthouse fences on August 2,
a boundary line for Rockwood Hoar on September 8, the town's

8. Cameron, *The Transcendental Climate*, II, 423–46
9. Harding, *Thoreau, Man of Concord*, 107

boundaries with the selectmen in mid-September, the boundaries of David Loring's property in mid-October, Reuben Brown's Fair Haven Hill lot on October 20, a line for Stow on the 28th, the "Ministerial Lot" for the Trustees of the Ministerial Fund in mid November, the Concord-Carlisle town line for the selectmen in early December, a wood lot for Samuel Barrett on the 6th, and the Ministerial Lot on the 8th and 9th.[1]

Of all these tasks, it was perambulating the town boundaries with the selectmen which most interested him. That was—and still is—an annual duty for selectmen in many New England towns. But because there had been quarrels and threats of lawsuits from neighboring towns, Concord, in 1851, for the first time asked a trained surveyor—Thoreau—to accompany them. He was delighted to be asked for he was always partial to "across-lot routes," and no route could be more "across-lot" than this one since the town's roads rayed out from the center and followed none of the boundaries. "It is a sort of reconnoissance of its frontiers authorized by the central government of the town, which will bring the surveyor in contact with whatever wild inhabitant or wilderness its territory embraces," he said.[2] Once out in the field he quickly got to the heart of the trouble, discovered that variations in the compass over the years had caused marked discrepancies, and promptly settled the matter to everyone's satisfaction.[3] But he had forgotten that the selectmen would be his constant companions in the work. By the time the task was over he was complaining that he had been "dealing with the most commonplace and worldly-minded men and emphatically *trivial* things." He felt "inexpressibly begrimed and almost as though he had committed suicide in a sense. For days after the task was over he wandered alone in the fields, trying to recover his "tone and sanity," trying "to perceive things truly and simply again."[4]

Surveying had its rewards, though, he found. It did provide him with a small but adequate income. It led him to new fields and woods where occasionally he was lucky enough to discover new flowers, new birds, new mushrooms, and even Indian relics

1. Cameron, *The Transcendental Climate*, II, 447–93
2. Thoreau, *Journal*, II, 498–9
3. Horace Hosmer, "Reminiscences of Thoreau," *Concord Enterprise*, April 15, 1893
4. Thoreau, *Journal*, III, 5

occasionally it brought him in contact with such colorful and congenial individuals as old Joseph Hosmer, who filled his ears with reminiscences of the Concord of bygone years—and Thoreau loved every minute of it. He discovered that while the physical labor of surveying might make him weary, it surprisingly made him more susceptible than usual to music and poetry when he returned to his home at evening. But even then he was not at all sure it was worth it, for he was often too busy surveying to do what he really wanted. The boys, he discovered on December 14, 1851, had been skating for a week, and he had not only not put his skates on, but he had been so busy surveying he had hardly been aware that there was ice. In his estimation it would take quite a sum of money to make up for the loss of a week's skating. But what disturbed him more was that surveying used only his lowest talents. He had more important things to do for his community, he thought, than running lines and measuring angles. Why was it, he wondered, that he was never invited to do anything quite worthwhile.

V

In mid-July, 1850, word reached Concord that the ship *Elizabeth*, bearing Margaret Fuller (now the Marchesa Ossoli), her husband and young son as well as Charles Sumner's brother Horace, had been wrecked on Fire Island just off Long Island. She had gone to Europe several years earlier as a foreign correspondent for Greeley's New York *Tribune* and there, covering the Italian revolution, had met and married Ossoli, a member of the minor nobility. She was returning to her native land with the manuscript of a book on the revolution ready for publication when the boat was wrecked and all four perished.

Emerson at first thought he would go himself to the scene of the wreck to recover the manuscript and any other personal property he could find. But he soon decided that Thoreau would be more competent about such matters and persuaded him on July 24 to make the journey; he obtained, through Ellery Channing, Margaret Fuller's brother-in-law, authorization for him to act for the family, and gave him seventy dollars to cover his expenses.[5]

5. Frederick T. McGill, Jr., Manuscript biography of Ellery Channing

Emerson also wrote Marcus Spring, the philanthropist and reforme
with whom Miss Fuller had originally gone abroad and who no
lived in New York, to ask him to assist Thoreau in any way neces
sary and to authorize him to supply Thoreau with further funds i
he needed them and then sent similar letters to William Emerso
and Horace Greeley.[6]

Setting out promptly for New York City, Thoreau tried un
successfully to find Greeley and then proceeded to Fire Island. Th
wreck had occurred five days earlier and by now there was littl
left. Vandals had poured on to the scene and walked off with ever
thing they could lay their hands on. On July 25 Thoreau wrot
Emerson that he was staying at the home of Smith Oakes, less tha
a mile from the wreck, and interviewing everyone possible fo
details. He had learned that a broken desk, a black leather trunk
both containing unimportant papers, and a carpet bag and a sho
that belonged to Ossoli had been found. There was no sign of th
bodies of the Ossolis nor of Sumner.

Then, learning that many of the pilferers had come fror
Patchogue, he persuaded three fishermen to take him there in a
oyster boat, but he had to wait three hours for the tides to floa
their boat. The fishermen meanwhile adjourned to a nearby taver
and were well under the weather when it was time to go. One o
them, "a Dutch sailor with a singular bullfrog or trilobite expres
sion of the eyes," as Thoreau described him, insisted upon carryin
Thoreau out to the boat on his back, reeling in the darkness as h
went. For the entire voyage, two of the men lay flat on the bottor
of the boat soaked by the bilge water and wallowing in their ow
vomit. The skipper steered for what he supposed to be a light
house five or six miles off in the mist, and almost ran aground befor
he discovered it was the light through a crack in a fisherman'
bunk not more than six rods off.

The trip to Patchogue was completely unsuccessful and Tho
reau returned to Fire Island to search the beach once more. Some
one had found a shift with Margaret's initials on it, a gentleman'
shirt, a child's petticoat and drawers, a nightgown, and a piece of
patterned cloth with a silk fringe on it, he learned.[7] He himsel

6. Sanborn, *Recollections of Seventy Years*, II, 415; Emerson, *Letters*
(New York, 1939), IV, 219, 220
7. Henry David Thoreau [Notes on Fire Island], MS, Morgan Library

ound Ossoli's coat and ripped off a button to take home. Later he
earned that a body, badly mangled by sharks, had been cast up
n the shore a mile or two from the lighthouse. When he reached
t, he found there was little more than a few bones with a little
lesh adhering to them. It was possible that it was the body of
Horace Sumner, but when he wrote of his discovery, he admitted
t was impossible to identify the remains with any certainty. His
thoughtfulness however won the friendship of Sumner, who thereafter made a point of sending Thoreau any government publications
that he thought might be of interest, from his own speeches against
slavery to patent office reports and accounts of explorations in the
West.

Thoreau eventually gave up on Fire Island and returned to
Concord, where he read his few notes on his findings to Emerson
and Elizabeth Hoar. There was pitifully little to report. It had
been a mission of mercy, but a singularly unsuccessful one.

VI

When the railroads announced a special excursion to Canada
at the cut-rate of seven dollars round-trip fare in the early fall of
1850, Thoreau and Ellery Channing, along with fifteen hundred
others, decided to go. They left Boston on September 25 and
journeyed up through Fitchburg, Ashburnham, Keene, New Hampshire (where Thoreau was happy to get a glimpse of the broad
main street of his mother's native town), Bellows Falls, Vermont,
Ludlow, and Burlington. There they boarded a steamer for a night
trip down Lake Champlain to Plattsburg, New York, and in the
morning crossed by train into Canada at St. John's. The bilingual
posters in French and English, the first sign of a foreign land, immediately caught Thoreau's eye when they crossed the border.

Arriving in Montreal in the early afternoon, they made the
church of Notre Dame their first stop and Thoreau found himself
impressed in spite of himself at the quiet, religious atmosphere of
the building. He was even led to admit that he was not sure but
that the Catholic religion might be an admirable one—if only the
priests were omitted. A good Yankee for once, he resented Britain's
show of military might. Wherever he went, he was struck with the

sight of soldiers—something unusual in his own country—and considered their presence a waste of time, money, and energy. Their work was destructive, he complained; what might be accomplished if they could be used for building up rather than tearing down?

Early in the evening the two took the steamer *John Munn* to Quebec and docked at six the next morning. Annoyed with the throngs of tourists, Thoreau and Channing took off by themselves and headed for the citadel, but when they learned the tourists were provided with guides, they forgot their annoyance and joined the crowd once more to pick up whatever tidbits of information they could. In mid-afternoon they broke off by themselves once more and hiked the eight miles out to Montmorency Falls. With only a twenty-five-cent palm-leaf hat and a thin brown linen sack for a coat, Thoreau soon began to notice the chill of the northern latitudes. It was not long before he had acquired a heavy cold.

When dusk came that evening they found to their chagrin and astonishment that they could not walk up to any farmhouse and rent a bed for the night as they always had in their tramps across New England. Not only were the Canadians unwilling to take wandering strangers into their homes for the night, but most houses simply lacked an extra bed. After much inquiry they finally found a public house half a mile from the falls and put up for the night. In the morning, to their amazement, they were offered brandy with their breakfast.

The Montmorency Falls were a great disappointment. Queen Victoria's father had built a great estate nearby and had fenced off all the good views for himself. Thoreau fulminated against those who would deprive the public of its God-given rights to the wonders of Nature. Though it was by now raining as well as cold, they continued their hike along the north bank of the St. Lawrence and by twilight had reached St. Anne, thirty miles downstream. When they visited the shrine in the morning, Thoreau suspected that the crutches hanging on the walls, inferring that the ill had been cured, had been manufactured to order by the carpenter who built the church. The Falls of St. Anne he found more rewarding, even though he had lost his way briefly in trying to find them. Clambering over wet and slippery rocks and logs to get as good a view as possible, he was thankful that he could examine them to his heart's content.

In the early afternoon they began retracing their steps. Heavy winds prevented their going out to the Isle of Orleans, but it gave them more time to explore the various falls. Every stream entering the St. Lawrence in that region, they found, had a great fall or a cascade, and they inspected each one until they had had their fill. "Falls there are a drug," Thoreau confessed, "and we became quite dissipated in respect to them."

Near Château Richer that night they found lodging in a house where the master to their surprise could speak a little English—though it staggered them more than any French they had heard. They spent the evening in the kitchen chatting merrily and drawing maps with chalk on the oiled tablecloth to make clear their questions. Their hosts they found markedly superior to most of the natives, whom they thought intellectually and physically inferior to those of New England, and incredibly filthy. Thoreau's low opinion of the natives was confirmed the next morning when he stopped on his way back to Quebec to ask a miller the age of his stone mill and the man demanded a coin before he would answer. Thoreau regretted that he did not know enough French to give him a piece of his mind but instead had to satisfy himself by looking all he would have said and departing without the information.

They took a calèche that afternoon to the Chaudière Falls, crossing the St. Lawrence on an inconvenient and dirty ferryboat. The next morning they toured the walls and fortifications of Quebec but were anything but impressed with the display of military power. "Does my friend there, with a bullet resting on half an ounce of powder, think that he needs that argument in conversing with me?" Thoreau queried. The inhabitants of the region he thought were caught between the twin fires of the soldiery and the priesthood. The blue flowers of the succory and the late goldenrods and buttercups on the summit of Cape Diamond impressed him far more than churches and fortifications.

Finding that he had an hour and a half to spare before his steamer left, Thoreau returned in the late afternoon to a restaurant where he had seen a large map of Canada on the wall. He obtained the permission of the proprietor, rolled up a mahogany table and, placing a handkerchief on it, clambered up and made a copy of the map. Just as he finished, a maid firmly announced, "Some gentlemen want the room, sir."

The two spent their last day in Montreal climbing Mount Royal. By evening of the next day they were back in Concord.

Thoreau's total expenses, including the purchase of two guide books and a map, were $12.75. But he was not happy with the trip. He told his friends, "What I got by going to Canada was a cold." And in his journal he lamented that he had been unable to take one honest walk there as he might in the Concord woods of an afternoon.

Typically he set immediately to work to harvest an essay from his excursion. He had taken the trip on too short notice to do much reading in advance, so now he journeyed into Cambridge and borrowed a goodly number of books on Canadian history from the Harvard Library. For some reason or other—probably chiefly because he was so markedly unenthusiastic about the journey itself —he could not seem to whip the essay into the shape he wanted it. All through the next year he continued to borrow and read more books on the subject and take more and more notes. Eventually he filled an entire notebook with quotations on Canada.

It was January 7, 1852, before he tried the essay out in lecture form before the Concord Lyceum. On March 17 he gave a second installment. When Emerson went to Canada in April, Thoreau asked him to check for him the meanings of various French-Canadian terms.[8] Meanwhile he had submitted his essay, now titled "A Yankee in Canada," to Horace Greeley for publication. Greeley suggested that Thoreau chop it into three or four pieces, omit the sections on Montreal and Quebec, obviously realizing that Thoreau's caustic comments on church and state would alienate both editors and readers, and emphasize the natural history. Thoreau soon resubmitted the essay to Greeley only to have it turned down first by the *Whig Review* and then by another magazine. But thanks to the intervention of his old Concord friend George William Curtis it was accepted by *Putnam's Monthly,* on whose editorial staff Curtis now served.

"A Yankee in Canada" appeared serially in *Putnam's* for January, February, and March 1853, but then publication was abruptly halted with less than half the essay in print. Curtis had insisted upon removing what he called "heresies" in the article— among them the statement that "I am not sure but this Catholic religion would be an admirable one if the priests were quite omitted" —and Thoreau would have none of it. He asked for the return of his

8. Ralph Waldo Emerson, *Journals,* VIII, 282–3

manuscript even though he fully realized, as Greeley quickly pointed out to him, that no other magazine would take it with half of it already in print.[9] To make matters worse, it was then discovered that more than half of the manuscript, including the entire unpublished portion, was missing. Thoreau wrote a polite but obviously angry letter to Curtis asking for the rest of the manuscript. It eventually turned up, but it was not published until after Thoreau's death when the complete essay was gathered into a volume with his anti-slavery and reform papers.

"A Yankee in Canada" is the least successful of Thoreau's various "excursions." He announced on the first page, "I fear that I have not got much to say about Canada, not having seen much," and most readers agree with him. Even the faithful H. G. O. Blake for once was unenthusiastic, and Thoreau apologized in a letter to him: "I do not wonder that you do not like my Canada story. It concerns me but little, and probably is not worth the time I took to tell it."[1] Thoreau quite openly displays his strong prejudices against both Roman Catholicism and British colonial militarism. At times he appears to be only a notch or two above the most chauvinistic of super-patriots, a strange role indeed for him. He himself later realized that he had chosen the wrong area of Canada to visit. What he had seen was the little of the country that was then urbanized. What he should have chosen was the great Canadian wilderness. He closed his essay with the hope that someday he might "make a longer excursion on foot through the wilder parts of Canada," but that wish was never fulfilled.[2] The only advantage he derived from "A Yankee in Canada" was a monetary one—the money he received from *Putnam's* enabled him to repay Greeley the seventy-five dollars he had borrowed the previous summer.

VII

In November 1848 the Alcott family, in desperate financial straits, moved to Boston. Bronson Alcott himself was proving

---

9. Gordon Milne, *George William Curtis & the Genteel Tradition* (Bloomington, 1956), 67

1. Thoreau, *Correspondence*, 299

2. Thoreau, *Writings*, V, 101

utterly inadequate to cope with the situation and Mrs. Alcott, to keep the family together, accepted work as a missionary to families even poorer than her own. Alcott blithely kept on reading, writing, talking, and, as usual, ignoring the situation. His only source of income was from the "Conversations" he occasionally held in his rooms. These Thoreau faithfully attended whenever he was in the vicinity.

In March 1849 Alcott embarked on another of his Quixotic schemes—he founded the Town and Country Club. He sent a circular letter to fifty-three friends, including Thoreau, to invite them to meet at his home on March 20 to "discuss the advantages of organizing a Club or College for the study and diffusion of the Ideas and Tendencies proper to the nineteenth century; and to concert measures, if deemed desirable, for promoting the ends of good fellowship."[3] Twenty-nine, including Thoreau, showed up for the first meeting. It was, as Ellery Channing said, "an impossible alliance between Boston lawyers who desired only a smoking room, and ... country ministers, who expected to be boarded and lodged, and to have their washing done, whenever they came up to the city."[4] Briefly the two groups managed to settle their differences, organize the club, rent rooms from Alcott for their meetings—thus giving him a source of income—and establish a monthly lecture series. But for Thoreau one such meeting was enough and he never showed up again. The club lasted a year and then, a complete financial failure, it was dissolved. By pure happenstance Thoreau was again in Boston visiting Alcott on May 2, 1850, the day of its legal dissolution, and so attended its requiem.[5]

Alcott missed his Concord friends and returned to visit them whenever he could find the opportunity, often stopping in to dine with the Thoreaus when there. In September 1849 he spent several weeks in Concord, walking, talking, and swimming almost daily at the "Fishing Place" with Thoreau and returned to Boston "refreshed, and repaired a good deal, spiritually and bodily." Concord he thought "classic land," for here, as he said, "dwell the poets, the Americans *par excellence* and men of the future, whose names shall render Harvard and Yale, with their professors and

3. Thoreau, *Correspondence*, 239–40
4. W. S. Tryon, *Parnassus Corner* (Boston, 1963), 28
5. Alcott, Journals

halls, one day ridiculous." "'Tis at heart my own home," he thought and he longed for the day when he could "draw closer to its bosom."[6] But such was not to be for some time.

Requests for lectures continued to come in and Thoreau was happy to fill them. He was invited to speak in Newburyport on December 6, 1850, and Thomas Wentworth Higginson, when he learned of the engagement, invited Thoreau to be his house guest. Higginson, one of the younger Transcendentalists, was then minister of the Unitarian Church in Newburyport. He had married Ellery Channing's sister-in-law and thus visited frequently in Concord. Happening upon Thoreau's *Week,* he enjoyed it as few others did and so called upon him one day in Concord, and found him engaged at the moment in the family pencil shop. He thought Thoreau "pure and wonderfully learned in nature's things and deeply wise," but also "tedious in his monologues and cross-questionings."[7] When later he talked with Mrs. Thoreau about her son, he learned that Thoreau was more domestic and filial than he appeared.[8] In Newburyport Higginson took Thoreau around to meet Dr. H. C. Perkins and there gave him his first opportunity to look through a high-power microscope and observe the circulation in the Nitella.

On January 1, 1851, Thoreau gave his Cape Cod lecture before the Bigelow Mechanic Institute in Clinton, Massachusetts, and while there took the opportunity to inspect the gingham mills at length. Mechanical ingenuity always fascinated him, and despite his occasional fulminations against the increasing mechanization of civilization, he was always eager to examine new and different machinery.

On January 22 he read one of his *Walden* lectures in Medford, Massachusetts, and stopped off in Boston to dine with the Alcotts on his way. When he read the lecture privately to Alcott, Alcott thought it "as refreshing a piece as the Lyceum will get from any lecturer going at present in New England—a whole forest, with forester and all, imported into the citizen's and villager's brain."[9]

---

6. Ibid.
7. Thomas Wentworth Higginson, *Letters and Journals* (Boston, 1921), 94
8. Mary Thacher Higginson, *Thomas Wentworth Higginson* (Boston, 1914), 98
9. Bronson Alcott, *Journals,* 238

On April 23 he tried out a new lecture, entitled "The Wild," on the Concord Lyceum and on May 31 repeated it in Worcester. It was to become one of his favorite lectures, one that he repeated many times, working it over and adding to it each time until eventually it became large enough to break into two, the new part entitled "Walking." Because he knew the market for it would vanish once it reached print, he was careful not to have either part published in his lifetime. But just before his death, he put the two back together again and sold the essay to the *Atlantic Monthly,* where it was published in the issue of June 1862 as "Walking, or the Wild." It is in actuality still two separate essays, the first section on the joys of walking and the second on "the wild." In the former he contends that he cannot preserve his health and spirits without spending at least four hours a day "sauntering through the woods and over the hills and fields, absolutely free from all worldly engagements" and confesses his astonishment at the power of endurance of those who confine themselves to shops and offices. In the latter he expounds one of his favorite theses—that "in Wildness is the preservation of the World." Man, Anteus-like, he believes, must return to the soil if he is to preserve his sanity, his morality, and his strength. The essay is a plea to save some of the wildness of the earth for future generations and has rightfully been recognized as one of the pioneer documents in the conservation and national-park movement in this country.

On January 6, 1852, Thoreau gave his first lecture in the neighboring town of Lincoln, after walking there from Concord in a snowstorm. In all probability he gave the Canada lecture that he delivered the next night in Concord. On February 22 he journeyed down to Plymouth to lecture at the invitation of Marston Watson, who had instituted a series of Sunday lectures in Leyden Hall for those "who for one reason or another do not attend church." Charging five cents admission to the hall, Watson promised to pay his speakers ten or fifteen dollars plus expenses.[1] Thoreau's lecture, one of his *Walden* chapters, was sufficiently successful for him to be asked to return and deliver another on May 22. This time he spent three days visiting with the Watsons and exploring the many ponds of Plymouth. The next winter

---

1. Marston Watson, Letter to Bronson Alcott of January 15, 1852. MS, Houghton Library

however, when Watson asked him to come back for a third lecture, Thoreau begged off, saying the only lectures he had ready were too secular and heathenish for a Sunday service and he had no leisure at the moment to prepare another.[2]

On March 17, 1852, he read another segment of his Canada paper to the Concord Lyceum and on the 22nd, at Bronson Alcott's invitation, he read a lecture on "Sylvan Life," undoubtedly a chapter from *Walden,* in Alcott's rooms in Boston.[3] Alcott had advertised it in the newspapers as a subject "peculiarly appropriate to Mr. Thoreau's experience and views," one in which he could "disregard conventionalisms without being driven into controversies." The audience of sixty or more, according to Alcott, was delighted.[4]

The success of this lecture led Thomas Wentworth Higginson, who had recently given up his Newburyport church, to arrange another lecture for Thoreau in Boston, this time on April 6 in Cochituate Hall on Tremont Street. Advertising it in the newspapers, Higginson urged those who wished to hear something fresh and invigorating to attend. Conventionalisms, he promised, had "about as much influence over [Thoreau] as over a forest tree or the birds in its branches." He would "entertain any one who is not muffled in more than ordinary dullness."[5] Unfortunately a furious snowstorm blocked the streets of Boston that day. Thoreau and Higginson plowed through the snow to find only Alcott, Dr. Walter Channing (Ellery's father), and three or four other ticket holders present. When Alcott learned there was a mechanics' reading room adjacent, he arbitrarily moved the meeting there and tried to persuade the young men present that here was a golden opportunity for them to hear a promising young writer. A few put their newspapers down but more retained them. The lecture proved introspective, even for Higginson. Some of the audience went to sleep, others rustled their papers, all were glad when it was over. So far as Higginson was concerned the only happy part of the occasion was the fact that Dr. Channing forced

---

2. Thoreau, *Correspondence,* 290
3. Alcott, Journals
4. Clipping pasted in Alcott's Autobiographical Collections, VI, 174, Houghton Library
5. Alcott, Journals

a five-dollar bill on him to help pay the expenses he had incurred.[6] Fortunately few of Thoreau's lectures were so disastrous.

VIII

Despite his writing, his lecturing, and his surveying, Thoreau still managed to spend a good part of each day tramping the fields and woods not only of Concord, but of the neighboring towns of Wayland, Bedford, Billerica, Lincoln, Boxboro, Sudbury, Stow, Natick, and Acton. He rejoiced that he could easily walk ten, fifteen, or twenty miles from his own door without going by any house or without crossing a road "except where the fox and mink do."[7] There were square miles in his vicinity, he boasted, that had no inhabitants, and no one else knew these areas as well as he. He set out each afternoon well prepared for his hikes. Under his arm he carried an old music book (his father's *Primo Flauto*) in which to press flowers. In his hand was a cane made of a gnarled stick, one side shaved smooth and its edge marked off in feet and inches for quick measuring. On his head was his size seven hat with a special shelf built inside on which to place interesting botanical specimens—his brains, he joked, helped to keep the specimens moist.[8] His clothes were chosen not for fashion but to provide a natural camouflage in the woods and fields—Vermont gray or, when he could find it, a mixture of browns and greens that made him look, he said, "the color of a pasture with patches of withered sweet-fern and lechea" so that he might more easily approach wild animals.[9] When his tailoress said, "They do not make them so now," his reply was, "It is true, they did not make them so recently, but they do now," and continued to wear his own individual fashion.[1]

Wasps, bees, and hornets interested him particularly for a time and he took every opportunity to observe them. He consulted the Concord farmers Pratt, Rice, and Hastings to learn the tech-

---

6. Thomas Wentworth Higginson, "Glimpses of Authors," *Brains*, I (1891), 105
7. Thoreau, *Journal*, II, 52
8. Thoreau, *Journal*, IV, 133
9. Ibid. XIII, 230–1
1. Thoreau, *Writings*, II, 27

niques of bee hunting and joined them in catching wild bees, letting them go one at a time and by their flight tracing down their nest in some hollow tree—though for Thoreau the exercise was purely academic since he had already found the bee tree itself in an earlier ramble. It was the technique he was interested in, not the find. He gathered abandoned hornets' nests as decoration for his bedroom museum; but once when he knocked on a nest too early in the fall "to see if anybody was at home," the whole swarm came out after him and he was forced to flee without dignity.[2] On another occasion when he brought a nest home, the heat of his room hatched the hornets and he was forced to toss the nest hurriedly out the window.

He spent a good deal of time in his boat on the river. When the annual floods were unusually high in the spring of 1852, he devoted days to visiting each of the various bridges and measuring its depths, then, hunting up the old-timers of the town, compared notes with them on all the floods of the past they could remember, and rejoiced that he was seeing something new in Concord. Frogs and toads particularly interested him that spring. He brought some peepers (*Hylodes Pickeringii*) home to study in a tumbler, but they promptly crawled out and he eventually found them peeping on the family piano. His rowboat finally disintegrated from old age and for a time he was forced to borrow whenever he needed one. But in mid-December of 1852 he acquired a new one of his own and boasted the next spring when he first used it, "Without being the owner of any land, I find that I have a civil right in the river,—that, if I am not a land-owner I am a water-owner. It is fitting, therefore, that I should have a boat, a cart, for this my farm."

When he spotted his first woodchuck of the 1852 season at Hubbard's grove on April 16, he reported in his journal that he succeeded in cornering it away from its hole:

I squatted down and surveyed him at my leisure. . . . When I moved, it gritted its teeth quite loud, sometimes striking the under jaw against the other chatteringly, sometimes grinding one jaw on the other, yet as if more from instinct than anger. Whichever way I turned, that way it headed. I took a twig a good

2. Thoreau, *Journal*, III, 34

long one and touched its snout, at which it started forward and bit the stick, lessening the distance between us by two feet, and still it held all the ground it gained. I played with it tenderly awhile with the stick, trying to open its gritting jaws. . . . We sat looking at one another about half an hour, till he began to feel mesmeric influences. . . . I walked round him; he turned as fast and fronted me still. I sat down by his side within a foot. I talked to him *quasi* forest lingo, baby-talk, at any rate in a conciliatory tone, and thought that I had some influence on him. He gritted his teeth less. . . . With a little stick I lifted one of his paws to examine it, and held it up at pleasure. I turned him over to see what color he was beneath (darker or more purely brown), though he turned himself back again sooner than I could have wished. . . . I spoke kindly to him. I reached checkerberry leaves to his mouth. I stretched my hands over him, though he turned up his head and still gritted a little. I laid my hand on him, but immediately took it off again, instinct not being wholly overcome. If I had had a few fresh bean leaves, thus in advance of the season, I am sure I should have tamed him completely. . . . I finally had to leave him without seeing him move from the place.[3]

Perhaps it was the result of his recent contacts with Louis Agassiz, perhaps it was because of the generally increasing scientific interest of the time, at any rate Thoreau found himself approaching nature more and more scientifically. He began to keep longer and longer lists of specimens he found and records of the budding of trees, the blossoming of flowers, and the arrival of birds. He began collecting, drying, labeling, and classifying botanical specimens until in a period of ten years he was able to locate more than eight hundred of the twelve hundred known species of Middlesex County.

More and more he consulted and collected for his own library the technical fieldbooks and handbooks of bird, mammal, insect, flower, tree, lichen, reptile, and moss identification that were just then beginning to appear—though often to his disappointment he was forced to do the best he could with British handbooks since the American were not yet available—a difficulty that occasionally and quite understandably led him into the misidentification of species.

---

3. Ibid. III, 421–3

When his townsman Perez Blood built a homemade telescope, Thoreau was quick to visit him and examine both it and the skies through it. Two days later, on July 9, 1851, he made a special trip into Cambridge to borrow books on astronomy from the college library for Blood, to take a look through Harvard's own new telescope at their observatory, and to talk with Bond, the astronomer. It did his heart good to learn that the naked eye still retained some importance in the estimation of astronomers, for like so many of his contemporaries—Poe, Emerson, Hawthorne, Whitman—he feared that science was destroying the beauty, the poetry of life. What was worse, he could observe in his own attitude a change that he felt was for the worse. "I fear," he complained in his journal of August 19, 1851, "that the character of my knowledge is from year to year becoming more distinct and scientific; that, in exchange for views as wide as heaven's scope, I am being narrowed down to the field of the microscope. I see details, not wholes nor the shadow of the whole. I count some parts, and say, 'I know.' "[4]

Two years later, when Spencer Fullerton Baird, the secretary of the [American] Association for the Advancement of Science, who had met Thoreau on a visit to Emerson in Concord in 1852, proposed Thoreau for membership in the association and asked him to fill out a questionnaire on his scientific interests, Thoreau noted in his journal:

> I felt that it would be to make myself the laughing-stock of the scientific community to describe or attempt to describe to them that branch of science which specifically interests me, inasmuch as they do not believe in a science which deals with the higher law. . . . The fact is I am a mystic, a transcendentalist, and a natural philosopher to boot. Now I think of it, I should have told them at once that I was a transcendentalist. That would have been the shortest way of telling them that they would not understand my explanations.[5]

When he finally got around to filling out the questionnaire and sending it in nine months later, he declined the honor of the membership, he said, because he would not be able to attend the

4. Ibid. II, 406
5. Ibid. V, 4–5

society's meetings, explained that it was "The Manners & Customs of the Indians of the Algonquin Group previous to contact with the civilized man" that most interested him, and added, "I am an observer of nature generally, and the character of my observations, so far as they are scientific, may be inferred from the fact that I am especially attracted by such books of science as White's Selborne and Humboldt's 'Aspects of Nature.' "[6]

His neighbors however gradually began to realize that they had an authority on natural history in their midst and looked upon him with a new respect. Whenever they discovered anything out of the ordinary in the world of nature about them, they turned to him for an explanation. Even those who had cold-shouldered him and denounced him for years as a ne'er-do-well began beating a path to his door with birds' nests or flowers or Indian relics in their hands and questions on their lips. Quietly and politely he answered their questions when he could, and when he couldn't, he researched until he found the answers. Emerson half-seriously proposed that the town should hire him as a consultant. If they had a town doctor and a town lawyer, he argued, why not a town naturalist? Or perhaps, he suggested, Thoreau should answer his neighbors' questions for stipulated fees—"new information paid for, as a newspaper office pays for news."[7] But Thoreau would have none of it. He was perfectly happy to answer their questions gratis and take as his pay their goodwill, the specimens, and the news they brought him.

But he was bothered with requests from his neighbors who wished to join him on his walks. That he felt he could not allow, as he explained in his journal: "They do not consider that the wood-path and the boat are my studio, where I maintain a sacred solitude and cannot admit promiscuous company. . . . Ask me for a certain number of dollars if you will, but do not ask me for my afternoons."

A few however, such as Ellery Channing and Edward Hoar, whom he could trust not to intrude into his observations and who with their alert eyes could aid him, he willingly took with him, but even these had to play the game according to his rules. Hoar later said if you were willing to walk long and far, have wet feet

6. Thoreau, *Correspondence*, 309–10
7. Emerson, *Journals*, VIII, 227

for hours at a time, pull a boat all day long, and come home late at night after many miles, Thoreau would take you with him, but if you flinched at anything, he had no more use for you. Once when Ellery Channing was done up with a headache, he begged off hiking, hoping to get a little sympathy from Thoreau. But Thoreau all too characteristically replied, "There are people who are sick in that way every morning, and go about their affairs," and marched off on his way alone. Yet Channing and Hoar and the few others who were accorded the privilege of accompanying Thoreau were happy to overlook his occasional disgruntlements. The rewards of his companionship were worth far more than the trouble.

IX

Thoreau took only one brief excursion in 1851, a journey on foot along the South Shore from Hull to Plymouth, Massachusetts. Setting out on July 25, he took the train to Boston, the Hingham boat as far down the harbor as Hull, and there started off on foot. Before he left on such a trip, he had collected every bit of information he could from maps, guide books, local histories, and gazetteers as to the routes and the places he was going. He had divided a large map of Massachusetts into sections so that he could take just that part appropriate to his trip and had made himself a knapsack of india-rubber cloth, partitioned to fit his books, papers, and other supplies. He included a botany book and *Primo Flauto* for pressing flowers, a measuring tape, and sewing equipment too. And almost inevitably a huge umbrella was hooked over his arm, ready for any eventuality.

At Hull, Thoreau explored the ruins of an old French fort with its ninety-foot well and watched for a while the operations of the semaphore telegraph to Boston. He walked along beautiful Nantasket Beach, years later to be a Coney Island madhouse, and watched riders cooling their horses in the sea. At Jerusalem Village he watched the natives gathering Irish moss along the shore before a storm. Spending the night at Cohasset, he called on old Captain Snow, who could remember outfitting as a young man at Thoreau's grandfather's store in Boston. He visited briefly

Ellen Sewall Osgood and her husband and searched for the wreck of the *St. John* he had seen in 1849, but could find no signs of it. In Scituate he called on Ellen's parents and then continued along his way to Duxbury. Here he took brief passage in a mackerel schooner setting out to sea, persuaded the captain to drop him off at Clark's Island in Plymouth harbor, where he put up for four days at the home of "Uncle Ed" Watson, sailed to the Gurnett, a seven-mile sandspit protecting the harbor, and visited the old fort, the lobster shanties, and the lighthouse there. He called on "Uncle Bill" Watson, in his schooner home half-keeled up on the mud, and roused him out of a sound sleep by thumping on the bottom of the vessel to borrow a shovel to dig clams. He sailed to Marshfield around Powder Point and chatted with Daniel Webster's neighbors. He watched the seals playing in the harbor and tried his hand at catching striped bass. He called on Marston and Mary Russell Watson, inspected their newly established nursery, and admired their arboretum of rare trees. He explored the early records in the Plymouth County courthouse, the relics in Pilgrim Hall, and as usual read every book and pamphlet on local history that he could lay hands on.

On August 1 he left Plymouth and traveled up through Kingston, Plympton, Halifax, Hanson, and Weymouth to Boston, where, stopping at the Boston Society of Natural History rooms, he talked for a while with Édouard Desor, the Swiss naturalist, and James Elliot Cabot about strange jellyfish he had found along the shore. (Desor the preceding November had made a special trip out to Concord to meet Thoreau—probably at Cabot's suggestion—to compare botanical notes with him and to report on his own experiences in collecting on the shores of Lake Superior.) From the amount of reading and note taking Thoreau did on this journey it seems likely he intended to write it up as another of his "excursions," but instead, for some unknown reason, he eventually added a few of his notes to the Cape Cod essays and left the rest untouched in his journal.

The next summer, 1852, his only excursion was a brief two-day trip to Mount Monadnock with a companion in early September. They left at 7:30 a.m. on the morning of September 6 by train for Mason Village, where they started off on a beeline hike across the tops of the intervening Peterboro hills. Their technique was to set their compass by the map or a distant peak on the horizon and start off on a straight line, across fields, through forests, and over brooks and swamps, stopping for nothing. (Legend has it that once when they found a farmhouse in their way, they went in the open front door, down the hall, and out the back, leaving the astonished farmer and his family speechless around their dining table.)

On their way to Monadnock they came across a lunatic being carried off to confinement. He insisted first on shaking their hands and told them that the spirit of God had descended upon him and had given him all the world. He shouted after them a promise to give them half a million dollars, but they ignored it for they were more interested at the moment in watching a male bald eagle in full plumage sailing over the village.

They spent the night in Peterboro where they found an old-timer who could tell them some of the early legends of the region, of wolves, and of the burning of the mountaintop. The next day they continued on their beeline and reached the summit shortly after noon, but their excursion came to an abrupt end. Since their train was scheduled to leave Troy at three, they raced down the mountainside, caught the train, and at quarter past five were back in Concord with the plants they had picked on the mountain still fresh in Thoreau's botany-box hat.

At thirty-four Thoreau began to realize his youth was behind him. Four days after his birthday he commented in his journal: "I think that no experience which I have to-day comes up to, or is comparable with, the experiences of my youth. . . . I can remember that I was all alive, and inhabited my body with inexpressible satisfaction."[8] Perhaps it was the loss of his teeth that first made him feel old, for early in May he had visited the dentist, gone under ether, and had them all removed. Subjecting himself to anaesthesia he found to be a unique experience and he recommended to his friends, "If you have an inclination to travel, take the ether; you go beyond the furthest star."[9] Quite typically, a few days after the operation he journeyed to the library to read up on dentistry. To his own amazement he was completely satisfied with his new false teeth and told Emerson, "What a pity that I could

8. Thoreau, *Journal*, II, 306–7
9. Ibid. II, 194

[295]

not have known betimes how much Art outdoes Nature in this kind of outfit for life, so that I might have spoken for such a set to start with!"[1]

And yet paradoxically at the very moments he was beginning to feel old, he was recording in his journal a sensuousness that any youth would envy. He was squeezing pokeberries and rejoicing to see their rich purple wine staining his hand. He noted the aroma of wild grapes on the wind and thought he possessed the sense of smell in greater perfection than usual. He took a boy's delight in swimming in the nude. As he walked through the woods on hot days, he made a ritual of shedding his clothes and bathing in every stream he came to. It then occurred to him it would intensify the pleasure to take his rivers "endwise," and so he began "fluvial excursions," wading down the rivers clothed only in a hat and occasionally a shirt to protect himself from the sun. He wondered if any Roman emperor had ever indulged in such luxury as this.[2] Ellery Channing, surprisingly, warned him that such behavior was not exactly conventional and, when he saw a young man on the bank with a gun in his hand, refused to join Thoreau in the water. But nothing came of it and Thoreau was not one to be daunted by conventionalism. Besides, the purity of water lilies interested him more than the impurities of his neighbors' minds. One of the purposes of his river walks was a gathering of the lilies so that he could experiment with their opening mechanisms in bowls of water at home.

When the first telegraph lines were strung through Concord in August 1851, Thoreau discovered a new musical instrument. He had long delighted in the aeolian harp—a tuning wire strung on a box and placed in a window to vibrate with the wind—and had built one for his own amusement. Now he discovered that the telegraph wires made a gigantic aeolian harp and he reveled in its sound. "I put my ear to one of the posts," he said, "and it seemed to me as if every pore of the wood was filled with music, labored with the strain,—as if every fibre was affected and being seasoned or timed, rearranged according to a new and more harmonious law."[3] Emerson and his friends could go to their con-

1. William Hague, *Life Notes* (Boston, 1887), 187
2. Thoreau, *Journal*, IV, 214
3. Ibid. III, 11

erts in Boston, if they wished, but Thoreau had no such need. He had music now every time the wind blew through the fields of Concord.

In June 1851 he was suddenly struck by the different look of the sandbank in the Deep Cut near Walden Pond at night and decided it was necessary to see his world by moonlight as well as sunlight to get a complete picture of it. Thus began a series of midnight hikes that lasted all summer long. Each month as the full moon approached he would tiptoe out of the house, sometimes as late as 1:30 a.m., and walking carefully down the streets to be sure not to wake his neighbors, he would wander out into the fields to see the world in this new light. "Will not my townsmen consider me a benefactor if I conquer some realms from the night, if I can show them that there is some beauty awake while they are asleep?" he asked. He noted that there was a type of stone, selenite, found in Arabia whose whiteness supposedly increased and decreased in phase with the moon, and thought his journal that summer could be termed *selenitic* in that sense.

It was while he was on these moonlight walks that he first heard the singing of a mysterious "night-warbler" as he called it, a bird which he heard frequently on warm summer nights but which he was never able positively to identify. Emerson warned him not to try too hard to solve the mystery, for it would take some of the poetry out of his life. Modern ornithologists, less poetic in their approach, have almost positively identified it from his notes as the ovenbird, a common wood warbler which he knew perfectly well from its daytime song and by sight.

Nature, in all its manifestations, was becoming the absorbing passion of Thoreau's life. More and more of his time was being devoted to its study and more and more of his journal to a cataloging of his observations in the fields and woods and rivers of Concord.

CHAPTER FIFTEEN
(1849–1853)

I

FOR SOME TIME there had been a gradual cooling of the friend
ship between Thoreau and Emerson. Whereas in the early day
neither could find anything but satisfaction in the other's way
and thoughts, they began to have differences of opinion and t
be more critical of each other. Emerson was coming to the en
of his great creative period. By the late 1840s he had said every
thing of importance he had to say. The rest of his life he was, fo
the most part, only to repeat himself or to retreat slowly from hi
most advanced positions. Thoreau on the other hand was jus
beginning to reach the peak of his creative powers. He was jus
beginning to turn out his masterpieces. And unquestionably, eve
if at first only subconsciously, he began to be aware of the chang
in their relative positions. It came almost as a shock to him tha
he could no longer find Emerson's writings as stimulating to hir
as they once had been.[1] He began to question Emerson's idea
more closely and to strike out on his own with more assurance

Emerson, on his side, was also finding himself disappointe
with Thoreau. Here Thoreau was in his thirties and had so littl
to show for it. Was he, like Ellery Channing, Jones Very, Charle
King Newcomb, and so many other young Transcendentalists
never going to fulfill the promise he had shown so strongly a
a young man? More than a decade before, Emerson had promise
Carlyle that Thoreau was to be *the* man of Concord, but wha
had he accomplished since? His only book had been a failure, hi
name was hardly known outside the bounds of Concord. Emer
son complained in his journal: "Thoreau wants a little ambitio

---

1. Thoreau, *Journal*, III, 134

n his mixture. . . . Instead of being the head of American engi-
neers, he is captain of a huckleberry party."[2]

To make matters worse, the old charges that Thoreau was
but an imitator of Emerson were still being bantered about. Ednah
Littlehale, who met Thoreau at one of Alcott's Conversations
in Boston on January 15, 1848, noted in her account of the
evening: "Thorault [sic] amused me. . . . He is all overlaid by
an imitation of Emerson; talks like him, puts out his arm like him,
brushes his hair in the same way, and is even getting up a caricature nose like Emerson's."[3] Such whisperings behind Thoreau's
back were bad enough. What really hurt was when James Russell
Lowell made the whisperings a matter of public record. On
October 31, 1848, he published his *Fable for Critics* and it
promptly became one of the best sellers of the day. Lowell bantered lightheartedly in doggerel verse all of his better-known
literary contemporaries. After discussing Emerson at some length,
he continued:

> There comes ——, for instance; to see him's rare sport,
> Tread in Emerson's tracks with legs painfully short;
> How he jumps, how he strains, and gets red in the face,
> To keep step with the mystagogue's natural pace!
> He follows as close as a stick to a rocket,
> His fingers exploring the prophet's each pocket.
> Fie, for shame, brother bard; with good fruit of your own,
> Can't you let Neighbor Emerson's orchards alone?
> Besides, 't is no use, you'll not find e'en a core,—
> —— has picked up all the windfalls before.[4]

Lowell, everyone agreed, was talking about Thoreau and Ellery
Channing, and which name went into which blank mattered little,
for he was making the same general charge of imitation of Emerson against both—and his charges were being broadcast across
the land. Perhaps—we cannot now be sure—that publication
marked the turning point in the relations of the two Concordians.
It imposed on Thoreau the need to break away, to show his independence.

2. Ralph Waldo Emerson, *Journals*, VIII, 228
3. Sanborn, *Recollections of Seventy Years*, II, 469
4. James Russell Lowell, *Poems* (Boston, 1890), 42

If Emerson's journal is an accurate indication, they saw markedly less of each other in 1849 than they had in previous years, and, if anything, even less in 1850. Emerson still hired Thoreau on occasion to be the handyman around his house, to trim the vines, repair the trellises, and set out new posts in the arbor, but there was little of the old closeness. On October 27, 1850, Emerson made an attempt at reconciliation and went particularly out of his way to invite his old friend in for a long talk —"the first for a long time"—but while they chatted for several hours about the difference between American and English scholars, they found little of the inspired enthusiasm of earlier days.[5]

By November 16 Thoreau was saying in his journal: "I love my friends very much, but I find that it is of no use to go to see them. I hate them commonly when I am near them. They belie themselves and deny me continually."[6] By February 15, 1851 the break was even greater and Thoreau was complaining: "I thought that friendship, that love was still possible between [us]. I thought that we had not withdrawn very far asunder. But now that my friend rashly, thoughtlessly, profanely speaks, *recognizing* the distance between us, that distance seems infinitely increased."[7] And on October 10 he added: "Ah, I yearn toward thee, my friend, but I have not confidence in thee. We do not believe in the same God. I am not thou; thou art not I. . . . Even when I meet thee unexpectedly, I part from thee with disappointment. Though I enjoy thee more than other men, yet I am more disappointed with thee than with others."[8] By December Thoreau had decided that no frankness would settle their differences. Any attempts to explain to each other seemed but to make them farther apart. When they met they seemed only to hurt each other. Even though Thoreau blamed himself as much as Emerson, he seemed unable to attempt a reconciliation. Perhaps it was better, he thought, to keep apart. At times he tried to rationalize that in peacefully parting company, they might achieve a better understanding than when they were more at one, that in not expecting essential agreement with one another they could each be more

5. Emerson, *Journals*, VIII, 135
6. Thoreau, *Journal*, II, 98
7. Ibid. II, 161–2
8. Ibid. III, 61

emselves. Nonetheless he continued to accuse Emerson of being patronizing and faultfinding.

Emerson on his side thought that Thoreau was affected and that he studiously avoided discussing anything personal or private when they were together. He complained to others that Thoreau was never frank, that there was no bow in him, that he never ought to please his friends, and that he never gave any social pleasure. In his journal he confessed, "As for taking Thoreau's arm, I should as soon take the arm of an elm tree."[9] And he quoted with approval Elizabeth Hoar's saying, "I love Henry, but I can never like him."[1] He charged that Thoreau's only value was that of a gendarme—"good to knock down a cockney with, but without that power to cheer and establish which makes the value of a friend," that at times he deliberately kept out of step with everyone else.[2] And he even wondered to Rebecca Harding Davis, when she visited him, if Thoreau were not pure animal, and thought perhaps he lacked a human soul.[3]

Ironically at just the time Emerson was complaining in his journal, "Henry does not feel himself except in opposition. He wants a fallacy to expose, a blunder to pillory, requires a little sense of victory, a roll of the drums, to call his powers into full exercise,"[4] Thoreau was complaining in *his* journal, "Talked, or tried to talk with R.W.E. Lost my time—nay, almost my identity. He, assuming a false opposition when there was no difference of opinion, talked to the wind—told me what I knew—and I lost my time trying to imagine myself somebody else to oppose him."[5]

There is a deep sadness about these years of estrangement. Neither man wanted it. Each could admit to himself but not to the other that he was at least partially at fault. Each felt a deep need for the other. Each felt closer to the other than to any other man. But when they met, they found only their sadness and their loneliness emphasized. Emerson in one of his earlier journals had remarked that in his relationship with some of his friends he

9. Emerson, *Journals*, VII, 498
1. Ibid. VI, 371
2. Ibid. VII, 303
3. Rebecca Harding Davis, "A Little Gossip," *Scribner's Magazine*, XXVIII (1900), 565–6
4. Emerson, *Journals*, VIII, 375
5. Thoreau, *Journal*, V, 188

felt as though they were "porcupines meeting with spines erect."
Such now had become his relationship with his dearest friend
And yet there seemed to be nothing either could do about it.

The break however should not be overstressed. It was nev
complete. They still continued to see each other. On the surfac
they were careful to make all appear well. When Emerson's moth
died in November 1853, it was Thoreau who journeyed over 1
Littleton to bring home Emerson's mentally retarded broth
Bulkeley and to watch him through the funeral while Thoreau
father acted as one of the bearers. And it was Thoreau who, c
March 30, 1854, wishing to have his townsmen hear more c
Emerson, drew up a petition requesting him to give a series c
lectures at the Concord Lyceum, and promising to pay him "on
with an eager attention," and then went around town and gathere
up forty signatures for it.[7] And later, in 1855, when Emerso
found that proofs of his *English Traits* would arrive while he w
away on a lecture tour, it was Thoreau he called on to correct th
proofs for him.

The estrangement continued over a number of years. As lat
as February 1856 Emerson complained in his journal: "If I kne
only Thoreau, I should think cooperation of good men imposs
ble. . . . Always some weary captious paradox to fight you with
and the time and temper wasted";[8] while a few weeks later Thorea
in his journal said:

> My friend offered me friendship on such terms that I could
> not accept it, without a sense of degradation. He would not
> meet me on equal terms, but only be to some extent my patron.
> He would not come to see me, but was hurt if I did not visit
> him. He would not readily accept a favor, but would gladly
> confer one.[9]

And two months later, "If my friend would take a quarter par
the pains to show me himself that he does to show me a piece c
roast beef, I should feel myself irresistibly invited."[1]

6. Emerson, *Journals,* V, 457
7. MS, Houghton Library
8. Emerson, *Journals,* IX, 15–16
9. Thoreau, *Journal,* VIII, 199
1. Ibid. VIII, 348

The rupture of their friendship reached a climax in February 857, when Thoreau on the 8th noted despairingly: "And now nother friendship is ended. I do not know what has made my riend doubt me, but I know that in love there is no mistake, and hat every estrangement is well founded. . . . With one with whom ve have walked on high ground we cannot deal on any lower ground ever after. We have tried for so many years to put each other to this immortal use, and have failed."[2] Two weeks later, as an afterthought he added: "At the instant that I seem to be aying farewell forever to one who has been my friend I find myself unexpectedly near to him, and it is our very nearness and dearness to each other that gives depth and significance to that forever. . . . While I think I have broken one link, I have been forging another."[3] The outburst proved to be a final outburst. Facing the issue forthrightly had a cathartic effect. Each was able at last to realize that he could not return to the original terms of friendship but that they could nonetheless build on new terms. Their new relationship did not have the warmth of the old, but now each openly appreciated the strengths—and the weaknesses—of the other and neither deferred to the other. In 1878 when Mrs. Gilchrist visited the aging Emerson, she found his memory fading. He turned to his wife and asked, "What was the name of my best friend?" "Henry Thoreau." "Oh, yes, Henry Thoreau."[4]

Oddly enough, while Emerson was losing his influence on Thoreau, Thoreau was, if anything, increasing his influence on Emerson. Emerson had always found Thoreau stimulating. But now more and more he found his conversations with Thoreau sources of inspiration for his own writings. In a matter of a few months in the spring of 1851 he was to write down in his journal notes taken from their conversations that he was later to incorporate into essays as varied as "Culture," "Poetry and the Imagination," and "Country Life." Earlier he had used such conversations with Thoreau as the basis of a paragraph in "The Poet" and later for one in "Quotation and Originality." He recognized that Thoreau was putting into practice what he himself preached, and agreed in his journal, "Thoreau gives me, in flesh

---

2. Ibid. IX, 249
3. Ibid. IX, 276
4. Canby, *Thoreau*, 455

and blood and pertinacious Saxon belief, my own ethics. He i[s]
far more real, and daily practically obeying them, than I."[5]

When visitors came to Concord, Emerson was still please[d]
and proud to introduce them to Thoreau. When he met Fredrik[a]
Bremer, the popular Swedish novelist, in Boston on January 17[,]
1850, he invited her out to Concord and saw that she met him[.]
(She however was so little impressed that when several years late[r]
she published an account of her American tour, *The Homes o[f]
the New World*, she spoke of Thoreau only as "F——" wh[o]
"went out into the wild woods and built himself a hut and live[d]
there—I know not on what."[6])

When Emerson's eccentric but brilliant Aunt Mary Mood[y]
Emerson came to Concord to visit in November 1851, the resul[t]
was very different. She found much the same to value in Thorea[u]
as she had found earlier in her nephew. She was shocked b[y]
Thoreau's religious unorthodoxy and did not hesitate to lectur[e]
him when he used the word "God" without sufficient solemnit[y]
of voice. But in spite of her orthodox biases, as Thoreau readil[y]
recognized, she could entertain large thoughts with hospitalit[y]
and was capable of what he thought of as "a masculine appreciation of poetry and philosophy."[7] He thought he had never talke[d]
with another woman who could accompany him so far as h[e]
described a poetic experience and concluded her to be the wittie[st]
and most vivacious woman he knew.

When Elizabeth Oakes Smith, a far more celebrated bluestocking of the time, visited Concord to lecture on December 31[,]
Thoreau was not nearly so impressed. Although she reporte[d]
that after the lecture Thoreau gave her his hand gravely, saying
with solemn emphasis, "You have spoken" (which Alcott explained to her meant, "You have brought an oracle"),[8] Thorea[u]
remarked in his journal that "she was a woman in the too common
sense after all," and laughed that though she was the championess
of woman's rights, she insisted he be a "ladies' man," and carry
her lecture for her to the hall. (His pocket, he complained after-

5. Emerson, *Journals*, VIII, 303
6. Fredrika Bremer, *The Homes of the New World* (New York, 1853),
I, 167
7. Thoreau, *Journal*, III, 114
8. Elizabeth Oakes Smith, *Autobiography* (New York, 1924), 140

wards, reeked of cologne.[9]) But he had a higher opinion of her
the next night when she showed spirit enough to join him in
walking out of one of John Gough's temperance lectures because
it was too emotional for either of their tastes.[1]

When John Albee, a theological student at Andover Seminary,
came to call on Emerson in May 1852, he met Thoreau and
found him so at home in Emerson's parlor that he decided he
was a regular member of the household. He was astonished that
Emerson seemed to defer to him, though he noted that at times
he seemed to be leading Thoreau on, to have a quiet laugh at
his negative and biting criticisms. When Emerson remarked on
the need for great poets, Thoreau said he had found one in the
woods but it had feathers on and had not been to Harvard. "Let
us cage it," said Emerson. "That is just the way the world always
spoils its poets," responded Thoreau, and had the last laugh.[2]

II

More and more Ellery Channing became the companion on
Thoreau's walks. In March 1849 Channing had given up his
house on Ponkawtasset Hill and moved to one on Main Street almost directly across the street from the house the Thoreaus shortly
thereafter acquired, and thus he was handier than ever. Channing's
garden sloped down to the Sudbury River and there, under a clump
of willows, Thoreau now kept his boat. Channing tried for a time
to adopt Thoreau's scheme of carrying a notebook along on their
walks, but to no avail. While Thoreau scribbled away at length,
Channing contented himself with scrawling a sketch of the landscape. And if Thoreau scribbled too long, Channing would petu-
antly remark, "*I am universal; I have nothing to do with the
particular and definite,*" and declare that he would confine himself
to the ideal and leave the facts to Thoreau.[3]

Channing was a moody soul, Thoreau recognized, and "as
naturally whimsical as a cow is brindled."[4] He could be incredibly

---

9. Thoreau, *Journal*, III, 168
1. Smith, *Autobiography*, 138
2. John Albee, *Remembrances of Emerson* (New York, 1903), 45
3. Thoreau, *Journal*, III, 99
4. Ibid.

selfish one moment and unexpectedly generous the next. He was horribly conceited, but Thoreau felt there was far more in him than usual to ground conceit on. Channing quarreled with every one but Thoreau. Once in his outspoken way he told Thoreau he did not like Mrs. Thoreau and to instruct her not to appear when he came to call. Thoreau quite naturally refused: "No indeed I shall not; it is my mother's house." The next time Channing came to call, Mrs. Thoreau by chance opened the door. Channing promptly turned his back to her but remained standing on the step. She, not to be outdone, turned her back to him and remained standing in the doorway. And so Henry found the two of them standing silently back to back when he happened by the open door some minutes later.[5]

Even Thoreau himself found Channing at times impossible to take and more than once sailed off in his boat, leaving Channing standing on the bank. Although Channing usually had only the best to say of Thoreau, once at least, on April 17, 1853, in one of the few extended entries in his usually cryptically brief journal, he stormed:

Behold H D T, he who believed in simplicity, he who has gone steadily along over the rough places and the thorns, in order to crucify and to kill out the human virtues, to render himself a Spartan. Each social faculty in which all others delight, he mortifies. Behold the victim of mortification. On him neither beauty nor goodness; you have him there, eminently chaste and abstinent, and at the same time dry as husks. His abstinence and his chastities have made him only doubly repulsive to his kind. What is his compensation [?] Eternal solitude, and endless blundering, blunder after blunder. And his is no favorable case. But it may be said, that he went according to his nature. Well! this is by no means doubtful, but his nature—how trifling a space in the great world.[6]

Although Channing was often outspoken about others, this is the only time on record he spoke so bitterly of Thoreau. It would be interesting to know what caused the outbreak, particularly since Thoreau at the moment and for several days past had been away in Haverhill surveying.

5. Brown, *Memories of Concord*, 101
6. Typescript of Channing's journal, Frederick T. McGill, Jr.

Channing's relations with his wife had deteriorated completely. He made no pretense of attempting to take care of either her or their children—or himself, for that matter. His only income was a small allowance his ever-tolerant father continued to give him and he made virtually no attempt to earn more. His wife's family, in desperation, finally intervened. Her brother-in-law Thomas Wentworth Higginson came to Concord in November 1853 and took her and the children home to Worcester with him. When, surprisingly, Channing threatened court action to get the children he had consistently neglected back, Higginson gathered up depositions from the neighbors—including Mrs. Thoreau—that he was unfit to be a father and the suit was quickly dropped. Mrs. Barzillai Frost wrote Channing's mother-in-law that Thoreau and Channing had "had a jubilee in the front parlor" to celebrate his wife's departure.[7] Channing for a time tried to persuade Thoreau to move in with him and wrote him: "I have an old house and a garden patch, you have legs and arms, and we both need each other's companionship."[8] But Thoreau wisely refused, knowing only too well that Channing's eccentricities could be tolerated only at a distance. Besides, despite the front parlor jubilee, he was more than sympathetic with Ellen Channing and disgusted with Channing's irresponsibility.

Emerson, thinking that at least some of Channing's problems were financial, had, in the spring of 1853, offered to pay him one hundred dollars for compiling an anthology of selections from the journals of Thoreau, Emerson, and Channing himself, to be entitled "Country Walking." The idea in all probability was originally Bronson Alcott's, for on February 12, 1850, he had come to Concord to dine with Emerson and to propose the establishment of a new periodical, the *Town and Country Magazine*, specifically to get the writings of Thoreau and Channing into print, and even more specifically to include excerpts from Thoreau's unpublished journals.[9] The magazine, like so many of Alcott's quixotic dreams, never materialized, but Emerson's interest was aroused and he jotted down in his own journal at the time for future action a suggestion for publishing a volume of the combined writings of Thoreau, Channing, and himself.

---

7. Frederick. T. McGill, Jr., Manuscript biography of Channing
8. Sanborn, *Henry D. Thoreau*, 178–9
9. Bronson Alcott, Journals

Much to everyone's amazement Channing for once settle
right down to work and by July 1, 1853, had completed a larg
enough segment of the work for Emerson to read sizable passag
to Bronson Alcott on a visit to Concord. The book was complete
by October 1 and Channing received his hundred dollars. But th
money did not solve his problems and the manuscript itself wa
shelved. Twenty years later, when Channing submitted his biograph
of Thoreau to Roberts Brothers of Boston for publication, the
complained that it was hardly book-length. Channing, rememberin
the "Country Walking" manuscript, chopped out a sizable chun
and inserted it with no explanation into the middle of the biog
raphy, and so a portion of it was published. Irresponsible as eve
Channing bothered neither to explain what the insertion was nor t
identify which portions were from Thoreau's journal, which fron
Emerson's, and which from Channing's. Most readers were un
derstandably confused and the section a loss. Ironically, if th
manuscript had been edited properly and published in 1853, a
originally intended, it could conceivably have helped along bot
Thoreau's reputation and Channing's, for it was the publicatio
of somewhat similar volumes of excerpts from Thoreau's writing
edited by H. G. O. Blake, in the 1880s that sparked a genuine an
widespread interest then in Thoreau as a nature writer.

On March 10, 1852, Nathaniel Hawthorne purchased Hillsid
from the Alcotts and, renaming it Wayside, moved back to Co
cord. Thoreau and Hawthorne promptly resumed their friendshi
on its old terms and Thoreau told Hawthorne an old legend abou
a man who had once lived there who believed he would never di
Recognizing at once the story potential of the legend, Hawthorn
tucked it away in his memory. Ten years later, after Thoreau'
death, he used it as the basis of his unfinished novel *Septimiu*
Felton, which he had hoped to preface with a sketch of Thoreau.

Julian Hawthorne, now seven years old, was as intrigued b
Thoreau as was his father. When Thoreau came to survey the ne
property, Julian followed him about, never losing sight of a move
ment nor asking a question nor uttering a word. Thoreau praise
him—"Good boy! Sharp eyes, and no tongue!"—and accepte
him as a friend and companion. He took Julian on his walks, taugh

---

1. Randall Stewart, *Nathaniel Hawthorne* (New Haven, 1948), 229

im how to snare chub and pickerel with a loop of long-stemmed
rass, called the beauty of dragonflies to his attention, and pointed
ut the strange shadows that water-skating insects made on the
ottom of a pool.[2] Taking him down to Egg Rock where the
Assabet and the Sudbury join to form the Concord River, Thoreau
ointed out acres of water lilies and told him that if he would go
here early enough some morning to see the first rays of the sun
trike them, he would see their closed buds suddenly flash open into
lorious blooms of white and gold. In later years Julian Hawthorne
rastically changed his opinion of Thoreau and in 1898 said:

> Thoreau was neither a child nor a man; he had the narrowness
> but not the ingenuousness of the former, and the vanity and
> self-consciousness of the latter, without the redeeming tolerance
> and common-sense. He had a good, though ultra-bilious, physical
> organization; his nature was bitter, selfish, jealous and morbid.
> His human affections were scarcely more than rudimentary; his
> intellect was sharp and analytical, but small in scope and re-
> source; he shunned society because he lacked the faculty of mak-
> ing himself decently agreeable; and yet no man ever hankered
> more insatiably after social notice and approbation.[3]

III

In the late summer of 1853 Thoreau determined once again
o visit the woods of Maine and left Boston on the steamer
Penobscot at 5 p.m. on September 13. There was a jovial group of
passengers on board, singing on the decks and in the parlors till
en o'clock. After watching the lights of Cape Ann and saluting
some mackerel fishers from Gloucester, Thoreau went below to
sleep, only to be awakened by a man who wished to black his boots.
Thoreau promptly informed him that his boots were not for black-
ing, and turned over. At the first sign of light he mounted to the
decks to discover that it was only midnight and it was the moon
he saw rising. He slunk back into the bowels of the ship once again

2. Julian Hawthorne, *Memoirs* (New York, 1938), 114–15
3. Rufus Griswold, *Correspondence* (Cambridge, 1898), 207

but was up early enough in the morning to see the lights of St. George's Island.

Arriving at Bangor at noon, he found Thatcher, his cousin, had already engaged Joe Aitteon, son of the Indian governor, for the expedition and sent him on ahead to make preparations. The two left Bangor on the 15th in the rain and spent the night at Monson, forty miles distant. At Moosehead Lake the next morning they found Aitteon waiting for them. He was a good-looking Indian, twenty-four years old, dressed in the red flannel shirt, woolen pants and black Kossuth hat typical of both the Indians and the lumbermen of the region. Thoreau was disappointed at first when he heard him say "By George!" and feared that he was already too civilized, but he soon learned that he was a true Indian and indeed one of the leaders of his tribe.

At 8 a.m. the three set out on a little steamer and reached the head of the lake about noon. There a rude log railroad drew their canoe and luggage over the carry to the banks of the Penobscot River, where, after Joe carefully pitched their canoe, they set out and reached Moosehorn Deadwater in time to camp at sundown. Thatcher, who wanted to do some moose hunting, persuaded Joe to set out in their boat by starlight. Thoreau was not anxious to go along for he did not approve of killing, but deciding it might be his only opportunity to see a moose, he finally joined them. Not a moose did they find. The only sound they heard, Joe explained, was the spontaneous falling of a dead tree, a sound which Thoreau found singularly grand and impressive on a perfectly calm night.

In the morning they continued along the Penobscot, glimpsing the summit of Katahdin in the distance. It was shortly after noon that they spotted their first moose—two of them standing on the edge of a meadow, peering through the alders. To Thoreau they looked like great frightened rabbits, with their long ears and half-inquisitive, half-frightened looks. Thatcher fired and the moose fled. Joe tried unsuccessfully to track them but soon gave up. Half an hour later, by pure chance they stumbled upon the body of the moose Thatcher had shot. Thoreau, recognizing an opportunity he was not likely to have again, set about carefully measuring it. For once, when he most needed it, he had not brought along his measuring tape, so taking the cord which served for the canoe's painter and with Joe's assistance, he measured each of the moose's dimensions, making a knot each time. Since they needed the painter that night, he then reduced these measures to lengths and fractions of his ubiquitous umbrella, untying the knots in the painter as he proceeded. The next day at Chesuncook, finding a two-foot rule, he reduced his measurements to feet and inches and took care to make a two-foot rule of his own out of black ash to be prepared against future eventualities. But despite all his pains, when he returned to civilization and checked the textbooks, he found out that somehow, somewhere he had slipped up. The measurements were obviously preposterously wrong.

When Joe proceeded to skin the moose, Thoreau found the sight heartrending. It was a tragical business to see the Indian's knife pierce the still warm and palpitating body and to see the warm milk stream from the torn udder. Later when Thatcher fired at a rustling in the woods Thoreau was happy to discover that it was not a moose but only a large porcupine he had killed this time. Thoreau had not come to the woods to kill moose nor had he foreseen that Thatcher would want to. It was a tragedy that destroyed the pleasure of his adventure and it particularly irked him that his cousin hunted merely for the satisfaction of killing the moose, for he gave the Indian the hide and abandoned the carcass. When they reached their camping grounds that evening, Thoreau refused to join in another hunt and instead devoted himself to examining the botanical specimens he had gathered and to writing up his notes for the day.

In the morning they continued on to Chesuncook Lake where they stopped at Ansell Smith's farm. The frontier houses built of great logs, the blacksmith shop, the barns, the cellars all impressed Thoreau. He saw how carefully Smith prepared himself against the sieges of winter as though he were in a frontier fort, and thought that here was a kind of primitive life he could admire.

The next day the three continued further up the Penobscot and camped that night with a group of Indians at a carry. Thoreau watched carefully as the Indians cured their moose hides and smoked the meat. They used, he noted with interest, the same techniques that DeBry had recorded in his *Collectio Peregrinationum* in 1588. When the Indians conversed in their own language, Thoreau tried to guess their topics. And although he was not particularly appreciative of their dirt, he slept with them, boasting that he lay that night as near to the primitive man of America as any of its discoverers ever had. For hours after they went to bed they talked, and Thoreau asked them the meaning of every Indian word that came to his mind. It was too good an opportunity to miss and he made the most of it while he could.

When morning came it was raining hard, so any thought of further travel was abandoned. The three took the steamer back to the foot of Moosehead Lake and reached Bangor a night later. Thoreau spent a day at Oldtown, the Indian village, interviewing old John Neptune, the patriarch of the tribe, and his son-in-law and studying closely the Indian techniques of manufacturing both batteaus, the boats of the Maine rivermen, and canoes. On September 26 he took the steamer *Boston* from Bangor and on the 27th was back in Concord where he boasted to Aunt Maria that he had had the fine opportunity of seeing the Indians and the forest in all their wild luxuriance.[4] Within a few weeks he was hard at work writing up his notes on the expedition into essay form.

IV

Thoreau, unlike most of his contemporaries, was concerned for the welfare of the downtrodden Irish immigrants who had poured into New England at the time of the great Irish potato famines of the 1840s and who, being hired as cheap labor to build the railroads that had rapidly spread their network over the area, had become resident in every village and city. At first Thoreau, like most Yankees, was scornful of the Paddies, as they were called. He thought they were dirty, shiftless, and unconcerned with spiritual values. When he took shelter from a sudden rainstorm in John Field's shanty in the Lincoln woods, he stuck up his nose at the leaking roof, the broken window, and the chickens scratching on the dirt floor. He thought Field had made a poor bargain when he bogged a neighbor's meadow for ten dollars an acre and was appalled when he learned Field spent his hard-earned money on such luxuries as tea, coffee, butter, milk, and beef. He gave Field a

4. Maria Thoreau, Letter to her nephew of October 4, 1853. MS, Mrs. Millicent Todd Bingham

ecture on the virtues of the simple life and a vegetarian diet and was disappointed and disdainful when he would not accept his advice.

But as Thoreau became better acquainted with the Irish, his opinions changed. He became aware that their poverty was not their own fault but that of their money-pinching Yankee taskmasters. When he found little five-year-old Johnny Riordan trudging a mile to school each day through the snow in patched and inadequate clothes and shoes with holes, he carried a new cloak for Johnny out to his house and found the Riordans far more literate and sociable than he expected. He loaned money to the Flannerys when they found themselves in a pinch. He wrote letters to the "old country" for the illiterate. When he learned that one was trying to raise money to bring his family across the Atlantic to join him, Thoreau got up a subscription paper and went from door to door asking for contributions or loans. He was shocked to discover that the local bank president and other of the town dignitaries refused to contribute. He was equally shocked to discover that still another Irishman, who rose at 4:30 each morning to milk twenty-eight cows, received only $6.50 a month pay while his employer prospered on his labors. When he discovered that another of his townsmen had deprived his Irish employee of a four-dollar premium won in a spading contest at the county cattle show, he thought the man "as mean as a slaveholder" and drew up a petition, which he circulated around the town:

Concord Oct 12th '53

We, the undersigned, contribute the following sums in order to make up to Michael Flannery the sum of four dollars, being the amount of his premium for spading on the 5th ult., which was received and kept by his employer, Abiel H. Wheeler.[5]

Rapidly and understandably the Irish learned that Thoreau was one Yankee they could depend upon. Many years later David Starr Jordan, the distinguished biologist and educator, in traveling across Wisconsin, happened upon one Barney Mullins in the village of Freedom Center and, learning that he had once lived in Concord, asked him if he had known Thoreau. "I knew him well," was the

---

5. MS, Barrett Collection

reply. "He had a way of his own, and he didn't care much abou money; but if there ever was a gentleman alive, he was one."[6] An the rest of the Irish of Concord agreed.

But if Thoreau was concerned for the welfare of the down trodden Irish, he was far more concerned for the welfare of th even more downtrodden Negro, free or enslaved. When Washing ton Goode, a Negro seaman, was sentenced to death in Boston fo the murder of another Negro, Thomas Harding, in a quarrel over prostitute, Thoreau, apparently feeling that Goode, because of hi race, was being railroaded to the gallows without sufficient evidence signed along with four hundred of his fellow Concordians, a two and-a-half-yard-long petition against the intended execution as " crime in which we would under no circumstances participate, whicl we would prevent if possible and in the guilt of which we will no by the seeming assent of silence, suffer ourselves to be impli cated."[7]

In the winter of 1851 the Fugitive Slave Law, granting South ern slaveholders or their agents the right to seize and carry back tc the South any runaway slaves they found in the North and promising them federal aid, was passed by Congress. Northern abolitionist were shocked and horrified. Even the gentle Emerson vowed tha he would not obey the law. When in February a Negro waiter ir Boston by the name of Shadrach was arrested for his Virgini: master, he was rescued by an abolitionist mob, taken to the home o Thoreau's friend and neighbor Mrs. Mary Brooks in Concord, anc from there conducted safely to Canada. This seizure of the initiative by the pro-slavery interests stirred the abolitionists to action. The ranks that had been split years before between the organizationa and the individualistic approaches began to feel that there was nc longer time for any argument over abstract philosophical principles Every day Negroes were being dragged back to the chains anc cruelties of slavery. It was time to act.

On April 3, 1851, Thomas Sims, a seventeen-year-old Negrc fugitive was also arrested in Boston. Once again the abolitionist: organized and attempted a rescue, but this time government official: were prepared with 250 troops on hand. On April 12 he wa: escorted by federal marshals and city militia to a ship waiting in the

6. David Starr Jordan, *Imperial Democracy* (New York, 1899), 280
7. MS, Thoreau Society Archives

arbor and shipped back to Georgia, where he was nearly lashed to death. Thoreau stormed in his journal: "I do not believe that the North will soon come to blows with the South on this question. It would be too bright a page to be written in the history of the race at present."[8] For days he filled the pages of his journal with diatribes against the South and slavery. On the 23rd, when he was asked to deliver his new lecture on "The Wild" before the Concord Lyceum, he opened the lecture by saying:

> I feel that I owe my audience an apology for speaking to them tonight on any other subject than the Fugitive Slave Law on which every man is bound to express a distinct opinion,—but I had prepared myself to speak a word now for Nature—for absolute freedom & wildness, as contrasted with a freedom and culture simply civil—to regard man as an inhabitant, or a part and parcel of nature—rather than a member of society. I wish to make an extreme statement, if so I may make an emphatic one—for there are enough champions of civilization—the minister and the school committee—and every one of you will take care of that.[9]

Why at the moment he did not speak out further against the Sims incident is not known. Certainly, as events proved later, it was utterly uncharacteristic of him. But Thoreau could act when the opportunity offered. On September 30, 1851, Henry Williams, who had escaped to Boston from slavery in Stafford County, Virginia, the previous October, learned that there were warrants out for his arrest and that the police had called for him when he was fortunate enough to be out. Accordingly he fled to Concord on foot, carrying with him letters of introduction to the Thoreaus from Mr. Lovejoy of Cambridge and William Lloyd Garrison. The Thoreaus lodged him for the night and collected funds to help him along his way. On the morning of October 1, Thoreau went down to the railroad station to buy him a ticket to Burlington, Vermont. He saw someone there acting so much like a Boston policeman that he retired and waited until the 5 p.m. train, when, with the coast clear, he got Williams safely on his way to Canada. Later arrangements were made to raise Williams's purchase price of six hundred dollars and

---

8. Thoreau, *Journal*, II, 174
9. MS, Houghton Library

he was able to return safely to Boston. So grateful was he that he purchased a china statue of Uncle Tom and Eva with his last pennies and walked out from Boston to Concord to present it to Thoreau.[1]

On July 28, 1853, Moncure Daniel Conway, a Harvard Divinity School student from Virginia, came to Concord to visit Emerson. The son of a well-to-do slaveowner, he had served for a time as a conservative Methodist circuit rider in Maryland after his graduation from Dickinson College but, happening upon Emerson's essays, had been converted to more liberal views on both slavery and religion and entered Harvard. Emerson promptly introduced him to Thoreau, who invited him to go for a walk the next day. When Conway arrived in the morning, he found Thoreau nursing a fugitive slave who had come in the night. The Negro was immediately alarmed, for he recognized Conway from Virginia and feared he was about to be seized. Both Conway and Thoreau quickly reassured him and Thoreau spent the day not only standing guard over him, but bathing and caring for him, astounding Conway with his tenderness. Only the next day after the fugitive had been safely sent along his way to Canada was Thoreau willing to redeem his promise to take Conway on a walk.[2]

On November 1, 1853, the Thoreaus lodged a free Negro woman at their home while she collected funds from the local abolitionists to buy her husband, a slave to a Mr. Moore in Norfolk, Virginia. She had persuaded Moore to buy her husband that he might not be sold further South. Moore had paid six hundred dollars for him, but now asked her for eight hundred. Thoreau thought such despicable behavior all too characteristic of a slaveholder.

Such incidents of Thoreau's kindliness to the Negro were innumerable. Mrs. Edwin Bigelow, the acknowledged leader of Concord's participants in the Underground Railroad, has testified that rarely a week went by without some fugitive being harbored overnight in town and sped along his way before daylight. Henry Thoreau more often than any other man in Concord looked after them, she said, caring for them for the night, purchasing their

1. Marble, *Thoreau: His Home, Friends and Books,* 198–9
2. Moncure Conway, *Autobiography Memoirs and Experiences* (Boston, 1902), I, 140–3

ickets, escorting them to the station—often taking them to West Fitchburg, where, since it was a smaller station, they felt safer— or for further protection accompanying them on the trains for a while, although taking care to sit in separate seats so as not to attract attention.[3]

Thoreau's indignation against the slaveholder reached its height with the Anthony Burns case. On the evening of May 24, 1854, Burns, who was a fugitive slave employed in a Brattle Street clothing store in Boston, was confronted by his former master, arrested, and told he was to be shipped back to Virginia. Abolitionists called a protest meeting at Faneuil Hall and Thomas Wentworth Higginson led an ill-fated attempt to rescue Burns from his Boston jail. President Franklin Pierce ordered out the militia and Burns was escorted under armed guard to a revenue cutter at Long Wharf, which took him back to Virginia and slavery. Fortunately he was quickly purchased by Northern philanthropists, freed, and sent to Oberlin College to study for the ministry.

The Burns incident was perhaps the turning point in Massachusetts in the anti-slavery fight. Many who had earlier shown little sympathy towards the activities of the abolitionists now supported their cause. United States Commissioner Edward G. Loring, who had ordered Burns sent back to slavery, was removed from office, his classes at Harvard were boycotted, and his appointment to the Harvard faculty was not renewed. The Massachusetts legislature passed a Personal Liberty Law which made the Fugitive Slave Law thereafter virtually unexecutable in the state.

When Thoreau learned of Burns's arrest, his wrath boiled over in his journal. When the local abolitionists called a meeting in Concord and then devoted it to denouncing the activities of proslavery men in Nebraska, Thoreau was disgusted and informed them that he was more concerned with what was happening right before their eyes in Massachusetts. A more radical group of abolitionists, led by William Lloyd Garrison, called a mass meeting in nearby Framingham for the Fourth of July. Thoreau, going back through his journal, culled out his comments on both the Burns case and the earlier Sims case, welded them at white heat into one of the most searing and devastating of his attacks on a government that would condone slavery, and entitled it appropriately enough

---

3. Edward Emerson, *Notes on Thoreau*

"Slavery in Massachusetts." Word had reached the crowd at Framingham that Thoreau had prepared a speech and he was clamored for. Ascending to the platform, he read his paper with great effectiveness.

Although less widely known, "Slavery in Massachusetts" is in many respects far more outspoken than "Civil Disobedience." Thoreau was not generalizing about the evils of government, but denouncing a particular incident of wrongdoing to a specific individual. The State could arrest him when wittingly he refused to pay his taxes and he would denounce government in general. But when it stepped in and took away the rights of an innocent individual, a Negro, Thoreau rose up in righteous wrath, shouting, "My thoughts are murder to the State." He swore, "The law will never make men free; it is men who have got to make the law free. They are the lovers of law and order who observe the law when the government breaks it."[4] Hitherto Thoreau had sided with the non-resistants as more consistent with his Transcendentalist philosophy. But now in his anger he came out with the activists and publicly denounced both Church and State for condoning and even supporting slavery. When Garrison ceremonially burned a copy of the United States Constitution at the meeting to symbolize his defiance, Thoreau now heartily approved.

Thoreau's speech attracted wide attention. Thomas Wentworth Higginson, who had led the ill-fated attempt to rescue Burns from his Boston prison, hailed it as surpassing everything else as a literary statement of the truth called out by the Burns arrest.[5] The *Anti-Slavery Standard* published an abbreviated version of the address, while Garrison's *Liberator* and Horace Greeley's New York *Tribune* published it in full on July 21 and August 2 respectively. Greeley accompanied the speech with an editorial entitled "A Higher-Law Speech":

> The lower-law journals so often make ado about the speeches in Congress of those whom they designate champions of the Higher Law, that we shall enlighten and edify them, undoubtedly, by the report we publish this morning of a *genuine* Higher Law Speech—that of Henry D. Thoreau at the late celebration of our National Anniversary in Framingham, Mass., when Wm. Lloyd Garrison burned a copy of the Federal Constitution. No

4. Thoreau, *Writings*, IV, 396
5. Thoreau, *Correspondence*, 336

one can read this speech without realizing that the claims of Messrs. Sumner, Seward and Chase to be recognized as Higher-Law champions are of a very questionable validity. Mr. Thoreau is the Simon-Pure article, and his remarks have a racy piquancy and telling *point* which none but a man thoroughly in earnest and regardless of self in his fidelity to a deep conviction ever fully attains. The humor here so signally evinced is born of pathos—it is the lightning which reveals to hearers and readers the speaker's profound abhorrence of the sacrifice or subordination of one human being to the pleasure or convenience of another. A great many will read this speech with unction who will pretend to blame us for printing it; but our back is broad and can bear censure. Let each and all be fairly heard.

It is significant however that though with the Burns incident Thoreau moved over more closely to an approval of William Lloyd Garrison's use of organizational action, he never actually joined an anti-slavery society. He could now approve somewhat of their doings, but he could not bring himself to act other than independently. It was deep in his nature, no matter how strongly he was stirred, to go his way alone.

V

Thoreau's sympathies for the downtrodden did not however extend to the professional reformers who often came to board at his mother's house on their visits to Concord and who insisted they shared a common interest with him in the welfare of the weak and unprotected. So far as Thoreau was concerned, they went at things backwards. They believed that if they succeeded in reforming society, society would then reform the individual. Thoreau, true Transcendentalist that he was, believed that all reforms must begin with the individual. So long as the individual was corrupt he would find ways and means of corrupting even the most ideal society, but if the individual were truly reformed from within, he would lead the good life in society, he thought.

Thoreau suspected that many a reformer needed far more reform himself than the society in which he lived, that their activities were often misdirected efforts to conceal their own personal weaknesses, and that oftentimes they were far more interested in achieving personal power than in truly bringing about a reformation. He much preferred an idealist like Bronson Alcott, who he thought the sanest man he ever knew, with the fewest crotchets of all, because he refused to pledge himself to any institution and devoted his attention to the reformation of himself. When Alcott told Thoreau that his proffered services as a lecturer for the abolitionist had been declined, Thoreau was certain that it was because of the littleness of such men as Garrison and Phillips who did not want leaders but small men to serve under them.

All Thoreau's ire at the professional reformers poured out in his journal when by pure coincidence three of them—A. D. Foss, a former Baptist minister in Hopkinton, New Hampshire; Loring Moody, "a sort of travelling pattern-working chaplain"; and H. C. Wright (not to be confused with Bronson Alcott's English friend H. G. Wright), "who shocks all the old women with his infidel writings"—landed at his house at once. Thoreau complained:

> They . . . rubbed you continually with the greasy cheeks of their kindness. They would not keep their distance, but cuddle up and lie spoon-fashion with you, no matter how hot the weather nor how narrow the bed,—chiefly [Wright]. I was awfully pestered with his benignity; feared I should get greased all over with it past restoration; tried to keep some starch in my clothes. He wrote a book called "A Kiss for a Blow," and he behaved as if there were no alternative between these, or as if I had given him a blow. . . . ———— addressed me as "Henry" within one minute from the time I first laid eyes on him, and when I spoke, he said with drawling, sultry sympathy, "Henry, I know all you would say; I understand you perfectly; you need not explain anything to me;" and to another, "I am going to dive into Henry's inmost depths." I said, "I trust you will not strike your head against the bottom."[6]

Thoreau's greatest antipathy was reserved for the clergy. So far as he was concerned they were chiefly hypocrites and he had nothing but contempt for them. It was his greatest delight to deflate their pomposity and he did it whenever the occasion arose. When he ran across his Harvard classmate, Rev. John Weiss, he asked him, "Have you ever yet in preaching been so fortunate as to say any-

6. Thoreau, *Journal*, V, 263-5

ning?" And when Weiss replied in the affirmative, Thoreau declared, "Then your preaching days are over. Can you bear to say again? You can never open your mouth again for love or money."[7] When Lovejoy, the preacher, came to Concord, he announced that he had written a sermon on purpose for Thoreau and expected to see him in church. When Thoreau's aunts informed him he would not come, he insisted on being introduced to him at home and greeted him with, "Here's the chap who camped in the woods." Thoreau looked around and said, "And here's the chap who camps in a pulpit" and their conversation came to an end.[8] Of another clergyman he complained, "Here's a man who can't butter his own bread, and he has just combined with a thousand like him to make dipt toast for all eternity."[9] When his Aunt Maria asked Thoreau to read a biography of Dr. Chalmers, he refused, and he later overheard her complaining to Aunt Jane, "Think of it! He stood half an hour today to hear the frogs croak, and he wouldn't read the life of Chalmers."[1]

Despite (or maybe because of) the missionary efforts of his aunts, Thoreau regularly refused to attend church. Only when someone as unorthodox as Father Edward Taylor, the minister of Boston's seaman's bethel and the original of Melville's Father Mapple in *Moby Dick*, came to preach in Concord would Thoreau go and even then the unusualness of his attendance led Emerson to remark it in his journal.[2]

Thoreau delighted in fact in shocking the orthodox. His favorite story was that of the little boy who was building a model of a church in the dirt as a minister walked by. "Why, my little lad," said the minister, "why, making a meeting-house of that stuff? Why, why!" "Yes," answered the boy; "yes, I am; and I expect to have enough left over to make a Methodist minister besides."[3]

Once his mother asked him to find and bring home a pine tree of a certain size to ornament the yard. It was a Sunday morning when he first happened upon one that met her specifications, so he promptly dug it up and started home with it in his hands, only to

7. John Weiss, "Thoreau," *Christian Examiner*, LXXIX (1865), 106
8. Emerson, *Journals*, VIII, 305–6
9. Channing, *Thoreau, the Poet-Naturalist*, 90
1. Thoreau, *Journal*, V, 58
2. Emerson, *Journals*, VII, 76
3. *Truth Seeker*, "Memories of Thoreau," November 20, 1897

arrive in front of the church just as the congregation was letting
out. He could easily have ducked down a side alley or have hidden
the tree momentarily behind some convenient bushes, but instead he
marched proudly down the center of the street, tree in hand, leaving the churchgoers gaping and horrified. When Aunt Louisa Dunbar hastened out to reprove him, he replied only, "Aunt Louisa,
I have been worshipping in my way and I don't trouble you in
your way."[4] (Aunt Louisa did not approve of her nephew's Transcendentalism either. He has recorded how she "spurned that innocent every-day book, 'Germany by De Staël,' as though a viper
had stung her.")

There were a few exceptions to Thoreau's disdain for the
clergy and they were all men who Thoreau thought practiced exactly
as they preached. One of these was the Reverend Daniel Foster
who came to Concord to minister for the Universalist church in
1852. When Foster prayed aloud on Boston's waterfront as the
militia carried Sims back to slavery, Thoreau was proud that he
came from Concord. He noted approvingly that Foster, even though
he openly opposed their traffic, got along well with the local
rumsellers because he was frank and manly with them. He was
delighted when he heard that Foster had said in a sermon, "Thank
God, there is no doctrine of election with regard to Nature! We
are all admitted to her."[5] He noted that such confirmed non-
churchgoers as Rice, Pratt, Barrett, Houghton, Hubbard, and
McKean—men whom Thoreau thought to be the salt of the
earth—were attracted to Foster's services whereas they were re-
pelled by the Unitarian and Trinitarian ministers. But even though
Thoreau was impelled to give Foster an autographed copy of his
Week, he still refused to attend his church. (Thoreau would have
been pleased to learn that Foster later served as chaplain for a
Negro regiment in the Civil War.)

VI

It was children and young people who particularly continued
to attract and delight Thoreau. He liked their informality, their

4. Edward Emerson, Notes on Thoreau
5. Thoreau, *Journal*, III, 234

lack of ostentation, their complete open-mindedness. If they were willing to show the least interest in nature, he was ready to tell all his secrets to them. Moncure Conway recalled that Thoreau often took children along on his walks and boat rides. He delighted particularly in reaching over the side of his boat and bringing up a fish in his hand, explaining later to the astonished children that it was a bream guarding its spawn and that they too could do such magic if they only watched to see where the bream's nest was and approached it carefully. Conway also recalled Thoreau's taking the Emerson children on a huckleberrying party. When little Edward Emerson, carrying a basket full of his harvest, tripped and spilled them all and burst into tears, none of the others could console him with offers of berries from their baskets. But Thoreau came up, put his arm around the boy, explained that if the crop of huckleberries were to continue, it was necessary that some should be planted and that nature had provided for little boys now and then to stumble and sow the berries. If Eddy would come back in a few years, he would find a grand lot of bushes and berries on this very spot. And Edward's tears turned to smiles.[6]

The Hosmer children were always happy when Thoreau dropped in to call for they thought the stories he told of the ways of birds and squirrels better than any fairy tale. When he found a rare plant he would call them around him and help them search it out in a botany book. He liked to read aloud to them from *The Canterbury Tales* and would often stop and think about a line, and say, "You can sometimes catch the sense better by listening than by reading." He discussed Scandinavian mythology so much that they all became adept in those legends. When he returned from his trips to Maine or Canada his tales were so fascinating that no child wanted to go to bed.[7]

Another Concord child has related anonymously Thoreau's often dropping in at dusk, settling down in the great green rocking chair before the dining-room fire, and telling her and her brother his adventures as a child—about each of the houses he lived in and what he could remember about each. He would delight them with the adventures of a brood of chickens which slept at night in a tall old-fashioned fig drum in the kitchen, and as their bed was not

6. Conway, *Autobiography*, I, 148
7. Brown, *Memories of Concord*, 96–7

changed when they grew larger, they grew up not shapely, but shaped to each other and the drum, like figs. He would often play juggler tricks for them, swallowing his knife and producing it again from their ears or noses. They would run to bring apples as soon as he came in and he would cut one in halves so skillfully that the break scarcely showed. The joke then was to ask their father to break the apple and watch it fall to pieces in his hands. She remembered his singing "Tom Bowline" for them and playing on the flute. He would arrange huckleberrying parties for them, loading up the hay rigging with children, joking and laughing with them as they jolted along the road. Either he had great tact, she thought, or great skill in managing the children, for she never recalled being reproved by him no matter how noisy they were. When he learned she had a wildflower garden, he often brought her seeds or roots of rare plants. And if they met him in the woods on a Sunday walk he would always stop long enough to point out a rare oak or the nest of some bird.[8]

Frank Brown, Emerson's nephew, had now grown up into manhood, but he remembered his long hikes with Thoreau as a boy when Thoreau had aroused his interest in natural history and birds in particular. Frank now often brought Thoreau unusual specimens he found in his hunting and told him of new birds he had seen. When Frank married and decided to settle down to life as a farmer, he took Thoreau with him on tours of the available farms of the area. Once Brown settled down in Framingham, Thoreau often went to call on him. Brown in later years remembered him as always good-humored, talkative, and ever willing to share his knowledge of natural history. Of his personal appearance, he recalled only his prominent nose and his skin darkened by out-of-door exposure. Brown's wife added that his look, complexion, and eye always reminded her of a longshoreman.[9] (Another neighbor is reported to have said that Thoreau with his hooked nose and big, round eyes always reminded her of an owl.[1])

8. Sanborn, *Henry D. Thoreau*, 270–3
9. Edward Emerson, Notes on Thoreau
1. Kenneth Walter Cameron, *Emerson, Thoreau and Concord in Early Newspapers* (Hartford, 1958), 71

VII

For more than a year and a half Thoreau had delivered no lectures. In the spring of 1853 Blake invited him to speak again at Worcester, but he declined, explaining that although he thought he had something to say on "Traveling, Vagueness, and Poverty," he preferred to wait until he was "fuller."[2] On November 2, 1853, he was elected curator of the Concord Lyceum once more but declined the office immediately because he did not know where he could find enough good lecturers to make up a course for the winter. Emerson, who was then elected in Thoreau's stead, called on Thoreau to deliver a lecture of his own, and so on December 14 he read his "Journey to Moose Head Lake." To celebrate, Emerson invited him for dinner before the lecture. Although only a few days before Thoreau had denigrated loudly any lecture that was aimed solely at pleasing an audience, when little Edith Emerson asked him if his lecture that evening would be "a nice interesting story such as she wanted to hear," or "one of those old philosophical things that she did not care about," he immediately tried to convince himself that his lecture would suit her.[3]

Thoreau was unquestionably disappointed not to be asked to lecture more and grumbled that while he offered himself much more earnestly as a lecturer than a surveyor, it was surveying, which he thought a hundred others in the county could do as well as he, which he was asked to do. Yet he underestimated his abilities as a surveyor, for his neighbors recognized that his plans were both exceptionally honest and accurate and they placed a constant demand upon his services. Although he grumbled, they knew he would do a conscientious job. Although he admitted that days spent in the field surveying were profitable to him in a pecuniary sense, they seemed highly unprofitable to him in any other way. He said, "All I find is old bound-marks, and the slowness and dullness of farmers reconfirmed." When Mr. Hoar, Concord's most influential citizen, hired him to survey some land in Carlisle, Thoreau boasted:

2. Thoreau, *Correspondence*, 304
3. Emerson, *Journals*, VIII, 425

> I rode with my employer a dozen miles to-day, keeping a pro-
> found silence almost all the way as the most simple and natural
> course. I treated him simply as if he had bronchitis and could
> not speak, just as I would a sick man, a crazy man, or an idiot.[4]

But despite such boorish behavior, the farmers came back to him
more and more.

The most important of his many surveying jobs at the time
was seventeen days of surveying in Haverhill for Duncan, White
& How in April 1853. It gave him an opportunity once again to
explore the historical sites of the city and he spent his Sundays
hunting up the few remaining brick houses of refuge built during
the seventeenth century. Haverhill however had become much too
urbanized for him. No one could tell him where to find the nearest
woods and on his return he was particularly charmed with the
quantity of forest in Concord after the bareness of the Haverhill
country.

In February 1853 Leonard Spaulding filed suit in the Middlesex Court of Common Pleas against William Benjamin of Lincoln
claiming that Benjamin had raised the dam at his mill illegally and
so had flooded and spoiled Spaulding's crops upstream. Benjamin
entered the defense that he and all previous owners of the mill had
had the right to maintain a sufficient head of water to keep the
mill running.[5] Before the case came up for trial, he hired Thoreau
to check the height of the dam. Thoreau was promptly served with
a summons as an expert witness and spent three days in court, but
to no avail. The jury found for the plaintiff and Benjamin was
assessed $25.00 damages and $128.33 court costs.

In October Thoreau found a more satisfying surveying job.
Marston Watson asked him to survey his farm in Plymouth and
Thoreau spent a week there enjoying the fellowship of the Watsons
and sharing a bedroom with Bronson Alcott, who was their house
guest at the same time. His survey, now framed, graces the wall
of the Watson home.

In the late fall Thoreau experimented briefly in gathering wild
cranberries and selling them on the Boston market. He received
four dollars for two and a half bushels. He abandoned the project

4. Thoreau, *Journal*, VI, 185
5. Kenneth Walter Cameron, "Thoreau in the Court of Common
Pleas," *Emerson Society Quarterly*, XIV (1959), 86

ere, but his experimentation gave him the idea of flooding bogs to
rotect the cranberries from frost—an idea that did not occur to
rofessional cranberry growers until many years later but is now
andard procedure.

Thoreau's busyness did not keep him out of the fields and
oods. He still managed to devote at least four or five hours of
very day to his self-appointed task. When he discovered a hawk's
est in a tall pine, he visited it day after day, watching the young
evelop and begging his hunter friends to keep away with their guns.
Ie told them, "I would rather never taste chicken's meat nor hens'
ggs than never to see a hawk sailing through the upper air again."

One day, out walking as usual, he heard strange noises in the
ushes. Investigating, he discovered they came from a hole in the
round, and looking down, he said: "I saw the tail and hind
uarters of a woodchuck, which seemed to be contending with an-
ther further down. Reaching down carefully, I took hold of his
ail, and, though I had to pull very hard indeed, I drew him out be-
ween the rocks, a bouncing great fat fellow, and tossed him a
ttle way down the hill. As soon as he recovered from his bewilder-
ent he made for the hole again, but, I barring the way, he ran off
lsewhere."[6] Such was an adventure really worth having, he thought.

He was astonished when one day his sister Sophia brought
ome the blossom of a wildflower he had never seen in Concord—
ie *Azalea nudiflora* or pinxter flower. He traced it first to a bouquet
: Mrs. Brooks's house, then to her son George, and then to
eorge Melvin, who, he said,

was sitting in the shade, bareheaded, at his back door. He had
a large pailful of the azalea recently plucked and in the shade
behind his house, which he said he was going to carry to town
at evening. . . . At first he was a little shy about telling me
where the azalea grew, but I saw that I should get it out of him.
He dilly-dallied a little; called to his neighbor Farmer, whom he
called "Razor," to know if he could tell me where that flower
grew. He called it, by the way, the "red honeysuckle." This was
to prolong the time and make the most of his secret. . . . Well,
I told him he had better tell me where it was; I was a botanist
and ought to know. But he thought I couldn't possibly find it
by his directions. I told him he'd better tell me and have *the*
glory of it, for I should surely find it if he didn't; I'd got a clue

---

6. Thoreau, *Journal*, V, 259

to it, and shouldn't give it up. . . . I could smell it a good way, you know. He thought I could smell it half a mile, and he wondered that I hadn't stumbled on it, or Channing. Channing, he said, came close by it once, when it was in flower. He thought he'd surely find it then; but he didn't, and he said nothing to him. . . .

We went on down the brook,—Melvin and I and his dog,—and crossed the river in his boat, and he conducted me to where the *Azalea nudiflora* grew,—it was a little past its prime, perhaps,—and showed me how near Channing came. ("You won't tell him what I said; will you?" said he.) I offered to pay him for his trouble, but he wouldn't take anything. He had just as lief I'd know as not.[7]

Melvin was one of the town ne'er-do-wells, like John Goodwin a Haynes. As unconventional in their way as Thoreau was in h they spent all their time hunting and fishing, living their lives fro one day to the next and enjoying every minute. The proper peop of the town, as a result, condemned them, but Thoreau didn't. H "thanked his stars" for Melvin and his like and trusted that tl Lord would provide him with another Melvin when he was gon Melvin might be a great trial to his mother, but to Thoreau was a pure joy because he had the courage to live the life he wante Thoreau was always on good terms with these village scamps a indeed recognized that it was because they regarded him as "t humblest, cheapest, least dignified man in the village"—after a as he readily admitted he was "a good deal of a scamp" himsel And as a result of his rapport with them he often profited fro their findings as he did on this occasion with the pinxter flower.

In mid-June 1853 Thoreau found a tremendous toadsto sixteen inches high, and proudly paraded it down the main street Concord, displaying it to the milkman, the butcher, the you ladies, and the children. He noted that several who had nev spoken to him before now came over to inspect his treasure. I promised faithfully to exhibit it at the flower show in the courthous but, to his disappointment and chagrin, it soon melted in the he even in his cellar, and before the day was over he found he h nothing but a dish of foul-smelling mold to show for it.

7. Ibid. V, 205–7
8. Canby, *Thoreau,* 304

He took Moncure Conway on one of his walks. Plucking an unusual grass, he offered it to his guest to chew, saying, "It is a little sharp, but an experience." When Conway asked where he might find the *Hibiscus* in flower, Thoreau quickly pointed out the spot near the river where alone it could be found, and said it would open about the following Monday and not stay long. Conway delayed returning until Tuesday or Wednesday and found he was a day too late, the petals were scattered on the ground.[9]

But despite Thoreau's joy in nature and his apparent ebullency, there cropped up here and there signs of an underlying melancholy and unhappiness. For the first and only time in his life he seems to have lost his faith in man and turned to nature not to fulfill his life but to escape from it. On January 3, 1853, he wrote in his journal: "I love Nature partly *because* she is not man, but a retreat from him. None of his institutions control or pervade her." On January 21: "Yesterday I was influenced with the rottenness of human relations. They appeared full of death and decay, and offended the nostrils." On March 12: "Men choose darkness rather than light." On April 3: "No fields are so barren to me as the men of whom I expect everything but get nothing." On November 15: "From hard, coarse, insensible men with whom I have no sympathy, I go to commune with the rocks, whose hearts are comparatively soft." Such disappointment with man is not characteristic of Thoreau. He was not generally a misanthrope. Although he could not live without nature, ordinarily he used her Anteus-like to return refreshed to man.

What caused this despair we can only guess. Was it an aftermath of his break with Emerson? Was he discouraged because his literary career seemed to have reached a stalemate with *A Week,* a failure, no publisher was interested in the manuscript of *Walden,* and the demand for his services as a lecturer was reduced to nil? Any of these—or all of them together—might have been the cause. But the melancholy fortunately did not last. His spirit was resilient and by another year he was walking through the streets and fields of Concord with as much joy as ever.

---

9. Moncure Conway, "Thoreau," *Eclectic Magazine,* LXVII (1866), 192

CHAPTER SIXTEEN
(1854–1855)

I

ALTHOUGH Thoreau had completed a first draft of *Walden* whi[le] at the pond, he was not at all satisfied with it. In 1848, while he wa[s] revising *A Week,* he also nursed *Walden* through a second dra[ft.] When in 1849 he signed his contract with Munroe for the publ[i-] cation of *A Week* and they agreed to publish *Walden* soon afte[r] he polished it again. Aunt Maria wrote Prudence Ward on Februa[ry] 28: "[Thoreau] is preparing his Book for the press, and the title [is] to be, Waldien (I don't know how to spell it) or life in the Wood[s,] I think the title will take if the Book dont."[1]

From 1849 on he tested many of the *Walden* chapters on th[e] lecture platform, revising them carefully on the basis of audien[ce] reception. Version number three he wrote in 1849 and versi[on] number four in 1852, adding such memorable passages as that on th[e] battle of the ants.[2] At Greeley's request he then culled out sever[al] short essays from the text and submitted them along with the "Ya[n-] kee in Canada" essay in early March. Greeley promptly forwarde[d] them to John Sartain, editor of the *Union Magazine,* on March 1[8,] telling him that he considered Thoreau one of the best youn[g] writers and that he had solicited the essays from him in order t[o] make him better known, adding that if Sartain used them be wou[ld] be expected to pay for them. He said Thoreau had more manu[-] script on hand that he would send along if Sartain wanted it[.] Sartain replied promptly on the 24th that he would pay three do[l-] lars a page for the essays and would be glad to consider more—

---

1. MS, George L. Davenport, Jr.
2. J. Lyndon Shanley, *The Making of Walden* (Chicago, 1957), 30–2
3. Horace Greeley, Letter to John Sartain of March 18, 1852. MS, Barrett Collection

hich Greeley, in his turn, promised to obtain. "The Iron Horse" ✿
om the "Sounds" chapter appeared in the July *Union* and "A
et Buying a Farm" from the "Where I Lived" chapter in the
ugust issue. Greeley proudly puffed them in the *Tribune* of June
) and July 22 as articles of which any magazine might well be
oud. But the *Union* ceased circulation with the August issue
d Thoreau not only never got paid for his contributions but
st some other manuscripts that he had submitted. ✿

In 1853 he wrote a fifth version of *Walden* using for the first
me the chapter divisions and titles he was to use in the final ver-
on. By the end of the year he had completed a sixth draft, still
olishing, revising, and adding new material from his reading
d from his journal. In February and March 1854 he wrote a
venth version and this he took to Ticknor & Fields of Boston,
ho had expressed an interest in publishing it in 1849 only to have
horeau insist on having them publish *A Week* first. In the inter- ✿
ening years Ticknor & Fields had risen to prominence as the out-
anding publisher of American literature, counting Hawthorne,
ongfellow, Lowell, Holmes, and Whittier among their prized
uthors. Although Ticknor was not particularly enthusiastic about
alden, Fields, the more literary of the two partners, was. He was
harmed with the author and thought he brought "a rural frag-
nce—spicy odors of black birch, hickory buds, and penny-royal
—with him from his native fields into the streets and lanes of
oston."[4] Ten per cent royalties—pretty much standard in those
ays—were what he gave most of his authors, but for *Walden*
e offered fifteen per cent, a figure he reserved for what he called
is "first class authors."[5]

Thoreau accepted with alacrity and set right to work making a
ir copy and sending it off to the printer in sections as he com-
eted it. "Fair copy," he called it, but his handwriting had de-
nerated over the years so that the baffled typesetter scribbled on
e proof, "Can't read the MS."[6] The manuscript was immediately
t up in page proof, skipping the usual galley stage, and returned
Thoreau in sections, the first batch reaching Concord on March

---

4. James T. Fields, "Our Poet-Naturalist," *Baldwin's Monthly,* April,
1877
5. W. S. Tryon, *Parnassus Corner* (Boston, 1963), 170
6. MS, Huntington Library

28. Anxious to see his book in print, Thoreau kept himself so bu
that for the first time in years he missed the breaking up of the i
on Walden Pond. The proof was comparatively clean and he h
to make nowhere near the number of corrections he had made
A Week. Here and there he made minor revisions, correcting t
train fare for the Fitchburg Railroad, for example, from seventy
ninety cents, and explaining in a note to the printer, "They ha
raised the fare within a week."[7]

At first it was planned to publish the book in May, then
June. Anxious to see that it, along with several other books, recei
English copyright as well as American, Fields set off for Lond
by steamer on June 7 with proof sheets in hand, but suffered
much from seasickness that he left the boat at Halifax, Nova Scot
and returned home. Emerson meanwhile had written Richa
Bentley, and suggested that he publish it in London, so Fields nc
followed up by offering Bentley the English copyright for o
hundred dollars. Unsuccessful at that, Fields then sent a copy
the book to his English agent, and asked him to see what he cou
get for it, but apparently no one was interested. All these unsucce
ful efforts delayed publication until August.[8]

Horace Greeley, concerned that Thoreau was not attaini
the fame he deserved, had written on March 6 suggesting that
gather together his various published essays and that Gree
would try his best to get them published as a book. When Thore
replied that the publication of *Walden* was at last really under wa
Greeley agreed that the volume of miscellanies could wait a
promised to give *Walden* all the publicity he could whether Tickn
& Fields did or not. He was as good as his word. All that spri
he touted the book in his popular lecture on "Self-Culture" and
July 29, under the heading "A Massachusetts Hermit," he ran
long series of excerpts from the book and announced its immine
publication.

Thoreau received a specimen copy of *Walden* on August
1854, and the book was officially published a week later on Augu
9 in an edition of two thousand copies. Of the thirty-nine ne
books Ticknor & Fields issued that year, it was destined by far

7. MS, Huntington Library
8. Herbert F. West, *Mr. Emerson Writes a Letter About Walden*
(Hanover, N. H. 1954)

*rs. Ralph Waldo Emerson
ith one of her children*

*Ralph Waldo Emerson with two of his children,
Edward and Edith*

THE EMERSONS

Nathaniel Hawthorne in 1846

Ellery Channing in old age

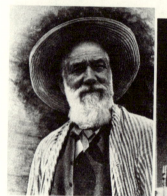

*Sam Staples,
the Concord jailer,
in old age*

Bronson Alcott in 1857

THOREAU'S CONCORD FRIENDS

ecome the most famous. Costing the publisher forty-three cents
copy and retailing for a dollar, it was brought out in the neat,
rown, blind-stamped buckram binding that Ticknor & Fields
hen used to identify all their books.[9] There were two illustrations
—Thoreau's own survey map of Walden Pond and his sister
ophia's drawing of the cabin on the title page. The latter, which
Ellery Channing thought had been included to satisfy Bronson
Alcott's demand for appropriate pictures for his autobiographical
notebooks, disappointed Thoreau. He thought the trees looked
more like firs than pines and that the roof of the cabin projected
too far above the door.[1] But nonetheless it was a great satisfaction to see the book in print after all these years, and Thoreau,
looking like "the undoubted King of all American lions," Emerson said, walked up and down Concord "in a tremble of great
expectation."[2]

Walden is, without question, Thoreau's masterpiece. It is
his account of the two years, two months, and two days he spent at
Walden Pond. For artistic purposes he condensed the narrative into
the circle of the seasons of a single year, opening with the building
of the cabin in the spring, continuing with gardening in the summer, housewarming in the fall, ice cutting and snow in the winter,
and ending with the reawakening of the world of nature in the
spring once more.

He wrote the book primarily to answer the questions of his
neighbors who were curious about his life in the woods, but he also
addressed it to those students who wished to know how to free
themselves from the seemingly endless toil necessary to keep themselves alive and to those people everywhere who were dissatisfied with their lives but did not know how to improve them. He
wished, he said, "to brag as lustily as chanticleer in the morning,
standing on his roost," hoping to wake his neighbors from the
somnolent lives of quiet desperation they were leading. Contrary to
popular opinion, he did not advocate that civilization be abandoned
and everyone flee to the woods. He stated very explicitly in the
book:

---

9. Warren Tryon and William Charvat, *The Cost Books of Ticknor
& Fields* (New York, 1949), 289
1. Sanborn, *The Life of Henry David Thoreau*, 338
2. Ralph Waldo Emerson, *Letters* (New York, 1939), IV, 460

I would not have any one adopt *my* mode of living on any account; for, beside that before he has fairly learned it I may have found out another for myself, I desire that there may be as many different persons in the world as possible; but I would have each one be very careful to find out and pursue *his own* way, and not his father's or his mother's or his neighbor's instead.[3]

Walden can be read on many levels. Like Gilbert White's *Natural History of Selborne* it is one of the outstanding nature books of all time. As such it achieved its first popularity and as such it still perhaps has its widest appeal. Like *Robinson Crusoe* it is a vivid exposition of the simple life that all of us at times yearn for. And like *Gulliver's Travels* it is a biting satire on the many, many flaws and foibles of the merry chase of life most of us are leading today. But above all *Walden* is a positive book. As earnest as John Bunyan's *Pilgrim's Progress,* it is a guide book to the higher life. On this level it is Transcendentalism in its purest form—a plea that would we but obey that light within us we could attain a fulfillment, a happiness, and a success such as man has never known. And Thoreau in his buoyant optimism believed that man would some day achieve that goal.

Apparently the earliest review to appear was a brief paragraph in the *Providence Journal* for August 11, which described Thoreau's philosophy as being "shrewd and eccentric" and the book "worth reading."

The next was one by John Sullivan Dwight in the *Journal of Music* for August 12, 1854. Dwight, a former Brook Farmer, had long circulated in Transcendentalist circles and had undoubtedly met Thoreau at Emerson's more than once. Dwight gave *Walden* a long paragraph in an article about his own vacation reading, and said that the book's "literary style is admirably clear and terse and elegant; the pictures wonderfully graphic; for the writer is a poet and a scholar as well as a tough wrestler with the first economical problems of nature, and a winner of good cheer and of free glorious leisure out of what men call the 'hard realities' of life."

On August 26 the Unitarian *Christian Register* said: "[*Walden*'s] opening pages may seem a little caustic and cynical; but it mellows apace, and playful humor and sparkling thought appear

---

3. Thoreau, *Writings,* II, 78–9

n almost every page. We suppose its author does not reverence
many things which we reverence; but this fact has not prevented
ur seeing that he has a reverential, tender, and devout spirit at
ottom. Rarely have we enjoyed a book more, or been more grate-
ul for many and rich suggestions."

The *Boston Atlas*, on the other hand, was devastatingly harsh:
"It is a sorrowful surprise that a constant communion with so
much beauty and beneficence was not able to kindle one spark of
genial warmth in this would-be savage. Pithy sarcasm, stern judgment, cold condemnation—all these abound in the pages of this
volume. . . . There is not a page, a paragraph giving one sign of
liberality, charitableness, kind feeling, generosity, in a word—
heart. . . . It is difficult to understand that a mother had ever
clasped this hermit to her bosom; that a sister had ever imprinted
on his lips a tender kiss."

In September came some friendlier reviews. *Graham's Magazine* gave it three full pages, quoting from it at length and saying:
"Whatever may be thought or said of this curious volume, nobody can deny its claim to individuality of opinion, sentiment,
and expression. Sometimes strikingly original, sometimes merely
eccentric and odd, it is always racy and stimulating. . . . Through
all the audacities of his eccentric protests, a careful eye can
easily discern the movement of a powerful and accomplished
mind."

The *National Magazine* thought it "cooling and refreshing," and
the *Southern Literary Messenger* said it was "a delightful companion for a loll under the rustling leaves of some old oak, far in
the country,"[4] while the abolitionist *National Era* said: "With all
its extravagances, its sophisms, and its intellectual pride, the book
is acute and suggestive, and contains passages of great beauty."

In October *Putnam's Monthly* devoted more than five pages to
a review entitled "A Yankee Diogenes," which said, in part:

> We infer from his volume that his aim was the very remark-
> able one of trying to be something, while he lived upon nothing;
> in opposition to the general rule of striving to live upon some-
> thing, while doing nothing. . . .

---

4. Walter Harding, "Some Forgotten Reviews of *Walden*," *Thoreau
Society Bulletin*, XLVI (1954), 2

There is nothing of the mean or sordid in the economy of Mr. Thoreau, though to some his simplicity and abstemiousness may appear trivial and affected; he does not live cheaply for the sake of saving, nor idly to avoid labor; but, that he may live independently and enjoy his great thoughts . . . and commune with the visible forms of nature.

The October *North American Review* however dismissed i in one brief paragraph: "The economical details and calculations in this book are more curious than useful, for the author's life in the woods was on too narrow a scale to find imitators."

One of the best reviews appeared in the *National Anti-Slavery Standard* for December 16:

If men were to follow in Mr. Thoreau's steps, by being more obedient to their loftiest instincts, there would, indeed, be a falling off in the splendour of our houses, in the richness of our furniture and dress, in the luxury of our tables, but how poor are these things in comparison with new grandeur and beauty which would appear in the souls of men. . . .

The striking peculiarity of Mr. Thoreau's attitude is, that while he is no religionist, and while he is eminently practical in regard to the material economies of life, he yet manifestly feels, through and through, that the loftiest dreams of the imagination are the solidest realities, and so the only foundation for us to build upon, while the affairs in which men are everywhere busying themselves so intensely are comparatively the merest froth and foam.

Thoreau thought, perhaps correctly, that it was written by his friend H. G. O. Blake.

Sophia Thoreau pasted into one of her scrapbooks a number of reviews of *Walden* which she had clipped out of various papers, although unfortunately she did not bother to identify them. One of them says: "In some things the Author of this work is a sort of Cynic philosopher; at all events he is pa[n]theistic in his religious notions. He is a man of original views, with an investigating mind." Another: "[*Walden*] is marked by originality, keenness of perception and observation, with a certain degree of quaintness and quiet humor running through its pages, which make it delightful reading." And a longer one begins: "This book breathes the freshness and vitality of the rustling pines which embowered the forest nook from whence it emanated. It contains momentous truths and noble thoughts, forcibly and succinctly expressed, and a searching analysis of the existing condition of society. The author mercilessly probes the shallow conventionalism, the shams of the day; he proclaims war to the knife with all snobism. Penetrating to the very pith and core of modern society, he lays bare the worm of corruption which preys upon its vitals—shows hideous rottenness concealed beneath a fair and alluring exterior. *Thoreau* is *Carlisle* simplified. The Anglo-German jargon of the latter is translated into pure English."[5]

In January 1855 a lengthy discussion entitled "Thoreau and His Books," by Edwin Morton, appeared in the undergraduate *Harvard Magazine.* Surprisingly it devoted almost its entire attention to *A Week,* rhapsodizing over the beauty of its nature passages, but it did agree that *Walden* "though less artistic than its predecessor, yet [is] in other respects superior, and in every way worthy the attention of all honest readers."

In March 1855 the *Knickerbocker Magazine* reviewed *Walden* along with P. T. Barnum's autobiography under the title of "Town and Rural Humbugs": "If any thing is calculated to induce a man to see how few beans will support animal life, we think it is a contemplation of the life and career of the great showman. If there is any thing calculated to reconcile us, not to the career of Barnum, but to whatever laborious drudgery may be necessary to procure good beef-steaks and oysters, with their necessary accompaniments, it is the thought of those inevitable beans, that constituted so large a part of the *crop* of Mr. Thoreau, and that extraordinary compound of corn-meal and water, which he facetiously called bread."

In mid-summer of 1855 Horace Greeley wrote to suggest that Thoreau send some review copies of *Walden* to England. He had found virtually no one who knew of the book when he visited London. The result was that Ticknor & Fields advertised the book through their London agent Trubner and two reviews appeared. The first was surprisingly enough by George Eliot and appeared in the January 1856 *Westminster Review:* "In a volume called *Walden; or, Life In The Woods,* published last year, but quite interesting enough to make it worth while for us to break our rule

5. MS, Raymond Adams

by a retrospective notice—we have a bit of pure American life (not the "go a-head" species, but its opposite pole), animated by that energetic, yet calm spirit of innovation, that practical as well as theoretic independence of formulae, which is peculiar to some of the finer American minds. . . . His observations of natural phenomena . . . are not only made by a keen eye, but have their interest enhanced by passing through the medium of a deep poetic sensibility; and, indeed, we feel throughout the book the presence of a refined as well as a hardy mind. . . . There is plenty of sturdy sense mingled with his unworldliness." The second, which appeared in Chambers's *Journal* for November 21, 1857, was a piece of hack work cribbed almost entirely from the American reviews in *Putnam's Monthly* and the *Knickerbocker*. *Walden* was also noticed with a lengthy excerpt and a biographical sketch in the *Cyclopaedia of American Literature*, which Evert and George Duyckinck edited for Scribner in 1855.

Reading all these evaluations of his own writing led Thoreau to make a self-evaluation of his own style. Scribbled on the inside cover of his manuscript journal for that fall is a note which reads:

My faults are:—

Paradoxes,—saying just the opposite,—a style which may be imitated.

Ingenious.

Playing with words,—getting the laugh,—not always simple, strong, and broad.

Using current phrases and maxims, when I should speak for myself.

Not always earnest.

"In short," "in fact," "alas!" etc.

Want of conciseness.[6]

Thoreau was harsher in evaluating his own style than any of his harshest critics—although it is perhaps significant that all his own criticisms are directed toward his style and not his content.

Thoreau gave copies of *Walden* to his mother, Mrs. Emerson, Ellery Channing, Bronson Alcott, H. G. O. Blake, Thomas Wentworth Higginson, Charles Sumner, Spencer Fullerton Baird, and A. R. Spofford (who had, as we have seen, sent him a check

6. Thoreau, *Journal*, VII, 7–8

appreciation of *A Week*.)[7] Alcott sat right down and read it through several times. When William T. Harris, later the first United States Commissioner of Education, came soon after to call, Alcott, filled with enthusiasm, urged him to read it immediately.[8] Sumner assured Thoreau in a letter that he had "made contribution to the permanent literature of our mother tongue."[9] John Greenleaf Whittier, who had received a copy from Fields at Thoreau's request, replied to Fields that he thought it "capital reading, but very wicked and heathenish." He thought its moral to be "that if a man is willing to sink himself into a woodchuck he can live as cheaply as that quadruped," but as for himself he preferred "walking on two legs."[1] Whittier then wrote his friend Harriet Prescott that he had enjoyed it as much as *A Week* but felt it "calmer, more *whole*, crammed with fine observation and thought, and rising into sublimity at the last."[2]

Ellery Channing's wife, who had received a copy from her brother Eugene for her birthday, said she really enjoyed it because it was so thoroughly characteristic and fresh.[3] When J. B. Hill of Bangor, Maine, Emerson's college classmate, after writing that he thought it "capital satire," added that he thought the map of the pond was not real but a caricature of the Coast Surveys, Thoreau was astonished.[4] But it was a real blow when five years later one of his townsmen innocently told him after riding through Walden woods in his sleigh that he had never seen anything so beautiful in his life and that if there had been men there who knew how to write about it, it would have been a great occasion for them. Such Thoreau thought was the smallness of his fame.

Nathaniel Hawthorne, on the other hand, now a consul in Liverpool, England, was most enthusiastic about the book, and

7. Barrett Collection; Berg Collection; Bronson Alcott, *Journals*, 273; Stephen Wakeman [Sale Catalog] (New York, 1924), #1007; Edgar L. McCormick, "Thoreau and Higginson," *Emerson Society Quarterly*, XXXI (1963), 76; Thoreau, *Correspondence*, 348
8. Social Circle in Concord, *Memoirs* (Boston, 1882–1940), V, 48
9. Thoreau, *Correspondence*, 348
1. Samuel T. Pickard, *Life and Letters of John Greenleaf Whittier* (Boston, 1894), I, 359
2. Thomas Wentworth Higginson, *Letters and Journals* (Boston, 1921),
3. MS, Frederick T. McGill, Jr.
4. Thoreau, *Journal*, VII, 103

when Lord Houghton asked him to recommend some goo[d]
American books, he had Ticknor ship him both of Thoreau's
When Houghton told Hawthorne he thought them delightfu[l]
Hawthorne replied:

> [Thoreau] despises the world, and all that it has to offer, and,
> like other humorists, is an intolerable bore. I shall cause it to be
> known to him that you sat up till two o'clock reading his book;
> and he will pretend that it is of no consequence, but will never
> forget it. . . . He is not an agreeable person, and in his presence
> one feels ashamed of having any money, or a house to live in, or
> so much as two coats to wear, or having written a book that
> the public will read—his own mode of life being so unsparing a
> criticism on all other modes, such as the world approves.[6]

But nonetheless Hawthorne was disturbed that Thoreau's wor[k]
was not better known in England and two years later ordered tw[o]
more copies of each of the books from Ticknor to present t[o]
Dr. Charles Mackay and Douglas Jerrold that they might furthe[r]
Thoreau's fame in England.[7]

A tribute that particularly pleased Thoreau was a letter i[n]
French from the Abbé Adrien Rouquette of New Orleans prais-
ing *Walden*. Rouquette, a Louisiana Creole and an authority on
monastic solitude, a friend of the Choctaw Indians, and a write[r]
on nature, also sent along a package of three of his own books—
La Thébaïde en Amérique, Wild Flowers, and *Les Savanes.*
Thoreau was prompt to return in kind with a copy of *A Week.*

Compared with those for *A Week,* the sales of *Walden* were
astoundingly good. In its first year it sold all but 256 copies of
the original printing of two thousand. On September 29, 1855,
Ticknor & Fields sent him a check for $51.60 for the sale of 344
copies and on February 16, 1857, $45.00 for the sale of 240
copies plus 12 copies of *A Week.* By 1859 it was out of print and
no longer available. It was not until just a few weeks before his
death that he was able to persuade Ticknor & Fields to reprint it
and this second printing did not actually appear until a few weeks

---

5. Caroline Ticknor, *Hawthorne and His Publisher* (Boston, 1913),
135
6. Edward Mather, *Nathaniel Hawthorne* (New York, 1940), 334
7. Nathaniel Hawthorne, *English Notebooks* (New York, 1941), 316

.fter his death. But since that date it has never been out of
rint again, it has been reprinted in more than one hundred and
fty different editions, has been translated into virtually every
najor modern language, and has sold untold millions of copies.

II

Thoreau decided to capitalize on the fame of *Walden:* he
decided to offer himself as a lecturer on a nationwide scale and to
try to arrange a tour through the Midwest where Emerson was
regularly so successful. He did not enter the project without
misgivings, for he confided to his journal:

> Thinking this afternoon of the prospect of my writing lectures,
> and going abroad to read them next winter, I realized how in-
> comparably great the advantages of obscurity and poverty which
> I have enjoyed so long. . . . I have given myself up to nature; I
> have lived so many springs and summers and autumns and
> winters as if I had nothing else to do but *live* them, and imbibe
> whatever nutriment they had for me. . . . If I go abroad lecturing,
> how shall I ever recover the lost winter?[8]

But he need not have worried. Despite the fact that Greeley in a
notice in the New York *Tribune,* offered Thoreau's services on the
lecture platform, he received only one firm offer—from Hamilton,
Ontario—and an inquiry from the Library Association in Akron,
Ohio. And so the project was abandoned.

Nearer at home however he was more successful. Marston
Watson and his friends in Plymouth asked him to return and give
a series of lectures there. Thoreau replied that he had only one
lecture to offer, and after a delay occasioned by a confusion over
dates, he delivered a new lecture there, "Night and Moonlight,"
on October 8, 1854. It was based on the many notes he had
taken on his moonlight walks in the summer of 1851. Probably
neither Thoreau nor his audience were satisfied with it, for there
is no record of his having repeated it and the printed version

---

8. Thoreau, *Journal,* VII, 46

that was published posthumously is over-effusive, rambling, and marred by a quite uncharacteristic sentimentality.

On November 20 he took the train to Philadelphia, where he delivered a lecture called "Moose-hunting"—apparently a portion of his Chesuncook essay—on the 21st. Here again he was unsuccessful. W. H. Furness wrote Emerson that the audience was stupid and did not appreciate Thoreau.[9] But the occasion did give Thoreau an opportunity to explore Philadelphia, climb to the cupola of Independence Hall, visit the Fairmount waterworks and Girard College, and examine the collection of bird skins at the Academy of Natural Sciences. On his way home he stopped over in New York City to see the Crystal Palace and to visit with Greeley at the *Tribune* office. Greeley took Thoreau to the opera house to hear Guiditta Grisi and her troupe, an Italian opera company then touring the States, and to visit Barnum's Museum where they saw a herd of giraffes and a diorama of the houses of the world. The opera did not impress him however. He preferred, he said, listening to the native wood thrush at Beck Stow's Swamp in Concord.[1]

On December 6, 1854, he read a paper at the Independent Lectures at Railroad Hall in Providence, Rhode Island. It was one he entitled variously "Getting a Living" or "What Shall It Profit [a Man if He Gain The Whole World But Lose His Own Soul]?"—an early version of one of the most cogent essays he ever wrote—and he delivered it as a lecture at least six times in the next several years. When he finally, in the last months of his life, edited it for publication, he entitled it "Higher Laws," but when it reached print in the *Atlantic Monthly* after his death, it was entitled "Life without Principle."

This essay epitomizes in a few pages the very essence of Thoreau's philosophy. It is his essay on self-reliance, and asks his audience to get down to fundamental principles and not to be led astray by public opinion, the desire for wealth or position, or any other diverting influence. It is pure Transcendentalism, a plea that each follow his own inner light. Although later it was to be considered one of his more successful lectures, on this first

9. H. H. Furness, *Records of a Lifelong Friendship* (Boston, 1910), 103
1. Thoreau, *Journal*, VII, 74–6

occasion in Providence it was a failure and Thoreau complained in his journal that night: "I feel that I am in danger of cheapening myself by trying to become a successful lecturer, *i.e.*, to interest my audiences. I am disappointed to find that most that I am and value myself for is lost, or worse than lost, on my audience. I fail to get even the attention of the mass. I should suit them better if I suited myself less."[2] But at least the visit to Providence gave him an opportunity to visit with Emerson's friend Charles King Newcomb, to inspect Roger Williams's rock in the Blackstone River and an old fort overlooking Narragansett Bay, and to take a hike out through the country west of Providence.

Lyceum curators continued to ask Thoreau for "humorous" lectures, but he refused to submit to what he called their "grovelling appetite for profitless jest and amusement."[3] They could take his Transcendentalist sermons or do without. Both the New Bedford and Nantucket, Massachusetts, lyceums announced themselves willing to hear him on his own terms, and so on Christmas Day, 1854, he set out by train for southeastern Massachusetts.

Within a few days of the publication of *Walden* in August, Daniel Ricketson, a wealthy New Bedford Quaker who had some slight acquaintance with Emerson, had read it and written Thoreau a letter gushing with enthusiasm. It was October before Thoreau replied and his answer was so short and cool that Ricketson for a time was frightened off. But then when he learned Thoreau was to lecture in New Bedford, he immediately extended an invitation for Thoreau to stay with him.

Ricketson, four years older than Thoreau and a diminutive five foot three, had studied law and had been admitted to the bar, but thanks to his private income was enabled to devote more time to his hobbies of historical research and writing than to his practice. In the mid-1840s he had built a rough cabin approximately the size of Thoreau's, christened "The Shanty," on a tract of land on the outskirts of New Bedford, had filled it with books, and had decorated its walls with his favorite quotations, and there spent much of his time reading and writing. Later he erected a large house nearby for his wife and four children and named the estate Brooklawn. A series of accidents in his

2. Thoreau, *Journal*, VII, 79–80
3. Ibid. VII, 89

youth had left him with weakened eyesight, an injured hip, and frequent headaches. By the time he met Thoreau he was a confirmed hypochondriac. Although he adored his children and spent much time with them, his marriage was not a particularly happy one and he preferred his shanty to his house. Like Thoreau he was an abolitionist. Although he published two volumes of verse and several of local history, he never achieved literary fame, but maintained friendships with many of the writers of his day including eventually most of the Concord writers, Whittier, and the British essayist William Howitt.

Ricketson expected Thoreau on the noon train but, when he did not arrive, gave him up for the day. Later in the afternoon, as he was cleaning the snow off his front steps, he noticed a man wearing a long dark overcoat and a dark soft hat and carrying a portmanteau in one hand and an umbrella in the other walking up his driveway. Thinking it was a peddler, he ignored the man, who, coming up to him said, "You do not know me." At once Ricketson realized it must be Thoreau whom he had imagined to be a stout, robust person rather than the small and rather inferior-looking man who stood before him. Concealing his disappointment, he replied, "I presume this is Mr. Thoreau," and conducted him into the house.

Once they started talking over the dinner table, Ricketson's disappointment over Thoreau's physical appearance disappeared. He became aware of the gentleness, humanity, and intelligence of Thoreau's blue eyes and noted that though his arms were long, his legs short, his hands and feet large, and his shoulders markedly sloping, he was strong and vigorous in his walk and bubbling over with good-natured humor.[4]

They spent the evening in Ricketson's library talking while Thoreau filled in the missing lines in his host's copy of *A Week* and Ricketson made a quick pencil sketch of Thoreau on the flyleaf. The next day they wandered together through the Tarkiln Hill woods, visited the Friends Meeting House, which Thoreau thought repulsively ugly, and rode round one of New Bedford's large factories. Thoreau gave his "What Shall It Profit?" lecture that evening, but Ricketson was kept home by illness. Although

4. Daniel Ricketson [Reminiscences of Thoreau]. MS, Abernethy Library

afterwards Ricketson heard several of his friends speak well of the lecture, he concluded that it had not been generally understood.

On the morning of December 27th, Thoreau went on to Hyannis and there embarked on a rough three-hour passage to Nantucket, once again being afflicted by seasickness. His host on the island was Captain Edward W. Gardiner, who took him on a tour of the island in his carriage and told him at length of his whaling experiences; they visited Sancoty Head lighthouse and inspected the South Sea artifacts at the Athenaeum museum. Thoreau gave his "What Shall It Profit?" lecture that evening and was astounded and delighted to find it a huge success. "I found them to be the very audience for me," he boasted to Ricketson later.[5]

Thoreau feared that he might get weather-bound on the island and his fears were nearly fulfilled. He encountered a pea-soup fog on the return trip. The ship lost its way, whistled for aid, and finally found its way into Hyannis harbor by the sound of a locomotive whistle and a lifeboat bell. Lecture tours did have their disadvantages.

The spurt of interest in Thoreau as a lecturer was unfortunately but a brief one. In 1855 he gave only two lectures— at Worcester on January 4 and at Concord on February 14. On both occasions he read "What Shall It Profit?" Then he did not lecture again for nearly a year and a half, despite the fact that Greeley continued to announce the availability of his services in the pages of the *Tribune*.

Thoreau himself was fully aware of what was wrong. A few days after his Concord lecture he stated the case in his journal:

> Many will complain of my lectures that they are transcendental. "Can't understand them." "Would you have us return to the savage state?" etc., etc. A criticism true enough, it may be, from their point of view. . . . If you wish to know how I think, you must endeavor to put yourself in my place. If you wish me to speak as if I were you, that is another affair.[6]

And that Thoreau was unwilling to do.

---

5. Thoreau, *Correspondence*, 362
6. Thoreau, *Journal*, VII, 197

It was also a fact that Thoreau simply was not a very good speaker. For one thing he had a minor speech defect, a peculiar pronunciation of the letter r—a sort of burr in it, Channing said.[7] His presence on the platform has been described as "not inspiring" and his voice as "not specially musical."[8] He tended to bury his nose in his manuscript rather than keep his eye on his audience and occasionally mumbled his words. Only when he was aroused in the fight for justice, such as on the occasion of his "Slavery in Massachusetts" speech in Framingham or, later, with his John Brown pleas, was he sufficiently dynamic to excite his audience. When he read his various excursions, it was the humor that carried him along. But the audiences missed the more subtle humor of the Transcendental lectures and so they often failed to go over.

III

In the autumn of 1854 Thomas Cholmondeley came from England to Concord to meet Ralph Waldo Emerson. A nephew of Bishop Heber, a graduate of Oxford University, and a friend of Arthur Hugh Clough, who had visited Concord and had met Thoreau several years before, Cholmondeley had read several of Emerson's works and was inspired to meet their author. He had lived for a time in New Zealand and had written one of the pioneer books, *Ultima Thule,* about that country. His arrival in Concord created a great stir for he brought with him ten pieces of luggage and his own bathtub. His high falsetto voice caused much amusement and it was whispered that his nightshirts were embroidered with his family crest.

When Cholmondeley informed Emerson that he wished a place to stay for several weeks, it was suggested that he board with the Thoreau family. Thoreau was invited to dinner with Cholmondeley at the Emersons, and was not at all impressed, though Cholmondeley immediately took to Thoreau and lost all interest in Emerson. But when Cholmondeley moved into the Thoreau

7. Channing, *Thoreau, the Poet-Naturalist,* 2
8. Sanborn, *The Personality of Thoreau,* 37

ousehold and became better acquainted, Thoreau found him more
o his liking and a warm friendship ensued.

In mid-October Thoreau, arranging for H. G. O. Blake to join
hem, took Cholmondeley by train to Westminster, Massachusetts,
nd from there hiked the six miles to the top of Mount Wachusett,
vhich they found sugared with snow. They stayed overnight at
'oster's, but rose early enough to return to the summit to see
he sun rise and the pyramidal shadow of Wachusett stretch clear
cross the state to the Hoosac Mountains. Later, when Chol-
nondeley removed to Boston, Thoreau wrote letters of intro-
luction for him to Bronson Alcott and to Thaddeus Harris of the
Iarvard Library. When Cholmondeley left eventually for his home
n England, he urged Thoreau to accompany him, but Thoreau
aid he was too attached to his native Concord to think of going
broad.[9]

The two started a correspondence that with some gaps was
ontinued for the rest of Thoreau's life. Cholmondeley, like Emer-
on, was not satisfied with Thoreau's way of life and urged him
o participate more in society. He thought life at a college would
e ideal for him and warned that unless he gave himself the
enefit of some such intellectual stimulation he was liable to
nolder away as he grew older. But Thoreau failed to be con-
inced and continued along his own way.

In the autumn of 1855 Cholmondeley gathered up a collec-
ion of forty-four Oriental books, including translations of the
Rig Veda Sanhita, the *Mandukya Upanishads,* the *Nala* and
Damyanta, the *Vishnu Purana,* the *Institutes of Menu,* the *Sankhya
Karika,* the *Aphorisms of the Mimasma* and *Nayaya,* the *Bhagavat
Gheeta, Sakoontala,* and the *Bhagavita Purana* as well as a num-
er of volumes of history and criticism of Indian literature, and
hipped them to Thoreau as a token of friendship. When Thoreau
earned of their imminent arrival, he gathered up appropriate
ieces of driftwood along the Concord rivers to make a special
ookcase. When they arrived in Concord on November 30, he
nade haste to write Cholmondeley:

After overhauling my treasures on the carpet, wading knee
deep in Indian philosophy and poetry—with eager eyes around

---

9. Emerson, *Letters* (New York, 1939), IV, 479

ready to admire the splendid binding and illumination at least, drawing them forth necessarily from amidst a heap of papers . . . I placed them in the case which I had prepared, and went late to bed dreaming of what had happened. Indeed it was exactly like the realization of some dreams which I have had; but when I woke in the morning I was not convinced that it was reality until I peeped out and saw their bright backs.[1]

Thoreau sent Cholmondeley a copy of Emerson's *Poems, Walden,* a book by F. L. Olmsted on the South, and a first edition of Whitman's *Leaves of Grass* in return and wrote boastfully to Ricketson of Cholmondeley's "royal gift": "I send you information of this as I might the birth of a child."[2]

    Although Thoreau was unquestionably delighted with Cholmondeley's present, which put him in possession of what has been called the largest collection of Oriental books in private hands in America at that time, the books had actually arrived some years too late to have any strong influence on Thoreau. In the early 1840s, when he had first discovered the Oriental books in Emerson's library, he had been deeply impressed. In the late 1840s, when he had begun drawing on the resources of the Harvard Library, he had been stimulated by a philosophy so close to his own. But as the years had passed, he became more and more sure of his own way of life and felt less the need for outside confirmation of his ideas. It is not at all certain that he ever finished reading all the books that Cholmondeley had sent him. Four years later he proudly showed the collection to Mrs. Caroline Dall when she visited Concord. She looked at some of the Sanskrit volumes and asked if he could read them. "Oh, no!" he said. "And will you not learn?" "For what good?" he answered. "Now this box holds everything; then I might find it very empty."[3]

    In late November 1858 Cholmondeley suddenly wrote from Montreal that he was on his way to the West Indies and would be spending a few days in Boston. Thoreau persuaded him to visit

1. Thoreau, *Correspondence,* 398–9
2. Ibid. 403; Sanborn, "Thoreau and His English Friend Thomas Cholmondeley," *Atlantic Monthly,* LXXII (1893), 752
3. Joseph Slater, "Caroline Dall in Concord," *Thoreau Society Bulletin,* LXII (1958), 1

Concord for a few days and then took him to New Bedford to see a typical whaling town and to meet Daniel Ricketson. They spent three days at Brooklawn talking "of mankind and his relationships here and hereafter."[4] Cholmondeley then asked Thoreau to accompany him to the West Indies, offering to pay all his expenses and suggesting that they go on to explore the valley of the Amazon where he might see the great *Victoria regia,* but he replied that he fully expected to find the *Victoria regia* someday on Concord River and added, "I think I had better stay in Concord."[5] Cholmondeley then changed his plans, went south as far as Virginia for a few weeks, returned to Concord briefly in January 1859, and returned to England.

It was the last time Thoreau was to see Cholmondeley. They continued to correspond and Cholmondeley tried frequently, but always unsuccessfully, to persuade Thoreau to visit England. Cholmondeley eventually inherited a large estate in Shropshire, was married in 1863, and died in Florence, Italy, of a malignant fever on his honeymoon. As Jane Austen would say, in their friendship Cholmondeley was the thicker of the two. He was conventional in his outlook and therefore often dismayed at what he thought Thoreau's wayward ways. When Cholmondeley once attempted to question him on original sin and future punishment, Thoreau replied only, "Those voluntaries [i.e. electives] I did not take." He was a patrician rather than a plebeian and in dress a fop—a charge that could hardly be leveled against Thoreau. But despite their differences they were both devoted idealists and that proved enough of a link to overcome their differences.

Thoreau noticed that some of Cholmondeley's clothes were made of corduory and it struck him as such serviceable material that he ordered a pair of corduroy trousers made. They cost him only $1.60. Their clay color, he thought, would not only help to camouflage him in the field but would not soil quickly. Besides, he found they wore exceedingly well. His friends however were disturbed. They thought of corduroy as "Irish clothing" and refused to wear it, while the Irish themselves thought of it as old-

---

4. Anna and Walton Ricketson, *Daniel Ricketson and His Friends,* 309–10
5. Charles J. Woodbury, *Talks with Ralph Waldo Emerson* (New York, 1890), 81–2

° country stuff and refused to wear it themselves. But suc
considerations bothered Thoreau not in the least and he con
tinued to wear corduroy for some years. (Thoreau came by hi
independence of dress naturally. The story is told that in 185
his mother at the age of seventy, wearing bright yellow ribbon
on her bonnet, called on Mary Moody Emerson. During the entir
conversation Miss Emerson kept her eyes tightly shut and whe
Mrs. Thoreau got up to leave, she remarked: "Perhaps you noticec
Mrs. Thoreau, that I closed my eyes during your call. I did s
because I did not wish to look on the ribbons you are wearing
so unsuitable for a child of God and a person of your years."

Cholmondeley and Ricketson were only two—but the mos
devoted two—of a group of admirers who gathered aroun
Thoreau after the publication of *Walden*. A young Providenc
banker, B. B. Wiley, started a correspondence with Thorea
after learning about *Walden* from the New York *Tribune* an
made at least one trip to Concord to meet him. Calvin Greene c
Rochester, Michigan, started a similar correspondence and pu
chased autographed copies of his books to send to others. Green
to express his admiration, had a cane made of Californian man
zanita wood, with a silver head and an engraved inscription.
Since Thoreau died before it was completed, Greene presented i
to Channing. Fairly frequently Thoreau received requests fo
autographs. And amateur naturalists in neighboring towns, such a
John Will Randall of Stow and Austin Bacon of Natick, bega
to exchange visits with him.

IV

In July 1853 Eben J. Loomis, a twenty-five-year-old mathe
matician for the *American Ephemeris and Nautical Almanac* i
Cambridge had married Mary Alden Wilder, the daughter of th
former Trinitarian minister in Concord and an intimate frien
of Thoreau's Aunt Maria and Aunt Jane. Mrs. Thoreau immedi
ately invited them to spend part of their honeymoon in Concor

6. Samuel A. Jones, *Some Unpublished Letters of Henry D. and
Sophia E. Thoreau* (Jamaica, N. Y., 1899), 64

nd they enjoyed themselves so much that they returned there
egularly for vacations for several years. Thoreau and young
Loomis quickly took to each other and spent much time together.
Loomis found Thoreau very hospitable to any new ideas. If he
happened to suggest some new thought, Thoreau would say little at
he time, but a day or a week later, after he had had time to think
t over, would suddenly announce whether he had decided to ac-
ept or to reject it. Loomis, as a result, thought Thoreau's
pinions "well-formed and clear."[7]

Thoreau developed the habit of dropping in on the Loomises
when he visited Cambridge. On one occasion in 1856, shortly
fter the birth of their daughter Mabel (who years later achieved
literary fame as the first editor of Emily Dickinson's poetry),
Thoreau came to see the new baby. The nurse, not knowing
Thoreau and thinking it a special treat, placed the infant in his
rms. He hardly knew which end was which and when Mrs.
Loomis walked into the room a few moments later she was
errified to see two wildly waving pink feet sticking out of the top
f a bundle of blankets, with the head nearly invisible at the
ower end. With a groan of relief, he quickly relinquished the
baby to her.[8]

Late in the summer of 1854 Samuel Worcester Rowse, then
a well-known portrait painter, came to Concord for a time and
boarded with the Thoreaus. He, Loomis, and Thoreau often
tayed up until after midnight talking, as Loomis remembered, on
" 'fate, free-will, foreknowledge absolute,' or other topics equally
r more interesting."[9] And Rowse gave Thoreau an engraving
f his portrait of Daniel Webster as a remembrance.

Mrs. Thoreau asked Rowse to do a crayon portrait of her son.
Thoreau did not care to pose, but since Rowse preferred to work
s much as possible away from his subject, there was no diffi-
ulty. For two or three weeks he did not put pencil to paper,
but studied Thoreau's face at every opportunity. Suddenly at
breakfast one morning, he jumped up from the table, excused

7. E. J. Loomis, Letter to A. W. Hosmer of June 1896. MS, Concord Free Public Library
8. Mabel Loomis Todd, *The Thoreau Family Two Generations Ago*
(Berkeley Heights, N. J., 1958) 1
9. E. J. Loomis, Letter to A. W. Hosmer of June 1896

himself, and disappeared into his room alone for the rest of the
day. The next day he brought down the now-well-known crayon
portrait in almost exactly its finished form and explained his
hurried departure from the table by saying that he had seen a cer
tain expression crossing Thoreau's face which he knew he wanted
to catch in the portrait.

Sophia Thoreau thought the portrait brought out the poet
in her brother. Loomis thought it the most satisfactory likeness
he ever saw for, even years later, it brought to him the Thoreau
he had known those summers. Mrs. Loomis thought it showed
Thoreau's real personality—"the purest-looking man that ever
lived."[1] Although Alcott at first complained that it made too
much of a gentleman out of its subject, later he agreed that it
was the best picture we have.[2] Only H. G. O. Blake seemed to think
it an unsatisfactory likeness.[3]

On November 2, 1854, Franklin Benjamin Sanborn, then
a student at Harvard, called on Emerson in Concord to discuss
Transcendentalism. They walked out to Walden Pond together
and before Sanborn returned to Cambridge, Emerson spoke of
Thoreau and gave him a copy of *A Week*. A few weeks later when
Sanborn met Bronson Alcott, he asked further about Thoreau
and was told, "[Thoreau] is a *fine beast*—the brutes ought to
choose him their king, so near does he live to nature and under
stand her so well."[4] Sanborn was editor for the undergraduate
Harvard Magazine and published in January 1855 Edwin Morton's
essay on "Thoreau and His Books." On his next visit to Cam
bridge Thoreau left a copy of *Walden* at Sanborn's room as a gift
for Morton. On January 30, Sanborn, writing Thoreau to say he
had passed the book along, added, "For my own part, I thank you
for the new light it shows me the aspects of Nature in, and for
the marvelous beauty of your descriptions," and then said, quite
frankly, "At the same time, if any one should ask me what I
think of your philosophy, I should be apt to answer that it is not
worth a straw." He concluded by asking if he might come out

1. Todd, *The Thoreau Family Two Generations Ago*, 19
2. Richard Herrnstadt, *The Letters of A. Bronson Alcott* (University
of Maryland, unpublished doctoral dissertation, 1960)
3. H. G. O. Blake, Letter to A. W. Hosmer of February 6, 1893.
MS, Concord Free Public Library
4. Cameron, *The Transcendental Climate*, I, 213

Concord to meet Thoreau.[5] Thoreau characteristically replied, "I shall be glad to see you whenever you come to Concord, and I will suggest nothing to discourage your coming, so far as I am concerned, trusting that you know what it is to take a partridge on the wing."[6]

Emerson, meanwhile, had proposed to Sanborn that he open a private school in Concord, assuring him that the Emerson, Hoar, and Ripley children would all be enrolled. After some deliberation, and after receiving assurance from the president of Harvard that he would still receive his degree, Sanborn left Cambridge and opened up his school in Concord in late March 1855. He and his sister made arrangements to room at Channing's house on Main Street and, soon thereafter, to take their dinner each day at the Thoreau table—a practice they continued until April 1858. Sanborn first met Thoreau on March 28 at the Concord Lyceum. Two weeks later, on April 11, Thoreau came to pay a formal call and spent two hours talking chiefly about Latin and Greek. Sanborn thought him "a sort of pocket edition of Emerson" so far as outward appearance was concerned. He jotted in his diary:

[Thoreau] is a little under size—with a huge Emersonian nose, bluish gray eyes, brown hair, and a ruddy weather-beaten face, which reminds one of that of some shrewd and honest animal—some retired, philosophic woodchuck or magnanimous fox—He dresses very plainly—wears his collar turned over like Mr. Emerson, and often an old dress coat, broad in the skirts and by no means a fit—He walks about with a brisk rustic air, and never seems tired.[7]

Sanborn found dining at the Thoreau table a pleasant experience. The room was made cheerful by Sophia's collection of potted plants. Mr. Thoreau sat silently at the head of the table, because of his deafness taking little part in the talk. Thoreau sat at his father's left hand and generally led the conversations toward his recent reading or his outdoor explorations. Often interrupted by his loquacious mother, he would pause and wait with courteous

5. Thoreau, *Correspondence,* 367
6. Ibid. 370
7. Cameron, *The Transcendental Climate,* I, 225–6

silence until the interruption ceased and then, bowing to h
mother, but without a word of comment on what she had said, h
would resume his discourse. Sophia, who had all the livelines
of her mother, but a broader interest in cultural matters, too
her own active part in the talk.[8]

Sanborn tried to persuade Thoreau to lecture at his scho
regularly once a week. He almost agreed but then on reflectic
decided he could not spare a day a week from his chosen task
Sanborn nonetheless planned a weekly excursion in the woods f
his pupils and occasionally was successful in persuading Thore
to accompany them.

Samuel Storrow Higginson, one of the pupils in Sanborn
school, later recalled Thoreau's friendliness:

> He was ... to us more than a charming companion; he became
> our instructor, full of wisdom and consideration, patiently listen-
> ing to our crude ideas of Nature's laws and to our juvenile
> philosophy, not without a smile, yet in a moment ready to correct
> and set us right again. And so in the afternoon walk, or the long
> holiday jaunt, he first opened to our unconscious eyes a thousand
> beauties of earth and air, and taught us to admire and appreciate
> all that was impressive and beautiful in the natural world around
> us. When with him, objects before so tame acquired new life and
> interest. We saw no beauty in the note of veery or wood-thrush
> until he pointed out to us their sad yet fascinating melancholy.
> He taught us the rich variety of the thrasher's song, bidding us
> compare with it the shrieks of the modern *prima donna*. The
> weary peep of Hyla had for us no charm until he showed us
> how well it consorted with the surrounding objects,—the dark
> pool with the andromeda weeping over it, as if in fear of the little
> "sea-monster." Nor did we fancy the flaming red-wing, with his
> anxious cry, the Perseus of the story, who makes his home near
> by, to keep the maiden company, until by his very love he caused
> us too to like him. Then we sought to know more of the young
> gallant, and saw how wonderfully well he built his home, and
> laughed at the grotesque markings upon the eggs. He turned
> our hearts toward every flower, revealing to us the haunts of
> rhodora and arethusa. . . .
>
> His ear was keenly alive to musical sounds, discriminating with
> astonishing accuracy between the notes of various songsters. This

8. Sanborn, *The Personality of Thoreau*, 11–12

discernment enabled him to distinguish at once the songs of many birds singing together, selecting each one with great nicety of perception. A single strain was enough for him to recall the note at once, and he always had some English translation, or carefully marked paraphrase of it, singularly expressive and unique.[9]

Later, as the school prospered, Sanborn expanded it, eventually employing five full-time teachers on his staff and persuading Emerson and others to be guest lecturers. Alcott, visionary and impractical as ever, proposed that Sanborn expand the school into a college and hire Agassiz, Hedge, Parker, Thoreau, and Alcott himself as a faculty, but understandably nothing came of his brief dream.

It is not surprising that young Higginson had found Thoreau so fascinating a companion. Thoreau was always a boy at heart. As he himself once commented, he never lost his sense of wonder. Channing noticed that, like a boy, he could never pass a berry without picking it. When Channing commented to him on his insatiable curiosity, Thoreau replied, "What else is there in life?"[1] He could never take anything for granted, and looking at the world about him with a questioning mind, he was constantly discovering things that others had not noticed. When from the top of a mountain he noticed the shadows of clouds in a valley, he quickly figured how to calculate their height accurately. When he noticed the pattern with which star fungi split, he puzzled out the reason. When he observed water squirting through leaks in a dam, he noticed their varying jets and reasoned that it was related to the varying heads of water above the leaks. When he discovered that turtles tended to bury their eggs three inches beneath the soil, he tested with thermometers and proved that the overall day and night temperature was greatest at this depth. And when he noticed that some of the shingles on his neighbor's roof were blacker than others, he figured out that those were the poorer or sappy shingles which absorbed the most water in a rainstorm. As Channing said of him, "He was alive from top to toe with curiosity."[2] And

9. [Samuel Storrow Higginson], "Henry D. Thoreau," *Harvard Magazine,* VIII (1862), 313–18
1. Channing, *Thoreau, the Poet-Naturalist,* 10
2. Ibid., 6

someone so insatiably alert always had something interesting to say. That, the children of the town had quickly discovered.

Many adults however were still skeptical. They simply could not understand why Thoreau exerted so much effort on labors which produced no money for him. They could not understand a search for knowledge for its own sake. And even when they could understand that, they could not understand why he seemed perversely to take the most difficult method of acquiring knowledge, overlooking, of course, that that was often the only dependable way. One day one of the villagers stopped him on the street. "Don't you ever shoot a bird when you want to study it?" he asked. "Do you think," Thoreau aptly replied, "that I should shoot you if I wanted to study you?"

CHAPTER SEVENTEEN
(1855–1857)

I

ALTHOUGH Thoreau had spent a vigorous winter, taking longer
ating excursions on the rivers than he ever had before, and
ending as much of the spring outdoors as he ever had, he was
truck down the spring of 1855 with a strange illness. All the
strength and vigor seemed to depart from his usually sturdy legs
and he found it almost impossible to continue his daily walks,
though he tried manfully. The Emersons were alarmed and
tried unsuccessfully to persuade him to spend a week resting at
their home.[1] On June 27, Thoreau wrote Blake:

> I have been sick and good for nothing but to lie on my back
> and wait for something to turn up, for two or three months. . . .
> I should feel a little less ashamed if I could give any name to
> my disorder, but I cannot, and our doctor cannot help me to it,
> and I will not take the name of any disease in vain. . . . I
> expected in the winter to be deep in the woods of Maine in my
> canoe long before this, but I am so far from that that I can only
> take a languid walk in Concord streets.[2]

When he visited Alcott in Boston on the Fourth of July, Alcott
noticed his illness and thought he acted "shiftless" for the first time
in his life.[3] His daily journal entries diminished often to but a
sentence and sometimes disappeared altogether for a week at a
time. He lost his ebullient optimism for a time and complained
often of his loneliness. He felt weak enough that he gave up
surveying almost entirely, doing only a little work for Emerson,

---

1. Ralph Waldo Emerson, *Letters* (New York, 1939), IV, 512
2. Thoreau, *Correspondence*, 376
3. Bronson Alcott, Journals

and leveling the land for an ornamental pond at the new Slee[
Hollow Cemetery.

But despite his weak legs and his depressed spirits, he lo
none of his enthusiasm for nature. He devoted himself for
time to a study of birds' nests. When he found a tanager's nest
the top of a pine tree too fragile to climb, he carried three ra[
and a rope a quarter of a mile into the woods and erected a mak
shift derrick so that he could see if there were any eggs in
When he found it empty, he retrieved it and carried it triumphan[
home for his collection. For a time mice were his enthusiasm a[
he set up a miniature trap-line to catch and examine the[
Later it was muskrats, and he consulted farmers and hunters [
details of their lives. In March he captured a flying squirrel
its nest in a rotten hemlock. Rolling it up in a handkerchief,
carried it home where he soon tamed it enough to stroke it a[
watched it attempt to sail in the confines of his room. The ne
day he returned it to the woods, released it, and watched it s[
from tree to tree.

Two months later, in investigating another hollow tree,
found a screech owl sitting on its eggs and reached in and strok
it repeatedly, the owl showing no resistance. When he return[
for later visits, the owl flew off at the sound of his approa[
which gave him the opportunity to examine the eggs and you[
The babies soon became so tame that he could handle them with[
their protesting. Although his friend Minott warned him that
knew of a man's losing his eyes from an owl's attack, Thore[
was not in the least deterred.

In mid-October, while boating near the Hemlocks, he spot[
another screech owl on a tree stump. After watching from [
boat for ten minutes, he landed and stole up behind the bi[
Springing around rapidly, he stretched out his arm and caught
in his hand. At first it was so surprised that it offered no resi[
ance, and only glared at him in astonishment. When it began
snap and hiss, Thoreau rolled it up in a handkerchief and put
in his pocket, it biting his finger slightly in the process. He carri[
it home and made a small cage in which to keep it for the nig
The next day he returned it to the woods but was astonish[
when the owl seemed not anxious to be released. He toss[
it up into the air and it flew off twenty rods, but he was eas[

[358]

le to pluck it off a branch and make it fly once more. Eventu-
ly it flew into a higher tree beyond his reach.

In November 1852, when Thoreau had been corresponding
ith George William Curtis of *Putnam's Magazine* about the pub-
cation of his "Yankee in Canada" essays, he had also submitted
 Curtis some of his Cape Cod essays which Curtis at first
ccepted, and then, apparently because of the controversy over the
'anada papers, put aside. In November 1853 Francis Underwood
ad written Thoreau for a contribution to an anti-slavery maga-
ine that he was hoping to establish under the aegis of John P.
ewett. Thoreau submitted a paper on December 2—possibly it
vas one of these Cape Cod papers—but Underwood's plans never
naterialized. (Thoreau did succeed in having his poem "My life
s like a stroll upon the beach" from his *Week* published in an
nthology, *Thalatta: A Book for the Sea-Side,* edited by Samuel
,ongfellow and Thomas Wentworth Higginson and published
•y Ticknor, Reed, and Fields in 1853.)

Then in April 1855 Curtis suddenly wrote that he was plan-
ing after all to publish the Cape Cod essays in *Putnam's* and
isked permission to revise a few sentences that he thought
ieretical. Since the change requested was trivial involving only
he dropping of the words "in Scripture" at one point, Thoreau
icceded so long as an omission was indicated at the appropri-
ite spot, and installments of the essays appeared in the June,
uly, and August issues.

Inspired perhaps by this long-postponed publication and
ioping that the sea air would help him recover his health, Thoreau
nade another journey to Cape Cod in July 1855. About a month
arlier Channing had proposed that they go to Truro and board
or a while but Thoreau declined. Blake and Brown in Worcester
eard of these plans and wrote that they would like to join the
xpedition. In the midst of a letter telling them he was not going,
Thoreau suddenly changed his mind, announced that he had de-
ided to leave for the Cape within a week, and invited the
Worcester folks either to accompany him from Concord or to join
iim at Truro. At such short notice they were unable to accept,
iowever.

On the morning of July 4, Thoreau and Channing arrived at
City Wharf in Boston in response to an advertisement that said

the schooner *Melrose* would make its first trip of the season t
Provincetown. There was no sign of activity about the ship an
Captain Crocker informed them that despite the advertisement h
had decided to lay over another twenty-four hours. With an u
wanted day in Boston on their hands, they visited the Athenaeu
gallery, watched a regatta, and then spent the night at Bronso
Alcott's. They sailed on the 5th at mid-morning and, arriving
Provincetown, put up for the night at Gifford's Union House. O
the 6th they took the stage coach to North Truro post offic
and then, walking across the Cape to Highland Light, arrange
with James Small to board at the Stage House, attached to th
light, for $3.50 a week.[4]

They spent an enjoyable two weeks at Highland Ligh
Thoreau botanized at length, although he was annoyed that it wa
so damp all the flowers he pressed mildewed on him. He examine
a large school of blackfish stranded by the tides, and picked up
fox skull for his collection and an eighteenth-century Frenc
crown piece. When a storm shifted a sandbar to make a protecte
pool, he and Channing enjoyed swimming together until they di
covered they were keeping company with a shark. Thereafter the
made certain the pool was not "preoccupied" before they venture
in. They watched menhaden rippling the ocean surface and stripe
bass playing along the shore. The quiet relaxation did Thorea
good and he felt better, at least temporarily, than he had i
months.

They left Small's on the 18th after a boy at the table an
nounced he had seen the *Olata* sail into Provincetown harbor. The
had a quick sail back to Boston, leaving the *Melrose* far behind an
nearly keeping pace with a steamer for a time. "To be continued
appeared at the end of the August installment of the Cape Co
essays in *Putnam's* and Thoreau submitted a newly revised manu
script for the September issue, but it never appeared. He an
Curtis had become embroiled in another controversy. This tim
there were a number of points at issue. Although Thoreau ha
received thirty-five dollars for the August installment, he felt h
deserved more. Curtis was afraid that Cape Codders might b

4. Grace Deschamps, "Plaque Once Marked Thoreau Room," *Provincetown Advocate*, September 27, 1962

ffended by the tone Thoreau had adopted toward them,[5] and he omplained that he had not realized before that Thoreau intended ventually to gather the essays together in book form. The real natter at issue was that Putnam's liked to publish their own nthologies of essays from their magazine in book form—and in act, in 1857, they did issue just such a volume, *Tales and 'ketches For the Fire-Side. By the Best American Authors. 'elected from Putnam's Magazine,* which included "The Plains of Nauset" installment of Thoreau's Cape Cod essays.[6]

Thoreau eventually asked Curtis to return the unpublished portion of the Cape Cod manuscript and no more of it saw print in his lifetime. His friendship with Curtis easily survived the quarrel. A year or two later, writing to Sanborn, Curtis asked to be remembered to Thoreau "if that Cato-Osceola does not despise such messages," and they met occasionally afterwards at Emerson's.[7] After Thoreau's death the whole Cape Cod manuscript was edited by Ellery Channing and published by Ticknor & Fields in book form.

Cape Cod is Thoreau's sunniest, happiest book. It bubbles over with jokes, puns, tall tales, and genial good humor. There is no preaching in it. Except for a few digressions on the history of the Cape, it is purely and simply a report on his various excursions to the peninsula, using his 1849 trip as the thread for the narrative and weaving materials from his 1850 and 1855 trips into it. The result is unquestionably the best book that has ever been written about Cape Cod and it is the model to which all new books about the Cape are still compared.

II

Daniel Ricketson went to Concord in late September 1855, hoping to persuade Thoreau to return with him for an extended

5. Francis H. Allen, *A Bibliography of Henry David Thoreau* (Boston, 1908), 71
6. I am indebted to Jacob Blanck for this information
7. Kenneth Walter Cameron, "Emerson Manuscripts—Ungathered and Migrant," *Emerson Society Quarterly,* VI (1957), 27

visit in New Bedford. They took several walks together and Ellen Channing joined them for a long evening's conversation, but most of the visit Ricketson suffered from his miserable headaches and Thoreau still complained of the weakness of his own legs. Ricketson returned to New Bedford alone after only a day and a half. But when he renewed his invitation by mail, Thoreau reconsidered, accepted, and on the 29th took the train to New Bedford, stopping off on the way at the Natural History Society library in Boston to talk with Dr. Cabot about thrushes.

Thoreau and Ricketson, accompanied by the Ricketson boys Arthur and Walton, explored the nearby Middleborough ponds, botanizing and gathering Indian relics on their shores. Happening upon an Indian fishing, Thoreau questioned her at length about the Indians of the area but found she knew little. On a rainy day they rode in a carriage to see the old houses of Fairhaven. Evenings they spent looking over Ricketson's extensive library, Thoreau dipping into many of the local histories. On occasion they joined the family around the piano, singing while the children accompanied them on the violin and flageolet. When Mrs. Ricketson asked Thoreau to sing, he said "Oh, I fear, if I do, I shall take the roof of the house off!" But when she urged him further and offered to accompany him on the piano, he sang his favorite "Tom Bowline" with spirit and expression.[8] Ricketson, who did not care for such festivities, soon retired to his shanty in the yard by himself.

On October 4, Thoreau was suddenly overcome with an urge to return to Concord; so on the 5th Ricketson drove him through Middleborough and Carver to Plymouth in his buggy, picnicking under the Carver pines on the way and stopping to call on Marston and Mary Russell Watson for tea. Thoreau took the train for Boston and Concord on the 6th and Ricketson returned to New Bedford. He found Thoreau, "upon an intimate acquaintance—modest and gentle in manner, the best read and most intelligent man I ever knew."[9]

Ricketson made plans to follow Thoreau back to Concord but later changed his mind and instead urged Thoreau to return to New Bedford for a longer visit. Thoreau replied that since he felt

8. Edward Emerson, Notes on Thoreau
9. Ricketson, *Daniel Ricketson and His Friends,* 283

early recovered from his long illness, he must at last settle down seriously once more to his work.

Actually Thoreau's full recovery was slow in coming. On September 16 he had noted, "After four or five months of invalidity and worthlessness, I begin to feel some stirrings of life in me."[1] But on the 26th he wrote Blake, "I do not see how strength is to be got into my legs again." In October 1856 he still spoke of being "run down" and in 1857 he referred to his "two-year-old invalidity."[2] What the illness was cannot be identified at this distance, although it was probably in some way related to his chronic tuberculosis, for Channing noted in his diary that summer that Thoreau's cough was particularly bad.[3] Why this time it seemed to affect his legs in particular is puzzling.

III

Once Thoreau thought he had good legs under him once again, he went back to his regular program of devoting each afternoon to long walks in the countryside. The winter of 1855–6 was marked with unusually deep snows and he spent hours and days in measuring depth, noting where the drifts occurred and wondering why. He consulted the old-timers of the town to see if they could recall another winter like this. Animal tracks in the snow caught his attention and he puzzled to identify them. Even he, with all his experience, was astounded at the amount of activity they revealed.

When workmen felled the huge elm in front of Charles Davis's house on Boston Road, he was there to watch every step of the process, systematically measuring the circumference of the trunk and every major limb as it came down, and mourning the passing of this, one of the most ancient residents of the town. He was annoyed when the townspeople argued at length over the age of the tree and showed them that it could be accurately determined simply by counting the growth rings in the stump. In his enthusiasm he studied the tree patterns of every stump and piece of wood he

1. Thoreau, *Journal*, VII, 417
2. Henry Salt, *The Life of Henry David Thoreau* (London, 1890), 189
3. Transcript of manuscript, Frederick T. McGill, Jr.

came across for a time. Examining the trees more closely remind
him of his old interest in birds' nests and once more he start
✲ collecting specimens for his attic museum.

Concern with trees led him in turn to a long series of expe
ments with tree saps and syrups. Early in March 1856 he beg
tapping sugar maples, learning by experimentation that uplar
✲ sumac made the best spouts. Once he slipped on the ice walki
home on the river and spilled all but a pint of a painstaking
gathered bucketful. Later he spoiled a batch by accidentally putti
in soda instead of saleratus. When he boiled the sap down on t
kitchen stove, his father tried to tell him he was wasting his tir
saying that he knew before he started it could be done and th
he could buy sugar at the grocery store cheaper than he cou
produce it. Besides, argued his father, it took him away from l
studies. Thoreau replied that *this* was his study and he was learni
✲ as much as he would at a university.

When warmer weather came, he began tapping other kinds
trees, particularly the birches—black, yellow, white, and canc
At Alek Therien's suggestion he tried making various birch wir
and drinking them with his meals but decided they were too "or
door-sy" in flavor for general use. When he aged them for sever
months, he found the flavor greatly improved and almost mea
like. When he emptied the last bottle in late July, he regrett
that there was no more, for he thought the taste would continue
✲ improve. After further experimentation in later years, he final
concocted a combination of the saps of the white, black, and yellc
birches that needed only the addition of sugar to make what eve
Daniel Ricketson admitted to be "a very pleasant acidulo
drink."[4] (His interest in sap wines is a little surprising in that I
rarely liked to drink even water and would sometimes try to reca
when he last had had a drink.)

In mid-June of 1855 he had discovered a painted tortoise la
ing its eggs in a sandbank near the hemlocks and spent thre
quarters of an hour bent over, his face eighteen inches from th
turtle, observing in minute detail the process of laying and buryi
the eggs. When he had returned to the site in September, he ha
been disappointed to discover the eggs had already hatched and th
young gone their way. Now a year later recalling his experienc

---

4. Harding, *Thoreau, Man of Concord,* 191

Daniel Ricketson

Harrison Gray Otis Blake

Thomas Cholmondeley

Theophilus Brown

"DISCIPLES"

*Thoreau's
birthplace
Virginia R*
Concord

From an
insurance-
company
calendar
of the 1880s

*The family home c
the Square*
Thoreau's grandfathe
purchased the buildin
on the right in 1799
and Henry's family li
there from 1835 to 18
It is now the
Colonial Inn

*The "Yellow House" on Main Street
where Thoreau died on May 6, 1862*

THOREAU'S HOMES IN CONCORD

with the painted turtle, he was delighted to come across a huge
napper in the river. Reaching over the side of his boat, he caught
it by the tail and pulled it into his boat only to discover that he had
more than he bargained for. He could not both row and keep
himself out of the range of the turtle's dangerous trap-like jaws.
Finally he turned it on its back, braced an oar from its sternum to
the bottom of the seat and held it down with one foot while he
paddled the boat to shore with a single oar. Once he got it home,
he measured and recorded its every detail and then let it go.

In the fall of 1856 his interest turned to wild fruit and he
gathered great quantities of cranberries, grapes, and barberries, and
brought them home to eat. Although he considered himself as
dextrous a barberry picker as one who had been "born in the
Barberry States," it was days before he got the prickles out of his
fingers. Herbs too he gathered in earnest and he was particularly
disappointed when he found pennyroyal tea "too medicinal" for his
taste.[5]

His townsmen took more and more of an interest in his
studies and apprised him whenever they discovered anything out of
the ordinary. Rice told him where to find a dove's nest. Minot Pratt
gave him a chimney swallow's nest and the wing of a sparrow hawk.
Frank Harding collected a cicada for him. Goodwin sold him a
muskrat he had just killed and later brought him a cinereous coot,
while Farrar gave him the wing and foot of a hawk. Thoreau
expressed his gratitude for each and carefully carried the treasures
home to add to his attic collections.

IV

On March 4, 1856, Horace Greeley suddenly wrote Thoreau
to suggest that he live with them on their farm at Chappaqua,
thirty-six miles north of New York City, and tutor the Greeley
children. He set the freest possible terms: the pay would be whatever Thoreau considered satisfactory; he would have time to write
or to go off on lecture tours as he saw fit; and the arrangements
could be terminated at any moment. Greeley, like Emerson when he

---

5. *Thoreau, Journal* IX, 85, 89

had arranged for Thoreau to go to Staten Island years befor
wished to bring his friend into closer contact with the publishing an
editorial world. Thoreau accepted and agreed that he would repo
to Chappaqua about the first of July, when Mrs. Greeley, who ha
already given her approval to the plans, returned from Europe wit
* the children. But then realizing that he could no longer be happ
in the classroom, that Concord was his whole world, he change
his mind and the plan was abandoned.

On March 27, 1856, Uncle Charles Dunbar died at the ag
* of seventy-six. With all his eccentricities and absolute independenc
of all conventions, he was unquestionably Thoreau's favorit
relative. His unpredictable comings and goings always added col
to the life of the Thoreau household. Many would—and did—n
doubt consider him a ne'er-do-well on the order of Robert Frost
"hired man." But Thoreau saw through his foibles, recognized hir
for the kindhearted soul he was, respected him, and, after his deatl
missed him. Uncle Charles, in his turn, had respected Thoreau, ha
quite understandably refused to worry about his eccentricities, an
with no little awe had looked upon him as a fount of all knowledge
More than once some of the more conservative Thoreau relatives—
Aunt Louisa Dunbar, for instance—must have thought of Thorea
and his Uncle Charles as two of a kind—and the thought implied n
compliment to either.

In June 1856 Thoreau made the longest visit of his life wit
his friends in Worcester, arriving there on Friday the thirteenth an
remaining for a week. The first four nights he spent with th
Theo Browns at 10 Chestnut Street, the last two with the Blakes a
3 Bowdoin Street.[6] It is said that he mortified one of his Worceste
hostesses because he never bothered with a valise or traveling ba
but brought his possessions wrapped up in a red bandanna or tie
up in a sheet of brown paper. His sister Sophia and the Thorea
aunts were, by coincidence, visiting the city too. Thoreau and hi
friends, often accompanied by Sophia, walked in the Hermitag
Woods, inspected a night-blooming cereus in blossom at the hom
of Mrs. Newton, examined the collections in the Natural Histor
rooms, rode around Quinsigamond Pond, studied Rev. Horac
James's collection of reptiles and stuffed animals, and called or

---

6. Ruth Frost, "Thoreau's Worcester Visits," *Nature Outlook*, I
(1943), 12

igginson and Edward Everett Hale. On the 16th they took a
ain to Sutton, where they explored Purgatory Chasm, a spec-
cular gorge which prehistoric earth movements had filled with
ouse-sized fragments of rock.

While he was in Worcester, Thoreau had his first picture taken.
Calvin H. Greene of Rochester, Michigan, who had corresponded
vith him after reading *Walden*, sent some money and requested a
photograph. Thoreau visited the Daguerrean Palace of Benjamin
D. Maxham at 16 Harrington Corner and had three daguerreotypes
made at fifty cents each. One he gave to Blake, another to Brown,
and the third he mailed to Greene. They show a sober-faced individual with turbulent hair and the Galway whiskers he had grown
under his chin during his illness of the year before, hoping to prevent further throat colds. Thoreau reported to Greene that his
friends thought the likeness "pretty good—though better looking
than I."[7] Horace Hosmer, who knew Thoreau well, thought it the
best picture of Henry he had ever seen.[8]

When Thoreau returned to Concord on June 19, he found
Daniel Ricketson awaiting him. Ricketson had arrived unannounced
on the 17th and Thoreau's parents had entertained him until their
son's return. They then spent three days sailing on the river,
bathing at Walden Pond with Emerson and his son, taking tea with
Mrs. Brooks, and discussing the foibles of Ellery Channing. When
Ricketson returned to New Bedford on the 23rd, he persuaded
Thoreau to accompany him and they stopped off in Boston to
visit the Natural History Society rooms on their way. On the 24th
they took a buggy ride to Tobey's Pond and Long Pond, stopping
for a picnic lunch under an apple tree in Freetown. The next day
Thoreau was taken to meet Thomas A. Greene, a local botanist, who
told him where to find the rarest plants in the vicinity. He then
visited the city library to identify in Audubon's "hundred-dollar"
Ornithology a sparrow he had seen in Ricketson's yard. On the
26th they explored Sconticut Neck, in Fairhaven, in search of
marine plants and discovered while eating their lunch that they
had seated themselves in the midst of clumps of star grass (*Aletris
farinosa*), which Greene had told them was one of the rarest plants

7. Thoreau, *Correspondence,* 426
8. Horace Hosmer, Letter to A. W. Hosmer of February 27, 1891.
MS, Concord Free Public Library

in the region. On their way home they stopped to call at the hut c
Martha Simonds, the last of the pure-blooded Indians of the are:
Thoreau was disappointed to learn that she could not speak a wor
of the Indian language and that she knew nothing of her race. Sh
answered his questions listlessly, indicating interest only when h
showed her the *Aletris*. That she informed him was "husk-root,
good to put into bitters for a weak stomach. He wished then tha
he had brought along a hatful of plants for her to identify. Despit
his disappointment with her, he was disgusted when a Quake
neighbor said sanctimoniously to him, "I think that the Indians wer
human beings, dost thee not think so?"[9]

On the afternoon of June 27 Thoreau and the Ricketsons too
the steamer *Eagle's Wing* out to visit Naushon, the largest of th
Elizabeth Islands, to explore its unspoiled wilderness. They wer
astounded to spot a deer shortly after their arrival and later Thorea
discovered a grapevine twenty-three inches in circumference tha
he thought might date back to the time of Gosnold. Two years late
when Ricketson published his *History of New Bedford,* he include
in it an account of their afternoon's visit.[1]

Thoreau remained in New Bedford five more days, botanizin
with the Ricketson boys, visiting an Indian burying ground, an
touring the Middleborough Ponds once again. When he notice
a haymaker working in the fields with his suspenders crossed befor
as well as behind, he made note of it in his journal as "a valuabl
hint" since he was much troubled with his own suspenders slippin
off his shoulders.

Ricketson later in the year paid two more visits to Thorea
in Concord. In September he spent three days, walking out t
Walden Pond and spending a morning in conversation at Chan
ning's, but he found his hotel room so uncomfortable that h
suffered from excessive fatigue and headache and cut his visit shor
In December he spent a day at Concord, visiting Walden Pon
again, listening to Thoreau reading Channing's poetry aloud
and sleeping the night at Emerson's house.

In September Thoreau accepted a long-standing invitation from
Bronson Alcott to visit him in Walpole, New Hampshire, where h

9. Thoreau, *Journal*, VIII, 390–2
1. Daniel Ricketson, *History of New Bedford* (New Bedford, 1858),
126–8

d settled with his family the year before. He set out by train on
e morning of the 5th, but when he discovered he had a three-
d-a-half-hour wait in Fitchburg, he walked five miles along the
ack to the next station at Westminster rather than waste his time
tting in the station. He had been corresponding with Rev. Addi-
n Brown, a former Unitarian minister who conducted a school for
ung ladies in Brattleboro, Vermont, and studied botany as a
obby, and so stopped off to see him. Brown promptly introduced
im to Charles Christopher Frost, a local shoemaker who had be-
ome the leading authority on the botany of Vermont, and for
ur days Thoreau roamed the woods, fields, and mountains of
e area with Frost, Brown, and Brown's children. They climbed
ount Wantastiquet, explored the Connecticut River, examined
e scars of a recent freshet, found leatherwood (Indian rope) grow-
g indigenously for the first time, and, after seeing the skull and
kin of a panther which had been killed a few months before on one
f the Saranac Lakes, went to some length to interview both the
an who had killed it and the taxidermist who had set it up.
Unfortunately he missed by a few hours meeting Dr. Elisha Kent
ane, the celebrated Arctic explorer, whose books he was familiar
vith, and who had been taking the water cure after returning
rom his second search for the lost English explorer Sir John
ranklin.

Mary Brown, who was fourteen at the time, was amused that
Thoreau overwhelmed her with questions about "all sorts of things"
o which she could only reply, "I do not know." It appealed to her
ense of humor that a person with such a fund of knowledge should
eek information from a young girl like her. She remembered that
vhen they stood on the summit of Wantastiquet he suddenly de-
ignated a distant spot on the landscape and asked, "How far is it
n a bee line to that spot?"[2] A year later Thoreau sent her a
pecimen of climbing fern for her herbarium and she in turn sent
im on two occasions boxes of mayflowers she had picked in the
Brattleboro woods.

On September 10 Thoreau took the train to Bellows Falls,
Vermont, where after exploring the rocks and potholes, he climbed
Fall Mountain with his valise on his back. Though the tollman at

---

2. Elizabeth Davenport, "Thoreau in Vermont in 1856," *Vermont
Botanical Club Bulletin,* III (1908), 38

the river warned him against the trip, he made the ascent wit
ease. Coming down however he found more difficult—often slippin
on the rocks, falling, and battering his valise. After bathing in th
Connecticut River to recuperate, he begged a ride into Walpol
New Hampshire, with a lumberer and inquired at length about th
techniques of the lumbering industry as they wended their way.

Thoreau spent the morning of the 11th in Alcott's study di
cussing Fremont's current campaign for the presidency, but in th
afternoon he was able to persuade Alcott to come outdoors lon
enough to climb Farm Hill and to investigate the monuments in th
local graveyard. That night he took to bed with him all he could fin
of local history in Alcott's library and filled his journal with note
He returned to Concord on the 12th, carrying sixty-six new spec
mens for his herbarium—fifteen of them a gift from Brown
herbarium. The *Aster ptarmicoides,* a rare Vermont species tha
he had particularly hoped to find, unfortunately was not amon
them.

V

In 1852 Margaret Fuller's one-time sponsor Marcus Spring
a wealthy Quaker abolitionist, had purchased a two-hundred acr
tract on the shores of Raritan Bay, a mile west of Perth Amboy
New Jersey, and incorporating as the Raritan Bay Union an
erecting a tremendous brownstone and brick phalanstery, 254 fee
long, three stories high, with dormitories, apartments, and school
rooms, he attempted to establish a co-operative community. Whe
the community did not prosper, he decided in 1856 to rename i
Eagleswood and to convert the property over into small estates fo
New York City commuters, hoping to attract them with pleasan
country living, a good school, lyceum lectures, and other cultura
activities, and good commuter service via steamboat to the city.
Bronson Alcott was visiting at Eagleswood at the moment an
suggested Thoreau as the ideal surveyor for the project.

Thoreau set out from Concord on October 24, stopping of
long enough in Worcester for an afternoon's visit with Higginso

3. Marcus Spring et al., *Eagleswood, Perth Amboy, N. J.* (Perth
Amboy, 1856), 1–2

and Theo Brown (Blake was out attending, of all things, a horse race) and then continuing by train and steamboat to New York City, where he once more visited the Barnum Museum and continued on to Eagleswood in the late afternoon in the company of Elizabeth Peabody, whom he had happened upon on his way.

On Monday morning he set about his surveying and found himself kept so busy that he had little time to write in his journal or elsewhere. The woods were filled with cat briers, mud, and beggars' ticks. It took him ten to fifteen minutes before each meal to pick the seeds and burrs off his clothing and longer to repair the tears. He learned that Spring also wanted him to set out a vineyard and an orchard and that some of the individual owners wished him to survey their properties, so his visit stretched out much longer than he had originally planned. His first Saturday night he was astonished to learn they expected him to attend the regular dance and he complained, "They take it for granted you want society!" Sunday morning he attended Quaker meeting, and when he was told that it was hoped he would speak, he said, as he wrote his sister, "just enough to set them a little by the ears & make it lively." Despite his protestations, they insisted he read a lecture to the children. He was pleased when they were delighted with his "moose story"—the report of his Maine Woods excursion. The following Sunday he read his essay on "Walking" and still later his "What Shall It Profit?" lecture and they were equally successful. The Eagleswood group with its unconventional bent and slightly radical sympathies turned out to be just the audience for him.

Bronson Alcott, who was spending the winter in New York City, went out to Eagleswood on November 1 to visit both Thoreau and the Springs. When he reported the next day to Greeley that Thoreau was that nearby, Greeley invited the two of them to his farm in Westchester for the next weekend. Thoreau came into New York on Friday, met Alcott at his rooms at Mrs. Anne C. Lynch Botta's, and there was introduced to William Swinton, the Scottish admirer of Walt Whitman. Mrs. Botta, a prominent bluestocking of the period who conducted a noted literary salon, promptly invited Thoreau to attend her soiree that evening, but he as promptly declined the invitation and spent the night at Dr. Trall's water cure with Alcott.[4]

4. Bronson Alcott, Journals

In the morning they met Greeley at the Harlem railroad station and journeyed the thirty-five miles out to his farm by train. After spending the day inspecting his agricultural experiments, they returned to the city in the evening with the poet Alice Cary, who also had been Greeley's guest.

On Sunday morning Alcott and Thoreau took the ferry to Brooklyn and attended Plymouth Church to hear Henry Ward Beecher. Thoreau was restive throughout the service and told Alcott he thought it pagan in its emotionalism. Later he added sarcastically in his journal, "If Henry Ward Beecher knows so much more about God than another, if he has made some discovery of truth in this direction, I would thank him to publish it in *Silliman's Journal,* with as few flourishes as possible."[5] (Elbert Hubbard has reported that Beecher invited Thoreau as a fellow abolitionist to sit up on the platform with him but there seems to be no foundation for his statement.[6])

Thoreau and Alcott dined at noon with Alcott's friends, the Mannings. Alcott had recently discovered Walt Whitman and now loudly sang his praises. Thoreau was already familiar with his work, having a copy of the 1855 edition of *Leaves of Grass* in his library and, as we have seen, having sent a copy to Cholmondeley. Alcott led Thoreau to Whitman's home on Myrtle Avenue, far out in the suburbs of Brooklyn. Whitman, unfortunately, was not there but his mother greeted them warmly. She was baking in the kitchen at the moment and treated them to cake hot from the oven, telling them meanwhile how good her son was and how wise and how much his two sisters and four brothers loved him.[7] She promised that, if they would return in the morning, Whitman would be happy to see them.

Thoreau and Alcott spent the night with the Mannings, devoting the evening to a discussion with the Welds of the Eagleswood community and a Mrs. Sarah Tyndale of Philadelphia (whom Alcott described as "a sort of Saintly Walrus of a woman, stuffed with goodness to the full"). Thoreau praised the wild, while Mrs. Tyndale defended the human and Alcott the divine.

---

5. Thoreau, *Journal,* XI, 438
6. Elbert Hubbard, *Thoreau* (East Aurora, 1904), 185
7. Horace Traubel, *With Walt Whitman in Camden* (Boston, 1906), I, 212

In the morning Alcott and Thoreau returned to Myrtle Avenue accompanied by Mrs. Tyndale and found Whitman awaiting them. He led them up two narrow flights of stairs to his bedchamber, which he shared with a feeble-minded brother, where they found the bed unmade, the chamber pot plainly visible, books strewn on the mantelpiece, and unframed pictures of Hercules, Bacchus, and a satyr pasted roughly on the walls. Whitman informed them of his bathing daily even in mid-winter, of his riding on top of an omnibus up and down Broadway from morning till night beside the driver and dining afterwards with the whipsters, of frequenting the opera in its season, of his editing the *New Orleans Crescent* for a time, and of his living to make his poems and "for nothing else particularly." He said that he devoted his mornings to reading and writing and his afternoons to walking—a program remarkably similar to Thoreau's own. When Alcott, looking at the pictures on the wall, asked "Which, now of the three, particularly, is the new poet here —this Hercules, the Bacchus, or the satyr?"[8] Whitman begged him not to question too closely and Alcott inferred he wished to take the virtues of all three to himself unreservedly. Whitman was very curious for criticism of himself and his book and, whenever the conversation wandered off that topic, hastened to bring it back.

When they descended to the living room below to continue their talk, Alcott tried his hand at starting a conversation between Thoreau and Whitman. Both acted reserved. Alcott thought they looked "like two beasts, each wondering what the other would do, whether to snap or run" and each thinking of the other, "Well, you're almost as great as I am!"[9] But after a while they fell into a pleasant talk. Thoreau, thinking he had noticed signs of an Oriental influence in *Leaves of Grass,* asked if Whitman were familiar with the great books of the East. Whitman answered, "No: tell me about them." They talked of *Leaves of Grass.* Whitman defended his controversial publication of Emerson's personal letter to him, "greeting him" at the beginning of a great career. Thoreau thought, "In his apologizing account of the matter he made the printing of Es [sic] letter seem a simple thing—and to some extent throws the burden of it—if there is any, on the writer." Thoreau told Whitman

---

8. Unidentified newspaper clipping in Bronson Alcott's autobiographical collections for 1880, Houghton Library
9. Alcott, *Journals*

that he thought the book something to be reckoned with, and then said, "There is much in you to which I cannot accomodate myself the defect may be mine: but the objections are there!"[1] But h added, "Whitman, do you have any idea that you are rather bigge and outside the average—may perhaps have immense significance? He referred to Whitman's critics as "reprobates," and when Whit man asked "Would you apply so severe a word to them?" h replied, "Do you regard that as a severe word? reprobates? wha they really deserve is something infinitely stronger, more caustic I thought I was letting them off easy."[2]

They talked of the mass of men. Thoreau said, "What is ther in the people? Pshaw! what do you (a man who sees as well a anybody) see in all this cheating political corruption?" Whitma thought that he did not like his Brooklyn spoken of in this way that Thoreau showed a disdain for men, an inability to appreciat the average life.[3] It seemed to him that Thoreau's was "a ver aggravated case of superciliousness," that he was surprisingl egotistic. The two could not at all agree in their estimate of th common man, of Tom, Dick, and Harry.[4]

Whitman gave Thoreau a copy of the 1856 edition of *Leave of Grass*, inscribing it "H. D. Thoreau from Walt Whitman. Thoreau, in turn, gave Whitman a copy of *A Week*, filling in th missing lines in his own hand. Despite their differences, each seeme to appreciate the other: Whitman admitted that Thoreau "was man you would have to like—an interesting man, simple, con clusive,"[5] and Thoreau told Alcott as they came away, "That a great man." Thoreau returned to Eagleswood, stopping off t visit the New York bookstores on the way. On November 25 he re turned to Concord.

The visit with Whitman made a profound impression o Thoreau. On November 19 he wrote Blake:

Whitman . . . is apparently the greatest democrat the world has seen. Kings and aristocracy go by the board at once, as they

1. Traubel, *With Walt Whitman in Camden*, III, 403
2. Ibid. III, 318–19
3. Herbert Gilchrist, *Anne Gilchrist: Her Life and Writings* (London, 1887), 237
4. Traubel, *With Walt Whitman in Camden*, I, 212–13
5. Ibid.

have long deserved to. A remarkably strong though coarse nature, of a sweet disposition, and much prized by his friends. Though peculiar and rough in his exterior, his skin (all over (?)) red, he is essentially a gentleman. I am still somewhat in a quandry about him,—feel that he is essentially strange to me, at any rate ... He said that I misapprehended him. I am not quite sure that I do.[6]

Reading over the more earthy 1856 edition of *Leaves of Grass* that Whitman had given him, Thoreau was shocked and disturbed. He wrote to Blake again:

That Walt Whitman, of whom I wrote to you, is the most interesting fact to me at present. I have just read his 2nd edition (which he gave me) and it has done me more good than any reading for a long time. Perhaps I remember best the poem of Walt Whitman an American & the Sun Down Poem. There are 2 or 3 pieces in the book which are disagreeable to say the least, simply sensual. He does not celebrate love at all. It is as if the beasts spoke. I think that men have not been ashamed of themselves without reason. No doubt, there have always been dens where such deeds were unblushingly recited, and it is no merit to compete with their inhabitants. But even on this side, he has spoken more truth than any American or modern that I know. I have found his poem exhilirating encouraging. As for its sensuality,—& it may turn out to be less sensual than it appeared —I do not so much wish that those parts were not written, as that men & women were so pure that they could read them without harm, that is, without understanding them. One woman told me that no woman could read it as if a man could read what a woman could not ...

On the whole it sounds to me very brave & American after whatever deductions. I do not believe that all the sermons so called that have been preached in this land put together are equal to it for preaching— ...

Since I have seen him, I find that I am not disturbed by any brag or egotism in his book. He may turn out the least of a braggart of all, having a better right to be confident.

He is a great fellow.[7]

6. Thoreau, *Correspondence*, 441–2
7. Ibid. 444–5

Emerson later told Whitman that Thoreau carried his new copy o
Leaves of Grass around Concord "like a red flag—defiantly, chal
lenging the plentiful current opposition there."[8] He thought
Thoreau's fancy for Whitman "grew out of his taste for wild nature
for an otter, a woodchuck, or a loon."[9] When Thoreau sent a copy
of *Leaves of Grass* to Thomas Cholmondeley in England,
Cholmondeley replied: "[Whitman] appears to me not to know
how to behave himself. I find the gentleman altogether left out of
the book! Although these leaves completely puzzle me."[1] But
Thoreau made no attempt to enlighten him.

Although Whitman in his later years spoke of several further
meetings with Thoreau, there is no definite record of any of them.
Thoreau visited New York City briefly in the spring of 1858, and
it is possible but unlikely they met then. Whitman was in Boston
for some time in the spring of 1860 correcting the proofs of the
ill-fated third edition of *Leaves of Graves* published by Thayer &
Eldridge. He walked on Boston Common with Emerson at least
once and attended Sanborn's trial in Cambridge, but we cannot
be certain that he met Thoreau. It is said that Thoreau, Emerson,
and Alcott then wished to join in inviting Whitman to visit Concord, but Mrs. Emerson, Mrs. Alcott, and Sophia Thoreau were
all so strongly prejudiced against him for his outspoken verse that
they joined in vetoing the invitation before it could be extended.[2]

When Emerson read his eulogy of Thoreau in 1862, he spoke
of the profound impression Whitman had made on Thoreau but
referred to him only as "a person not known to this audience."
When Sanborn asked his identity, Emerson replied, "Walt Whitman." But when Sophia Thoreau learned of this, she strongly protested and the sentence was dropped when the eulogy was printed.[3]

Blake had asked Thoreau to lecture in Worcester on his way
home from Eagleswood, but Thoreau was not at all enthusiastic and
finally went straight home to Concord without stopping over to see
his friend. His only lecture of the year was one that he gave on
December 18, 1856, in Amherst, New Hampshire, where he read

8. Traubel, *With Walt Whitman in Camden*, III, 405
9. Ralph Waldo Emerson, *Journals*, IX, 401
1. Thoreau, *Correspondence*, 481
2. Sanborn, *The Personality of Emerson*, 128
3. F. B. Sanborn, "Emerson and His Friends in Concord," *New England Magazine*, III (1890), 430–1

s paper on "Walking" in the vestry of the orthodox church and usted he "helped to undermine it." The audience gave him heir close attention, but no one spoke to him afterwards and he oncluded that, although they had liked it, they did not dare admit . An earlier attempt to arrange a lecture in Harrisburg failed. ◦

On February 3, 1857, Thoreau delivered a lecture in itchburg, Massachusetts, and ten days later read "Walking" in Vorcester. He informed Blake that he had read the same paper ◦ here six years before but in the meantime had expanded and altered so much that he would have enough for a full evening even after mitting what he had read previously. ◦

CHAPTER EIGHTEEN
(1857–1858)

I

O N MARCH 28, 1857, Thoreau suddenly wrote Daniel Ricketson
that he would like to come to New Bedford for a visit. He had
still not recovered fully from his illness and thought the earlier
spring in New Bedford would be cheering. It snowed and turned
cold however the morning of April 2 as he left Concord and, passing
through Cambridge, he picked up a frozen toad from the sidewalk
hoping the heat of his body would thaw it back to life in his pocket.
In New Bedford he found not only Ricketson but Alcott and
Channing awaiting him and they talked late into the night.

Thoreau spent two full weeks in New Bedford. The Ricketson
boys had acquired a large fishing boat and he helped them repair
and refurbish it. He went over their natural history collections and
assisted them to identify difficult species. When he learned that Mrs.
Ricketson liked bayberry candles, he helped her gather the berries
and boil them down to obtain wax and then took several of the
little golden nuggets of wax back to Concord with him for his
museum.[1] He was amused when one night a thunderstorm came up
and Ricketson, thoroughly frightened, dashed about the house
calling his sons down from the attic where they slept, and insisting
that Thoreau keep a light burning in his bedroom.

Together they visited the New Bedford Library to discuss
frog spawn with its librarian, Mr. Ingraham, and to consult various
books on natural history. They watched fishermen seine alewives
from the cove south of town and catch smelts at the head of the
river. They toured the Middleborough Ponds, and when Thoreau
found a strange-looking turtle, he made a waterproof box for it

---

1. Edward Emerson, Notes on Thoreau

ut of birchbark and so carried it home later to Concord, where
proved to be nothing more than an odd variation of the common
stink turtle." When Ricketson heard the turtle scratching in
Thoreau's coat pocket that evening, he was convinced that mice
had invaded his shanty. Thoreau, amused, did not bother to en-
ghten him.

They had lunch one day with the Brady sisters whom Thoreau
had met the year before as maids in the Ricketson household. Kate
Brady, twenty years old, had read *Walden* "with great pleasure"
he said and now proposed to live alone in the family homestead,
n abandoned ruin, and support herself by farming, sheepkeeping,
pinning, and weaving. The next day she called at the Ricketsons
nd took a long walk in the country with Thoreau. Alcott thought
ter quite enamored of Thoreau, and Thoreau, if we judge correctly
rom the long effusion he entered in his journal more than a week
ater, was quite taken with her. But he, after all, was twice her
ge and his brief interest soon vanished.[2]

One evening as the family gathered around the piano,
Thoreau sang Moore's "Row, Brothers, Row" and Dibdin's "Tom
Bowline" to Mrs. Ricketson's accompaniment. When she struck
p "The Campbells Are Coming," he suddenly launched into a
dance by himself, keeping time to the music perfectly, but exe-
uting steps more like Indian dances than the usual ballroom
igures.[3] He continued the performance for five or ten minutes and,
when Alcott looked less than enthusiastic, took pains to tread
n his toes to liven him up.

Thoreau's visit, thanks to Ellery Channing, who was at the
moment employed by the *New Bedford Mercury,* was recorded
n the social columns, where he was described as "well known
n reform and literature."[4] When he finally left for Concord on
he 15th, the 6 a.m. train failed to stop long enough for him to
board and he had to wait four and a half hours for the next train.

Finding Thoreau's companionship so stimulating, Ricketson
hought seriously for a time of pulling up stakes and moving to
Concord. He talked it over at length with Alcott, who, thinking

---

2. Walter Harding, "Thoreau and Kate Brady," *American Literature,*
XXXVI (1964), 347–9
3. Sanborn, *Recollections of Seventy Years,* II, 397
4. Clipping in Bronson Alcott, Journals

Concord the hub of the universe, encouraged him. Ricketson wro
Thoreau, asking him to find an appropriate farm to purchase, b
Thoreau, practical as ever, urged him to try renting first, to t
sure that he did not regret leaving New Bedford. He visited Co
cord for a few days in late May, sleeping at Channing's and dini
at the Thoreau's. They took several boat rides on the Conco
River, but he complained so chronically of headaches that Thorea
annoyed, fussed in his journal, "I have noticed that notion
nervous invalids, who report to the community the exact conditi
of their heads and stomachs every morning, as if they alone we
blessed or cursed with these parts . . . improve the least oppo
tunity to be sick."[5]

Later in September Ricketson suggested that Thoreau vis
New Bedford again, but he replied that he had already spent t
much time away from Concord that year. In December Rickets
made another brief visit in Concord after attending an anti-slave
bazaar in Boston. Once again he slept at Channing's and too
his meals with the Thoreaus, where he met Parker Pillsbury, t
anti-slavery orator. Thoreau took Ricketson with him while
surveyed a Walden woodlot, and spent the evening until elev
talking with him. Thoreau had recently grown a full beard a
Ricketson thought it much improved his appearance;[6] Channin
on the other hand, thought the new beard "terrible to behold.

II

Bronson Alcott's long-precarious financial situation w
somewhat improved in the spring of 1857 when Emerson and h
friends established a life-annuity fund for him, taking ample pr
caution that he not be able to touch the principal. Emerson an
T. Davis contributed a hundred dollars each to the fund; Lon
fellow, Starr King, Cheney, and Wendell Phillips fifty dollars eac
F. Beck, forty; C. F. Hovey, ten; and Thoreau, one dollar.[8]

5. Thoreau, *Journal*, IX, 379
6. Daniel Ricketson [Notes on Thoreau]. MS, Albert Lownes
7. William Ellery Channing, Diary. Transcript of MS, Frederick T.
McGill, Jr.
8. Bronson Alcott, *Journals*, 300

In September 1857 Alcott returned to Concord to live and felt like an exile returning to his native land. Although his wife was not particularly happy at the prospect, for she had never liked Concord and thought some of the people there bad influences on her ever-impractical husband, he purchased a run-down farm on Lexington Road from John Moore and, naming it Orchard House, proceeded to repair, remodel, and beautify it as he had Hillside next door a decade before. Thoreau, on occasion, helped him to terrace it and to plant the grounds with locusts and fruit trees and made a careful survey of the property.

In the spring of 1858 Alcott's daughter, Elizabeth, the Beth of *Little Women,* always frail, slowly faded away, dying on March 14 at the age of twenty-three. Thoreau called that evening to offer his condolence. At the funeral the next day he helped Sanborn, Emerson, and John Pratt carry her casket to the carriage and he rode in the first carriage with the family in the funeral procession.

With better health and stronger legs, Thoreau once more actively resumed surveying, doing work for Daniel Shattuck, Louis Surette, George Heywood, George Brooks, Stedman Buttrick, Gordon, Bateman, John Moore, Sam Staples, Rufus Morse in Lincoln, Miss Bigelow, the Richardsons, George Brooks, Ellis, Samuel Bancroft, Cyrus Hosmer, Abel Brooks, Emerson, Charles Bartlett, and the town of Concord.[9] When in March his father purchased a small piece of land to straighten the lines of their property, Thoreau surveyed the plot, and in May built a fence around the entire yard.

The surveying for Bartlett and Emerson climaxed a long-standing controversy over their respective wood lots near Walden. In 1845 Emerson had purchased a second wood lot at the pond and, as we have seen, Thoreau witnessed the deed. Bartlett, whose own wood lot adjoined Emerson's, soon after walked the boundary and accepted Emerson's marks as fair. A year or two later when Edmund Hosmer reported that Bartlett had cut trees on Emerson's land, Bartlett apologized that it was an error and gave the wood to Emerson. Then Bartlett found an old deed and claimed that it was Emerson who was infringing on *his* wood lot. Emerson proposed that Thoreau be hired jointly to run the lines anew and Bartlett agreed. But since Thoreau had earlier sold Bartlett some

hay for Emerson and Bartlett had refused to pay for it until
lawyer was authorized to collect it, Thoreau now refused to surve
for Bartlett unless he were paid in advance. Bartlett refused t
pay for work before it was done and so they reached a stalemat
and the lines were not run. There the matter rested until 185
when Bartlett filed suit against Emerson for cutting trees on h
land. When the case was tried, the court found for Bartlett an
assessed Emerson fifty dollars damage. Emerson appealed th
decision and asked Thoreau to survey the line with Bartlett an
Emerson himself as witnesses. This Thoreau did in December 185
and, not trusting Bartlett, wrote up the survey in his field boc
with far more meticulous detail than usual. Yet he increased th
size not only of Bartlett's tract but also of Emerson's—for the lin
on both sides of Emerson's piece he found had been wrong
When the case came up again in June 1858, on the basis of th
new evidence it was agreed that Emerson had unwittingly cut som
of Bartlett's wood and he was assessed twenty-five dollars an
costs.[2] But since Emerson, thanks to Thoreau, was able to demon
strate that he had been given a faulty deed in the first place,
was those who had sold him the land in the first place that final
had to pay.[3]

III

On June 12, 1857, Thoreau set out alone on what proved
be his last visit to Cape Cod. He had hoped to have Ellery Chan
ning accompany him, but Channing, undependable as ever, backe
out once again. Taking the train to Boston, Thoreau made h
usual visit to the Natural History Society rooms and then con
tinued on to Plymouth to spend three nights with the Marsto
Watsons. On the 14th he thought to visit "Uncle Ed" Watso
on Clark's Island in the harbor and tried to cross from Captain
Hill in Duxbury to the north shore of the island on the flats a
low tide. But the tide came up more quickly than he thought an

1. Ralph Waldo Emerson, *Letters*, (New York, 1939), V, 95
2. Kenneth Walter Cameron, "Emerson's Fight for His Walden Wood-
lots," *Emerson Society Quarterly*, XXII (1961), 90–5
3. Ralph Waldo Emerson, *Journals*, VIII, 580

rtunately a fisherman, Sam Burgess, happened along in his
oat, collecting his lobster pots just in time to come to the
scue, and delivered him safely at last to the island. Uncle Ed,
ho had since the last visit read Thoreau's *Walden,* greeted him
ith the query, "I've read . . . that you 'lost a hound, a horse, and
dove.' Now what do you mean by it?" "Well, Sir, I suppose we
ave all had our losses," was all that Thoreau would say, and
Jncle Ed had to satisfy himself with grumbling, "That's a pretty
ay to answer a fellow."[4]

Thoreau sat around the living room that evening talking
ith Uncle Ed and his four stalwart sons, telling them tales
f the ancient Norsemen, and the sea voyages of the Vikings. In-
pired by their questions and the arrival of one after another of the
ther islanders, who as word spread flocked around to hear his
ales and even leaned in through the open windows, he talked
ar into the night, thrilling his impromptu audience with his nar-
ation. In the morning he was safely returned to Plymouth by
oat at high tide.

He toured Marston Watson's Old Colony Nursery, taking
nany notes on rare trees and shrubs therein, watched for a time
 new-born colt in the pasture, and queried his host on the folk-
ore of the area, puzzling over the origin of a local place-name,
'Shall I go naked?"[5] After visiting briefly at the farm of James
pooner, he set out with Watson and his wife by carriage on the
fternoon of the 15th for Manomet Point, about eight miles
outh of Plymouth, and there, shouldering his pack and bidding
is hosts good-bye, he set out on foot, at times walking along
he shore, at other times cutting through swamps and fields, avoid-
ng the capes and points. After hiking six or seven miles, he put
p for the night at the home of Samuel Ellis, just beyond Salt
'ond, and spent the evening talking with a sixteen-year-old peddler
rom Conway, Massachusetts, who arrived soon after with horse
nd cart. Thoreau thought his host, a loud-praying Methodist,
o be a Philistine whose single purpose in life was to scrape more
ennies together, but the youth he found attractive.

In the morning he walked through an Indian village, bathed

---

4. Ellen Watson, "Thoreau Visits Plymouth," *Thoreau Society Bulletin,* XXI (1947), 1
5. Thoreau, *Journal,* IX, 420

along the shore, and at eleven took the train from Scusset to Sand
wich. Hiking through Yarmouth, he asked the way to Friend
Village, but since he could convince no one that he wanted to go
there cross-lots, he finally had to find his own way by compass
and chart. He was astounded when he saw hardly an able-bodied
man all day, until he suddenly realized that they all had gone to
sea. After having walked nearly thirty miles that day, he put up
for the night at Isaiah Baker's in West Harwich, and dined on
herring for supper and fresh eels from the Herring River for break
fast.

In the morning he walked along the shore for a mile and then
turned inland to Harwich center. Near Hinckley's Pond, he saw his
first cultivated cranberry bog and stopped to inspect it closely—
professional cranberry raising had just come to the Cape. When
a native gave him what he believed to be incorrect directions, he
climbed a tree but, seeing nothing identifiable on the horizon, set
out by compass once more and put up that night at Cobb's Trav
eller's Home, near the Eastham Camp Ground, having covered
about twenty miles that day.

June 18 was a mizzling day, as he called it. The rain soaked
his clothes through and the wind-blown sand stuck to his pant
legs. Picking up a dead Mother Carey's chicken he found on the
beach, he tied it to the tip of his umbrella, letting it dangle outside
The natives, he was sure, thought him demented. At noon he
stopped to inquire for John Newcomb, the Wellfleet oysterman,
but learned that he had died the previous winter at ninety-five.
At 2 p.m. he reached the Highland Light, and was greeted by Uncle
Sam Small, who picked up the conversation where they had
dropped it two years before.

Thoreau spent three days at Highland Light, visiting the
new telegraph station and roaming the dunes looking for wild-
flowers, but rain and fog every day made the visit a miserable one.
Sunday, the 21st, when it at last cleared, he set out directly cross-
country for Provincetown, stopping only long enough to uncover
some arrowheads on the shore, to inspect the washed-up ribs of
a whale, and to climb Mt. Ararat, the highest dune in the area.
That evening he called on Mr. Atwood, the state representative,
to talk about fish and fishing. He spent the night in a tiny attic
room at the Pilgrim House, fearful that stray cats would crawl in

rough the one tiny window. He had over the years, he said,
ent four nights at the Pilgrim House and thereby "had added con-
derably to his knowledge of the natural history of the cat and the
edbug."[6]

Monday morning, he took the steamer *Acorn* to Boston in
e fog and arrived back at Concord at 5 p.m. Although this was
ne of his longest visits to the Cape, he unfortunately never got
round to writing it up for his Cape excursions. His only account
f the journey is in his journal.

IV

On July 20, 1857, he took off from Concord once more,
is time to visit the Maine Woods again. He had asked Eben
oomis to accompany him, but Loomis was not free. Blake hinted
at he would like to go along, but Thoreau thought him not sturdy
nough to stand the rigors of the trip nor knowledgeable enough
bout woodcraft to be much help. He finally settled upon Edward
oar, who had just returned to Concord after a long sojourn in
alifornia.

They took the train from Boston to Portland and then a
eamer to Bangor but were delayed for hours in a dense fog and
id not reach port until late in the afternoon of the 21st. The next
orning Thoreau's cousin, George Thatcher, took them down to
ldtown to find an Indian guide. Thoreau had hoped that George's
n Charles might accompany them on the trip, but he had made
ther plans. The first man they saw on the Oldtown island was
oseph Polis, a stoutly built, forty-eight-year-old Indian, "with
erfect features and complexion." Thatcher had known him for
ears and recommended him as being particularly steady and
ustworthy. Polis at first asked two dollars a day for his services
ut finally compromised on a dollar and a half and fifty cents
xtra a week for his canoe.

The Indian arrived in Bangor that evening, carrying his
ghteen-foot canoe on his head, and put up for the night with
horeau and Hoar at the Thatchers'. In the morning the canoe

6. Ibid. IX, 453

was lashed to the top of a stagecoach and they started off. They were delayed for several hours when a dog belonging to a fellow traveler wandered off. When found, he was tied on top of the coach, only to fall off several times and dangle by his neck. Despite their mishaps, they reached Moosehead Lake about half past eight in the evening, and since it was raining hard, put up at a tavern for the night, though Thoreau said he preferred to camp out.

At four the next morning they launched their canoe, packed as tightly as a market basket with their 166 pounds of luggage. Part way down the shore near Deer Island, they ate a breakfast of hardbread, fried pork, and strong coffee. Thoreau soon learned that Polis had an extensive knowledge of the Indian language and extracted a promise from him to teach Thoreau all he knew. From that point on Thoreau demanded to know the Indian name for everything he saw from herbs to streams and from mountains to paddles.

Their canoe, they soon discovered, was so low in the water that they were forced to skirt the edges of the lake rather than risk the high waves in the center. Once when Thoreau moved suddenly to watch a fish leap, he took in a gallon or two of water, filling his lap. By noon they had reached Mount Kineo, and after having some difficulty finding a suitable camp site, they left Polis sleeping under his turned-up canoe while they botanized up the slopes of the mountain. They returned to find Polis had caught a three-pound lake trout.

That evening as they lay in their tents, Polis entertained them with his nasal but musical Indian chants. When Thoreau got up in the middle of the night to tend the fire, he discovered fox fire (phosphorescent wood) for the first time in his life. How he had missed it in all his years of walks in the Concord woods after dark is hard to explain, for it is a phenomenon familiar to the most amateur of woodsmen.

Since the weather was good the next morning, they set out early to finish their voyage on the lake before the wind came up. They cooked their dinner at Northeast Carry and, after portaging, started down the Penobscot River at four o'clock. An hour later they pitched their tent just in time to crawl in out of a sudden thunder shower. Mosquitoes plagued them all night long.

[386]

Thoreau awoke in the morning to the plaintive notes of the ìite-throated sparrow. Polis, announcing that it was Sunday, ought that they should lie by for the day. When Hoar and ìoreau insisted they go along, he quickly acceded, saying that f he no takum pay for what he do Sunday, then ther's no rm." Thoreau told him he was stricter in his religion than ìite men—but noticed that he did not deduct his Sunday pay the end of the trip. They took the Caucomgomoc River up to e Umbazookskus and pitched their tent at one of Polis's old mp sites. Most of the afternoon, in deference to Polis's religion, ey rested, botanizing close to the site of the camp.

On Monday they continued up the Umbazookskus. Once lis accidentally spat on Thoreau's back. Wiping it off, he said it is a sign Thoreau was about to be married. When they portaged the Allagash watershed, Polis set off ahead of them, carrying e canoe and telling them to follow in his tracks. They promptly st their way, stumbling through foot-deep water and mud. When e Indian finally found them, they were miles off their route and ey decided to carry on to Chamberlain Lake rather than Mud nd, their original destination, though they found their path lay rough a swamp filled with fallen trees. Reaching their goal late r supper, having already gone without their noon meal, they alked into the lake clothes and all to wash themselves clean. ìoreau, in disgust, concluded:

If you want an exact recipe for making such a road, take one part Mud Pond, and dilute it with equal parts of Umbazookskus and Apmoojenegamook; then send a family of musquash [muskrats] through to locate it, look after the grades and culverts, and finish it to their minds, and let a hurricane follow to do the fencing.[7]

idges pestered them when they tried to sleep that night and the ud, raucous laughter of a loon filled the air.

In the morning they continued on their way through the llagash lakes to an island on Caucomgomoc, where, concluding ey had gone far enough for this trip, they decided to turn back. sudden thunder shower threatened to trap them on the island,

---

7. Thoreau, *Writings,* III, 244

but the waves soon flattened out and they paddled rapidly bac
through Chamberlain Lake, reaching the Chamberlain farm, whe
they camped out in the rain, at dusk.

On Wednesday, the weather having cleared, they crosse
Telos Lake and portaged to Webster Pond, the headwaters of tl
East Branch of the Penobscot. While Polis shot the rapids of Wel
ster Stream in the canoe, Thoreau and Hoar carried all the
baggage along the shore, often far out of sight of the India
Once Thoreau stripped off all his clothes to ford a deep strea
while Hoar stumbled along until he finally found a rude log bridg
Later Hoar suddenly disappeared. Thoreau and Polis searche
until dark but could find no trace of him. They feared for
time that he had walked off one of the many precipices. The
doubted whether he could hear the firing of a gun above th
roaring of the stream and they feared that if they lighted
fire he might break his neck trying to reach them. Finally the
concluded that since he had both blankets and matches with hin
he was safe though supperless for the night. Nonetheless Threa
worried through the darkness how they could find him in that va
wilderness and how his family would feel should he retur
without him.

In the morning however, when they portaged to the Eas
Branch, they soon heard him calling and found him calmJ
smoking his pipe at the mouth of Webster Stream. He had mis
understood some of Thoreau's signals to Polis the afternoo
before and had wandered off in the wrong direction. He ha
passed a comfortable night and now was ready for a hearty break
fast, after which they continued on their way to Second Lake
Polis, suddenly spotting a moose, stood up in the stern of th
boat and shot it. Thoreau measured the carcass carefully for hi
notes and then went off fishing while Polis skinned it. The hide
according to custom, was theirs, but they gave it to Polis, whc
could sell it for seven or eight dollars. The additional hundrec
pounds of weight in their canoe they found considerably increasec
their danger of swamping.

Continuing along through the outlet to Grand Lake, they
stopped to eat lunch on a rocky island soon after entering
Matungamook Lake. They camped early for once to give themselves an opportunity to explore the wilderness by daylight. When

oreau asked Polis for a new tea, he made them one from eckerberries. While they wandered the "mossy and moosey" ods, Polis by unaccountable good fortune rolled over a log d found under it a cache of thirty or forty steel traps which immediately claimed for himself.

Most of Friday Thoreau and Hoar spent clambering around pids while Polis shot the canoe through. "There were more rand or Petty Falls than I can remember," Thoreau complained, it there were advantages to their portaging, for everywhere they alked they found ripe blueberries and raspberries. At one falls here Polis was forced to carry the canoe, he showed them first caribou track and then one of a cougar. When they stopped for e night, he demonstrated how to make a candle from a tightly lled strip of birch bark.

On Saturday they had intended to climb Katahdin, but oar's feet were so sore from the long hiking of the day before at he decided he couldn't make it and the climb was abandoned. lis cheered them up by making hemlock tea for Thoreau and birch-bark pipe to replace one Hoar had lost. When they came their first carry of the morning, Polis challenged Thoreau to a ce. Thoreau afterwards wrote:

As his load, the canoe, would be much the heaviest and bulkiest, though the simplest, I thought that I ought to be able to do it, and said that I would try. So I proceeded to gather up the gun, axe, paddle, kettle, frying-pan, plates, dippers, carpets, etc., etc., and while I was thus engaged he threw me his cowhide boots. "What, are these in the bargain?" I asked. "Oh, yer," said he; but before I could make a bundle of my load I saw him disappearing over a hill with the canoe on his head; so, hastily scraping the various articles together, I started on the run, and immediately went by him in the bushes, but I had no sooner left him out of sight in a rocky hollow than the greasy plates, dippers, etc., took to themselves wings, and while I was employed in gathering them up again, he went by me; but hastily pressing the sooty kettle to my sides, I started once more, and soon passing him again, I saw him no more on the carry. . . . When he made his appearance, puffing and panting like myself, in answer to my inquiries where he had been, he said, "Rocks (locks) cut 'em feet," and, laughing, added, "Oh, me love to play some-

[389]

times." . . . I bore the sign of the kettle on my brown linen
sack for the rest of the voyage.[8]

They camped in the rain that night two miles below Nicketow
the south side of the West Branch.

When they awoke in the morning, Polis was ill with the col
Thoreau, convinced that he had devoured too much moose me
tried first to get him some brandy in Lincoln. Failing this,
apothecary offered Brandreth's pills, but Polis refused to ta
them and spent most of the day groaning under his canoe.
twilight he finally mixed himself a tonic of gunpowder and wat
To Thoreau's astonishment, he was enough better in the morni
for them to continue on their way down the river.

Polis had often complimented Thoreau on his ability with
oar, giving him an Indian name meaning "great paddler," but n
stopping in mid-stream, he suddenly said, "Me teach you paddl
Turning toward the shore, he got out, came forward, and plac
Thoreau's hands, one of them quite outside the boat and the oth
parallel with the first, telling him to grasp the paddle near t
end, not over the flat extremity, and to slide it back and for
on the side of the canoe. Thoreau found it to be a great improv
ment, saving him the labor of lifting the paddle each time a
wondered that Polis had not suggested it earlier.

By four that afternoon they had traveled forty miles a
reached Polis's home at Oldtown. Their whole canoe journe
had covered 325 miles. Before they took the last train to Bang
Polis tried to sell Thoreau his canoe, promising that it would l
seven or eight years, but Thoreau would have none of it. Thore
and Hoar spent three days in Bangor with the Thatchers, drivi
through the countryside, visiting an Indian village site, and tryi
their hand at fishing. On Friday, August 7, they took the tra
to Portland and a night boat to Boston, Hoar carrying with hi
a pair of moose horns, a gift from George Thatcher. The trip ha
cost the two of them about forty dollars apiece.

It was Thoreau's last visit to the Maine Woods and it ha
been made particularly memorable by his acquaintance with Pol
He wrote Blake:

8. Ibid. 314-15

[390]

[The Indian] begins where we leave off. It is worth the while to detect new faculties in man,—he is so much the more divine; and anything that fairly excites our admiration expands us. The Indian, who can find his way so wonderfully in the woods, possesses so much intelligence which the white man does not,—and it increases my own capacity, as well as faith, to observe it. I rejoice to find that intelligence flows in other channels than I knew. It redeems for me portions of what seemed brutish before.[9]

hen the following March Thoreau attended an Indian lecture Concord, he was delighted to discover one of the speakers s Polis's brother. Polis himself remained one of Thoreau's ajor heroes, on a par with, though very different from, Walt hitman.

Edward Hoar found himself newly impressed with Thoreau's ilities and years later wrote Henry Salt, Thoreau's biographer, s to Thoreau's courage and manliness, nobody who had seen m among the Penobscot rocks and rapids, the Indian trusting s life and his canoe to his skill, promptitude, and nerve, would er doubt it."[1]

Later Thoreau talked at length with John Langdon Sibley, arvard's new librarian, of his journey, and Sibley recorded in his urnal:

To-day [Thoreau] enlarged to me somewhat on the mistake of men of science in not giving more attention to the Indians & their languages & habits. In relation to geology, botany, zoology, &c., they stand between the men of science and the subjects which they study, and much may be learned from them, who have no books, that will surprise people. For instance, the Indians have more than fifty names for the cedar. Of it they make boats, paddles, bows, strings, &c., & the names which they give to it, are descriptive of its various properties & uses. Father Rasle's Dictionary, published in the Memoirs ot the American Academy is very valuable in this respect, & Mr. Thoreau has carefully compared much of it with the words in use at the present day & finds it very accurate. In his last excursion he was accompanied by a son of the Indian governor at Old Town. He was intelligent & had

9. Thoreau, *Correspondence*, 491
1. Salt, *The Life of Henry David Thoreau,* 179

[391]

acquired a property of some six thousand dollars, chiefly by letting himself to travellers for $1.25 or $1.50 per day & his canoe for fifty cents, & accompanying them. He never would get lost in the wilderness. He could always tell the points of the compass by the appearance of the hills & a multitude of other signs which he told Mr. Thoreau he could not describe, but which to Mr. T. seemed a kind of instinct. Mr. T. mentioned a case where with an old settler they had a very irregular chase all day after a moose. When the game was secured the white man could not tell which way to go home. The Indian took a direction as straight through the wilderness as a bee would to its hive. It made no difference whether he had been over the wilderness before; he would always take the right direction home. The effect of the sun on the south side of hills &c, was particularly noticed by the Indians. When travelling, the Indian stopped short: "Me hear snake"—"rain." "Do snakes make a noise?" "Yes." The noise was a little whistle. This fact is not generally known to naturalists. The Indian could talk the language of many animals. He would call a wild musquash to him by imitating his notes & sounds. Naturalists make no mention of the habit of the pout in leading about young pouts as a hen does its chickens. Mr. Thoreau says he observed this before any person mentioned it to him. He named it to Mr. Agassiz who had a faint recollection that he had seen the statement somewhere in Aristotle. Mr. Thoreau subsequently found that the word for pout in one of the Indian dialects was descriptive of this habit of the fish. The mother keeps driving or drawing into a compass of some two feet in diameter, by means of her tail & swimming, around them, all her young, & a rod or two before them is another pout, probably the male, to protect them from outside enemies. Thus men of science might learn best through Indians many of the properties &c of the subjects of their studies.[2]

V

The *Atlantic Monthly* had been established in 1857 a James Russell Lowell, as its editor, promptly approached Thore to be a contributor. In September 1857 he asked Emerson if

2. Cameron, *The Transcendentalists and Minerva*, II, 485–6

ould not persuade Thoreau to submit a piece and in November, nore specifically, if Thoreau would not write up an account of his nost recent trip to Maine. Thoreau himself replied in January 858 that his report, already written, contained so much about oe Polis that he would be embarrassed for Polis's sake to see it in rint—though he did deliver it as a lecture before the Concord yceum on February 25, 1858. He added, however, that he did ave the account of his 1853 excursion to Maine, which, originally repared as a lecture, he could easily convert to an essay suitable or publication. Lowell said he was interested and Thoreau sub- nitted the essay in installments from March 5 to May 18. He asked o be paid at the same rate as Emerson, but finally had to be atisfied with the six dollars a page paid to rank and file contribu- ors.[3]

The first installment appeared as the lead article in the June 858 number. Although it was unsigned as was the custom with he magazine, its authorship was pretty generally known and no ne was surprised when Greeley announced it as Thoreau's n May 21 in his *Tribune*. When the July installment appeared, Thoreau was chagrined to discover that Lowell had omitted a entence without his knowledge or approval. He angrily wrote owell:

When I received the proof of that portion of my story printed in the July number of your magazine, I was surprised to find that the sentence—"It [a pine tree] is as immortal as I am, and perchance will go to as high a heaven, there to tower above me still."—. . . [had] been crossed out, and it occurred to me that, after all, it was of some consequence that I should see the proofs; supposing, of course, that my "Stet" in the margin would be respected, as I perceive that it was in other cases of com- paratively little importance to me. However, I have just noticed that that sentence was, in a very mean and cowardly manner, omitted. I hardly need to say that this is a liberty which I will not permit to be taken with my MS. The editor has, in this case, no more right to omit a sentiment than to insert one, or put words into my mouth. I do not ask anybody to adopt my opinions, but I do expect that when they ask for them in print, they will print

3. John Trowbridge, "An Early Contributor's Recollections," *Atlantic Monthly*, C (1907), 588

them, or obtain my consent to their alteration or omission. I should not read many books if I thought that they had been thus *expurgated*. I feel this treatment to be an insult, though not intended as such, for it is to presume that I can be hired to suppress my opinions.

I do not mean to charge you with this omission, for I cannot believe that you knew anything about it, but there must be a responsible editor somewhere, and you, to whom I entrusted my MS. are the only party that I know in this matter. I therefore write to ask if you sanction this omission, and if there are any other sentiments to be omitted in the remainder of my article. If you do not sanction it—or whether you do or not—will you do me the justice to print that sentence, as an omitted one, indicating its place, in the August number?

I am not willing to be associated in any way, unnecessarily, with parties who will confess themselves so bigoted & timid as this implies. I could excuse a man who was afraid of an uplifted fist, but if one habitually manifests fear at the utterance of a sincere thought, I must think that his life is a kind of nightmare continued into broad daylight. It is hard to conceive of one so completely derivative. Is this the avowed character of the Atlantic Monthly? I should like an early reply.[4]

The expurgated sentence Lowell had apparently thought too pantheistic for his readers. But he made no correction of the omission when he printed the final installment in the August number nor, apparently, ever gave Thoreau even the courtesy of a reply. To make matters even worse, he was dilatory in paying Thoreau the $198 he had been promised for the articles and Thoreau had to dun him twice. Although there had been some talk of following the Chesuncook series with a modified version of the Allegash papers Thoreau would have nothing more to do with Lowell and refused to submit anything to the *Atlantic* so long as he remained on the staff.

Lowell, according to Emerson, never forgave Thoreau for wounding his pride.[5] Three years after Thoreau's death he took his revenge by reviewing Thoreau's posthumous books for the *North American Review* and therein not only denouncing Thoreau

4. Thoreau, *Correspondence*, 515–16
5. Charles Woodbury, *Talks with Ralph Waldo Emerson* (New York, 1890), 62

nce more as an imitator of Emerson but dismissing his works as one more symptom of the general liver complaint." Unfortunately or Thoreau, Lowell was by this time the most influential of American literary critics and his denunciation, it has been frequently verred, set back a general appreciation of Thoreau and his writing or many decades.

Thoreau's Allegash River essay remained unpublished at the me of his death. Then, in 1864, his sister Sophia and Ellery Channing gathered it and the accounts of his two earlier trips o Maine together and published it as *The Maine Woods,* with everal appendixes listing the trees, flowers, shrubs, plants, birds, nd quadrupeds he had found there, a description of an outfit he uggested for such an excursion, and a list of Indian words. Although the Allegash section and the appendixes suffer from careess editing—in the first edition two and a half pages of material vere misplaced by three days—the book as a whole gives an efective bosky and moosey picture of the deepest wilderness Thoreau was ever to explore. If *Cape Cod* tastes of salt, *The Maine Woods* smells of hemlock and balsam.

VI

Thoreau delivered a lecture in John B. Alley's parlor in Lynn, Massachusetts, on January 13, 1858, and found "a good company" in attendance.[6] Jonathan Buffum, a sixty-year-old Lynn spiritualist nd friend of Bronson Alcott, invited Thoreau to stay on for everal days. He took Thoreau to Nahant to see the ducks wintering there and to Little Nahant to examine masses of puddingstone. They visited Samuel Jillson, a taxidermist, who showed them a even-foot glass blowgun he had invented, with which he declared e could easily kill birds at six rods. They also visited Alonzo Lewis, who lived in a cottage he had built and clapboarded himself ith hemlock bark and who proudly showed a collection of egg-naped pebbles of sienite fifteen to eighteen inches long that he ad picked up on the beach at Kettle Cove. With Parker Pillsbury

---

6. Alcott, *Journals,* 304

and Benjamin Mudge, a local lawyer and amateur geologist, they rode to Danvers, where Mudge showed them many boulders o sienite and of porphyry. They examined a ledge where pioneer had quarried millstones and Thoreau discovered the rare dyers' green-weed (*Genista tinctoria*), which had become naturalized i the area.

Buffum told of having seen a sea serpent in Swampsco harbor twenty times, but Thoreau, recalling Buffum's belief i spiritualism, was not convinced. He was amused when Buffur warned him never to eat sea clams without first removing what h thought to be the clam's penis. He left Lynn carrying specimen of jasper, graywacke, amygdaloid, asbestos, hornstone, porphyr epidote, and argillaceous slate given him by Mudge and Buffur for his mineral collection. Although Jones Very had written askin him to stop off for a visit in Salem, Thoreau apparently was no able to find the time.

On his way back to Concord he stopped as usual at the Natura History Society rooms in Boston where he talked with Dr. Samue Kneeland about the ducks he had seen at Nahant and inspected live young bald eagle they had caged in their cellar. He also visite Dr. Durkee in Howard Street to discuss some rare glowworm Marston Watson had sent him from Plymouth the previous sum mer and others he himself had later found in Lincoln. (The forme were *Phengodes* and his description of them in his journal is sai to be the earliest known to entomologists.)

In May 1858 Thoreau made one last brief visit to New Yor City. He left Concord on the 22nd and stopped over for a day i Worcester, to visit Blake, Brown, and Rogers, to walk out t Quinsigamond Pond for breakfast, and to climb Wigwam Hill. H was astounded to see a muskrat swimming across a pool as the trai entered Manhattan. He spent the evening examining the aquariu at Barnum's Museum and the next morning visited the Egyptia Museum. The afternoon he spent visiting the William Emerson on Staten Island.

The purpose of Thoreau's trip concerned the family graphit business. The Munroes, cutting the price of black lead, ha become serious competition for the Thoreaus again. Thorea succeeded in making arrangements with what he thought one o the best agents in New York City to handle their business, bu

e had to cut their price in half in order to do it.[7] Having completed his business in New York, on the 26th he returned to Concord via Boston. Thoreau's father was growing feeble with the
passage of years and more and more Thoreau himself took over the
details of the business. He did what overseeing was necessary at
the mill, brought the lead back to the house on Main Street, and
did the heavier work of boxing and packing. But he still found
plenty of time for his own activities.[8]

VII

In June 1858 Thoreau made another visit to Mount Monadnock in the southwestern corner of New Hampshire. He left
Concord by train on the morning of the 2nd and by prearrange-
ment joined H. G. O. Blake at Fitchburg. When they arrived at
the Troy station shortly before noon, they immediately shouldered
their packs and headed northeast toward the mountaintop four
miles away. In mid-afternoon they chose a sunken yard in a rocky
plateau about half a mile southeast of the summit for their camp
and, cutting spruce branches, proceeded to make both a bed and a
roof of spruce twigs to protect themselves from the elements, but
since their roof was but eighteen inches high and their feet stuck
out the bottom, their lean-to was hardly palatial.

Proceeding to the summit to watch the sunset, they spotted a
slate-colored junco and soon found its nest. The few of the previous
year's crop of mountain cranberries still remaining were, Thoreau
discovered, agreeably acid to the taste. But the eggshells, newspaper fragments, and the names and initials painted and even
chiseled on the rocks were unpleasant reminders of tourist crowds
that often flocked to the summit. They were glad that none had
remained to spoil the night for them. Returning to their camp site,
they briefly lost their way in the haze but found it again in time to
brew tea and sit on the edge of a rocky plateau in the twilight,

---

7. John Thoreau, Letter to George Thatcher of June 9, 1858. MS,
Raymond Adams
8. Edward Emerson, *Henry Thoreau as Remembered by a Young
Friend*, 36–7

drinking their tea and listening to the calls of the chewink and the nighthawk.

They arose at three in the morning in order to see the sunrise from the top and to prepare their breakfast there. Unfortunately it turned out to be hazy again, so they devoted their time to botanizing, finding more than forty species of plants on the rock summit. The remainder of the day they devoted to exploring thoroughly the top of the mountain, clambering over rocks, wading through miniature bogs, examining glacial scratches on the ledges and inspecting tadpoles in the rain-water pools. When they boiled rice for dinner, their fire threatened to get out of hand, but Thoreau put it out with a spruce bough soaked in a pool.

At six the next morning they began their descent, taking the road to the State Line Station and Winchendon through the west part of Rindge. Walking along the railroad right-of-way, they were astonished to discover huge white pines, far more impressive than any Thoreau had ever seen in the wilderness of Maine, rising perfectly straight without a limb of any kind for sixty or more feet. By evening Thoreau was back in Concord.

Late in June, when Edward Hoar announced that he was considering botanizing in the White Mountains, Thoreau remarked that he too would like to go if he could afford it. Hoar replied that if Thoreau would accompany him, he would hire a horse and wagon and the excursion would cost Thoreau nothing. Thoreau accepted and the next morning proposed that Blake and Brown of Worcester be added to the company. When Hoar readily agreed, Thoreau wrote suggesting they meet in the mountains.

Thoreau and Hoar started out from Concord in their private carriage on July 2, stopping at noontime to bathe in the river at Dunstable, Massachusetts, and spending the night at a tavern in Merrimack, New Hampshire. On the 3rd they continued on through Bedford, Manchester, Hookset, Allenstown, and Pembroke to Loudon in the drizzling rain. On the 4th they went on through Canterbury and Gilmanton, eating their noon lunch on the shore of Lake Winnepiseogee. That night they camped just outside Senter Harbor. Thoreau thought traveling by horse far less independent than traveling by foot. They often found it difficult to locate appropriate camping sites. The horse kept them awake with his whinnering and pawing the ground. Even their stops for noonday lunches

ad to be chosen for the convenience of the animal rather than
hemselves.

On the 5th, upon reaching Moultonboro, they climbed Red
Hill to see the famous view of Winnepiseogee and Squam Lake,
carrying up water so that they could boil tea for lunch. Botanizing
for a time on the summit, they discovered and examined a huge
hill of red ants and then descended in time to drive to Tamworth
Village to put up for the night. On the 6th they breakfasted on
the shore of one of the Ossipee Lakes, continued on past Mount
Chocorua, nooning on the bank of the Ellis River near Jackson
Centre, and camped for the night at the home of William H. H.
Wentworth, about four miles from Jackson.[9]

The next morning, after Hoar had hired Wentworth to carry
their baggage and keep their camp, they rode eight miles on to
the Glen House. At 11:30 a.m. they began their ascent of Mount
Washington on foot. Much to Hoar's chagrin, Thoreau insisted
each man carry his own pack and dismissed contemptuously Hoar's
complaints. They spent the night in a collier's shack near the
present site of the Halfway House, and dined on boiled beef tongue
and milk from the colliers' goats. Wind blowing down the chimney
tunnel scattered their fire and nearly burned down the shanty. The
building, the colliers told them, sometimes rocked as much as four
inches in the wind.

In the morning Thoreau started off alone for the summit,
Wentworth and Hoar following later with the colliers and their
goats. Thoreau was rewarded with a good view from the top; the
clouds had closed in and there was a driving mist by the time the
others arrived. They talked with the landlords of the Tiptop and
Summit Houses and watched a Mr. White taking views from the
summit. After trying unsuccessfully to hire one of the colliers to
guide them through the dense fog, Thoreau produced a map he
had made the day before at a roadside inn, where, practicing his
old trick, he had climbed up on a table and traced a map of the
region mounted on the wall. Although the summit landlords tried
unsuccessfully to convince him that the map was faulty, he announced, "Well, if we cannot have a guide we will find it ourselves,"
and started off on a compass line for Tuckerman's Ravine in a fog

9. Jeannette E. Graustein, "Thoreau's Packer on Mount Washington,"
Appalachia, XXXIII (1957), 414–17

so dense that the landlords were sure some harm would come to them. Despite the fog they botanized nonchalantly as they went Crossing the snow in the ravine was difficult they found, and Thoreau tore his nail trying to save himself from sliding. They examined the famed Snow Arch and then cleared a space in the dwarf firs for a campsite. Wentworth, against Thoreau's advice built a fire which promptly got out of control, made them jump for their baggage, and eventually burned over several acres before going out itself. They finally made camp on a slight rise of ground near a small body of water Thoreau mistakenly took to be Hermit Lake.

In mid-afternoon they heard a noise which Wentworth thought was made by a bear, but Thoreau, skeptical of his decision, investigated and found his friends Blake and Brown, wet, ragged, and bloody with flies. He had left a note at Glen House telling them to look out for smoke and a white tent. "We had made a smoke sure enough," Thoreau remarked, thinking of Wentworth's fire. The five slept that night in their six-by-seven tent while it rained hard enough to put out their fire.

By leaving the summit Thoreau and his party had missed meeting a group of nearly one hundred editors, lawyers, and politicians who had been brought up from New York City to celebrate the opening of a carriage road to the top. Actually the road was not yet completed. The party had to trudge the last three miles to the summit and arrived there well after Thoreau had started down into Tuckerman's Ravine. But the reporters learned of Thoreau's presence and when a lengthy account of the celebration appeared in the New York *Tribune* for July 17, 1858, it announced:

That night of fog and rain Mr. Thoreau, the Concord Pan, spent in Tuckerman's ravine with Judge [sic] Hoar, his companion on the Chesuncook tour, now being described in The Atlantic Monthly, two other gentlemen and a guide. [We] have been assured by one of the party that the[y] woke up in the morning perfectly dry, although they had only a cotton tent for shelter. The water ran down hill under them, through the crevices of their bed of fir and spruce boughs, without damping the highest stratum. Mr. Thoreau doubtless understands as well as any mountaineer how to make himself comfortable under such circumstances, but we could not help shivering, as we looked down the ravine the next morning and saw the banks of snow that are all but eternal, and the little black pools a mile below, beside which the party camped for four nights.

On the morning of July 9 Hoar fished while Thoreau botazed. In the afternoon Thoreau explored the upper reaches of e ravine, gathering chiogenes for tea. Returning, he sprained his ot jumping down the brook and was unable to sleep that night or walk the next day. He plunged his foot in the ice-cold stream reduce the swelling[1] and, remembering he had seen some *Arnica ollis* the day before on the side of the ravine, sent his companions r it and packed it round his foot. That evening as they sat before e fire, a curious screech owl flew down, landed within twelve et of them, and watched them inquisitively.

The next day, because of his foot, Thoreau was forced to end in camp. A mysterious bird intrigued him by constantly nging just out of sight, but he was unable to pursue or identify Black flies pestered him and he had to spend most of the day tting in the smoke of the campfire. Meanwhile, Hoar, Blake, and rown botanized up the ravine. Sunday, the 11th, they were all onfined to camp all day by mizzling weather, though Thoreau ondered afterwards why he had not thought to strip the bark om a spruce and make a natural raincoat for himself.

On Monday it was clear and they tramped down the new arriage road, and dined by the Peabody River, south of the Glen ouse. In the afternoon they rode northward around the base f the mountain and camped on the bank of the Moose River near orham. Tuesday it rained and, after waiting a while for the skies clear, they started along, dined at Wood's Tavern in Randolph, nd stopped for the night at a store on Jefferson Hill. When it eared that evening, they climbed the hill and found a splendid iew of the range from Madison to Lafayette.

On Wednesday, July 14, they rode on through Bethlehem ito Franconia Notch, past the Profile House, and camped half a ile up the side of Lafayette. Hoar shivered all night long, gazing akefully up at the full moon while Thoreau slept peacefully at is side.[2] On Thursday they climbed to the summit of Lafayette,

1. Channing, *Thoreau, the Poet-Naturalist,* 38
2. Sanborn, *Henry D. Thoreau,* 254

and had their tea for dinner at the headwaters of the Pemigewass
They lost Hoar briefly on the way up but met again at the sumn
Thoreau was impressed with the dwarf firs and spruces and, cutti
one a half an inch in diameter, was astounded that it show
seventy annual rings of growth. On their way down they fou
pine grosbeaks so fearless that they perched within four feet. T
night they spent at Morrison's Inn in West Thornton.

On the 16th they headed homeward through Thornton a
Campton, ate their lunch on the banks of the Pemigewasset ne
New Hampton, and spent the night in a tavern in Franklin. Co
tinuing on through Weare, New Boston, Amherst, and Holl
they finally arrived back in Concord at noon on the 19th, havi
been gone seventeen days. Before reaching the mountains, Ho
and Thoreau had marked in their books forty-six species of pla
they hoped to find. They found forty-two of them.

Three years later when Thoreau was suffering his final i
ness, a group of eight Worcester ministers who were planning
week's hike through the White Mountains wrote to inquire wl
supplies they would need. Thoreau carefully detailed all the nec
sary equipment for them, including a full menu, and even add
instructions on erecting a tent and making a twig bed. Maki
converts to an appreciation of the natural wonders of his count
he thought well worth the effort.

VIII

On September 21, 1858, Thoreau left Concord for a bri
excursion to Cape Ann. He met John Russell in Salem and tour
Essex Institute, examining the Indian relics, the birds' eggs, a
the herbarium. In the afternoon they walked to Marblehead ar
back, botanizing along the way. On the 22nd they started for tl
cape on foot, walking along the shore from Beverly onward. The
ate their lunch on a rocky cliff on the west side of Manchest
Harbor, boiling their tea over dead bayberry bushes they ha
gathered. In the afternoon they scuffled their feet on Manchest
Beach to hear the famed musical sand and beyond Kettle Co
took to the road so that they might visit a magnolia swamp. Th

ening they cooked their supper with driftwood in a salt marsh
tside Gloucester and then sat until starlight on flat stones they
d gathered. They roomed for the night in Gloucester.

On the 23rd they continued on to Rockport, watching men
ther seaweed in carts and asking a hunter's permission to examine
e bird specimens in his bag. As they ate their lunch opposite
raitsmouth Island, they watched the sea breaking over the Sal-
ges that Eliot was to make famous a century later. At Annisquam
ey turned inland, strolling through fields of huge boulders. When
ey boiled their evening tea, two oxen came up to reconnoiter
eir fire. They spent the night again in Gloucester, looking out
om their windows to see the moonlight lighting the harbor and
e fishing vessels. On the 24th Thoreau returned to Concord.
ther than their breakfasts which came with their lodging, they
d eaten a pound of ship-bread which cost seven cents, six herring
hich cost three cents, and the sugar and tea they had brought
th them.

Despite his many excursions, Thoreau still devoted the major
art of his time to the natural history of Concord. In the spring of
858 he made a study of the ova of fish and amphibians, searching
e ponds, streams, springs, and puddles for eggs and bringing
em home in bottles so he might observe their development. He
amined some of the spawn under Hoar's new microscope, watch-
g the beating of the heart and the circulation of the blood. Often
e was surprised that what he assumed to be the ova of one species
rned out to be that of something quite different, but it made an
teresting guessing game he thought.

With the coming of warmer weather he turned his attention
frogs and found that if he had the patience to sit by the side of a
ool long enough, the frogs that first disappeared from sight would
oke their noses quietly out of the water to stare curiously at him
nd eventually would come hopping up to within a foot and permit
im to scratch their noses with his finger and to examine them
his heart's content. Emerson, as usual, was astonished when
horeau demonstrated his technique, but some of the other Con-
ordians were not as impressed. One farmer, seeing him standing
ill in the midst of a pool, concluded that it was his own father
ho had been drinking and lost his way home, and was astounded
discover when he investigated more closely that it was Thoreau

studying bullfrogs. Another, years later, told Mrs. Daniel Chest
French:

> Why, one morning I went out in my field across there to the
> river, and there, beside that little old mud pond, was standing
> *Da*-a-vid Henry, and he wasn't doin' nothin' but just standin'
> there—lookin' at that pond, and when I came back at noon,
> there he was standin' with his hands behind him just lookin'
> down into that pond, and after dinner when I come back again if
> there wasn't *Da*-a-vid standin' there just like as if he had been
> there all day, gazin' down into that *pond,* and I stopped and
> looked at him and I says, "Da-a-vid Henry, what air you a-doin'?"
> And he didn't turn his head and he didn't look at me. He kept on
> lookin' down at that pond, and he said, as if he was thinkin' about
> the stars in the heavens, "Mr. Murray, I'm a-studyin'—the habits
> —of the bullfrog!" And there that darned fool had been standin'
> —the livelong day—a-studyin'—the habits—of the *bull*-frog![3]

Even Emerson reportedly told Thoreau that if God had intende
him to live in a swamp, He would have made him a frog.[4] B
the children of the town thought differently. Abby Hosmer to
Raymond Adams that from her home near the Assabet she sa
Thoreau standing all day long by the river's edge. Knowing sh
should not disturb him, she waited patiently and at suppertime h
came up to the house to report that he had discovered a duck th
had just hatched a nest of eggs and that he had watched all da
to see her teach the little ducks about the river. "And while w
ate our suppers there in the kitchen," she recalled, "he told us th
most wonderful stories you ever heard about those ducks."[5]

One day in June as Thoreau was wading in Wyman meado
looking for bullfrog spawn, he noticed a pout poking her head o
of a hole in the bottom three or four feet from shore. Thrustin
his arm down into the hole, he felt first a gelatinous mass of wh
he took to be spawn, but then feeling further, he touched the horn
of the pout and, deliberately taking hold of her by the hea

3. Mrs. Daniel Chester French, *Memories of a Sculptor's Wife* (Boston, 1928), 95
4. Edward Wagenkneckt, *Nathaniel Hawthorne, Man and Writer* (New York, 1961), 65
5. Raymond Adams, "Thoreau and His Neighbors," *Thoreau Society Bulletin,* XLIV (1953), 3

ifted her out of the hole and the water. She offered not the least resistance, even when he held her up close to his face, and only darted away suddenly when he dropped her back into water.

In November when he went back to examine the pout's nest, he discovered a multitude of tiny minnows there. Looking at them closely, he decided they were nothing he had ever seen before and collected specimens. When he failed to find anything like them in his handbooks, he took them along with some pickerel and some amphibians into the Boston Society of Natural History. Drs. D. H. and H. R. Storer and Messrs. Baird, Girard, and F. W. Putnam were all called in to examine them. They concluded the minnows were a new species of bream and so announced it to the Boston newspapers. For a time they thought the pickerel was new too, but later Putnam announced that it coincided with the *P. obesus* of Girard.

As Thoreau observed the streams more closely, he became more and more puzzled by heaps of stones he found on the bottom. He had noticed them for years and knew they were the work of some water creature but could not make up his mind which. He consulted some of the old-timers of the town. One told him they were the work of lamprey eels, another said they couldn't be because he had seen them in the Saco River in the White Mountains where there were no lampreys, and a third said they were made by suckers.

When a group of the Concord boys, their own curiosity aroused, asked Thoreau about them, he replied, "I asked a Penobscot Indian that question and he said, 'The musquash did,' but I told him that I was a better Indian than he, for I knew and he did not," and with that walked off. The boys were understandably annoyed with Thoreau and one, John Pratt, muttered, "That is just like him, he never will tell a fellow anything unless it is in his lectures, darn his old lectures about chipmunks and Injuns, I won't go to hear him."[6] Apparently Thoreau was not certain of the truth at the moment and hated to admit it, for years earlier when he had thought he had known the answer, he had readily told Horace Hosmer that they had been built by lamprey eels.[7] As a matter of fact Thoreau never did know the correct answer, for

6. Sarah Hosmer Lunt, "Memories of Concord," MS, Evald Lawson
7. Edward Emerson, Notes on Thoreau

modern ichthyologists say that while the lamprey eels do construct stone nests, the type that Thoreau saw were the work of the fall-fish, a species that he was familiar with and had described as a "soft fish [which] tasted like brown paper salted."[8]

It was indeed unusual for Thoreau to be so haughty with the children. Much more typical was his reaction when the young Carr boy working at Samuel Barrett's grist mill asked him one day, "Mr. Thoreau, can the snakes in the mill pond hurt me if I go in [swimming] where they are?" "No," replied Thoreau, "they cannot; if you can find me one I will show you why not." Carr said he was sure they could find one sunning itself at the reservoir dam. Sure enough there was a big one fast asleep and Thoreau quickly caught it and held it in his hands. Showing it carefully to the boy, he said, "You see he has no jawbones; he cannot bite; he sucks in his food; and as for a sting in his tail that you may have heard the boys talk of,—you can see for yourself there is none. So you may be assured you will get no harm if you come in contact with the very king of the water snakes."[9] (Carr's recollection was probably faulty. The water snake unquestionably has a jawbone and can bite. What Thoreau probably pointed out was that it has no fangs and therefore can inject no poison.)

The collecting of birds' eggs became a fad among the children of Concord that summer. Edward Emerson, Storrow Higginson, and Edward Bartlett were the leaders and scarcely a week went by that they did not bring a specimen to show Thoreau—hawk, bittern, warbling vireo, purple finch, veery, and Virginia rail eggs; hawk, crow, bobolink, hermit thrush and goldfinch nests; and, as a real triumph, a live little green heron. Thoreau carefully identified their treasures, warning them always to leave eggs for the mother bird.[1] When they showed him the Virginia rail nest in Cyrus Hosmer swamp, that was unusual enough that he took an egg from the nest himself, blew it carefully, deposited it in a bandanna handkerchief in the crown of his botany box hat, and took it home for his own collection.[2] Later he made a special trip into

8. Edwin Way Teale, Letter to Walter Harding of December 15, 1963
9. Sanborn, *Recollections of Seventy Years*, II, 389–90
1. Social Circle in Concord, *Memoirs*, V, 113
2. Ibid. 103

Boston to talk at length with Mr. Brant at the Natural History Society about the eggs the boys had collected. Thoreau so aroused young Edward Neally's interest in studying natural history that he later became an official observer in the area for the Smithsonian Institute.[3]

Edward Simmons, who later became an internationally known artist, had an unpleasant memory of Thoreau though. He was playing on the grass in front of the Old Manse one day when Thoreau, walking by, noticed he had a great crested flycatcher egg in his hand. He asked if he could have it, but when Eddie did not want to give it up, Thoreau promised to show him a live fox in exchange. The boy gave him the egg and Thoreau promised to show him the fox. The next Sunday Thoreau devoted the whole afternoon to taking him on a long walk through the woods. At one point they got down on their stomachs and crawled what seemed to the boy for miles. But no fox did they see and Eddie did not get his egg back. He confessed he always held a grudge against Thoreau for that.[4]

Adults were just as eager to show Thoreau their discoveries. Jacob Farmer gave him a sharp-shinned hawk and showed him where a bittern was nesting. Puffer, one of the town ne'er-do-wells, tried to convince him that eels copulated with clams. Mr. Warren brought him three rails, two sandpipers, and a snipe he had shot on the Great Meadow. A neighbor brought in a Carolina rail their cat had caught. Goodwin brought him a rare red-throated loon he had killed on the river. Caroline Pratt told him of seeing an albino bobolink and showed him a strange luminous bug she had found in her shed. And Minot Pratt showed him some rare plants he had discovered in Boulder Field. (Mrs. Pratt confessed later that she liked Thoreau better than his books. She thought they did not do him justice. She thought him religious—"more like the ministers than others; that is, like what they would wish and try to be." She "loved" him but always felt a little in awe of him. "He loved to talk, like all his family, but not to gossip," she remembered. "He kept the talk on a high plane.")[5]

3. Edward Emerson, Notes on Thoreau
4. Edward Simmons, *From Seven to Seventy* (New York, 1922), 5–6
5. Edward Emerson, *Henry Thoreau as Remembered by a Young Friend*, 80

CHAPTER NINETEEN
(1859–1860)

I

THOREAU'S FATHER'S HEALTH had gradually been fading over a period of years. A severe attack of jaundice in October 1857 nearly carried him off and his sisters Maria and Jane were summoned posthaste from Cambridge. He recovered somewhat but a bad cough troubled him now and he spent more and more time sleeping in his chair, rarely trying to go outside.[1] For a time a daily glass of bourbon seemed to help him, but he still grew weaker and weaker.[2] After January 13, 1859, he was confined to his bedroom although he still insisted on sitting in his chair each day. It was obvious he could not last many days and Thoreau became his most devoted nurse. Mrs. Thoreau later said, "If it hadn't been for my husband's illness, I should never have known what a tender heart Henry had."[3]

By January 31 Mr. Thoreau was confined to his bed and coughed and expectorated a great deal. Several times he thought he was dying and took leave of his family, eventually expressing a slight impatience at the delay. The end finally came on February 3, at the age of seventy-one, so peacefully that the family gathered around his bed were hardly aware that he had gone. Thoreau, in his journal, said, "I have touched a body which was flexible and warm, yet tenantless."[4]

Rev. Grindall Reynolds of the First Parish Church conducted

---

1. Sophia Thoreau, Letter to Mary Anne Dunbar of December 31, 1857. MS, Thoreau Society Archives
2. John Thoreau, Letter to George Thatcher of June 9, 1858. MS, Raymond Adams
3. Brown, *Memories of Concord*, 92
4. Thoreau, *Journal*, XI, 435

e funeral services, though for years Mr. Thoreau had absented mself from the church because he thought it endorsed slavery.[5] he next evening Thoreau called on Reynolds to express his ap- :eciation and ended by spending two hours telling the story ∶ his Canadian journey of 1850 in a far livelier fashion, Reynolds ιought, than he had in his essay.[6]

Thoreau immediately assumed his position as head of the ιmily. In the 1860 national census he was listed as head of the ɔusehold ("occupation: surveyor"), with real estate valued at 4000 and personal property at $1500. On March 1, 1859, after ɔsting bond for $10,000, he was appointed executor of his father's ːtate by the county probate court.[7] He also assumed manage- ιent of the family graphite business and acquired a copy of the *ιsinessman's Assistant* to help himself on proper procedures.   ❋ /ith his renewed interest he re-examined the whole manufactur- ιg process and, at Warren Miles's suggestion, decided that stone ither than the traditional iron balls might be more effective in the ‐inding mills.[8] After searching for most of a forenoon in Acton, e finally found a stone to his liking and tried it out. It turned out ɔ be a great improvement. He took over the planting of the family   ❋ ιrden and in the fall of 1860 built a new fence between their :operty and Shattuck's, boasting that if he had hired it done it ɔuld have cost at least four dollars. He also assumed his father's aily chore of walking to town for the family mail. Thoreau was illed to testify in court twice that year. On February 4, 1856, he, is father, and two others had witnessed the signing of Rev. arzillai Frost's will. Frost died on December 8, 1858, and on ɑnuary 11, 1859, Thoreau was the only one of the four available ɔ testify as to the genuineness of the will.[9] In October 1859 he as asked to testify on behalf of his aunts, Jane and Maria. heir neighbor, Eliza Pallies, had invaded their yard, thrown down ιeir fence, and erected a spite fence within a foot and a half

---

5. Unidentified clipping in the collection of Raymond Adams
6. Edward Emerson, *Henry Thoreau as Remembered by a Young Friend,* 148
7. Cameron, *The Transcendentalists and Minerva,* I, 80
8. Edward Emerson, Notes on Thoreau
9. Kenneth Walter Cameron, "Thoreau and Barzillai Frost," *Emer· son Society Quarterly,* X (1958), 44

of their door. She claimed a right of way through their yard, bu the court threw her case out and charged her court costs an damages of one dollar.

When Emerson's mentally retarded brother Bulkeley died o May 27, 1859, at the age of fifty-two in Littleton, Massachusett, where he had for years been in the care of a local farmer, it wa Thoreau who took over handling all the arrangements for bot the funeral and the burial.[1] Earlier, on March 22, he had bee one of the few outside the family asked to attend the privat funeral services for the seventeen-year-old Theodore Parker Prat son of Minot Pratt, who had been buried under an oak near th family homestead.[2]

In May 1857 Thoreau and Emerson had taken a walk to gether around Walden Pond. Thoreau said the barren sand at the sit of his old cabin disturbed him and proposed to plant it with trees. It was two years before he got around to doing anything about it but in the spring of 1859 he gathered up all the acorns he coul find for the task. Having to separate the sound acorns from th rotten ones bothered him for a while, until he discovered tha if all were immersed in water, the good ones would sink and th poor ones float. As a result he offered the children of the neighborhood five cents a quart for acorns that would sink.

On April 21, 1859, with two men, a horse, and a cart, he se out four hundred pines, fifteen feet apart, on two acres of the Walden property. While one man dug up the trees, another dug new holes and Thoreau himself did the planting. On the 29th he added a hundred two-year-old larch trees imported from Eng-
land; later he added some birch trees. To make absolutely certain they would have a forest, Emerson purchased a quarter pound of white pine seed, and Thoreau sowed it for him. Regularly thereafter for some time Thoreau walked out to Walden to check on the condition of the seeds and trees, which eventually became an outstanding grove. The white pines in particular became a Concord showpiece. Part of the grove was destroyed by a fire in 1872, but the greater part remained until well into this century.

In June 1859 Thoreau was hired to make a study of the

---

1. Ralph Waldo Emerson, *Letters* (New York, 1939), V, 148-9
2. Bronson Alcott, Journals
3. Ralph Waldo Emerson, *Journals*, IX, 96

pths of the Concord River and its dams and bridge abutments.
e had been surveying wood lots and house lots as much as ever,
ough with little enthusiasm, but this new project immediately
roused his interest. A controversy had arisen over the flooding,
aused by the raising of dams, of the haying land in the river
eadows. The various owners of the Concord meadows claimed
at the proprietors of the Richardson grain mills in Billerica had
legally raised their dam by three feet and three inches and so
ad precipitated the problem of useless, soggy meadows, once
heir chief source of hay.[4]

All summer long Thoreau worked avidly at the project, not
nly surveying and measuring, but spending a good deal of time
nterviewing the older residents of the town about the earlier
istory of the river. He made charts, showing its depth, its rise
nd fall, and the rapidity of its current. He journeyed into Cam-
ridge to borrow Comte Louis Gabriel Dubuat Nancay's *Principes
l'Hydraulique* and translated a number of pages of notes from it
nto English.[5] Emerson, amused at Thoreau's energetic enthusiasm,
vrote Elizabeth Hoar, then touring England, "Henry T. occupies
imself with the history of the river, measures it, weighs it, and
trains it through a colander to all eternity."[6] When the case came
o court, it aroused such ill-feeling that Thoreau thought the river
"damned at both ends and cursed in the middle."[7]

On September 7, 8, and 9, 1859, the Commonwealth of
Massachusetts sponsored an elaborate muster in Concord. It was
the talk of the state. Local militia units swarmed into town; tourists
swarmed after them. Most of Concord was understandably excited,
but Thoreau himself was unimpressed. He wrote to warn his
cousin George Thatcher that visitors to Concord that week would
find it "more like Discord" and he feared scamps would be "all
over the lot."[8] When he stopped at the hardware store a few
days before the event, he told the clerk he wanted a bolt for his

---

4. [Ruth Wheeler], "Concord River Rolls for 22 Quiet, Lazy Miles,"
Concord Journal, December 3, 1959
5. Kenneth Walter Cameron, "Thoreau's Notes from Dubuat's
Principles," *Emerson Society Quarterly*, XXII (1961), 68
6. Ralph Waldo Emerson, Letter to Elizabeth Hoar of August 3,
1859. MS, Morgan Library
7. Thoreau, *Journal*, XIII, 149
8. Thoreau, *Correspondence*. 555

front door because the Governor was coming. When the cler reminded him that the legislature would be there too, he ordere a second bolt for the back door. He complained, when the mu terers arrived, that Concord was more full of dust and more uni habitable than he had ever known it. On the last day of the er campment, he climbed one of the neighboring hills with or of the visiting militiamen, and after looking some time at th panorama of tents and men spread below, he turned to the ma and said, "Mr. D——, did it ever occur to you what a small plac in Nature a camp fills?"[9]

In December 1859 Caroline Dall, who had married Thoreau college classmate Charles Dall, came to Concord to lecture. A bluestocking who modeled her life quite consciously on that c Margaret Fuller, she was one of the leading feminists of her day When Thoreau was asked if he would attend her lecture, he tol Emerson that he thought women never had anything to say. H did nonetheless attend, arriving late and seating himself on th end of the very last bench by the door. He had been on the river al day and dropped in on his way home to see what she had to say When Emerson chided him at the end of the lecture, "Why Thoreau I thought you were not coming," Thoreau for once graciously ad mitted, "But *this* woman had something to say!" He was, in fact so impressed that he went up to speak to Mrs. Dall on the platform persuaded her to stay over in Concord for the next day, invite her to spend it with him and his family, and so thoroughly charmed her that she long recalled it as one of the most memorable days o her life.[1]

II

After a long dearth, there was a sudden surge of interest in Thoreau as a lecturer. He delivered more lectures in 1859 than in any other year in his life.

In January Bronson Alcott had visited St. Louis, Missouri, on a lecture tour in the Middle West and there had spoken before

9. Harding, *Thoreau, Man of Concord*, 87
1. Joseph Slater, "Caroline Dall in Concord," *Thoreau Society Bulletin*, LXII (1958), 1

illiam Torrey Harris and his circle of friends. Although the
ctures there had been a financial failure, Harris was convinced
at with better publicity they would have been a success and
romised not only to bring Alcott back another year but to bring
ut Thoreau and Emerson too for a whole series of lectures. Un-
ortunately his plans did not materialize until years after Thoreau's
eath. Blake invited Thoreau to speak in Worcester, but he post-
oned accepting because of his father's illness. It was arranged
or February 15 and then postponed again for another week.
inally on the 22nd he arrived in Worcester and gave lectures
oth that evening and the next. The former was called "Autumnal
ints," a lecture he had been preparing for several years, gathering
aterial on foliage coloration each fall. In it he attempted "to
escribe all these bright tints" of autumnal foliage "in the order
 which they present themselves." He included not only the
ees, but the grasses and the shrubs. As he lectured he often
eld up various specimens of colored leaves.

"Autumnal Tints" was not published until October 1862 in
 e *Atlantic Monthly,* after his death. It is generally considered one
 f his most successful nature pieces. He complained in his journal
 at all the criticism he ever got on the lecture was that he had
 ssumed that his audience had not seen so much of the autumnal
 nts as they had. But Sallie Holley, who heard the lecture in
 Vorcester, reported that it was a "beautiful and, I doubt not, a
 aithful report of the colours of leaves."[2] And Caroline Dall, who
 as in the same audience, said: "Never since have I been in the
 ountry at that season when his description of the royal ranks
 f the purple poke berries and the steady beaming of the yellow
 awk weed on the hillside has not risen in my mind. He fascinated
 very one of us."[3]

Another member of Thoreau's Worcester audience was young
 . Harlow Russell, a protégé of Blake who many years later in-
 erited Thoreau's manuscript journals from Blake. Russell has
 ecalled:

[Thoreau] seemed rather less than the medium height, well-
proportioned, and noticeably straight and erect. . . . His head

---

2. John White Chadwick, *A Life for Liberty* (New York, 1899), 167
3. Joseph Slater, "Caroline Dall in Concord," 1

was not large, nor did it strike me as handsome. It was covered with a full growth of rather dark hair somewhat carelessly brushed after no particular style. His face was very striking whether seen in the front or profile view. Large perceptive eyes—blue, I think, large and prominent nose; his mouth concealed by a full dark beard, worn natural but not untrimmed; these features pervaded by a wise, serious and dignified look. The expression of his countenance was not severe or commanding, but it certainly gave no hint of shallowness or trifling. In speech he was deliberate and positive. The emphatic words seemed to "hang fire" or to be held back for an instant as if to gather force and weight. . . . Thoreau was always interesting, often entertaining, but never what you would call charming.[4]

On March 2 Thoreau gave the same lecture before the Concord Lyceum and a week later repeated it for a group of young people gathered at Emerson's house. Alcott noted: "Certain is we had never seen leaves before, the chemistry of evenings mornings, or twilight, of autumn's comings and goings, h opulence of foliage, the ways she woos and wins the moral sen ment and the mind through all her changes of leaf and lan scapes."[5] And Sanborn wrote Theodore Parker that he thoug the lecture "as good as anything [Thoreau] ever wrote."[6]

The last week of April Thoreau gave the lecture again, t time in Lynn and once more it was a success.[7] He took advanta of the visit to spend several days roaming the North Shore countr side. Meanwhile, since Theodore Parker had gone abroad for health, his congregation was searching for substitutes in his p pit. Emerson recommended that they ask Thoreau to give "Autumnal Tints" lecture.[8] They shortly got in touch with hi but he, while accepting, said he would prefer "Life Misspent"- his old "Life without Principle" lecture—apparently thinking more appropriate for the pulpit. October 9, 1859, was agre upon and the lecture was well advertised in the Boston newspape Emerson confessed himself anxious that Thoreau should succe for it had been some time since he had appeared before a metr

4. Harding, *Thoreau, Man of Concord*, 97–8
5. Alcott, Journals
6. F. B. Sanborn, Letter to Theodore Parker of March 13, 1859. MS, Concord Free Public Library
7. Alcott, Journals
8. Sanborn, Letter to Theodore Parker of March 13, 1859

litan audience. But he need not have worried—the audience
as very happy with the result. One Boston newspaper reported
at Thoreau had "a fine voice, and a prompt, effective style of ora-
ry that fixes the attention of the hearer."[9] The *Banner of Light,*
spiritualist journal, said that the lecture "notwithstanding its
ry peculiar views, elicited much interest from the epigrammatic
yle in which it was clothed."[1] And the ever-faithful New York
ribune said that it "was an original, racy, and erratic production,
d was listened to with close interest."[2]

But it was Thoreau's John Brown lectures that created a
al impact. Thoreau had first met John Brown in the late winter
1857 when Brown had visited F. B. Sanborn in Concord.[3]
rown had been one of the leaders of the anti-slavery forces
the Kansas Territory, and had battled with the Border Ruffians,
ho swarmed over from Missouri and hoped to make Kansas
other slave state. His activities had brought him to national
tention and he had come east to raise more funds for his
erilla troops. Sanborn, one of his most active supporters, in-
oduced him to the Massachusetts legislature and then brought
m out to Concord for a brief stay. Since Sanborn was at the time
ill taking his noon meal with the Thoreaus, he brought Brown
ith him for lunch and left him there for the afternoon while he
nded his school. Thoreau and Brown talked at length, Brown
lling Thoreau the details of the battle of Black Jack in Kansas,
here he with only nine men had captured more than twenty
nder the command of Henry Clay Pate, and of his childhood
d young manhood. Emerson, who had just returned from a lec-
re tour in the West, dropped in to visit Thoreau and so was in-
oduced to Brown.

That evening Brown spoke at the Concord Town Hall, dra-
atically displaying a bowie knife he had taken from a Border
uffian and a chain with which his son had been bound prisoner
y the slavery forces.[4] When Brown pleaded for funds, Sanborn
ave one hundred dollars, Emerson fifty, and Thoreau's father

---

9. Clipping pasted in Alcott, Journals
1. Clipping pasted in Bronson Alcott's Autobiographical Collections,
Houghton Library
2. New York *Tribune,* October 12, 1859
3. Leo Stoller, *After Walden* (Stanford, 1957), 144
4. Ruth Wheeler, "John Brown in Concord," *Concord Journal,* October, 15, 1959

ten. Thoreau himself contributed "a trifle" because he was irritat
that Brown was not willing to take his supporters more into l
confidence and explain what he wished to do with the funds.[5]

Brown returned to Concord on May 7, 1859, to visit wi
Sanborn. Meanwhile in January 1859 George Luther Stearr
a well-to-do abolitionist and supporter of Brown from Medfor
Massachusetts, had spent an afternoon skating with Thore
and Emerson at Walden Pond, and devoted a good part of h
time extolling Brown's virtues to Thoreau, apparently convinci
Thoreau of Brown's heroism.[6] On May 8 Brown spoke at leng
at Concord Town Hall, giving further details of his Kansa
activities and pleading for more funds. Thoreau was in the aud
ence again and was more impressed than he had been at the tin
of Brown's first visit.

Thoreau knew nothing in advance of Brown's plans fo
raiding Harpers Ferry. He and Alcott happened to be at Emerson
house on October 19, 1859, when word of the raid first reache
Concord, and his reaction was immediate.[7] As much as he dis
liked the use of force and violence, he saw Brown now as a tru
Transcendentalist, a man who was willing to sacrifice everything
even his life, for his principles. For days Thoreau could think c
nothing else. Even nature temporarily lost its appeal and he con
fessed, "I was so absorbed in him as to be surprised whenever
detected the routine of the natural world surviving still." H
breathed a fire into his journals even greater than that at th
time of the Burns incident. At night he went to bed with a penci
and notebook on his table so that he might write down his thought
of the moment.

Thoreau was not surprised that many of his neighbor
dismissed Brown as a fool nor that most of the newspapers de
nounced him, but he was shocked that none of the abolitionist
seemed willing to come to Brown's defense. Their only reaction wa
that Brown had been inexpedient. Even Garrison's usually out
spoken *Liberator* called the attack a "misguided, wild, and ap

5. Thoreau, *Journal*, XII, 437; [Pledge to pay sums for relief of the
Free State Citizens of Kansas], MS, Concord Free Public Library
6. Frank Stearns, *The Life and Public Service of George Luther
Stearns* (Philadelphia, 1907), 181
7. Sanborn, *The Personality of Emerson*, 87-8

arently insane . . . effort."[8] Someone must speak out in Brown's
efense, Thoreau decided. He sat up most of a night organizing
is scattered journal comments into a lecture, and in the morning
e announced at breakfast that he was to read it in public. Two
members of the family supported him; one opposed. He then sent
word around the town that he would deliver a defense of Brown
a Concord Town Hall on October 30. Both the members of the
Republican Town Committee and the local abolitionists sent word
hat they thought his action inadvisable; a defense of Brown at
his point would only further arouse opposition to all anti-slavery
ctivities, they feared. But Thoreau replied, "I did not send to you
or advice, but to announce that I am to speak."[9]

Since he was a citizen of Concord, the selectmen could not
leny him the use of the Town Hall, but they did refuse to ring the
own bell to announce the meeting, so Thoreau rang it himself.
The hall was filled—many who had no sympathy for Brown came
o scoff. Brown's few supporters came in shyly as if afraid to be
een there. Edward Emerson thought Thoreau read his paper "as
f it burned him" and noted that "many of those who came to
coff remained to pray."[1] Minot Pratt, as soon as he returned
tome at ten that night, sat down and wrote his wife:

> Henry spoke of [Brown] in terms of the most unqualified eulogy.
> I never heard him before speak so much in praise of any man.
> . . . The lecture was full of Henry's quaint and strong expres-
> sions: hitting the politicians in the hardest manner, and showing
> but little of that veneration which is due to our beloved President
> and all the government officials, who are laboring so hard and
> so disinterestedly for the welfare of the dear people. The church
> also, as a body, came in for a share of whipping, and it was laid
> on right earnestly. . . . The lecture was full of noble, manly ideas,
> though, perhaps, a little extravagant in its eulogy of Capt. Brown.[2]

"A Plea for Captain John Brown" is the most eloquent of
all Thoreau's occasional addresses. Though Brown and his attack

---

8. Thoreau, *Journal,* XII, 407
9. Ralph Waldo Emerson, *Complete Works,* X, 460
1. Edward Emerson, Notes on Thoreau
2. *Concord Journal,* "When Thoreau Lectured on John Brown,"
December 8, 1932

are now buried more than a century in the past, Thoreau's plea
is still vibrant and alive.

There is unquestionably a definite progression in Thoreau's
three major statements on the anti-slavery issue, from "Civil
Disobedience" through "Slavery in Massachusetts" to "A Plea
for Captain John Brown." It is a progression of increased resistance to the State as an institution. In the first his resistance
was "civil" or "polite" and consisted of his refusing to pay taxes.
In the second he encouraged violation of a specific law—the Fugitive Slave Law. In the third he endorsed one, that is, John
Brown, who had openly rebelled not just again one law but
against the whole State. But it is a progression, not a break with
the past as some of Thoreau's critics have maintained who thought
his stand with Brown inconsistent with his earlier remarks against
slavery. Although he had become more aroused by Brown's action
than by any other incident of his later years, and although Brown
unquestionably became one of the heroes highest in his personal
pantheon, Thoreau did not lose sight of his Transcendentalist
principles. It will be noted that Thoreau has little to say specifically about Brown's attack on Harpers Ferry. He was more attracted by Brown's ideals than by his actions, by his courage than
by his deeds. He pleaded not for Brown's life, but for his character
and he denounced those who spoke timidly against slavery but
were afraid to say a word in defense of Brown. And the highest
praise he gave to Brown was that he thought of him as a Transcendentalist—that is, one who followed the voice within himself
even though it led him into opposition with the State.

Had Thoreau known of Brown's perpetration of the bloodthirsty Pottawatomie massacre in Kansas, he might never have
endorsed him and might have been convinced of his insanity.
But Brown was sane enough to know what it was expedient to
publicize and what to keep silent about. Thoreau never knew about
Pottawatomie and even Sanborn, who was of course much more
in Brown's confidence, denied that he had had any part in it or any
other of the inexcusable acts that have since been assigned to
Brown.[3]

Having aroused the people of Concord, Thoreau was now

3. Gilman Ostrander, "Emerson, Thoreau, and John Brown," *Missis-sippi Valley Historical Review*, XXXIV (1953), 719

tisfied to let the matter drop. On October 31st he wrote
lake and offered to repeat the lecture in Worcester if only his
xpenses would be paid. Before the day was out, a telegram
rrived from Charles W. Slack, director of the Fraternity Lectures
a Boston, asking if he would repeat the lecture in Boston on
November 1. Frederick Douglass, the Negro orator, had originally
een scheduled for the date, but when federal officers searched
Brown's headquarters near Harpers Ferry, they found cor-
espondence that incriminated Douglass and he, forewarned, had
led to safety in Canada.

Thoreau immediately accepted the invitation and spoke at
Tremont Temple. The lecture was well advertised in the Boston
papers and tickets were only twenty-five cents. The auditorium, one
of Boston's largest, was filled and Thoreau spoke again with
great success. The lecture was reported and discussed in all the
major Boston newspapers. The *Traveler* printed the speech almost
verbatim. The *Boston* Journal noted that many of his statements
had been greeted with applause. The *Boston Atlas & Daily Bee,*
a pro-slavery paper, after devoting a number of columns to
reporting the speech, denounced it as the views of a fanatic. Another paper, complaining that Thoreau extolled Brown above every
other man that ever lived, thought his views "high-wrought."[4]
Garrison's *Liberator,* annoyed that Thoreau had singled it out for
particular censure for not defending Brown, dismissed the lecture
in three short paragraphs, but acknowledged bitingly that "this
exciting theme seemed to have awakened 'the hermit of Concord'
from his usual state of philosophic indifference."[5] The New York
Tribune, equally annoyed at his chastising, dismissed his ideas as
"foolish and ill-natured" and complained, not without justice,
"Editors like those of The Tribune and The Liberator, . . . while
the lecturer was cultivating beans and killing woodchucks on the
margin of Walden Pond, made a public opinion strong enough
on Anti-Slavery grounds to tolerate a speech from him in defense
of insurrection."[6]

On November 3 Thoreau repeated the lecture in Worcester

---

4. Clipping pasted in Alcott's Autobiographical Collections
5. November 4, 1859
6. Helen Morrison, "Thoreau and the New York Tribune," *Thoreau
Society Bulletin,* LXXXII (1963), 2

and was again favorably received. Blake had rented Washbur
Hall and announced that ten cents admission would be charge
The *Worcester Spy* urged its readers to attend because they thoug
Thoreau never dealt in commonplaces and "what he has to sa
is likely to be worth hearing."[7]

On November 9 Thoreau told Alcott that he thought som
one should make a trip to Virginia to see Governor Wise an
plead mercy for Brown. Sanborn suggested Alcott for the erran
and said he might thus ascertain whether an attempt to rescu
Brown would be feasible, but the plan was soon dropped. Thorea
meanwhile journeyed into Boston and tried unsuccessfully t
persuade various publishers to bring his "Plea" out in pamphl
form to be "sold for the benefit of Capt. Brown's family."[8]

When it became obvious to all that Brown was doome
Thoreau called a meeting in the Town Hall on November 28 t
arrange appropriate services for the day of Brown's executio
Some who had originally denounced Thoreau's "Plea" no
had changed their minds and spoke out in Brown's favor. Th
reau, former Lieutenant-Governor Simon Brown (no relation
Emerson, and John Shepard Keyes were chosen to arrange t
details.

For the next few days Thoreau worked at fever pitch maki
arrangements for the services. He had a broadside announci
the meeting printed, including in it the words of a dirge writt
for the occasion by Sanborn.[9] He hired Frank Pierce and h
father to have a piano moved into the hall for the meeting.[1] H
applied to the selectmen for permission to toll the town bell
the hour of Brown's execution, but they refused their assent. D
Bartlett warned that he had heard five hundred damn Thore
for suggesting the action and that a counter-demonstration wi
a firing of minute guns was planned if he insisted on going throu
with it.[2] It was decided not to force the issue, Alcott arguing th

---

7. Ruth Frost, "Thoreau's Worcester Visits," *Nature Outlook*, I
(1943), 14

8. Thoreau, *Correspondence*, 566; Henry David Thoreau, "A Plea f
Capt. John Brown." MS, Huntington Library

9. Walter Harding, "A Rare Thoreau Broadside," *Thoreau Society
Bulletin*, LIV (1956), 3

1. Harding, *Thoreau, Man of Concord*, 192

2. Thoreau, *Journal*, XII, 457

was more appropriate to signify their sorrow in subdued and
ent tones rather than by "any clamor of steeples and the awaken-
g of angry feelings."[3] It was also decided to have a simple
emorial service rather than any inflammatory speeches.

December 2, the day of Brown's execution, was a strangely
ltry day with threatening clouds overhead and an ominous
eling in the air. The Concord meeting was conducted by Simon
rown, Thoreau, Keyes, Rev. Edmund Sears, Charles Bowers, and
lcott. Thoreau, for his part, after a few brief comments, read
veral appropriate poems, including Sir Walter Raleigh's "The
ul's Errand," and his own translation of a selection from Tacitus.
ater that evening John Brown was burned in effigy in Concord
y those who opposed the memorial service.[4]

Hardly were the services over when Sanborn received word
at one of the fugitives from Brown's band was at the home
f Dr. David Thayer in Boston and needed aid in escaping to
anada. It turned out to be Francis Jackson Merriam of Boston,
ho had already fled once to Canada but who had become un-
alanced with all the excitement and had returned to Boston to at-
mpt to raise another expedition like Brown's against the slave-
olders. Sanborn, Wendell Phillips, and Thayer joined in per-
uading Merriam to take a train back to Canada, but by accident
e took one that ran no farther than Concord and so showed up
t Sanborn's door. Sanborn obtained from Emerson the promise of
 horse and covered wagon to be used the next morning at dawn
nd then asked Thoreau to drive Merriam to the South Acton sta-
on four miles away and to see that he got on the next train to
anada. Because he feared Thoreau might be asked to testify at
le Senate hearings on Brown, Sanborn identified Merriam to
horeau only as "Mr. Lockwood" and did not reveal Thoreau's
lentity to Merriam, nor tell Emerson why they borrowed his
agon.

Thoreau thought that his passenger was an accomplice of
rown and immediately suspected his insanity. Merriam kept in-
isting that he be taken to see Emerson so that he might persuade
im to back the plans to reinvade the South. Thoreau continued
n quietly towards South Acton. For a few minutes Merriam

---

3. Alcott, *Journals,* 323
4. Canby, *Thoreau,* 391

[4 2 1]

thought Thoreau was Emerson, but when Thoreau denied Merriam was satisfied, for he was certain that Emerson would n lie. At one point Merriam jumped out of the wagon, but someho Thoreau persuaded him to get back in and finally got him on the train for Canada. By thus wittingly aiding a fugitive fro justice he unquestionably had opened himself to criminal pros cution, but fortunately the act was never uncovered by the a thorities. It was not until two years later on his deathbed th he finally learned the identity of "Mr. Lockwood," when Sanbo revealed that it was the grandson of Mrs. Thoreau's old frier Francis Jackson.[5]

James Redpath, a reporter for the New York *Tribune* wh had become an ardent defender of Brown, appeared at the Co cord memorial services for him and announced that he had preparation both a volume of tributes to Brown and a biograph Mrs. George L. Stearns of Medford had been trying to persuac Thoreau to write a biography of Brown, but he had pleaded th he was too busy with his studies.[6] Redpath now gathered up a the papers read at the Concord meeting and incorporated ther along with other papers including Thoreau's "Plea," into *Echo of Harper's Ferry,* which was published early the next year. sold 33,000 copies in less than a month and its profits were turne over to the Brown family. Redpath apologized to Thoreau fr the many errors in the first edition and offered him the opportun of correcting the text of his lecture for future printings. Redpa also spent a number of days in Concord interviewing Thorea and others for details of Brown's life. In mid-February he ser Thoreau a cryptic letter asking for details Brown had given of tr Battle of Black Jack and included his return address in a seale envelope to be opened only by Sanborn so that in case Thorea was called to Washington to testify before the Senate committe he could honestly say that he did not know Redpath's whereabout When Redpath published his *Public Life of Captain John Brow* he dedicated it to Thoreau, Emerson, and Wendell Phillips– "Defenders of the Faithful, who, when the mob shouted, 'Mac man!' said, 'Saint!' "—and sent Thoreau an autographed copy.

When Brown's daughters were enrolled in Sanborn's scho

---

5. Sanborn, *The Personality of Thoreau,* 52–7
6. Sanborn, *The Life of Henry David Thoreau,* 509

February 1860, they confided to Alcott that Thoreau reminded
em of their father. Thoreau's sister Sophia rounded up the ladies
f the village to make a bed quilt or comforter for Mrs. Brown,
ach square embroidered with an appropriate quotation.[7] The
rowns, in gratitude for Thoreau's aid, are said to have presented
im with a huge knife that had belonged to Brown.[8]

On February 17 the Senate committee, chaired by Senator
Iason of Virginia, that investigated Brown's raid on Harper's
erry issued an order for Sanborn to appear in Washington and
 testify as to his part in the affair, but no attempt was made to
ibpoena him until the evening of April 3, when a deputy United
tates marshal and four assistants appeared at his front door across
 e street from Thoreau's home. Under the pretext of asking for
harity, they were able to get into the house and there announced
anborn's arrest. His sister ran from the house screaming, "Mur-
er! Murder! Five men are arresting my brother."[9] She pulled one
 arshal's beard and whipped the horses while Sanborn kicked,
 truggled, and spread-eagled his long legs to prevent being put
 to their carriage. Someone rang the fire alarm and soon more
 han a hundred people, Thoreau among them, appeared.[1] Sanborn,
 encompassed by a throng of men, hoarse with passion, and of
 omen shrieking with frenzy; now struggling convulsively with
 he officers and now rattling his manacles above his head, [called]
 n all present to witness the penalty imposed by slavery on free
 peech."[2] Judge Hoar quickly made out a writ of habeas corpus,
 nd when it was served on the marshals, they were forced to re-
 ase Sanborn, although only after the deputy sheriff, Mr. Moore,
 alled on the assembled citizens to take him by force. Once San-
 orn was free, the townspeople chased the marshals out of town
 ith sticks, stones, and violent threats.

Fearing that the marshals might return, Mr. Bull, the chair-
 an of the selectmen, gave Sanborn a loaded revolver and sug-
 ested he spend the night at the home of George Prescott. Thoreau

---

7. Alcott, Journals; Annie Bartlett, Letter to Ned Bartlett, MS, First
Parish of Concord Archives
8. Richard Bailey, Letter to Walter Harding of March 1964
9. Sarah E. Sanborn, "Sanborn's Arrest," *Concord Journal,* December 24, 1959
1. Edward Emerson, Notes on Thoreau
2. Howard S. Mott, *Catalogue 182A* (Sheffield, Mass., 1963), 50

volunteered to spend the night at Sanborn's house to protect h
sister.

The next day Sanborn was rushed to Boston and at a speci
session of the state supreme court was discharged from arrest l
the full bench. A large crowd of citizens, among them Walt Whi
man, gathered at the courthouse prepared to rescue him by for
if the court did not release him. When Sanborn returned
Concord that evening, he found the town wildly celebrating h
victory. Cannons were thundering and a crowd huzzahing at tl
station.[3] A meeting was announced for the Town Hall, and o
their way the crowd stopped to hiss and groan at the homes o
Colonel Joseph Holbrook and Postmaster Charles B. Davis, bo
of whom it was rumored had assisted the marshals in findir
Sanborn the night before.

Dr. Josiah Bartlett chaired the meeting. Sanborn narrate
the events of his arrest. Rev. Grindall Reynolds got up to expre
his joy at Concord's latest victorious battle for freedom. He w
followed by Thoreau, whose speech was reported in the Bosto
papers:

> Henry T. [sic] Thoreau, a genius and a philosopher, and
> reputed to be a man of practical sense and tact—his business a
> surveyor—said he heard the bells ringing last night, as he
> supposed for fire, but it proved to be the hottest fire he ever wit-
> nessed in Concord. He denounced what he termed the mean and
> sneaking method the United States officials took to accomplish
> their purpose. Early in the evening there appeared a poor boy,
> under a forged name, seeking aid. This is the course the Senate
> of the United States took to arrest one of their fellow citizens. The
> kidnappers, he said, should have been in their place. (Applause.)
> He thought somebody should have taken the responsibility to
> arrest them at the time of the arrest of Sanborn. That was a
> mistake. Many had been congratulated because the affair had
> been conducted in a lawful and orderly manner, and their friend
> was now free according to law. He did not agree with them.
> No. The Concord people didn't ring the fire alarm bells accord-
> ing to law—they didn't cheer according to law—they didn't groan

---

3. F. B. Sanborn, Letter to Theodore Parker of April 8, 1860. MS,
Concord Free Public Library

according to law—(loud applause)—and as he didn't talk according to law, he thought he would stop and give way to some other speaker.[4]

oreau was followed to the platform by Alcott, Emerson, Thomas entworth Higginson, and others.[5] When the meeting was finally ljourned, it was announced that Sanborn would be arrested on arges of assaulting federal officers, a legal device to keep him in e control of the Massachusetts courts. He spent that night and few succeeding nights sleeping in different homes—spending at ast one night at Thoreau's—to prevent another attempt at arrest v the federal marshals.[6] Senator Mason and his committee fumed Washington and referred the matter to the judiciary committee, hich in turn reported out a special bill legalizing Sanborn's arrest. ut before the bill could be passed, the South had seceded and inborn's crisis was over.

Thoreau was invited to attend and speak at the John Brown lemorial Celebration in North Elba in the Adirondacks on the ourth of July, 1860. Brown's sympathizers were dedicating a onument over his grave. But when R. J. Hinton, the secretary : the meeting, stopped off in Concord on his way, he found horeau unwilling to make the journey. Thoreau did however rite out and give Hinton a brief paper to be read at the meeting id Hinton prefaced its reading with the comment:

The manuscript I hold . . . was handed to me at Concord . . . by one whom all must honor who know him—Henry D. Thoreau. Of a fearless, truthful soul, living near to Nature, with ear attuned to catch her simplest and most subtle thought, and heart willing to interpret them to his eager brain, he often speaks undisguised, in most nervous Saxon, the judgment upon great events which others, either timid or powerless of speech, so long to hear expressed. So it was last fall Mr. Thoreau's voice was the first which broke the disgraceful silence or hushed the senseless babble with which the grandest deed of our time was met.[7]

4. Clipping pasted in Alcott, Journals
5. Anon. "Mr. Sanborn's Case," *Thoreau Society Bulletin,* LXXVI (1961), 4
6. Sanborn, *Recollections of Seventy Years,* II, 515
7. *Liberator,* XXX (1860), 118

"The Last Days of John Brown" was published in the *Liberat* for July 27, 1860. In it Thoreau traced briefly the change in mi of the people who at first violently denounced Brown's raid b who gradually became aware of its heroic characteristics. Elle Channing has said that Thoreau's pulse accelerated and his han involuntarily clenched whenever Brown's name was mentioned later days.[8] Brown had a profound influence on Thoreau, but was his courage and his idealism that Thoreau most admired, n his recourse to violence. Brown, according to Emerson, had join Whitman and Joe Polis in Thoreau's private pantheon.

III

The reason Thoreau had given for not writing a biograpl of John Brown was that he was now too busily engaged in I Indian researches. The American Indian had fascinated hi ever since childhood. It has been said that as a boy he love to search for their relics along the Concord riverbanks, althou he himself said he had never found any arrowheads until 183 the year he graduated from college.[9] But then he rapidly d veloped an astonishing facility for finding them. One Sund evening in the fall of 1837 he and his brother John strolled the mouth of Swamp Bridge Brook, and as they neared t brow of the hill forming the bank of the stream, he playfu broke forth into an extravagant eulogy on the ancient Indian "There on Nawshawtuct was their lodge . . . and yonder, Clamshell Hill, their feasting ground. . . . Here stood Tahatawa and there . . . is Tahatawan's arrowhead." At that instant th sat down on the spot Thoreau had pointed to and, to carry o the joke, he picked up the first stone he laid hands on—whic to his complete astonishment, turned out to be the most perfe arrowhead he had ever found.[1]

He soon learned from experience just which were the mo "arrowheadiferous" sands in Concord and pored over them

---

8. Channing, *Thoreau, the Poet-Naturalist*, 262
9. Thoreau, *Journal*, VIII, 66
1. Ibid. I, 7–8

e hour each spring as soon as the snows had melted or when-
ver their surface was broken by a farmer's plow. He became
) adept at finding the relics that he boasted to Grindall Reynolds
hat if he could sell them at six cents apiece he could make a
omfortable living out of them.[2] By the time of his death he had
ccumulated a collection of about nine hundred pieces, including
xes, pestles, gouges, mortars, chisels, spear points, ornaments,
nd a large number of arrow points of varied patterns and
aaterials, which his mother and sister then presented to the
oston Society of Natural History and which is now in the Fruit-
nds Museum in Harvard, Massachusetts.

His brother John had done much to stimulate Thoreau's in-
rest in the Indian. In 1838 John had shipped him a large box
f relics that he had picked up in Taunton, where he was teach-
ng at the time, and the two corresponded in mock Indian dialect
s a joke. Earlier, while at Harvard, Thoreau had composed a
atin cenotaph for the ancient Concord Indian Tahatawan for
is own amusement.[3]

It is thought that about 1848 Thoreau first began collecting
aaterials for a book about the American Indian.[4] At first it was
very amorphous project and he did little more than copy down
uotations that interested him from the books he was reading
n early American history. When Indians visited Concord in
November 1850, he took pains to interview them at length on
heir hunting techniques, their clothing, and their knowledge of
woodcraft. In 1852 he discovered the many volumes of *Jesuit
Relations* in the Harvard Library and from then on read volume
fter volume for the insight they gave into the lives of the
ndians. As we have seen, when he rejected Spencer Fullerton
Baird's invitation to join the Association for the Advancement
of Science in 1853, he pointed out that his major scientific interest
t the time was centered on the Indian, and that fall, when he
nade his second journey to the Maine Woods, he told friends
hat one of his major purposes was to get to know the Indian

2. Edward Emerson, *Henry Thoreau as Remembered by a Young Friend,* 147
3. Kenneth Walter Cameron, "Thoreau's Early Compositions in the Ancient Languages," *Emerson Society Quarterly,* VIII (1957), 20
4. Albert Keiser, "Thoreau's Manuscripts on the Indians," *Journal of English and Germanic Philology,* XXVII (1928), 184

better. He inquired among his townsmen for Indian burial site
and was particularly impressed when J. Hosmer showed him a
Indian pestle that had a bird's head carved on its handle, fo
it was the first indication he had found of any aesthetic intere
* on the part of Indians.

His 1857 visit to Maine and his meeting with Joe Polis gav
his interest in the Indian his greatest impetus and his conversa
tion with Polis gave him his greatest accumulation of primar
material. By 1860 he had filled eleven good-sized notebooks o
the American Indian—a great welter of material, largely quota
* tions, jotted down simply in the order he found it. In the lat
fall of that year he began to check periodicals systematically fo
information about the Indian and to organize the material he ha
on hand. He made a table of contents for his projected book
listing such topics as ante-Columbian history, physique, musi
* food, funeral customs, manufactures, government, relics, and arts

On January 24, 1860, after Thomas Wentworth Higginso
lectured in Concord on barbarism and civilization, defendin
civilization against what Alcott described as "Thoreau's prejudic
for Adamhood," Higginson, Alcott, Anna Whiting, and Thorea
all adjourned to Emerson's house to discuss the lecture. Thorea
stressed that the Indian filled a vital niche between civilize
man and nature.[6] More than a year later, in the fall of 1861
George William Curtis happened upon Thoreau one day in Emer
son's library and their conversation turned to Indians. Thorea
spoke at length of the white man's obligations to the red man an
of his ingratitude. Curtis thought it by far the best talk abou
Indians he had ever heard or read and hoped that a book migh
come out of Thoreau's researches.[7] But by that time Thoreau'
health had gone and he had been forced to abandon the project
All that is left is a monumental pile of unorganized notes. Ha
he had the opportunity to complete his book, it would have
offered an entirely new view of Thoreau—Thoreau the anthro
pologist. Since most of his material was gained at second hand
it is doubtful whether he would have made any startlingly new

---

5. Ibid. 197
6. Alcott, *Journals,* 325
7. George William Curtis, "Editor's Easy Chair," *Harper's Monthly,*
XXV (1862), 271

WALDEN;

OR,

LIFE IN THE WOODS.

By HENRY D. THOREAU,

AUTHOR OF "A WEEK ON THE CONCORD AND MERRIMACK RIVERS."

I do not propose to write an ode to dejection, but to brag as lustily as chanticleer in the
morning, standing on his roost, if only to wake my neighbors up. — Page 92.

BOSTON:
TICKNOR AND FIELDS.
M DCCC LIV.

The title page of the first edition of WALDEN
with Sophia Thoreau's drawing of the Walden cabin

Concord in 1841

A view from the steps of the Thoreau home on the Square. The church on the
is the First Parish, where Thoreau was baptized

The Mill Dam, the shopping center of Concord

Thoreau lived in the brick house at the far right from 1823 to 1826. It has lor
since been torn down

CONCORD IN THOREAU'S DAY

ntributions to our knowledge of the Indian. But since he was
ie of the first Americans to view the Indian with anything other
an disdain, his projected book might have hastened the day of
cognition of the Indian's cultural contributions and of his rights.

IV

On January 1, 1860, when Charles Brace came to Concord
o speak about his Children's Aid movement in New York City,
ie brought with him a copy of Charles Darwin's *Origin of Species,*
vhich had been first published only five weeks before and which
ie had picked up just that day from Asa Gray, the botanist,
n Cambridge.[8] Alcott, Brace, and Thoreau dined at Sanborn's
ind their talk centered primarily on Darwin's new book and his
heories of evolution. Thoreau was so impressed that he quickly
got hold of a copy, took six pages of notes on it in one of his
commonplace books, and told Sanborn that he liked the book
very much.[9] When Emerson told Thoreau that Agassiz had
scoffed at the new theories, Thoreau replied: "If Agassiz sees
two thrushes so alike that they bother the ornithologist to dis-
criminate them, he insists they are two species; but if he sees
Humboldt and Fred Cogswell [a dim-witted inmate of the Concord Almshouse], he insists that they come from one ancestor."[1]
But despite the fact that Thoreau was impressed with Darwin's
theories, they had appeared too late to have any significant influence on his own thinking.

On January 4 young Samuel Ripley Bartlett, a Concord
boy, proudly delivered a poem on "The Concord Fight" before
the Concord Lyceum. Led by the enthusiasm of his audience to
over-evaluate his effort, he asked Thoreau to help him find a
publisher for the poem. Thoreau wrote a letter of introduction to
Ticknor & Fields for the boy, then frankly warned him: "I would
advise you, if it is not impertinent, not to have it printed, as
you propose. You might keep it by you, read it as you have done,

8. F. B. Sanborn, Letter to Theodore Parker of January 2, 1860. MS,
Concord Free Public Library
9. F. B. Sanborn, Letter to Theodore Parker of March 11, 1860. MS,
Concord Free Public Library
1. Emerson, *Journals,* IX, 270

as you may have opportunity, and see how it wears with your self."[2] But the young man ignored Thoreau's sage but rather chilling advice, eventually persuaded another Boston firm, A. Williams & Co., to publish it, and then found to his dismay that Thoreau's word had been wise, for the poem in print proved to be a tediously sentimental affair and it fell stillborn from the press.

Thoreau had mellowed with the years. He found time to stop and gossip with his townsmen on his daily journey to the post office. Emerson now kept a rowboat on Walden Pond and the two often spent their afternoons rowing meditatively together on the pond. Thoreau told Alcott that he thought Emerson's newest volume, *Conduct of Life*, lacked the "fire and force of the earlier books," but he said nothing of it directly to Emerson to spare his feelings.[3]

When Sam Staples bought property adjacent to Emerson's that spring, he asked Thoreau to survey it. Thoreau discovered to his amusement that Emerson's boundary hedge was several feet over on Staples's property. Calling the two men together, he charged that Emerson's appropriation of the land had been intentional, only Staples had proven too sharp to be imposed upon. He declared that Emerson had for years been holding up his nose as an upright citizen and an example to everybody, yet every time he reset his fence, he shoved it a little further onto Staples's property until he had stolen enough land to feed a yearling heifer. Although it was an awful disappointment to him, he said, he was glad to have a hand in exposing his dishonesty. Thoreau shouted loud enough to be heard out on the road and Emerson looked as though he had been caught picking pockets at town meeting. Staples was so embarrassed that he stared at the floor. When Thoreau made one of his harshest charges, Staples looked up, and when he saw Thoreau's eye twinkling, he let out a laugh that could be heard across town and Emerson at last realized Thoreau had been pulling his leg. The boundary "dispute," needless to say was quickly settled amicably.[4]

When the Hawthornes arrived back in Concord after many

---

2. Thoreau, *Correspondence*, 572-3
3. Alcott, *Journals*, 331
4. Samuel A. Jones, "Thoreau's Incarceration," *Inlander*, IX (1898), 97-8

ars abroad, Thoreau attended a strawberry party at Emerson's
n June 29, 1860, in their honor and thought Hawthorne looked
pretty brown after his voyage" and "as simple & child-like as
ver."⁵ They soon resumed their old friendship and Hawthorne's
aughter Rose later recalled that Thoreau "used to flit in and out
f the house with long, ungainly, Indian-like stride, and his pierc-
ıg large orbs, staring, as it were in vacancy."⁶ He was probably
ever aware that Hawthorne had quite obviously used him as the
asis of the character Donatello in the novel *Marble Faun,* pub-
shed a few months before.⁷ Thoreau almost never read novels,
ven those of as close a friend as Hawthorne.

In January 1860 Bronson Alcott made another abortive at-
:mpt to start a club, the "Concord Club"—which would meet
reekly for conversation and apparently be limited to the intel-
:ctuals resident in the town—Emerson, Alcott himself, Thoreau,
Channing, David Wasson, Sanborn, and Hawthorne. But listing
ıeir names was as far as he got and there the matter died
-borning.

When Alcott's daughter Anna and John Pratt were married
n May 23, 1860, Thoreau was sent a last-minute invitation to
ttend. Members of the Pratt, Alcott, and Emerson families,
'phraim Bull, Sanborn, Elizabeth Peabody, and Thoreau were
ıvited; only Thoreau did not bring a gift for the bride.⁸ After
he formal ceremonies, the guests danced around the bridal
:ouple on the lawn and feasted on cake and some of Mr. Bull's
;rape wine. Unlike Emerson, Thoreau did not take advantage
f the opportunity to kiss the bride.⁹

V

Early in the summer of 1860 Thoreau decided to make an-
»ther excursion to Mount Monadnock in New Hampshire. He

5. Thoreau, *Correspondence,* 582
6. Harding, *Thoreau, Man of Concord,* 78
7. Moncure Conway, *Life of Nathaniel Hawthorne* (New York, 1890), 165
8. Anna B. Alcott, Diary for August 15, 1860. MS, Houghton Library
9. Madeleine Stern, *Louisa May Alcott* (Norman, Okla., 1950), 97

asked Channing to accompany him, but Channing, undependab
as ever, at first refused to commit himself one way or the othe
then suddenly he decided to go and wanted to leave immediatel
Thoreau hurriedly invited Blake and Brown to join them only
find they had already made plans to spend a few days on Mou
Washington and so could not come. On August 4, though tl
day was rainy, Channing and Thoreau started off by train an
arriving at Troy, New Hampshire, set off on foot. As was the
custom, once they had determined the compass direction of tl
summit, they set off cross-country on a beeline, going throug
rather than around any obstacle in the way.

It was so foggy that for a time they mistook the small
Gap Monadnock for the true mountain. By the time they ha
reached the actual summit it was three in the afternoon and the
were soaked to the skin. Choosing a site near the spot where l
had camped two years before, Thoreau cleared the area ar
quickly built a lean-to with a thatched spruce roof, which Cha
ning declared the handsomest he had ever seen. Building a fi
at its door, they slowly turned around like meat on a spit ar
dried themselves out. By 8 p.m. the skies were clear and tl
booming of the nighthawks sang them to sleep.

After gathering blueberries for breakfast before sunrise, the
spent the day exploring various spurs of the mountain, returnir
to the summit only after the day's hundred tourists had descende
On the 6th, they built a new camp in a more secluded spot
quarter of a mile to the east on the edge of a plateau, so tha
they need not worry about tourists pawing over their possessio
in their absence. So successfully was it hidden in the spruces tha
Channing had to ask Thoreau to guide him to it on occasio
Realizing that they were sleeping in an unprotected spot, he aske
Thoreau what was the largest beast that might nibble his le
there. Thoreau's answer was not at all reassuring and Channin
slept but fitfully thereafter.

Keeping out of sight of the constant stream of tourists, the
devoted their time to cataloging the flora and fauna of the summi
Thoreau made a rude map of the area, measuring his distances b
casting stones—one easy cast, he found, measured ten rods. Whe
they descended from the mountain on August 9 and took th
train from Troy back to Concord, he had taken enough note

fill more than forty printed pages of his journal.[1] It was his
plan to write a book on the mountain—a plan that unfortunately
was never to be fulfilled. He called on Alcott soon after he arrived to report on his trip and spoke so entertainingly that before
he had finished the entire family had gathered around his chair
to listen.[2]

On his return Thoreau found awaiting him, appropriately
enough, a copy of *The Mountain,* sent to him by the author,
Robert Montgomery Smith Jackson, the proprietor of the Allegheny Mountain Health Institute in Cresson, Pennsylvania.
Jackson had probably heard of Thoreau through Senator Charles
Sumner, who had recuperated in the institute from the brutal
beating given him by Preston Brooks in the Senate in 1856.
The Mountain is a strange book, a wild, uncontrolled panegyric
to the health-giving virtues of the Allegheny Mountains, but full
of digressions. Its third and longest epigraph is an extensive
quotation from the final chapter of *Walden.* It took Thoreau
nearly two months to acknowledge the book and he apologized
that other engagements had up until then prevented his reading
it through. He found it the best specimen of Carlyle's style outside of Carlyle's own books and added that he detected a similarity
in ideas between Jackson's central theme and that of his own unpublished essay on "The Wild."[3] By then Thoreau was getting
quite used to receiving such gifts from complete strangers. In
1858 Henry Stephens Randall, the author of a biography of
Jefferson, had sent him through Emerson the huge four folio-
volume set of the *Documentary History of New York.* And in
April 1859 a Benjamin Smith Lyman of Huntingdon, Pennsylvania, had visited Concord to present him with a copy of Peter
Lesley's *Manual of Coal* as a token of his regard.[4]

A few days after Thoreau's return to Concord the twenty-
three-year old William Dean Howells arrived to call. He was making a pilgrimage to the homes of the literary lights of the Boston
area. In 1859, when Thoreau had come to the defense of Brown,

---

1. Thoreau, *Journal,* XIV, 8–51
2. Alcott, *Journals,* 329
3. Emil Freniere, "The Mountain Comes to Concord," *Thoreau Society Bulletin,* LXXV (1961), 2–3
4. Walter Harding, *Thoreau's Library* (Charlottesville, 1957), 45,
66

[433]

Howells, an ardent abolitionist himself, had been particular
pleased at Thoreau's action and now wished to express his a
preciation. Unfortunately the visit he had so long looked forwar
to turned into a debacle. Howells described it in his aut
biography:

> Thoreau came into the room a quaint, stump figure of a man,
> whose effect of long trunk and short limbs was heightened by his
> fashionless trousers being let down too low. . . . He tried to place
> me geographically after he had given me a chair not quite so far
> off as Ohio, though still across the whole room, for he sat against
> one wall, and I against the other; but apparently he failed to
> pull himself out of his revery by the effort, for he remained in a
> dreamy muse, which all my attempts to say something fit about
> John Brown and Walden Pond seemed only to deepen upon him.
> I have not the least doubt that I was needless and valueless about
> both, and that what I said could not well have prompted an
> important response; but I did my poor best, and I was terribly dis-
> appointed in the result. The truth is that in those days I was a
> helplessly concrete young person, and all forms of the abstract,
> the air-drawn, afflicted me like physical discomforts. I do not
> remember that Thoreau spoke of his books or of himself at all,
> and when he began to speak of John Brown, it was not the warm,
> palpable, loving, fearful old man of my conception, but a sort of
> John Brown type, a John Brown ideal, a John Brown principle,
> which we were somehow (with long pauses between the vague,
> orphic phrases) to cherish, and to nourish ourselves upon.
>
> It was not merely a defeat of my hopes, it was a rout, and I
> felt myself so scattered over the field of thought that I could
> hardly bring my forces together for retreat. I must have made
> some effort, vain and foolish enough, to rematerialize my old
> demigod, but when I came away it was with the feeling that there
> was a very little more left of John Brown than there was of me.[5]

Howells went on to say that he did not blame Thoreau for th
debacle, for "his words were addressed to a far other understand
ing than mine, and it was my misfortune if I could not prof
by them." But it is obvious that Thoreau had gone little out c
his way to reassure the young man.

5. William Dean Howells, *Literary Friends and Acquaintances* (New
York, 1900), 58–60

On September 11, 1860, George Melvin reported to Thoreau that a strange animal had been killed near the north line of the town of Concord on the 9th. From the description Thoreau judged it to be a Canada lynx and immediately went out to the home of John Quincy Adams, who had killed it, to see it. For weeks there had been rumors of a strange animal haunting the area, though most had dismissed it as the product of children's or old wives' imaginations. But when Adams lost some hens, his son set out with a gun in search. The animal jumped at him from a tree and he struck at it with the butt of his gun; then, firing at it, he killed it. By the time Thoreau arrived, the animal had been skinned and the skull boiled for mounting. Thoreau measured the skin carefully and wrote down a detailed description, but could not decide when he consulted his textbooks whether it was a lynx or a wildcat. On the 13th Thoreau visited Adams again and this time examined the carcass as well as the hide, opening the stomach to discover its contents and cutting off a leg to add the bone to his collection. Adams later sold the skin and skull to Thoreau, who, with the help of Baird's *Mammals,* was finally able to identify it as the Canada lynx. He then wrote a lengthy letter to the Boston Society of Natural History describing the animal, which was read at their meeting on October 17 and incorporated into their proceedings. Several months later, when Thoreau boasted to a friend of his find, he was asked if he had collected the state bounty on lynxes. "You might have inferred that ten dollars was something rarer in his neighborhood than a lynx even," Thoreau lamented in his journal. "I have thought that a lynx was a bright-eyed, four-legged, furry beast of the cat kind, very *current,* indeed, though its natural gait is by leaps. But he knew it to be a draught drawn by the cashier of the wildcat bank on the State treasury, payable at sight. . . . But the fact was that, instead of receiving ten dollars for the lynx which I had got, I had paid away some dollars in order to get him."[6]

---

6. Thoreau, *Journal,* XIV, 282–3

VI

On February 8, 1860, Thoreau delivered what was to prove to be his final lecture before the Concord Lyceum. It was a new paper on "Wild Apples" and was an immediate success. Frank Preston Stearns thought it "the best lecture of the season" and recorded that "at its close there was long continued applause." Alcott said that he listened to it "with uninterrupted interest and delight."[8] And young Annie Bartlett said she liked it "pretty well," though she confessed that after being out to a ball at Mr Sanborn's school the night before until two, she had really been too sleepy to listen.[9] On the 14th Thoreau repeated it in nearby Bedford, and although he had complained in his journal, "Always you have to contend with the stupidity of men. . . . Halve your lecture, and put a psalm at the beginning and a prayer at the end of it and read it from a pulpit, and they will pronounce it good without thinking," he made no such concessions and was pleased to have several hundred people show up and enjoy it just as much as his own townsmen had.[1]

Thoreau had been working on the "Wild Apples" essay for many years, and much of it is derived from journal entries of the early 1850s, but even after its success on the platform, he continued to revise and improve it until the end of his life. It was not published until November 1862, after his death, when it appeared in the *Atlantic Monthly*. It is his most successful "familiar essay," a delightful blending of wit and wisdom, filled with whimsical humor and facetious catalogs of imaginary species of fruit. A high point is a vivid and amusing description of a wild apple's fight for survival against the continued browsing of pastured cattle.

In July, Theodore Parker's parishioners—Parker had died in Italy in May—invited Thoreau to speak at their picnic in Waverley, but he declined, saying that it was entirely out of his

7. Frank P. Stearns, *Sketches from Concord and Appledore* (New York, 1895), 28
8. Alcott, *Journals,* 326
9. Annie Bartlett, Letter to Ned Bartlett of February 10, 1860. MS, First Parish in Concord Archives
1. Thoreau, *Journal,* XIII, 145

e: he didn't attend picnics even in Concord. In the fall F. B.
nborn attempted to line up guest laymen, Thoreau and Ellery
hanning among them, to preach in Parker's old church in Bos-
n, with Sanborn himself acting as a sort of master of ceremonies,
it Channing said that it was too much like being a second mate
a ship, and Thoreau apparently agreed with him, for he too
rned the offer down.[2]

In mid-summer Thoreau began negotiations for a lecture tour
the Middle West. He corresponded for a time jointly with
harles Morse of Rochester, New York, and Benjamin Austin
Buffalo. When they asked him to speak on a subject of a sci-
itific nature, he replied frankly that his topic would be tran-
endental rather than scientific and thus "to the mass of hearers,
robably *moonshine.*" Morse and Austin were frightened off by
ich frankness and the plans for the lecture tour were abandoned.
horeau wrote to the *New York World* on September 17 and
sked them to announce his availability as a lecturer generally,
ut nothing came of it.

Correspondence with Charles P. Ricker of Lowell, Massa-
husetts, however was more successful and Thoreau delivered
vo lectures there on September 9. Z. E. Stone, who heard him
ead his "Life without Principle" paper there, thought it "a most
intertaining denunciation of those who find satisfaction in read-
ig the mere news of the day." He commented that Thoreau with
is interest in "squirrels, fishes, bugs and things . . . had a right
) be indifferent to what was going on in the world among his
ellow-men, and to spend his time as he pleased, if he paid taxes,
vhich he didn't—willingly."[3] While in Lowell, Thoreau explored
ne banks of the Merrimack for botanical specimens and carefully
xamined the dams of the lower Concord River in the light of his
ecent researches upstream.

On September 20, 1860, he read a paper on "The Succession
f Forest Trees" before the Middlesex Agricultural Society in the
Concord Town Hall on the occasion of their annual cattle show.
t was a stormy day and the rain fell in torrents; nonetheless he

---

2. Kenneth Walter Cameron, "Thoreau and Emerson in Channing's
Letters to the Watsons," *Emerson Society Quarterly,* XIV (1959), 82
3. Laurence E. Richardson, "Thoreau Notes," *Thoreau Society Bulletin,* LXXVIII (1962), 4

lined up with the officials of the society at their hall and marche under escort of Gilmore's Band to the Town Hall. There he sa on the platform with C. C. Felton, his old Greek professor, no President of Harvard University, and ex-governor George Boutwell of Massachusetts, now president of the society. Boutwe introduced Thoreau. Although Thoreau's subject was serious, h approach was light and humorous. He introduced himself as man "distinguished for his oddity" and closed his paper wi an amusing account of his winning a prize at the 1857 cattle sho (He had obtained six seeds of a new large yellow squash, th *Poitrine jaune grosse,* from the Patent Office in Washington, an through treating them with tender, loving care, had succeede in raising one that weighed 123.5 pounds and four others th together totaled 186.25 pounds. He not only took the premiu at the fair, but his achievement was written up in the *Bosto Herald* and he sold the squash to a sharp businessman who im mediately announced he would sell the seeds inside for ten cen each.[4]) At the conclusion Boutwell congratulated the audienc on hearing an address "so plain and practical, and at the sam time showing such close observation and careful study of natur phenomena."[5]

For years Thoreau had pondered the puzzle of the successio of trees, wondering why and how trees and plants seemed to sprin up when there seemed to be no obvious source for their seed. A early as 1850 he had noted that a pitch pine had sprung up in h yard though there was not another such tree within a half a mil In 1851 he observed that squirrels were capable of carryin seeds surprisingly long distances, that milkweed down could carr its seeds hundreds of miles under optimum conditions, and th the railroad seemed to aid the spread of plants through seed blown off in the dust from freight cars. For the next few year he jotted down many such observations on the dispersal of seed of various plants. But his real impetus came on April 28, 1856 when he was surveying along the Marlborough Road and Georg Hubbard remarked that, if pines were cut down in a wood lot

4. September 30, 1857
5. Hubert Hoeltje, "Thoreau as Lecturer," *New England Quarterly,* XIX (1946), 492

aks often came up in their place. Immediately they checked
Loring's recently cut white pine lot together and found the ground
covered with healthy young oak seedlings. From then on Thoreau
took care to make specific notes of every occasion on which he
saw any indication of the dispersal of seeds by animal, bird, wind,
or man. Gradually he came to the conclusion that many kinds of
seeds were constantly being dispersed in all directions, but only
comparatively few were able to take root and, of those, even fewer
found the conditions suitable for maturation. He found, for example, that in any pine grove, a multitude of tiny oaks could be
discovered, but that they matured only when and if the covering
shade of the pines were removed. Out of this discovery, after much
further research, his lecture had been written.

"The Succession of Forest Trees" is Thoreau's major contribution to scientific knowledge. Although others simultaneously
were making the same discovery, Thoreau's research was independent and the conclusions he reached are still accepted. Most
important to Thoreau himself was the fact that his discoveries
solved the dilemma he had long faced when through his surveying
activities he brought about the destruction of Concord's woods.
Now he could point the way towards proper forest management,
which would yield lumber and profit for the landowner and at the
same time bring about proper reforestation and so preserve the
woods.

Thoreau immediately sent his paper off to Horace Greeley,
who rather surprisingly, considering its rather narrow range of
interest, published it in its entirety in the New York *Weekly
Tribune* for October 6, 1860. Shortly afterwards it was reprinted
in the *Transactions of the Middlesex Agricultural Society* for 1860
(a copy of which Thoreau promptly donated to the Boston Society
of Natural History library), and later, in "expurgated" form (with
the humorous passages censored) in the *Eighth Annual Report of
the Massachusetts Board of Agriculture*. Moncure Conway, who
had established a new *Dial* in Cincinnati and had already unsuccessfully tried to persuade Thoreau to contribute an essay, now
tried to obtain his permission to reprint the "Succession" essay,
but was again unsuccessful. It was however summarized at length
in the *New England Farmer* for February 1861, in the *Century,*

and apparently in other publications. It thus achieved the wide circulation of any of Thoreau's shorter essays in his lifetim (Benjamin Tolman who set the first printing of the essay in typ found Thoreau "agreeable & pleasant" to work with, but felt tha he was "so superior a man" that he was not at ease to talk wit him much.[6])

Thoreau looked upon the "Succession" essay as only a sma part of a much larger study on the dispersion of seeds and h had already embarked on further research. In the winter of 1859 1860 he had studied the structure of tree buds, leaves, and seeds. I June 1860 he had concentrated on pollens, particularly those c the pines, and had pioneered in pointing out the possible relatio ship between pollens and human allergies, or "diseases of th season" as he called them.[7] Gradually he gathered together manuscript some 575 pages in length called "Notes on Fruits an Seeds."[8] Although he never was able to complete the manuscri nor polish it for publication, it contains some of his best writin Someday, it is to be hoped, it will be edited and published.

When on October 23, 1860, Anthony Wright told him of th existence of a large tract of virgin forest, Inches' Woods, onl eight miles away in Boxboro, Thoreau promptly made two jou neys to inspect it at length. He thought it was like finding a undiscovered country in his back yard and could not understan how he had overlooked anything so grand so near for so lon It was as exciting as any discovery he had made in the wilds c Maine and he was as ebullient in his enthusiasm as a child wit a new toy. "Far the handsomest thing I saw in Boxboro was i noble oak wood," he said. "Let her keep it a century longer, an men will make pilgrimages to it from all parts of the country.'

Tree growth patterns, exemplified in the annual rings of the stumps, had long interested him. Now he returned to this stud with renewed vigor. He soon realized that through them he "coul unroll the rotten papyrus on which the history of the Concor forest is written," that through their patterns he could "not onl detect the order of events but the time during which they elapsed,

6. Edward Emerson, Notes on Thoreau
7. Thoreau, *Journal*, XIII, 366
8. MS, Berg Collection
9. Thoreau, *Journal*, XIV, 304

d thus he anticipated by many decades the discoveries of sci-
ntists in our Southwest that Indian ruins could be dated by the
rowth patterns in the timbers they had used.[1]

In November he began making studies of tree growth pat-
erns of specific species of trees in specific groves, and thus it
was that he spent the afternoon of December 3, 1860, counting
rings on the stumps of trees on Fair Haven Hill. It was a bitterly
cold day and before it was over he had contracted a severe cold
—the beginning, as it turned out, of his final illness. When he got
home that evening, instead of taking care of himself, he spent
his time arguing with Sam Staples and Walcott as to the rightness
or wrongness of John Brown's actions.

On September 22, he had written to the lyceum in Waterbury,
Connecticut, to offer his services as a lecturer. After some nego-
tiation, it was arranged that he would speak there on December
11. His cold had rapidly developed into bronchitis. His friends
and the family doctor all urged him to cancel the lecture, but he
insisted that he had an engagement to fulfill and journeyed to
Waterbury to read "Autumnal Tints" despite their advice. He
was worn out and delivered the lecture in such a monotone that
a reporter in the *Waterbury American* thought it "prevented the
audience from duly appreciating whatever of real merit [the
lecture] contained as a composition" and dismissed it as "dull,
common-place and unsatisfactory . . . [with] nothing of the poeti-
cal discoverable in it."[2]

The strain of the journey worsened Thoreau's condition and
he returned to Concord a seriously ill man. He was confined to
the house for most of the winter but wandered out occasionally
on brief experimental trips to the post office. For the first time
in years he left large gaps in his daily journal, sometimes going
as much as two weeks without a single entry. Just before he had
fallen ill he had begun work on a new lecture on wild fruit, particularly huckleberries. Halfheartedly he continued working on it
for a time, but eventually he gave it up and never finished it. His
productive days were over.

---

1. Ibid. XIV, 152
2. December 14, 1860

CHAPTER TWENTY
(1861–1862)

I

As the winter of 1861 progressed, Thoreau's health deteriorated. On January 28 Alcott called on him and found him busily working on his journal but too hoarse to think of going out. Alcott expressed the hope that fair weather would prove his best physician and that with the coming of spring he would get out doors once more.[1] On February 3 Ellery Channing reported that Thoreau had been confined to the house for ten weeks and that cold air brought on attacks of coughing. Ten days later he wrote Mary Russell Watson that Thoreau had lost a great deal of weight and his pulse was down to fifty-six. He added, in a confusing bit of medical double-talk, "His system suffers a retardation, it ceases to make blood, hence adipose tissue which is formed of the elements of blood ceases to be found and the lack of respitory oxygenation combined with the lack of supplying sufficient stimuli to the blood-corpuscles, produce a semi state of metastic dyscarasia."[2] On March 1, when Blake and Brown walked over from Worcester for a visit, Thoreau reported that his "pipes were not in good order."[3]

In 1859 Bronson Alcott had been appointed superintendent of Concord's schools. He immediately invited Thoreau to visit the schools occasionally and talk to the pupils. When in April 1860 he published his first annual report as superintendent, he suggested that a small textbook on the geography, history, and antiquities of Concord be prepared for the pupils and proposed

1. Bronson Alcott, *Journals*, 333
2. Kenneth Walter Cameron, "Thoreau and Emerson in Channing's Letters to the Watsons," *Emerson Society Quarterly*, XIV (1959), 78–9, where the letter of February 13 is, I believe, misdated 1862
3. Henry David Thoreau, *Correspondence* (New York, 1958), 609

horeau as the most appropriate author.[4] (Simon Brown, the ditor of the *New England Farmer,* had also been encouraging horeau to write a book on the natural history of Concord.[5]) When on February 4, 1861, Alcott called to see the ailing Thoreau, e found him busily "classifying and arranging his papers by sub- cts, as if he had a new book in mind," and expressed the hope at the new book might be the "atlas of Concord" that he had roposed the year before.[6] When Thoreau replied that he had ther projects in mind, Alcott refused to give up hope and in his April 1861 report suggested that since Thoreau was already "a ort of resident Surveyor-General of the town's farms, farmers, nimals, and everything else it contains," he should "set his ten enses at work upon an illustrated Atlas for the citizens, giving uch account of the world they inhabit, with such hints concerning he one he lives in, as he pleases." Such a book, Alcott thought, would suit us all, and become a model text book for studies out f doors, and a gift to our children for which they could not be oo grateful."[7] It is a book that would have been close to Thoreau's eart. Even as early as the 1840s he had thought of writing "a oem to be called 'Concord.'" It would concern, he said, the river, woods, ponds, hills, fields, swamps, meadows, streets, build- ngs, villages, morning, noon, evening, spring, summer, autumn, winter, night, Indian Summer, and the mountains in the horizon. And for years he had been constructing charts of the Concord seasons that would have made appropriate illustrations. Regretting that Thoreau had been unable to fulfill his promise of speaking to the school children "on his favorite theme of Nature as the friend and preceptor of man." Alcott looked forward to a day when he would lead the children "along our fields, wood-paths, river- lands, brook-sides, and the plain landscape" and help them "to seize at once and at first hand their mysteries and uses."[8]

Alcott also buzzed with a new idea—the compilation of a "Concord Book" from the writings of the town's authors through the years. "There seems no reason," he thought, "why a volume

---

4. Bronson Alcott, *Essays on Education* (Gainesville, 1960), 90–1
5. Edward Emerson, Notes on Thoreau
6. Alcott, *Journals,* 334
7. Alcott, *Essays on Education,* 174
8. Ibid., 175

of this attractive character should not be published at once," and he immediately set about interviewing Sanborn, Emerson Channing, Thoreau, and Hawthorne for suggestions. He eventuall gathered together a scrapbook which he labeled "Papers from which selections are to be made for The Concord Book" and included in the Thoreau section "The Natural History of Massachusetts," "A Winter Walk," "Chaucer," "Walking," "Life without Principle," and a number of poems.[1]

Unfortunately nothing came of any of these ideas. Thoreau was invited to speak at the annual school exhibition on March 1€ and his name was announced on the printed program, but he was too ill to attend. It was not long before it was obvious to ever such a perennial optimist as Alcott that he would never be able to compile the "Atlas of Concord." And a year later Alcott was forced to announce in his annual report that the war had forced postponement of the "Concord Book." By the time the war had ended, Alcott was no longer superintendent and so the book never was published.

On February 27 and 28, 1861, Thoreau was well enough to take brief strolls along the Boston road in the shelter of the hill and to enjoy the early arrival of bluebirds. On March 4 he ventured out again, joining with Alcott to call on Mr. Barker, a Leominster clergyman who was spending the winter in Concord. It was the day of Lincoln's inauguration, and Thoreau announced himself as "impatient with the politicians, the state of the country, the State itself, and with statesmen generally." He roundly accused the Republican Party of duplicity and called Alcott to account for his favorable opinion of the new administration.[2] In mid-March, with new snows, he was confined to the house once more for a time, but on April 6 he was out investigating the spring floods and on the 7th he was well enough to hike the "two-mile square" of Monument and Liberty streets and Lowell Road.

His recovery however was not as rapid as all had hoped. He found himself intensely sensitive to cold. The doctor suggested that he try a warmer climate and recommended the West Indies, but Thoreau thought it would be too muggy there. Southern Eu-

9. Ibid. 164
1. MS, Houghton Library
2. Alcott, *Journals*, 337

ope was next suggested, but Thoreau replied that that would be oo expensive. Finally, probably because a distant cousin, Samuel Thatcher, Jr., of Bangor had moved there ten years before because of lung trouble and had found himself improved, Thoreau decided to try the dry air of Minnesota. (Minnesotans had already begun to advertise widely the therapeutic values of their climate.) He had never been west of the Alleghenies and thus could combine the journey for his health with a further study of the American Indian and the flora and fauna of the Middle West.

It was obvious to all that Thoreau was not well enough to make the trip alone. He turned first to Ellery Channing as a companion, but Channing characteristically refused day by day to make up his mind. On May 3 Thoreau wrote Blake to see if he were interested, but Blake replied that he could not free himself for such a long journey at such short notice. Thoreau then turned to the seventeen-year-old Horace Mann, Jr., son of the famed educator.

Young Mann had recently moved to Concord with his widowed mother and younger brother. Supposedly he was studying to enter the Lawrence Scientific School at Harvard in the fall, but he was far more interested in collecting specimens for his various natural-history collections than in brushing up on his Greek. He had been dropping in regularly to talk with Thoreau and to show him specimens he had collected in his walks ever since he arrived in Concord. Mrs. Mann, thinking Thoreau a good influence on her son, had him in to dinner to meet Mrs. Josiah Quincy, daughter-in-law of the late president of Harvard, and described Mrs. Quincy as an ardent admirer of Thoreau's writings.

Mann quickly accepted Thoreau's invitation and the two busied themselves with preparations for the journey. On May 10 they each purchased through railroad tickets to Chicago for $25.25. Thoreau, methodical as ever, made out a checklist of his baggage: "carpet bag, umbrella, half-thick coat, plant book, blotting paper, writing paper, waist coat, cap, botany book, twine, cards, pencils, buttons, scissors, thin coat, trochees, envelopes, tape, dipper, bottles, pins, needles, thread, stamps, jackknife, watch, ticket, guidebook, shoestring, map of the United States, notebook, matches, letters, best pants, socks, shirts, drawers, cotton batting, hand-

[445]

kerchiefs, towel, soap, medicine, compass, microscope, spy glas: insect boxes, clothes brush, slippers, neckerchiefs, ribbon, bosom and $78.10 in left pocket, $60.00 in right, and $40.00 hidde in bosom."[3]

They left Concord on May 11 after Emerson had droppe in to say good-bye and give Thoreau letters of introduction t friends along the way. After a two-day stop-over in Worcester visit Blake and Brown and to drive around Lake Quinsigamone they continued on to Albany, where Thoreau found the Delava House "not so good as costly" (they charged him $2.50 for th night).[4] Mann noticed that Thoreau was already "pretty tired from his journey.

On the 14th they continued on through Syracuse and Roche ter to Niagara Falls, where they put up at the New York Centr: House. Again Thoreau thought he was being overcharged an the next day, after insisting on visiting every boarding house b one in the town, finally settled on the American House at a doll: a day. Hoping vainly that Channing might catch up and join the: on their journey, they spent five days at the falls, botanizing o Goat Island and on both sides of the river. Finally on the 20t they gave up hope and took the train to Detroit; the next da they continued on to Chicago. There Thoreau looked up Eme son's friend Rev. Robert Collyer, the Unitarian minister, wh said:

> [Thoreau's] voice was low, but still sweet in the tones and in- flections, though the organs were all in revolt just then and wasting away. . . . His words also were as distinct and true to the ear as those of a great singer. . . . He would hesitate for an instant now and then, waiting for the right word, or would pause with a pathetic patience to master the trouble in his chest, but when he was through the sentence was perfect and entire, lacking nothing, and the word was so purely one with the man that when I read his books now and then I do not hear my own voice within my reading but the voice I heard that day.[5]

---

3. Walter Harding, *Thoreau's Minnesota Journey* (Geneseo, N. Y., 1962), 29
4. Thoreau, *Journal*, XIV, 340
5. Robert Collyer, *Clear Grit* (Boston, 1913), 294–6

hen they parted, Collyer urged Thoreau to return via Chicago
d spend a few days with him.

Chicago was, at the moment, in the midst of a financial panic
ovoked by the war, and the travelers were for a time worried
out their funds, but they called on B. B. Wiley, a Chicago
anker, and were able to obtain a hundred dollars in gold to carry
em along. Wiley, formerly of Providence, had corresponded with
horeau for some years and at least once visited him in Concord.
espite his profession, he found Thoreau's philosophy appealing
d was one of his more devoted admirers.

On May 23 they purchased tickets to St. Paul for $5.60 and,
ter taking the train across the Illinois prairie to Dunleith (now
ast Dubuque, Illinois), boarded the steamer *Itasca* on the Mis-
ssippi. Thoreau noted as they arrived at each village that every
habitant including the dogs and pigs rushed down to the wharf
 see the excitement. Below Wabasha he spotted an Indian en-
ampment with "Dacotah-shaped wigwams." They had two beau-
ful, warm spring days on the boat and arrived at St. Paul early
n the morning of the 26th. After they put up at the Tremont
Iouse in sight of the Falls of St. Anthony, they called that evening
n Samuel Thatcher only to learn that he had been thrown from
is carriage in an accident a few days before and had been seri-
usly injured. (Thatcher died on August 31, some weeks after
horeau had returned to Concord.)

For the next nine days Thoreau and Mann botanized at
icollet Island, Lake Calhoun, Minnehaha Falls, Hennepin Is-
and, and along the banks of the Minnesota River. Thoreau was
ascinated by the prairie gophers and succeeded in seeing three
pecies—the striped gopher, the Missouri gopher, and the Franklin
round squirrel. He had lunch on May 28 with Dr. Charles L.
Anderson, the Minnesota state geologist, to whom Samuel Thatcher
ad given them a note of introduction, and Thoreau read widely
n the Minneapolis libraries.[6] He saw six hundred volunteers
raining at Fort Snelling but thought Minnesotans generally apa-
hetic about the war. Mann thought that Thoreau was showing
 marked improvement; he had a good appetite, his cough was

---

6. Samuel Thatcher, Jr., Letter to Charles Anderson of May 26,
1861. MS, Robert Rulon Miller

better and did not hinder his sleeping so much, and he had r
covered from a bowel complaint he had picked up in Chicag

On June 5 the two moved out to live at Mrs. Hamilto
"exclusive boarding house" set in the midst of woods betwee
Lake Calhoun and Lake Harriet. Huge mosquitoes swarm
around them in thick clouds but failed to keep them from furth
botanizing and from swimming in the lakes. Thoreau had lo
wanted to find a wild crab apple in its native haunts; at one tir
he had even considered making a special trip from Concord
Pennsylvania where it was said to grow to perfection. On t
train trip through Michigan he had seen it from the windo
but began to fear that like Tantalus he would never succeed
touching it. At St. Paul he was told he was too far north to fi
it. Mrs. Hamilton then claimed it grew on her premises b
Thoreau searched and could find only the shadbush. Jonathan
Grimes, a nurseryman in the neighborhood who was called
said that he had set out a number of trees in the spring and
had died, but together they finally succeeded in finding o
withered flower on a recently transplanted tree and Thore
plucked it triumphantly for his herbarium.

On June 10 Mann reported cheerfully that Thoreau seem
to be recovering and thought that he would be "entirely well befc
a great while,"[7] but on the 12th, he announced that Thoreau w
still "pretty well," and informed his mother that they could
expected home before the middle of July, even though they h
originally planned to stay three months. Thoreau himself w
already aware that his trip had been futile and it was doing h
no good to remain in the area.

On June 12 when they read an announcement in the St. Pา
Pioneer and Democrat of an excursion on the steamer *Fra
Steele* three hundred miles up the Minnesota River to the Low
Sioux Agency near Redwood, they decided to go if they cot
get good accommodations and the fares were not too high. Wh
they found the round-trip fare would be only ten dollars, th
bought their tickets and embarked on the afternoon of the 17
It was a fantastic trip they had up the narrow and winding riv
Often the boat deliberately ran aground to navigate sharp turr
Occasionally it was forced to break its way through overhangi

7. Harding, *Thoreau's Minnesota Journey*, 52

ees. Once they rammed a concealed rock and the mate rushed
below with a lamp, expecting to find a hole, but did not. Sometimes the passengers would land and walk across a narrow neck
while the boat was forced to steam two or three miles around.

They arrived at the agency on the morning of the 20th. The
Indians had gathered from miles around on their ponies to receive
their regular payment from the federal government. The ceremonies were formal and both the Indians and the white officials
made long speeches. The Indians, Thoreau thought, had the advantage in truth, earnestness, and eloquence. He was particularly
impressed with Chief Little Crow, who a year later was to lead
the great Sioux uprising there in which eight hundred Minnesota
pioneers were killed. When the Indians complained of the white
man's treatment, Thoreau suspected they had reason enough for
dissatisfaction.

In the afternoon, at the request of Governor Ramsay, the
half-naked Indians performed a ceremonial dance. Thirty men
danced while twelve played on drums and the rest struck their
arrows against their bows. The dancers blew flutes and moved
their feet and shoulders in time to the music. Afterwards they
feasted on roasted ox. Thoreau learned with excitement that
a herd of buffalo was feeding within twenty or thirty miles, but
there was no time to go to see them. He satisfied himself with
purchasing three Indian garments of buckskin and a pair of Indian
snowshoes as souvenirs.

They started back downstream that very evening, leaving
behind them a flock of gamblers, who Thoreau was sure would
soon fleece the Indians of their money. They reached St. Paul
on the 22nd and, after putting up at the Merchant's Hotel for the
night, started downstream by boat the next morning. The Minneapolis *State Atlas* soon noted that "a very choice and select
company [including] Horace Mann, Jun., son of the lamented
statesman and Henry D. Thoreau, Esq., the 'celebrated abolitionist' " had enjoyed the excursion on the *Frank Steele*.[8] They
stopped for four days at the Metropolitan House at Red Wing,
botanized the area, climbed the famed Red-Wing Bluff, visited
the grave of Chief Red Wing for whom the town was named, and
swam in the Mississippi.

8. July 3, 1861

On June 26 they embarked on the *War Eagle* downstrea
and the next morning took the train at Prairie du Chien, Wisco
sin, for Milwaukee. They arrived to find the city virtually in
state of siege. Three days earlier, after ten banks had announce
their failure, the working men of the city had revolted, broke
into the banks, demolished furnishings, and set fires. Police, the
firemen, and finally state guards were called out before order w
restored.[9] Thoreau and Mann put up at the Lake House fc
seventy-five cents that night and found the city surprisingly qui
after the recent violence. The next morning they purchased ticke
home to Boston for $20.15 and embarked on the propellor shi
Edith, which sailed up through Lake Michigan. They arrive
at Mackinaw City, Michigan, on the morning of the 30th and pu
up at the Mackinaw House. Mann botanized for five days o
Mackinaw Island, but Thoreau, suffering from chills, spent mos
of his time close by the fire.

On the evening of July 4 they took the propellor shi
Sun and, sailing down through Lake Huron, arrived at Goderich
Ontario, the next evening. They took a train to Toronto, spen
a day touring the city, continued on to Ogdensburg, New York
and after an eleven-cent lunch and a ten-cent supper, took a fifty
cent berth on the Vermont Central Railroad to Boston. The
were back in Concord on the morning of July 9.

The Minnesota journey had been a tragic failure. Thoreau'
health was no better; in fact, strained and tired by the long journey, he was if anything in poorer condition than when he had
left Concord in May. He had been too ill to make any more than
a perfunctory study of the flora and fauna of the Middle West.
His few contacts with the Indians of the Plains had been too staged
to be satisfactory. He had succeeded in finding the wild crab apple
—but only a withered blossom, an all-too-appropriate symbol
of the whole trip. He returned to Concord with a full realization
of the futility of the journey and an awareness that the end
could not be far off. The New York *Tribune* on July 26, 1861,
shortly after his return, publicly confirmed the reports of his

9. Harriet M. Sweetland, "Why Thoreau Spent One Night in Milwaukee," *Historical Messenger of the Milwaukee County Historical
Society,* XVIII (1962), 3–9

poor health. Stoically he faced the facts and straightforwardly prepared to wind up his affairs.

Although much to his mother's dismay Mann had neglected studies on his journey west, he succeeded in entering Harvard in the fall; and majoring in botany under Asa Gray, he received a bachelor of science degree with a thesis on Hawaiian plants based on a summer's expedition to the islands. He became curator of the Harvard Herbarium and was being groomed to succeed Gray as head of the botany department when, at the age of only twenty-four, he died of tuberculosis. It is thought by some that he acquired the tuberculosis from Thoreau on their journey west.

II

Although war had been sundering the country for many months, Thoreau was too ill to raise but little interest. When the fiery old abolitionist Parker Pillsbury asked his opinion, Thoreau replied: "I do not so much regret the present condition of things in this country (provide I regret it at all) as I do that I ever heard of it. . . . I am reading Herodotus & Strabo, Blodgett's Climatology, and Six Years in the Deserts of North America, as hard as I can, to counterbalance it."[1]

When Moncure Conway visited Concord shortly after the Battle of Bull Run, he thought Thoreau, despite his ill health, the only cheerful man in Concord. Yet Channing thought "the country's misfortunes in the Union war acted on [Thoreau's] feelings with great force: he used to say he 'could never recover while the war lasted.' "[2]

Daniel Ricketson had been disturbed for some time at what he thought Thoreau's neglect. He had written a lengthy epistle on January 15, 1860, and had received no answer. On October 14 he wrote again and asked: "Am I to infer from your silence that you decline any farther correspondence and intercourse with me?"[3]

---

1. Thoreau, *Correspondence*, 611
2. Channing, *Thoreau, the Poet-Naturalist*, 8–9
3. Thoreau, *Correspondence*, 593

Thoreau, refusing to be rebuked, waited three weeks and then replied: "Not to have written a note for a year is with me a very venial offence. . . . I do not feel addressed by this letter of yours. It suggests only misunderstanding. . . . I have a very pleasant recollection of your fireside, and I trust that I shall revisit it."[4] Ricketson, mollified, resumed the correspondence, but still they did not see each other. Then suddenly on August 15, 1861, Thoreau wrote: "If you are to be at home, and it will be quite agreeable to you, I will pay you a visit next week, & take such rides or sauntering walks with you as an invalid may."[5]

Thoreau arrived in New Bedford on August 19 and Ricketson met him at the station. For five days the two old friends talked together and toured the countryside in Ricketson's carriage or took short walks while Thoreau gathered specimens for his herbarium, finding to his surprise nine species of plants he had not collected before. But his invalidism restricted his activities. He refused to go in swimming and at night requested a secluded bedroom so that his coughing would not disturb the others.[6] Ricketson noted:

> In relation to my friend Thoreau's health my impression is that his case is a very critical one as to recovery; he has a bad cough and expectorates a good deal, is emaciated considerably, his spirits, however, appear as good as usual, his appetite good. Unless some favorable symptom shows itself soon I fear he will gradually decline. He is thinking of going to a warm climate for the winter, but I think a judicious hydropathic treatment at home would be much better for him.[7]

Ricketson persuaded Thoreau to have his picture taken by Dunshee, a local ambrotypist. It is the last likeness we have. Sophia Thoreau thought it "very lifelike and one of the most successful likenesses we ever saw." She thought it remarkable because "it shews scarcely at all Henry's loss of health."[8] Walton Ricketson,

4. Ibid. 599–600
5. Ibid. 625
6. Walton Ricketson, Letter to F. H. Allen of April 16, 1917. MS, Thoreau Society Archives
7. Ricketson, *Daniel Ricketson and His Friends*, 318
8. Ibid. 146

on the other hand, while agreeing that it was one of the best of Thoreau, thought it lacked the "clear-eyed courage and directness, qualities so dominant in his personality."[9]

Thoreau returned to Concord on August 24. A week later Ricketson, still worried about his friend's health, wrote that he had persuaded Dr. Edward E. Denniston, a "water-cure" physician, to stop in to see Thoreau on his way from New Bedford to his spa at Northampton, Massachusetts. Apparently fearing that Thoreau might not have anything to do with Denniston, Ricketson at the last moment decided to accompany the doctor to Concord. Thoreau, with misgivings but not wishing to hurt Ricketson's feelings, did permit Denniston to give him an examination and then walked with the two men to see the Concord battleground. Denniston invited Thoreau to spend a fortnight as his guest in Northampton and dissuaded him from seeking relief in the West Indies, which Thoreau once again was considering visiting, but he was unable to awaken any interest on Thoreau's part in taking a water cure. After the doctor's departure, Thoreau informed Ricketson that he was not interested in being examined any further by quacks. Ricketson, hypochondriac that he was, however, could not resist. The next April, only a few weeks before Thoreau's death, he wrote and insisted that if Thoreau would only move where he could breathe in the fragrance of the pines, even suggesting a particular grove of pine trees near Plymouth, some seventy miles from Concord, he was certain he would find his health improved. By that time Thoreau was too weak even to reply. In fact, in the last few months of his life Thoreau would have nothing to do with any doctors, apparently feeling they could be of no help.[1]

On August 31 the Emersons invited Channing and Thoreau to a dinner in honor of their son Edward's impending departure for Harvard College. As they left the table and were passing into the parlor, Thoreau, realizing the mental turmoil young Edward was going through at this turning point in his life, took him aside and, with a serious face but a quiet, friendly tone of voice, reassured him that after all he would still be really close to home

---

9. Walton Ricketson, Letter to F. H. Allen of April 16, 1917
1. *Boston Transcript*, "More Views of Concord Men," August 10, 1906

and that most likely after his college days he would return to his beloved Concord to live just as Thoreau himself had. Edward found the words of comfort a great relief.[2]

In mid-September 1861 Ricketson extended an invitation for another visit to New Bedford, but Thoreau could not gather the strength for even that short journey. The circle of his walks in Concord gradually narrowed. Once he walked out to Flint's Bridge with Channing. Speaking of some minute thing he had observed, he told him that it was the art of genius to raise the little into the large and Channing thought that a remarkably good summation of Thoreau's own best capabilities. Near the end of the month he made a final visit to Walden Pond with his sister Sophia; he gathered wild grapes and dropped them one by one into the water while Sophia sketched.

In October there seemed to be a brief improvement in his health. The Hoars offered the use of their horse and wagon and Thoreau took a ride every day or two. Hoar's dog threw himself into the bargain, Thoreau noticed, and went along to do scouting duty. Earlier Simon Brown, the editor of the *New England Farmer* and a former lieutenant governor of Massachusetts, had taken pains to call on Thoreau and take him for a ride in his carriage.[3]

Channing reported to Mary Russell Watson that though Thoreau's cough was still formidable, he had shown so much improvement that should it continue for a month they could hope for his ultimate recovery.[4] But the recovery was brief and illusory. Cold weather set in and he rapidly lost all the ground he had gained. On November 3 he made the last entry in the journal that he had kept so faithfully for so many years. Noticing the pock marks made by a violent rain in the gravel of the railroad causeway, he quickly deduced the quarter from which the rain had come, and closed his journal with the singularly appropriate words, "All this is perfectly distinct to an observant eye, and yet could easily pass unnoticed by most."[5] Later in the month George

2. Edward Emerson, *Henry Thoreau as Remembered by a Young Friend*, 147
3. Simon Brown, Journal for July 14, 1861. Transcript courtesy Laurence E. Richardson
4. Cameron, "Thoreau and Emerson in Channing's Letters to the Watsons," 79
5. Thoreau, *Journal*, XIV, 346

William Curtis, now an editor of *Harper's Monthly,* dropped in for a visit in Concord. He was in Emerson's library when Thoreau came in to borrow a volume of Pliny's letters. Curtis noticed that Thoreau was "much wasted" and "his doom . . . clear." But he thought he "talked in the old strain of wise gravity without either sentiment or sadness"[6] and maintained "the same habitual erect posture, which made it seem impossible that he could ever lounge or slouch."[7]

Thoreau continued to fail rapidly. An old friend of the family, dropping in for a visit, noticed that "by evening a flush had come to his cheeks and an ominous brightness and beauty to his eyes, painful to behold. His conversation was unusually brilliant, and we listened with a charmed attention which perhaps stimulated him to continue talking until the weak voice could no longer articulate."[8] Sanborn and Alcott had dinner with him on December 2 and found him "lively and entertaining, though feeble and failing."[9] Later Thomas Wentworth Higginson came for a visit and they talked at length about birds, Thoreau pointing out that, while red-tailed hawks were common in Concord, they were unknown at the seashore twenty miles away and that white-throated sparrows, rare in Concord, were common in Ashburnham, thirty miles to the west. Higginson had been doing a series of nature essays for the *Atlantic.* In September, in "My Out-door Study," he had singled out Thoreau for praise, saying that before *Walden* "absolutely nothing in Nature had ever yet been described."[1] When he learned later that Thoreau had particularly liked his essay on "Snow" in the January 1862 issue, he replied that he thought him "the only critic whom I should regard as really formidable on such a subject."[2]

The death of George Minott in December was a blow to Thoreau. With the cold weather his cough increased. In mid-December he had an attack of pleurisy which confined him to

---

6. George William Curtis, "The Editor's Easy Chair," *Harper's Monthly,* XXV (1862), 271

7. Ibid. XXXVIII (1869), 415

8. *Outlook,* "Reminiscences of Thoreau," LXIII (1899), 920

9. Alcott, *Journals,* 341

1. T. W. Higginson, "My Out-door Study," *Atlantic Monthly,* VIII (1861), 305

2. T. W. Higginson, *Letters and Journals* (Boston, 1921), 114

the house, though his sister wrote Ricketson on the 19th, "His spirits do not fail him, he continues in his usual serene mood, which is very pleasant for his friends as well as himself."[3]

When Bronson Alcott called on New Year's Day, 1862, bringing cider and apples, he found Thoreau failing and feeble, but talkative and "interested in books and men." They discussed Pliny, Evelyn, and the rural authors. When Alcott mentioned the war, Thoreau spoke impatiently of the temporizing policy of the government and blamed the people too for their indifference to the true issues of national honor and justice. But despite Thoreau's brave talk, Alcott thought it obvious that his days were numbered.

A week later Daniel Ricketson wrote to invite Thoreau to visit him again in New Bedford. But Alcott at Sophia Thoreau's request, replied:

> He grows feebler day by day, and is evidently failing and fading from our sight. He gets some sleep, has a pretty good appetite, reads at intervals, takes notes of his readings, and likes to see his friends, conversing, however, with difficulty, as his voice partakes of his general debility.[4]

His old Worcester friends, H. G. O. Blake and Theo Brown, skated down the river from Framingham to visit him in mid-January—a journey they repeated several times in the succeeding months. Brown said of the visit:

> We found him pretty low, but well enough to be up in his chair. He seemed glad to see us; said we had not come much too soon. . . . There was a beautiful snowstorm going on the while which I fancy inspired him, and his talk was up to the best I ever heard from him,—the same depth of earnestness and the same infinite depth of fun going on at the same time.
>
> I wish I could recall some of the things he said. I do remember some few answers he made to questions from Blake. Blake asked him how the future seemed to him. "Just as uninteresting as ever," was his characteristic answer. A little while after he said, "You have been skating on this river; perhaps I am going to skate on some other." And again, "Perhaps I am going up country." . . .

3. Ricketson, *Daniel Ricketson and His Friends,* 135
4. Ibid., 188

He seemed to be in an exalted state of mind for a long time before his death. He said it was just as good to be sick as to be well,—just as good to have a poor time as a good time.[5]

Thoreau received a letter from Myron Benton, a young poet from Leedsville, New York, saying that news of his illness had affected him as if it were that of a personal friend whom he had known a long time. He said he had read and re-read Thoreau's books with ever fresh delight and asked what progress Thoreau had made on a work in "some way connected with natural history,"—which Emerson had mentioned in a short interview two years before in Poughkeepsie.

It was mid-March before Thoreau was able to answer Benton's letter, and dictating to his sister, he said:

> I have intended to answer before I died, however briefly. I am encouraged to know, that, so far as you are concerned, I have not written my books in vain. . . . You ask particularly after my health. I *suppose* that I have not many months to live; but, of course, I know nothing about it. I may add that I am enjoying existence as much as ever, and regret nothing.[6]

As ill as he was, Thoreau nonetheless continued his literary work. Early in February a request came from James T. Fields for him to submit some of his writings to the *Atlantic Monthly.* Ticknor & Fields, the publishers of *Walden,* had purchased the *Atlantic* in 1859 from Phillips, Sampson & Co. In June 1861 Fields had taken over its editorial direction. Since James Russell Lowell now no longer had any connection with the magazine, Thoreau was happy to accede, but, remembering his unpleasant experience with Lowell, he said, "Of course, I should expect that no sentiment or sentence be altered or omitted without my consent," and then carefully asked how much Fields would be willing to pay.[7]

Fields replied with the offer of a rate well above that for most contributors and Thoreau immediately started to work on his various manuscripts.[8] According to Channing he erased many of

---

5. Ibid. 214
6. Thoreau, *Correspondence,* 641
7. Ibid. 63
8. W. S. Tryon, *Parnassus Corner* (Boston, 1963), 264–5

the humorous lines, saying, "I cannot bear the levity I find."
On February 20 he submitted a manuscript based on his lecture
"Autumnal Tints." Fields accepted it and asked for another essay
more appropriate to the spring season. He also suggested that
he would be interested in bringing *Walden* back into print. Thoreau
immediately replied that he would soon send along another essay
and that not only would he be very happy to see *Walden* back
in print, but he had 146 bound copies and 450 unbound copies of
A Week in his attic—an obvious hint to Fields that he would like
to see the earlier book republished too.

On February 28 Thoreau submitted an essay which he had
entitled "The Higher Law." It was derived from his old "What
Shall It Profit?" lecture. After paying Thoreau one hundred
dollars for the essay, Fields, perhaps fearing that it might be confused with the chapter entitled "Higher Laws" in *Walden,* complained that he did not like the title. They soon agreed on a new
title—"Life without Principle"—but the essay was not published
in the *Atlantic* until October 1863. They also agreed to the re-
printing of *Walden* in a new edition of 250 copies (actually 280
were printed just a few weeks after Thoreau's death) and Thoreau's
request that the subtitle "or Life in the Woods" be dropped was
followed.

On March 11 Thoreau returned the proofs of "Autumnal
Tints" (it was published in the October 1862 *Atlantic*) and submitted his essay on "Walking." It was immediately accepted and
published in the June 1862 *Atlantic.* On April 2 he submitted
"Wild Apples," which also was accepted and was published in
November 1862, and asked Fields if he had come to any decision
about republishing *A Week.* On the 12th Fields came to Concord
and purchased all the unsold copies—bound and unbound—and
two months later reissued them with a new title page as a second
edition.

At Fields' request, Bronson Alcott wrote out a tribute to
Thoreau and it was published in the April *Atlantic* as "The
Forester." It said in part:

> I had never thought of knowing a man so thoroughly of the
> country as this friend of mine, and so purely a son of nature. . . .

9. Channing, *Thoreau, the Poet-Naturalist,* 34

He has come nearer the antique spirit than any of our native poets, and touched the fields and groves and streams of his native town with a classic interest that shall not fade. . . . One shall not meet with thoughts invigorating like his often: coming so scented of mountain and field breezes and rippling springs, so like a luxuriant clod from under forest-leaves, moist and mossy with earth-spirits. . . .

He seems one with things, of Nature's essence and core, knit of strong timbers, most like a wood and its inhabitants. . . .

I know of nothing more creditable to his greatness than the thoughtful regard, approaching to reverence, by which he has held for many years some of the best persons of his time, living at a distance, and wont to make their annual pilgrimage, usually on foot, to the master,—a devotion very rare in these times of personal indifference, if not of confessed unbelief in persons and ideas.[1]

Although Thoreau was not mentioned directly by name in the essay, the many references to Walden Pond and to a book on the rivers made its subject perfectly obvious to his friends and acquaintances. A contemporary newspaper commented:

"The Forrester" [sic] is a touching, interpretative and beautiful tribute to the genius of Henry D. Thoreau, of Concord,—a man now failing, we fear, under the insidious disease peculiar to New England, but whose works prove him to be the subtlest of all observers of New England scenery. Few men have ever observed nature so exactly, ever entered so thoroughly into the interior life which her outward form partly expresses and partly conceals to ordinary minds, as this brave and poetic naturalist; and the lyric extravagance which marks some of the phrases of the poet-philosopher who here celebrates his virtues will be as readily pardoned by criticism as they are excusable on the ground of friendship and sympathy.[2]

Daniel Ricketson, reminded of Thoreau by the appearance of the "Forester" and the announcement of the forthcoming republication of *Walden*, started a weekly series of letters to Thoreau reporting the progress of the spring. On March 23 he wrote of

1. [Bronson Alcott], "The Forester," *Atlantic Monthly*, IX (1862), 443–5
2. Unidentified clipping in the collection of George L. Davenport, Jr.

the arrival of the robin, bluebird, song sparrow, and cowbird, and on the 30th, the coming of the purple finch and some of the warblers.

On April 6 Sophia Thoreau replied to Ricketson, reporting of her brother:

> Now the embodiment of weakness; still, he enjoys seeing his friends, and every bright hour he devotes to his manuscripts which he is preparing for publication. For many weeks he has spoken only in a faint whisper. Henry accepts this dispensation with such childlike trust and is so happy that I feel as if he were being translated rather than dying in the ordinary way of most mortals.[3]

On the 13th, Ricketson wrote:

> Truly you have not lived in vain—your works, and above all, your brave and truthful life, will become a precious treasure to those whose happiness it has been to have known you, and who will continue to uphold though with feebler hands the fresh and instructive philosophy you have taught them.[4]

Thoreau, though, was disturbed that Ricketson did not come to Concord to see him. When he learned that it was because Ricketson feared his "own ability to endure the strain of his nerves at seeing Thoreau's then emaciated appearance, and the leave-taking that would follow," he whispered to his sister, "Now Ricketson ought to come and see me; it would do him good."[5]

But Thoreau's other friends and neighbors did not shy away. Emerson dropped in frequently to talk of chickadees, the behavior of the river, the ice on Walden Pond, and the arrival of the spring birds. On March 23 Sam Staples dropped in for a visit and later told Emerson that he had "never spent an hour with more satisfaction. Never saw a man dying with so much pleasure and peace." He thought Thoreau "serene and happy" and lamented that "very few men in Concord know Mr. Thoreau."[6]

Thoreau was pathetically interested in the world of nature

---

3. Ricketson, *Daniel Ricketson and His Friends*, 136–7
4. Thoreau, *Correspondence*, 649
5. *Truth Seeker*, "Memories of Thoreau," November 20, 1897
6. Ralph Waldo Emerson, *Journals*, IX, 405, 413, 415, 416

A photograph of Walden Pond in May

Handbill announcing
Thoreau's availability
as a surveyor

From the original in the
Berg Collection of the
New York Public Library

LAND SURVEYING

Of all kinds, according to the best methods known; the necessary data supplied, in order that the boundaries of Farms may be accurately described in Deeds: *Woods* lotted off distinctly and according to a regular plan: *Roads* laid out, &c., &c. Distinct and accurate Plans of Farms furnished, with the buildings thereon, of any size, and with a scale of feet attached, to accompany the Farm Book, so that the land may be laid out in a winter evening.

Areas warranted accurate within almost any degree of exactness, and the Variation of the Compass given, so that the lines can be run again.   Apply to

HENRY D. THOREAU.

Label for a box of
Thoreau pencils

THOREAU'S

IMPROVED

DRAWING PENCILS,

FOR THE NICEST USES OF THE

Drawing Master, Surveyor, Engineer, Architect,
and Artists generally.

GRADUATED FROM

1 to 4,

IN PROPORTION TO THEIR HARDNESS.

MANUFACTURED BY

JOHN THOREAU & Co.

CONCORD, MASS.

/passing him that spring. On a cold morning he tried vainly to
scrape the frost from the windowpane, saying with utter sadness,
as he failed, "I can not even *see* out-doors."[7] He often asked his
sister to throw open the doors to the adjacent room so that he
could admire her conservatory of potted plants. Learning that
young Edward Emerson was planning a trip to the Far West, he
urged him to find an Indian who could tell the secret of the making of stone arrowheads.[8] When he heard that some boys in the
neighborhood had been robbing birds' nests, he requested that
they be called into his sick room and asked them "if they knew
what a wail of sorrow and anguish their cruelty had sent all over
the fields and through the woods."[9]

But he did not lose his sense of humor. He told Sanborn that
whenever his corpulent, full-faced aunt came to his chamber door
to inquire about his welfare, he thought her to be "the rising full
moon."[1] When someone commented how little his hair had grayed,
even in his illness, he replied:

> I have never had any trouble in all my life, or only when I was
> about fourteen; then I felt pretty bad a little while on account
> of my sins, but no trouble since that I know of. That must be the
> reason why my hair doesn't turn gray faster. But there is Blake;
> he is as gray as a rat.[2]

When Grindall Reynolds called and found him still working on
his manuscripts, Thoreau looked up cheerfully and, with a twinkle
in his eye, whispered, "You know it's respectable to leave an
estate to one's friends."[3] In going over his writings he noted mis-
takes in his published books and asked Ellery Channing to have
an error in *A Week* corrected. As late as thirteen days before his
death, finding it difficult to rouse himself for work, he complained
that he could not see to correct his Allegash paper—the final

---

7. [Hannah Hudson], "Concord Books," *Harper's Monthly*, LI (1875),
31
8. Emerson, *Letters*, V, 279
9. *Truth Seeker*, "Memories of Thoreau"
1. C. T. Ramsey, "A Pilgrimage to the Haunts of Thoreau," *New
England Magazine*, L (1913), 435
2. *Truth Seeker*, "Memories of Thoreau"
3. Edward Emerson, *Henry Thoreau as Remembered by a Young
Friend*, 117

chapter in *The Maine Woods:* "It is in a knot I cannot untie."

He realized fully that the end was near. He told Channir that he could never feel warm again, that he had no wish to liv except for the sake of his mother and sister, and that, "It is bett« some things should end."[5] To Bronson Alcott he said, "I sha leave the world without regret."[6] And when Edmund Hosmer tol him of seeing a spring robin, Thoreau replied, "Yes! This is beautiful world; but I shall see a fairer."[7]

He was greatly moved by the attentions of his friends an neighbors. He came to feel very differently toward people an« said if he had known he wouldn't have been so offish. He had go into his head before that people didn't mean what they said.[8]

His sister Sophia reported:

The devotion of his friends was most rare and touching; his room was made fragrant by the gift of flowers from young and old; fruit of every kind which the season afforded, and game of all sorts was sent him. It was really pathetic, the way in which the town was moved to minister to his comfort. Total strangers sent grateful messages, remembering the good he had done them. All this attention was fully appreciated and very gratifying to Henry; he would sometimes say, "I should be ashamed to stay in this world after so much had been done for me, I could never repay my friends."[9]

Remembering how much he had enjoyed their music box when they had first moved to Concord twenty years before, the Haw-thornes brought it to his sickroom. Mrs. Alcott sent over some spearmint from her garden to be used as a tonic, saying in a note to Mrs. Thoreau, "I wish I had some delicacy for the dear patient —but we have none of those things usually so grateful and ap-petising to the sick."[1]

When he learned that some of the boys of the neighborhood

4. Sanborn, *The Personality of Thoreau,* 70
5. Sanborn, *Henry D. Thoreau,* 180
6. Ibid. 307
7. Emily Lyman, *Thoreau* (Concord, 1902)
8. Harding, *Thoreau, Man of Concord,* 188
9. Ricketson, *Daniel Ricketson and His Friends,* 142–3
1. Walter Harding, "Mrs. Alcott Writes Mrs. Thoreau a Letter," *Thoreau Society Bulletin,* LXIX (1959), 1

ad brought him some game to eat, he asked, "Why did you not
vite them in? I want to thank them for so much that they are
ringing me," and added, "Well I declare; I don't believe they are
oing to let me go after all."[2]

A neighboring child has remembered:

> In his last illness it did not occur to us that he would care
> to see us, but his sister told my mother that he watched us from
> the window as we passed, and said: "Why don't they come to
> see me? I love them as if they were my own." After that we went
> often, and he always made us so welcome that we liked to go. I
> remember our last meetings with as much pleasure as the old
> play-days.[3]

When he heard a wandering street singer playing some old tune
of his childhood on a hand organ in the streets outside, tears came
to his eyes and he said, "Give him some money! give him some
money!"[4]

As long as he could possibly sit up, he insisted on his chair
at the family table, and said, "It would not be social to take my
meals alone."[5] When he could no longer negotiate the stairs even
with assistance, he requested that the little cane bed he had used
at Walden be brought down and placed in the front parlor.

> "This room did not seem like a sick-room," said his mother.
> "My son wanted flowers and pictures and books all around here;
> and he was always so cheerful and wished others to be so while
> about him."[6]

Sleeplessness often bothered him. He wished his bed were in
the form of a shell so that he might curl up in it. At night he asked
that the lamp be set on the floor and the furniture arranged so
that he could amuse himself watching the fantastic shadows.[7] He

---

2. *Truth Seeker,* "Memories of Thoreau"
3. Sanborn, *Henry D. Thoreau,* 273
4. Channing, *Thoreau, the Poet-Naturalist,* 323
5. Ibid.
6. Samuel A. Jones, *Some Unpublished Letters of Henry D. and Sophia
E. Thoreau* (Jamaica, N. Y., 1899) 75
7. Ibid.

refused opiates, telling Channing that "he preferred to endure wit
a clear mind the worst penalties of suffering, rather than be plunge
in a turbid dream of narcotics." When he did sleep, he wa
troubled with strange dreams. "Sleep seemed to hang round m
bed in festoons," he told Channing, and he reported a pitifu
dream he had "of being a railroad cut, where they were diggin
through and laying down the rails"—the place being in his lungs.

Nevertheless he kept up his good spirts. He told Alcott h
° would leave the world without regret, and Sophia said:

> Henry was never affected, never reached by [his illness]. I
> never before saw such a manifestation of the power of spirit over
> matter. Very often I have heard him tell his visitors that he
> enjoyed existence as well as ever. He remarked to me that there
> was as much comfort in perfect disease as in perfect health, the
> mind always conforming to the condition of the body. The
> thought of death, he said, could not begin to trouble him. His
> thoughts had entertained him all his life and did still. . . .
>
> During his long illness I never heard a murmur escape him, or
> the slightest wish expressed to remain with us; his perfect content-
> ment was truly wonderful. None of his friends seemed to realize
> how very ill he was, so full of life and good cheer did he seem.
> One friend, as if by way of consolation, said to him, "Well, Mr.
> Thoreau, we must all go." Henry replied, "When I was a very
> little boy I learned that I must die, and I set that down, so of
> course I am not disappointed now. Death is as near to you as
> it is to me."[9]

Some of his more orthodox friends and relatives tried to prepare him for death, but with little satisfaction to themselves. When
an old friend of the family asked "how he stood affected toward
Christ," he replied that "a snow-storm was more to him than
Christ."[1] When his Aunt Louisa asked him if he had made his
peace with God, he answered, "I did not know we had ever
quarrelled, Aunt."[2] Just a few days before the end, Parker Pillsbury
visited the sickroom:

8. Channing, *Thoreau, the Poet-Naturalist*, 319, 320, 322
9. Ricketson, *Daniel Ricketson and His Friends*, 141–2
1. John Weiss, "Thoreau," *Christian Examiner*, LXXIX (1865), 112
2. Edward Emerson, *Henry Thoreau as Remembered by a Young Friend*, 118

He was very weak and low; he saw but very few more setting suns. He sat pillowed in an easy chair. Behind him stood his patient, dear, devoted mother, with her fan in one hand, and phial of amonia or cologne in the other, to sustain him in the warm morning. At a table near him, piled with his papers and other articles related to them and to him, sat his sister, arranging them, as I understood, for Ticknor and Fields, who had been to Concord and bought the copyright.

When I entered Thoreau was looking deathly weak and pale. I saw my way but for the fewest words. I said, as I took his hand, "I suppose this is the best you can do now." He smiled and only nodded, and gasped a faint assent. "The outworks," I said, "seem almost ready to give way." Then a smile shone on his pale face, and with an effort he said, "Yes,—but as long as she cracks she holds" (a common saying of boys skating).

Then I spoke only once more to him, and cannot remember my exact words. But I think my question was substantially this: "You seem so near the brink of the dark river, that I almost wonder how the opposite shore may appear to you." Then he answered, "One world at a time."[3]

On May 4, Alcott and Channing came to call. Alcott came away certain that Thoreau had "not many days of his mortality to give us."[4] On the 5th they returned and found that he was very weak but suffered nothing and talked in his old pleasant way. He said it took Nature a long time to do her work but he was most out of the world.[5] As they left, Alcott stooped over and kissed him. "It was affecting," said Channing, "to see this venerable man kissing his brow, when the damps and sweat of death lay upon it, even if Henry knew it not. It seemed to me an extreme unction, in which a friend was the best priest."[6]

That evening Thoreau received a last letter from Daniel Ricketson, which his sister read to him. Ironically it said: "I hope this will find you *mending,* and as I hear nothing to the contrary, I trust that it may be so that you are."[7] A "Mr. B——" had volunteered to sit up the night with him, but Henry wanted his

3. Sanborn, *The Personality of Thoreau,* 68–9
4. Alcott, *Journals,* 346
5. Walter Harding, "Thoreau's Feminine Foe," *PMLA,* LXIX (1954), 115
6. Sanborn, *The Personality of Thoreau,* 67
7. Ricketson, *Daniel Ricketson and His Friends,* 143

old friend Edmund Hosmer and he was sent for. In the mornin
when Hosmer was ready to leave, Thoreau called his sister an
asked her to give him a copy of one of his books.[8]

At seven o'clock he became restless and asked to be move
Judge Rockwood Hoar arrived with a bouquet of hyacinths fro
his garden. Thoreau smelled them and said he liked them. H
self-possession did not forsake him. A little after eight he asked
be raised up. The last few weeks of his life he had been workin
over his Maine Woods papers and his thoughts continued on h
writing to the end. The last sentence he spoke contained but tw
distinct words: "Moose" and "Indian."[9] As his mother, his siste
and his Aunt Louisa watched, his breathing grew fainter and fainte
and without the slightest struggle, he died at nine o'clock, May
Sophia said, "I feel as if something very beautiful had happened–
not death."[1]

Word of his passing soon spread around the village. Elle
Channing said: "Just half the world died for me when I lost M
Thoreau. None of it looks the same as when I looked at it wit
him."[2] Even Daniel Shattuck, the president of the Concord ban
a man who has been described by one who knew him as "positive
antipodal to Thoreau," wrote a friend:

> Mr. Thoreau was a man who never conformed his opinions after
> the model of others; they were his own; were also singular. Who
> will say they were not right? He had many admirers, and well he
> might for, whatever might be the truth of his opinions, his life
> was one of singular purity and kindness.[3]

Plans were immediately started for the funeral. Emerson in
sisted that it be held in the First Parish Church, though many c
his friends protested that he would have felt such a service in
appropriate after his "signing-off" from the church as a youn
man.[4]

---

8. Brown, *Memories of Concord,* 105–6
9. Channing, *Thoreau, the Poet-Naturalist,* 319
1. Marble, *Thoreau: His Home, Friends and Books,* 180
2. Sanborn, *Recollections of Seventy Years,* II, 368
3. Clipping pasted into Bronson Alcott, Journals. MS, Houghton Library
4. Harding, "Thoreau's Feminine Foe," 115

Alcott planned the service, patterning the arrangements on those Thoreau himself had made for the John Brown memorial service in Concord three years before. When Alcott called at the home to talk over the plans, Sophia "showed him Thoreau's face." He thought he looked as he had last seen him, but of "a tinge of paler hue."[5]

The service was held at three on the afternoon of May 9. Alcott instructed his teachers to dismiss all the children from the schools, and many of them attended the funeral. The church was filled. As Louisa May Alcott ironically pointed out to her friend Alfred Whitman, "Though he wasn't made much of while living, he was honored at his death."[6] Hawthorne and his family were there, as were the faithful Blake and Brown from Worcester, James T. Fields and his wife, and Bronson Alcott and his daughters Anna and Louisa May, among others. Daniel Ricketson, too appalled with grief, did not attend.

The casket was in the church vestibule covered with wild flowers. Inside the coffin was a wreath of andromeda—"his favorite flower"—and three mottoes gathered and inscribed by Ellery Channing.

As the bell tolled his forty-four years, the mourners walked in procession to the church. The service opened with selections from the Bible read by the Rev. Grindall Reynolds, minister of the church. A hymn written by Channing and printed for the occasion was sung "plaintively" by the choir. Emerson read an extensive eulogy ending:

> The scale on which his studies proceeded was so large as to require longevity, and we were the less prepared for his sudden disappearance. The country knows not yet, or in the least part, how great a son it has lost. It seems an injury that he should leave in the midst his broken task, which none else can finish,—a kind of indignity to so noble a soul, that it should depart out of Nature before yet he has been really shown to his peers for what he is. But he, at least, is content. His soul was made for the noblest society; he had in a short life exhausted the capabilities

---

5. Alcott, *Journals*, 347
6. E. B. Schlesinger, "The Alcotts Through Thirty Years," *Harvard Library Bulletin*, XI (1957), 375

of this world; wherever there is knowledge, wherever there is virtue, wherever there is beauty, he will find a home.[7]

Alcott read some passages from Thoreau's writings and the servic closed with a prayer by the Reverend Mr. Reynolds.

A new procession was formed to follow the coffin as it w carried by six of his fellow townsmen to the grave. More tha three hundred of the town's four hundred school children walke in that procession.[8]

He was buried in the New Burying Ground, at the foot Bedford Street. As Emerson turned away from the newly fill grave, he murmured, "He had a beautiful soul, he had a beautif soul."[9]

Louisa May Alcott afterwards wrote to Sophia Ford (who many years before had proposed marriage to him):

It seemed as if Nature wore her most benignant aspect to welcome her dutiful & loving son to his long sleep in her arms. As we entered the church yard birds were singing, early violets blooming in the grass & the pines singing their softest lullaby, & there between his father & his brother we left him, feeling that though his life seemed too short, it would blossom & bear fruit for us long after he was gone, & that perhaps we should know a closer relationship now than even while he lived.[1]

---

7. Ralph Waldo Emerson, "Thoreau," *Atlantic Monthly*, IX, (1862), 239–40, 249
8. Elbert Hubbard, *Thoreau* (East Aurora, N. Y., 1904), 188
9. Unidentified clipping in author's collection
1. Alcott, *A Sprig of Andromeda*, 9–10

EPILOGUE

ᶠOR ONE who is thought to have been little recognized in life, Thoreau received wide notice at death. Obituaries appeared in the Concord Monitor, the Boston Advertiser, the Boston Transcript, the New York Tribune, the Liberator, the New Bedford Standard, the Banner of Light, the Atlantic Monthly, the Christian Register, the Harper's Monthly, the Harvard Magazine, the National Almanac, and the Annual of Scientific Discovery. Walden and A Week were both brought back into print within a few weeks. "Walking" was the lead article in the June Atlantic Monthly and was followed by "Autumnal Tints" in October, "Wild Apples" in November, "Life without Principle" in October 1863, "Night and Moonlight" in November, "The Wellfleet Oysterman" in October 1864, and "The Highland Light" in December. In 1863 a collection of his travel essays was published under the title Excursions in Field and Forest; in 1864, The Maine Woods; in 1865, Cape Cod and Letters to Various Persons; and in 1866, A Yankee in Canada, with Anti-slavery and Reform Papers.

Sophia Thoreau and her mother were flooded with letters of consolation, many of them from complete strangers. So many asked for his picture that they finally arranged for I. E. Tilton, a Boston photographer, to sell copies of the Rowse crayon portrait for twenty-five cents each. Admirers began to make pilgrimages to Concord as to a shrine and often called on his mother and sister to speak of their devotion.

The rest of the story of his slow climb to posthumous fame and recognition has often been told elsewhere; it need not be reiterated here. But it was not until nearly a century after his death that he finally achieved his present rank as one of the greatest American authors.

[469]

A Bibliographical Note

he standard edition of Thoreau's *Writings* is the Walden or Manuscript Edition, twenty volumes including fourteen volumes of the
Journal (Boston: Houghton Mifflin; 1906). The *Journal* has recently
een reprinted separately (New York: Dover; 1963). The *Collected
Poems* have been edited by Carl Bode (Baltimore: Johns Hopkins;
1964); the *Correspondence*, by Walter Harding and Carl Bode (New
York: New York University Press; 1958); and the "lost volume" of
the journal, *Consciousness in Concord*, by Perry Miller (Boston:
Houghton Mifflin; 1958).

Among the more important critical studies of Thoreau are *Passage
to Walden*, by Reginald L. Cook (Boston: Houghton Mifflin; 1949);
Thoreau: A Century of Criticism, edited by Walter Harding (Dallas:
Southern Methodist University Press; 1954); *Henry David Thoreau*, by
Joseph Wood Krutch (New York: Sloane; 1948); *The Shores of
America*, by Sherman Paul (Urbana: University of Illinois Press;
1958); *The Making of Walden*, by James Lyndon Shanley (Chicago:
University of Chicago Press; 1957); *After Walden*, by Leo Stoller
(Stanford: Stanford University Press; 1957); and *Thoreau: the Quest
and the Classics*, by Ethel Seybold (New Haven: Yale University Press;
1951). Thoreau scholarship is summarized and evaluated in *A Thoreau
Handbook*, by Walter Harding (New York: New York University
Press; 1959).

The major collections of Thoreau's manuscripts are to be found
in the Pierpont Morgan Library and the Berg Collection of the New
York Public Library in New York City; the Huntington Library in
San Marino, California; the Houghton Library of Harvard University
in Cambridge; the Abernethy Library of Middlebury College in Middlebury, Vermont; and the Barrett Collection in the Alderman Library
of the University of Virginia at Charlottesville. Notable collections of
Thoreau memorabilia are to be found in the Free Public Library and
the Antiquarian Society in Concord, Massachusetts.

The early years of scholarship on Thoreau are covered in *A Bib-

liography of Henry David Thoreau, by Francis H. Allen (Bostor Houghton Mifflin; 1908); "A Contribution to a Bibliography from 190 to 1936 of Henry David Thoreau," by J. S. Wade (*Journal of the Ne York Entomological Society,* XLVII, 1939, 163–203); *A Henry Davi Thoreau Bibliography 1908–1937,* by William White (Boston: Faxo 1939); and "Contribution to a Bibliography of Thoreau, 1938–1945 by Philip E. Burnham and Carvel Collins (*Bulletin of Bibliograph* XIX, 1946, 16–18, 37–40). Since 1941 the quarterly *Thoreau Socie Bulletin* (Geneseo, New York) has had a running bibliography in ea issue.

Afterword to the 1992 Edition

t has been more than a quarter of a century since *The Days of Henry Thoreau* was first published (New York, 1965). In the intervening years interest in Thoreau has continued to grow and his spirit seems more alive now than it did then. Much new work has been accomplished in the field of Thoreau scholarship.

Unquestionably the most important has been and is the ongoing publication of the Princeton University Press edition of *The Writings of Henry D. Thoreau* (1971–), with new volumes appearing regularly and with an eventual goal of more than twenty-five volumes. Scholars and enthusiasts are now for the first time gaining access to accurate texts of Thoreau's writings edited according to modern standards. But even more important, we are now seeing for the first time a complete edition of his *Journal*, including many, many pages that either Thoreau himself or his various editors had deleted and which are now being restored, and which help greatly to fill out the picture of their author. The additions to the first three volumes of the new edition already published nearly double the text for that period and give us many new insights into his techniques as a writer as well as into his personality. They whet our interest in anticipation of the still forthcoming volumes. It is a continuing feast.

Since the original publication of *Days* new biographical studies of Thoreau have appeared which should be called to your attention. First is Richard Lebeaux's two-volume *Young Man Thoreau* (Amherst, 1977) and *Thoreau's Seasons* (Amherst, 1984), a psychological study in the tradition of Erik Erikson. Although I feel that Thoreau does not always fit comfortably into Eriksonian analysis, Lebeaux's work has been diligent, imaginative, and enlightening. He has some very thoughtful and perceptive things to say.

A second biography is Robert Richardson's *Henry Thoreau: A Life of the Mind* (Berkeley, 1986), a study of Thoreau's adult intellectual life, a beautifully written book that is a joy to read. I emerged from reading it with a far deeper understanding of Thoreau's place in the intellectual currents of his day. (One should also note Robert Sattelmeyer's superb *Thoreau's Reading: A Study in Intellectual History with Bibliographical Catalogue*, Princeton, 1988, a comprehensive listing of all of Thoreau's

[473]

known reading.) Raymond Borst's *A Thoreau Log* (New York 1992) offers the first comprehensive checklist of Thoreau's daily activities throughout his life, and so is a particularly useful reference work. While there have been many other volumes on Thoreau published in recent years, they, unlike the above, are chiefly devoted to literary criticism rather than biographical study, so I shall make no attempt to discuss or evaluate them here.

Many scholarly articles on different facets of Thoreau's life have appeared in the past twenty-five years, far too many to even try to enumerate here. (They are all catalogued in the "Additions to the Thoreau Bibliography" which has appeared regularly in the quarterly *Thoreau Society Bulletin* for more than fifty years now. These add many new details to our knowledge of Thoreau's life, though *in toto* they change the picture surprisingly little. For the most part they serve to confirm and enlarge what was already known. I do however want to single out particularly the outstanding work of Bradley Dean and Gary Scharnhorst in their several publications in bringing to light much new detailed information culled from nineteenth-century newspapers and records both on Thoreau's lecturing career and the reviewing of the first edition of *Walden*. Their ferreting out of these details has been most remarkable. Robert Sattelmeyer's "Thoreau's Projected Work on the English Poets" (*Studies in the American Renaissance* [1980]: 239–58) brings to light a facet of Thoreau's early studies that I had completely overlooked, I am sorry to say. I would also like to cite Thomas Woodson's "Thoreau's Excursion to the Berkshires and Catskills" (*ESQ* 21 (1975): 82–87) as a model of scholarship in which he recovers many lost details of that almost forgotten trip.

Michael Meyer has been equally successful in bringing up new information in his several articles on Thoreau's defense of John Brown. I would like to disagree, however, with one suggestion he makes. In his "Thoreau's Rescue of John Brown from History" (*Studies in the American Renaissance* [1980]: 301–16) he points out convincingly that Thoreau was eventually unquestionably aware of the charges that Brown had murdered five men in cold blood in the so-called Pottawatomie massacre in Kansas and wonders how Thoreau then could continue to endorse Brown as an heroic and even Christ-like figure. Meyer, it seems to me, overlooks the fact that while Thoreau did know of these charges, did not believe them and dismissed them as the propaganda of slave owners trying to destroy Brown's reputation. Nor was Thoreau alone in this disbelief. Rightly or wrongly Brown remained a hero for Thoreau and many of his abolitionist friends.

One may very well ask if all the records about Thoreau hidden in attics, on library shelves, and in historical society archives have after all these years been at last ferreted out. I am certain they have not. New materials keep turning up, often in the most unexpected places, and I am certain they will continue to do so for years to come. I therefore urge all students of Thoreau to continue the search for more information that will add to our knowledge of this challenging and enigmatic man.

I would now like to confess to a major lacuna in *The Days of Henry Thoreau*—a gap which was of my own creation and done quite wittingly. That is a discussion of Thoreau's sexuality. One reviewer of the first edition of *Days* quite rightfully pointed out when the book first appeared that it was written as though Sigmund Freud had never lived. I had done this quite deliberately. *The Days* was written before the gay revolution of the late 1960s. It was a time when to state that a person was homosexual was accusatory, even libelous. A man could be destroyed by being so labeled. To state *then* that Thoreau had homoerotic inclinations would have turned many people against him. That that was so is proven, I think, by the fact that when as late as 1978 I stated in a paper read at a scholarly conference that there were homoerotic overtones through much of Thoreau's writing, another scholar immediately jumped up and shouted that I had "destroyed" both Thoreau and my own reputation by making such a statement. Thus, while writing *Days* and talking the situation over with many of my friends among Thoreau scholars, I thought it best to play down any commentary on his sexuality. I did not, though, play it down completely. There is a least one direct reference to it, but it is admittedly a gingerly one. Whether I did rightly or wrongly then, I am not trying to justify my actions here.

Fortunately the situation has changed almost completely in recent years. When I was asked recently to write the Thoreau entry for the forthcoming *American National Biography*, I was instructed, as were all other contributors, not to ignore any homosexuality on the part of the subject. We are now well aware of the fact that a thoughtful discussion of a person's sexuality, whether heterosexual or homosexual, can lead to a much fuller understanding of his or her motivations and accomplishments. I would like therefore to add to this text a brief summary of an article on "Thoreau's Sexuality" which I recently published in the *Journal of Homosexuality* (21 [1991]: 23–45), and refer the reader who wishes further discussion and documentation to that article.

Thoreau's attitude towards women was almost entirely negative and his pages are filled with denunciations and denigrations of them both as individuals and as a group. He thought "the society of young women . . . the most unprofitable that [he had] ever tried." Typical of those young men who wished to avoid marriage, he seemed interested by only those women who were patently unavailable—married women such as Lidian Emerson and Lucy Jackson Brown, or the elderly such as Mary Moody Emerson.

Ellen Sewall was a special case. Despite Perry Miller's ponderings to the contrary, there is solid evidence that Thoreau did propose to her. But virtually every single biographer of Thoreau who does discuss their "romance" makes note of the lack of any emotional depth on Thoreau's part. As Henry S. Canby has suggested, it was more of an experiment in the philosophy of love than true love, that Thoreau had come to feel that society expected him to marry like any "normal" young man, and so he wrote out his proposal. But note that he sent it by mail rather than presenting it in person and that he confided to his journal that he did not expect it to be accepted. He was undoubtedly relieved when it was turned down. Marriage was not for him. He never again showed the least interest in proposing marriage to anyone else. And when Sophia Ford proposed marriage to him, he reacted with atypical violence.

On the other hand, he did feel a deep need for love and companionship, a need he often expressed in the privacy of his journal. But it was invariably to members of his own male sex that he was attracted. It was something deep within him and all-compelling, something he was not at ease with, something he felt he must hide—not only from others, but even at times from himself.

He found young men particularly attractive and often com-

nented to that effect in his journal. What is astonishing is that on
several occasions he even compared specific individuals he saw to
well-known homosexuals of the classical past. There are also, as
further evidence, the "Lately, alas, I knew a gentle boy" poem
Thoreau wrote about Ellen Sewall's younger brother and the se-
cretive series of passages in his October, 1840, journal about his
love for an unnamed male.

There are many other clues: his penchant for wide reading in
homosexual literature, his recording of homoerotic dreams, his
use of homoerotic imagery in his writings, and his frequent
"Freudian slips." All of these I have documented in my article.

It should however be emphasized that while all these can be
indications of homoerotic *inclinations* on Thoreau's part, no one
has as yet, to my knowledge, found any concrete evidence on
Thoreau's part of homosexual *activity*. While it is of course impossible to prove that he was never homosexually active, it seems
highly unlikely that he could have engaged with any great frequency in such activity without some evidence of it turning up
over the years.

What pertinence does all this discussion have to a study of
Thoreau's life? His, it would seem, is an outstanding example of
Freud's theories of sublimation. Thoreau apparently diverted his
sexual energies to a love of nature, which became the dominating
interest of his life and resulted in the production of the more than
three million words of polished, professional, publishable prose
that made him one of the great masters of American literature.
Had he not redirected those energies, it is possible he might never
have become the literary master he was. It explains quite conclu-
sively why he never married—and as has often been pointed out,
a married Thoreau would have been a very different Thoreau. It
helps to explain why he went to Walden to live alone at just that
point in his life when most men are marrying and settling down to
raising a family. It may help to explain some of the sense of guilt
which haunts so many of his pages. It undoubtedly explains the
astounding frequency of comments on handsome young males in
his pages and conversely the paucity of comments on young ladies. I would also suggest that possibly some of Thoreau's lifelong radicalism, the completely different angle of vision with
which he viewed the world around him, and his perennial habit of

questioning all things, may have derived in part at least from hi
realization that he was different from others. Thoreau's sexualit
was of course by no means his only driving force, but, as with a
of us, it was an important factor in making him the man he was
It in no way diminishes his stature.

If you have been interested enough in Thoreau to read this biography of him, you might like to know of the existence of The
Thoreau Society, an "informal gathering of students and followers of Thoreau," now numbering more than fifteen-hundred members scattered both across the country and around the world, who
publish a quarterly bulletin of notes and articles about Thoreau
and who each year in July hold an annual meeting in Concord,
Massachusetts, to discuss Thoreau and to visit the Thoreau country. Membership is open to anyone interested. Simply write to me
at the State University College, Geneseo, New York 14454 or
write our office in Concord.

In closing I wish to thank the literally thousands of persons—
readers of earlier editions of this book, members of the Thoreau
Society, and other Thoreau enthusiasts—who have taken the time
to write me about our mutual interest. They have added much to
the joy of my life and to the accuracy of my books.

Geneseo, N.Y.
May 13, 1992

Notes Added to the
1982 Edition

following notes are keyed by page
ine number. Thus "13-26" means
he accompanying note glosses page
ine 26 of the text. An asterisk has

been placed in the margin next to each
line of the text for which a note has
been added to the 1982 edition.

CHAPTER I

bid., II, 81
.horeau, Journal, IX, 132
.B. Sanborn, The Life of Henry David Thoreau
ston: Houghton Mifflin, 1917), 5
.uth Robinson Wheeler, Our American Mile
ncord: Privately printed, 1957) 34
.horeau, Journal, X, 252
Ibid., 526
.rs. Caleb Wheeler, "Thoreau Farm," Thoreau
.iety Bulletin, XLII (1953), 2
Sanborn, The Life of Henry David Thoreau, 530
Thoreau, Journal, XI, 436
Sanborn, Henry D. Thoreau, 251
Concord Freeman, August 14, 1840
Samuel Arthur Jones, Thoreau: A Glimpse
ncord, 1903), 31
Thoreau, Journal, IX, 381
Edward Emerson, Notes on Thoreau; Kenneth
.lter Cameron, The Transcendentalists and
nerva (Hartford, 1958), II, 459-460
Ibid.
.-Mrs. Caleb Wheeler, "Thoreau Farm," 3
.6-Sanborn, The Life of Henry David Thoreau, 36
.9-Thoreau, Journal, VIII, 64
.9-Thoreau, Journal, VIII, 64
2-Thoreau, Journal, VIII, 65
7-Henry Seidel Canby, Thoreau (Boston, 1939), 32
.8-William Ellery Channing, Thoreau, The Poet
.aturalist (Boston, 1873), 250
31-Sarah Gertrude Pomeroy, Little-Known Sisters
f Well-Known Men (Boston, 1912), 256-257
21-Sanborn, The Life of Henry David Thoreau, 34
26-Thoreau, Journal, VIII, 65
31-Sanborn, The Life of Henry David Thoreau, 35

CHAPTER II

10-Social Circle in Concord, Memoirs (Boston,
.882-1940) II, 297-8
14-Ibid., 297-8
.31-Mrs. Caleb Wheeler, "The Thoreau Houses,"
Thoreau Society Bulletin XXXI (1950), 2
34-Social Circle in Concord, Memoirs, II, 298
2-Milton Meltzer and Walter Harding, A Thoreau
Profile (New York, 1962), 138
11-F.B. Sanborn, The Life of Henry David Thoreau
(Boston, 1917), 212; Hildegarde Hawthorne,
Concord's Happy Rebel (New York, 1940), 80
18-Edward Emerson, Henry Thoreau as Remembered
by a Young Friend (Boston, 1917), 134
7-30-Social Circle in Concord, Memoirs, V, 72
3-13-Moorfield Storey and Edward W. Emerson,
Ebenezer Rockwood Hoar: A Memoir (Boston, 1911),
23-24
8-16-Sanborn, The Life of Henry David Thoreau, 39
9-16-Joseph Hosmer, "Henry D. Thoreau," Concord
Freeman: Thoreau Annex, 1
.9-30-Thoreau, Writings, I, 222-224
.9-30-Thoreau, Writings, II, 200
21-14-Sanborn, The Life of Henry David Thoreau, 388
21-29-Henry Seidel Canby, Thoreau (Boston, 1939), 22
22-3-Sanborn, The Life of Henry David Thoreau, 46
23-25-Thoreau, Journal, VIII, 65
24-7-Townsend Scudder, Concord: American Town
(Boston, 1947), 150
24-19-Ibid., 21
25-20-Social Circle in Concord, Memoirs, II, 258-9
25-23-Kenneth Walter Cameron, "Historical Notes on
the Concord Academy," Emerson Society Quarterly,
XIX (1960), 49
26-19-Dorothy Nyren, "The Concord Academic Debating
Society," Massachusetts Review, IV (1962), 83

26-21 Yeoman's Gazette, September 8, 1827
26-31-Kenneth Walter Cameron, "Young Henry Thoreau
in the Annals of the Concord Academy," Emerson
Society Quarterly, IX (1957), 4-14
28-2-Ibid., 105

CHAPTER III

32-5-Henry Seidel Canby, Thoreau (Boston, 1939) 28
32-9-Edward Emerson, Henry Thoreau as Remembered by
a Young Friend (Boston, 1917), 125
32-12-F. B. Sanborn, Henry D. Thoreau (Boston, 1882)
51
32-20-Canby, Thoreau, 40
32-25-John Olin Eidson, Charles Stearns Wheeler:
Friend of Emerson (Athens, Ga., 1951), 7, 102
33-8-James Russell Lowell, Fireside Travels
(Boston, 1904), 15-16
34-8-Canby, Thoreau, 43
34-20-Christian P. Gruber, The Education of Henry
Thoreau, Harvard 1833-1837 (Princeton University,
1953, unpublished doctoral dissertation), 25
35-7-Edward Everett Hale, James Russell Lowell and
His Friends (Boston, 1899), 15-16
35-26-Wendell Glick, "Three New Early Manuscripts
by Thoreau," Huntington Library Quarterly, XV
(1951), 59
37-2-Cameron, "Chronology of Thoreau's Harvard
Years," 1-108
38-7-Kenneth Walter Cameron, Emerson the Essayist
(Raleigh, N. C., 1945), 191-208
38-33-Cameron, "The Solitary Thoreau of the Alumni
Notes," 2
39-2-Henry David Thoreau, Correspondence (New York,
1958), 175
41-20- Kenneth Walter Cameron, "Thoreau Discovers
Emerson," Bulletin of the New York Public Library,
LVII (1953), 328
41-29-Edwin I. Moser, Henry David Thoreau: The
College Essays (New York University, 1951), unpublished master's thesis), 7
43-36-Ibid., 352
43-38-F. B. Sanborn, Recollections of Seventy Years
(Boston, 1909), II, 319
44-6-McGill, "Thoreau and College Discipline," 349
44-24-Canby, Thoreau, 41
45-7-Thoreau, Correspondence, 8
45-10-Henry David Thoreau, Journal (Boston, 1906),
VIII, 66
45-31-Ralph Waldo Emerson, Journals (Boston, 1910),
VI, 297
46-1-Cameron, "Chronology of Thoreau's Harvard
Years," 16
46-21-Ibid.
47-3-Sanborn, Recollections of Seventy Years, II,
457
48-9-Ralph L. Rusk, The Life of Ralph Waldo Emerson
(New York, 1949), 274
48-13-Louis A. Surette, By-laws of Corinthian Lodge
(Concord, 1849), 274
48-18-Rusk, The Life of Ralph Waldo Emerson, 274
49-3-Hubert H. Hoeltje, "Thoreau in Concord Church
and Town Records," New England Quarterly, XII
(1939), 353
49-8-Henry David Thoreau, Writings (Boston, 1906),
VI, 58-59
49-19-Cameron, "The Solitary Thoreau of the Alumni
Notes," 22
50-22-Walter Harding, "Thoreau's Diploma," Thoreau
Society Booklets, V (1948), 1
50-34-Harding, "Thoreau's Diploma," 1
51-27-Edgeley W. Todd, "Philosophical Ideas at Harvard, 1817-1837," New England Quarterly, XVI
(1943), 88-89

CHAPTER IV

52-25-Townsend Scudder, Concord: American Town (Boston, 1947), 159
53-13-Annie Russell Marble, Thoreau: His Home, Friends and Books (New York, 1902), 78-79
53-31-Henry Williams, Memorials of the Class of 1837 of Harvard University (Boston, 1887), 83
55-33-Ibid., 19-20
56-17-Edward Emerson, Notes on Thoreau, MS
56-21-Edward Emerson, Henry Thoreau as Remembered by a Young Friend (Boston, 1917), 32
56-24-Ibid., 135
56-35-Ibid., 33
57-5-Hildegarde Hawthorne, Concord's Happy Rebel (New York, 1940), 80
57-11-Henry David Thoreau, Writings (Boston, 1906), II, 219
57-12-Ibid.; Edward Emerson, Notes on Thoreau
58-3-Thoreau, Correspondence, 24
58-6-Social Circle in Concord, Memoirs (Boston, 1882-1940), II, 330
58-20-Thoreau, Correspondence, 25-26
59-2-F. B. Sanborn, Henry D. Thoreau (Boston, 1882), 58
59-4-Mark Van Doren, Henry David Thoreau (Boston, 1916), 88-89
59-8-Thoreau, Journal, I, 47
59-16-Ibid., I, 48-49
60-18-Kenneth Walter Cameron, The Transcendentalists and Minerva (Hartford, 1958), I, 86
67-6-Abba May Alcott, Diary, MS, Houghton Library
67-10-Perry Miller, Consciousness in Concord (Boston, 1958), 154
67-12-Ralph Waldo Emerson, Letters (New York, 1939), II, 343-344
68-8-Thoreau, Correspondence, 32
71-4-Ralph Waldo Emerson, Letters, II, 324
71-30-Ibid., I, 1
72-10-Ibid., I, 36-37
72-12-Ibid., VIII, 66
72-28-Kenneth Walter Cameron, The Transcendental Climate (Hartford, 1963), III, 691
72-33-Walter Harding, "Thoreau and the Concord Lyceum," Thoreau Society Bulletin, XXX (1950), 3
72-35-Huffert, Thoreau as a Teacher, Lecturer and Educational Thinker, 483
73-2-Cameron, The Transcendental Climate, III, 695
73-5-Thoreau, Journal, I, 64
73-9-Henry David Thoreau, The First and Last Journeys, I, 117
73-19-Thoreau, Correspondence, 27
74-7-F. B. Sanborn, Recollections of Seventy Years (Boston, 1909), II, 378; Wendell Glick, "The Native Background of Thoreau's Early Radical Thought," Report to the American Literary Group (MLA), February 10, 1954
74-35-Canby, Thoreau, 109

CHAPTER V

76-8-Henry David Thoreau, Correspondence (New York, 1958), 656
76-28-Kenneth Walter Cameron, "Historical Notes on the Concord Academy," Emerson Society Quarterly, XIX (1960), 51
77-1-George Hoar, Autobiography of Seventy Years (New York, 1903), I, 70; Edward Emerson, Notes on Thoreau; Social Circle in Concord, Memoirs (Boston, 1882-1940), IV, 258
77-2-Henry David Thoreau, Writings (Boston, 1906), VI, 24
77-5-Clayton Hoagland, "The Diary of Thoreau's 'Gentle Boy,'" New England Quarterly, XXVIII (1955), 480
77-13-Edmund Sewall, Diary, MS, T. S. Abbott (Transcription by courtesy of Clayton Hoagland)
81-13-Thoreau, Writings, VI, 24; Mary Hosmer Brown, Memories of Concord (Boston, 1926), 90; Edward Emerson, Henry Thoreau as Remembered by a Young Friend, 128; Edward Emerson, Notes on Thoreau
82-12-Sanborn, The Life of Henry David Thoreau, 204
82-19-Ibid., 206-207
83-1-Perry Miller, Consciousness in Concord (Boston, 1958), 184
83-9-Sanborn, The Life of Henry David Thoreau, 209
86-12-Cameron, "Thoreau Bills His Pupils at the Concord Academy," 47-48

88-29-Thoreau, Writings, I, 12-13
89-9-Ibid., X, 59
89-12-Prudence Ward, Letter to Dennis Ward of 29, 1838, MS, Abernethy Library
89-26-Thoreau, Journal, XII, 298-299
90-37-Ibid., I, 118-119
91-21-Ibid., I, 179
92-5-Ibid., I, 322
92-7-Thoreau, Writings, I, 334-335
96-3-Ibid., I, 420

CHAPTER VI

97-14-Ibid.
98-13-Ibid.
99-1-Florence Becker Lennon, "The Voice of th Turtle," Thoreau Society Bulletin, XV (1946)
99-24-Davenport and Koopman, "Henry D. Thoreau 1839-1840"
100-13-Davenport and Koopman, "Henry D. Thoreau 1839-1840"
103-7-Raysor, "The Love Story of Thoreau 1839-1
103-34-Davenport and Koopman, "Henry D. Thoreau 1839-1840"
104-5-Walter Harding, Sophia Thoreau's Scrapboo (Geneseo, New York, 1964), B
104-27-Thoreau, Journal, IX, 146
105-4-Ralph L. Rusk, The Life of Ralph Waldo Em (New York, 1949), 216
105-7-Ibid., 220-221
107-9-Ralph Waldo Emerson, Letters (New York, 1 II, 116, 203; Henry Seidel Canby, Thoreau (Bo 1939), 467-468
107-21-Thoreau, Writings, VI, 329
108-24-Thoreau, Correspondence, 63

CHAPTER VII

114-1-Henry David Thoreau, Journal (Boston, 189 I, 117
114-3-Emerson, Letters, II, 259
114-5-Ibid., II, 280-1
114-7-Ibid., II, 293
114-10-Ibid., II, 317; Thomas Wentworth Higginso Margaret Fuller Ossoli (Boston, 1884), 155; Co An Historical and Biographical Introduction to Accompany the Dial, II, 187-188
114-20-Ibid., II, 315, 322
114-22-Ibid., II, 320
115-35-Norton, The Correspondence of Thomas Carly and Ralph Waldo Emerson, I, 366
116-8-Emerson, Letters, III, 47
116-28-Cooke, An Historical and Biographical Intr duction to Accompany the Dial, I, 96
116-33-Cooke, An Historical and Biographical Intre duction to Accompany the Dial, II, 188-189
117-22-Emerson, Letters, III, 106
118-3-Ibid., 90
118-6-Ibid., 89
118-21-Ibid., 102
118-23-Ibid., 107
118-24-Ibid., 118
119-7-Ibid., 145
119-13-Henry David Thoreau, The First and Last Journal (Boston, 1905), 142-146
119-14-Henry David Thoreau, Writings, (Boston, 1906), V, 176
119-16-Emerson, Letters, II, 320
119-19-Thoreau, Correspondence, 126-127, 138
119-21-Ibid., 133
119-23-F. B. Sanborn, Henry D. Thoreau (Boston, 1910), ix
119-27-Thoreau, Correspondence, 149
120-31-Ibid., 198-200
120-33-Ibid., 200
121-8-H. H. Furness, Records of a Lifelong Friend-ship (Boston, 1910), 33
122-10-Ibid., I, 176
122-12-Ibid., I, 201
122-14-Ibid., I, 214
122-27-F. B. Sanborn, Recollections of Seventy Year (Boston, 1909), II, 392
122-29-Thoreau, Journal, I, 211
122-30-Ibid., I, 241-244
123-10-Thoreau, Writings, II, 92
123-16-Annie Russell Marble, Thoreau: His Home, Friends and Books (New York, 1902), 115
123-18-Thoreau, Correspondence, 57
127-25-Thoreau, Writings, I, 324

30-Ibid., I, xxii-xxiii
33-Norton, The Correspondence of Thomas Carlyle
d Ralph Waldo Emerson, I, 335
2-Thoreau, Journal, I, 243
4-Emerson, Letters, II, 394
4-Edward Emerson, Notes on Emerson, MS,
ymond Emerson
3-Emerson, Journals, VI, 152-153
5-Emerson, Complete Works, IX, 454
6-Edward Emerson, Notes on Thoreau
11-Emerson, Letters, II, 436-437
13-Thoreau, Correspondence, 47
22-Thoreau, Correspondence, 54
35-Ibid., II, 433
1-Kenneth Walter Cameron, Ralph Waldo Emerson's
eading (Raleigh, 1941), 141
21-Emerson, Letters, II, 449
25-Margaret Bell, Margaret Fuller (New York,
930), 129
28-Emerson, Letters, II, 450
18-Emerson, Letters, III, 17
35-Thoreau, Writings, V, 133-152
13-Ibid., 74
16-Ibid., 74
26-Ibid., 48
22-Marble, Thoreau: His Home, Friends and
Books, 51
3-Edward Emerson, Henry Thoreau as Remembered
by a Young Friend, (Boston, 1917), 26
8-Emerson, Letters, III, 4
9-Thoreau, Correspondence, 66
10-Emerson, Letters, III, 47
15-Anna and Walton Ricketson, Daniel Ricketson
and His Friends (Boston, 1902), 14
29-Emerson, Letters, III, 8-9
35-Edward Emerson, Emerson in Concord (Boston,
1888), 128-129
7-9-Emerson, Letters, III, 53
9-12-F. B. Sanborn, "A Concord Note Book," Critic,
XLVII (1905), 267
10-24-Thoreau, Correspondence, 77
11-36-Thoreau, Correspondence, 142
2-4-Ibid., 147
42-22-Walter Harding, "A Check List of Thoreau's
Lectures," Bulletin of the New York Public
Library (LII (1948), 79
43-19-Ibid.

CHAPTER VIII

45-8-Henry David Thoreau, Correspondence (New York,
1958), 89
45-13-Emerson, Letters, III, 158-9
46-19-Ibid., III, 162-3
47-3-Ibid., 180
47-7-Henry David Thoreau, Journal (Boston, 1906, I,
317
47-10-Thoreau, Correspondence, 98, 106
47-25-Ibid.
47-28-Thoreau, Correspondence, 99
148-2-Thoreau, Correspondence, 114
148-12-Henry David Thoreau, Writings (Boston, 1906),
I, 190-191; Thoreau, Journal, XII, 111
148-14-Thoreau, Correspondence, 105
148-22-Thoreau, Writings, I, 253
148-34-Ibid., IV, 185-186
149-5-Ibid., 107
150-13-Ibid, 111
150-16-Ibid., 128
150-26-Ibid., 104, 142
150-34-Thoreau, Correspondence, 141
151-5-Kenneth Walter Cameron, "Annotations on Thoreau's Correspondence," Emerson Society Quarterly,
XXIV (1961), 37
151-14-Henry David Thoreau, The First and Last Journeys (Boston, 1905), I,76ff
151-31-Ibid., 139
151-34-Emerson, Letters, III, 124
152-1-Thoreau, Correspondence, 105, 107
154-27-Thoreau, Correspondence, 122
154-29-Ibid., 129
154-36-Thoreau, Correspondence, 106
155-23-Ibid., 142
155-26-Kenneth Walter Cameron, "Thoreau in the Papers

of Nathan Brooks and Abel Moore," Emerson Society
Quarterly, XIX (1960), 45; Edward Emerson, Notes
On Thoreau, MS, Raymond Emerson
155-30-Thoreau, Correspondence, 148, 149
155-33-Walter Harding, "A Check List of Thoreau's
Lectures," Bulletin of the New York Public Library, LII (1948), 79
155-36-Thoreau, The First and Last Journeys, I,
XXVIII
156-7-Thoreau, Correspondence, 151

CHAPTER IX

157-4-Sherman Paul, The Shores of America (Urbana,
1958), 181
157-24-Edward Emerson, Henry Thoreau as Remembered
by a Young Friend (Boston, 1917), 34
158-16-Edward Emerson, Notes on Thoreau, MS, Raymond
Emerson
159-23-Ralph Waldo Emerson, Letters (New York, 1939),
II, 267, 273
160-7-Henry David Thoreau, Journal (Boston, 1906),
II, 22
163-14-Henry David Thoreau, Correspondence (New York,
1958), 152
166-5-Ibid., 157-158
166-12-Ibid., 159
168-13-George F. Hoar, Autobiography of Seventy
Years (New York, 1903), I, 55
168-26-Emerson, Letters, III, 245
168-29-Edward Cary, George William Curtis (Boston,
1894), 29-30
169-13-George Willis Cooke, Early Letters of George
William Curtis to John S. Dwight (New York, 1898),
37
169-17-"Emerson's Club," May 19, 1859
169-30-Emerson, Letters, IV, 302
170-14-Ibid., III, 80
170-16-F. B. Sanborn, Hawthorne and His Friends
(Cedar Rapids, 1908), 21
170-20-F. B. Sanborn, Bronson Alcott at Alcott House
(Cedar Rapids, 1908), 35; Nathaniel Hawthorne, The
American Notebooks (New Haven, 1932), 175
170-26-Thoreau, Correspondence, 96-97
171-3-Townsend Scudder, Concord:American Town (Boston
1947), 179
171-8-Emerson, Letters, III, 247
171-11-Henry David Thoreau, The First and Last Journeys (Boston, 1905), I, 30
171-14-Thoreau, Journal, X, 474
171-21-Ibid., I, 213
171-30-Ibid., I, 193
172-3-Ibid., I, 196
172-16-William Ellery Channing, Thoreau, the Poet-
Naturalist (Boston, 1873), 26
172-19-Thoreau, Journal, I, 361
172-24-Channing, Thoreau, the Poet-Naturalist, 26
174-7-Milne, George William Curtis and the Genteel
Tradition, 25
174-23-Milne, George William Curtis and the Genteel
Tradition, 23; Ralph Waldo Emerson, Complete Works
(Boston, 1903), XI, 527
175-2-F. B. Sanborn, The Personality of Emerson
(Boston, 1903), 14
175-10-Emerson, Journals, IX, 507
175-19-Glick, "Thoreau and the 'Herald of Freedom,'"
201; Anna Alcott, Diary, MS, Houghton Library
176-5-Scudder, Concord: American Town, 202
176-18-Walter Harding, "Thoreau and the Concord
Lyceum," Thoreau Society Bulletin, XXX (1950), 2
176-23-Thoreau, Writings, IV, 311-314
176-32-Walter Harding, "A Check List of Thoreau's
Lectures," Bulletin of the New York Public Library,
LII (1948), 79
178-1-Sanborn, The Life of Henry David Thoreau, 328
178-4-(Hannah Hudson), "Concord Books," Harper's
Monthly, LI (1875), 32
178-8-Louis A. Surette, By-Laws of Corinthian Lodge
(Concord, 1859), 169
178-10-Sanborn, The Life of Henry David Thoreau, 328
178-17-Annie Russell Marble, Thoreau: His Home,
Friends and Books (New York, 1902), 265; Henry
Seidel Canby, Thoreau (Boston, 1939), 210
178-19-Thoreau, Journal, XIV, 99

CHAPTER X

181-10-Roland Robbins, Discovery at Walden (Stoneham, 1947), 9
181-21-George Willis Cooke, Early Letters of George William Curtis to John S. Dwight (New York, 1898), 81
183-4-Henry David Thoreau, Journal (Boston, 1906), I, 387
186-28-Walter Harding, "Our Thoreau Collectors," Thoreau Society Bulletin, XXXIX (1952) 4; Kenneth Walter Cameron, "Thoreau in the Papers of Nathan Brooks and Abel Moore," Emerson Society Quarterly, XIX (1960), 44-45
186-34-Leo Stoller, After Walden (Stanford, 1957), 74
187-11-Thoreau, Journal, I, 336
187-12-Walter Harding, "A Check List of Thoreau's Lectures," Bulletin of the New York Public Library, LII (1948), 80
187-16-Thoreau, Journal, I, 485
187-26-Harding, "A Check List of Thoreau's Lectures," 80
188-11-J. Lyndon Shanley, The Making of Walden (Chicago, 1957), 24, 27
188-21-Emerson, Letters, III, 338
188-23-Margaret Lothrop, The Wayside (New York, 1940) 63
189-23-Thoreau, The Variorum Walden, 312-313
191-2-Kenneth Walter Cameron, "Thoreau Witnesses Emerson Purchase Land at Walden," Emerson Society Quarterly, XI (1958), 15
191-24-Stoller, After Walden, 53
192-11-F. B. Sanborn, Henry D. Thoreau (Boston, 1882) 278
192-15-Bronson Alcott, Journals (Boston, 1938), 185, 175-176
195-6-Thoreau, Journal, I, 368-369
195-22-Thoreau, Correspondence, 179, 181, 183
197-24-Thoreau, Correspondence, 181
197-30-Emerson, Letters, III, 415

CHAPTER XI

202-21-John Broderick, "Thoreau, Alcott, and the Poll Tax," Studies in Philosophy, LIII (1956)
203-18-Thoreau, Writings, IV, 377-379
204-5-H. G. O. Blake, Letter to Alfred Hosmer of May 14, 1894, MS, Concord Free Public Library
204-5-Samuel Arthur Jones, Letter to Alfred Hosmer of May 8, 1894, MS, Concord Free Public Library
204-6-E. Rockwood Hoar, Letter to Alfred Hosmer of May 14, 1894, MS, Concord Free Public Library
204-6-Bronson Alcott, Journals (Boston, 1838), 239
204-6-Edward Emerson, Notes on Thoreau, MS
204-35-Walter Harding, Thoreau: Man of Concord (New York, 1960), 78
206-10-Ibid., IX, 413n
206-20-Anton Huffert, Thoreau as a Teacher, Lecturer and Educational Thinker (New York University, 1951, unpublished doctoral dissertation), 476
206-30-Henry David Thoreau, Correspondence (New York, 1958), 242
208-11-Thoreau, Writings, III, 3
211-3-Walter Harding, "A Check List of Thoreau's Lectures," Bulletin of the New York Public Library, LII (1948), 80
212-3-Thoreau, Correspondence, 170-171
212-18-Ibid., 174
212-21-Thoreau, Journal, I, 431-433
212-29-Thoreau, Correspondence, 217, 218
212-35-Ibid., 222-225
214-28-Ibid., 228
215-2-Thoreau, Writings, IV, 320
216-6-Ibid., III, 370
216-9-Thoreau, Correspondence, 226
216-22-F. B. Sanborn, Henry D. Thoreau (Boston, 1882), 194
217-2-Emerson, Journals, VII, 307; Alcott, Journals, 196
217-16-Alcott, Journals, 196
217-24-Ibid., Julian Hawthorne, Memoirs (New York, 1938), 57
217-27-Edward Emerson, Notes on Thoreau, MS

CHAPTER XII

221-7-Ralph Waldo Emerson, Journals (Boston, 1910) VII, 241
221-10-Thoreau, Correspondence, 188
221-11-Thoreau, Correspondence, 193
221-15-Emerson, Letters, III, 462
222-9-Edward Emerson, Henry Thoreau as Remembered by a Young Friend, (Boston, 1917), 1-7
222-11-Thoreau, Correspondence, 189
222-14-Emerson, Letters, III, 455
222-19-Henry Seidel Canby, Thoreau (Boston, 1939), 243
225-13-Walter Harding, "Thoreau's Feminine Foe," PMLA, LXIX (1954), 110
225-19-Margaret Lothrop, The Wayside (New York, 19 73
225-23-Emerson, Letters, III, 347-348
226-4-Emerson, Letters, III, 358
226-5-Ibid., III, 390; Canby, Thoreau, 260
227-30-Milton Meltzer and Walter Harding, A Thoreau Profile (New York, 1962), 66
228-29-Walter Harding, "A Check List of Thoreau's Lectures," Bulletin of the New York Public Librar LII (1948), 80; Anton Huffert, Thoreau as a Teach Lecturer and Educational Thinker (New York Univer sity, 1951, unpublished doctoral dissertation), 475
229-2-Ibid., 218
229-8-Thoreau, Correspondence, 231-323
230-22-Ibid., 232
230-26-Ibid., 232-233
233-21-Thoreau, Writings, I, 325
235-1-Thoreau, Correspondence, 226
236-17-Thoreau, Correspondence, 230
237-21-Samuel Longfellow, Life of Henry Wadsworth Longfellow (Boston, 1891), II, 136; Canby, Thoreau 251-252, 474
238-14-Harding, "A Check List of Thoreau's Lectures, 81
238-17-Thoreau, Correspondence, 238-239
238-27-Harding, "A Check List of Thoreau's Lectures, 81
238-38-Thoreau, Correspondence, 240-241
241-30-Harding, "A Check List of Thoreau's Lectures, 81

CHAPTER XIII

244-31 Henry David Thoreau, Correspondence (New York, 1958), 181
244-34-Ibid., 173 (where letter should be dated June 14, 1847)
244-34-Ibid., 184
245-20-Thoreau, Correspondence, 185
245-25-Thoreau, Correspondence, 191
245-29-Ibid., 195
245-34-Ibid., 204
246-2-F. B. Sanborn, Henry D. Thoreau (Boston, 1882), 304
246-10-Ibid., 236
246-12-Ibid., 238
246-27-Thoreau, Correspondence, 240
246-29-Walter Harding, A Thoreau Handbook (New York, 1959), 52
246-31-Alcott, Journals, 209
246-31-Emerson, Letters, IV, 145
247-13-H. M. Tomlinson, Waiting for Daylight (New York, 1922), 29-30
252-21-Thoreau, Journal, V, 459
254-7-Thoreau, Journal, V, 512
254-11-Henry Seidel Canby, Thoreau (Boston, 1939), 278
256-3-Thoreau, Correspondence, 465
256-24-Thoreau, Correspondence, 114
256-30-Ibid., 237
258-1-Emerson, Letters, IV, 153

CHAPTER XIV

261-18-F. B. Sanborn, The Life of Henry David Thoreau (Boston, 1917), 325-6
263-1-Sanborn, The Life of Henry David Thoreau, 212
263-5-Social Circle in Concord, Memoirs (Boston, 1882-1940), III, 72
263-24-Emerson, Notes on Thoreau, MS

27-Annie Russell Marble, Thoreau: His Home, ends and Books (New York, 1902), 37-38
28-Sanborn, The Life of Henry David Thoreau, 7
30-Henry David Thoreau, Journal (Boston, 1906), II, 67
20-Alcott, Journals
3-F. B. Sanborn, The Personality of Thoreau oston, 1901), 11
6-George W. Cooke, "The Two Thoreaus," Independent, XLVIII (1896), 1671
10-Truth-Seeker, "Memories of Thoreau," November , 1897
12-William Ellery Channing, Thoreau, the Poet-Naturalist (Boston, 1873), 247
14-Ibid., 5
27-Channing, Thoreau, the Poet-Naturalist, 34
7-Channing, Thoreau, the Poet-Naturalist, 107
25-Thoreau, Journal, I, 288
8-Kenneth Walter Cameron, Emerson the Essayist Raleigh , 1945), 195
12-Henry David Thoreau, The Transmigration of he Seven Brahamans (New York, 1932)
11-Ibid., 480
35-Kenneth Walter Cameron, "Emerson, Thoreau, and the Society of Natural History," American iterature, XXIV (1952), 21-23
4-Henry David Thoreau, Writings, (Boston, 1906), V, 5
2-37-Cameron, The Transcendentalists and Minerva, II, 378-379
3-4-Walter Harding, "A Check List of Thoreau's ectures," Bulletin of the New York Public Library LII (1948), 82
3-17-Thoreau, Writings, IV, 3
4-32-Thoreau, Journal, II, 7-8
7-7-Ibid., III, 126
7-12-Ibid., III, 137
8-8-Thoreau, Correspondence, 261
8-17-Ibid., 262-263
78-31-Thoreau, Journal, II, 49-51, 79-80
79-7-Thoreau, Correspondence, 263
79-15-Rusk, The Life of Ralph Waldo Emerson, 378
79-20-Thoreau, Journal, II, 73
79-24-Thoreau, Writings, V, 3
82-11-Cameron, Emerson the Essayist, 195
82-19-Harding, "A Check List of Thoreau's Lectures," 83
82-27-Thoreau, Correspondence, 277
82-29-Ibid., 281-282
82-31-Ibid., 289-290
83-17-Ibid., 299
283-29-Thoreau, Correspondence, 301
284-3-Bronson Alcott, Journals (Boston, 1938), 198
284-7-Bronson Alcott, Journals, MS, Houghton Library
284-16-Alcott, Journals
285-6-Harding, "A Check List of Thoreau's Lectures," 82
285-7-Thoreau, Correspondence, 269
285-20-Thoreau, Journal, II, 121
285-24-Ibid., II, 134-135; Harding, "A Check List of Thoreau's Lectures," 82
285-30-Harding, "A Check List of Thoreau's Lectures," 82
286-2-Harding, "A Check List of Thoreau's Lectures," 82
286-28-Ibid., 83
286-36-Alcott, Journals
287-6-Harding, "A Check List of Thoreau's Lectures," 83
288-14-Channing, Thoreau, the Poet-Naturalist, 36
289-10-Ibid., III, 34
289-12-Ibid., XI, 245
291-3-Ibid., II, 288
291-7-Ibid., II, 294
294-2-Ibid., II, 347-348
294-25-Ibid., II, 367
294-37-Ibid., IV, 342-347
295-29-Ibid., II, 306-307
295-36-Ibid., II, 208

CHAPTER XV

300-6-Ralph Waldo Emerson, Letters (New York, 1939), IV, 187
300-29-Ibid., III, 139
301-1-Ibid., III, 214
301-8-Kenneth Walter Cameron, Emerson, Thoreau and Concord in Early Newspapers (Hartford, 1958), 45
302-10-Emerson, Letters, IV, 402
304-21-Ibid., III, 114
307-8-Emerson, Letters, IV, 404
307-36-Emerson, Journals, VIII, 90
308-4-Bronson Alcott, Journals (Boston, 1938), 269
309-23-Gorham Munson, Penobscot (New York, 1959), 15
309-31-Henry David Thoreau, Writings (Boston, 1906), III, 94
310-14-Fannie Hardy Eckstorm, The Penobscot Man (Bangor, 1924), 67
313-3-Thoreau, Writings, II, 226-229
313-6-Frank Buckley, "Thoreau and the Irish," New England Quarterly, XIII, (1940), 389-400
313-11-Thoreau, Journal, III, 241-289
313-12-Henry David Thoreau, Correspondence (New York, 1958), 295
313-13-Ibid., 324
313-18-Thoreau, Journal, V, 438-439
313-21-Ibid., II, 351
315-35-Thoreau, Journal, II, 37-38
316-29-Thoreau, Journal, V, 472
317-32-Thoreau, Writings, IV, 388
318-4-Conway, Autobiography, I, 184-185
318-30-Ibid., 337
320-9-Ibid., V, 365
320-31-Ibid., V, 263-265
322-20-Ibid., III, 230
322-23-Ibid., III, 234
322-29-Albert Lownes, Letter to Walter Harding of March 30, 1964
325-8-Thoreau, Journal, V, 506
325-11-Walter Harding, "A Check List of Thoreau's Lectures," Bulletin of the New York Public Library, LII (1948) 83
326-4-Ibid., VI, 185
326-16-Ibid., V, 111-128
326-26-Thoreau, Correspondence, 318
327-4-Ibid., V, 508
327-21-Ibid., V, 259
328-20-Ibid., IX, 148
328-37-Thoreau, Journal, V, 272-274

CHAPTER XVI

331-1-Henry David Thoreau, Correspondence (New York, 1958), 278
331-8-Ibid., 290, 294
331-16-Shanley, The Making of Walden, 31-32
332-1-Henry David Thoreau, Journal (Boston, 1906), VI, 176
332-24-Thoreau, Correspondence, 323
332-28-Ibid., 324
332-33-Thoreau, Journal, VI, 419
333-9-Ralph Waldo Emerson, Journals (Boston, 1910), VIII, 485
336-27-Thoreau, Correspondence, 358
337-33-Thoreau, Correspondence, 380
337-34-Nicholas Trubner, Trubner's Bibliographical Guide to American Literature (London, 1859), 456
339-27-Ibid., XI, 405
340-25-Thoreau, Correspondence, 349
340-32-Ibid., 387, 465, 553
341-4-Walter Harding, A Centennial Check-list of the Editions of Henry David Thoreau's Walden (Charlottesville, 1954)
341-22-Carl Bode, The American Lyceum (New York, 1956), 166; Thoreau, Correspondence, 367, 352
341-28-Thoreau, Correspondence, 337-340; Note on front cover of Journal XXVIII, MS, Morgan Library
342-5-Journal XXVIII, MS, Morgan Library
342-21-Walter Harding "An Unnoticed Early Review of Walden," Thoreau Society Bulletin, XVI (1946), 3
342-22-Thoreau, Correspondence, 332-335
342-24-Ibid., 344
343-31-Anna and Walton Ricketson, Daniel Ricketson and His Friends (Boston, 1902), 308
344-33-Now owned by Albert E. Lownes
345-3-Thoreau, Correspondence, 363
345-24-Walter Harding, "A Check List of Thoreau's Lectures," Bulletin of the New York Public Library, LII (1948), 84

346-24-Mary Hosmer Brown, Memories of Concord
(Boston, 1926), 106
346-26-Mabel Loomis Todd, The Thoreau Family Two
Generations Ago (Berkeley Heights, New Jersey,
1958), 9; F. B. Sanborn, Recollections of Seventy
Years, (Boston, 1909), II, 476
346-29-F. B. Sanborn, "Thoreau and His English
Friend Thomas Cholmondeley," Atlantic Monthly,
LXXII (1893), 741
347-2-Sanborn, The Life of Henry David Thoreau, 337
347-9-Thoreau, Journal, VII, 64-65
347-12-Thoreau, Correspondence, 350
347-22-Thoreau, Correspondence, 452
347-31-Ibid., 395-396
347-34-Thoreau, Journal, VIII, 18
348-34-Thoreau, Correspondence, 528-529
349-12-Thoreau, Writings, VI, 343
349-30-Sanborn, The Personality of Thoreau, 24
350-1-Thoreau, Journal, IX, 359
351-2-Todd, The Thoreau Family Two Generations Ago,
1-2
351-28-Hildegarde Hawthorne, Concord's Happy Rebel
(New York, 1940), 140
351-32-Brown, Memories of Concord, 108
352-2-Todd, The Thoreau Family Two Generations Ago,
3
352-6-Walter Harding, "The Rowse Crayon of Thoreau,"
Thoreau Society Bulletin, XX
352-8-Anna and Walton Ricketson, Daniel Ricketson
and His Friends, 147
352-10-Harding, "The Rowse Crayon of Thoreau," 4
352-24-Ibid., I, 213
352-28-Sanborn, The Personality of Thoreau, 5-6
353-11-Cameron, The Transcendental Climate, I, 219-
220
353-15-Ibid., I, 241; Thoreau, Writings, VI, 253
354-8-Ibid., 21
354-11-Sanborn, Recollections of Seventy Years, II,
517
355-16-Thoreau, Journal, IX, 145
355-19-Ibid., 10
355-24-Thoreau, Journal, X 475
355-26-Ibid., VIII, 298
355-28-Ibid., VIII, 324
355-31-Ibid., XIII, 379
355-34-Ibid., XIII, 423

CHAPTER XVII

357-2-Henry David Thoreau, Journal (Boston, 1906),
VII, 155
358-2-Thoreau, Journal, XIV, 109
358-10-Ibid., VII, 418
358-11-Ibid., VII, 247
358-18-Ibid., VII, 263-267
358-27-Ibid., VII, 365-390
359-2-Ibid., VII, 522-525
359-8-Thoreau, Correspondence, 288
359-13-Ibid., VII, 306, 308
359-21-Ibid., 374
359-37-Ibid., 376
360-7-Thoreau, Journal, VII, 431-432
360-22-Henry David Thoreau, Writings (Boston, 1906),
IV, 112-113
360-36-Thoreau, Correspondence, 379
362-4-Henry David Thoreau, Undated letter to (George
William Curtis), MS, University of Texas Library
362-9-Thoreau, Journal, VII, 463
362-19-Thoreau, Correspondence, 389
363-2-Thoreau, Correspondence, 393
363-22-Thoreau, Journal, VIII, 152, 176, 186
364-3-Ibid., 116, 125, 146, 147
364-7-Walter Harding, Thoreau, Man of Concord (New
York, 1960), 191
364-16-Thoreau, Journal, VIII, 209, 217, 225
364-25-Ibid., VIII, 274, 429
365-3-Thoreau, Journal, VIII, 345-346
366-6-Thoreau, Correspondence, 411, 419, 422
366-10-Thoreau, Journal, VIII, 229
367-4-Thoreau, Journal, VIII, 378-380
367-8-Thoreau, Correspondence, 426
367-11-Frost, "Thoreau's Worcester Visits," 13-14
367-23-Anna and Walton Ricketson, Daniel Ricketson
and His Friends, 284-289

368-26-Thoreau, Journal, VIII, 396
368-34-Anna and Walton Ricketson, Daniel Ricketson
and His Friends, 295-298
369-5-Thoreau, Journal, IX, 61-62
369-23-Elliott S. Allison, "Thoreau in Vermont,"
Vermont Life, IX (1954), 11-13
369-34-Thoreau, Correspondence, 472, 510, 551
370-6-Thoreau, Journal, IX, 74-77
370-11-Bronson Alcott, Journals (Boston, 1938), 284
370-15-Thoreau, Journal, IX, 78-80
370-24-Maude Greene, "Raritan Bay Union, Eagleswood,
New Jersey," Proceedings of the New Jersey Historical Society, LXVIII (1950), 4-5
371-5-Thoreau, Journal, IX, 133-134
371-26-Thoreau, Correspondence, 439
372-9-Alcott, Journals, 288
372-24-Alcott, Journals, 289
374-21-Walter Harding, Thoreau's Library (Charlottesville, 1957), 98
374-23-Leo Stoller, Henry David Thoreau 1917-1862
(Detroit, 1962), 8
376-12-Traubel, With Walt Whitman in Camden, I, 213
376-19-Ralph Rusk, The Life of Ralph Waldo Emerson
(New York, 1949), 403
376-33-Thoreau, Correspondence, 441-442
377-5-Thoreau, Journal, IX, 187-188
377-8-Walter Harding, "A Check List of Thoreau's
Lectures," Bulletin of the New York Public Library, LII (1948), 85
377-11-Thoreau, Correspondence, 465

CHAPTER XVIII

378-4-Henry David Thoreau, Correspondence (New
York, 1958), 470, 473
378-7-Henry David Thoreau, Journal (Boston, 1906),
IX, 315
378-9-Bronson Alcott, Journals (Boston, 1938), 298
379-26-Henry David Thoreau, Writings (Boston, 1906),
VI, 307
379-32-Anna and Walton Ricketson, Daniel Ricketson
and His Friends (Boston, 1902). 301
380-1-Alcott, Journals, MS, Houghton Library
380-4-Thoreau, Correspondence, 479
380-17-Thoreau, Correspondence, 492-494, 499
381-10-Annie Russell Marble, Thoreau: His Home,
Friends and Books (New York, 1902), 4
381-14-Alcott, Journals, 307
381-16-Ednah D. Cheney, Louisa May Alcott (Boston,
1889), 98
381-26-Thoreau, Journal, IX, 350, 357
382-25-Thoreau, Correspondence, 484
385-12-Thoreau, Correspondence, 486
385-15-Ibid., 486, 491
385-20-Thoreau, Journal, IX, 485
387-30-Ibid., 244
391-11-Thoreau, Journal, X, 293
393-10-Thoreau, Correspondence, 504, 505, 509, 514
394-29-Ibid., 520-521
394-33-Austin Warren, "Lowell on Thoreau," Studies
in Philology, XXVII (1930), 452
396-14-Thoreau, Journal, X, 243-248
396-16-Thoreau, Correspondence, 503
396-29-Ruth Frost, "Thoreau's Worcester Visits,"
Nature Outlook, I (1943), 14
397-12-Thoreau, Correspondence, 514
397-20-Allen Chamberlain, The Annals of the Grand
Monadnock (Concord, New Hampshire, 1936), 71
398-19-Thoreau, Journal, X, 452-519
398-27-Thoreau, Correspondence, 516-519
399-18-Thoreau, Writings, VI, 336
399-20-Christopher McKee, "Thoreau: A Week on Mt.
Washington and in Tuckerman's Ravine," Appalachia,
XXX (1954), 17th
400-11-Ibid., 174
401-22-Thoreau, Journal, XI, 57
402-13-Thoreau, Journal, XI, 3-62
402-15-Thoreau, Writings, VI, 335
402-23-Thoreau, Correspondence, 623-624
403-17-Thoreau, Journal, XI, 170-180
403-22-Ibid., X, 370
403-24-Ibid., X, 368
403-34-Ibid., X, 375
403-36-Emerson, Journal, IX, 154

5-3-Thoreau, Journal, X, 483-484
5-15-Ibid., XI, 348-349
5-18-Ibid., IV, 221; V, 125
5-21-Ibid., X, 406
5-23-Ibid., X, 417
5-24-Ibid., XII, 268
7-2-Thoreau, Journal, X, 503
7-22-Thoreau, Journal, X, 429

CHAPTER XIX

3-4-Henry David Thoreau, Correspondence (New York,
1958), 495
8-17-Thoreau, Correspondence, 546
9-14-Walter Harding, Thoreau's Library (Charlottesville, 1957), 37
9-20-Thoreau, Journal, XII, 203
0-3-Thoreau, Correspondence, 559-560
0-22-Thoreau, Journal, XII, 150
0-26-Ibid., XII, 152
0-28-Ibid., XII, 166; F. B. Sanborn, Recollections
of Seventy Years (Boston, 1909), II, 392
0-30-Thoreau, Journal, XII, 153
1-1-Thoreau, Correspondence, 552
3-7-Alcott, Journals
3-9-Thoreau, Correspondence, 541, 542
3-11-Walter Harding, "A Check List of Thoreau's
Lectures," Bulletin of the New York Public Library, LII (1948), 86
13-23-Thoreau, Journal, XI, 457
14-16-Harding, "A Check List of Thoreau's Lectures,"
86
14-32-Thoreau, Correspondence, 557
15-1-Emerson, Letters, V, 176-177
15-29-Sanborn, Recollections of Seventy Years, I,
103-104, 111
16-14-Sanborn, Recollections of Seventy Years, I,
163-164
17-1-Ibid., XII, 407
17-15-Henry Seidel Canby, Thoreau (Boston, 1939),
391
17-17-Emerson, Complete Works, X, 460
17-18-George W. Cooke, "The Two Thoreaus," Independent, XLVIII (1896), 1671
19-6-Thoreau, Correspondence, 563-564
19-13-Clipping pasted in Alcott's Autobiographical
Collections
19-17-Clipping pasted in Alcott, Journals, MS, Houghton Library
19-18-Ibid.
19-20-Kenneth Walter Cameron, "Annotations on
Thoreau's Correspondence," Emerson Society
Quarterly, XXIV (1961), 98
20-2-Harding, "A Check List of Thoreau's Lectures," 87
20-10-Bronson Alcott, Journals (Boston, 1938), 321-322
20-21-Alcott, Journals, 322
21-7-Emerson, Journals, IX, 253
23-4-Thoreau, Correspondence, 547-575
24-5-F. B. Sanborn, "A Concord Arrest in 1860,"
Middlesex Patriot, March 29, 1901
26-10-F. B. Sanborn, "Emerson and His Friends in
Concord," New England Magazine, III (1890), 430
26-15-Annie Russell Marble, Thoreau: His Home,
Friends and Books (New York, 1902), 57
27-11-Third Annual Report of the Trustees of the
Peabody Museum of American Archeology and Ethnolo-
gy (Boston, 1870), 6-7
27-16-Thoreau, Correspondence, 16-18, 24
27-26-Thoreau, Journal, II, 112-115
27-29-Kenneth Walter Cameron, Emerson, the Essayist
(Raleigh, 1945), 196
28-5-Thoreau, Journal, V, 525
28-11-MS, Morgan Library
28-16-Keiser, "Thoreau's Manuscripts on the
Indians," 197
31-18-Alcott, Journals, 325
31-21-Thoreau, Correspondence, 580
32-6-Thoreau, Correspondence, 598
33-32-Ralph Rusk, The Life of Ralph Waldo Emerson
(New York, 1949), 404
35-23-Thoreau, Correspondence, 591-592
36-11-Alcott, Journals
37-1-Thoreau, Correspondence, 582
37-18-Thoreau, Correspondence, 548- 590
37-21-Anton Huffert, Thoreau as a Teacher, Lecturer
and Educational Thinker (New York University, 1951,

unpublished doctoral dissertation), 477
437-31-Thoreau, Journal, XIV, 75-76
438-5-Hubert Hoeltje, "Thoreau as Lecturer," New
England Quarterly, XIX (1946), 492-493
438-14-Thoreau, Writings, V, 203
438-26-Stoller, After Walden, 79
438-31-Thoreau, Journal, II, 446; III, 19, 31
439-3-Ibid., VIII, 315
439-17-Edward Deevey, Jr., "A Re-examination of
Thoreau's 'Walden,'" Quarterly Review of Biology,
XVII (1942), 8
439-37-Thoreau, Correspondence,, 601
441-3-Ibid., XIV, 290-291
441-14-Thoreau, Correspondence, 591

CHAPTER XX

443-20-Henry Seidel Canby, Thoreau (Boston, 1939), 186
444-3-John C. Broderick, "Bronson Alcott's 'Concord
Book,'" New England Quarterly, XXIX (1956), 369
444-12-Alcott, Essays on Education, 222
444-16-Ibid., p. 260
444-21-Henry David Thoreau, Journal (Boston, 1906),
XIV, 320, 321
444-32-Thoreau, Journal, XIV, 334-336
444-34-Cameron, "Thoreau and Emerson in Channing's
Letters to the Watsons," 79
445-2-Thoreau, Correspondence, 615
445-5-Newspaper clipping of an obituary notice for
Samuel Thatcher, Jr., property of Mrs. Henry
Wheelwright
445-15-Thoreau, Correspondence, 615
445-29-Ibid., 614
446-18-Harding, Thoreau's Minnesota Journey, 47
447-2-Thoreau, Correspondence, 617
448-20-Harding, Thoreau's Minnesota Journey, 17
449-4-Thoreau, Correspondence, 619-622
451-2-Louise Hall Tharp, Until Victory (Boston,
1953), 317
451-22-Moncure Conway, Autobiography, Memories and
Experiences (Boston, 1904), I, 335
452-16-Anna and Walton Ricketson, Daniel Ricketson
and His Friends (Boston, 1902), 16
453-8-Thoreau, Correspondence, 626
453-20-Anna and Walton Ricketson, Daniel Ricketson
and His Friends, 320-231
453-26-Thoreau, Correspondence, 642-644
454-1-F. B. Sanborn, The Life of Henry David Thoreau (Boston, 1917), 345
454-14-Ibid., 483
454-19-Thoreau, Correspondence, 628
455-22-T. W. Higginson, Out-Door Papers (Boston,
1863), 312
455-31-Ralph Waldo Emerson, Letters (New York,
1939), V, 259
456-5-Ralph Rusk, The Life of Ralph Waldo Emerson
(New York, 1949), 413
456-11-Alcott, Journals, 343
457-19-Ibid., 641
458-3-Thoreau, Correspondence, 636
458-10-Ibid., 637-368
458-12-Ibid., 638
458-22-Ibid., 639
458-25-Ibid., 640
458-29-Ibid., 645
461-5-M. A. DeWolfe Howe, Memories of a Hostess
(Boston, 1922), 62
462-3-William Ellery Channing, Thoreau, the Poet-
Naturalist (Boston, 1902), 118n
462-4-Sanborn, The Personality of Thoreau, 66
462-26-Rose Hawthorne Lathrop, Memories of Hawthorne
(Boston, 1897), 420
463-27-Anna and Walton Ricketson, Daniel Ricketson
and His Friends, 141
464-9-Sanborn, Henry D. Thoreau, 307
466-6-Anna and Walton Ricketson, Daniel Ricketson
and His Friends, 143
466-13-Anna and Walton Ricketson, Daniel Ricketson
and His Friends, 143
466-19-Frederick T. McGill, Jr. unpublished biography of Ellery Channing
467-18-Lathrop, Memories of Hawthorne, 431
467-20-Harding, "Thoreau's Feminine Foe," 115
467-22-William Rounseville Alger, The Solitude of
Nature and of Man (Boston, 1871), 338
467-2 -Boston Transcript, May 10, 1862

Index